Concept of Freedom

Edited by

REV. CARL W. GRINDEL, C.M., PH.D.
Professor of Philosophy, St. John's University Graduate School

HENRY REGNERY COMPANY
Publishers *Chicago*

MANUFACTURED IN THE UNITED STATES OF AMERICA

Library of Congress Catalog Card Number: 55-10062

Foreword

Quite naturally one may inquire about the considerations which induced St. John's University to undertake this project titled "Concept of Freedom." Certainly no single motive occasioned this lengthy study. Rather it was an accumulation of motives that influenced the University and the individual contributors. Freedom is the great topic of the day. Consequently, a community of scholars has the right and duty to examine it and to apply their conclusions to those areas in which there is apt to be controversy. In a word, to freedom has been attached so many meanings, at times apparently contradictory, that it was the desire of St. John's and the members of the Humanities Research Board to endeavor to clarify the significance of true freedom as it is applied in so many different ways.

The philosophy of totalitarian government has spread all too widely throughout the world. Yet many of its excesses have been justified in the name of freedom. Human beings are, by nature, free. The human desire to exercise freedom can never be eradicated. Yet there is the consciousness that freedom can be abused. The absolute freedom irrationally desired by some can result not in liberty but in license, not in order but in chaos. During the past fifteen years, especially, freedom has been debated by statesmen, politicians and philosophers. Yet careful examination of what has been spoken and written discloses the astounding fact that much of it has no sound philosophic or practical foundation. The moral and social anarchy which is rampant in many countries today is the direct result of the false premises concerning the objectives of man, his obligations to God, to himself and to society and to the purpose and scope of his freedom.

Freedom is the very cornerstone of man. Without it man cannot remain human. Destroy man and society is meaningless. There is no time more profitable than the present to consider the irreparable ravages of the loss of the precious jewel of liberty. Men are dying to retain it. The whole world is bitterly divided over it. In such a basic struggle peaceful co-existence is an underestimated myth.

Consequently, there is a definite obligation on the part of a faculty of a University to investigate exhaustively the manner in which man is and should be free. We received an added impetus when our sister university, Columbia, announced as the theme for her bicentennial celebration "Man's Right to Knowledge and the Free Use Thereof." We were convinced, however, that we could not begin to discuss this topic until we had made a basic philosophical and psychological study of man's freedom—an attempt to discover its primary meaning. Having accomplished this, we endeavored to investigate the application of the concept of freedom to such strategic areas as theology, economics, law, international relations, education, government, and labor.

Throughout this series of studies, our sole objective was to capture Truth. In faith and science, we attest to the supreme validity of the clear and wise words of the Divine Teacher: "The truth shall make you free."

VERY REVEREND JOHN A. FLYNN, C.M.
President, St. John's University

Special Award

ST. JOHN'S UNIVERSITY

For St. John's University, whose faculty group has written the volume "Concept of Freedom," Freedoms Foundation at Valley Forge at the direction of the distinguished Awards Jury does strike a new George Washington Honor Medal.

With vigorous, profound language, their new literature on freedom contributes mightily to the knowledge of men who study freedom's hard and glorious path. *May their chapters stir Americans to defend this land of God and Freedom valiantly and fervently, with wisdom and clarity.*

IMPRIMI POTEST:

Sylvester A. Taggart, C.M., S.T.L., S.S.B.
Visitator Provinciae Orientalis

NIHIL OBSTAT:

Martinus S. Rushford, Ph.D.
Censor Librorum

IMPRIMATUR:

✠ Thomas Edmundus Molloy, S.T.D.
Archiepiscopus-Episcopus Brooklyniensis

BROOKLYNII

die VII Octobris, 1954

Contents

Concept of Freedom

Introduction

Freedom and Human Knowledge

by Dr. William E. Carlo
Professor of Philosophy,
Graduate School, St. John's University

The aspiration towards freedom, though rooted in human nature, unfortunately does not flower in a political society without careful cultivation. The visible blight that has fallen on modern civilization is proof enough of this. Entire nations are casually surrendering their God-given freedoms, or, what appears to be the same thing, are so indifferent as to allow an inconsequential minority to deprive them of their personal freedoms. This decay of political virtue can be attributed to a deadening of enthusiasm for freedom, and the actual rejection of it for a precarious economic security. Equality and fraternity are still magic words, but liberty has yet to fire a contemporary revolution.

This deadening of enthusiasm for freedom is the result of a confusion in the understanding of the nature of freedom. All are agreed as to the value and desirability of freedom, and yet so many difficulties arise in its pursuit. One reason for this is that freedom does not mean exactly the same thing to all men. Freedom exists in different ways and under different conditions in the several spheres of human activity. Not only does freedom seem to vary in meaning, but at times it seems to be self-contradictory, and we witness the spectacle of freedom pitted against freedom.

Let us take an example from economics and politics. Never before have such great numbers of human beings lived together in harmony and order. Never before have so many shared in the direction and fruits of the state. It is certainly a new era in history. But there is another side to the coin. For the first time in history, the poor have their hands on political power through the vote, and they are not going to let the wealthy keep what they have. A wave of socialism has swept the entire world, and left us struggling in its wake. The economic and political changes of the last thirty years have resulted in a social transformation which would shock a banker of 1900, what with social security, unemployment insurance, the strength of organized labor, and the like.

Of course, behind all this is a good motive, the crying need for a more equitable distribution of wealth. Unfortunately, communism is capitalizing on an economic good. Otherwise it would not have spread so rapidly throughout Europe and Asia. Social justice is a necessity. But is the method of the communists, state action or socialization, the best way to accomplish it? If so, how can the bureaucratic regimentation that seems inevitably to accompany historical socialism be prevented? Must the price of social justice be the loss of our freedoms? This is the difficulty that confronts us in politics and economics. Social justice must be achieved, or the whole world will go communistic. But if we attempt to accomplish it by means of the only instrument that seems to be effective against human greed, by means of government, then we are confronted with a dilemma. As government increases in scope, it encroaches further upon individual privacy. Even in these inflated times the loss of freedom is too high a price for economic equality.

Now this problem is precisely one instance of the self-contradiction of freedom that concerns us. For example, if freedom is identified with the political order, then when it is applied to economics, economic freedom must be interpreted in terms of a *laissez faire* capitalism. If freedom is identified with the economic order, as the liberation of a human being from the bondage of brute nature (for to be free, a man must have certain material goods or he cannot achieve his proper perfection) then when this notion of economic freedom is applied to the political sphere, socialism and communism result, namely a policy in which the achievement of freedom is identified with liberation from servitude to the wants of brute nature.

One of the present sources of conflict is the tendency of some to justify a *laissez faire* type of capitalism by an appeal to freedom as it is defined in the political order, while others seek to justify a socialism or communism on the basis of the freedom from slavery to brute nature, which has a natural fascination for so many of the poverty-stricken peoples of the world. Freedom that comes with the possession of necessary material goods seems to have a more universal appeal precisely because it is a more fundamental need in human nature. It is difficult for a starving man to enjoy his political freedom. This is something for those who are concerned with the loss of political freedoms to ponder. A certain measure of economic freedom seems necessary for the preservation of political freedom. Man wants not only to be a free citizen, he wants to be a free man, free to pursue his total perfection.

Not only is it true that freedom is so complex a thing as to appear in different fashion in different areas of knowledge, but even a cursory examination will reveal that many of the current dangers to freedom arise from ideas dominant in these knowledges. In fact, we might go so far as to say that it is the lack of self-awareness, the absence of self-recognition on the part of the various knowledges that have made them actually dangerous to human freedom—they who should be the guardians of our freedoms. For it is through knowledge that freedom is to be attained. "You shall know the truth and the truth shall make you free."

Human beings by the use of their intelligence have freed themselves in great measure from the first tyranny, the tyranny of brute nature and the despotism of their fellow men. All the types of human knowledge have contributed to this advance from barbarism to culture. The recognized instruments of this transformation have been for the most part mathematics, physics, chemistry, biology, psychology, education, sociology, economics, and politics. Our debt to them is immeasurable. They have transformed the slave into the master and given him almost infinite aspirations and ambitions. But it is in precisely these instruments, the sciences, which have molded modern life, that we see a certain fundamental pattern, frightening, but intelligible.

To recognize our vulnerability, we have only to visualize the future development of physics. In addition to bestowing benefits, it has inflicted certain evils. By the employment of atomic weapons, it has transformed war from a kind of sporting event to "total" war. But will human genius stop here? Man has not learned the secret of matter, but he has learned the secret of the destruction of matter. The day may come when he who is able to wire the planet, can explode it. Modern science is like the baby, who tugging at the tablecloth is stunned and frightened to find his own strength pulling the world down upon his head.

This has been the era of mathematical physics. Tomorrow will be the era of biochemistry. Just as the union of mathematics and physics gave us the modern industrial age, so the union of chemistry and biology will result in a science that may utterly transform the social fabric as we know it. The silent assault of bacteriological warfare will be more terrifying than atomic blasts. What effect will the prediction and determination of the sexes before birth have on the existing social structure, for instance, the family? Genetic mutation could supply the foundation for an occupational breeding. Human beings may be determined before birth to be hewers of wood and drawers of water, perfectly modified for their life's work. What totalitarianism is so dangerous to human freedom as this type of regimentation?

The same dangers to freedom present in politics, economics and science are also to be found in the fields of psychology, education and sociology. One dangerous area is that of testing, both intelligence and aptitude tests. From a purely psychological standpoint, such tests do not do what they claim. A test, of course, tests only knowledge, not intelligence. Thus, intelligence tests actually reduce themselves to some elementary knowledge common to all, in the attempt to eliminate the advantages of education and special training. The anomaly which the aptitude test presents is that it claims to test something which does not exist, but could exist. What it is actually testing is knowledge and experience. A real danger to freedom lurks here. Some ardent proponents of such tests seek to determine human lives on the basis of these devices. They would make auto mechanics of boys who could be surgeons. Human capacities are unlimited. The normal human being can become almost anything, given sufficient incentive. These tests may be handy ways of controlling large groups of people, but they are not reliable enough for individual evaluation. Yet the layman and the uninitiated attribute to them an infallibility which professional psychologists do not disown, but rather foster. For all too many educators, the school is not an institution for the communication of knowledge, but for equipping the student for life, meaning a job. Any form of liberal education for the masses must be subordinated to showing them how to make a living! Only the few aristocratic intellects should have the cultural courses that produce free men. There are some who would make the majority of the human race merely slaves to the economic needs of mankind.

A corollary of this notion of the school is its role as an *adjustorium*. Its purpose is to adjust. Such educators may not be quite sure what they are adjusting, but, at any rate, they adjust. They train character. They develop personality—all without knowing, much less agreeing on, what character is, or what personality is.

The head of the education department of a large university was recently quoted to the effect that his university was reducing its methods courses, and adding more liberal arts courses to the curriculum, in order to achieve a better balance. He is even considering the advisability of lessening the hours of practice teaching demanded. Some educators look on this as an improvement. But who was responsible for a curriculum stretched and distended by methods courses in the first place? They do not realize that they are tending back to something most people were aware of long ago. To them it is a new conclusion scientifically established by the science of education!

The frightening thing about all this is that their every whim, sometimes with little actual scientific basis, can determine the indoctrination of tens of thousands of teachers—and then the experiment devolves upon millions of malleable human beings. What sort of freedom is compatible with the role of the guinea pig?

Another example is the infant science of psychoanalysis. Handled properly, it is a useful aid to medicine. But there are great dangers inherent in the way some practitioners use it, especially in the theory that underlies certain of its techniques. One of the needs of modern psychoanalysis is a shortened form of analysis, in order that it may be more universally applied. In fact, there is a large business organization which demands a certain type of psychoanalytic analysis, under the name of psychiatry, of course, and it is the aim of some to have every single individual tested for the good of the business, the country, and themselves as well. It seems logical, for are they not the scientists of the mind? Therefore, they are the ones to explain the laws of mind and personality. Consider the dangers inherent in much of modern psychoanalytic theory. Imagine the day when the campaigner for public office must undergo a psychoanalytic evaluation! Imagine such results: he believes in God—escape from reality—not at all the tough-minded realist needed to hold public office! The diabolical part of all this is that you are told you do the things you do without being aware of the real reason for doing them.

Your action is really determined by the unconscious, or, at least, the subconscious. You are told that you do something because you had an unholy love for your mother. How do you answer such a charge? You are not supposed to know it. Only they know it. But who will analyze the analyst? If an analyst is obsessed by sex, then he is going to see a sex association in your every image, even the Church spire. Is there any political tyranny as ghastly as this tyranny of the mind and heart?

We are not asserting that all these evils exist today. We are not asserting that they are pure evils unmixed with any good. What we are asserting is that if the various knowledges are left to go their own way without any sort of theological and philosophical guidance, then the day may come when the human being, trapped Frankenstein-like by the monstrous offspring of his own intelligence, will look up at the stars from out of his physical, mental and moral cage, and curse the day he was born. Is this the legacy of the human race? It may well be. It is almost a fact in some parts of the globe. Why should such dangers exist? What do we know about the structure of the human mind and its knowledges which would free us from the tyranny that they can exert over us? An analysis of the nature of knowledge, the nature of science, and the limitations of the specific knowledges is absolutely necessary if man is to use them for his good rather than for his destruction. Will they be masters or slaves? In order to answer some of these eminently vital problems facing the human race, we undertake this analysis of the nature of knowledge and the function of the different types of knowledges, not only to understand what freedom is, but most important of all, to preserve freedom.

In analyzing any part of reality, we must take cognizance not only of the thing we are investigating, but also of our proper mode of inquiry. If there were but one, single, homogeneous knowledge which differs only by reason of the object it investigates, then the difficulties of human knowing would be simplified immeasurably. If all the limitations of human knowledge are ignored, as has been the case since Descartes, then a homogeneous knowledge is distinguishable only by its application. Mathematics differs from grammar because one deals with numbers, and the other with speech; chemistry deals with the elements and their compounds, whereas spelling deals with words. If this were the case, then any human mind, no matter what the method of its proper discipline, would be free to analyze freedom with equal prerogative. But since knowledge is not homogeneous, since knowledges do differ as knowledges, and not only by reason of their subject matter, certain complications arise. The professional mathematician can study a book on diving all winter long, but, when he first steps out on the board in the middle of June, the results are rather disastrous. Experience is witness to the fact that no matter what the mental development in one area of human knowledge, it can never be adequately transferred to a different area of knowledge. *Knowledges differ by an inner, intrinsic differentiation, and it is due to this fact that one knowledge cannot be used as a substitute for another, because it is incapable of doing the work of another.* Descartes was only being consistent when he attempted to instruct Harvey in the workings of the circulatory system, a substitution of the deductive method proper to mathematics in an area where, by its very nature, the inductive method must be primary. If there is only one homogeneous knowledge distinguishable by reason of the object to which it is applied, then there is no reason why Descartes could not do so, even though the results were ludicrous.

To understand further the fundamentally different structures of the various knowledges, we need only point to the fact that many knowledges deal with man, but their definitions of man as defined within the scope and methods of their own fundamental movements will vary. For the physicist, man is an articulating system of stresses and strains. For the chemist, man is a complexus of elements and their compounds. For the mathematician, man is a quantity. For the biologist, man is a mammal of the order of primates. For the economist, he is a producer and consumer. Whatever else we may say about these knowledges, we must recognize their structural differences since they deal with the same thing, and yet ignore so completely aspects of this thing rich in intelligibility for other knowledges.

The conclusion is evident then, that the human intellect, when it comes to investigate a reality such as freedom, must be aware of the natures and limitations of the different kinds of knowledges if it would escape a multiplicity of diverse and contradictory answers to the question of freedom. We must understand something about the basic exigencies of the various knowledges if we are to evaluate and profit by what they have to contribute to the total understanding of freedom. And we can make disastrous errors by substituting the results of one knowledge for another. If, for instance, physics has as its object, matter in its motions, then the physicist, as physicist, working completely within his own method and immersed in the procedures of measurement, an immersion which is absolutely necessary if he is to do original work in his field, in attempting to understand freedom will be in danger of analyzing it within the proper method and according to the techniques which have become the habitual mode of operation of his scientific life. But if this method and these techniques were constructed to know matter and know it exhaustively, then whatever does not fall within the laws of matter must be either materialized or denied. Thus a physicist completely immersed in a method made to know matter and matter alone, blind to the nature of his own knowledge, and unaware of the existence of other knowledges with objects proper to themselves, must of necessity answer in terms of atheism and materialism, when he attempts to answer the question of the existence of God and the spirituality of the soul. Every man must be the master of some knowledge. But he cannot afford to be ignorant of all other knowledges, or he will find himself attempting to answer questions that confront him as a man in terms of the only material he has, the methods and techniques of his own knowledge. Most of the great philosophical errors of history have been due precisely to such a mistake. It is the tendency of every man to exalt *his* knowledge as the answer to the ultimate questions of reality. If he has no other knowledge, and is, nevertheless, seeking ultimate answers, what else can he do? So Descartes tried to interpret all reality in terms of mathematics, Kant of physics, Comte of sociology, and Marx of economics. They tried to interpret all reality in terms of the law of their own particular area of reality.

It is in the awareness of these pitfalls, then, that we as theologians, philosophers, historians, economists, biologists, sociologists, lawyers, educators or psychologists, attempt to analyze freedom in some total fashion. We want our knowledge to be ordered and supplementary, not confused and contradictory. Therefore, before we examine freedom in its proper operations and nature, we want first to lay out in general fashion the boundaries of the different knowledges and their lines of demarcation, so that direction and order may govern our analysis from the beginning.

In constructing a Thomistic classification of the human knowledges we may, at times, appear to be rather far away from our principal preoccupation, the analysis and application of freedom. But this is not a digression, it is a geography. In order to locate the precise role that freedom plays in the different knowledges we must first understand something of the natures of these different knowledges. Our task is, then, to examine knowledge in its intrinsic dynamics, in order to discover its proper movements and the laws under which it operates.

A good way to initiate an investigation into knowledge is to use as a guide the genius of Aristotle, as Saint Thomas Aquinas does. Aristotle begins his *Metaphysics* with the words: *All men by nature desire to know.* We can see what this means, he tells us, by an examination of the sense of sight which is the highest of all the sensory powers and the most akin to intellectual knowledge. It is certainly true that we desire to see, even when we have no care to match shirt and tie or to transfer food from plate to mouth, but just for the pure joy of seeing. The same is true of human knowledge, Aristotle tells us. For a man wants to know even when no practical end is in sight, even when there is nothing to make or do. Knowledge is its own delight. The value that the human being confers upon knowledge becomes evident when we examine that most powerful of all human drives, the instinct of self-preservation—so strong, that it is capable of turning mother-love into cannibalism. This instinct which is so fundamental is not a drive for life itself in a human being, but for a certain type of life, human life. It is awareness or knowledge that is sought, not the unthinking processes of nutrition, growth and reproduction by which life is characterized. If a man had to choose, in a hypothetical case, between dying immediately or contracting a form of sleeping sickness, being unconscious for the remainder of his life, and then dying (the hypothesis being that there is no possible cure or regaining of consciousness), we venture that the average man would prefer to die immediately. Man does not place primary value on the aspects of existence that he has in common with the vegetable. When he wants to live, he wants to be aware of things. He wants to know for the sheer joy of knowing! The life of the cauliflower has no attractions for the human being.

Thus in knowledge itself we find the basis for the first distinction among knowledges, a distinction without which all order in knowledge is impossible: the distinction of speculative and practical knowledge. This is what we mean by speculative knowledge, knowledge for its own sake. It is the supreme physical good of human existence. Imagine the wonder of it, if a man could be produced in the full possession of his faculties who had never before experienced this relation to things that we call knowledge. Just the colors of a room would fascinate him, the shape of things, the various ways that man has organized matter, as well as the works of nature in its infinitely greater productions. Imagine the thrill with which he would see another human being, walking, talking and moving! It would be like a million moving pictures wrapped up into one in its dramatic impact. This is the natural movement of the intellect, even before it cares to make or do anything. By a natural, almost gravitational inclination, it seeks its object, and in knowing things, in a way it possesses them. For it is certainly true that the beauty of the peacock and the sunset, the strength of the lion, the dancing fleetness of the antelope and the soaring flight of the eagle, do exist for the knowing being in a way that they do not exist for the stone or the tree. By knowing things, they, in a way, become yours. That is why a man will turn to look at a beautiful thing. It explains also the fascination of spectator sports; for the grace of the infielder, the skill of the pitcher, and the power of the batter become yours, in a way, when you know them, with the consequent delight that follows on the possession of any perfection and the satisfaction of any appetite.

Practical knowledge on the other hand, is not the natural movement of the mind seeking its object and resting in the delight of its possession, than which there is no greater physical good on this planet. In practical knowledge the intellect is used for a purpose outside its own inner, intrinsic constitution, which is a *speculum* or a mirroring of the thing. Instead, it is made to know in order to make or do something—some thing which the human being wants becomes the object of his movement. But here the intellect is not moving in accordance with its natural momentum. Another faculty or desire calls it into existence, sustains it at every step, and only permits it to rest when the car has been bought, the steak consumed, or the girl wed. The intellect is operating at the command of some appetite or desire, and the object of this appetite becomes its own object. This is the evidence, sketchy and in part, upon which scholastic thinkers, historically, have based their assertion of the primacy of speculative knowledge. Not that by this assertion they intend to demean in any way practical knowledge. One has to be a man to be an artist; art and practice are manifestations of a rational intellect and flow from the dignity of humankind. It is not the lack of a thumb or a hand that makes the brute incapable of artistic production but the absence of rationality, despite certain similarities to rational behavior which instinct possesses. But a man with the body of a dog would still be an artist, although under certain difficulties. Practical knowledge is most important to human existence. We call it practical simply because, in it, knowledge has as its own object, not its own natural movement, but the object of another appetite which is using knowledges to gain its own end. The artist does a great deal of intellectual work. If a man wants to make a statue, he has to think: this wood would be best for a large statue; this for a small one. This type of wood, due to its grain, is better for curves; this type for angles. This kind would be better for outdoors; this for indoors—a tremendous amount of technical knowledge which takes the best years of a lifetime to accumulate. An artist can well spend a lifetime learning how to depict water and rocks. The knowledge involved is inexhaustible. All knowledge is specifically human and worthy of the dignity of the intellectual being, but this practical knowledge is not for the sake of knowledge itself, but for the sake of some thing, some artifact like a chair or an automobile.

We should note that this distinction of speculative and practical, this inner differentiation within the knowledge itself by reason of its end, is not due to the whim of the knower, but has its roots in the very nature of the knowledge under investigation. But speculative knowledge does not mean that we study medicine for the sake of merely knowing it, never intending to practice, or that, by the simple expedient of studying medicine with the intention of practicing it, we thereby make it a practical knowledge. We know how to do something. We know how to restore the harmony of a physical organism. Even when we never practice, we still learn how to do something, to cure the sick, even though we do not intend to do it. The distinction of speculative and practical is thus not based on the intention of the knower but on the direction of the knowledge itself. Despite certain inadequacies, speculative knowledge is the highest type of knowledge because it is the fulfillment of man's highest faculty, the intellect, and his most basic appetite, to know.

If our immediate purpose is to know freedom, to understand its nature, then we are concerned primarily with speculative knowledge. But if we want to do something about freedom, if we want to defend it, to preserve this precious possession, then we must look to the practical knowledges for help. Those practical knowledges in which freedom plays so important a part are medicine, or more properly, psychiatry, law and art.

Since medicine is characterized in large measure as art, therefore freedom enters into its scope only in the way that it is common to any strictly human activity. Both doctor and patient are aware of their freedom as men. If the empirical methods and observational modes of procedure of this knowledge are not meant to attain to human freedom in some proper and profound way, why is it that in our society there is a branch of medicine that is especially concerned with freedom? It is the board of psychiatrists that certifies responsibility. A human being can be committed to an institution for life on the word of medical men. This certainly seems to imply a real insight into the nature of freedom as a function of psychiatry, since one should know the nature of that which one judges. What kind of knowledge of freedom does the psychiatrist really possess? Does he know what freedom is ultimately or the fundamental nature of freedom? The methods and techniques of his knowledge seem to argue against such a claim. But does that mean that his power of certification of the mentally irresponsible is invalid? It is true that the court and not the psychiatrist makes the legal decision and orders the execution of the committal, but does so on the basis of the knowledge of the psychiatrist. Does the psychiatrist know the nature of freedom, or does he rather recognize the influence of specific organic and functional diseases on the normal behavior of man? Through his experience and practical knowledge gained from the examination of a variety of cases, he can determine whether or not the conditions of freedom are present, a domination of passions and emotions by the intellectual powers. All this can be done, and very effectively, without the proper knowledge of the nature of freedom. However, curative treatment might be more effective in mental cases if the nature of man's intellectual powers and their free exercise were better understood by the psychiatrist.

Since the professional jurist (by jurist we mean all those involved in the construction and operation of a legal system), the lawmaker, the judge, the lawyer also work in the practical order, they do not investigate within their own proper field the nature of freedom anymore than the geometer questions his first principles, for instance, that the whole is greater than any of its parts. They start with the fact of freedom, an irreducible datum of reality and proceed from there. If freedom is questioned by the legist, then the whole structure of responsibility and punishment collapses. To demand responsibility for an uncontrollable action is unjust. Even if we consider the role of punishment to be merely that of a deterrent, freedom must be assumed as a necessary constituent of human actions.

To look upon the law positivistically as the mere practical instrument for the preservation of order, possessed of no ontological roots, with an appeal to precedent as the ultimate authority, is not to deny the fact of freedom, though its nature may be ignored. The very fact that a legal system can work even when it prescinds from a scientific knowledge of the nature of freedom, is a significant indication that perhaps such an examination does not fall within the authority of the jurist. A common sense knowledge of the results and conclusions of freedom is the general framework of law, and a practical, prudential judgment is the characteristic core of legal decision. That is why precedent, although without value to science, can perform so valuable a service in law. What was done intelligently in the past is perhaps a practical guide to what should be done today in the area of individual and social behavior. The fundamental legal structure, the court, is a good example of the exercise of the precise type of knowledge involved in the law. In the court, the prosecuting attorney and counsel for the defense each presents his case in all possible strength, so that the judge or jurist may make a concrete prudential judgment on the basis of the facts involved. In such a situation, the office of the attorneys is concerned primarily with presenting the strongest points of their clients, not in making a personal moral judgment in respect to the case. That is the primary function of the jurist.

Thus, the role of the psychiatrist and psychologist as strictly consultants to the court is an eminently sensible one. Their knowledge of freedom, basically non-scientific as it must be, does not possess the certainty and necessity to give it absolute authority. And although certain members of the medical profession have been very vocal in their dissatisfaction with their present consultative status, the fact remains that their knowledge is just as much a knowledge of results and conclusions as that of the experienced jurist, and it is of greatest value when used in conjunction with the jurist's own practical knowledge, at his own discretion.

It is not the duty of the jurist then, to explain what freedom is, to analyze its nature, but it is his obligation to provide in the construction and operation of a legal system, the profoundest guarantees and the most effective protection for the freedom of his fellowmen. What are the limitations that society can place upon individuals consonant with the dignity of free men? It is important to note that the only reason for placing limitations on the freedom of individuals is, paradoxically, to gain for him the greater freedom that he possesses as a member of a just, smoothly articulating society.

Perhaps one of the most hotly contested areas of freedom is that of the arts. Art must be free. Censorship and control stifle artistic genius, we are told. Time and again daily newspapers, and especially their Sunday supplements, repeat the slogan. Controversial cases of censorship make excellent copy, at times meriting headlines. Of course, art should be free, but there is no such thing as an absolute freedom in a contingent world. Can a man sculpt any statue he wishes, or paint any canvas as the whim moves him? Can he produce lewd and vulgar representations as he wills? If art is one intellectual operation of man, having as its object the perfection of man, the ministering to his wants, and the fine arts, in particular, to the more spiritual and aesthetic needs,—then any artistic production that is in conflict with man's perfection is by that fact invalidated. Such production does not further the end of art as an operation of man contributing to the perfection of the whole man, including his moral exigencies.

In theory, therefore, although art is not possessed of some fictitious absolute freedom, in practice, however, man must bend over backwards in order not to infringe on the free artistic exercise. One must be very careful lest one transgress the legitimate liberties of the artist. But legitimate authority has not only the right, but even the obligation of censorship. Men of a practical common sense who know their people, their level of education and customary modes of thought and expression, are in a very good position to make a prudential judgment on whether such and such a work of art will be definitely harmful.

Speculative knowledge is, itself, of two types: *science,* and the *knowledge of common sense.* That type of knowledge which we call *science* is distinguished from the knowledge of common sense, the knowledge of the man in the street, inasmuch as it deals with causes, while the *knowledge of common sense* is concerned with conclusions. When you boil an egg, you know that in three minutes it will be soft boiled, in five, hardboiled. You have real knowledge and certainty of that fact, but you have not scientific knowledge. You do not know the causes of this operation going on before your eyes. Unless you know the laws of heat in relation to water and protoplasm, you do not know, scientifically, what you mean when you say something is cooked. Cooked? What does that mean? Is it the application of heat? What then is heat? What is the difference between a hot piece of metal and the same piece when cold? Many are puzzled when confronted by such questions. You must know the scientific laws of chemical reaction. You have to know the causes of a thing or the reasons why it is what it is. No one in his right senses would step in front of a speeding car. But why not? It hurts, bones would be broken, the result might be death. But just what happens when a car strikes a man or a dog? Why should a moving body have such an effect on another? We know that it does—from experience. We know the results of such an accident. We know conclusions, but we do not know the causes of the event. One avoids a speeding car, not because one knows the physical, chemical and biological reactions which would take place at the impact of car and body, but because one knows that, failing to do so, the conclusion would be most disastrous. Unless we know the physical laws of matter in motion, we cannot explain what happens when a car strikes us. Another example: If a bomb were set in the center of an assembled group, the place would be instantly vacated. But why? Do we know just what happens when a bomb explodes? We know the results, the effects of a thing, but unless again we know the laws of matter in motion, the causes of an event, we have not scientific knowledge. By common sense, of course, we do not mean a hard-headed business sense or a practical prudential judgment. Even though many elements of practical knowledge are interwoven, the knowledge of common sense is not a practical knowledge. We need not learn it by doing. We need not fall from a ten story building in order to discover what happens. We know the results.

It is in this common sense knowledge that we find the recognition of freedom which is needed for the direction of the practical knowledges. The psychiatrist, the lawyer, the artist, the moralist, even the psychologist need not have scientific knowledge of the nature of freedom. They do not have to know the definition of freedom, in order to attain their end of protecting and preserving it. Their common sense experience of freedom from its effects is sufficient. They begin with the fact of freedom as an ultimate datum of reality, and from that starting point pursue effectively their separate ends.

Scientific knowledge of freedom becomes necessary only if there is confusion or substitution of this fundamental knowledge by a science (such as physics), which has no business to be analyzing the nature of freedom because it does not fall within its proper sphere. Then one must go to the scientific examination of freedom in order to counteract such an error. But ordinarily, the common human experience of personal freedom and the control over the effects of our human actions is sufficient for the starting point of the practical knowledges in their relations to freedom.

The other type of speculative knowledge is Science, which has been defined as a certain knowledge through causes. There has been a great deal of human energy expended in an analysis of the nature of science and we do not intend to try to give a definitive and exhaustive treatment to a subject on which men like Descartes and Kant have blunted their genius. On the other hand, it is a matter of fact that there are certain fundamental patterns of intelligibility evident in this complex mental operation. There are certain basic laws that have stood the test of time since Aristotle, and what is just as important, have served to illumine whatever deviations have occurred. When we assert the certainty and necessity of the character of scientific knowledge, we are merely reiterating a common intellectual experience. The status of science has been attached invariably to those knowledges that demonstrate an invariable power of prediction. Historically, the precise knowledges to which were assigned the dignity of science have varied, but the reason for the conferring of such a title has always remained the same. Science is a necessary type of knowledge.

There was a time in the history of man's intellectual endeavors when the title of science with all its dignities and privileges was invested in metaphysics. Today, metaphysics is the transcendental illusion, and it is physics which comes to mind when we hear the word science. This does not mean that the criteria of scientific knowledge have changed, but merely that man has become accustomed to certitudes of another type. Yesteryear and today, there is no quarrel about the scientific status of mathematics. It is science par excellence, the ideal type of human knowledge. Why has its dignity never been challenged? Precisely because of the certainty of its laws. Mathematicians do not dispute the Pythagorean theorem that the square of the hypotenuse equals the sum of the squares of the other two sides. Thinkers do not quarrel over whether two plus two equals four. It is this certitude that Descartes had in mind when he chose mathematics as the archetype of all scientific knowledge. And it is this same characteristic that even today causes men to model economics, sociology, psychology and education upon mathematics, in order that through the copious sprinkling of numbers and quasi-mathematical formulas, it may share in the scientific values of mathematics itself. This would be the proper procedure if the mere presence of numbers was the cause of certainty. But the certitude of mathematical science comes from a source other than the physical fact of numbers. This we shall explain at its proper place in our discussion.

There is no doubt, however, that at every period of history, it is because of its certainty and necessity that a scientific character is bestowed upon any knowledge. Certainty is a characteristic of scientific knowledge because it is concerned with the necessary in the objects of knowledge. The certainty of the science flows from a necessity in the thing. In turn, the necessity of physical operation depends on the causes involved, the necessity of effects following invariably on their causes. For example, water always boils at one hundred degrees centigrade under standard conditions. There is something in matter by reason of which solids always expand under heat and contract when cooled.

If science is concerned with causes, if it is a *cognitio certa per causas,* then sciences will be distinguished by reason of the kinds of causes they are concerned with. Our first task, then, is to clarify just what we mean by a cause. When a principle, i.e. something first, has a positive influx on its consequent, that is, when it leaves something of itself in its consequent, it is called a cause. For example, a father leaves an imprint of himself on his child, a poet on his poem, fire on the wood it burns. If one came upon a chair in the middle of a desert island, one would know immediately that a man had been there. A chair embodies in itself something of the spiritual intellect that conceived and produced it. Every effect resembles its cause since something of the cause itself is clearly present in the consequent.

Therefore, you can reason back from effect to cause and ahead, from cause to effect, in prediction. Thus, you can know something when you know it according to its causes. For Aristotle, in order really to know a substance in any basic fashion, we must know the four causes that explain it. He lists these as the efficient cause, the maker; the final cause, the end for which the thing is made and the maker acts; the formal cause, that which makes a thing the kind of thing it is; the material cause, that out of which the thing is made.

In regard to existence, the efficient cause of a thing is, of course, the most important, but for the purposes of knowledge, the formal cause is the primary object. For once the formal cause is known, you can work back to the efficient cause, and ahead to the final cause. It gives the knowing being a power over things, a control of their intelligible aspects.

To locate this formal cause in reality, to understand just what it is that we mean when we speak of form or essence or nature, principles that are the key to the understanding of knowledge, an analogy may prove useful. Analogies have a certain importance in philosophy. Not that they provide in themselves an illumination of those intelligibilities which are so immersed in concrete, individual reality, that they cannot be intelligently disengaged, but must be experientially communicated, as in practical, poetic knowledge; not in this direct fashion is the analogy of value to the philosopher as it is to the poet. But it does serve to rivet the attention of the mind on the precise aspect of reality to be investigated; to provide the rich imagery and emotional resonances psychologically necessary to rational activity to keep it revolving about its exact object, and thus to make possible the eventual intellectual penetration of a problem to intelligible depths at which otherwise it is very difficult to arrive. It is only in this fashion that we make use of images, metaphors, and similes, not for the intelligibilities they occasion more directly in their proper role in a practical knowledge such as poetry.

If we consider the dissolution of three representative life forms, a man, a dog and a rose bush, we find that they may be reduced to the same kind of synthesis in organic chemistry, carbon and its compounds, and to exactly the same materials in inorganic compounds. If the material to which these things may be reduced in their dissolution is the same, and if the elements out of which they are constructed are similar, the same basic elements, then how do we account for the differences among a man, a dog, and a rose bush? The differences of things demand some basic principle of difference. There must be something different in a man and a dog, if the same meat and cheese when eaten is woven in one case into a hand, in the other, a paw. Matter alone cannot account for the differences of things. There must be some principle of organization which makes a man a man, a dog a dog, and a rose bush a rose bush. There must be some principle of organization that takes the zygote or primary living cell of a human being and moulds it, shapes it, organizes it into a man. Likewise, it is the same for the dog and the rose bush. This is what the scholastics meant by form:—that by which a thing is what it is, that by which a man is a man, a dog a dog, and a rose bush a rose bush. And this is what we mean by the soul of things. A soul is simply a certain kind of form, the form of a living body, a form from which flows the immanent operations that characterize living beings, nutrition, growth, reproduction, sensation, locomotion, intellection, and volition.

If this is what it means to be a soul, then the canard, "I never found a soul under my scalpel," becomes ridiculous! Where does the heart come from? What organizes lungs out of the bread and butter we eat? What systematizes protoplasm into the awesome complexity of the human brain tissue? Every time you shake hands with a man, you touch his soul. In his five fingers with their protective nails, we see the stamp of the soul on the body, the principle of organization that makes a thing to be what it is.

This, of course, is not a proof for the existence of forms in things. We simply mean to point out the intellectual absurdity of a speculative materialism. We do not mean practical materialism. That is very understandable. Man has always been attracted and torn asunder within himself by the compelling beauties and delights of the material things that beckon to the hungers of his own nature. All of us well know the fascination of this type of materialism. But a speculative materialism, an intellect that can reduce all the complexities of reality into one basic homogeneous stuff, matter, that can ignore the obvious differences in things, so that a man, an automobile, the sun blazing out the sky, and the rose bush it warms and vivifies, are all made of but one homogeneous, basic stuff, this we find absurd. It is the differences of things which are more important than that which they have in common, and it is their differences by which they are specified when they are known to us as a man, a dog, or a rose bush. We shall have more to say about this later.

Since science is properly a knowledge of causes, then the different sciences will vary by reason of the kind of causes they seek. In the philosophical ones we are concerned with the ultimate causes of all things. We are looking for the most basic principles which make things what they are, and, consequently, explain them. The philosophical sciences deal with what a thing is in its last analysis. Because they are concerned with ultimate causes, the philosophical sciences study essences directly; and since they know essences, the method of procedure must be deductive. From the application of these general principles, they arrive at knowledge in particular cases. For example, once we know that in essence man is body and soul, if we know that Reginald is a man, we know that he is composed of body and soul. If we see the essential relation of speech to man's essence, then the same type of deduction follows. Man has a body and more specifically, lungs and vocal cords by reason of which he can produce sound. He is also possessed of an intellect that produces concepts which find their verbal expression in these sounds. Once we see the essential connection of man's fundamental constitution and the power of speech, we know that wherever we encounter a human being, he will have the power of speech, by which, however, we do not mean the actual exercise of speech as in conversation, so that the dumb man would lack the power of speech. By the power of speech, we mean rather the inner structure or faculty by reason of which man can speak. A doctor who is skillful enough could make a dumb man speak. Man has the power of speech even when he is silent, just as the swimming champion has the ability to swim even while sunning himself on the sands. Also, since these philosophical sciences tell that things are and attempt to explain the essences of things, they are called explanatory in mode.

On the other hand, in mathematical sciences we are concerned with proximate causes, i.e., the quantities of things abstracted from concrete things. Quantity is the accident from which flow size, weight, dimension, measurability and divisibility. However, although abstracted from concrete things, nevertheless the objects of mathematics exist only in the mind. We abstract roundness from an apple or squareness from a table top, and mentally construct a circle and a square which do not exist outside the mind. Only the roundness and squareness exist in reality as a real accidental characteristic of real things. Like the point, which takes on height, width, and thickness when drawn, the circle and square can only exist in their simplicity and perfection in the mind. They are intellectual constructs and this is precisely the reason for the celebrated certitude of mathematical thought. Since the objects of mathematics exist in the mind, since they are produced by the mind, since they are cut of the same cloth as the mind, we can know them exhaustively. And since we know them exhaustively we can deduce from them with absolute certitude. We deal with the essences of these accidents which we have constructed mentally. We can know the essence of a square, though not the essence of a square thing. From this we can see the fallacy of those knowledges like education, sociology, and economics which, in order to become sciences, model themselves upon mathematics. In order to attain a share of the certainty of mathematical knowledge, some are of the opinion that all they have to do is to sprinkle their work with numbers, graphs, and esoteric definitions, the nearest thing in words to mathematical formulae. They fail to realize that the source of mathematical certitude is neither the mere presence of numbers nor the rigor of deductive procedure, but rather the simplicity of the objects involved. Mathematical entities, since we make them, are known exhaustively. When we know that the triangle is a three-sided figure, the sum of whose angles equals one hundred and eighty degrees, then we have captured a triangle; everything else can be deducted from the first principles of geometry. But real things are much more complex than abstract quantity. There is a whole wealth of intelligibility that we ignore when we designate a thing as two, or circular. We cannot know the essences of real things so exhaustively because the human intellect cannot possess absolutely all that is knowable in things. However, the fact that just because education and sociology cannot arrive at the same degree of certitude as mathematics does not mean that they are unimportant by comparison, as some pseudo-scientists today seem to think. When Aristotle said that a little knowledge about the highest things is more valuable than a great deal of knowledge of the lowest things, he put his finger on the point at issue. Since man is of such importance, anything that we can know about his development, relationships and well-being is by that fact very valuable. Even the little that is known becomes of much more importance than a mountain of mathematical fact about lower things. This realization should give the social scientist a conception of his own dignity independent of a slavish humility to mathematics and physics, a sense of the worth of his own knowledge. Because his insights are incapable of exhausting the richness of human nature, must he reduce this richness to the barrenness of quantitative relations?

The natural sciences on the other hand deal with proximate causes, the accidents of things. They do not care what things are. They do not know essences immediately. If we ask of the various sciences: "What is man?," we receive the answers we saw earlier. For the physicist, man is an articulating system of stresses and strains; for the chemist, man is a complexus of elements and compounds;

for the biologist, he is a mammal of the order of primates, that is, he has a vertebra so constructed that he walks upright, and a certain type of gland by which he is enabled to suckle his young; for the economist, he is a producer and consumer; for the philosopher he is a rational animal. All these sciences except philosophy define the things they deal with in terms of accidents, whether of quantity or otherwise. One thing we do know is that philosophy, when, for instance, it defines man as a rational animal, whether right or wrong, is at least attempting to tell us *what* things are, something that not one of the other sciences alone, or all of them together, attempt to do.

When the physicist, in illustration of the law of acceleration, drops objects from the Empire State Building, as long as the objects have the same weight and dimensions the results then will be the same. It makes no difference whether this article is a man, a sack of potatoes, or a barrel of flour. The job of the physicist is not to tell what things are but only how they operate. He is concerned only with matter in motion. Now although we do not know essences in the way that we do in the philosophical and mathematical sciences, essences, however, cannot be completely eliminated from the natural sciences. For if we deny the very existence of essences, then we find it impossible to preserve the scientific character of the natural sciences. If there are no essences in things, then the inductive method is reduced to a raw enumeration which in no way carries with it the principle of its own necessity. If we deny the existence of essences, it follows therefore that certainty and necessity so necessary to scientific method have no basis. Simply because a given number of instances have been examined, as in examining ten men we see that they have the power of speech, are we then justified in formulating the general law that all men have the power of speech? If we find that in each case water boils at one hundred degrees centigrade under standard conditions, are we justified in stating that in all cases water boils at one hundred degrees centigrade under standard conditions? Does this simple enumeration carry any more weight than the fact that since we have found in every case that broomsticks have red bands, the next time we come across a broomstick it is going to have a red band? Why cannot the next man we meet not have the power of speech?

It is only if there is something about man by reason of which he has the power of speech and if there is something in his inner structure from which this characteristic flows, that we can preserve the scientific character of induction. Unless there is some essential connection between the thing and its characteristic property, there is consequently no foundation for the certainty of scientific knowledge. Therefore, although the natural scientist does not deal with essences immediately, he cannot deny their existence, otherwise he cuts away the scientific character of his own knowledge. Certain modern scientists have seen the problem in just this way and suicidally followed out the consequences of their denial of essences. The result has been that they have actually denied the certainty of their own knowledge and reduced scientific law to mere probability, a conclusion that contradicts both science and experience.

If the natural sciences do not know essences, then of course their method cannot be a deductive one whereby one works from the essence to the properties that flow from it; rather the method they use must be inductive, and they proceed from the particular to some sort of general conclusion, a progressive approximation of the essence, an approximation which, for their purposes, can be used as a substitute for essence in their scientific advancement.

Freedom will never enter into the natural sciences as a constitutive element of the object of these sciences. Freedom as a spiritual reality lies outside the scope of knowledges such as physics, chemistry, and biology. If the physical scientist does attempt to include freedom within the sphere proper to his knowledge, the presumption is inexcusable and the result disastrous. The culmination of such a misapprehension of the nature and method of the natural sciences is of course the complete elimination of freedom and the substitution of the necessity of physical law to a field of human behavior utterly foreign to it. If the physicist is concerned with matter and motion, then freedom must be reduced to a function of matter or vacate its claims to reality. This is the origin of a determinism that would resolve all free action into a multiplicity of causes so complex that since we are not able at one particular moment to discover and evaluate the precise contribution of each to any human action, we, consequently, substitute the freedom of action for our ignorance of its real causes. Therefore, we reiterate, freedom is not a constituent of the object of the natural sciences, and, as a result, the natural scientist is not qualified in his office of scientist to judge of the existence or non-existence of freedom as a basic component of reality. This does not mean that as a man, in his daily experience of common sense knowledge, he ignores the obvious presence of freedom as an experiential datum. He well knows that he can or need not, as he wills, reserve a hotel room at the end of his trip. He is perfectly aware of his ability to take the car or walk to work. We have again that basic contradiction of two legitimate knowledges indicating the erroneous conclusion of one. But the precise knowledge for which the natural scientist is respected and from which flows whatever authority is attached to his statements, has no bearing on the question involved. We might as well ask the professional mathematician the best method of high diving. True, he might know, but then he would have to be a diver as well as a mathematician. Thus, the scientist rejects free will because it introduces an element of disorder into the universe, an element which is not predictable. But freedom is not anarchy, and in casting a doubt on the absoluteness of whim or noting the absurdity of uncontrolled behavior, the free man is by no means losing sight of the everyday meaning of freedom. He is merely doubting or denying the existence of any such thing as a core of indetermination at the root of an ordered, orderly thing. In this sense he agrees with the scientist who refuses to admit in a measurable, predictable world the presence of a fundamental anarchy or disorder at the heart of that supreme artistic production of nature, the human being. But such an indetermination does not make sense because it does not exist. Freedom is harmony, not anarchy. The anthem of freedom is not sung off key; it is in tune with the universe. It is an ignorance of the true nature of freedom that causes so many erroneous notions of freedom.

Along with the common experience of the fact of freedom that the physical scientist shares with the rest of mankind, there is a precise and important way in which freedom does enter into his office as a scientist, but not as a constitutive element of the object of his science. For freedom does enter into the initiation and direction of research into the control that he exercises over his productions. Science is not an autonomous being pursuing its own solitary aims; nor is it some juggernaut that must advance even though it entails the destruction of every obstacle. Science is an operation of the human being and like all the operations of man it has as its end and purpose the perfection of man. Therefore, the pattern of control is laid very clearly. If this instrument will be disastrous for man, should I produce it? When the scientist can make a bomb that will destroy the world, is he free to make it? It is here that the problems of freedom with their inextricably tangled implications are to be found. This is one of the crucial decisions of our age.

The physicist seems to have greater personal freedom in his rejection of scientific theory, but only because his scientific judgment lacks the urgency of the concrete prudential judgment with its necessity of action. A man who is standing on the edge of a cliff awaiting the charge of an angry bull cannot remain indifferent or in a state of suspended judgment like the scientist. The particular circumstances of his situation make a decision imperative. Likewise in the political and social areas the urgency of a situation demands immediate assent or dissent. Therefore, the freedom proper to the professional physicist within his own field could never be extended absolutely to the area of political and social affairs. Such an extension would be disastrous. Certain eminent physicists seem to be completely unaware of this fact.

Economics, psychology, sociology and education are not sciences, but rather the application of the methods of the natural sciences to realities and areas of investigation which lie outside these methods. The great scandal of our day has been that these knowledges have modeled themselves on mathematical physics in order to partake of its scientific stature. But, as we have seen, it is not possible to make sciences out of these knowledges by the mere insertion of numbers.

In order that economics might become a science it would have to operate in an absolute planned society. The sociologist would have deliberately to disrupt families under artificial conditions to be able to predict the outcome of social forces as they operate, for instance, in divorce. Psychology must reduce man to a determined effect of determinable causes in order to arrive at any satisfactory so-called scientific knowledge of his behavior.

Freedom enters into the subject matter of economics, for instance, as a constituent variable and it is for this reason that economics can never achieve scientific stature. As long as human beings have the power, despite coercive advertising and propaganda, to say yes or no, to buy or to refuse to buy, then the so-called laws of economics can never become necessary or certain. Free human acts can never become predictable in any absolute fashion, no matter how eager its ardent proponents are to make a science out of such a body of knowledge. And here a danger exists. For the attempt to make a science of economics usually follows one of two roads, each entailing the elimination of human freedom. One, by a certain absorption of individual free actions into an almost mystical mathematicism, a corruption of the proper role of statistical knowledge. This is very dangerous when the statistics are used as directive of action without sufficient corroboration.

The second or alternative method of removing the frustrating inadequacy of modern economics is by a direct attack on freedom itself. In the completely planned economy, economics would be possessed of an absolute value. In a society in which the economist possessed an exact index of production (because the worker was told where to work, what to produce and how much) and in which he also had at his command the precise consumption (because each worker was given just so many tickets and so could consume just so much and not more), there is a real temptation for the professional economist. He may possess an exhaustive index of necessary economic facts. He may predict in absolute fashion like that paragon of scientific knowledge, the mathematical physicist. He may become a scientist. There is a terrible temptation to power and a very real fascination in the planned economy which we must keep in mind when consulting the economist on the proper direction of economic progress and achievement.

But economics, although it is not concerned with the nature of freedom, is interested in the precise structure for attaining freedom in the economic order. Both phases of freedom, both choice and autonomy, are necessarily represented. Freedom of choice finds its natural expression in the self-determination of the worker to choose his work and his employer, while autonomy is found in the obligation of the entire society to bring about those material conditions consonant with the highest development of the specifically human powers of man. Consumption implies need and thus is an instrument for freeing man from the slavery to his material wants. Thus advertising, in its effects on consumption should not enslave man by an excitation of desire and emotion to a point where he can never free himself from these artificial needs, terrible in their obsession. Production, likewise, is bound up with competition, price policies and regulations, saturated with the stuff of freedom. Monetary economics, finance, profits, investment, taxation, interest, all of these have a profound bearing on human freedom, and since money is the standard means of acquiring economic goods, it must be handled so as to free all, not only the favored few.

It is here that the economist and kindred thinkers such as the sociologist and the political scientist make their contribution to human freedom, for example, the labor relations expert is almost completely dedicated to preserving freedom in employment. The conditions of workers, labor problems, wages, unions are all devices to gain and preserve the liberty of human beings.

Since psychology has attempted to model itself upon the methods and techniques of physics, to the extent of its success in doing so, it has been deprived of the ability to analyze freedom as a proper object; in fact it has cut itself off from the interpretation of any immaterial reality. Evidence of this is the disproportionate amount of space in contemporary psychology texts devoted to the treatment of sensation as compared to the pitifully inadequate treatment of what is called "imageless thought." What is so tragic is not only that immaterial operations such as freedom do not fall within the proper scope of psychology thus conceived, but that psychologists believe this ignorance to be all that our knowledge can attain to, in understanding itself. They do not realize that there is a scientific knowledge of man's intellectual processes about which entire volumes have been written and to which men of genius have dedicated their entire lives. That is the price that a man of one knowledge must pay. But the shame of it is that society must subsidize his intellectual bankruptcy.

Contemporary psychology is a hybrid knowledge. It is composed of many techniques and methods drawn from several knowledges, possessing only the artificial unity of a common subject matter. Part of it falls under the natural sciences along with sociology, economics and education, especially experimental psychology. Adolescent psychology, child psychology and much of the study of personality actually belong to the knowledge of common sense and, at times, practical knowledge. Thus, the dicta of the child psychologist should not be given the authority of the scientist. When we are told that we should not spank our children, this is not a certain conclusion of the science of psychology but rather the considered judgment of a prudent, experienced mind. Although we owe these judgments respect, we should not accord to them a necessity even when they contradict common sense.

These people—sociologists, psychologists, educators—are not scientists. They have not a method which they can rely on completely—and yet they run our lives. They do valuable and necessary work which we could not do without. But their contribution is in a different order. They are not scientists, they are sages. An educator of experience, his harsh iconoclasm and academic dogmatism mellowed by time, a man of great intelligence who has centered his intellectual powers constantly upon the problems of this field, whose life has revolved around the difficulties of the classroom, he or she should be able to see more deeply and with clearer insight into the confusion of human relations. He is not a scientist, he is a sage. And his opinion should have a high value and carry great weight. If any one is to know the answers, he should, and so his advice should be sought and should play a part in every major decision. He is a sage, the wise man who has prudential wisdom. But he is not a scientist, his judgments do not carry the necessity of physical law. They are not always right; they may be half wrong. They may be completely wrong. Therefore, such judgments should not rigorously determine the actions of men. We should not be controlled and determined by the latest fad of progressive educators. Occasionally they themselves do see their mistakes. But all too often we find the same rigorous exercise of a method which they would be the last ones to claim infallible, and the same dogmatic imposition of personal opinion and insight, which no matter how well trained it is, is still not scientific law.

Since psychology, like economics, models itself on physics, the problem of freedom will present itself in the same way. One of the reasons for the success of the Freudian interpretation of psychological phenomena lies in its reducing all human operations to some determined, albeit unknown, concatenation of causes. The superego, the ego and the id, are concepts more abstract than metaphysical notions. Freud has transliterated the very facts of which ancient and medieval psychologists were very much aware into a denial of human freedom. This reconciliation of the conclusions of psychology with its own materialistic methods and techniques is in good part responsible for the fame of Freud. Every trace of the immaterial has been eliminated from fundamental human behavior.

Education, likewise, is not a science, and its conclusions do not carry the authority that scientific conclusions do. Yet such is the confusion sometimes evident in the behavior of professional educationists that they seek to impress on millions of malleable human beings as absolute fact what may have only the certitude of opinion. Drastic and revolutionary changes in these fields should be undertaken very cautiously and deliberately in conformity with the type of knowledge that we have of these areas. For our knowledge here does not possess the certainty it does in science and therefore is not as reliable a guide. Thus the relatively contemporary innovation of public education should proceed cautiously and be very loathe to discard the lessons learned from the history of education which has been private and religious. I am holding no brief against public education, of course, but it is amazing to find some of its advocates who do not realize the comparative inexperience and apprenticeship of the state in education. The inability to locate religion in its proper place in our school systems is merely one example. We must proceed slowly and be willing to learn from the past.

It is in a recognition of the fundamental freedom of the human being and an attempt to preserve its dignity, that the so-called progressive education has found so much of its strength and appeal. But the spontaneity of progressive education must be restricted and channeled by the rules of discipline. A progressive education with its loose curriculum and the traditional education with its planned curriculum based on the development of the whole man, are but one phase of the relations of initial freedom and freedom of autonomy.

Just as there are different types of knowledges, science being the highest, and different kinds of science, among which philosophy holds a prominent place, so also there is more than one philosophical science. These divisions of philosophy may be distinguished by the degrees of materiality consonant with their mode of operation. If a thing is intelligible in proportion to its immateriality, then the more immaterial the knowledge, the more perfect it is. The degree to which the mind departs from the materiality of things is the basis of distinction between the different philosophical sciences. The philosophy of nature deals with things that cannot exist without matter nor be thought of without matter. That is why the object of this science is moving or changing being, matter and motion, because matter is the principle of change in things. The philosophy of mathematics is concerned with things that cannot exist without matter but can be thought of without matter; for example, the circle abstracted from an apple. But metaphysics, the highest of the philosophical sciences, has as its proper object things that can both exist and be thought of without matter, such as God, angels, honor, love.

The relationships between the philosophy of nature and natural science are precise ones. The philosopher of nature cannot afford to ignore the discoveries and achievements of the natural science of his day. He must be steeped in it. For example, the periodic chart is a much better illustration of the theory of matter and form than the famous four elements of antiquity, earth, air, fire, and water; nor on the other hand can the natural sciences ignore the philosophy of nature. One of the most critical problems that faces the modern scientist is the question of the unity of the sciences. How can the various natural sciences be unified and their mountainous collection of data be coordinated? One way of achieving such a unity entails the choice of one science as the principle of unity of the others. But there is no one natural science that includes within its object the proper objects of the other sciences in order to serve as a unifying instrument. The search is frustrating when it is for a principle of unification on the level of the methods and techniques of the natural sciences for a kind of universal natural science. But the philosophy of nature can be a principle of unification for the natural sciences. Being outside of them, it can provide direction and order. For example, the alchemists in their reputed search for the philosopher's stone, maintained that a base metal could be transmuted into a precious metal. At a time when the chemists and natural scientists of the day generally ridiculed their efforts in view of the theory that the elements were supposed to be the ultimate indivisible units of reality, the alchemists knew that it could be done because they had learned from Aristotle the structure of material substance. The natural scientist was not aware of this until the actual transmutation of certain periodic elements was accomplished in the nineteen-thirties, and most convincing of all, the production of new substances as an accompaniment of atomic fission. The philosophy of nature in this way is capable of giving direction and order to the natural sciences and thus of acting as the principle of unity for all.

This does not mean that we would have just one science, the philosophy of nature, with all the so-called natural sciences as mere applications of this universal knowledge, more artistic then scientific. It is certainly true that art plays an important role in the natural sciences. It takes the skill of an engineer to perform many experiments even in biology, the least organized of the sciences. But the natural sciences do possess an autonomous scientific character, and this must be maintained against those who would attack the natural sciences and categorically deny their proper autonomy. The philosophy of nature and the natural sciences deal with one and the same set of principles; for instance, that it is the soul from which flow life itself and also the local motion that the physicist studies. Therefore, should we have only one science, the physical of the ancients and medievals? This is not a position to be lightly dismissed for it dominated men's minds for centuries.

But ontological principles are not necessarily the principles of a particular science. The intellect makes precisions in the things it studies; that is precisely what we mean by the formal object of a science. The natural sciences have their own type of formal object, the proximate causes of things as we have seen, which is a legitimate area of investigation. They are capable of a unified treatment of their proper object, self-sufficient and independent of philosophical procedure. The law of acceleration and Boyle's law are evidence that it is possible scientifically to delimit one's field of operation. The possibility of such a phenomenon as the atomic theory or the theory of evolution suggests the autonomous nature of these knowledges. They find principles of unity within their own proper spheres. We do not mean that the atomic theory and the theory of evolution are philosophical substitutes. Actually, they are not, in spite of the fact that many scientists do not seem unaware of that fact. But they do show how, on the level of the natural sciences, they, themselves, can provide the unification of their own knowledge so necessary for scientific progress. The fact that so many advances have been made by scientists wholly unaware of even the possibility of philosophical thought, argues a certain autonomy of procedure; otherwise how could they have accomplished any genuine scientific work, if while they denied essences, they needed essences as a constituent of their proper object?

Of all the human knowledges, there is none more abstract and difficult to comprehend than metaphysics. It is from its exalted position as the supreme achievement of the human intellect in the natural order that its difficulties flow. The more profound a science, the more difficult of comprehension. And it is precisely because of these difficulties that metaphysics has fallen into such disfavor today. I am certain that a survey of philosophy courses throughout the country would find less time and effort spent on metaphysics than any other branch of philosophy. Then, too, the objection might well carry weight: how can certain parts of psychology, for example, the immortality of the soul, be intelligible without metaphysics, or how can one discuss the nature of philosophy itself? How can an ethics be taught without a thorough grounding in the notions of essence and nature?

There is a real need then to make metaphysics comprehensible, and to make it intelligible without doing violence to its nature. This study is an experiment in the satisfaction of this need, not so much by an adequate treatment of the principles and structure of metaphysics, as a means of indicating the framework of its application. Our purpose is to show not what metaphysics is (a difficult enough question), but rather what metaphysics does,—which explains in a way what it is.

Metaphysics is not merely a collection of insights on the level of the deepest penetration into reality. It is a science, and as such, it begins some place and goes somewhere. There is an initial starting point and a necessary direction. The scientific sequence of problems is not an arbitrary one. When the speculative mind enters within the structure of being there is a dynamic pattern or geography that it must follow. The movement of a metaphysics is as rigorous as that of a geometry or a logic. The science of being is very far from being a fanciful production of the creative imagination, fluid and amorphous. It is stiffened with the iron of a mental discipline, the certainty and necessity of the scientific character it eminently possesses.

Looking back over our analysis of the nature of knowledge and the application of the different knowledges to freedom, we realize that if we are to initiate our examination with the nature of freedom, then these first papers must be philosophical because philosophy, alone of all the forms of knowledge, is properly concerned with essences or natures; and the foundation of psychology, for instance, and indeed of all knowledges, is laid in metaphysics.

Thus far, we have been using the word, *free,* to designate a being that is master of itself though influenced by external things and jostled by irrelevant events. Of course, rather than a definition, this is the mere beginning of a description on the level of common sense. In order to describe more fully the whole realm of freedom, we must explore those recesses of human behaviour open only to philosophical science.

It is not within the scope of this introductory study to begin the analysis of freedom itself. However, we should like to call attention to the division of the first two philosophical treatments of freedom.

Much of the confusion and difficulty that surrounds modern questions of freedom flow precisely from the twofold aspect of freedom itself, due to which freedom seems often to be in conflict with itself. This mortal contradiction is revealed on all levels of human thought and activity. Although it has been the object of a variety of names and distinctions, the terms, Initial Freedom and Freedom of Autonomy, seem to be as accurate as any.

Basically, freedom is something that an intellectual being possesses and expresses in its ability to make choices. Human acts are termed free acts because of the relation they have to an intellect. It is precisely in the ability of the human mind to form the concept of Goodness that we discover one of the elements of freedom. The transcendental concept of Goodness is the very distillation of whatever good there is in the universe, and as such it is precisely the crystallized object of the profoundest yearnings and deepest hungers of this human nature of ours. Having once lost itself in this vision of total splendor to which all the rest of the universe is blind, the will, because it is enamored of all Good cannot be completely ensnared by any partial good. This freedom of choice, however, is not an unmixed perfection. The ability to do what is contrary to the exigencies of nature is not entirely enviable. Freedom is a responsibility of frightening proportions. For a being of finite, limited intelligence to be able to will exactly as it wishes, leaves it with a basic insecurity and fear of the results of its actions. To be faced with a world that I can and will change, for better or worse, when I am not sure of what better or worse actually is, presents a problem of disquieting implications. Freedom, in that sense, is a painful thing and a liability to the creature that is free. Thus, this initial plunge into motion by a being hitherto under the rule of the determination and necessity that flow from non-intellectual nature must find its completion or fruition in the achievement of that Good which is proper to man and in which his perfection consists, what has been known as freedom of autonomy. The virtuous man, for instance, has brought the entire complexus of causes of human behavior into harmony with the end perceived by his intellect, so that the dissonances of appetite are reconciled in the symphony of the soul where every faculty is intent upon its contribution to the whole without violation of its due autonomy. That man, then, is truly free who restricts freedom of choice to the choice of means consonant with his end, and there is a progressive advance in freedom paralleling the progressive achievement of his destiny.

Freedom is not merely and exclusively freedom of choice; nor is it only the exercise of a choice of means, each of which can be assigned the character of Goodness itself by a being that looks through a partial goodness to the vision of absolute Goodness of which it is the expression. In a fuller and more complete sense, freedom is found in the realization of the end of the nature wherein the person is independent of the remainder of reality, as only a being which has realized its perfection is free and thus no longer is enslaved by the means through which it achieved its autonomy. Thus, in the examination of the nature of freedom both these aspects must be studied.

Because the analysis of freedom will vary with the particular metaphysics involved, the metaphysical location of freedom, therefore, is of prime importance. It is no secret that there is a plurality of metaphysics. A metaphysics of essence will emphasize the proper role of intelligence in the specification of the will and the spontaneity of the volitional act will be explained as an ultimate operation of nature, a tendency flowing from the immanent principle of immanent action of a spiritual being. The ultimate explanation of freedom is thus, in fact, located on the level of the philosophy of nature.

On the other hand, an existential metaphysics provides the explanation of the autonomous operation of the will, the ultimate spontaneity of the volitional act on a properly metaphysical level. The act of existence, the fundamental metaphysical principle, is the dynamic aspect of being that expresses itself in human acts in the spontaneity of the will. The ultimate, irreducible fact of freedom is this ability of the will to be the source of its own movements. The freedom of an act is possible because of the dynamism of existence, the source of its own energy expressing itself through the specification of the intellect just as essence delimits existence, so in the free act, the intellect specifies the operation of the will.

It is the office of philosophy to examine the nature of things while the other knowledges, as we have seen, are more concerned with freedom in practice, they want to know how to attain and conserve freedom. In the larger perspective of things these knowledges are all complementary and supplementary. They are not mutually exclusive or contradictory.

Granted the Christian economy, theology, too, must be a science precisely because it is the most certain and necessary of all knowledges since it is founded on the Word of God. In the light of this fact, the relations between freedom and authority are clearly delineated. The charge that the Church is undemocratic makes sense only to a mentality that exalts the socio-political order to the supreme pinnacle of reality, that makes politics a metaphysics by which it judges all things. Democratic is an adjective that belongs to the order of politics and applies especially to that method of deciding issues by the vote of the majority, claiming this to be the best way of preserving the freedom and dignity of the individual citizen. It rebels against political coercion.

But to call a church undemocratic because it does not permit opinion to run roughshod over religious truths is to make that same mistake of confusing two orders of knowledge. Do we settle the time of the rising of the sun by the vote of the majority,—or the rate of acceleration of a falling body, or the boiling point of water? It is a fact that God either exists or He does not. Can that be settled by the vote of the majority? The vote is of value only in concrete prudential decisions where certitude cannot be arrived at and a course of action must follow.

If we lived in a world where there was no revelation, then an absolute and unbridled freedom both of thought and religion might be countenanced. But if Revelation is a fact, then never again can man reason as if he were unaware of these same fundamental truths. We do know that God exists, that He created the world and that, as a part of creation we owe Him love and obedience. In this lies our fulfillment and the completion of our natures. It is ignorance that is the worst slavery, because when you do not know something, then precisely you do not know. The most terrible thing about ignorance is that the ignorant man does not know what he does not know. He is not even aware of his own ignorance, because otherwise he would know in some way that which he does not know.

Dogma, therefore, instead of being an obstacle to man's freedom, is, in reality, an aid, precisely because it frees him from that ignorance which makes freedom impossible. Man must know what he is and how to act in accordance with what he is, if he is to achieve the estate of a free man. Dogma does not coerce and enslave the mind. It guides it. The history of the councils of the Church is there to show us that the definition of doctrine was made precisely when great danger of error was present, when men needed guidance to see the truth. In this sense, dogma, as paradoxical as it may sound to the contemporary mentality, is an instrument of freedom, especially of the freedom of autonomy.

The fact of freedom is evident and is written on the hearts of all men as a basic human value unless obscured by an erroneous theory of freedom. But to understand the nature of freedom is a complete scientific and intellectual venture of which not all are capable. Therefore, they must accept the results of those who ought to know, that is, the scientists. This places a sobering responsibility on the intellectual and the scientist. He cannot follow any intellectual will-of-the-wisp he pleases. He cannot scribble off any chance phrase simply because it delights the ear and tickles the sensibilities. He is thinking for the human race and his thought, whether he will or not, is affecting the lives of many more people than he suspects. The parading of one's ignorance in public as the height of scientific method is unforgivable.

We do not ask anyone to bolt this entire intellectual structure in one swallow. Enough if he chews awhile on this or that. But we do demand that he recognize the unity of our thought. What we have to say about freedom is not a collection of chance conclusions and random recollections centered about one topic. These conclusions are drawn from principles synthesized into a total view of reality, judgments that include within themselves a perspective of the problems under consideration from all aspects. We do not amputate the arm in order to examine, in scientific isolation, a broken finger. We observe the movements of the finger as the culminative articulation of the entire body. And it is for this reason that our analysis of freedom is of prime importance, because we shall not sacrifice one freedom while pursuing another, because we see all the articulations of freedom in one grand, intelligible pattern, wherein even their conflicts when not resolved, are reconciled, the first step to resolution in practice.

Part I

The Metaphysics of Freedom

The Initial Freedom

by JOSEPH G. SCULLY
Professor of Philosophy,
University College, St. John's University

The world is divided today into two opposing ways of life: one recognizes the freedom of the individual to make the decisions that shape and direct the course of his life and development; the other denies and suppresses that freedom and makes the human individual a mere cog in a social machine designed and operated by an elite of social engineers. The former way of life is that of the Democratic West; the latter way of life is that of the Communist World Revolution.

> Every day makes more evident the fact that two strong essentially incompatible ways of life will divide the loyalties of men and nations in the political world of tomorrow. They are genuine Democracy and Marxian totalitarianism.[1]

This paper is addressed to those who accept as beyond question the value and desirability of individual freedom and to those who reject from the depth of their souls any social order which reduces man to the level of a mechanical cog in a social machine. It is also addressed to those who love freedom and who regard life without freedom as something less than human.

This paper is written with the sad realization that individual freedom, precious as it is, is something that can be abused, and in its abuse can generate the conditions that lead millions to fear it and flee from it and then seek relief in the glowing promises of its opponents.

It is written, finally, in the hope that modern man of the mid-twentieth century, seeing individual freedom abused, may be brought to the realization that if freedom is to be preserved, it must be exercised in accord with its own nature as proceeding from the nature of man. That we should understand as accurately as possible the nature of freedom and the nature of the rational individual who exercises it, is of basic importance.

It is in the light of the principles of the philosophy of Western Judaeo-Christian tradition that we shall examine the nature of man and of his freedom. It appears to be wisdom to go to the mother and generator of our freedom and our free institutions to learn both what they are in their nature and how they can be exercised and preserved.

We shall proceed in a certain order in this paper so that we shall know not only what freedom is, but also what must exist in order for freedom to exist. We shall begin with the notion of an individual thing and proceed to the individual human being. In passing, we shall take notice of the origin of the question of the *one* and the *many* and the solution as presented by the doctrine of Aristotle and Aquinas. With the principles of that solution we shall depend upon the "matter-form theory" as explaining the ultimate nature of all material things. We shall then be ready to consider St. Thomas' concept of incommunicable individuality—subsistence—and the subsistence of the rational soul and its importance in the metaphysical structure of man. We shall then undertake to relate the activity of the rational individual and individuals that do not possess rationality with free activity, as contrasted with necessary activity. We shall then be in a position to make an analysis of the free act and consider precisely what it means to be free. Finally, we shall turn to the extrinsic root of freedom, to the question touching on the relation of the free secondary, created cause, to the First Cause, God.

"What makes a man a man?" is a simple normal question for a child to ask. Yet, the answer to this and to that of how a man or any thing can be, must be found in a most necessary science, Metaphysics. The metaphysical structure of a thing is simply what must be in a thing in order for it to exist. Metaphysics is an account of reality in terms of being. Being is the first notion the human mind attains and our first judgments are judgments of being.

A man is a being existing in himself. He is not a part of the reality of something else, as the leg of a chair is a part of the reality of the chair or as the color of the rose is a part of the reality of the rose. To deny this fact in the structure of man would establish him with a structure in being not unlike that of a single leaf of a tree, deriving its status from the great organism, the tree. There are those who regard men as so constituted and find the State as the great organism to which and from which man has his *raison d'être*. Others who regard men as beings with a status in being such as colors have, must consequently regard them as merely passing aspects of some national or class reality.

Those who do admit in man's structure the paramount fact of existing in himself, may err by not seeking more in the structure than those factors which constitute any thing as an individual of the species. A horse is an individual of the species "horse" and is of no special importance beyond that of being a representative of a species that is realized in the multitude of horses. The multitude never exhausts the species but establishes the whole of the species at any instant. Man, though similarly an individual of the species "man" which is not exhausted by the totality of men, is so constituted as to be a structural whole in himself. The totality of men is a totality of wholes, because there is that in the structure of man that makes him a person. The person is the most perfect thing in nature.

To take the position that man in his structure exists in himself is merely to say that he is a substance. Here the child might pose another question. Why are there many things? Why are there many trees; many horses; many men? This is no idle question. It must be answered; otherwise, we can not give an intelligent account of the most striking fact of experienced reality, its plurality. This question was first raised in the fifth century, B.C., by Parmenides, to whom Plato gave the title "Father of Philosophy" because he raised the question.

Parmenides put the question this way: How can two beings differ from one another? They can not differ by the fact that they are being, since that is why they are alike, and not different. The only alternative appeared to Parmenides to be that they would have to differ by nothingness. Nothingness can not serve to distinguish two beings since nothing does not exist, and, therefore, it can not serve as a principle of distinction or multiplicity. To Parmenides, the solution was that multiplicity is an illusion; thus his philosophy of the structure of reality contradicted his experience.

The genius of Plato and Aristotle rescued Metaphysics from this impasse. Being, they pointed out, is not as simple as it first appears; we must distinguish in being, between that being which perfectly is, actual being, and that being which is more than mere nothing yet is not all that it can be. This latter being, this capacity for perfection or actuality, Aristotle termed potential being or potentiality. The great tradition in Philosophy has employed this fundamental distinction in being of *Potency* and *Act,* thus making multiplicity intelligible and developing the metaphysical structure of reality in accord with experience. Beings are not distinct from one another simply because they are being. They are distinct from one another and multiplicity is possible, because each one of a plurality is partly potential in its structure. It is a composite of being and a certain capacity for sharing in being. To state it succinctly: beings are composed of *Potency* and *Act.* The rational individual, accordingly, is a substance existing in himself and composed of Potency and Act.

Any material being whose metaphysical structure is under consideration must be viewed as doubly composite, of an *essence* and an *existence,* the *essence* of which is itself a composite of *matter* and *form.* Accordingly in material things, the *Potency,* the passive determinability is *primary matter* while the *Act* or definite perfection of the matter is the *substantial form.* The perfections in the world of material beings which we wonder at and strive to understand are sometimes generic, at other times specific, and frequently they are individual. What exists absolutely is, of course, the individual substance which reveals the generic or the specific as well as its individual perfections. We look at, for example, John Smith who, while possessing the specific perfection of humanity in common with many other individual men, possesses at the same time perfections which belong to him as the individual *John Smith.* He is also in possession of the generic perfections of animality in common with all sentient things.

Human beings, as we know, are in the order of material substances. It might seem a simple, straightforward, intelligent explanation of the possibility of their individuality to say that the perfection (*form*) of humanity in them is able to be multiplied in many individuals because it is received in *primary matter.* This explanation, true as far as it goes, seems to have satisfied a great thinker like Aristotle. But in a Christian atmosphere, rational individuality is too precious to be explained as deriving merely from matter as a determinable, passive principle. The great Schoolmen profoundly investigated the problem, and each of their solutions preserved the unique value of rational individuality. The solution of Thomas Aquinas is outstanding for its simplicity and clarity. We may summarize it as follows:

The principle of individuation is matter. That is to say, it is impossible for a form to be multiplied and to be realized in many individuals of the same species, unless it be a form received in matter and limited by the matter. This, of course, follows from the fact that an act is limited by the potency in which it is received. This Aristotelian teaching which, as can be seen, is a particular application of *Act* and *Potency,* is adopted by St. Thomas even in the case of the human soul.

> Although the intellectual soul, like the angel, has no matter from which it is produced, yet it is the *form* of a certain matter; in which it is unlike an angel. Therefore, according to the division of matter, there are many souls of one species; while it is quite impossible for many angels to be of one species.[2]

St. Thomas made no essential change in the doctrine of Aristotle on matter, yet we must be alert to the deeper and more profound clarification it receives from him because of certain truths of Revelation. To Aristotle, matter is necessary, eternal, independent of the First Cause; to Thomas it was contingent, temporal, and freely created from nothing. Thus does freedom enter into the picture of the world. The world was freely created. Again, on the teaching of matter as the principle of individuation, especially on that concerning the rational individual, St. Thomas goes far beyond the speculation of the Greeks.

By the teaching of matter as the principle of individuation, St. Thomas explained the possibility of multiplying forms in the same species. However, he was far from considering this principle as a sufficient explanation of what constitutes the individual substance as an individual substance, that is, as the immediate and incommunicable subject of independent existence.

The multiplication of individuals in the same species considered simply and solely as multiplication implies limitation, and hence can derive only from the potential principle of composite natures, namely, from the matter. Similarly, multiplication of individuals in general can derive only from a potential principle, namely potentiality to existence.

On the other hand, incommunicable individuality which formally constitutes the subject of independent existence, is of the nature of a perfection, of that sort of perfection which in its formal concept includes no limitation. Hence, it can not derive from a potential principle, but must have its foundation in that which is most perfect in the individual; for it is a participation in that which is absolutely perfect.

The principle of incommunicable individuality, or, more briefly, the principle of individuality as distinguished from the principle of mere individuation or multiplication, is not matter but *subsistence.* It is *subsistence* which constitutes the individual as incommunicably individual, whether the individual be of a composite nature with a form individuated by matter, or of a simple nature (like the angel) with a form independent of, separated from and having no relation whatsoever to matter. To *subsist* in any kind of nature, whether simple like the angel, or composite like all material things, means to be an incommunicable subject of independent existence. To subsist means to be an individual in the full sense of the term. The perfection of subsistence is that perfection which makes an individual substance incommunicable. Because of subsistence it is the subject of independent existence. It is not a part of any other substance, but it is *subject* whole, complete and independent in its own right.

If this is so, it follows that whatever has subsistence is an individual. Subsistence is found first of all in the order of being in the Trinity of Persons in the Divine Nature. It is next found, analogically participated, in the various orders of creation. Each of the angels is a subsisting species. In material created things, the species as such does not subsist but only in the individuals in which the species is realized: this individual man, this individual brute, this individual plant, etc.

Human subsistence, however, is unique among composite natures. For, in every composite nature, except man, subsistence belongs only to the composite of matter and form. The forms of those things can not subsist separated from matter. Hence, the forms of those things are not individuals. Only the composite thing is an individual in such natures. In man, however, subsistence belongs not only to the composite substance made up of body and soul, but also to the soul alone, for the soul being spiritual is able to subsist apart from matter. Indeed, since subsistence is indivisible, it is the subsistence of the soul that is communicated to the composite of body and soul in the human individual. Hence the soul of every individual man is individual in itself, not by reason of any formal or material difference from other human souls, but solely by reason of its subsistence.

> The soul communicates that being in which it subsists to the corporeal matter, out of which and the intellectual soul there results one being; so that the being of the whole composite is also the being of the soul. This is not the case with other non-subsistent forms. For this reason the human soul retains its own being after the dissolution of the body; whereas it is not so with other forms.[3]

Hence, man's individuality derives from his rational soul, whose subsistence is the subsistence of the human composite. Individuality in other composite natures derives from the composite of matter and form, to which alone can subsistence belong in such natures. In these other composite natures individuality is dependent on the union of matter and form; hence, in these natures the individual is less important, less valuable, than the species, which is relatively permanent since it perdures so long as the individuals reproduce other individuals. In human nature, individuality is independent of the union of matter and form, once the form has been individuated by matter.

We say that human individuality is independent of the union of matter and form, *once the form has been individuated by matter.* By this we mean to say that according to St. Thomas, there could not be many individuals with the same specific nature or form unless this form were received in the material determinable substratum and limited by it, but, at the same time, that in the very instant the human individual begins to exist, his spiritual soul—the form of his complete human nature—possesses in itself the perfection of subsistence, which in other subrational individuals of the material world belongs only to the composite and which ceases to be with the natural corruption of such a composite. Man, also, as a member of the order of material reality, suffers corruption, death; but with the separation of his soul from the material substratum, which originally made it possible for him to be one of many in a species, his subsistence perdures, since it is the subsistence of a spiritual soul which was lent, so to speak, to the body during the course of his mortal life.

Hence, in human nature individuality is incorruptible, permanent. In human nature the individual is important in himself; he has inherent nobility and dignity. As a permanent individual he is among the primary objects or intentions of God's creative wisdom and power; he does not exist in a passing way merely for the continuation of a specific type.

We are now in a position to see that a complete account of the metaphysical structure of the rational individual includes, not only his substantiality and his composition of material determinability and a formal perfection, but also his subsistence, a subsistence, unique among material things, since it is a subsistence that is permanent.

The Activity of the Rational Individual

In our first section we detailed the metaphysical structure of the rational individual. If we are to regard such a nature as possessing dignity, we must find that dignity within the structure manifesting itself in the permanence of human individuality and in the excellence of human activity, for human activity is free. The human individual is not necessitated like the brutes to seek after particular goods, but only after the good in general, universal good. The human individual freely determines himself with respect to the seeking of particular goods. Thus he has dominion over his own acts. This freedom, rooted as it is in his spiritual, rational soul (and thus reducible to the same source whence derives his permanent individuality), invests the human individual with a dignity which demands a special name. Thus it is that the human individual and all individuals of a spiritual, rational nature are called *persons*.

We shall turn now to a consideration of the free activity of human persons, beginning first with that of the rational individual from a standpoint of finality. The principle of finality states: *every agent acts for the sake of an end*. Finality itself is an ordering of an agent to an end, the end being some good in accord with the nature of the agent or at least some part of the nature. The principle of finality has often been misunderstood by those who have not kept in mind that every agent acts for an end but not in the same way. There are in general three ways in which different agents act for an end:

1. Agents that lack knowledge can act for the sake of an end only executively. That is to say, they merely perform the action which conduces to the end. Natural agents do this by reason of an *intrinsic finality,* i.e., a direction towards a determinate end, which direction is implanted in their very nature. An example of this is found in the seed that develops into the perfect organism, the acorn into the

oak. Other non-cognitive agents may act towards an end by reason of an extrinsic finality, i.e. a direction towards a determinate end which direction is imparted from without, as a bullet is directed to the target.

2. Agents endowed with sense knowledge can act for the sake of an end which they apprehend as desirable and useful. They can do this only in an imperfect manner, however, recognizing by instinct the concrete desirability or usefulness of the good apprehended, but without being able to give a reason for its goodness or usefulness. Such agents do not direct themselves to an end. Instead, they are directed to their end, or are directed to employ certain means to an end, by the direction to their end implanted in their very nature. These agents are said to act for an end *executively* and *apprehensively* but not *formally* or perfectly because they do not determine themselves to the end. Thus it is that the bee, the ant, the bird building its nest, the spider constructing its web, any animal seeking food, reproducing its like, etc., all of these activities are instances of this second manner of acting for the sake of an end.
3. Only agents that have intellectual knowledge act perfectly for the sake of an end, for they alone recognize the nature of the end as the perfection of their being. They alone are able to grasp the essence of a means and unite it with end in a single act of understanding. They alone are able to determine themselves to particular ends by freely choosing to act for the attainment of this or that good.[4]

Thus we see the gradation of material things into the *natural,* the *sensitive,* the *rational* on the basis of the evident operations and activities of a higher order. There are higher forms, the sensitive forms, which possess some knowledge of the particular good perfective of the agent. Thus it is that the forms of perfecting goods are first apprehended before they become *movers* through desire. St. Thomas describes this more aptly:

> But it must be noted that, since every inclination results from a form, the natural appetite results from a form existing in the nature of things; while the sensitive appetite, as also the intellective or rational appetite, which we call the will, follows from an apprehended form. Therefore, just as the natural appetite tends to good existing in a thing, so the animal or voluntary appetite tends to a good which is apprehended.[5]

The perfection of each of the agents, natural, sensitive, rational, depends upon the operations of the nature necessary to the agent. Thus the tree grows and is perfected in response to being acted upon by the warmth of the sun and the presence of the moisture surrounding the roots. The animal nourishes itself and grows by responding to the sense apprehension of those particular goods to which its nature tends through the form ordinated precisely to those particular goods. Thus it is, that some animals are moved by some things as food, whereas the same foods are in no wise attractive to other animals. One might explain this fact analogically either as a type of magnetization such that the nature of the animal is magnetized by its perfecting goods; or else as the result of forces in which the balance of power is in the perfecting good, the pull of which the animal has no power to resist, once the "magnet" of the "balance of power" comes within the sense perception of the animal.

The story of Buridan's ass comes to mind here as possibly helpful to illustrate the point in question. The hypothesis is that of a hungry ass situated between two bales of hay that are similar in every respect. There is nothing of sensible goodness in one that is not in the other. Each bale of hay is exerting an equal pull on the ass. As a result, the poor ass starves to death because it does not possess any power within itself whereby it could determine itself to move to one bale or the other. In other words, it lacks a power that is found in man, the power to determine himself to an apprehended good, namely the will.

The will, the rational appetite of man, is the power whereby man moves himself to act. Like any other power, it is found in a nature, and is itself a nature determined to an object. Here "potency" is used in the sense of active potentiality, i.e. a capacity to do or to make, rather than a mere passive potentiality to be determined, such as the passive determinability of matter discussed above in the metaphysical structure of the individual. Since every faculty or power is a potency, the act (perfection) of such potencies is called its object. Since that which perfects is good and the good is that which all things desire, the object of every faculty is always called the good of the faculty. Every potency, every faculty, is perfected by some specific good: Sight for example, is perfected by the color in an object; smell is perfected by the odor in an object; taste by the flavor in an object. Each of man's powers is perfected by its proper object that necessarily moves the power.

The human will is rooted in the intellect. The object that is perfective of the will must be an apprehended good, a good which has been apprehended as a good. However, its object is not this particular good, such as color etc, nor that particular good, such as knowledge, health etc, but rather any good, whether it is color, health, wealth. Aristotle and the Schoolmen after him designate this as *universal good.* The intellect likewise is perfected by an object of similar amplitude, *universal truth,* not this particular truth of being, nor that particular truth of being, but rather, *any truth of being.*

The world, however, overflows with particular finite beings no one of which contains the fulness of truth for the intellect nor the fulness of goodness for the will. This capacity for universal truth, which is the intellect, and the capacity for universal goodness, which is the will, is ordinated to Infinite Being, Unlimited Truth, Unlimited Goodness as their adequate and proper object. This is the thought expressed by St. Augustine when he said: "For thou hast made us for Thyself and our hearts are restless until they rest in Thee" [6] and Gerard Manley Hopkins sang: "The world is charged with the grandeur of God." [7]

However, the human will which is the tendency of the human person can not be determined necessarily by any particular apprehended good: any good less than infinite, less than unlimited, leaves the will *unmoved, undetermined.* This fact, this power in man in virtue of which he remains unmoved, undetermined in the presence of any or all finite goods, is *initial freedom.*

We can regard this *initial freedom* as the *status libertatis,* from which man moves, acts. The acts or movements are for that reason called deliberate, since they proceed from this status of freedom. This *status libertatis* of the will, its *initial freedom* finds it necessitated neither *externally* by any of the other faculties and appetites nor *internally* in the will itself as e.g. a determination necessitating the will to be moved by a greater of two goods. On analysis there are three possible moments we must note:

1. To will or not to will.
2. To will this apprehended particular good rather than that one; to do this rather than to do that. Since they are particular goods they are not as such the proper object of the will.
3. To will to do something that is good for the person or to will to do something that is harmful to the person.

The Schoolmen have labeled these respectively: 1. Freedom of Contradiction; 2. Freedom of Specification; 3. Freedom of Contrariety. We might pause for a moment to hear St. Thomas on this matter:

> Man does not choose of necessity. And this is because that which is possible not to be, is not of necessity. Now the reason why it is possible not to choose, may be gathered from a twofold power in man. For man can will and not will, act and not act; again he can will this or that, and do this or that. The reason of this is seated in the very power of reason. For the will can tend to whatever the reason can apprehend as good. Now the reason can apprehend as good, not only this, viz., *to will,* or *to act,* but also this, *not to will* or *not to act.* Again, in all particular goods, the reason can consider an aspect of some good, and the lack of some good, which has the aspect of evil: and in this respect, it can apprehend any single one of such goods as to be chosen or to be avoided.[8]

An Analysis of the Free Act

The question proposes itself: how does man exercise the power of choice? How does the will, when undetermined in the presence of an apprehended good, become determined? The will, as appetite, follows the intellect; consequently, if there is indifference in the will such indifference follows the intellect. How can there be indifference in the intellectual act since the intellect is not free but rather necessitated to act in the presence of its object? There can be no indifference on the part of the intellect, as we have just noted. The indifference must come from the side of the object about which the intellect judges. The intellect formally possesses truth, necessary, eternal and immutable in its act; the object presented, through which it has gleaned the truth, and now the object of the will, is contingent, temporal, mutable. The judgment of the intellect reveals about the object different aspects of its reality, such as usefulness or non-usefulness; its limited goodness and at the same time its lack of goodness which can be apprehended by the intellect as an evil which is pleasurable but morally reprehensible. So, likewise, may the intellect present the object as a means necessary or indifferent to the end; as easily or as difficultly obtained.

It is quite evident then that none of these judgments have any necessary connection with the will in determining it. They are called *free judgments* by analogy, because they leave the will free, free to choose that *free judgment* which will determine or actuate the will after the manner in which matter is determined by form. This elected judgment is known as the *determining motive* of the will and is generally defined as that motive (practical judgment) which the will selects to be the determining motive.

Hence it is that at that metaphysical moment, in the most immanent action found in corporeal reality, the will moves from *initial freedom* and actuates itself, determines itself, with regard to a good perfective of the agent, man. Consequently, by maintaining, supporting this elected motive as the actuating motive, the whole unified person moves to the acquisition of the apprehended good because the soul, now actuated by this choice, is the formal cause for the activity of all the other powers subordinate to the will. St. Thomas has said this rather briefly:

> Consequently, when the operation of the will by its election is centered on something, the irascible and concupiscible [appetites] follow the movement of the will.[9]

It is for this reason that other powers in man are capable of performing free acts, not as proceeding freely from these powers, but as proceeding from the will actuating them.

We might pause here for a reorientation. We have been soaring in the heights of metaphysical reflection and analysis. Our purpose was to enable us to obtain a greater insight into the nature of man and his freedom. For it is the man, the person, who is free. It is the man who exercises choice. It is the unified being who acts. The metaphysical structure as herein unfolded should enable us to better understand the operations which we find in the human being. It likewise enables us to realize the value of freedom in our concrete existence and the consequent value of the human individual. The whole metaphysical structure, beginning with essence and existence, act and potency, matter and form, through finality of being, ordering things to their own perfection, and the tendency of created beings to seek their various perfecting goods in keeping with the demands of their natures; all these insights we shall find to be in keeping with our own every day living and experience.

All beings, as we have seen, seek their own perfection. Man is no exception. What is exceptional, what is dumbfounding, is that man is self perfecting. The power enabling him to perfect himself is the power of *initial freedom*. Hence, freedom is a means, not an end. It is the means whereby a being having received an existence that is personal, is able thereby to further perfect the person; to enhance and ennoble it beyond the original grant of power. This is at once the grandeur and misery of his freedom. Man can humanize himself. He can also dehumanize himself. This is the power of initial freedom in the concrete order of human existence. Hence it is that the world of freedom grows. It grows as the world of persons grows in age and wisdom and grace.

This is the dynamism of freedom. The human person acquiring the perfection of self through his own efforts by choosing the individual and common goods necessary to his nature. Hence his social needs and the institutions of society are naturally and freely established, only that the individual, the person might ultimately achieve and increase the grandeur of his person in the nobility of his self mastery. A free world! A world in which every man is able to acquire for himself the needs of his nature so that he might actualize to its fullness the dignity of his person. Man is not brought up. He brings himself up—or down—noble or debased. This is freedom! Metaphysics is circling the ethical and moral world here in its flight. We must return to our base, the metaphysics of freedom.

Freedom of choice is based on man's final determination. That determination is manifest by his will, the rational appetite for the good as such. The will is his "drive" for happiness, his supreme good. Man as a happiness-seeking animal, is therefore necessitated to seek happiness. He would therefore be absolutely necessitated to choose the Supreme Good, if so apprehended by his intellect. However, he is not necessitated to choose the supreme good when presented under any other aspect, even though he may realize that it is eminently reasonable to do so. This is, as we have seen, because the Supreme Good is only inadequately apprehended by man. When man is confronted by Supreme Good, he will move necessarily. At that moment he will not need freedom. Freedom is necessary to man only in those moments when he is in the presence of goods that are not supreme . . .

St. Thomas in this context says:

> The perfect good alone, which is happiness, can not be apprehended by the reason as an evil, or as lacking in any way. Consequently, man wills happiness of necessity, nor can he will not to be happy, to be unhappy. Now since choice is not of the end, but of the means, as was stated above, it is not of the perfect good, which is happiness, but of other and particular goods. Therefore, man chooses, not of necessity, but freely.[10]

The Extrinsic Basis of Freedom

We turn now, briefly, to the final consideration of the Metaphysics of Freedom, namely its extrinsic cause, which is of course, God, the First Cause of all things. We shall again rely on the Aquinate writings as the outstanding expression of the great Christian philosophic tradition. St. Thomas is quite explicit on the manner of God's causality. He compares, since there is no other way for man to know how God operates, God's causality in creating, to the causality of the artist in producing his artifact.

> The knowledge of God is the cause of things. For the knowledge of God is to all creatures what the knowledge of the artificer is to the things made by his art. Now the knowledge of the artificer is the cause of the things made by his art from the fact that the artificer works through his intellect.[11]

However, the intelligent causality of the artist is not simply the operation of the intellect. If the idea (form) in the mind of the artist is to be translated into actuality it must receive a determination that can only come from the free determination of the will. Comparably, it is manifest that God's knowledge is the cause of things in so far as His will is joined to it.[12]

A difficult problem presents itself here. It is the problem of reconciling the Divine Causality with the Freedom of the created agent. Certain thinkers, overambitious in their desire to understand the Divine Causality were so impressed by the universal efficacy of the First Cause that they were led to a denial of human freedom. We may call this view Theological Determinism, ranging all the way from Calvin to Spinoza. However, just as Parmenides' views on the structure of reality were rejected because they were in apparent conflict with experience, so Theological Determinism must be rejected as in evident contradiction with experience. Men, in the commonsense view of their reality, know from their own personal experience that they are free.

The problem is a formidable one. Even within the Christian tradition there are various solutions proposed. However, despite their disagreements, all of these solutions are satisfactory, because they preserve in their framework both the universal efficacy of the First Cause and the genuine freedom of the rational creature. It is true they leave a mystery. The problem, below a certain depth, escapes human understanding, but this must be so in any genuine metaphysical solution of the problems concerning the efficacy of the Infinite Incomprehensible (by creatures) First Cause.

St. Thomas probes to a depth of understanding that has not been surpassed. We merely summarize here his teaching as found in the first part of the *Summa Theologica* on the knowledge that God has of future contingents and of their relationships to the act of God's Will.

In the comprehension of Himself, God knows all things actual or possible. Hence He knows the extent of His Power and all the things to which His Power extends. Nothing can be except through this Power, the power of the Primary Artist. His knowledge of future contingents does not, like human knowledge, look to the future. It is a knowledge that is sweeping in its glance and embraces the creatable, possible and actual. God's glance at all possible things is *His knowledge of Simple Intelligence;* His glance at all actual things is *His knowledge of Vision.* It is in the latter that God infallibly knows the future contingent things. In time, the future contingent things become actual successively, though God knows them simultaneously in their own being in that glance that is carried from eternity over all things in their presentiality.

It is pertinent here to point out that in creating, God's will is the cause of things and that He acts by His will and not through a necessity of His nature. St. Thomas' argument to prove this, is based on the priority of the intellectual and voluntary agent over the non-intellectual, non-voluntary agent.

> Since both *intellect* and *nature* act for an end, the natural agent must have the end and the necessary means predetermined for it by some higher intellect; as the end and definite movement is predetermined for the arrow by the archer. Hence the intellectual and voluntary agent must precede the agent that acts by nature. Hence since God is first in the order of agents, He must act by intellect and will.[13]

Whatever God causes, He causes by His will and He causes *freely.* What God wills necessarily is His own Goodness. All other things He wills through a free choice. Since the divine will is perfectly efficacious, it follows that things are done in the way he wills them. Some are to be done necessarily . . . some freely.[14] God, who is free, with sovereign freedom, has freely willed to give His creatures a share in this precious attribute. He has made intelligent creatures.

If the world of tomorrow is divided into two essentially incompatible ways of life, it very well may be because our educators, entrusted with answering the questions of children, have become philosophical narcissists at the very moment when the so-called practical man of the West should be alert to the greatest conspiracy of history, that of spending the patrimony of the West on communistic baubles in the name of education and academic freedom. It may be advantageous for us to restate some of the basic concepts that we have considered in our examination of *initial freedom*.

Primary in that consideration was the metaphysical structure of the rational individual. Here the substantiality of man was opposed to Phenomenalism. The problem of the "man," the plurality of individuals of a species was considered to be in opposition to any type of Monism. Finally, we emphasized the uniqueness of the rational individual by indicating that the reason of its uniqueness and nobility, namely, its spirtuality, was to be found in his metaphysical structure. Only in such a being is found personal dignity and wholeness; whereas, the modern insight of Collectivism views man as the puppet of the social engineer. Collectivist man exists only as a functional worker on the level with the bee who must be provided with the security of a hive at the price of his person and freedom.

Secondly, we considered the manner in which the rational individual acts for an end known as such and willed as such. Here we also emphasized the contrast between man as a real agent in the universe and other individual material beings that are more acted upon than act. Thus was brought into contrast the modern thinkers who fail to distinguish differences while they are noting common properties in things. It is for that reason that many thinkers have made no distinction between the rational and the irrational animal. The activities of the latter are all reduced to a commonality and are exactly the same. Accordingly, we found ourselves in opposition to the Behaviorists, the Mechanists and the Materialists.

In the third section of the paper we analyzed the free act itself and took a position in opposition to any and all groups of thinkers who would eventually destroy man's freedom in a Physiological or Psychological Determinism.

Our conclusion advanced the position of God as the external cause of man's freedom. Such a position places us in opposition to any Theological Determinism as well as Atheism. Here, also, we are in opposition to any limited Theological Determinism such as is found in the Philosophies of J. S. Mill and of William James.

The world is divided, it is true, and the unity it seeks must be a unity through freedom, a freedom that begins in *initial freedom* and ends in a *freedom of autonomy.*

Freedom of Autonomy— The Terminal Freedom

by Rev. Carl W. Grindel, C.M., Ph.D.
Professor of Philosophy, Graduate School, St. John's University

The saint, the man who uses his will ever in accord with the natural and divine law, is the man who is free in the highest sense that freedom can have! This is a statement that I am certain would shock the modern "liberal," perhaps bring to his lips a patronizing smile. Yet, for one who has plumbed the meaning of this much-abused word and has studied the nature of the faculty in which it formally resides, i.e. the human will, there can be no other conclusion. To arrive at this conclusion, however, we must study the nature of the will and the difference between *free will* and *free choice.* Although these two freedoms are often confused, there is a fundamental difference between them. Freedom of the will is a quality that belongs to the will by its very nature as a spiritual faculty; freedom of choice, on the other hand, is, in the final analysis, a means only to the attainment of the fuller and more perfect freedom which the will must attain if it is to achieve its perfection.

It is true that the medieval philosophers were not called upon to discuss many of the modern questions which have made necessary an emphasis upon this distinction. We do not, therefore, find in medieval authors, or even in many moderns, a specific treatment of *freedom of autonomy,* a fact which contributes to the difficulty of an analysis such as this. We do, however, find a satisfactory basis for our discussion. Admittedly, medieval scholastics are not in entire agreement in their treatment of the will and its freedom. The development of this article will proceed from the background of the doctrine of St.

Thomas which distinguishes with striking clarity between freedom of the will and freedom of choice. In his treatise, *On Truth,*[1] he discusses these two freedoms in different questions and, as a result, draws a careful distinction between them.[2]

In his treatment of *free will,* St. Thomas first distinguishes the various types of natural appetite. He shows that when reason is not involved the appetite can never be called *free* in any proper sense of the term. The inclinations of bodies lacking knowledge are impressed on their very natures in such a way that, given the proper circumstances, they give rise necessarily to corresponding activities. We need refer only to the phenomena of gravitation. Furthermore, even in the case of the brute animal which does possess sense knowledge and an appetite or inclination consequent to that knowledge, the animal does not *choose* or *not choose* to follow the inclination. When made conscious, through sense knowledge, of something attractive to any of its faculties, the animal, again necessarily, follows that inclination unless prevented from doing so by something from without the animal itself. We have instances of this in the instinctive activities of animals. On the other hand, man, the rational animal, placed in precisely the same circumstances as the brute, can *choose* or *not choose* to follow that inclination. If food be presented to a hungry dog, he will invariably and inevitably seize it and eat it; man, however, experiencing the same inclination of sense consequent to hunger, may refuse to accept the food; witness, for example, the hunger strikes of Gandhi and others, as well as the practices of many ascetics. The rational appetite or will is ever in man's power, i.e. he is able to seek or not seek a good that has been perceived and recognized as a *good.* This power in man arises from the fact that man knows the end and can *understand* the relation of *this good* as a means to that end. Man can do this because he alone is endowed with reason.[3]

Now, can we say that this rational appetite is free? To answer this question we first distinguish between the will as *nature,* since it does belong in the category of natural things, and the will as a *rational tendency.* The will as nature has a natural and necessary inclination towards its last end, i.e. happiness and all that it implies. This inclination, however, is in no way submitted to a necessity of coercion, for that would be contrary to the very notion of natural appetite.[4]

As a rational tendency, on the other hand, the will is not determined with regard to the *means* for attaining the end. This lack of determination can be seen clearly in three different ways. First of all, the will is not determined to any particular object which is a means: there are a variety of means for arriving at the end and these may be utilized in various ways as they are used by different persons. If, for example, it seems good to me to make a trip to Europe (an intermediate end), I could go by plane or ocean liner, or even by freighter or private yacht; I can take the quickest way or the longest way; I may go First-Class or Tourist-Class, etc. Unlike the brute who, in the presence of a pleasurable good, must seek it in a certain way, I am free to choose any one of the means that I have mentioned.

Again, the will is not determined even to the act of willing. Even though the object of the will may be determined, even though that object is presented to me as good, I can will it or not will it. Even though a trip to Europe does appear to me as good (in this case, the trip itself is a means), I need not will to take the trip. Unlike bodies which seek the earth without any mastery over this inclination, the will has the power of self-determination which permits it to will or not will the determined object.

Finally, the will is not determined with regard to the moral agreement of its act with its last end. The object may be good or evil in itself and it can be apprehended as good or evil because of a false conscience (in which latter case, the person may, of course, still be responsible). This act of fornication, for example, as pleasurable to a sense faculty, can here and now be apprehended by me as a good. As such I may choose it even though objectively it will not lead me toward my last end but rather away from it and even though, theoretically, I may recognize that fact. So consequently we may say, too, that the will has the power of doing moral good or evil. As we will point out later, however, this is no necessary part of the liberty of the will although, as St. Thomas notes, it may be a sign of liberty.

There is, then, in the will a threefold liberty: (1) liberty to will or not will a determined object. This liberty is inseparable from the will in whatever condition man may be found; it applies to every object, means or end. We note, however, that with regard to the Supreme Good, although there is freedom from coercion, the will as nature has a necessary inclination toward that object. (2) The will is free to choose this or that object. This, too, is inseparable from the will but applies only to means. (3) The will is free to do good or evil. This, we know, does not apply to man in every state as is clear from the condition of those who see God face to face; for they can choose only the morally good.[5]

Although, according to St. Thomas, the above discussion reveals that the will is not determined, it does not prove that the will has freedom of choice. How does the will leave its indetermination? If the will act is to exist at all, it must exist as a determined act. Since the will is a *rational* appetite, its act and choice ought to be reasoned; we cannot say that its movement to determination is the result of chance. Is there, then, a necessary connection between the determination of the will and the decision of reason which precedes it? Do we not, all things considered, always will that which our reason has decided to will? In other words, does not the will always follow the decision of the intellect?

"In human actions," St. Thomas writes, "we must distinguish three things: knowledge, appetite, and the action itself." But the action proceeds necessarily from the appetite: when the will is determined to such an act, this act proceeds from it inevitably unless there be some extrinsic interference. But in its turn and just as necessarily, the voluntary appetite is linked to the knowledge preceding its operation: when a man has judged that this act is, here and now, his good and, at the end of his deliberation, the only good which interests him, the will, made for the good, cannot but will it. Doubtless a man can judge speculatively and in the abstract that such a good is, in itself, evil; but if, under the influence of passion or any other influence, he judges practically and in the concrete that this act is for him, here and now, his good, his will cannot remain indifferent to it; he must seek it. If, then, man is free, we must seek that freedom in the judgment which precedes the act of the will.[6]

By this judgment or *arbitrium,* we certainly do not mean the abstract speculative judgment of which we have just written. Neither do we mean the concrete speculative judgment of conscience on the morality of the concrete act proposed to the will. We mean the practical decision of the reason which immediately precedes the act of choice. Thus the will is free if the practical judgment, its *arbitrium,* is free. St. Thomas then goes on to show that man alone is master of his judgment because he alone has reason which permits him to judge of his own judgment.[7] And why can man do this? It is because "he knows the nature of the end and the means as well as the relation of the one to the other," or again because "the reason reflects on its act and knows the relations of the things which it judges and of the things by which it judges." [8]

Man is, then, free in his choice of means that will lead him to his final happiness. He tends necessarily, however, toward this final end. Can this necessity be reconciled with true liberty of the will? St. Thomas thinks so.

> The natural necessity under which the will is said to will a thing of necessity—happiness for instance—is not incompatible with free will: but free will is opposed to violence or compulsion. Now there is no violence or compulsion when a thing is moved in accordance with its nature, but there is if its natural movement be hindered, as when a heavy body is prevented from moving down toward center. Hence the will naturally desires happiness, although it desires it necessarily: and thus also God by his will loves himself freely, although he loves himself of necessity.[9]

"With regard to the last end," he writes again, "we do not have free choice, but a free will." [10] In tending necessarily toward his last end in general, man is just as free as the angel who adheres to God necessarily. For he keeps, in the presence of the end, this self-determination of the rational appetite which alone suffices to destroy any coercion imposed from without, a self-determination which guarantees the liberty of exercise, necessary and sufficient for liberty.[11]

The distinction between *free will* and *free choice,* although vital as a preliminary step, does not give us, however, the full explanation of *freedom of autonomy*. We must digress a little to consider what we mean by the *perfection* of man. Although it is beyond the scope of this paper to discuss at length the question of man's ultimate end, yet we can say that man, like all natural beings, tends to his full perfection. Since man is a person, that means the perfection of that person. A person, however, is a complete individual of a rational nature. Now the person will be the more fully developed as all his faculties are more fully developed, for that is the proximate purpose of man's faculties. This total development of man's faculties is the work of education both at home and in the school. Parents endeavor to insure the development of the physical faculties of the child from birth by providing good food and suitable exercise. As he grows, he is taught through careful observation to develop his external senses; these in turn supply material for the development of his internal senses, especially the imagination. Good companions, good books aid in the development of his emotions, for, although the emotions, at times, prove a source of difficulty, they also are operations of man and the ideal is not their suppression but their proper development. All of these faculties are man's faculties and he will become the more perfect as a person as they are more fully developed. Since man, however, has a rational nature, his perfection will depend more especially upon the fuller development of those faculties which constitute him as a being of rational nature, i.e. his intellect and will.

The intellect by its nature seeks truth. It will therefore become more and more perfect as it is able more and more to attain to truth without error. The less that the intellect can err, the more perfect will it become. In like manner, the will seeks the good—and it becomes more perfect as the good that it chooses conforms the more closely or is better adapted to man's ultimate end. It is, therefore, no perfection for the will to be able to choose moral evil; for evil does not bring it closer to its end but rather makes it more difficult to obtain that end. This point seems to offer special difficulty to many modern advocates of freedom who although often willing to admit that he who chooses moral evil is less perfectly human—is inferior as a man—than he who chooses the morally good, still at the same time they seem unable to understand that such a man is also less *free*. Although they may speak of the "slavery of vice," they would seem to demand for man the "freedom" to become such a slave! Now we have already pointed out that the will is free in its choice of particular goods. However, if these goods are really to perfect the will, they should be means that lead to the end. But, as has been noted by Professor Yves Simon,[12] we must not lose sight of "the immediately evident principle that a means which does not lead to the end is no longer a means and is not desirable in any sense." If not desirable, then it cannot be a good and can in no way perfect the will. As our discussion proceeds this fact will become more manifest.

Since, then, the intellect by its nature seeks truth, and the will by its nature seeks the good, man, it follows, will attain the perfect fulfillment of his nature only when the intellect grasps perfect Truth intuitively and, in consequence, the will chooses only the perfect Good; thus only can we have perfect freedom of autonomy. This, however, will be possible only through supernatural aid in a future life. This being a theological rather than a philosophical question, it is not our purpose to discuss it here.

Man can, however, achieve a measure of freedom of autonomy in so far as here and now, his choices approach that perfection to which we have referred. How is this to be accomplished? We have already distinguished between *free will* and *free choice* and have noted that man has free will with regard to his end and free choice with reference to the means to that end. We have further shown that, with regard to the end, this free will is a *freedom of exercise.* It would, perhaps, be well now to explain another kind of freedom, namely *freedom of specification,* and to distinguish it clearly from freedom of exercise. Thereby we may be able the better to understand how man uses free choice, the initial freedom, as a means toward the greater fulfillment of his person in the freedom of autonomy. This distinction is emphasized by St. Thomas, especially in his treatise *On Evil.*[13]

Freedom of exercise, as we have already noted, implies that the will is free to seek or not seek any end. Now we must point out that just as the speculative reason is moved to its conclusions from principles, so also is the will moved to its choice of means from its choice of the end. A man is moved to take a dose of bad-tasting medicine because he wishes health. This determination of the will to act, however, does not take place in any particular case without preceding deliberation; it is through deliberation that the will acts in the order of means. This deliberation, however, does not conclude in the same way that a demonstration concludes; it is rather an inquiry that leaves the way open to contradictory solutions. I am ill, for example, with a certain disease, and wish to regain health. Deliberation reveals that there are several different courses of treatment that will bring about the desired result. I may choose one of them. The will, then, cannot be said to be moved necessarily because of the deliberation.

Furthermore, the deliberation itself proceeds from a previous will act. If I deliberate, it is because I have willed to deliberate, for the will has the primacy in efficient causality. The will, however, is not always willing; it must be moved to activity. Unless we are ready to concede an infinite process of intellectual and volitional acts—and this would explain nothing—we must admit that the first movement of the will comes from a First Mover, God. He, however, does not necessitate the will: just as He moves all things according to their natures, He moves the will to will freely.[14]

With regard to the exercise of the will, therefore, whether we consider its proximate cause, deliberation, or its First Cause, God, this exercise is free.

There remains, now, the question of the specification of the will act. It takes a specific form; it has a specific object. Could it be otherwise specified? Could it have another object?

The will clings to an object, presented by the reason, only in so far as this object appears fitting or suitable to it. Man inclines to a good only to the extent that this good, here and now, is personally appropriate for him. The deliberation and the choice have no other purpose than to make concrete the ideal of happiness that each individual pursues. If, then, an object is presented to the will as realizing in every way all these conditions of adaptation—this would be perfect happiness—clearly the will cannot not will to consider it. This would be a question of freedom of exercise. Once such an object is presented to the will, the will is drawn toward it inevitably; there is no question of freedom of specification. On the other hand, if the object presented by the reason does not realize in every way these conditions of adaptation—if, for example, it be the practice of a virtue which may imply denial of sense pleasures—then the man, considering the deficiencies in the object, need not be inclined toward it and the will can choose another object.

The fact that the will does reach out for any certain object does not happen without a cause. St. Thomas enumerates some of the things that have an influence on the determination of the will. Sometimes it is the reason that dictates the direction for the will to take; thus, for example, because of reason we may choose that which is useful for health rather than that which serves only for pleasure. At other times, there may be certain accidental circumstances which serve as occasions to draw attention to one or another aspect of the object presented. Finally, there may be subjective dispositions in a man who fixes his ideal on an object conformable to these dispositions. *De facto,* we know that we often judge according to our passions or subjective dispositions.

Can we say that these influences determine the will? St. Thomas speaks only of the third set of influences, i.e. the subjective dispositions. If the subjective disposition, i.e. the passion or emotion, which dictates the judgment is entirely beyond the control of the will, the man is drawn along with it necessarily; hence in such a case there is no freedom of the will. If, for example, a man through no fault of his own is aroused to extreme anger entirely beyond his control, consequently strikes and injures another, there is no freedom of the will and therefore no human act or responsibility. For in this case, the deliberation, if there can be said to be any deliberation, does not result in showing several solutions. There is one only:—that dictated by the passion, which has prevented true deliberation from taking place. If, on the other hand, this passion as a motive of action remains under the control of the will, then responsibility remains to the extent that there is this control. The man has only to change the disposition to avoid the moral repercussions. If, for example, I am injured by someone and, in consequence, I am aware that I am becoming angry, as long as I am able truly to deliberate, as long as I can see more than one possible conclusion to that deliberation, I am responsible. On the one hand, the passion urges me on to revenge and deliberation presents that revenge to the will as a good that can be sought; on the other, as a result of my knowledge of moral principles, my intellect also presents to the will the good that will result from the observance of the moral law—and this is also a good that can be sought by the will. It is, then, incumbent upon me to repress the passion and to act according to my moral principles.

The second set of influences mentioned above, i.e. the accidental circumstances that draw attention to certain aspects of the object, can be resolved in the same way. With regard to the first, there is no difficulty. When the will follows the directives of reason, it is playing its proper role as the rational appetite.

To sum up: *freedom of specification* is not complete since it is concerned only with concrete goods which are not the ultimate end; but *freedom of exercise* is complete even with regard to the ultimate end.[15]

It should be clear from what we have written of freedom of specification that the use of the initial freedom or freedom of choice can result in the terminal freedom—freedom of autonomy—only when these choices are properly specified, i.e. only when the will, in its choosing, chooses a *real* good, one which will actually perfect the human person, and not an *apparent* good, one which, while satisfying some special faculty of the human person, is actually detrimental to the person as human. Suppose, for example, that a man wills to commit adultery. Certainly he wills this as a *good,* and it *is* a *good,* but one that will perfect only his lower or animal faculties. In as far as he is a person, i.e. a rational being, it is only an apparent good, for it will not perfect him as a person. As a person, as a reasonable being, he knows that what he wills to do is contrary to the natural law, to justice and to chastity and, therefore, an unreasonable act. As such it does not lead him toward his ultimate end of perfect happiness but rather withdraws him from it, and therefore does not perfect him as a person. Certainly he has freedom of choice in this case: he *can will* to perform the act. But just as certainly, it is not a freedom of choice that will perfect him as a person and thus lead him on to the perfect freedom of autonomy. How, then, can we assure that our choices will be properly specified so that they may truly be means to the terminal freedom of autonomy?

We have seen that the choice of the will is ultimately due directly to the intellect or indirectly to the dispositions or the passions. If, then, the choice is to be a real good, a good that will actually perfect the human person by leading him toward his ultimate perfection, then there must be rectitude in the judgment of the intellect and control over the passions.

For a proper understanding of the difficulty that we are now facing, we must understand man's nature and his consequent natural tendencies. Although man is not just an *animal,* neither is he purely *rational*—he is aptly defined as a *rational animal.* Since his nature is a composite, although single, nature participating, as it were, in the nature of both brute and angel, he has *natural* tendencies that result from both natures. So he tends naturally to the conservation of his own being and that of his species just as he tends naturally also to understand and to will. Although man has the faculties possessed by the brute, unlike in the latter, they do not operate in a fixed and necessary manner. Thus if a brute animal finds himself in a situation involving danger to his life, he will experience the emotion of fear and flee the situation if it is at all possible. In contrast, an Army nurse under fire in a front-line dressing station will also experience the emotion of fear but she will remain at her post and carry out her duties. Why is this? Man can understand the purpose of his lower faculties and, through the proper use of his will, can utilize these faculties according to their purpose, always, however, with a view to his own proper end as a *rational* animal, i.e. in such a way that he may perfect himself as a person. Here we have both the strength and the weakness of man. It is no imperfection in man that he is subject to the passions, for man can and should use his sense faculties as means toward the fuller perfection of his rational faculties. His intellectual knowledge begins with the senses, and the passions, properly controlled, may act as strong incentives to the right use of his will. On the other hand, the sense faculties by their nature are attracted to *any* concrete good that will bring satisfaction and, as we have already seen in the case of the man who wills to commit adultery, in a particular case this concrete good of sense may not be a real good for man as a person, may not lead him toward his end as a person. Thus the passions may so affect the choices of the will that they will not be in accord with man's end. This is possible because, as we have already explained, the will, in its choice depends upon the judgment of the intellect, on deliberation. The intellect resides in this man, subject to passion. If the passion be uncontrolled, it can easily bring it to pass that the deliberation will not result in several possible solutions but in one only, that dictated by passion. The choice of the will, therefore, will not be in accord with reason rightly used and will not lead man to the perfection of his person. Only the choice of a real good can lead him to that perfection. That the choice of the will falls upon a real good can be assured then, only by the cultivation of the virtues:—the virtue of prudence in the intellect, and the moral virtues for the control of the passions.

At the beginning of this discussion we said that the saint is the only man who possesses freedom in the highest and truest sense of this word. He alone uses his freedom of choice in a manner that approaches closest to freedom of autonomy, that freedom that will best advance his perfection as a person. But how does he accomplish this? Only through the practice of what is called *heroic virtue*. It is, then, by the practice of virtue that man can assure that his will acts are properly specified, that he, in short, is actually using his freedom of choice as a means to freedom of autonomy.

It is not our purpose at present to discuss at length the question of virtue and the virtues although it is closely related to the topic of this article. We have already seen that the human person is endowed with freedom of choice: he is not determined to any special class of objects, nor is he determined to achieve any particular object in any special way. In this choice the human person is fallible; he can, and often does, err. His choices will be correct and in accord with his nature only when they are truly reasonable and, if there be question of his sense faculties, only when they seek their objects under the direction of right reason. This control of the reason over the sense faculties cannot be totally imposed from without, as it were, for this would be a sort of violence. In a sense it must be impressed on the faculties themselves in such a way that it becomes almost a second nature for them. If this can be brought about, the human person will find it easier to perform his actions so that they will the more easily lead him to his ultimate perfection—at least as far as it is possible in this life, and not forgetting the wound to human nature discussed by the theologian as *original sin*. This sort of activity, however, is possible for us only to the extent that it becomes natural for us to act in a truly reasonable manner even when our sense faculties are involved.

St. Thomas tells us that virtue *is natural,* that the roots of these good dispositions are within us,[16] but these dispositions must be perfected so that they become habitual, i.e. good habits or virtues. This will bring about a condition midway between natural properties over whose outcome we have no control and that in which we must constantly and laboriously watch over our sense faculties, ever making a new beginning. St. Thomas accepts, with some modification, St. Augustine's definition of virtue: *Virtue is a good quality of mind by which we live righteously, of which no one can make bad use, which God works in us, without us.* He substitutes *habit* for *quality* and, to make the definition generally applicable, omits the final words with reference to God, since they apply only to infused virtue.[17]

Habits, as has been pointed out by Jacques Leclerq [18] and others, are the basis for all human development. It is only because of the cultivation of physical and psychical habits that we are able to produce acts that are truly human, i.e. involving intellect and will. It is only because we have developed the physical habit of walking that we can, without any attention to the physical details of the walking, direct ourselves to our destination; in reading, we do not stop to spell out the words. Since we have developed the habit of reading, we can devote our intellectual faculties to the thought being conveyed by the words. One who has not made habitual the mechanical details involved in driving an automobile will never be a good driver, for he cannot concentrate on directing the machine. We might multiply instances, e.g. speaking, swimming, typewriting, etc. Now this truth also holds good as far as the actual exercise of intellect and will are concerned. It is the cultivation of the virtues, morally good habits, that makes it possible for us to insure that our choices will more and more fall upon *real* goods and not *apparent* goods—and thus more and more contribute to our development as human persons. When I have developed the virtue of prudence to such an extent that my practical judgments are always naturally produced in such a way that the means will actually lead to my end, when the moral virtues of justice, fortitude and temperance naturally incline me to keep my emotions under the control of reason, only then am I making progress in my development as a person, i.e. as a being of a rational nature.

It is needless to point out that, with the exception of certain radical materialists, men generally consider that he is the more perfect man, i.e. is more truly human, who is able to make reason rule more completely in his life; not indeed by the total suppression of his emotional life, but by the fuller control of reason over emotion. Even the Freudian psychologist has rejected the pure animalism of the Kinsey Reports.[19] This rule of reason over emotion, however, is precisely the outcome of the cultivation of virtue. The temperate man, i.e. he who submits the desires of the body to the control of law both natural and positive, is considered to be a more perfect individual and a better member of society. Only the most perverted society has ever regarded the uninhibited indulgence of passion as a good. Drunkenness is generally regarded as a vice—and not by Christian moralists alone. And why? Because the man who permits his desires for strong drink to rule his conduct loses to a greater or lesser extent the power of reason; he becomes less human.

Habits result from repeated actions and good habits or virtues are the result of repeated morally good actions. The continued and conscious effort to make our choices in accord with reason gradually brings it to pass that the choice of a real good becomes almost automatic or, as medieval philosophers and even James have said, "a second nature." The prudent man now naturally acts in a prudent manner, i.e. in such a way that he naturally chooses the means that will lead him to his end; the temperate man naturally acts temperately; the just man is naturally inclined to give to every man what belongs to him, etc. The virtuous man seeks the real good naturally; he is not so strongly drawn to the apparent good by his emotions that, in consequence, he cannot or can only with difficulty discern the real good. In this way every good habit or virtue develops my humanity, brings a perfection to my person, and results in an action that is more human, i.e. more conformable to reason. Briefly, we may say that perfection consists in making the choice of the real good become automatic. This, however, presents us with a problem.

When a man has developed a virtue to such an extent that, as far as is possible, he seeks the real good in an automatic fashion, what becomes of freedom? Can he be said to possess freedom of choice?

Just as passion formerly obscured real good, does not virtue now prevent the consideration of the good that may be present in its opposite? Is the deliberation now truly free, i.e. does it leave the way open to contradictory solutions?

In answering this objection, we must keep in mind the true nature of freedom of choice and its limitations that have already been discussed. Freedom of choice is not the *essential* freedom: it is freedom of autonomy that constitutes a man as truly free. Freedom of choice is limited, as we have indicated, to the means leading to the end. As Professor Simon puts it:

> The choice and the operations which immediately precede it (Consent, deliberation, use of means) presuppose the establishment of a relation between the will and its end. We choose only on the basis of an adhesion previously given to the end. We can choose only in view of an end already willed, just as we can reason only by beginning with a principle already admitted.[20]

Man's true perfection, however, consists in the full development of his intellectual faculties, i.e. his intellect and will. He is truly free in so far as he is able to act more reasonably. Virtue certainly makes it easier for him to do this.

Let us consider briefly a man addicted to the vice of drunkenness. This vice makes it extremely difficult for him to resist the inclination to take strong drink. When he is completely under the influence of this vice, his liberty is entirely suspended as soon as temptation presents itself because the temptation unleashes a passion so strong that he can consider no other good than this drink. He tends to alcohol as his absolute good. If the temptation should not be so great that it destroys his liberty, it nevertheless demands the application of all his presence of mind, his capacity for reflection and willing, in order to fight against this temptation. Each time that he gives in to the temptation, during the interval that he remains under the influence of liquor, he loses the use of his reason. When the passion for strong drink becomes habitual, reason has less and less influence over all the actions of his life, even when he is not drinking.

The sober man, on the contrary, enjoys the use of reason at all times and so he is always in a condition in which truly free acts may be performed. The more perfectly that he has acquired this virtue, the easier it becomes for him to reject almost instinctively any suggestion of excess in the use of strong drink. In his case, all of his intellectual faculties, his capacity for reflection and willing, may be employed on the further development of his human personality.[21]

It should be clear, then, that the less time that I am forced to spend in overcoming my passions, the more leisure do I have for true reflection and for making choices that will contribute to my development as a person. Vice lessens my freedom to perform rational acts; virtue increases it. We have seen that, if freedom of choice, the initial freedom, is to lead to freedom of autonomy, the terminal freedom, the choice must be properly specified; it must be the choice of a good that will actually lead to the end. We have seen, too, that this specification depends upon a judgment of the intellect and it will be a good choice only when that practical judgment presents a real good to the will. This it is which is assured by the cultivation of the virtue of prudence. The prudential judgment specifies the choice. It has become habitual with the prudent man to choose means that will always lead to the end. The prudent man cannot act prudently, however, unless he has also cultivated the moral virtues. It is because of the moral virtues that the will is disposed to act according to reason because these virtues restrain the passions and prevent them from obscuring the judgment of the intellect. St. Thomas writes:

> . . . prudence is right knowledge about the things to be done, and not merely in the universal sense but in the particular which is the order of actions. . . . Consequently, just as by the habit of natural understanding or of science, a man is made to be rightly disposed in regard to the universal principles, so, in order that he be rightly disposed with regard to the particular principles of action, viz., the ends, he needs to be perfected by certain habits, whereby it becomes connatural to man, as it were, to judge rightly about the end. This is done by moral virtue, for the virtuous man judges rightly of the end of virtue because such as a man is, such does the end seem to him. Consequently, the right reason about things to be done, viz., prudence, requires man to have moral virtues.[22]

But, if the virtue of prudence needs the moral virtues, so also do the moral virtues have need of prudence. Prudence judges correctly of the things that are related to the end. If the act of choice is not specified in accord with right reason, it is not a morally good act and so does not lead to the end. Its repetition, therefore, would result in the destruction of the moral virtues.[23] In the truest sense it therefore follows that I am the more free as reason increasingly dominates my life; for the true perfection of a person consists in the perfection of his rational faculties. The less that a person is under the domination of his passions, the more easily will his intellect be able to grasp truth and so the more surely will his will seek the true good—and thus will he become the more human. Man is certain to develop habits. If he is to act as man, i.e. reasonably, he must see to it that these habits are habits in accord with his nature as a human being. Virtues are such habits.

The nature of *freedom of autonomy* has now been revealed by our study of the will. Man has free will, i.e. he is able to seek or not seek a good, perceived and recognized as a good. When we consider the will as nature, it has a natural and necessary inclination toward its last end, happiness, but this inclination is not forced upon the will: it is consequent to the nature itself. The will, as a rational tendency, however, is not determined with regard to the means for the attainment of the end. It is free to choose this or that object as a means; it is free to will or not will a determined object, either as an end or a means; it is free to will good or evil human acts, except when face to face with the Supreme Good.

The will is undetermined. But is it free in its choice, i.e. in determining itself? This depends upon the deliberation preceding choice. If this deliberation results in a judgment permitting more than one solution, and it ordinarily does when there is question of means, the choice is free; if not, then the choice is not free. Man is free in his choice of means; he does not choose his end freely. With regard to the end, he has free will, i.e. he is not coerced; he has free choice with regard to the means to the end.

But man is most properly free when his choices are such that they will lead him to his end, i.e. when they will actually perfect him as man. This is possible only when his choices are so specified that they fall upon a real good and not upon an apparent good. Since the specification of the will act depends upon a practical judgment of the intellect, the act will be so specified that it will lead to man's true end only when the practical judgment of the intellect is in accord with truth and therefore presents the real good to the will. This demands rectitude in the judgment, obtainable only through the virtue of prudence. The passions must be controlled so that they do not obscure the true good; this is had by means of the moral virtues. Freedom of autonomy, then, is dependent upon truth: "The truth shall make you free." It is the freedom of the perfect man who has perfected himself as a human person; his intellect recognizes the truth, i.e. it judges of things as they actually are, and the practical judgment of the intellect presents this truth to the will as a real good, i.e. one that will lead man to his last end, his supremely real Good.

We began our discussion by saying that only the saint enjoys freedom in the truest sense of the word. Although not even the saint will find complete freedom of autonomy until his enlightened intellect can intuitively grasp Truth Itself, he has made at least a beginning here and now by his heroic cultivation of the natural and supernatural virtues. He alone understands that freedom does not consist of a succession of isolated acts; that freedom of choice, when correctly understood, is a choice between real goods that will lead him to his last end; that it is but a means leading him to his human perfection, an end that will be achieved only when he has reached full freedom of autonomy.

Freedom of Thought

by Rev. Edward P. Farrell, O.P.
Assistant Professor of Philosophy,
Teachers College, St. John's University

Metaphysically considered the essence of the problem of freedom of thought is the relation of the mind to reality. Is the mind the measure of reality; or does reality measure the mind? On the one hand, if reality measures the mind, then the mind is dependent upon, and must be subject to, reality. Briefly, reality imposes a limit upon the freedom of thought. On the other hand, if the mind is the measure of reality, if it be true as Parmenides claimed that "nothing can be but what can be thought," a dictum incorporated in the ancient axiom, *esse est percipi,*[1] then the mind is free from the obligation of subjection to reality and enjoys the full liberty of creating its own world.

The ancients were well aware of the implications of their answer to the question: *Is the mind the measure of reality?* The affirmative answer, apparently given by Protagoras, freed him from the necessity of investigating reality and made all knowledge relative to the knower. It was recognized that the position leads to the denial of objective truth and to the reduction of certitude to personal opinion. In this way Protagoras laid the foundations for the Sophists of a later day. Grant Protagoras' principle that the mind molds and measures reality and there follows immediately the conclusion that any proposition and its opposite are equally true should they appear to different persons to be true. Prodicus, the Sophist, drew out of the principle its logical consequence in the field of ethics. If there is no truth, there is no good and hence no law to do good. If that alone is true which seems to be true, that alone is good and lawful which seems to be good and lawful. In short, because the mind makes its own truth, the mind is completely free to make whatever it cares to be truth in both the speculative and practical orders. No authority need be consulted, for none is greater than man's own mind; no limits could be placed on this freedom of thought, for there was no one and no thing to impose any limits.

The answer that reality measures the mind, on the contrary, imposed definite limits upon freedom of thought. Now the mind to perfect itself with truth must first subject itself to reality, an intellectual humiliation not readily accomplished without a previous moral humiliation, as Socrates and Plato so vividly demonstrated against the Sophists. Where there is this subjection, where truth captivates the mind first, there could be the true freedom of thought to range within its proper fields without fear of destroying itself.

The answer given to this question of the relation of mind to reality is the basis upon which the problem of free thought is solved in the field of metaphysics. Obviously enough, if reality measures the mind and truth consists in conforming the mind with reality, then truth establishes a limit to freedom of thought. On the contrary, however, make mind the measure of reality and make truth whatever the mind conceives, then the limits of truth are removed. Accordingly, we may formulate the problem of the limits of free thought in this question: Does truth compel acceptance, or is the mind free to reject truth?

For clarification of the question, it is worthwhile to come to terms quickly by examining the immediately obvious possible meanings of freedom of thought. The phrase means different things to different philosophers and schools of philosophy. In the technical terms of scholastic philosophy the predication of freedom of the mind is analogous, for freedom is properly or formally predicated of certain acts of the will and only causally or radically of certain acts of the reason, namely the practical judgments concerned with definite means to an end. Now, in its proper sense as applied to acts of the will of man, freedom is distinguished primarily into liberty from coaction and liberty from necessitation. The first is immunity from violence or external determination and is known also as the freedom of spontaneity,[2] which is characteristic of all activity that proceeds from some principle intrinsic to man. Therefore, according to natural inclination as applied to freedom of thought, liberty of spontaneity is indicative of the natural desire of the intellect for its proper object, truth. It is this freedom of thought that is incorporated into the formula: all men naturally desire truth. Negatively, this freedom excludes things done from force contrary to natural inclination. In this sense, therefore, freedom of thought would exclude the use of violence either to prevent a man from learning the truth or to induce him to accept a truth or falsehood. We shall not be concerned here with this meaning of freedom of thought, for this is a matter of morality and not of metaphysics. Suffice it to say that it is a right, flowing from nature, to know and to have access to those truths necessary to lead a full human life, and violent obstruction of the exercise of this right would be immoral. Recognizable without too much difficulty is the fact that this right does not extend to all truth, e.g., the secrets of others; and the use of violence to prevent the acquisition of such knowledge would be judged by moral principles.

The second freedom of the will, freedom from necessitation, involves three elements: freedom of contradiction, of specification, and of contrariety. The first denotes the power to will or not to will; in brief it is the will's freedom of exercise. Assuredly, it would be absurd to apply this freedom directly to thought to indicate that the thinking faculty is free to know or not to know. Such choice remains the proper function of the will, which moves all faculties, the intellect included, to their proper acts.

Both freedom of specification and of contrariety are pertinent to the matter at hand. Freedom of specification signifies that the will can will this or that particular object as means to an end, as it chooses. It implies negatively, lack of restraint and positively, self determination to a particular course of action. Freedom of contrariety is present when the will is free physically (not morally) to choose evil as well as good. This liberty, as scholastic authors indicate,[3] is not essentially distinct from freedom of specification, and hence can be considered together with this latter liberty. As applied to the intellect, this freedom of specification would signify that the intellect is free to accept or reject truth or even to accept error in preference to truth. More specifically, this liberty, inasmuch as it implies positively, self determination and negatively, freedom from necessitation, would involve a power of intellect to determine for itself what is true and what is false, independently of any external reality and any inclination in its own nature to a definite object. It is in this sense that the problem of freedom of thought can be discussed metaphysically as opposed to ethical or moral considerations.

Since it would be quite impossible within the scope of this paper to restate in its entirety the problem of knowledge, the nature of the intellect and its validity, the validity of sense knowledge, and other allied theses, we shall have to assume as our starting point that man has an intellect, that this intellect has a natural and necessary inclination to know reality, and that when it has attained to reality, it has attained its proper object, which is truth. Assumed also is the principle, namely, that faculties are specified immediately by their acts and mediately and ultimately by their objects. Thus, by force of this principle it is necessary to affirm that if the intellect is to act at all it must act to know its proper object, truth; just as it is necessary to maintain that if the faculty of sight see, it must see its proper object, namely, a colored thing. There are indeed other assumptions made which are not immediately obvious. It is hoped that the astute reader will recognize that as these assumptions appear they are not mere gratuitous statements, but rather cherished scholastic theses, subject to proof.[4]

Having assumed everything necessary for this paper on the part of the intellect, we need now be concerned solely with the object of the intellect, that is, truth, and its relation to the intellect of man. Needless to say, the truth involved is *logical* truth, defined traditionally as the adequation of the intellect with reality.[5] In brief, truth is present when thought corresponds to reality. That the mind or intellect actually does attain truth is a common assumption of the generality of men evident in their ways of distinguishing the various states of mind in relation to truth. The mere lack of truth is called ignorance; the acceptance of falsehood for truth is called error. Again, when truth is attained a twofold state of mind is distinguished: opinion with its inseparable fear of error, and certitude with its consequent firm acceptance excluding all fear of error.[6]

It is particularly these latter states of mind, doubt or opinion and certitude, that are pertinent to the discussion of freedom of thought. While the generality of men are convinced of the existence and distinction of both states of mind, many modern philosophers are openly critical of the possibility of ever attaining to certitude. Urged on by their questions, difficulties, objections, and denials, scholastic authors have made explicit what was implicit in the Aristotelian-

Thomistic tradition concerning the ultimate criterion of certitude.[7] As scholastic authors indicate, the existence of this criterion is beyond doubt:

> That we actually possess a criterion of truth, must be obvious. This is proved by the fact that we change and correct our judgments after having become conscious of error. We would not correct an error, were we not conscious of error; and we could not be conscious of error, if we were not able to distinguish it from truth; and we could not distinguish it from truth, if there were no means or rule or test enabling us to discover both and discriminate them. The fact of discrimination, then, proves that we possess a criterion of truth and actually use it.[8]

What is the ultimate criterion of truth? A unanimous answer given is that it is the *objective evidence of reality*. Why is my judgment true? Because things outside the mind are exactly as they reveal themselves to the intellect. That is the scholastic answer to the seeker of the measure of truth and certitude: reality, objective evidence, measures the mind. This is an immediate truth, a fact of intellectual experience that can not be demonstrated without begging the question. As Fr. Bittle aptly explains it:

> In proposing this proof (that objective evidence is the ultimate criterion of truth), we must bear in mind that a strict demonstration is impossible. Primary facts cannot be demonstrated, but are shown to be true by an appeal to fundamental experience and reflections; what can be shown to be true by a mere exposition of the facts needs no strict demonstration. I cannot demonstrate, for instance, that I actually can see; the fact of seeing is its own proof. Similarly I cannot "demonstrate" that evidence is the criterion of truth, because such a demonstration would require the criterion of truth to prove that it is true: that means that I would prove a thing by itself, which would be a begging of the question. . . . It is only by seeing what actually induces the intellect to accept judgments as true and what actually determines it to give a firm assent to the judgments as true, that I can decide what constitutes this criterion and motive. Now, *experience* and *reflection* clearly show that as a matter of *fact* objective evidence is our criterion of truth and our motive of certitude.[9]

Experience and reflection upon this experience are the sole keys to this problem of truth and certitude. And what is this experience of men? Here the metaphysician joins hands with the man in the street. Our certitude or lack of certitude does not come primarily from our minds; we can always check our judgments by turning again to the reality involved. We look for a ground or reason outside ourselves to check our judgments. When this judgment conforms to the evident reality, and the intellect recognizes this conformity, then objective evidence is present for a true judgment. In brief, the mind is measured by reality and must conform to it, if truth is to be possessed. This is our experience and the Scholastics rest their case on this fundamental experience.

Since the criterion of truth is objective reality, immediately obvious, then, is the fact that the intellect does not enjoy what has been called liberty of specification. Although logical truth resides in thought, and in thought alone, thought does not create its own truth; it discovers truth, but does not make it. The mind is not free from reality; it is very much subject to it. In all truth, truth enslaves the mind.

Truth, however, does not involve a degrading slavery or subjection. It is unfortunate that today we think of subjection as a loss of something necessary for our true dignity. Subjection is an insult to our hopes of being our own bosses. We have lumped together in the idea of subjection all the tyranny and injustice involved in the slavery based on brute force and its consequent fear, and these are, of course, opposed to the true dignity of man. We forget that there is another kind of subjection that increases rather than decreases this human dignity. For one thing, there is subjection to God, subjection of citizen to the State, subjection of children to parents, etc., all of which perfect man by putting him right where he belongs in a position to receive some of the perfection of superiors. In fact, whenever man is placed in his proper place—the real meaning of true subjection—then the subjection is one that nature itself demands for the perfection of the individual. In each instance, the more perfect is the more subject. In matters of truth, the mind more subject to reality is the more perfect mind, the more truthful interpreter of reality. It is more perfect, because it was made to obtain truth precisely by subjecting itself to reality.

Not a small part of the perfection coming to the mind is the consequent freedom that the mind enjoys. It remains always true: "The truth shall make you free." [10] Speculative truth sets the mind free from the darkness of error and ignorance, floods it with the light of knowledge to see more clearly truths already known and to light the way to new truth. Practical truth gives eyes to the blind appetites to see the goals of human life and to avoid the obstacles and pitfalls encountered on the way to that goal. It is truth that the mind wants; it has a burning thirst for reality. Once attained by subjection to reality, truth slakes that thirst and brings a greater thirst for more truth. Here there is no violence, no forcing of the intellect, no going contrary to what it desires. It was made for truth, now it has attained its goal and can rejoice in that attainment.

This freedom of truth is realized most perfectly when objective evidence is most clear and apparent to the intellect. Reality, however, does not always impress itself with equal force and clarity upon the intellect, precisely because the very being of things is different with differences that in many instances impede a certain judgment. Consider, for example, the different kinds of acts discoverable in nature. As St. Thomas states:

> In the acts of nature we discover a threefold diversity. For in some nature acts from necessity and in such a way that it cannot fail. In others, however, nature operates in its own proper way more frequently than not, since at times it can fail to produce its proper act. Accordingly, two different acts are to be found in these operations: one which happens for the most part; the second, when nature fails to produce what is convenient to itself. An example of the first occurs when a perfect animal is generated from the seed; an example of the second is had when a monster is generated from the seed because of the corruption of some principle of generation.[11]

Corresponding to these acts of nature are three acts of mind, three judgments. The first is necessarily true; the second, not necessarily true, but true with varying degrees of probability; and the third is erroneous, since it fails to attain truth.[12] Men recognize these different qualities of their judgments and ultimately trace the difference back to the realities, or at least to a different understanding of the realities. Thus Aristotle and St. Thomas observed:

> The disciplined or well instructed man seeks only as much certitude in each science as the nature of the reality studied permits. For there cannot be as much certitude in variable and contingent matter as there can be in necessary matter which is invariable.[13]

This correlation of objective reality (objective evidence) with the various states of certitude, doubt or probability on the part of the intellect is most important for a more accurate determination of the limits of freedom of thought as well as the proper field where such freedom can be thoroughly enjoyed. Up to this point it has been seen that in terms of liberty of specification the intellect must recognize the limits to its freedom imposed by objective evidence. Now it is a question simply of showing where and why scholastics impose these limits and where the restraints are withdrawn in whole or in part. We have already indicated, in passing, one of the principles upon which the scholastic tradition is based: the kind of reality determines the quality of the judgment as certain or probable. More specifically, the necessary in nature is the basis for certain knowledge; the contingent, the fundament for probable knowledge or opinion.[14]

The necessary in nature, when it is properly understood by the mind, gives rise to two kinds of certain intellectual knowledge: understanding and science. The first is concerned with the primary principles of thought, whether these principles be absolutely first or only relatively so, i.e., first in a particular science or field of knowledge. Known variously as first principles, immediate propositions, self-evident truths, analytic judgments, or suppositions, these judgments are formed by the intellect through an analysis of the subject and the predicate of the proposition without the aid of any strict demonstrative process.[15] Thus, if I know what a whole is and what a part is it is evident to me that the whole is greater than the part.[16] Principles of this kind are at the roots of all intellectual convictions and are used, consciously or unconsciously, in every act of reasoning, thus guaranteeing by their own universal, necessary truth the possibility of obtaining further truth.

Following Aristotle, St. Thomas distinguished these immediate truths into two classes: the Dignities and Positions.[17] The first, called also Axioms, *Maximae Propositiones,* are concerned with the most universal concepts, e.g., being, unity, and the other transcendentals, which are known by all men at least implicitly and cannot be denied by them mentally but only verbally.[18] The second, Positions or Suppositions, include the first principles in the particular sciences which are *supposed* in the particular sciences. They cannot be demonstrated in the particular sciences but can be demonstrated in a superior science. Included also are propositions used in reasoning processes and containing the definitions of the subject matter proper to each science.

By way of summary, then, the necessity characteristic of certain realities imposes itself upon the intellect in its formulation of the first principles of thought, both absolutely first or relatively first in the particular sciences. Accordingly, concerning these necessary realities and the corresponding intellectual principles known as Dignities (Axioms), necessary Suppositions, and Definitions (when expressed as a proposition in a reasoning process) there can be no question of liberty of specification. The intellect was made to assent to these principles as the primary instances in which its proper object, truth, is to be found. It has a natural inclination to assent to these truths, once it has examined the objective evidence thoroughly and recognized the necessity inseparable from this evidence. Only by acting contrary to this natural inclination or desire of the intellect can one claim to be free from the necessity of accepting these truths, and this would be a most strange kind of freedom. Bluntly stated, this is violence depriving the intellect of its desired perfection. At its worst, when error is substituted for truth, it is then a violent shackling of the mind, an enslavement of an enemy. Fortunately, in regards to the first Dignity, the principle of contradiction, it is impossible to do this kind of violence to the intellect, for this principle can be doubted only orally, not mentally.[19]

Derived by a rigid process of demonstration from these self-evident truths, the conclusions of science (in the Aristotelian sense) share in the evidence and necessity of the first and immediate principles and consequently are capable of engendering certitude in the intellect that fulfills all the conditions of demonstration, particularly that of resolution back to first principles. An effect in the intellect of first principles, these conclusions share in the properties of the principles that caused them; like the principles, the conclusions are also necessary and capable of causing a similar certitude in the intellect. Hence, scientific knowledge must also be included among the truths necessitating the intellect, and in regards to these conclusions the intellect does not enjoy liberty of specification.[20]

While the matter of certain knowledge, such as found in the understanding of first principles and in the scientific knowledge of derived conclusions, is admittedly complex, there is a general principle underlying the whole subject: there can be certain knowledge only of what is necessary in nature.[21] The application of this principle to the problem of liberty of specification of the intellect produces a conclusion that serves admirably as a summary of this part of the discussion. The objective evidence of necessity in reality imposes a limit upon the freedom of the mind. Paradoxically, when an individual seeks to free the mind from the necessity of assenting to the truths reflecting the necessity of nature, he is not liberating the mind. Rather, he is doing violence to the natural desire of the intellect and at times, when error is embraced in favor of truth, he is enslaving the mind by forcing it to accept something contrary to its desire.

When then is the mind free, or is it ever free? These questions may well be asked, now that the limits of freedom of thought have been established. The area of freedom of thought may be rather easily determined in a general fashion. As necessity imposes limits, so too the absence of necessity removes the chains from the intellect. Wherever nature lacks necessity, whether totally or partially, there the intellect may have (we can not say enjoy) freedom of specification. In other words, objective evidence of contingency in reality is the essential condition for the mind to be free to accept or reject whatever truth it may have attained. The relationship of necessity in reality to certainty in the intellect is analogous to the relationship between contingency and doubt or opinion. Necessity engenders firm assent without fear of error; contingency, to the degree that it is present, evokes weak assent with fear of the opposite (opinion) or fails to gain any assent at all but leaves the intellect wavering between two possible positions (doubt).

There is a vast field of knowledge concerned with the contingent in nature and consequently a vast field for freedom of thought. In the practical order are the various kinds of prudence, both individual and social, developed by man to handle the concrete affairs of human life. Contingency marks also the representations of truth found in poetry and rhetoric. There is, too, the vast field of the particular sciences that seek to perfect the knowledge acquired in the universal science or philosophy of nature. Worthy of special mention is the topical, opinionative, or dialectical portion of logic that serves as a methodology to the discovery of first principles and to the elaboration of scientific conclusions.

Within the scope of this paper it would be impossible to consider all these fields of probable knowledge in which freedom of thought prevails. For our purposes it will suffice to disengage the element common to all, analyze it to discover its latent principles, and then apply them to one branch of knowledge in which freedom of thought is most perfectly realized and bears its most precious fruits.

The element common to all these various kinds of knowledge of the contingent in nature is doubt, the lack of determination of the intellect to one of several alternatives. Connatural to the human intellect whenever it is confronted with an event, situation, or problem that is in any way strange or unusual, this doubt, called by St.

Thomas the doubt of admiration,[22] is composed integrally of two elements, admiration and cogitation. In its simplest manifestations admiration is characterized by curiosity provoked by knowledge of an effect whose cause is unknown to the intellect. "Admiration is a kind of desire for knowledge; a desire which comes to man when he sees an effect of which the cause is unknown or surpasses his faculty of understanding." [23]

It is to be noted that admiration presupposes both in time and by nature the actual attainment of some truth by the intellect. Nature does not reflect upon itself to cast doubt upon the validity of its own proper activity. Likewise, this doubt presupposes the capacity of the intellect to perfect its general and confused knowledge with clear and particular knowledge, and in this regard admiration stimulates the intellect to undertake a process of intellectual development. Through admiration, the desire of the intellect to attain to truth, nature ensures, or at least attempts to ensure, an ever expanding knowledge of reality.

When admiration endures in a mind for any length of time, it brings into existence cogitation, i.e., an act of mind deliberating and investigating in order to come to the knowledge of truth.[24] In the generation of science cogitation has an important role to play in causing assent to the conclusion of a demonstrative syllogism. The exercise of its causality is found in the resolution of conclusions to prior and ultimately to immediate principles thus establishing as certain a rational medium truly representative of real causes existing in a thing on the basis of which the intellect assents to a proposition affirming the existence of an attribute in a subject.[25] The doubt of admiration, then, nature's stimulus to the acquisition of truth, has the remarkable property of being the point of departure in every new scientific inquiry. Aristotle and St. Thomas have viewed it as the psychological source from which philosophy and science have taken their origin.

> It is owing to their wonder that men at the very beginning of philosophy began, and at the present time begin, to philosophize. In the beginning they wondered at a few obvious difficulties in order that they might come to a knowledge of their causes; afterwards they advanced little by little from knowledge of the obvious to a search for the hidden causes. It is clear that this process of doubting and admiring springs from ignorance, and it is clear that the ancients were inspired to philosophize in order to escape their ignorance.[26]

This text of St. Thomas indicates both the starting point and goal of the doubt of admiration. The source from which it flows is conscious ignorance; the term to which it is ordered is science, or knowledge through causes. Just as no natural motion reflects upon its principle or denies its goal, so too the doubt of admiration does not fall upon any already acquired knowledge nor upon the possibility of the attainment of science. The precise function is to focus the attention of the intellect upon the search for the existence of a hidden cause and for an as yet unknown demonstrative medium linking an effect with its proper causes.

By way of summary, then, of the nature of the doubt of admiration, we may list the following properties:

1. Its principle is ignorance or imperfect knowledge.
2. Its term is scientific knowledge.
3. It is not concerned with previously acquired knowledge; nor does it question reason's ability to know truth.
4. Its precise role is to focus the mind's attention upon the search for a demonstrative medium.

Intended by nature as an instrument to be used by the intellect in its struggle to attain truth, the doubt of admiration is worthy to be called a liberator; for in exercising its function of focusing the attention of the mind upon the difficulties of a question and in impelling a rational inquiry into these difficulties, this doubt gives to the mind the freedom of thought necessary for reaching a true conclusion. The difficulties surrounding a problem, both those that arise from subjective causes and those which flow from the very nature of the problem, were likened by St. Thomas to bonds encircling and enslaving the intellect. That the intellect may recover that liberty of movement and impartiality of judgment required for an objectively true discussion, these chains must be burst asunder. Delivery demands that:

> . . . just as he who wishes to break a chain binding the body must first of all inspect the bond and the manner in which it has been forged, so too he who wishes to solve the difficulties must first examine all the difficulties and their causes.[27]

Since the difficulties of a problem frequently prove too strong to be easily solved, their power of enslaving the mind to the state of ignorance is not always broken. The liberator, admiration, desperately needs help to free the mind in its search for truth, and reinforcement was given to it in the form of an artificial mode of doubt molded according to the pattern of admiration. The purpose of the methodology is to reinstate the elements of natural doubt whenever necessary, and to bolster them up during the intellectual search for truth by pointing out the path to be taken to gain the goal. Fundamentally this process is nothing more than a transformation of natural and spontaneous doubt into an artificial one, one truly methodical.

The method of this doubt has been carefully outlined by Aristotle in his *Topics* and its purpose is clearly indicated. Whereas the wonder of the first philosophers was directed at the obvious difficulties, the master of dialectical or topical reasoning would be able to "raise searching difficulties on both sides of a question," an accomplishment that would enable them "to detect more easily the truth and error about the several points that arise." [28] Briefly, doubt was to be induced strongly to keep the mind free to discover truth. Although the process of methodical doubt outlined by Aristotle in the *Topics* has several uses, as he himself indicates,[29] its most fruitful use is in philosophical investigations to discover a medium of demonstration for science, or a way to prepare the mind to see the necessary connection between subject and predicate in immediate propositions that constitute first principles. In these inquiries thought possesses full and perfect freedom of specification. In regards to the finding a way to manifest first principles, since the principles cannot be demonstrated from a superior principle, since no reasoning process is the cause of their truth, there is no real relation existing between the arguments offered to establish the principles and the acceptance of the principles by the intellect. It is the intellect itself which sees the necessity of assenting to the principles; it alone is the cause of the truth of these principles, and no argument offered causes the mind to assent to these truths. Arguments at best dispose the mind, principally by way of removing impediments, to see the truth of these principles. Accordingly, the mind in forming arguments designed to prepare the way for the acceptance of first principles may employ any of the techniques of dialectical reasoning. It may affirm or deny either part of a contradiction, regardless of the truth or falsity of the side selected. Unlike the demonstrator who must pick true premises to get a true conclusion, the dialectician is indifferent to truth or falsity, because there is no causal link between his premises and the conclusion.[30] At best, in order to merit some assent the dialectician's premise must have some probability, at least it should be a proposition not contrary to the general opinion of men.[31]

In the attempt to discover a scientific medium of demonstration, the dialectician's indifference to truth or falsity permits him to construct difficulties to be doubted on either side of the question. Since he seeks only to pick out probable media of demonstration to be tested scientifically by reduction to first principles, he may assume his premises on the basis of opinion or probability. Since he is not concerned with producing objective evidence of necessity, he may employ even the principles of logical beings based upon the concepts of genus, species, difference, identity, contrariety, etc. Thus, he proceeds from principles extraneous to the reality being investigated.[32]

The use of arguments constructed upon premises of this kind, when the premises are true, helps to establish a probable medium of demonstration, an encouraging sign to a wearied investigator. By their very nature too they serve as psychological forces impelling the reason to continue the search for a real medium of demonstration, a medium which will stand the test of resolution to the ultimate term, the understanding of principles in the light of which the conclusion may be judged.

> Whenever the inquisition of reason does not lead to the ultimate term, but reason persists in the inquisition itself, namely when the inquirer remains indifferent to either part of a contradiction—and this happens when reason proceeds through probable principles— . . . then the rational process is distinguished from demonstration. And in this way one can proceed rationally (dialectically) in every science, in order that from probables the way to necessary conclusions may be prepared.[33]

Thus while reason persists in the inquisition, its natural, physical properties of admiration and cogitation continue to exercise their causality on the mind. The methodical doubt made possible by dialectical reasoning takes its effect of reinstating, or at least, reinforcing the natural doubt of admiration.

In this search for a demonstrative medium and in the attempt to find a way to manifest first principles, thought uses and actually enjoys the use of full liberty of specification. The mind doubts, and really doubts each possible medium or way it can conjecture. Indeed, the more possible positions it can conceive of, the better the process of doubting. It is free and remains free until it encounters the limits of freedom, the objective evidence of necessity that can be recognized as such by the mind itself.

By way of summary it may be said that in the scholastic theory, necessity in reality establishes the limits of freedom of thought; whereas contingency, the lack of necessity, permits the intellect to exercise freedom in its activity. Obviously enough, on the one hand, the denial of all necessity in reality involves logically the denial of all limits of freedom; on the other hand, the denial of all contingency involves the denial of all freedom of mind. Both positions have been proposed in these modern days: *instrumentalism* liberates mind by denying all necessity; *dialectical materialism* enslaves mind by denying all contingency.

The principal tenet of instrumentalism as proposed by John Dewey is the identification of the "true" with the practical.[34] This position presupposes the rejection of all speculative truth and all necessity in nature. Nature is an "unfinished, and ambiguously potential world." Man's purpose is to control and mold this potential world through the use of Dewey's method of inquiry. In this area of thought man exercises full freedom. His knowledge is only an event within nature and follows nature's law of constant expansion. More explicitly, nature is in constant evolution and change; its counterpart, knowledge, is equally variable and relative to the nature it explores. Thus, at one time philosophers were concerned with immutable objects in nature and eternal truths in mind. But now, according to Dewey, scientific method has replaced "fixity" with flux, and eternity with change. The logical consequence of the denial of necessity in nature and the endorsing of the relativity of knowledge must always be, as it is with Dewey, the debasing of the goal of intellect from the noble pursuit of speculative truth to the more humble role of an instrument of production. Man is then, an artist, not a thinker.

Clearly, there is perfect freedom for the mind in Dewey's system; not however the freedom to think, which is the true perfection of intellect, but the freedom from the necessity of thinking, which can hardly qualify as a perfection worthy of man. Dewey truly brought man down to earth from the heights of speculative truth and really set him free in the realm of practical things. But, it has been suggested, that the cost of this freedom is too much—a life without truth to guide it and hence, aimless and without a goal.

Although the principal emphasis in Dewey's thought on the practical and the "this worldly" values in human life makes it extremely difficult for one to see how his philosophy differs radically from the economic and atheistic thought of Communism, still in regards to freedom of thought, Communism's dialectical materialism is contrary to Dewey's instrumentalism. Whereas Dewey completely liberates mind from its true perfection, i.e., truth, Communism enslaves the mind to half-truths and errors. The totalitarian features of Communism extend not only to the basic tenets of dialectical materialism but also to the conclusions of all processes of thought and scientific investigations. In the present era, for example, the world has seen that Soviet scientists have been limited to pointing out in their respective fields evidence for the initial assumptions of the Communist philosophy. Thus, Soviet psychologists must hew to the determined line of Pavlov's experimentation in reflexes to the exclusion of all investigation of psychoanalysis. Reflex activity manifests the continuity of mind and matter far more perfectly than the less predictable results of psychoanalysis. In the field of genetics, too, the Lysenko school's dictum that environment, not heredity, is responsible for human personality must be accepted by all scientists, for this is in accord with Marx's teaching that man is the totality of his surroundings. Briefly, slavery of mind is complete in philosophy and science. As one author has stated in regards to physics:

> The Soviet view of empiriological physics seems often twisted and sometimes even naive. The so-called scientific premises which Communism arrogates to itself often appear like nothing but Procrustean after-thoughts to bolster a preconceived revolutionary theory that casts doubt on the scientific honesty and philosophical open-mindedness of its adherents. An Italian writer recently remarked about the dogmatism which enshrouds the dialectical first principles. They are not even considered questionable, and the effort of present Soviet thinking is only to confirm and illustrate them, never to recall them to the forum of discussion and submit them to rational analysis.[35]

Although many elements of Marxism and instrumentalism may well be singled out for criticism, scholastic philosophy readily and easily renders a judgment on their teaching about freedom of thought. Scholastic philosophy has its principle of judgment: thought is free wherever there is contingency in nature; thought is not free in the presence of necessity in reality. Dewey, accordingly, errs in attempting to free thought completely by denying all necessity in nature. Marxism is defective in enslaving thought by making everything necessary, even the two elements which in scholastic thought are most potential and contingent, matter and motion or process.

Truly, scholastics have been very much concerned with freedom of thought. For them the all important problem has been to keep the mind always free *for* truth, never free *from* truth. The following statements, which serve admirably as a summary of this study, constitute the more important contributions of scholastic philosophy to true freedom of thought:

1. Scholastic philosophy presents a clearly defined concept of the meaning of freedom of thought. As has been indicated freedom of thought, like freedom of specification in the will, implies negatively freedom from restraint and positively self determination. Specifically the intellect is free when it enjoys the power of determining for itself what is true and what is false.

2. Scholastic philosophy offers a basic principle determining the limits and scope of freedom of thought: Necessity in reality establishes the limits; contingency determines the proper field of intellectual freedom. The application of the principle has been made to the various kinds of knowledge attainable: certain and probable.

3. Not the least of the scholastic's contribution is a detailed analysis of the instrument to be used by the intellect in exercising its freedom, and a methodology to sharpen the instrument. The instrument is the doubt of admiration, the methodology is the process of dialectical reasoning outlined by Aristotle in the *Topics*.

Part II

The Psychology of Freedom

The Acts of Freedom

by Dr. Casimir J. Czajkowski
Associate Professor of Philosophy,
St. John's College, St. John's University

In considering the "acts of freedom" in the present article, the term "freedom" is taken in the special meaning of "psychological freedom" as distinguished from "physical" and "moral" freedom. The starting point of this article, therefore, is a review of the meanings of the terms "freedom" and "liberty," for the purpose of clarifying the meaning of "psychological freedom."

Freedom or liberty, taken in its widest supposition, contains a basic concept of indifference, that is, an absence or lack of determination to one effect or to one course of action. From a consideration of the objects of our experience, we find that this indifference or lack of determination may be found either in a passive or an active way. Some beings are passively indifferent in the sense that they have an indetermination in regard to undergoing many changes or modifications. Passive indifference, therefore, is a potentiality *to be acted upon,* to be determined or modified in many ways, just as water is passively indifferent to the temperature that it may receive, or marble to the shape that it may be given. Some beings, on the other hand, are actively indifferent in the sense that they have a capacity *for acting* in many ways, a power of producing many effects. It is this type of indifference that is contained in the concept of freedom, and hence it is the one that requires further consideration.

Attending again to the objects of our experience, a further examination reveals that active indifference may be possessed by beings in two ways. Some beings are immune in their activity from determination by an external agent. The absence of such external determination or compulsion is designated as physical freedom, freedom from coercion or external restraint, or freedom of spontaneous action. A bird in a cage or a horse confined within a pasture has limited physical freedom, for each can move without external restraint but within a restricted sphere. A man in a strait jacket has no such freedom at all. This spontaneity of action does not constitute the essence of *human* freedom, for it is something common to both rational and non-rational animals. The essence of human freedom is immunity not only from external determination or compulsion, but also from internal causes. This type of active indifference, the absence of external and internal determination or compulsion, is designated as psychological freedom or freedom of choice. This is liberty taken in the strict sense, and it is a property belonging only to a rational substance. The essence of psychological freedom is that the activity proceeds from within the agent but without being determined from within. It is the phrase, "determined from within" that distinguishes the physical freedom of the non-rational animal from the psychological freedom of man. Animals, as such, may enjoy physical freedom in so far as there is an absence of external compulsion or restraint, and inasmuch as their activity proceeds from within, but they do not possess psychological freedom because their actions are determined internally by their nature and instinct. Psychological freedom has been defined, therefore, as that active indifference from within in virtue of which an agent has dominative power over his own act, so that, when all the requisite conditions for acting are present, he can act or not act.[1] Viewed from a negative aspect, psychological freedom denotes the absence of determination or compulsion by external and internal agencies. Viewed positively, it implies an active power to act in many ways.

Moral freedom means immunity or exemption from obligation of law. Generally considered, man does not possess moral freedom for the obvious reason that the obligation imposed by the moral law (divine, natural, human) bind with necessity. Man is not exempt from the obligation of doing good and avoiding evil. The fact that he *can* act contrary to the obligation of law is a consequence of man's psychological freedom, of his freedom of choice. The relationship between moral and psychological freedom may be summarized as follows: man *may* not act contrary to moral law (denial of moral freedom), but he *can* do so (assertion of psychological freedom).

To develop more fully the notions presented above concerning human or psychological freedom, we shall next focus our attention on the conditions requisite for the exercise of man's freedom of choice. Philosophical psychologists generally enumerate the following as indispensable ones: 1. attention; 2. presence of a particular good; 3. immunity from compulsion; 4. choice based on reason; 5. active or dominative indifference.

The first condition that is required not only for an act of free choice but for every intellectual activity, is the active functioning of consciousness and attention. Actions which are performed unconsciously, without any internal awareness, lack freedom; for as a free act must be one which is under our control, we cannot therefore, control that of which we have no awareness. Since there are varying degrees of consciousness and attention, we may distinguish varying degrees of freedom, and hence varying degrees of responsibility.

The second requisite condition for the exercise of a free act is that the object of the volitional activity be a particular good, or that there be objective indifference. Because "good, as such" is its proper formal object, man's will, therefore, tends necessarily toward that which is presented as good and desirable from every aspect and without any admixture of undesirability.

It is only in relation to particular goods, such as those which are apprehended as good and desirable under one aspect and not good or undesirable under another, that there is a possibility of choice. More specifically, freedom of choice is not related to an end, as such, but to the various means for the attainment of an end.

The third necessary condition for freedom is immunity from compulsion. A free act is one which is performed without determination, compulsion, or necessitation by external and internal agencies. If the efficient principle of an action is external force or coercion, like the movement of a person who is pushed forward in a crowd, or internal determination, as is the case with the actions of brutes which are internally, instinctively determined, the activity is not free but determined. Here the distinction must be stressed between *compulsion* and *influence*. Psychological freedom requires absence of compulsion and not influence. Man is a composite being, a material organism animated by a non-material rational soul. Although he is formally or actually rational, he is virtually vegetal and sentient. The latter are as truly a part of his essence as is his rationality. This body-soul composite lives in a material world with which it comes into direct and immediate contact. Whatever affects man as part of corporeal nature, and whatever occurs within his own bodily organism, do have a decided effect upon his rational activity, and particularly upon his volition and choice. In making his decisions, therefore, and in determining his actions, man is guided not only by reason, but he is also influenced by his habit, environment, emotions, physical dispositions, and by the external physical agencies about him. Thus psychological freedom demands not the absence of influences, but rather immunity from necessitation.

The fourth requisite condition for the exercise of psychological freedom is that the choice be based on reason, that is, that it be a choice with motives. The term "motive," taken nominally, is "that which moves" man's will. Now what moves man's will is an object intellectually apprehended under the aspect of goodness. So it is not the object as such, but the object apprehended as in some way suitable or desirable that constitutes the motive. It is, in simple terminology, a man's reason for choosing or for acting in a particular way. Human freedom implies the power of determining one's choice according to a judgment of reason. A psychologically free act is one which man chooses to perform for reasons which he knows, when he could choose otherwise since he is also aware of the reasons for the alternate course of action. If man's choice were not directed by reason, it would be motiveless and hence irrational. If the guiding and dominant factor of human choice and action were not reason, man would be acting on blind impulse or instinct, or his activity would be under the dominance of some hidden and unknown agencies which would not be subject to man's individual control since man can only control what is known to him. Modern psychologists speak at times of "unconscious motivation" designating thereby the effect on human actions of past experiences of which a person is totally unaware. It may be noted that the various factors unconsciously determining human action are not motives in the strict psychological sense, for, as was indicated above, motive refers to intellectual *awareness* of the goodness of an object.

The fifth requisite for human freedom is an active or dominative indifference on the part of man's will.[2] To be free, the will cannot be passively indifferent, that is, capable merely of receiving various determinations. Passive indifference is opposed to freedom, for what is capable of receiving determinations from external agents is under the domination of that which determines it. It is only to the extent that external domination decreases that the possibility of freedom increases. Psychological freedom requires an active indifference, a power or potency for acting in many ways, or of producing many effects. But this active potency, as just defined, is not of the essence of human freedom, for the power of acting in many ways may also be found in necessary or non-free agents. It is a mere indifference for acting in many ways, in the sense that the agent can produce not only one effect but many effects of different species. Such is the active indifference that can be attributed, for example, to the sun which produces heat and light; or to the intellect which can perform the acts of apprehension, judgment, and reasoning. For psychological freedom, there must be a dominative indifference, one which contains such an excellence in regard to the possibility of acting in several ways that the agent cannot be necessitated or coerced to act. Even, it may be added, when the requisite conditions for acting are present, he can either act or not act. From the psychological point of view, this indifference means that not only does man's will have power over its own act and effect, to which it moves, but also dominion over the judgment by which it is moved. The will has the active power of directing the intellect in the formation of the judgment according to which it is going to act.[3] In the last analysis, therefore, liberty or freedom means the *power of self-determination,* or, as it has been descriptively phrased: "the ability to settle the issue between conflicting motives by the active interposition of the Ego." [4] Aristotle accurately described the central point of human freedom when he said that "man is the origin and the parent of his actions, as of his children." If man's will is free, he continues, "virtue also must be in our power, and in like manner vice: for wherever we have the power to do, we have also the power not to do; and wherever we have the power not to do, we also have the power to do." [5]

The third condition for human freedom was *objective* indifference; that is, the object had to be apprehended as a particular good, as desirable from one aspect and undesirable from another. The fifth requisite condition was *subjective* indifference, a power residing in man for acting or not acting even when the requisite conditions were present. Now, corresponding to these two types of indifference, philosophers distinguish between indifference or determination as to specification, and indifference or determination as to exercise. The former refers to the movement of the will by an object, the latter to the movement of the will by an agent or an efficient cause. Before applying these notions specifically to man's will, let us consider an example. If I want my child to come to where I am now sitting, I can accomplish this in one of two ways. First, I can pick up the child bodily and carry it over. Here I am the efficient cause of the child's movement, for it is by my own effort that the effect, the movement, was produced. The determination *as to exercise* of the act did not come from the child but from an external agent. Secondly, I can pick up a chocolate bar so that the child can see it, and it will come forward to get it. The efficient cause of the movement was the child, for it was by its own effort that the effect was produced. It was not determined as to exercise by an external agent. There is here, however, another type of determination, one of object. The chocolate bar determined the movement in the order of specification.

Applying these notions to man's will, the will is indifferent in the order of exercise if it is immune from determination by an efficient cause or external agent. Such an indifference plays an essential part in man's freedom, for if the efficient cause of the movement of the will is not the will itself but some external agent, then there is neither self-determination nor psychological freedom. The will is indifferent in the order of specification if it is immune from determination by an object. Referring again to the third requisite for human freedom, the will is indifferent as to specification in regard to a particular good which does not have an invincible attraction for the will since it contains desirable and undesirable aspects.

After such consideration of the factors requisite for psychological freedom, including an analysis of the important psychological concepts of "specification" and "exercise," the question of the limits of psychological freedom follows in logical sequence. From a consideration of the nature of man's will and its formal object, the good as such, it follows that there can be no liberty of specification in regard to an object which is apprehended as good and suitable from every aspect, without any admixture of undesirability. In terms of our own human psychology, what man naturally desires is happiness. Since it is a part of man's nature, so far as his ultimate end in general is concerned, to desire to be completely happy, man, therefore, cannot be indifferent to this state; hence, there can be no liberty of specification in that regard. Furthermore, in relation to those objects which are concretely apprehended as necessarily related to happiness, it appears that there is no liberty of specification. Such things as existence, life, use of our faculties, are desired naturally and, considered in themselves, cannot displease us or seem useless.[6]

Although there is no liberty of specification in regard to happiness and those goods which concretely appear as indispensable conditions of happiness, yet some freedom of choice is left to the will, according to Thomists, in the order of exercise. The reason for this position is that, while we cannot be indifferent when these goods are concretely presented to us, we can will in concrete circumstances not to think of them. By such willing, we do not have to desire them.[7] But even this liberty is very relative, for although we can will not to think of happiness in concrete circumstances, yet at the same time, we cannot will anything without virtually desiring to be happy.

In regard to particular goods, those which are not, here and now, perceived as good and suitable in every respect, but suitable and desirable from one aspect, and unsuitable and desirable from another, the will retains an indifference as to specification and exercise, and so it enjoys freedom in both respects.

Having enumerated the general conditions requisite for human freedom, and having examined the scope of this freedom, we now proceed to an examination of the implications of the fourth requisite condition: namely, that choice be based on reason. Implicit in this condition is that there are two powers or faculties involved in a psychologically free act, the intellect and will, and that there is some interaction between them. However, this problem of the reciprocal activity of the intellect and will cannot be treated in isolation, that is, without considering it in relation to the totality and unity of man's nature. Failure to consider this problem in its proper perspective can only lead to confusion and to difficulties which cannot be intelligibly solved.

The traditional Aristotelian concept of man is the application of his cosmological, hylomorphic principles to Psychology. Man is a bodily being, and like all bodily beings, he is composed of two essential and substantial constituent elements, Prime Matter and Substantial Form. The element present in bodily substances, which makes them capable of undergoing substantial changes, is Prime Matter. This, the substrate common to all bodies, is a passive and indeterminate substantial principle which is the subject of all substantial determinations and substantial changes. It is also the presence of Prime Matter in a substance that serves as the basis of such bodily properties as quantity, extension, divisibility, mensurability, occupation of space, and impenetrability. Although all bodies possess this passive and potential element, which is the subject of corruption and generation, they must also possess something actual, for all bodies have a determined nature, that is, they are actually this or that specific kind of body. Again, in addition to the common element, there must also be a differentiating element for not all bodies are essentially the same. The stone, the plant, the animal, are all alike in being bodies, but each is a specifically determined type of body, and an essentially different kind of body. The principle that constitutes a body in its essence, which is the source of essential differences in bodies, is the substantial form. So the answer to the question: What are the essential constituents of bodies? can be summed up in three statements: 1. There is in bodies a substantial material principle, and a substantial formal principle; 2. Although both these principles are incomplete substances, by their union they form one complete bodily substance; 3. The material principle has the same relation to the formal as potentiality to actuality.

Man is a bodily being, and so he too is a composite of prime matter and substantial form. The substantial form in living bodies is the vital principle, or the soul. What distinguishes man from the lower forms of life is his possession of a rational, non-material soul. The soul, considered entitatively, is that which makes the body a living body of a specific type; considered operationally, it is the root-principle or fountain-head of all vital operations. Although the soul is a basic principle of vital operations, it is not the organism, the agent. The agent or *that which* acts, in terms of human psychology, is the man, the composite, the Ego. It is not the soul that walks, sees, thinks, and wills, but the man, the agent. There are, however, certain principles *by which* this agent acts; the remote principle is the soul; the proximate or immediate principles are the potencies or faculties.

There is a tendency, at times, when discussing the determination of the intellect by the will, and the will by the intellect, to personify these two faculties; that is, of regarding them not as principles, nor as that *by which* man acts, but as agents, as *that which* acts. Sometimes the interaction of intellect and will is compared to a joint action of a cripple, who can see, being pushed in a wheelchair by a blind man, who can walk. This comparison may serve some purpose of initial enlightenment, but such personification can only lead to insoluble difficulties. Intellect and will are not two separate, distinct, substantial entities without any basic unity. They are powers or faculties of one and the same individual.[8] It is not, strictly speaking, the intellect that knows and judges, nor the will that desires and chooses, but it is the man himself who knows and judges, who desires and chooses. It is the man who chooses what he intellectually determines to be here and now suitable and desirable. The intellect and will are the proximate principles *by which* man, the agent, performs these operations.

The will and intellect are powers residing in one agent, but they are essentially distinct faculties. Faculties, in general, are distinguished by their operations, which, in turn, are distinguished by their formal objects, that is, that aspect of a reality which moves the power and makes it operative. The formal object of any faculty, therefore, is its moving cause or principle. Thus, sight, which is moved to the operation of seeing by colors of bodies, is distinguished from hearing, which is moved by sounds of bodies. Now, whereas the function of the intellect is to perform a knowing and judging operation, the function of the will is to perform an appetitive operation. Whereas the intellect is moved by being, as such, the will is moved by being under the aspect of goodness. So that by having essentially different operations and formal objects, intellect and will must be essentially different faculties.

Although the intellect and will are specifically different faculties, this does not prevent them from exercising a mutual or reciprocal influence in the production of a psychologically free act. In beings endowed with knowledge appetition follows some consciousness of goodness, and according as this knowledge is of a sensible or intellectual nature, there is a distinction between sense and rational appetite. Since will or rational appetite is the faculty of tending toward an object intellectually apprehended as good, the operation of the intellect is a prerequisite condition for will activity. Furthermore, because the power by which man wills and chooses is not a cognitive or a knowing power, it cannot be attracted by an object unless it is first presented as good by that power by which man does know. Not being a knowing faculty, the will is not the principle by which man can judge about the goodness of an object. Man must depend, therefore, on the intellect for knowledge of objects and their suitability. Without the apprehension of an object and its goodness the will would remain without a sufficient reason for acting in one way rather than another. Thus, from the point of view of causality, the intellect moves the will in the order of specification as a final or formal cause; for the will is attracted by what is proposed by the intellect as good. To be consistent with our conception of the unity of man, it should rather be said that it is the man who by his intellect knows and judges about the suitability of an object, and by his will chooses it. The cognitional activity which precedes the act of willing, not with a priority of time but with a priority of nature, and which determines the will in the order of specification, is referred to by Scholastic philosophers as "practico-practical judgments." To understand the nature of these judgments which play such an important role in psychological freedom, we shall examine, first, the structure of judgments, and secondly, the various types of judgments which are proper to man.

Judgment is usually defined as the pronouncement by the mind upon the agreement or disagreement of two objective concepts.[9] In more traditional terminology, it is the act by which the mind unites two objective concepts by affirmation, or separates them by negation. To clarify this definition, we must examine the elements of which a judgment is composed. It is made up of two parts: a material element, called enunciation, and a formal element, a mental assent. Before the intellect can exercise its operation of judging or assenting, it must construct for itself something to which assent could be given. Accordingly, it must construct for itself an enunciation, which itself is composed of a material and a formal element. The material element consists of two objective concepts in the relation of subject and predicate, and the formal element is the uniting of these concepts by the copula "is," or separating them by the copula "is not." [10] The members of a jury, for example, who have to make a judgment about the guilt of an accused, must give their mental assent to one of two enunciative propositions: "The man is guilty" or "The man is not guilty." In each case we find two objective concepts united in their relationship of subject and predicate, but they are held in composition in the first one by the copula "is," and in division in the second one by the copula "is not."

Not every union or separation of concepts constitutes a judgment, which requires, in addition to the division or separation, that the mind give its assent; its affirmation or denial that such is the case. In the enunciation the copula, which does not have assertoric force, exercises merely a joining function. It is only after the mental assent that the copula takes on the character of affirmation and exercises a properly judicative function. It is only after the members of the jury, in the example above, give their mental assent to an enunciation that they form a judgment.

Before considering the various types of judgments exercised by man and their relation to volitional activity, it may be noted that appetition in animals follows what is sometimes called "instinctive judgments." These are not judgments in the strict sense for they are not the products of an abstractive and universalizing faculty of the intellect, but of an internal, organic estimative sense or instinct. They are called judgments only by metaphorical analogy, the resemblance being that sense appetition follows this cognitional activity in a way that rational appetition follows rational judgments. The animal instinctively perceives the insensate qualities of usefulness or harmfulness of a sensible object, and the inclination to or away from the object necessarily follows. Neither the action, nor the appetition, nor the judgment, is free, for the animal does not determine its own judgment, nor does it have any control over it. These instinctive judgments are determined by the nature of the animal and the species.

Turning now to judgments which are proper to man, the first type is the speculative judgment, one in which the mind pronounces upon the natures, qualities, or causes of things. In these judgments what draws the assent of the intellect to an enunciation is objective evidence. The subject and predicate are clearly apprehended as related, either in themselves, as in self-evident propositions, or by means of a middle term necessarily joining them, as in demonstrated propositions.

The second type of judgment, the speculativo-practical, is not concerned with the natures and qualities of things but with actions and behavior; not with what things are, but with what ought to be done. They are called speculativo-practical because they are pronouncements about actions in the abstract, independent of subjective dispositions and individual, concrete circumstances. The intellect, either immediately or mediately, perceives that a certain mode of activity or behavior conforms both to the objective order of reality and to the rational nature of man. The intellect assents necessarily to such immediately evident moral principles as "good should be done and evil avoided," and to such mediately evident or demonstrated moral conclusions as "the act of justice in itself is good."

The final type of human judgment, the practico-practical judgment, is a pronouncement about action and behavior in the concrete, as distinguished from the speculative type which is concerned with the abstract or general. By this judgment the mind pronounces as to what is here and now, that is, in these particular, actual circumstances, suitable or desirable. In relation to man's will, it is this type of judgment that plays the part of "motive," for it serves as the determining factor in the order of specification. The fact that it is this judgment, and not the speculative type, that moves the will is due to the unity of man's conscious life. What is desirable to a particular *man,* as the agent, is what suits his particular, concrete condition in concretely determined circumstances. This cannot be determined by the intellect judging in the abstract, without any relationship to man's personal dispositions and concrete circumstances. This is verified by experience which testifies to the fact that what is accepted in the abstract as being good and desirable, may not be accepted as such in the concrete. So a man may judge speculatively that the acquisition of knowledge is good and desirable in general for it perfects man's intellectual nature, but in a given set of concrete circumstances the action of acquiring knowledge may be inconvenient and even distasteful. Although to point out to one's employer the less lovable aspects of his personality may appear as good in the abstract, it fails, however, to move the will for the reason that it appears as unsuitable in the concrete.

Since appetition in knowing beings follows cognitional activity, the nature of the appetition depends on the type of knowledge that precedes it. Since man's choice is consequent upon a practico-practical judgment, in order that it may be free, the judgment which precedes and guides the choice must be initially indifferent or undetermined. Referring to our analysis of the structure of the judgment, to be free, our choice must be preceded by an enunciation, that is, a composition or division which lacks the formal element of assent. Active, dominative indifference, the fifth requisite for psychological freedom, would be impossible if the judgment which precedes the act of willing were determined by causes other than the will itself. Obviously, if the will were determined by a judgment of the intellect which, in turn, was determined by external factors, there would be no self-determination, which is of the essence of freedom. This brings us to a consideration of the reason for the indifference of the practico-practical judgment which precedes volitional activity.

As was indicated above, the modality of an act depends on the type of form from which it proceeds. In beings which lack knowledge, the actions proceed from their natural form or constitution. According to the universal principle of finality, every natural agent tends toward and acts for a definite end or good. The natural tendency, called natural appetite, of every being is determined by its form, which in determining the thing's nature, gives the thing an inclination toward what is suitable for that nature. The seed, because of its nature, will necessarily grow when the suitable conditions are present; the eyes will see; the stomach will digest; the tree will send out its roots to obtain water. These actions are not free because they are predetermined in their causes and inevitably proceed from a determined nature when the requisite conditions are present.

Non-rational animals tend necessarily toward objects which are presented by the instinctive power as useful or suitable. Although sometimes the actions appear as though they proceeded from reasoning, the principle of their activity is an experienced succession of sensory images, subject to the law of association. This accounts for such animal behavior as when a chimpanzee procures a banana hung beyond his reach by piling one box atop another, or inserting one stick in the end of another.[11] The representations determining animal activity are concrete and individual and in no way abstract and universal. The animal by its instinct perceives in an empirical way the insensate qualities of the usefulness or harmfulness of a sensible object in a given concrete situation according as the object does or does not conform to the concrete, physical dispositions of its appetite. The animal perceives some things as good in a sensible manner, but lacking intellect and the power of forming abstract concepts, it does not know them as contained within the extension of the universal idea of good; nor can it reflect upon its instinctive judgments to determine the basis of it.

Man, a rational animal, in possession of a non-organic intellect, is capable of forming abstract and universal concepts among which is the universal concept of "good." Our mental representation of goodness is a metaphysical concept, and like many other such concepts, such as truth, cause, being, it is a representation of a pure perfection. Metaphysical concepts are those which do not involve materiality in their representations, that is, materiality is not an essential note of the represented object. These objects may be positively non-material in so far as matter does not enter objectively into the composition of the object, as is the case with God and spiritual substances, or negatively non-material because materiality has been discarded by the mind through a process of abstraction, that activity of the mind by which it discards the differences among the objects of its attention and attends to their common characteristics. The mind, for example, may disregard the differences among things existible and attend to their one common element, being. Although in reality beings may be material or immaterial, the idea of "being," as such, implies neither, for it contains merely a reference or relation to existence. Metaphysical concepts include, therefore, objects which can exist, and which can be thought of as existing, without matter.[12] A pure perfection is one which not only excludes materiality from its concept, but also every limitation and imperfection. "Substance," for example, is a metaphysical concept and a pure perfection, for in itself, it does not contain either materiality or imperfection and limitation. It is, in traditional terminology, an essence to whose being is due existence in itself and not in another. "Accident," on the other hand, is a metaphysical concept for in its definition as an essence to whose being is due existence in another, there is no materiality involved, but it is not a pure perfection for it contains the imperfection of dependency upon something else. As was noted above, our concept of *good* is a metaphysical concept, and a representation of a pure perfection. But as is the case with many other such concepts, although there is no limitation or imperfection contained within the concept itself, the perfection represented by the concept may be realized in a limited and imperfect way, which is to say that the manner of its existence may be limited and imperfect. Again, the idea of substance contains neither materiality nor limitation, but substances may exist in a more or less limited and imperfect way. An incomplete substance is less perfect than a complete one; a material substance has limitations not found in an immaterial one; a created substance is radically different from an uncreated one. The same applies to the concept of "good." The concept does not contain any materiality or imperfection, but what is represented in the concept may be realized in objects in varying and limited degrees.

Man's possession of the universal idea of good is the basis for the indifference of man's practico-practical judgment in regard to any concrete particular good which may be presented for his consideration. Unlike the brute animal, a rational one can compare the concrete good presented, with goodness, as such, and the result is a consequent awareness that the idea is realized in it only imperfectly and to a limited degree, that in some respects it falls short of the pure perfection. The state of man's mind, framed syllogistically, may be phrased somewhat as follows: My idea of good is what is totally desirable, without any limitation or imperfection. This object or course of action which is presented for my consideration is, from one point of view, desirable or good, and from another point of view, it is undesirable or non-good. Hence the initial state of mind is indifference or indetermination, an indifferent practico-practical judgment.

It is the non-material or non-organic nature of the intellect that enables man to form abstract and universal notions, including such metaphysical concepts as that of goodness, and, in addition, it gives man the capacity to reflect, to examine his own ideas, to judge about his own judgments. Consequently, when a man is inclined to make a judgment upon the desirability of a particular object or act, the potential judgment can itself be brought up for judgment. It is through this power of reflection that man can realize that the reasons which inclined him initially are not compelling, and that there are reasons for making an opposed judgment. Animals cannot do this because they lack intellect, and therefore cannot reflect upon their own judgments and know the reasons why they made them. So the reflective power of man's intellect is also the basis for the initial indifference of the practical judgment. Man's universal conception of goodness is primarily an abstractive goodness, a negatively perfect good, rather than a positively perfect good, which is God. Such being the case, even God himself, in our present earthly existence, may be compared with our abstract concept of goodness, and be found to be not wholly desirable, but desirable from one point of view and undesirable from another. On the basis of faith and reason, man may conceive of God as the Infinite Good, the love of Whom alone can satisfy man's highest aspirations. On the other hand, in a given concrete situation, God may appear as one good in competition with others; the demands of God may seem to be obstacles to happiness rather than conditions for it. Because the act of loving God may involve a practical inconvenience, effort, or physical hardship, it may therefore have, in concrete circumstances, aspects of undesirability. In the speculative and abstract order, therefore, loving God may be judged as good, but if there is a question of a here and now practical judgment, loving God may have aspects of undesirability, leaving the judgment indifferent.[13] The basis of psychological freedom lies, therefore, in the intellect which conceives the abstract metaphysical concept of good, and its judgment is consequently indifferent in regard to every object and act which is not free from every admixture of evil, reluctance, or imperfection.

Since the practico-practical judgment of the intellect which precedes the act of choice is, of itself, initially indifferent or undetermined, remaining an enunciation without the formal element of assent, it must in some way become determined if it is to exercise any determination on the will. On the principle that a being cannot give what it does not have, what is of itself indifferent, cannot exercise any determination upon something else. From the point of view of specification, the judgment cannot be determined by the object, which, being a particular good, is perceived under a twofold aspect of desirability and undesirability, and hence the object is insufficient to compel the assent of the mind. Accordingly, if the intellect is to play a part in the determination of the will in the order of specification, in the order of formal causality, the will must also play a determining part, for it has to intervene to make up for the insufficiency or indifference of the object in the order of specification. The intervention of the will is necessary for overcoming the initial indifference of the practico-practical judgment. The will moves the intellect, as it does most of the other faculties, as an agent, or, in other words, in the order of efficient causality. The reason for this is that whenever there is order among a number of active powers, that one which is concerned with the universal end moves those which refer to particular ends. In like manner, the general of the army who is responsible for the final end of the army, victory as such, may direct and move the lesser officers who direct their subordinates to those particular victories which contribute to the final one. So a king, to use St. Thomas' example, who aims at the common good of the whole kingdom, by his rule moves all the governors of cities, each of whom rules over his own particular city.[14] Now although the will is only one among the several active powers in man, it has as its object the highest end, the good or happiness as such. The other powers are directed to some suitable good proper to it, as sight is directed to color, and the intellect to the knowledge of truth. Whereas the will has a natural tendency towards the absolute good, the other powers tend toward particular goods. So the will, as an agent, controls or moves all the other powers of the soul, except the vegetal ones, whose ends are particular goods included in the universal good.

The fact that the practical judgment which determines the will as to specification owes its determination to the will itself in the order of exercise, is due to the unity of man's conscious life. It is an individual *man* who judges what suits his particular state in a given concrete situation. As was indicated above, the agent of the vital operations is the human person, the faculties being only the proximate principles by which this human person performs his operations. If we consider the nature of the intellectual faculty in itself, we find that it can only judge what is theoretically desirable, i.e., desirable in general or abstract. The truth of a purely intellectual judgment, whether it be the simply speculative or the speculativo-practical, depends upon some objective conformity. In the former, there is truth if there is a conformity between what a thing is and what we judge it to be. In the latter, confining ourselves to moral judgments, there is truth if there is conformity between our judgment of what ought to be with the divinely established objective order. The motive for assent of the intellect in both types of judgments is objective evidence. The practico-practical judgment, on the other hand, does not depend for its truth upon conformity with reality, or upon the objective order of things, nor is objective evidence, as such, the motive for assent. There is a radical difference between the motives for assent in such propositions as: "A straight line is the shortest distance between two points," "Man should not steal," and "I should stop writing for a while." We assent to the first two propositions because the mind clearly understands the reasons for them, knowing that the opposite judgments would be contrary to the nature of a straight line and man. We are conscious that they are purely intellectual judgments, that no other powers played any determining role in our assent. In the third judgment, the mind may have hesitated initially because it was conscious of reasons for continuing to write. Neither continuing nor stopping to write presents itself as absolutely necessary to the intellect. We are conscious, therefore, that the determination to stop writing was not a purely intellectual judgment, but that the human personality, the Ego, played some part in its determination. Since the practico-practical judgment is concerned with what is desirable, here and now, for an individual man, the truth of this practical judgment is a relative truth depending upon its conformity with right appetite.[15] The determination of this judgment must come, therefore, from the active interposition of a particular Ego.

Consequently, the intervention of man's will in the order of specification is explained by its tendency, by reason of which the object enters into a relationship of either fittingness or unfittingness with a particular subject in a given concrete situation.[16] So "the last practical judgment is not merely and wholly intellectual, but contains a large admixture of volition; for if of the two particular goods proposed in the deliberation which thus ends, the will chooses one; it only does so, and puts an end to the deliberation, when one or the other of these goods sufficiently appeals to it, and suits its taste, for it to be satisfied with. The goodness of the object is judged in relation to the appetite which it attracts."[17] The intellectual assent in a practico-practical judgment is connected with volitional consent.

This control or dominative power that man can exercise over his practical judgment is the basis of his psychological freedom. Since man's will is directed necessarily by its nature toward the good, as such, as its formal object, no external factor, whether it be reason, passion, habit, or previous volition, can necessitate it to choose a particular good which has some aspects of undesirability. When man does determinately will or choose, it is only because he himself has determined the judgment in accordance with which he is going to act. It remains a psychologically free act because it is a self-determined one. Man himself has made up his mind what to do.

The position presented above, concerning the mutual interaction of intellect and will, maintaining that the intellect determines the will in the order of final causality, and that the will determines the intellect in the order of efficient causality, seems to involve us in a vicious circle. If man's intellect is moved to form its practico-practical judgment by the will, then the determining activity of the will moving the intellect must itself be preceded by a judgment of the intellect, in virtue of our principle that nothing is willed unless first known as desirable. The judgment of the intellect must, in turn, be determined by the will, in virtue of our position that the will determines, as an agent, the practico-practical judgments of the intellect. But, again, this determination by the will must be preceded by a judgment of the intellect, in virtue of the principle indicated above. Consequently, we seem to be faced with a dilemma, and an infinite series of subordinated acts of intellect and will. If, in an effort to extricate ourselves from this dilemma, we remove the dependency of the will upon the intellect, then we run counter to our fourth requisite for freedom and encounter the difficulties presented in that section. If, on the other hand, we remove the intellect from dependency upon the will, then we are faced with psychological determinism, the absence of self-determination, which is opposed to our fifth requisite for freedom.

The source of the above difficulty seems to be the attribution of temporal priority of one determination over another. It is not, as some philosophers point out, that the will first determines the intellect, and then, in the order of time, the intellect determines the will. It is one and the same act of the will which determines the practico-practical judgment, and is itself determined by it, though in different respects. Hence when a man makes up his mind in regard to a choice of a given good, there is a simultaneous determination both of judgment and appetite. There is no priority of time of the determination of one faculty over the other, but both determinations take place simultaneously. We have here an instance of mutual or reciprocal causality, and the application of Aristotle's axiom concerning the ways in which the different kinds of causes are interrelated, causes which are causes of one another but in a different order of causality.[18] So, for example, matter receives form and makes it individual, while at the same time form determines matter and makes it specific. In this mutual reciprocal causality there is no priority of time, for neither the matter nor the material form can exist without the other. If we try to determine which has the priority, we can only refer to a mental priority, a priority of nature. So from one point of view, we conceive of matter as logically prior for we consider it as the subject which receives form. From another point of view, we conceive of the form as prior for it is the "first act," which constitutes a being in its essential perfection. The same applies to the causality of intellect and will. In the determination of the practico-practical judgment, the act of will determining it, and being determined by it, there is no priority of time. "Here, then, at the point when the last practico-practical judgment is about to be made, the will applies the intellect to judge determinately what is to be done, and receives thereby from this determinate judgment, so instantaneously formed, the guidance and determination of the intellect in choosing that this is to be done." [19] So when the will determines the judgment of the intellect, it is *simultaneously* directed by the intellect in its choice. There is only a priority of nature of one determination over the other, depending on the aspect from which it is viewed. In the order of extrinsic formal causality, there is a priority of the judgment of the intellect, for nothing is willed unless first apprehended as desirable. The intellect gives the psychologically free act its specification by actually directing the will that it may choose in a certain manner. In the order of efficient causality, there is priority of the will, for the will directs the intellect which specifies.

The mere elimination of priority of time, however, does not completely resolve the problem of psychological freedom. In order to avoid intellectual determinism, it remains to be established that the will retains absolute priority or initiative, even though it bears a relation of dependence upon the intellect for specification, for formal causality. If we examine the relation between efficient and formal causality in any activity, it is evident that both are necessary for an action. The formal is required from the point of view of specification, the efficient from the point of view of exercise. Before an action can take place, for example, before an artist can begin to paint, he must first specify or determine his action by a mental image of what is to be painted. He must have some idea of what he is going to portray. But this mental representation is not, of itself, sufficient for the action of painting. Formal causality is never operative in any action unless it is adopted, as such, by an efficient cause. So the idea of the artist will exert its formal causality only if the artist, as the efficient cause makes use of it as the director of his activity. The causality of the idea actually exerts its influence only in virtue of an application of it to action, which depends upon efficient causality. Consequently, although formal and efficient causality are mutually dependent, the efficient cause has absolute priority in the order of causality, for the formal cause exercises its causality only in so far as the agent, the efficient cause, applies it to his activity, by acting under its formal determination.

Applying these observations to a psychologically free act, the will as the efficient cause would have priority of causality over the judgment of the intellect, the formal cause. Although the will cannot be operative unless it is determined by the judgment of the intellect, the formal causality of the intellect is made effective only if the will itself, as the efficient cause, by its own action enters into a relation of dependence on the intellect. In a given concrete situation, when a choice is to be made, the will submits itself to the determination of the intellect by moving the intellect to pronounce the final practico-practical judgment, by which it itself becomes determined. The act by which the will moves the intellect to form the ultimate practical judgment is merely one phase of the one total act, the psychologically free act, the determined practical judgment and the consequent but simultaneous act of choice being the other phases. It must be stressed again that there are not three agents—will, intellect, and will again—producing three distinct acts—movement, judgment, and choice. There is one agent, the human person, moving himself to judge and to choose in accordance with this judgment. As was stated above, it is the man who makes up his mind what to do.

Having considered the role of the intellect and will in a psychologically free act, their reciprocal causality, and the causal priority of the will as the efficient cause, we now come to the problem of the origin and structure of this psychologically free act. How did the whole thing start? What are the series of intellectual and volitional operations which precede the act of choice, and which are, at least with a priority of nature, the immediate preparation for such an act?

The initial step must undoubtedly be the apprehension and volition of an end. It is by willing the end that the will moves itself to the willing of the means. The end is the starting point in the appetitive order in a way that a principle is in the intellectual order. So just as the intellect, through its knowledge of principles, reduces itself from potentiality to act in regard to its knowledge of conclusions, thus moving itself, so the will, through its volition of the end, moves itself to will the means. Through the actual knowledge of principles, the intellect proceeds to an actual knowledge of conclusions, thus being initially in act in regard to principles and in potentiality in regard to conclusions. Thus, with the principle of causality as my basis, I may proceed to the conclusion that there must be a first cause. The intellect is not, therefore, mover and moved, in act and in potentiality in the same respect. The same applies to the will. In so far as it actually wills an end, it proceeds to actually willing the means, being, therefore, initially in act concerning the end and in potentiality concerning the means.

Although the will moves itself to the means through its volition of the end, the question is: whence comes the movement of the will toward the end? Movement is the passage from potency to act, from the undetermined to the determined. Consequently, to be moved is to be in potency, and to move is to be in act. Now a thing cannot be in potency and act at the same time and in the same respect; for example, if I am actually writing now, I cannot be simultaneously potentially writing. So it is impossible that something should be the mover and moved in the same respect, that is, that it should move itself. Therefore, whatever is moved must be moved by another. On this basis we must conclude that the first movement of the will in the order of exercise must come from an exterior principle.

Furthermore, as St. Thomas observes, when a man wills an end, he employs counsel and deliberation about its attainment, and eventually concludes that it can be attained by certain determinate means, which he wills. Through the volition of the end the will moves itself to the willing of the means. But since man begins to will an end, which previously he did not will, he must of necessity have begun to will it through something moving him. Now if the movement of the will toward an end came from the will itself, this could only be possible after a process of deliberation following some previous volition, because self-movement of the will is directed only to the means, which presupposes a prior volition of the end. In other words, if the will determined itself to an end, it is only because the end is actually a means to a previously willed end, and from the volition of the latter it moves itself to a volition of the former.[20] So when a young man wills to go to a medical school, he does so from a previous decision to become a doctor. Such an intention may spring from his desire to serve humanity, a volition which may have as its basis the fulfillment of the Christian precept of love of neighbor. Since this process could not go on to infinity, it must necessarily be supposed that the will advanced to its first movement in virtue of some exterior mover. In this connection it may be observed that although it is of the essence of psychological freedom that the principle of the movement be within the agent, it is not necessary that this intrinsic principle of movement be the absolutely first principle unmoved by another. So although a voluntary act has an internal proximate principle of movement, its first and remote principle is from the outside.

If the first movement of the will as to exercise comes from an exterior principle, it can only come from that which is in some way the cause of the will's nature. The reason for this lies in the fact, as St. Thomas points out, that although it is possible for an agent to move a natural object, yet that alone which is in some way the cause of the object's nature can cause a *natural movement* in the object. Although a man could cause a stone to move upward, such activity is not natural to the stone whose natural activity proceeds from within and is communicated to it by the cause of its nature. The same applies to man's will. The natural movement of the will is from within. If the will were moved by an external agent which is not the cause of the will, it would not be a voluntary movement, and hence not a natural one. So man's *natural* voluntary movement can only come from an exterior principle which is the cause of the will.[21]

The first and natural movement of the will as to exercise can only come from God. The first reason for this conclusion is that the will is a spiritual faculty of an immaterial soul, and the only way that a spiritual reality can come into existence is through God's creation. Being the efficient cause of the will's existence, He is the cause of the natural movement of the will. The second reason is based on the universality of the object of the will. Since the will is ordained by nature to the universal and absolute good, the only possible cause of the will's movement is God, Who is the objective universal and absolute good. Every created good has its goodness not by its essence (for then it would be unlimited goodness), but only by participation, receiving the goodness from God, Who has it by His essence. Every created good is, therefore, not an absolute good but a limited or particular good, and a particular good cannot give a universal inclination, that is, it cannot be the cause of the will's movement to the absolute good. If it were, the effect would be greater than the cause, which is just as impossible as a material faculty producing an immaterial representation, or a plant producing a man. So God moves man's will, as the universal mover, to the universal object of the will, the absolute good. Without this universal motion man would not be able to will anything; for prior to any movement of the will by which it determines itself, there is a movement which is imparted to it by an external agent. The whole series of acts in which the will successively determines itself to new acts, begins from the movement of the will to which it does not determine itself but to which it is moved by an extrinsic agent, God.

Considering the acts of the will and intellect which follow the initial movement by God, psychologists divide them into two general classes: the elicited acts, which originate and terminate in the will; and the commanded acts, which originate in the will but are executed by man's other internal or external powers. Since the commanded acts are merely a prolongation or extension of man's psychological freedom of the will, we shall limit our observations to the elicited acts, of which there are six. Three of these acts are concerned with the end itself: volition, intention, and enjoyment or fruition; and the other three are concerned with the means to the end: consent, choice, and use.

The first in a series of acts which the human will exercises is volition. It is a desire of the end itself, and it is necessarily specified by the first act of the intellect presenting the end as good and desirable. This first apprehension of the end by the intellect and this first act of volition is followed by a second act of the intellect which conceives the end as attainable or realizable. It differs from the first intellectual apprehension in the fact that the first did not include the aspect of the end as attainable, but merely as good and desirable. This apprehension of the desirable end as attainable is followed by a second act of the will, intention. This second act of the will also differs from the first inasmuch as in the first act the will is related to the end absolutely or abstractly, whereas in the second, it is related to the end concretely as the term to which something is ordained. Whereas volition involves the perception of the end as good, and a simple inclination or movement of the will toward it, intention, preceded by knowledge of the end as attainable, is a purposive movement of the will to the end. The difference is clearly indicated in the following expressions: "I wish I were a doctor," and "I intend to be a doctor." In the first expression of volition, there is a simple, abstract inclination toward an end conceived simply as good. In the second, there is a perception of the end as realizable, with a consequent determination to move toward its attainment.

The next act of the will concerned with the end is fruition or enjoyment. Since, however, it is the terminal act of the will, we shall consider next the successive acts which follow volition and intention, and which precede this act of fruition or enjoyment. These acts, which are concerned with the means to the end, are intimately connected with the psychological freedom of man. Resuming the orderly succession of the acts of the intellect and will, we are at a point where the end has been apprehended, loved, and intended. But the question arises: how can this end be attained? Obviously, another intellectual act is required, an act of inquiry into the possible means for the attainment of the intended end.

In matters of action, as was so often indicated, choice is guided by the judgment of the intellect. Since it is here a question of a practico-practical judgment concerning the concrete means for the attainment of an end, and since these means are contingent, variable, and uncertain, the intellect cannot come to any decision without some previous inquiry. It must, of necessity, institute an inquiry before passing judgment on the suitability of the means in relation to the end. This inquiry is known technically as counsel. So counsel, as an integral part of a psychologically free act, is an intellectual inquiry which is limited in scope to human action, and it is basically concerned with the means for the attainment of an end in concrete, determined, here and now, circumstances. Being an inquiry, counsel is directed only to those things that admit of doubt or uncertainty. Now there are several instances pertaining to human acts, where, because of the absence of doubt or uncertainty, an inquiry is not necessary. First, there are instances where there are certain determinate means for the attainment of a determinate end, where the end is attainable by certain fixed rules of action, as happens in the arts. So when a person is writing, there is no doubt, and hence no deliberation or inquiry as to how he should form his letters, for that is determined by art. Secondly, the intellect does not take counsel in matters that are trivial, where it makes little or no difference whether something is done in one way or another, for it plays an insignificant part in the attainment of the end. So if a person has decided to walk to a certain place, it is of little significance whether his first step should be taken with the right or the left foot. Consequently, counsel or inquiry is instituted by the intellect when there are no fixed means or determined ways of employing the means; and finally, when the means have a sufficient importance or bearing on the attainment of the intended end. The basic purpose of counsel is to determine what, in concrete circumstances, it is possible for a man to do in order to attain the intended end.[22]

After the intellectual inquiry or counsel has taken place, the will follows with an act of consent. The term, "consent" as here employed, is really different from the term, "assent." Assent, derived from *assentire,* a shortened form for *ad aliud sentire,* means, literally, "to sense toward something else." The *ad aliud* implies a certain aloofness from that to which assent is given. To consent, *consentire,* means "to sense with," and implies a certain union with the object of consent. Thus, the tendency of the will toward the object is, properly speaking, consent. The act of the intellect, which does not consist in a movement to the object, but rather the reverse, is called assent. Consequently, consent, as a component part of a psychologically free act, is the application of the appetitive movement to the means presented by reason as suitable for the attainment of the intended end. It is, therefore, the desire of the means *in toto*.[23]

To recapitulate, in the series of intellectual and volitional operations which precede the final practico-practical judgment, there is first the apprehension of the end as good, which is followed by an inclination toward it, i.e., volition. This is followed by the intellectual realization of the end not only as good but also as attainable, with the concomitant desire of the end as the term toward which something is ordained, i.e., intention. Next comes the inquiry of the intellect about the general means for the attainment of the end, counsel. This is followed by the will's desire for the means in general, i.e., consent. The next step in the succession of acts is the selection of one definite means to be preferred to the others, constituting the act of choice.

Choice has something that consent lacks, namely, a certain relation to something which is preferred to something else. What usually happens is that in the act of intellectual counsel several means are apprehended as suitable for the concrete attainment of the intended end. Since each of the means is found conducive to the end, and since each meets with approval, package consent, as we may call it, has been given to each. So even after the will has given a general consent or approval to the means presented through counsel, there still remains the necessity of choice, a preference of one means over the others. After approving of the many, a preference has to be given to one by *choosing* it. Of course, if there is only one means apprehended as suitable for the attainment of the end, which alone meets with approval, then consent and choice are not really distinct acts but only mental or logical ones, that is, in our different way of looking at them. We call the act "consent" inasmuch as there is volitional approval of the one particular means. We call it "choice" inasmuch as it is preferred to those means which did not meet with approval or consent. Strictly speaking, however, choice implies a preference among means which did meet with approval.

Choice is the movement of the will to one means in preference to others under the guidance of the practico-practical judgment of the intellect. Consequently, the term "choice" expresses something that belongs both to the cognitional and the appetitive order. When the operations of two powers are related or ordered to one another, we find that in each of the powers there is something belonging to the others. As a result, the act, taken in its totality, cannot be said to proceed exclusively from one or the other power. In the act of choice itself, the operation of the intellect which determines the possible means and judges about their suitability, and the operation of the will which tends to these means, are related or ordered to one another. Therefore, in the volitional act of choice there will be found something of the cognitional order, for the will is guided by reason which alone can know and judge. Counsel, on the other hand, which is an operation of the intellect, contains something of the volitional order, for the following reasons. First, because it is the basic purpose of counsel to determine what man can will to attain the intended end. Secondly, because it is from willing the end that man is moved to make an inquiry about the means. In other words, as Aristotle phrased it, choice is either "intellect influenced by appetite, or appetite influenced by intellect." [24]

So the answer to the question—is choice an act of the will or of the intellect?—is, apparently, that it is the act of both faculties, but in a different manner. Materially, it is an act of the will because the proper object of choice is that which is ordered to an end, that is, that which is a useful *good,* and goodness is the object of the will. Formally, however, choice is an act of the intellect inasmuch as there is a mental comparison and preference of one means over another. The intellect presents something to the will as suitable for the attainment of the intended end. Tying this in with what was previously said about the mutual causality of intellect and will, from the point of view of formal causality, intellectual operation precedes and guides volitional activity. The intellect which determines the will in the order of specification does so by the ultimate practico-practical judgment which, judging on the preferability of means, formally moves the will to the acceptance of certain determinate means. Substantially, however, choice is a movement of the will. In the formation of the ultimate practical judgment, the intellect depends upon the determination of the will in the order of efficient causality. It is this dominative indifference of the will that makes free choice possible, and free choice constitutes psychological freedom. The choice is free because its determination in the order of exercise as well as in the order of specification, is dependent on the will itself. The will directs the cognitive faculty which specifies, and the will elicits the act of choice in the order of exercise.

Following the act of choice, the preference of one means in relation to others, is *use,* which, in general, means the application of something to an operation, and the operation to which it is applied is called its use: e.g., the use of a pencil is to write. In the present context, it is the movement of the will to the employment of the means chosen. Since the will, as the efficient cause, moves the other powers of the soul, use means the will's movement to operation of man's internal and external powers toward the employment of the means chosen for the attainment of the end.

Finally, the termination of volitional activity, which comes appropriately with the termination of this article, is fruition or enjoyment. As is the delight or satisfaction that accompanies the realization of the intended end, this enjoyment is not to be identified with *Joy,* which is an emotion of the sense appetite. The difference in the two is based on the difference in the knowledge of the end and the good. Knowledge of the end may be either imperfect or perfect. In imperfect knowledge, the end is known only in a concrete, sensible way. Such is the knowledge found in non-rational animals, who are moved by natural instinct to whatever they perceive. The possession of a sensible good is accompanied by the sense emotion of joy. In perfect knowledge, the rational being knows not only what it is that is the end and the good, but also the universal nature of the end and the good. This perfect knowledge of the end gives rise to perfect enjoyment in its attainment.

Part III

Internal Freedom (The Freedom of the Individual)

The Proper Concept of Freedom in Individual Acts

by REV. JOHN V. BURNS, C.M.
Professor of Philosophy,
St. John's College, St. John's University

MORAL LIMITS TO THE PERSON'S USE OF FREEDOM

This article makes no claim either to be exhaustive or original. The principles here re-stated and the ideas expressed represent the perennial position outlined in the mind of man from the dawn of reason and promulgated with the Ten Commandments on Mount Sinai.[1]

Characteristic of our mid-century materialism is its complete lack of sympathy with any type of restraint. In an era which identifies liberty with license and in which every prohibition is interpreted as an unjust invasion of the individual's rights, it may come somewhat as a shock and a surprise to the exponents of Modern Liberalism to be told that there are limitations upon the use of freedom. The purpose of this article is to indicate one of the areas in which man's moral freedom is limited and the reasons for such limitations.

Moral freedom "consists in immunity from a moral bond, or from any law restricting the will to one course of action: and in this sense anyone is said to be free to do or to omit anything because this is not forbidden or commanded by any law." [2] Moral freedom, therefore, is the permission to exercise our rights within the limits set by law.

It must be emphasized that moral freedom is to be distinguished carefully from mere physical freedom. Physical freedom is the absence of restraint—the freedom, for example, to sit or to stand—while moral freedom is the absence of a prohibition. There is a prohibition in the Natural Law against murder. Hence while a man may have the physical freedom to kill a child, he does not have the moral freedom to do so, because of the prohibition against murder. "The office of the moral law is that of a *pedagogue,* to protect and to educate us in the use of freedom." [3]

> Law is a rule and measure of acts, whereby man is induced to act or is restrained from acting; for *lex* (law) is derived from *ligare* (to bind), because it binds one to act. Now the rule and measure of human acts is the reason. . . .[4]

Hence, a *law,* in the classic definition of St. Thomas "is nothing else than an ordinance of reason for the common good, made by him who has care of the community, and promulgated." [5]

Law may be either eternal, natural, or positive. The supreme care of the community is in the hands of its Creator. God, Our Creator, bears to those things He has created the relation of an artificer to the works of his art; furthermore He governs all the acts and movements to be effected in each of His creatures.

> Wherefore as this type of the Divine Wisdom, inasmuch as by it all things are created, has the character of art, exemplar, or idea; so the type of the Divine Wisdom, as moving all things to their due end, bears the character of law. Accordingly the eternal law is nothing else than the type of Divine Wisdom, as directing all actions and movements.[6]

Law is considered natural or positive according to its manner of promulgation.

> In order that a law obtain the binding force which is proper to law it must needs be applied to the men who have to be ruled by it. Such application is made by its being notified to them by promulgation.[7]

Law, promulgated by positive statements of the Divine Legislator, is termed Divine Positive Law. These same commands of the Divine Legislator, when made known by the light of reason, make up the Natural Law.

The Natural Law

"We have not here a lasting city but we look for one that is to come." [8] Because man is destined for a world hereafter, God has given him a law to direct him to that end. Lest man object to being governed by the laws of another world when he is still living in this world, God has seen fit to implant in his very nature directions sufficient for his guidance. Inseparable from his nature, this direction is called the Natural Law; and because man is a rational animal this law which guides him must be based on reason to conform to his nature. Consonance with reason, therefore, is the formal constituent of moral action.[9]

Only those men who have lost their reason are no longer governed by the Natural Law. For them the law is as it were suspended. Hence those human beings who have lost the use of reason, or who never attained it, are not executed or imprisoned for their transgressions, but cared for in asylums. Not having reason they cannot be held accountable for their acts.[10]

> Every rational creature has a certain light from God that is totally lacking in the lower animals, and in those deprived of reason; a certain tendency in the will toward moral goodness and an aversion toward all evil. This apprehension is not studied but spontaneous, and it is before any knowledge that comes from study or revelation or human law and customs, although it exists side by side with them. It comes to us from our nature to enable us to lead a higher life than the animals, who are guided simply by sense. Some people refer to it as the Natural Moral Law.[11]

The Natural Law is man's participation in the Eternal Law, hence its authority comes from God. No one can say that there is no absolute standard of morality which is everywhere and constantly identical. If this were true, civilization would cease. Morality is not made by Kings or Councils, nor does it depend on popular opinion or the customs and traditions of men. No human sanction, whatever be its power or however vast be the extent of its influence, can turn wrong into right. The reason it is so hard to blot out truth is because the conscience of mankind as a whole has a true instinct that prevails in the long run over any perverting of the moral code. For a time perhaps, due to extraordinary conditions, the moral sense of a community or a country may be darkened; wicked fashions, for example, may become more or less general; but the conscience of men in general is usually right. Practices such as polygamy or euthanasia, that are at variance with the divine code of Moral Law, do not become right from the fact that the state sanctions them and everybody is doing them; neither will the fact that they have become common, exempt transgressors from punishment in this world or the world to come. When men choose to ignore principles so that they may enjoy unlawful pleasures, such actions do not abrogate those principles or render men less guilty in the eyes of God. The results of such actions teach us to judge which are false and which are true, regardless of custom.[12]

Just as the Ten Commandments can be summed up into love of God and the love of neighbor, so also are the dictates of the Natural Law reducible to one general principle: "Good must be done; evil must be avoided." Using his reason fully man can live a morally just life based on that principle. However, in order that there be no uncertainty on man's part as to what God expected of him, God gave man clearer and more positive expression of what He expected of our weakened human nature in His Ten Commandments and through human positive legislation. In order that man might have no excuse for evading or avoiding God's law, lest man protest that the Natural Law was too vague, and hence inoperative and invalid, God gave it clarification in more elaborate detail.

> But all those positive laws which direct man to his final end are based on the Natural Law and can be learned from reason by a normal individual. Human lawmakers have, of course, not attempted to codify virtue in their legislation, and for this reason man in his journey to his final end will not always find a complete set of signposts along the way. Wherever the road is not marked by statutes of the positive law, man's reason must supply him with the necessary knowledge. In other words the Natural Law must supply signs for whatever roads have been left unmarked by the positive law, *and must even determine when a sign is turned the wrong way and may lead the traveler astray.*[13]

In a unique way, therefore, the Natural Law fulfills the role of pedagogue assigned to it by St. Paul and Aquinas to protect and to educate man in the right use of his freedom.

Admittedly the Natural Law may not always be sufficient for man's guidance, so varied are the degrees of civilization, so varied the degrees of learning, so varied the individual differences of individual personalities, not to mention man's inherent weakness and his tendency to avoid those things which are difficult. Hence the Divine Positive Law, given by direct revelation, and Human Positive Law, both ecclesiastical and civil, are needed to give man more specific guidance as a means whereby he may direct his life to its final end.

> A single example of how the principle of the Natural Law has filtered down into human positive law might be shown thus: The Principle, "Do good and avoid evil" is made more specific in the Commandment, "Thou shalt not kill." In turn this prohibition is enacted into human

positive law which forbids murder and other forms of homicide. And it is further elaborated in divers statutes, such as those regulating the sale of firearms, and even those regulating traffic, for it is admitted that the latter statutes lessen the loss of lives resulting from the use of motor cars. But without any of these last mentioned laws, normal man knows from the dictates of reason that it is unlawful for him to kill.[14]

On the other hand subjection to law, whether it be Divine or Human, Natural or Positive, does not mean the loss of freedom. True freedom, it will be recalled, is the permission to exercise one's rights within the limits set by law. Such freedom consists in the power to choose between *good* objects, not between good and evil. The law, our pedagogue, has told us the difference between good and evil and forbids that evil be chosen. The law, once known, leaves no freedom to choose between good and evil. We may be physically free, psychologically free, to make such a choice, but not morally free. Moral freedom, true liberty, is the freedom to exercise our rights within the limits set by law.[15]

What kind of freedom is this which the law allows? Nothing else than the freedom to choose between or among many good things, among the many things conformable to our nature and capable of conferring good upon it. Law marks off the boundary lines that parallel life's broad highway. Outside these margins is evil, within are numberless spheres of legitimate choice: "the path of legitimate free choice is as broad as reason–that is, correct reason–itself, as broad as the fullness of life." [16]

Needless to say those limits marked off by law are not accepted by all. Modern Liberalism offers its false notion of freedom "conceived as the absolute autonomy of the human will, not only in the physical but also in the moral order, . . . complete independence from all human and divine authority." [17] It is the purpose of the succeeding portions of this article to examine some of the exaggerated claims of modern liberalism in the area of freedom of speech, which means for the modern liberalist "the moral power of teaching, by the spoken or written word, whatever one wishes." [18]

Basic Philosophical Differences

The conflict between right reason and modern liberalism begins at the point at which philosophies begin. The Christian philosopher starts with God, and having accepted God as the Creator of the human race accepts likewise that He has charged man with obligations arising from his personal dignity, his immortal destiny, and his relationship as a social being. These obligations are in reference to the Creator, to his family and fellowman, to the State and to the community of states; for the fulfillment of these obligations and rights form the substance of the Natural Moral Law which can be known by reason. One of the greatest points in this philosophical framework is the conception that obligations and rights are correlative, for at all times the obligations to respect the rights of others operate against the arbitrary use of rights.

Extreme liberals, on the other hand, may begin with the deification of the individual whose wishes, whims, and caprices must be the starting point of all else. In such a set-up the individual is thought to have the absolute and unlimited right of a god. For those whose convictions are so construed, there can be no understanding how an ideal order with its roots in the nature of man and of human society can impose moral requirements universally valid in the world of experience, of history and of facts, and can lay down alike for the conscience and the written law, the permanent principle and the fundamental and universal norms of right and duty.[19]

Because the true concept of freedom is centered in God, the interest, therefore, of all Christian peoples both in preserving true freedom and correcting the misunderstandings concerning it, rises above any purely natural consideration and rests on the fact that man is destined by God to enjoy a supernatural end.

Freedom of Speech

Among man's most priceless prerogatives is his ability to express his thoughts to his fellow-men. Not even the angels enjoy the power of speech; of all God's creatures, only man has received this faculty. When the animals emit sounds, these are not the outward expressions of ideas but mere indications of sense needs. Man, because he is intelligent, is able to form concepts not only of bodily things but even of realities, abstract and immaterial, transcendental and spiritual. Not only has man the power to form ideas, but he has been equipped to express them. He can unpack his soul in words. His God-given faculty of speech enables him to acquaint others with the sensations he experiences and the concepts he forms. Through arbitrary signs and letters, man can confirm his ideas and feelings in writing. The dictaphone and the recording machine enable him not only to preserve his ideas but even the sound and tone of voice in which they were uttered.

In our day there are scarcely any physical limitations to the power of communication. Not even the invention of printing five centuries ago represents the ultimate means of expressing thought and preserving ideas. In more recent times, the telephone and the telegraph have eliminated even the distance problem as an obstacle to human conversation, and the radio with its national networks and short-wave transmissions has overcome the last barriers to man's power of communicating with his fellow-men. Today it is possible for a single individual to speak directly and personally to anyone who may choose to listen on any part of the earth.[20]

The power of speech as well as the devices invented to aid it can be used for good or for evil. They may ennoble man or degrade him; they may be sources either of peace and harmony or of discord and hatred. Hence, these added improvements and increased facilities of communication bring with them added responsibilities and increased obligations to use these benefits only within the limits set by law. God who has given the power to speak has imposed also the obligation of using that power for purposes that are morally good, while refraining from any use that would be morally evil.[21]

Because no reasonable person would advocate freedom of speech, "if this is understood to mean that everyone may say what he wishes under any circumstances," [22] it is therefore obvious that there is no such thing as absolute freedom of expression. As Mr. Justice Holmes so strikingly remarked "the most stringent protection of free speech would not protect a man in falsely shouting fire in a theatre and causing a panic." [23] There have to be some limitations to freedom of speech. Even when a man is convinced of a truth of a statement, he does not thereby necessarily become immune from correction or the obligation of retraction. There is no freedom for error, only for truth. A school boy may be quite convinced that three and three make seven but his conviction does not gain him a perfect mark in solving his problems. Consequently, in this discussion of freedom of speech it will be more profitable to consider what one is not allowed to say rather than what one may say. Again we call upon the law—Divine and human, natural and positive—to guide and educate us in the use of this freedom as in all others.

The law of God imposes definite restrictions on freedom of speech.

What are they? First, *lying*, for deliberately speaking against one's mind is never permitted. No one is entitled to tell a lie; not even the fact that some good is anticipated could excuse a falsehood. The end cannot justify the means and it is evident even from reason that society would suffer immeasurably if misuse of the God-given gift of speech were not in every instance forbidden. The natural law, which insists that faith in human communications be observed, tells us that if it were allowable to indulge freely in lying, confidence in the truth of words exchanged between members of society must almost immediately disappear. If in any set of circumstances a man were allowed to lie, his associates could never be sure on any occasion that he was telling the truth, for they could never be certain that, unknown to them, those conditions might prevail which would justify a lie on his part.[24]

Furthermore, there is no freedom to misuse the gift of speech by discussing or disclosing the real or imaginary faults of others. *Calumny* injures the reputation of another unjustly by telling a lie concerning him—imputing to him faults he never committed. *Detraction* is an equally unjust injury to the neighbor's reputation through the revelation of his true, but hitherto unknown, faults, weakness, or difficulties. Even civil law holds us responsible for statements, oral or written, which defame another's character; and the offender may have to answer the offended party's law suit in a libel or slander action. However, this can hardly be construed as an unjust limitation to the right of free expression; rather is it a recognition of the right of others to maintain their reputation free from vilification.

What right has a man to his good name? If his good reputation is genuine, he has an absolute right to its possession and no one can justly take it from him. Even if his reputation is a false one, his right to it, though secondary to the common good or the necessity of protecting the rights of an innocent third party, is still inviolable as far as another individual is concerned. St. Thomas refers to a man's reputation as the most precious among temporal goods, and his words will support his analogy of reputation as a "social life" next in order to man's physical life and integrity.[25]

Now while every right contains the property of coercion, not every right carries with it the right to the exercise of coercion; this belongs *first* to constituted authority, and only *secondarily* to the individual, and then only in default of the primary. Hence, "every person has the right to be esteemed as good until *proved* to be bad." [26] A man, therefore, may defend even his false reputation; and no private individual may take it from him without being guilty of an act of injustice equal to stealing another's goods.

An argument parallel to this would be that a man's reputation, although false, has been acquired through his efforts, and is therefore his property by the title of labor. No one therefore may presume to take it from him, except from a more fundamental title, equally just, namely, the common good or possible injury to third party.

Finally, the common, or social good, which lives and thrives on the currency of reputation, could not survive if each individual could presume to adjust and readjust properties, such as reputations. Man therefore has a right even to his apparently good reputation, and unless a prior right prevails, no one can take it from him.

Blasphemy—insulting language about God and holy things—is forbidden by Divine and positive law: "Thou shalt not take the name of the Lord Thy God in vain." Blasphemy adds a note of contempt, insolence or rebellion against God. It is therefore a form of sacrilege, and as such, the civil law prohibits language of this type. Recently, however, there has been some confusion in the interpretation of the civil law, on this point, as well as laxity in enforcing it. For example, it is obvious that on the stage profane expressions are tolerated that deeply shock the sensibilities of any who cherish reverence for religion. Modern fiction writers, too, sometimes consider it a sign of cleverness to cast crude slurs on religious beliefs or practices that are held in veneration by good Christians.[27]

Freedom of speech gives no one a real right to express himself in obscene or indecent language. The extent to which the radio broadcasting companies have gone in preventing such an abuse is highly to be commended. Father Connell notes, however, that "it may also happen that restrictions will have to be put on radio commentators, some of whom are most unjust and unreliable in their remarks about governmental policies and persons in public life." [28] Many moderns complain that motion pictures are too well censored; however, a large part of the motion picture audiences have been children in their impressionable years. These are entitled to exceptional safeguards against lewdness and obscenity. Merely to punish the exhibitors of indecent pictures and suggestive dialogue after the fact, is scarcely the way to protect and preserve the morals of children.

The objection is frequently offered that the theatre and television are expressions of art; that art and morality enjoyed definite and perpendicular existences without any interrelation; and that even the great St. Thomas himself insists that art does not come under the rule of moral science. Here again we meet with the view of the extreme liberalist.

When St. Thomas says that art does not belong to moral knowledge, he means, as Jacques Maritain has shown, that the goodness or badness of a work of art, *as such,* does not depend upon the virtue or depravity of the artist. Indeed, the private lives of some of the world's great artists have not been models of right living. It is not the job of the artist, as such, to give moral edification but *to make something that is beautiful.* No doubt great artists might have been better artists if they had been better men, but it is irrelevant to pass judgment on their work on account of the shortcomings of their private lives.

Does this mean that there is, then, no relationship between art and morality? By no means. One of the four moral virtues which must govern the activities of man is the virtue of prudence, which directs everything to one's final end—God. *Now, while art, as such, is independent of prudence, the artist himself is not.* The artist, like every other man, is a rational being, created by God and must act prudently in the light of the moral law, so that he will ultimately attain his last end.

Prudence, unlike Art, presupposes the rectitude of the will with regard to eternal verities. Its task is to reduce all our subordinate activities, even artistic, to conform to the moral law. It does not, of course, prescribe the rules of a particular art, but it demands that the artist should behave, even when engaged in his art, as a responsible moral agent. The exercise of prudence, however, does not mean that the artist's work should be religious or even morally edifying. But it means that it must be executed in subject and treatment with an eye to the effect of the work, first on the artist himself, and secondly, on the community at large.

This responsibility of the artist is borne out by the Christian purpose of art, which is to aid the spiritual and moral well-being of man. Because its purpose is not solely to produce intellectual or sense delight, it cannot therefore contemplate or include anything which under the test of sound moral judgment or experience is calculated to be harmful to the welfare of souls.

Consequently, the radio or television artist may not scandalize an audience by presenting a situation of depraving realism which he seeks to justify on the grounds that because it mirrors the world as God made it, it therefore is legitimate art. Because the entire method of art is one of selection, this argument is fallacious and deceptive.

There is no such thing as exact realism in any art: the work of an artist must necessarily be highly selective. After first selecting the subject that is to be treated, he then determines the procedure to be followed in treating it. For an intelligent and faithful Christian artist, every step of his process will be taken in the light of the true purpose of art. He will see to it, for example, that the artistic task to which his talents are dedicated, even in the field of entertainment, will tend to better, not weaken, the moral well-being of the audience.

Every work of art is a creation of a person whose life must be lived under the eternal mandates of the moral law and every work of art is intended for an audience of persons who similarly are under the eternal mandates of the moral law. Hence, while the quest for artistic perfection should receive every reasonable aid, encouragement and opportunity, it must be remembered that the artist himself enjoys no unique, sole or extra-territorial rights. His position is subordinate in that domain of human affairs in which the moral law, divinely imposed, is supreme.

This applies particularly to the screen and television because they are powerful magnets which strongly attract to their graphic message the young, the impressionable, and the innocent—those whose protection against moral evil is both a grave obligation and a supreme objective.[29]

Perhaps it was the realization of this principle that caused the National Association of Radio and Television Broadcasters to endorse a code of ethics designated to eliminate obscenity, pre-occupation with sex, horror dramas, and other abuses in video programs. This code was approved on December 6, 1951, and became effective March 1, 1952.

Television, busy and excited as it is at the moment, has taken time out to watch where it is going. Since its inception, there have been lapses in taste and judgment which if they were not checked promptly, could have serious consequences on the industry. It had rapidly become apparent that television was going to have to watch with the greatest of care the evaluation of its own standards of conduct if only because what it presented before the camera carried such an impact in the home.

It did not come as any great surprise, therefore, that television broadcasters themselves, in an effort to forestall action by Congress and the Federal Communications Commission, drafted their own code. This code served in itself as an answer to a bill before Congress that called for a National Advisory Board to act as a watch dog over abuses in television.

Preamble of the Code

In their preamble, the code drafters reminded broadcasters that they were "obligated to bring their positive responsibility for excellence and good taste in programming to bear upon all who have a hand in the production of programs," including sponsors, advertising and talent agencies. Program materials should provide "wholesome entertainment and remind the viewer of his responsibilities towards society," the preamble said.

Proscribed under the code are profanity, obscenity, smut and vulgarity. Use of a long list of words and terms prohibited on radio as obscene and vulgar is barred. Attacks on religion and creeds are banned.

Divorce is not to be treated casually; illicit sex relations may not be treated as commendable; sex crimes and abnormalities are unacceptable material for programs; reference to sex perversion is forbidden; drunkenness and narcotic addiction may not be presented as desirable or prevalent; illegal administration of narcotics may not be shown; the use of liquor in American life, except for plot or proper characterization, is not to be shown, and gambling devices may not be displayed in a manner to excite interest or foster betting.

Fortune telling, astrology, phrenology, palm-reading and numerology exhibitions are barred for television under the code.

With regard to crime and mystery programs, the code prohibits the presentation of criminality as desirable; the condoning of crime or presenting it in a frivolous, cynical or callous manner; the presentation of techniques of crime in such detail as to invite imitation; the use of horror for its own sake; the use of visual or aural effects that would shock or alarm the viewer, and the detailed presentation of brutality or physical agony.

Officers of the law are to be portrayed with respect and dignity;

suicide is not to be depicted as an acceptable solution for human problems, and exposition of sex crimes is banned. With regard to responsibility to children, the code calls on broadcasters to avoid material that is excessively violent or that creates morbid suspense. The code prohibits references to kidnapping of children or threats of kidnapping.

A section on "decency and decorum" calls for costuming of all performers "within the bounds of modesty."

Ridicule of race or nationality is prohibited. Morbid, sensational or alarming details in newscasts "should be avoided," the code says.

Political television programs are to be identified as such. While sponsored religious broadcasts are not forbidden, the code discourages acceptance of pay for them.

With regard to advertising, the code asks broadcasters to bear in mind that television is intended for the home and family, including children. Thus it proscribes advertising of hard liquor, firearms and fireworks—subject to Federal and local laws—intimate personal products, tip sheet and race track publications and advertising and other organizations promoting betting or lotteries.[30]

Morality of Comic Books and Strips

A similar code and more stringent censorship should have been applied long ago to comic strips and comic books. Many of the former in daily papers are objectionable in one way or another; for example, almost all the fantastic hero-comics deal in crime. This can have serious consequences. To many children whose home and religious training is defective, such comics appeal strongly as an incitement to crime, if they do not even furnish ways and means of criminal action.[31]

Crime comics are especially damaging to children in grade school. These youngsters ought to be taught early in life both by precept and example a respect for property and life; respect for the police and other duly appointed guardians of the law. *Many fantastic crime comics glorify the fantastic hero, not the police.* In such comics the latter appear dumb, lazy, inefficient. Furthermore, the amount of crime in crime comics gives very young children a dangerously false notion of the world in which they live. Most serious of all, crime comics show graphically the excitement, publicity, and profit to be had from a life of crime.

Supermen are *fantastic* comic book heroes. The regular routine of these heroes is a violent conflict with gangsters and thugs, usually involving considerable damage to life and property, with the "hero" winning out at the end through the use of superhuman, fantastic powers. Violence, publicity, sensationalism, are the trademark of these supermen types of heroism. They deal almost exclusively in crime and matters which are far removed from youngsters' or adults' daily life. They solve their problems with means entirely beyond human reach. They operate outside the law as self-appointed additions to the police force.[32] Youngsters realize this. What can they learn of order in the matter of public law enforcement when parents or teachers approve unauthorized super-sleuthing by presenting such comic book characters as heroes?

The smashing of buildings, automobiles, bridges, and things in general, plus the wholesale damage to human life in such comics is, to put it mildly, a negative contribution to a child's sense of life and property values.

In Christ's life we find wonders which more than surpass the exploits of all the imaginary comic book heroes—but without the headline heroics, the thugs, the deadly weapons, the capes and fanfare. In Christ we have the perfect hero—the superhuman and yet human; perfectly imitable both in the problems He faced and in the means He used to solve them. As a means of travel He walked though He could have flown; when his enemies attacked Him, He appealed, not to force, but to reason; when the devil tempted Him to cast Himself down from the temple tower—a superman stunt—He refused. Though He could have used His startling divine power at any moment of His life, He chose, almost without exception, the human solution to problems—to give us a perfect example.

War Comics

War comics are decidedly harmful to youngsters. They teach hate while exerting all the damaging influences of other fantastic hero comics.

War comics thrust on young minds the critical problem of evil in its worst manifestation, international anarchy. They present the picture of mass destruction to life and property. Whether or not the admiration which older grade school children gain for real war heroes from reading such comics is worth the accompanying horror of death and destruction is questionable. Even with older children, the less war comics, the better.

Undue and Untimely Emphasis on Sex

The true Christian attitude toward sex has always been idealistic, candid, and—in proper circumstances—sincerely outspoken. It has been productive of personal integrity and peace of mind. The Christian standard of sex-control calls for proper sex-instructions by proper persons adapted to needs as occasions arise. It requires a program of living which fills a youngster's time and thoughts with so many active, worthwhile pursuits that the sex appetite is reduced to a negligible factor of disturbance in the pre-adolescent life. It also calls for training in modesty. Necessary but negative elements in modesty are the avoidance of speech, abbreviated clothing, and posture in ways calculated to arouse sex. It is evident, most of all to the publishers who play up sex, that nudity and exaggerated sex characteristics have the sole purpose of arousing sex. All such comics are unconditionally condemned.

In this matter, as in so many others,

> . . . the Catholic Church is neither prudish nor reactionary, but her attitude toward the disgusting flood of filth that some would have us believe is an evidence of a healthy trend toward realism, is an unqualified condemnation. The Church is conscious of Her mission to preserve and to develop in the minds and hearts of her children that glorious virtue of Which Christ and His Virginal Mother are resplendent exemplars, and which He extolled so highly when He said: "Blessed are the clean of heart, for they shall see God." [33]

Some crime comics have furnished children with ideas which resulted in self-destruction. A case in point is that of Edward England of Chicago who strangled himself in bed trying to imitate what he had read in a comic book.

Children given to fantastic crime comic addiction tend to develop the habit of escapism—seeking to dodge life's real duties and difficulties by flight to the world of imagination. Dr. Kenneth E. Appel, M.D., Assistant Professor of Psychiatry, University of Pennsylvania Medical School, says:

> One million children in The United States public schools today will some time go to mental hospitals if we follow the patterns of the

past . . . these mental failures are, in large measure an indictment of the too soft, indulgent, and unrealistic rearing and education of our youth in home and in school.[34]

Christ as an ideal appears pale and puny to a comic addict fed on the headline heroics revealed in *Supermen, Wonderwomen, Batmen, Black Terror* and the rest of their fantastic brood. The age-old miracles of Christ look trifling and meaningless beside the up-to-the-minute antics of the comic super-sleuths. Such everyday heroism in the Christian mode of conquering schoolwork instead of gangsters, cleaning out a playroom instead of a machine-gun nest, is a dull letdown for children gorged with war and fantastic crime comics.

It is a matter of fact vouched for by leading juvenile authorities and supported by testimony of delinquents themselves, that crime comics are far from negligible among the factors which cause *juvenile delinquency*. Judge Harold Scoville of Phoenix, Arizona, affirmed that it had been not only his experience, but also, in his opinion, that of every judge handling juvenile cases, that from time to time very young children, after being brought to court as a result of serious conflict with the forces of law and order, admitted that they gleaned information and guidance for some of their anti-social activities from the more lurid type of so-called funny book. Judge Braude of Chicago Boys' Court declared that he felt all along that the objectionable comic strips which appear in most of our newspapers can be said, in a sense, to be factors which predispose towards delinquency in juvenile and adolescents. There have been, he maintained, actual cases where the difficulty of the boy could be traced directly to some idea which he got through either such comic strips or some objectionable radio program.

An examination of a few of these cases of juvenile delinquency indicates that younger children are committing more and more serious and violent acts. Dr. Fredric Wertham, a leading criminal psychiatrist, offers some striking examples to confirm and support this assertion.

1. Three boys, six to eight years old, took a boy of seven, hanged him nude from a tree, his hands tied behind him, then burned him with matches. They could not find their first choice for this treatment—a girl of six. Probation officers investigating found that they were re-enacting a comic book plot.

2. A boy of eleven killed a woman in a holdup. When arrested he was found surrounded by comic books. His twenty-year-old

brother said, "If you want the cause of all this, here it is: It's these rotten comic books. Cut them out, and things like this wouldn't happen."

3. A boy of thirteen committed a "lust murder" of a girl of six. After his arrest, in jail, he asked for comic books. "I refused, of course," said the sheriff. A boy of thirteen who spent "most of his time looking at comic books" committed a "sex murder" of a girl of four.

4. In order to prove that he was "no sissy," a boy of fourteen garroted and killed a boy of eleven.

5. A boy who had participated when a group attacked and seriously stabbed another boy was found with a knife which had a legend inked on the sheath: "Kill for the love of Killing."

6. A boy of twelve and his eight-year-old sister tried to kill a boy of six. They threatened to knock his teeth out, stabbed through his hands with a pocket knife, choked him, kicked him and jumped on him. The police captain said, "It is the worst beating I've ever seen, child or adult." [35]

Dr. Wertham writes,

> My investigation and those of my associates have led us, very unexpectedly at first, but conclusively as the studies went on, to the conclusion that crime comics are an important contributing factor to present-day juvenile delinquency. Not only are crime comics a contributing factor to many delinquent acts, but the type of juvenile delinquency of our time cannot be understood unless you know what has been put into the minds of these children. It certainly is not the only factor, nor in many cases is it even the most important one; but there can be no doubt that it is the most unnecessary and least excusable one.[36]

Summation

The purpose of this article has been to indicate one of the areas in which the freedom of the individual is limited. These limits may arise from the natural or positive law, the rules of ordinary decency, the sensibilities of our fellow-men, or the effect of one's actions on the moral standards of the community. In restricting this topic to the sphere of communication, it seems advisable to insist once more that its treatment makes no pretense of being either original or exhaustive. The pertinent and authoritative testimony advanced, however, will give food for thought to those who insist that every one is free to speak or write whatever he wishes.

The easiest way to lose freedom is to claim too much of it. The extreme liberalist who wishes no restraint and acknowledges no curb to his freedom is well on the way to losing this priceless privilege. Those very factors which limit freedom are the roots also which sustain it: namely God, conscience and the natural law. When one denies the existence of God, he stifles also the idea that man was made for God, that he has an inalienable right to seek Him and the freedom to carry out his aspirations unhampered and unhindered. When one denies the existence of that objective standard of conduct called the "Natural Law," morality becomes the common denominator of what people usually do—a form of moral relativism which will eventually destroy the most elementary of moral standards and freedom as well.

Deprive a man of his soul, or its immortality, and you cut off the idea of inalienable rights; man then becomes a machine, a bundle of reflexes, a robot without intelligence and without responsibility. Man's rights and freedom are, as a result, at the mercy of other men and he is no longer a creature of God with an eternal destiny, but rather a chattel of the state, a mere cog in a social machine.

Conscience, the stern voice of duty, tells each man that he cannot live according to his whim, that he has a work to do, a destiny to achieve, and that he ultimately is responsible for the fulfillment of his life's work. Man cannot abdicate this responsibility; neither can he make it over to the state nor to any temporal authority. Such responsibility, however, is unthinkable without inalienable rights and powers. When each person has the inescapable responsibility of achieving his personal destiny, he must also have the inalienable rights and unhampered freedom to do everything necessary for that purpose; *because no one can be bound to do what he is unable to do.*

Conscience, then, far from lessening man's freedom is one of the strongest roots which nourish it.

BIBLIOGRAPHY

Appel, Kenneth E., "How Parents Change Children into Mental Misfits," *Your Life* (Dec. 1944), p. 88.

Banay, Ralph S., "2d Psychiatrist Joins Attack on Comic Books," *Herald Tribune,* Jan. 4, 1948, Sec. 2, p. 11, col. 2.

Baucher, J., "Liberte" *Dictionnaire de Theologié Catholique,* 14 Vols., Paris (1909-1939), Tome 9, cols. 660-703.

Bittle, Celestine N., *Man and Morals,* Milwaukee, 1950.

Connell, Francis J., "Catholic Church and Freedom of Speech," *Catholic University Bulletin,* Vol. 17 (July 1949); "Freedom of Worship," *The Catholic Position,* New York, 1944; *Morals in Politics and Professions,* Maryland, 1946.

Cushman, Robert E., *Our Constitutional Freedoms,* Indiana, 1944.

Grenier, Henri, *Thomistic Philosophy* (tr. by J. P. E. O'Hanley), Vol. 3, Canada, 1948.

Healy, Edwin F., *Moral Guidance,* Illinois, 1942.

Hochwalt, Frederick G., "Human Rights," *China Missionary Bulletin* (Aug.-Sept. 1951).

Lehmkuhl, Augustine, *Theologia Moralis,* 10th ed., Vol. 1, Switzerland, 1898.

Leo XIII, Pope, *The Great Encyclical Letters,* 3d., New York, 1903.

MacGuinness, John, *Commentarii Theologici,* Dublin, 1910.

MacIver, Robert Morrison, *Conflict of Loyalties,* New York, 1952.

Manion, Clarence, *Lessons in Liberty,* Notre Dame, Indiana, 1939.

Maritain, Jacques, *Freedom in the Modern World* (tr. by Richard O'Sullivan), New York, 1936.

Matt, Walter L., "Crime Comics and Your Child," *The Wanderer,* Vol. 23, Nov. 5, 1953.

McCann, John, "The Purpose of Liberty," American Catholic Philosophical Association *Proceedings,* Vol. 16 (1940), pp. 130-143.

McIntyre, Francis J., "Liberalism Leads U. S. to Disaster," The *Wanderer,* Vol. 23 (May 28, 1953).

Molloy, Thomas Edmund, "Mission Sunday Pastoral," *The Tablet,* Oct. 18, 1952, pp. 1, 2.

O'Hara, John Joseph, "Archbishop Emphasizes Obedience to Natural Law at Bar Association Mass," The Philadelphia *Catholic Standard and Times,* March 14, 1952, pp. 1, 7.

Prisco, Giuseppe, *Principii di Filosofia del diritto,* Naples, 1872.

Quigley, Martin, "Purpose of art, Movies defined—Martin Quigley asserts Moral Perfection is their end," *The Tablet,* March 13, 1953, p. 20, col. 1-3.

Southard, Robert E., *Our Comic Book Children,* St. Louis, 1950.

Taparelli, D'Azeglio, *Essai theorique de Droit Naturel,* 2nd. ed. Tome premier Tournai, 1875.

Thomas Aquinas, Saint, "Treatise on Law" (*Summa Theologica,* Ia-IIae, qq. 90-97), Chicago, Ill.

Wertham, Fredric, "What Parents Don't Know About Comic Books," *Ladies' Home Journal* (Nov. 1953), pp. 50, 53, 214, 220.

Part IV

External Freedom (Social Freedom)

Freedom and Government

by Dr. Irving G. Williams
Professor of History,
Teachers College, St. John's University

Whatever else may be said of the Twentieth Century, it is apparent that it ushered in a new historical world epoch. For if the antecedent period (modern history) had any meaning at all it was that it had been primarily an era of the rise, development, and generally successful achievement of political freedom for more and more nations. From the breakup of manorial particularism during the late Middle Ages to World War I, the significant movements of world history hinged directly or indirectly around the concept of the overthrow of the *status quo* in order to enlarge the area of man's initiative.

Of course, over such a long time span and under such varying local conditions, generalization becomes hazardous, but two main trends of the movement are readily apparent and may be fruitfully examined. The dissatisfaction with things as they were polarized around the effort to throw off foreign domination (nationalism) or to throw off inhibiting internal despotic régimes (liberalism). Down to the Nineteenth Century, which was itself the culminating age of the twin movements, four political revolutions served as prototypes of all revolutions for freedom: the English Revolution of the Seventeenth Century, the American Revolution and the French Revolution of the Eighteenth, and the Latin-American Revolutions of the early Nineteenth Century.

In all these is seen the dichotomy already referred to above, for two of them, the English and French Revolutions, commenced primarily as internal affairs of the nations concerned, and the other two were struggles for freedom from foreign domination—from an absentee ruler motivated by concepts that a later age would call colonial imperialism. However, regardless of the specific causes for revolt for freedom, none of them remained solely the domestic concern of the principals involved. The export of revolution occurred in all cases, and the principles of the original English Revolution as refined and adapted to meet later times and conditions, ricocheted alternately back and forth from Europe to the New World. No one doubts the influence of John Locke's justification for the transfer of effective power from King to Parliament on the American *Declaration of Independence,* just as no one doubts the influence of both Locke and Jefferson on the *Declaration of the Rights of Man* in revolutionary France. The twin examples in one generation of the thirteen British colonies in North America and of France throwing off absentee despotism on the one hand and indigenous despotism on the other, proved too much for Spain's America to resist; and thus her colonies too raised the standard of revolt in the name of liberty, accompanying it with mainly North American republican constitutional principles.

Of the above noted revolutions for freedom, only the English and American have resulted in any long-time stability of governmental forms and substance. The English alone retained monarchy, ultimately more as a symbol of the national unity, and the North Americans alone retained their Federal Constitution, drawn up after a short unsuccessful period of confederation. The French have experimented with constitutional monarchy, republicanism, and crowned or uncrowned despotism ever since, whereas the Latin-Americans, while retaining their republican constitutional forms, have, nevertheless, been characterized by the authoritarian *caudillos* in all but a few areas for relatively short periods ever since their independence was won.

This is not to suggest any inherent superiority in the Anglo-Saxon to gain and maintain political freedoms under effective representative forms. Rather it is to point out the real difficulty of winning over history by means of the revolutionary method. The English (and their American cousins) had been the beneficiaries of the long evolutionary struggle to contain political power of which Magna Charta (1215) was one of the early written manifestations. Thus viewed, both the Seventeenth Century English and the Eighteenth Century

American Revolutions were further advances in the struggle for freedom of the people. But neither France nor the Latin-American colonies of Spain had any real precedents in ancient liberties periodically proclaimed or fought for. The measure of post-revolutionary difficulties faced by these areas is explainable, at least in part, by their heritage. Thus must revolutions for freedom be viewed, not as one homogeneous kind, but as a phenomenon whose long-term results may depend on what has been that area's prior governmental experience. Even in the name of revolutions for freedom, tyranny may be exchanged for tyranny, as witness present day Russia and China.

In an important measure then, is a nation the prisoner of its historical past, and though it is relatively simple to commence revolutions for the purpose of destroying root and branch the old régime, the process is often attended by reactions, restorations, white terrors, and political confusions that may result in the last state being worse than the first. Timely education is still a better reformer than revolution.

As the Nineteenth Century advanced, the shock waves of nationalism, liberalism, and attendant republicanism reverberated in ever widening circles, resulting in the efforts at national unification in Central and Eastern Europe. Sometimes the efforts succeeded (Germany, Italy), sometimes they did not (Austria-Hungary and parts of the Turkish Empire). But the important thing was the persistence of the effort, and the consistency of approval of the aims of self-rule on libertarian principles.

From this point of view the former modern historical epoch carries down into our own newer age, with the battleground now in the hitherto somnolent continents of Asia and Africa. But the rise of nationalism and the revolutionary spirit seeking to overthrow foreign rulers in those continents is not the key to our own age. That must be looked for in another direction. For though, in a sense, the movement of the non-white areas of the world for political self-expression is an extension of the Western Revolutions, it operates in a wholly different political climate fraught with danger to those who are really friends of freedom.

If we must label our latest epoch of history, it might well be called "The Age of Totalitarianism," and however long it may last, it seems pretty apparent that it commenced with the onset of the First World War. For that war created conditions that permitted the first of the current totalitarian states to arise—the Union of Soviet Socialist Republics. And the main distinguishing feature of the Red Revolution of 1917 that placed it outside the framework of the older internal revolutions in England or France was its complete denial of the principles of religious, political, economic, and social polity that had hitherto governed men's affairs in the modern world. The accession of the Bolsheviks was not just the triumph of another point of view in running the affairs of state, it was the triumph of anti-State, the enemy of all existing political organizational forms. It deemed them all to be exploiters of "enslaved" workers and by Communist theory vowed to obliterate them all in the interests of creating a universal classless society. Thus here was a threat not in the line of political reformism as it had developed over the centuries of the modern age, but a threat from outside the world's political development and destructive of all forms of freedom, however politically expressed. Theoretically kings, presidents, and parliaments were all alike in being anathema to Communism; and constitutions, bills of rights, political freedoms, and freedom of religion were all "opiates" to lull the workers into thinking they had rights, but really to ensure the continued political dominance of the economic overlords of the world, the "capitalists." Thus was the entire world, national and colonial alike, threatened in its very existence by the new totalitarianism of Marxian Communism achieving its first political success in Russia in 1917.

World War I itself was not particularly an ideological war at its commencement. Prussian autocracy seeking world-wide domination may or may not have been a correct estimate of Germany's intentions, but at all events it was old-style absolutist-tending monarchy, too much discredited by 1914 to hope for long-term success, even if it should have won a military victory. The world knew well how to battle overweening kings seeking to impose themselves over non-nationals. This feeling of limited aims in Germany even if victory came, may have accounted for the necessity of injecting an Allied ideology to which all men of good will on both sides could subscribe. At all events Woodrow Wilson, the President of the United States, destroyed the mortar holding the Central Powers together and, probably unwittingly, countered the "new principle" of Communist totalitarianism by the idea of "the self-determination of peoples." Here was bait to hold out to the subject peoples of the multi-national Austro-Hungarian and Turkish Empires, which would spur internal revolution by the promise of recognition by the free world of nationalistic freedom. Here was the moral justification for the Allies in fighting what heretofore had been really considered a war for maintenance of the balance of power. Now World War I became the "war to end wars" in order to "make the world safe for democracy" and to advance the cause of human freedom all over the world. The ideology of world democracy had been set forth hard on the heels of political success for the totalitarian ideology of the Communist left.

In the period of the long armistice (1919-39) which followed the first defeat of Germany, the totalitarian ideology of the right was posited and executed in both Italy and Germany. This "wave of the future" was deemed by some to be the only effective answer to international atheistic Communism, since "decadent democracy" was unfit either to rule its own people or to defend the frontiers from the pressures of the Third International. However, Nazi-Fascist concepts were themselves so destructive of individual human freedom that, coupled with a program more aggressively belligerent toward western representative states than totalitarian Communistic Russia, the democracies again found themselves at war with Germany; a war made possible only by the live-and-let-live Nazi-Soviet Non-Aggression Pact of August 23, 1939. The anti-liberal ideologies of right and left had established their own *modus vivendi*. Nazism should attack and destroy liberal nationalism and its democratic ideology, while Communism should stand clear of the débâcle and reap the rewards. Because Hitler refused to allow this possibility to result, and invaded Russia (1941), the Communist left was perforce thrown into operational consonance with the West.

The failure—at least for the time being—of the bid for universal power by the totalitarian right has only cleared the ring of one of the main contenders seeking to make totalitarianism triumph. The older, tougher, and more subtle Communism remains, while at the same time the democratic West, weakened by two World Wars in one generation, seeks to maintain not only its freedom—collectively and individually—but also an accompanying security. Thus the "cold war" of the present time is the definitive struggle which will determine whether Western Judeo-Christian civilization with its concepts of freedom from despotism, whether foreign or internal, will continue, or whether the black night of atheistic nihilistic Communism will conquer. Over all is the further possibility, no longer remote, that in the process of determining the outcome there will be in the hands of the combatants the means of obliteration of both sides.

In such a state of affairs, a re-examination of the bases for our political beliefs is not only wise but also mandatory. For it is not enough to know one's enemy—world Communism; one must also know one's self, his own nature and ideals, his own strength and weaknesses. It would be fatal to waste our energies merely in exposing Communism for the fraud that it is, while at the same time letting the positive basis for our demonstrably successful way of life be dissipated by a vapid anchorless insistence on the rights of individuals. It is often asserted that the present conflict between the West and Communism is a struggle for the possession of men's minds, the only safe form of conquest there is. If such be the case, then it is imperative that we be sure we understand our own ideology before we try to win others to it. What follows, then, is an effort to re-state the principles governing the reciprocal relations of the human being to the State and its government, and a summary inspection of the American experience with the problem. However, before commencing, it would be well to illustrate the anchorless thought of the present day which, if not rejected, must surely lead to the triumph of materialistic Communism. One of America's most respected jurists, who has had the function over the years of interpreting the concrete application and meaning of many of our most cherished civil rights, recently spoke of the difficulties in determining questions of rights. Judge Learned Hand offered the opinion that:

> It is the voters, speaking through their delegates, who . . . can and will preserve our liberties, if preserved they are to be. For their guidance there are no *vade mecums,* no handbooks, no manuals; they must depend upon such enlightenment as they can muster from within, and upon their conscience, so far as they have one. That enlightenment and that conscience they may indeed find in divine revelation; but when they do, they tap sources that I am not qualified to discuss: not any better qualified than I am to discuss what doctrines are inherent in the nature of Man in Society. I know of none of either sort, nor can I find direction from those who profess to know. . . . There appears to be no escape in each situation from balancing the conflicting interests at stake with as detached a temper as we can achieve.[1]

It is just such "learned" observations which emphasize that the pragmatic view dominates American thought. That it is putting us on the defensive in the world-wide struggle for freedom, scattering and confusing us so that we are not sure of anything's validity, are all inevitable consequences of the denial of the relevance of revelation and the natural law to political philosophy. When man's liberties depend on the whims of voters at the polls, then indeed will America's political freedoms exist by unstable sufferance only. And for the present, if Judge Hand's principle of judicial action is usual with the courts, then our political liberties depend on giving conflicting interests some proportionate advantages rather than resolving those conflicts according to ageless principles.

The proper beginning, then, of any discussion of political science is the First Cause and the Last End of all persons and things—God, Personal and Unitary. Creator of the world and all things in it, God fashioned man as a whole person, endowed him with a reasoning mind and an immortal soul, and because of his very dignity as a human being, gave him inalienable freedoms.[2] Thus are these latter held, not because of the beneficence of any earthly authority (not even Judge Hand's "voters, speaking through their delegates"), but because of the fact of man's having been created. Thus is a man, regardless of his race, color, creed, national origin, economic or social status, entitled to the respect of all other men and human agencies because of his origin, his nature, and his final end.[3] No omnipotent individual or State can intervene to block or divert the direct flow of communion between Maker and creature, because to do so is to contravene the Divine Purpose for man, which is the attainment of eternal supernatural happiness by living according to man's own nature and God's own law while here on earth. To violate revelation or natural law by statutory enactment or by pragmatic regulatory ordinance is to make it unduly difficult, perhaps even impossible, for the individual to attain his earthly purpose, which is the salvation of his soul. Therefore, those in positions of authority must be extremely cautious lest they, even unwittingly, maim or destroy the clear yet delicate channels of relationship between Heaven and earth.[4]

Yet if the individual is thus of such supreme worth and so richly endowed with the means of successfully attaining his natural and supernatural ends, it is likewise true that everywhere he lives—not by himself alone—but also in society—in association with other individuals.[5] All his life he may have been a member of a family, first as a child of his father's family, later as the father of his own. Additionally, the individual may have a variety of other associations with what may be collectively termed private institutions: a church, labor union, civic organizations, social and fraternal clubs, trade associations, or alumni groups. Finally the individual is associated with public institutions: the organs of political governance established in the State to promote its ends. Thus does the individual, in the United States for example, have his associations with a variety of public institutions that may include all of the following: village, town, school district, fire district, sanitation district, county government, state government with its variety of special bureaus, and federal government with its ever-growing complexity of boards, agencies, and commissions. Thus is it apparent that even just physically speaking, the problem of maintenance of the just respect for the individual is growing more difficult as government itself proliferates in an increasingly industrialized society.

In such a welter of associations, not to mention the association of an individual with other individuals in their non-institutional capacities, it is clear that any study of man's freedom as a social being must be delimited for purposes of such a paper as this. Thus we are concerned here not with any problems of "Man's inhumanity to Man" in the individual, familial, or private institutional areas, but only with those in the public institutional one. Furthermore, though the principles of the due limits of the rights of individuals and of public authority as hereinafter described are timeless and geographically universal, the discussion of their history and application must perforce be limited primarily to our own country's experience.

The dynamic principle of political organization in the world has long been the State, and as the usual form for the political association of God-made individuals, it also is of God. This is what Pope Pius XI meant when he said: "God . . . destined man for civil society according to the dictates of his very nature . . . society is a natural means which man can and must use to reach his destined end. Society is for man and not *vice versa*." [6] The State is often conveniently described as a body of people permanently occupying a definite territory, politically organized and relatively independent of external control. Thus, to qualify as a State, five elements must all be present: population, a definitely bordered geographical area, relative permanence of existence, a government, and sovereignty. The first three offer little difficulty of understanding: obviously to have a state there must be people, and the number is immaterial. Population-wise, Vatican City with its few thousands is as much a true State as India with its three hundred million inhabitants. But not all populations are States. True nations may be lacking one or a combination of the other elements characteristic of Statehood (usually the missing element is sovereignty), in which case whatever else they are, the populations are in some other status than a State. It is this aspect of community life that attracts the sociologist, who prescinding from political considerations and concentrating on people as a social group, aptly defines a nation as a group of people bound together by common language, tradition, culture and aspirations, and enjoying a subjective sentiment of unity or consciousness of kinship. Thus India was always a nation but did not become a State until the Republic of India was proclaimed in 1947, and thus the Jews of Palestine until the establishment of Israel in 1949. Contrariwise, the Eskimos are still a true nation, but no State.

As with population, so also with territory it is relatively immaterial in theory how large a particular state is. What is important is that the boundaries of the State be certain. Since the State has the right to the allegiance of all its people and the further right to rule throughout its extent, it is indispensable that it know where its rights end in a territorial sense. Hence the delimitation of borders of states, exactly and unambiguously, has always been a basic concern of all nation-states, and no people is so peaceful that it lightly regards what it views as a violation of its borders. No boundary dispute has ever been other than a "vital interest" to the nation adversely affected, and history indicates the primary place boundary questions have as breeders of tension and conflict. The current dispute between the new States of India and Pakistan over the disposition of the Kashmir Valley is illustrative of the persistency of the problem.

The quality of permanence in the State is of course not absolute, for states have risen only ultimately to disappear; but a relative degree of continued life forms a part of the concept of the State. The connotation of permanence also includes a distinction between the State and its form of government at any one time. The State is "eternal," the government is not. From this point of view, France as a State is the same today after four republics as she was in the days of Louis XIV. The State is permanent, the governmental form may be impermanent, but the qualities of the State are unaffected. It is this aspect of the matter which is technically at the base of the current question regarding Chinese representation in the United Nations. The question is not one of admitting China into the UN, for China is a State and is a charter member of the world organization. The question is one of which government shall represent the State of China there: the one that still does (the Nationalist government established on Formosa) or the Communist government on the mainland.

However abstract in general the concept of the State is, there is nothing abstract about its fourth element—government. Government is the authorized agency of the State, expressing and exercising its authority. Thus, at any particular time the State will exert its will by means of the agency of government. The form of the governmental institutions may vary from state to state and within the state from time to time, but in general it is true to say that whoever controls the government controls the state, especially in the absence of a clearly written constitution or tradition of limited state power. So when Louis XIV, the prime example of the monarch who said he ruled by divine right, avowed "I am the State," he was really wrong in principle, though right as far as the exercise of power was concerned. It is this fact of the theoretical agent actually controlling the principal unless or until revolution breaks up the process, that accounts for Anglo-Saxon suspicion of strong government with its centering of power in one or a few men.

The Americans' chief contribution to political theory was their separation of powers principle embodied in the Federal Constitution, whereby they divided such governmental power as was given the central government into legislative, executive and judicial power, and provided for separate, coordinate, and independent branches in government to exercise their respective grants within a further framework of checks and balances. Here, carried to the furthest restrictive point that the political world had yet seen,[7] was the mistrust of the tendency of government to tyrannize emphasized.

The final element of the State is sovereignty, at once the most simple and the most complex of characteristics. In the definition of the State already given, the emphasis was placed on external sovereignty—the relative freedom from foreign control, the relative absence from foreign domination. What the dividing line for "relative" may be in particular situations, is often hard to determine. But obviously there is a difference between the United States limiting herself in the methods she employed to wage the Korean War due to the views of her UN partners there, and the limitations exercised by a Balkan satellite state due to the views of the U.S.S.R. Whatever may be said with regard to the latter's sovereignty, it is clear that the sovereignty of the United States is unimpaired. Perhaps the line of relative external freedom is best drawn along an axis that includes the nature of the limitation on freedom of action and its voluntariness on the part of the nation being limited.

Sovereignty, as an internal aspect of the State, means the supreme will of the State to command obedience, to the point, if necessary, of overriding the will of all other associations within the State. Internal sovereignty is thus the paramount fact of the State, domestically considered, which again, in the absence of correct moral principles, accounts for the totalitarianism of both Fascism and Communism. For the supreme overriding will, above spoken of, must be harnessed to Divine Law; else it is arbitrary, unprincipled, and tyrannical. Failure to recognize that the State, like its government, is a means for accomplishing the Divine Purpose for man, leads to the totalitarian error of which the following is an example:

> For Fascism, society is the end, individuals the means, and its whole life consists in using individuals as instruments for its ends. . . . Fascism . . . faces squarely the problem of the right of the state and the duties of individuals. Individual rights are only recognized in so far as they are implied in the rights of the state . . . the individual must be allowed to develop his personality in behalf of the state.[8]

Nor is Communism, with its theoretical distrust of the State, but its actual glorification of it, any different in the outcome with respect to the place of the individual in the scheme of things. As Pope Pius XI so rightly observed:

> Communism . . . strips man of his liberty, robs human personality of all its dignity, and removes all the moral restraints that check . . . blind impulse. There is no recognition of any right of the individual in his relations to the collectivity; no natural right is accorded to human personality, which is a mere cogwheel in the Communist system.[9]

Thus let it be repeated that the correct Western democratic view avers that

> Society is a natural means which man can and must use to reach his destined end. Society is for man and not *vice versa* . . . only . . . by means of an organic union with society and by mutual collaboration [is] the attainment of earthly happiness . . . placed within the reach of all. . . . Society . . . affords the opportunities for the development of all the individual and social gifts bestowed on human nature.[10]

Thus is it clear that the supreme overriding will of the state is not absolute and unlimited, but stops short, as it must, before the God-given, inalienable rights of its inhabitants, whose rights are anterior and superior to the State's. This is why it has been so clearly stated in the Preamble to the American Constitution that "We the people of the United States . . . do ordain and establish this Constitution for the United States of America"; for in the final analysis, internal sovereignty here rests with the populace who can perform their constituent function in the ways that same document prescribes; it further means, therefore, that no government acting for the State can act to invade, mutilate, or abolish the rights of the people as a whole or as individuals, no matter how large a political majority it may possess at the moment.

Within the limits above expressed, civil society is supreme, and may properly proceed to pursue its rightful ends. These are primarily "social order and public prosperity," or as Pope Leo XIII called them "public well-being and private prosperity." [11] Thus is the American Union conformable to these ends, for as the Preamble stated it, the ends of establishing the American State are "to form a more perfect union, establish justice, insure domestic tranquility, provide for the common defense, promote the general welfare, and secure the blessings of liberty."

In the pursuit of its Constitutional ends, the American government has the right to the obedience of all those subject to its laws, provided those laws themselves are conformable to the grant of power given, and are not violative of man's natural rights. Thus is the reciprocal obligation present for the individual to obey just law: "Man cannot be exempted from his divinely-imposed obligations toward civil society, and the representatives of authority have the right to coerce him when he refuses without reason to do his duty." [12] Therefore, the compulsive power of the State is properly used when an individual fails in his duty to serve the rightful ends of the State, as is the right of effective protest by the people necessary when the State fails in its duty to serve the rightful ends of the individual.[13]

The general conceptual framework noted above may be more particularly explained in terms of a closer examination of human nature. By that nature, man is both a person and a citizen, has both a personal and a social aspect. This is another way of saying that he is a creature composed of soul and body. It is with regard to his material (non-soul or non-rational) part that we recognize man's dependence on society, his being a part of the whole. Thus to say as would the philosophical Liberal that "man is born free" and thereby mean that he is a self-contained individual, independent of society, is patently false. Liberalism, at least in this sense, shuts its eyes to the facts of life, and exalting only the personal aspect of man's nature, harps on man's "freedom and liberty" until these are equated with the idea of "doing as one pleases." In such fashion is true liberty endangered by its most vocal defenders, who because they avow aberrant Individualism, tend to atomize society and to disrupt its rightful operation for the common good. The co-existence of a civil society and its membership doing as each pleases is a contradiction; it just cannot be.

The prime fact of the matter is that society exists, and thus the dependence of the individual on society likewise exists. Further, the complexities of societal operation multiply, and give every indication of continuing to do so, which increases the dependence of the individual on society for the goods and services he needs to sustain life. The interdependence of man in society, never more apparent than in our own time, is rendered more intense by the dawn of an atomic civilization. However present or future developments may further intensify this collective aspect of man, it must never be forgotten that the basis of it is that material element in man, his body. Having been created by God with a body, it is this which makes him a part of society, a member of the human race, a man among men, a citizen in a State, a soldier in an army, a unit in a social organism—in short, an individual in a group bound to the social whole for the sake of the common good.

But when all of the above is said, it is necessary to recall that it is only part of the complete picture. Man also has a soul, and being spiritual, the soul cannot be part of anything. It is itself a whole, total and integral. And it is because man has a soul that he can choose his own end and the means to achieve it. Man has rights which flow from this spiritual aspect of his nature; he likewise has liberty as the heritage of his spirit. This is what the Catholic Church means when it says that man is a person. It is because man is a person that he has rights, rights which are claims of moral beings on one another. Thus does the State come into this picture only as the conservator and protector of these "person-al" rights, these natural rights. Thus is it seen that these rights are inextricably bound up with the spiritual aspect of the human person, and their external manifestations (political, religious, and economic freedoms) are to be secured and enlarged because the development of human personality demands it. Or to repeat the words of Pius XI, "Society [the State] . . . affords the opportunities for the development of all the individual and social gifts bestowed on human nature."

Philosophic Collectivism is shown thus to be erroneous because it exalts man's social aspect alone, treats him only as a cog in the collective machine and an expendable one at that. Since in this viewpoint man is only an organism, a member of a herd, he can have no personality, no rights bound to be respected by the collectivity (the State). But we affirm the dualism of man's nature whereby he is both a part of the whole—a citizen in the State—but is also possessed of rights independent of the State. Man is thus bound to the State and yet free of it.

Christ's answer to those who asked whether it was lawful to pay tribute to Caesar perfectly answered the matter of the relationship of man to the State: "Render unto Caesar the things that are Caesar's, and to God the things that are God's." Man as a bodily creature, dependent upon society and earth-bound, must work for the common good of the State; but man as a spiritual creature is heaven-bound, and must work for that ultimate end with which the State may not interfere. Further than mere non-interference in "the things that are God's," the State—itself the result of action of human nature totally considered—must foster man's end as a person by providing the material setting necessary for its attainment. The State was founded to arrange temporal matters for the common good of men who are on their way back to God. The State results not from the common consent of the governed, but rather because of the fact of human nature. The State did not create human nature; therefore it may not nullify its rights.

Throughout the above discussion of the proper concept of the person and his relationship to the State, there has been occasion to use the phrase "the common good." It may well be asked what the common good is and how it is to be correlated with the individual good. The Federal Constitution accepts the common good as an end of the American State when it speaks of promoting "the general welfare" as a reason for adopting that instrument of government and as a legitimate end of the taxing power. Leo XIII defined the common good as that which "is concerned with the interest of all in general, albeit with individual interests in their due place and degree." Thus to say that the State exists for the common good is not to say that the State exists for itself whether itself is viewed as a race (as in Nazism), or as a class (as in an oligarchy, which in this sense the Communist "worker" is), or as an abstraction (as in Fascism). It is to say that the State exists for the welfare of the people, and, let it be emphasized, of all the people. Nor is the common good to be considered in such a general way that it may ignore the welfare of individuals. It is to say that the State is also concerned with the individual wellbeing of its people, all its people, but in particular those who are on the lowest rungs of the economic ladder (the poor, the sick, the aged, and the unemployed). Thus is the common good, not only the good of the whole and of its parts, a good which subordinates man to society insofar as man is social, but also a good which respects man as a person destined for God and eternity, and thus acknowledges that man is independent with regard to his personal supernatural end.

With regard to the relationship of individual good to the common good, the latter is superior. In case of need, society may for the common good set aside the interests of individual citizens. Viewed in this way, the common good subordinates man to society (as the part is subordinate to the whole) insofar as man is a social being. But the common good is also that which respects man as a person because of his origin and ultimate end, and thus this personal "inalienable" part can never be subordinated to the "good of the whole." Because of a misconception of the terms, "common good" and "individual good," the difficulty usually arises; actually, conflicts between the two are more apparent than real. Thus, although the right to life is certainly a basic inalienable part of the individual good, yet the state may for the common good (preservation of public order) inflict the death penalty for a capital crime. Why? The answer rests in the fact that civil society (the State) is natural, therefore from God, and in so doing is in effect commissioned by Him with that authority. The criminal has forfeited his inalienable right by his misdeed, has subverted his end in life, attacked the rightful end of the State, and thus the State has the authority to pursue its rightful purpose. An inalienable right can only be taken away by God or by one delegated by Him. In this aspect the State is acting within its authority for the common good.

Aside from forfeiting life for misdeed, individuals may have to forego private advantages in order to serve the common good, as when a citizen is called to military service in defense of his country. Certainly his life is thus endangered, and he may be killed, but if so, his right is not violated by the State. It did not take away his life though it did oblige him to expose himself to danger for a greater good, in accordance with the demands of duty.

Individual good and common good, rights and duties, liberty and responsibility—all these terms are not mutually exclusive, but correlative. And no proper understanding of the term "freedom" is possible unless one sees that basically it means not to do what one pleases but to do what one ought. Thus is true freedom born of the recognition of personal rights and nourished on the recognition of social responsibilities.

Nothing was more shattering to American aplomb and confidence in recent times than the realization that some of their soldiers, after capture by the Communist forces in Korea, had espoused the Totalitarian cause. President Eisenhower ruefully admitted that American soldiers had received a "meager education . . . in Americanism." The Defense Department was shaken into galvanic action and announced that it was "revamping the . . . military education program to make sure that fighting men were taught . . . what it meant to be an American." The spokesman for the Pentagon further said: "Teaching such fundamentals should be the job of the home and school," but since these were not sufficiently stressing them, the armed services provide "the last chance for society to do the job." The new program is to stress "four cardinal points . . . the dignity of the individual . . . respect for the truth . . . sovereignty of the people . . . [and] spiritual values." [14] If the content of the above-listed fundamentals squares with their titles, then indeed a revolution by education will have been accomplished in this country.

Readers of these pages should therefore appreciate that the type of knowledge exposited in this symposium is not "ivory tower" thinking, but represents the cutting edge of democracy in a world of heavy psychological warfare. If we fail at home to appreciate what freedom means, we fail throughout the world, not only ideologically but also militarily. We can only wish the armed forces the best of luck in their new venture and pray God that there is still time left to accomplish it successfully. For those of us at home, we had better take it as a personal job to see to it that a proper understanding of freedom is ingrained both in the family and at the school. Religion, properly speaking, has all along stressed the truth in this regard.

Having completed the general study of the conceptual framework within which both man and the State operate, with each recognizing the rightful place of the other, and with each respecting the duties he owes to the other, we are now in a position to assess aspects of the history of political freedom in the United States.

In the American theory of government, civil rights have a major role. Conditioned by the centuries-long struggle Englishmen waged to limit their own government's power to interfere arbitrarily with the lives and liberties of Englishmen, it was only natural that American Revolutionary theory should champion the individual against government. The original state constitutions of the rebellious colonies all listed prominently the freedoms of individuals with which state governments were not to interfere. When the Federal Constitution as drafted at Philadelphia in 1787 failed to express these or similar freedoms, the popular opposition forced the promise of their inclusion. Thus resulted the first ten amendments (the Bill of Rights) in 1791. Certain later amendments, notably the Thirteenth and Fourteenth, have added to this constitutional protection.

The court system of the United States is the primary protector of the rights of Americans, and within it the United States Supreme Court has come to be regarded as "the last safeguard for civil liberties." [15] It is the courts who must interpret and enforce the Constitutional rights. Furthermore, because of the doctrine of judicial review, they protect the individual's freedom from possible legislative encroachment. In this the American system departs from the British, because in the latter, courts have no alternative to enforcing legislative enactments. Thus the English citizen must depend on Parliament's self-restraint, whereas the American looks to the courts.

The problem of protecting American civil rights is further complicated by the federal system under which we operate. Governmental power is divided between nation and state, each a separate and distinct entity and each exercising a separate set of powers, with each separately subject to limitations. Some rights of Americans are thus protected from the interference of the national government; some are protected from state interference; and some are protected from the interference of both state and nation. Thus there is no wholly national system of rights. Moreover, since much legislation interferes with the freedom of the individual, it is important to note the different way in which the federal division of governmental power operates. The national government has only delegated powers, i.e. those expressed or implied in the Constitution, while the states have reserved powers. This means that the police power has been left with the states, and thus no specific justification for a state law is required beyond proof of its relation to the common interest in matters of health, safety, morals, and welfare. There is no such general authority granted to the national government, and thus when it seems to be exercising a police power it is acting really in accordance with a delegated power like the interstate commerce, taxing, or appropriating powers.

A further fact to be noted regarding powers in the American federal system has to do with the variety of limitations placed on the national and state levels of government. Although certain restrictions apply to both agencies, a few apply only to the states; most were originally designed to apply solely to the national government. Thus, the Constitutional Bill of Rights was directed toward the single purpose of restricting the national government, as the Supreme Court long ago held.[16] State Constitutions might or might not contain similar provisions to restrict state governments, but in any event varieties of guarantees existed, as did the interpretations which state courts might give them. Thus for example, while the First Amendment provided that "Congress shall make no law respecting an establishment of religion, or prohibiting the free exercise thereof," the states could and did have state churches in some areas well into the Nineteenth Century.[17]

There is little doubt that in some respects the Fourteenth Amendment (1868) is the most significant of all the Amendments. Among other things it says that no state shall "deprive any person of life, liberty, or property without due process of law." At the time and for years afterwards, it was felt that this language, identical with the Fifth Amendment as a stricture on the Federal government but now extended to state governments, was to assure Negroes of a fair trial in state courts. That it had a substantive meaning was denied. As late as 1922, the Court could say that "neither the Fourteenth Amendment nor any other provision of the Constitution . . . imposes upon the states any restrictions about freedom of speech." [18] But commencing in 1925, the Court began to think differently, and in considering a New York seditious utterance law averred: "For present purposes we may and do assume that freedom of speech and of the press—which are protected by the First Amendment from abridgement by Congress—are among the fundamental personal rights and 'liberties' protected by the due process clause of the Fourteenth Amendment from impairment by the states." [19] Subsequent decisions have so broadened the term "liberty" as used therein that state actions limiting assembly, the press, and the free exercise of religion have all been held invalid. Thus it would appear that the Fourteenth Amendment has made the Federal government (or at least the judicial branch) the protector of the great rights of the First against adverse state action. To this extent, at any rate, have the four basic freedoms (religion, press, speech, and assembly) been nationalized. This does not mean that the rest of the Federal Bill of Rights have been likewise nationalized. The Supreme Court has refused to do this *en bloc,* and indeed, in distinguishing between "fundamental" and "formal" rights of the Bill of Rights, without completely enumerating either, has held that the Fourteenth Amendment's due process clause covers only those felt by it to be basic and fundamental to liberty.

While emphasizing the role of the courts as the official interpreter and protector of civil rights, one should also be aware that executive agencies and legislatures also play a role. For example, local opinion may demand that the community curb the sale of those "comic books" that are felt to contribute to juvenile delinquency. In debating the measure it would undoubtedly be objected that such an ordinance would violate "the freedom of the press." The town council may or may not accept the argument. If it does and defeats the proposal it has clearly acted as an interpreter of this freedom; if, on the other hand, it does not accept the argument and adopts a measure, it is only then that the courts may have an opportunity to interpret the Constitution as it applies to this particular enactment, if suit is brought to test its validity. In similar fashion are executive authorities actually enforcers and interpreters of the specific application of basic liberties. As a police power regulation a community may have restricted the distribution of handbills as a way of cutting down litter. The publisher of a new newspaper as an advertisement may decide to distribute a free copy to every householder by means of leaving it on the doorstep. If then a rival publisher were to appeal to the mayor to invoke the anti-litter ordinance, the former would undoubtedly assert such action would violate his freedom of the press. The political authorities of the town would have to make a decision one way or the other. A refusal to enforce the ordinance would ordinarily end the matter, and in that case, not the courts but the executive would have interpreted the specific content of the freedom. If, on the other hand, the ordinance was enforced, and there was no subsequent costly and time-consuming suit to get the court's opinion, that, too, might end the matter. It is clear, therefore, that in many instances administrative and legislative actions in the field of enforcing and interpreting individual freedoms may be final, regardless of the actual and theoretical primacy held by American courts in this matter.

What are the freedoms, their connotations and delimitations, of an American? In any attempt to answer this important question it must always be remembered that basic to an individual's rights in a society of limited government such as ours, is the right to freedom itself. Yet despite both the brave words of Patrick Henry who preferred liberty to death, and of the *Declaration of Independence* which spoke of liberty as an inalienable right, there was human slavery in the United States until 1865 as complete and abject as any known to history. It was only with the passage of the Thirteenth Amendment then, that the supreme law of the land expressly stated that ours is a society of free men only. Unlike most of the other rights guaranteed by the Constitution, this one operates against its encroachment by private individuals as well as governmental organs. Slavery and "involuntary servitude, except as a punishment for crime," is forbidden to exist "within the United States or any place subject to their jurisdiction." Further the Congress was charged to protect the right "by appropriate legislation." Most subsequent controversies have centered around questions of involuntary servitude and, in general, attempts to force a debtor or a party to a contract to fulfill his obligations by involuntary labor are outlawed in America. However, where the occupation involves the public safety, the courts have made exceptions. Thus, seamen may be compelled to complete a term of service to which they agreed, and railroad workers may not strike until they have brought their passengers to their destination. However, apart from such instances, courts feel they cannot compel workers to return to or remain on the job. As was said recently: "The undoubted aim of the Thirteenth Amendment . . . was not merely to end slavery but to maintain a system of completely free and voluntary labor throughout the United States." [20]

Second only to the right of personal freedom is the right to equality—equality as to the protection provided by the law, and equality of opportunity to enjoy the advantages, cultural and economic, existing in a free, God-fearing civil society. By the Fourteenth Amendment such equality under the law was guaranteed in the clause, "No State shall . . . deny to any person within its jurisdiction the equal protection of the laws." Though the Fifth Amendment did not provide a specific counterpart, it has been generally accepted that its due process clause serves much the same purpose with regard to the Federal government.[21]

Equal protection does not prevent legislatures from classifying people for purposes of reasonable and necessary regulation. Thus a statute denying minors under fourteen the right to drive an automobile is hardly to be considered as unequal treatment under law. But that such a statutory classification may be so deemed is reflected in the 1948 Supreme Court decision that a California law which prohibited the issuance of commercial fishing licenses to persons ineligible for American citizenship was unconstitutional because it denied such persons equality of treatment under the law.[22]

No more controversial aspect of judicial interpretation of equality has arisen than stemmed from the doctrine announced in *Plessy vs. Ferguson* (1896). This decision upheld a state law enforcing racial segregation in public places and conveyances such as railroads, busses, hotels, theaters, parks, and schools. The Supreme Court felt that segregation was not discrimination within the meaning of the equal protection clause and that as long as equal facilities were maintained for the Negroes they could be facilities separate from those used by the whites. The Court asserted that the plaintiff fallaciously assumed "that the enforced separation of the two races stamps the colored race with a badge of inferiority. If this be so, it is not by reason of anything found in the act, but solely because the colored race chooses to put that construction upon it." [23]

Though never reversed, the Plessy doctrine has been rather consistently attacked as un-American and un-democratic, which it apparently is, and un-Christian, which it certainly is. In more recent years, the Court has been looking behind the façade of "separate but equal facilities" in states where segregation is practiced, and where it finds that no substantial equality of public facilities exists, has demanded that Negroes be admitted to the regular "white" ones. Thus, in 1938, Missouri was ordered to maintain a separate graduate school of law for Negroes or else permit them to attend the law school at the state university. Not even the state's offer to pay the plaintiff's tuition at another institution outside the state was acceptable as an alternative solution.[24]

In no other regard is the United States so vulnerable in the international propaganda struggle as in this discrepancy between American theory and fact respecting interracial relations. It does no good to repeat that we have come a long way from lynchings and armed mobs attacking minorities. As long as more subtle but equally effective measures exist which in fact promote the stigma of second class citizenship, we shall continue to be on the defensive throughout the world. Asiatics in particular will continue to be suspicious of our ultimate aims and purposes there. It is incomprehensible to them that we mean our protestations of equality and hand-clasping friendship abroad, when here at home we have territorial enclaves where discrimination and segregation are practiced. If we hold true to our national ideals and move toward their effective implementation, we shall be the gainers not only in conscience, but also in the cold war.

Specific political freedoms enjoyed by Americans also include the following: freedom of expression (speech and the press), freedom of assembly and petition (including the right to political association), and freedom of political activity. These will be briefly treated in turn, but one general remark is valid, and it is that no one of them is an absolute and unlimited freedom. As the president of St. Louis University said recently in discussing academic freedom, "Any human freedom which is based on reason has its limits in reason. By its very nature, no human right is unlimited because human rights are essentially social and limited by the rights of others." [25] This is not very different from the Court's view that:

> Liberty of speech, and of the press, is . . . not an absolute right, and the State may punish its abuse. . . . Liberty, in each of its phases, has its history and connotation and, in the present instance, the inquiry is as to the historic conception of the liberty of the press and whether the statute under review violates the essential attributes of that liberty.[26]

Thus, with regard to freedom of speech and press, government may not lay on "previous restraint" or censorship in advance of publication. This prohibition on government to curb ideas before they are expressed is so taken for granted by Americans that they fail to appreciate its significance. In any totalitarian or authoritarian-tending country, state control of all organs of public expression is imposed on the populace. Thus is thought control instituted and propagated, with a concomitant secret police force set up to "measure" the effectiveness of this previous restraint policy. Neither should it alarm Americans that on grave occasions a form of censorship has been imposed in the United States. Chief Justice Charles Evans Hughes said:

> Protection even as to previous restraint is not absolutely unlimited. . . . "When a nation is at war many things that might be said in time of peace are such a hindrance to its effort that their utterance will not be condoned so long as men fight and that no Court could regard them as protected by any constitutional right." [27]

If then, such a large measure of freedom of expression is rightfully an American's it follows that he should be willing to be responsible for his utterances. Thus it is a long-established Anglo-Saxon principle of law that words used with a malicious intent to defame the character of an individual are harmful both to the person attacked and to the public welfare, and are therefore punishable. It follows then that libel (printed words) and slander (spoken words) are not protected by the First Amendment. Neither is obscenity nor blasphemy, and any reasonable law restraining speech or publications along these lines is quite likely to be upheld by the courts. Contempt of court is also an allowable device for validly restricting freedom of speech and the press. Judges have the power to cite individuals and to impose punishment on them for remarks or publications which are thought to impede their judicial work. Thus were some of the lawyers for the eleven top Communists in the United States so cited by Federal District Judge Harold Medina in 1949 for their unbridled remarks in and out of court during that gruelling but significant trial.

Perhaps the most important type of allowable interference with freedom of expression is in laws aimed against sedition. Such laws prescribe punishment for words that incite to unlawful action. The first federal law of this type was the famous Sedition Act of 1798, containing an extreme clause providing that any speech or writing which intended to defame or bring into contempt or disrepute the President or Congress was punishable. Twenty-five prosecutions and ten convictions took place under the act. Historians are unanimous in declaring that this law was probably unconstitutional (the Supreme Court never ruled on it) and that, as enforced, it was a partisan measure that the Federalists used to contain their Jeffersonian rivals. In fact, all those convicted, were members of Jefferson's party.

Sedition laws were thereafter unimportant until World War I when understandably both an espionage and a sedition act were passed. Since then, federal sedition laws have been periodically revamped in order to keep pace with the techniques of totalitarianism whose main aim abroad is to "bore from within" in a country marked for destruction or inimical to its own aims. Thus, the Alien Registration Act of 1940 (the Smith Act) and the McCarran Internal Security Act of 1950 are efforts to prevent "fifth columns" from effectively arising by making conspiracies words, printed or uttered, that are intended to lead to the downfall by violence of the American government.

Paralleling federal activity in this field, the states, over the years, have enacted numerous statutes aimed against "criminal syndicalism," "criminal anarchy," and similar offenses. In general, the Federal government has fared better than the states in this problem; neither has a federal statute been overthrown, nor has the Supreme Court set aside convictions under federal laws. But many of the state laws have either been so loosely drawn, or so wildly enforced, that they have been upset.

Courts have found it very difficult in knowing where to draw the line between allowable free speech and speech that threatens society. Actually, only one principle of determination has been set up so far to guide it. This principle is the "clear and present danger" test, which, as first announced by Justice Oliver Wendell Holmes in 1919, maintained that:

> The question in every case is whether the words used are used in such circumstances and are of such a nature as to create a clear and present danger that they will bring about the substantive evils that Congress has a right to prevent. It is a question of proximity and degree.[28]

A number of cases have since been so decided, the most recent and most important being the eleven Communist leaders already mentioned. These were prosecuted under the 1940 law which made it a crime to conspire to "teach and advocate the overthrow and destruction of the government of the United States by force and violence." [29] Speaking for the majority, Chief Justice Fred M. Vinson said:

> In this case we are squarely presented with the application of the "clear and present danger" test, and must decide what that phrase imports. We first note that many of the cases in which this Court has reversed convictions by use of this or similar tests have been based on the fact that the interest which the State was attempting to protect was itself

> too insubstantial to warrant restriction of speech. . . . Overthrow of the Government by force and violence is certainly a substantial enough interest for the Government to limit speech . . . if a society cannot protect its very structure from armed internal attack, it must follow that no subordinate value can be protected. . . . Obviously, the words [clear and present danger] cannot mean that before the Government may act, it must wait until the *putsch* is about to be executed. . . . If Government is aware that a group aiming at its overthrow is attempting to indoctrinate its members and to commit them to a course whereby they will strike when the leaders feel the circumstances permit, action by the Government is required. . . . The formation by petitioners of such a highly organized conspiracy, with rigidly disciplined members subject to call when the leaders . . . felt that the time had come for action, coupled with the inflammable nature of world conditions, similar uprisings in other countries, and the touch-and-go nature of our relations with countries with whom petitioners were . . . ideologically attuned, convince us that their convictions were justified.[30]

It is apparent, therefore, that from here on out the "clear and present danger" test can be effectively utilized to curb the internal menace of Communism, without, however, endangering the precious rights to freedom of speech, press, association, and true political activity.

By the First Amendment, "Congress shall make no law . . . abridging . . . the right of the people peaceably to assemble, and to petition the government for a redress of grievances." Broadly considered, this provision guarantees the right of the people to engage in political activity, for under it they may assemble to discuss political questions, and organize with a view to securing political action. More specifically, they may form political parties and work to bring about the adoption of specific governmental policies, form pressure groups, and petition public officers in an attempt to influence the governmental program.

However, as with all rights, these are subject to reasonable regulation, and consequently, cannot be used as to endanger public safety or to disrupt traffic. What is usually involved in cases arising under this provision is whether the regulation is a *bona fide* exercise of the police power or an effort under the guise of allowed regulation to curb political activity. The courts will decide as the weight of evidence presented seems to indicate.[31]

Obviously, in a democratic society, citizenship lends meaning to one's political rights. As the symbol of full membership in the society, it customarily includes such rights as voting or holding public office.

Moreover, it is often true that non-citizens are excluded by law from certain trades and professions. Yet, despite the fact that the right to citizenship is axiomatic in American political thought, it is nevertheless true, paradoxical as it may seem, that the highest expression of citizenship, the right to vote, is not expressly recognized in the Constitution. It is to be remembered that universal *white male* suffrage was the rule as early as 1840, that the Fifteenth Amendment (1870) sought to eliminate the "white" qualification, while the Nineteenth Amendment (1920) forbade states to deprive women from voting merely because of their sex. In general it can be said that, except for the Negro in certain southern states, political democracy in the United States is more truly available to all mature Americans than anywhere else in the world.

Today more than at any time in our history our political liberties are threatened from without and, unfortunately, from within by a small (it is hoped) but well-knit group of subversives who are not merely engaging in political activity, but also serving as the advance guard of international Communism. For this reason, the Communist Party, USA, is not a true political party within the meaning of allowed freedoms under the American Constitution, but as the Subversive Activities Control Board decided on April 20, 1953, is rather a group which has as its objective "the overthrow of the United States Government," and exists to effectuate policies "for the purposes of defending and protecting the Soviet Union." [32]

How are Americans to meet this external and internal threat to our freedom? The main lines of the counter-offensive have already been set forth. These include: both to remember and to act upon the correct basis of all political life—God the Creator, to Whom we are all responsible for our every act, Who has ordained and established civil society and the due rights and duties of State to man, and of man to State; to live Christian and act Christian, which in this context means to apply without equivocation the full meaning of the Bill of Rights and the later Constitutional Amendments; and to recall that this Nation was founded as a God-believing and God-fearing State and to act on that basis, rejecting the interim, shifty, pragmatic, materialistic approach whose shoddiness is apparent even before the policies based upon it are half-executed. By remembering our origin and last end, and acting accordingly, we can prevent a totalitarian enemy, whether foreign or domestic, from prevailing against us. Then, and only then, in Lincoln's words, will "this nation, under

God, . . . have a new birth of freedom; and that government of the people, by the people, for the people, shall not perish from the earth."

BIBLIOGRAPHY

Primary Sources:

The Papal Encyclicals
Statutes at Large of the United States
The Brooklyn Tablet
The New York Times
United States Reports

Secondary Sources:

Beard, Charles A., *The Republic,* New York, 1943.

Brinton, Crane, *Ideas and Men,* New York, 1950.

Commager, Henry S., *Majority Rule and Minority Rights,* New York, 1944.

Coppens, Charles, S.J., *A Brief Text-Book of Moral Philosophy,* New York, 1924.

Gosnell, Harold F., *Democracy—The Threshold of Freedom,* New York, 1948.

Hand, Learned, "Freedom and the Humanities," *Bulletin* American Association of University Professors, XXXVIII, no. 4 (Winter 1952-3), 521-7.

Hocking, William E., *Man and the State,* New Haven, 1926.

Kerwin, Jerome, *The Great Tradition: The Democratic Idea,* New York, 1948.

MacIver, Robert M., *The Web of Government,* New York, 1947.

Merriam, Charles E., *Systematic Politics,* Chicago, 1945; *Political Power: Its Composition and Incidence,* New York, 1934.

President's Committee on Civil Rights, *To Secure These Rights,* Washington, 1947.

Rocco, Alfredo, "The Political Doctrines of Fascism," *International Conciliation,* no. 223 (1926), 401-20.

Vanderbilt, Arthur T., *The Doctrine of the Separation of Powers and Its Present-Day Significance,* Lincoln, Nebraska, 1953.

Freedom and the Law

by DR. HAROLD F. MCNIECE,
Assistant Dean and Professor of Law,
School of Law, St. John's University

INTRODUCTION

This paper is concerned with what might be called "legal control of voluntary action," or, stated another way, "freedom under law." The very existence of law is a recognition of the obvious fact that freedom to act cannot be absolute, for absolute freedom is synonymous with anarchy.[1] Man is a social being, and the existence of society presupposes the imposition of some restraints upon the scope of voluntary action. The quantity and quality of these restraints is, in our society, measured roughly by resort to a kind of legal "golden rule"—*sic utere tuo ut alienum non laedas* (so use your own as not to injure others).

The effort here is to paint in broad strokes a canvas which pictures the limitations upon individual conduct constructed in the United States by the formally organized agencies of legal control—the legislative, executive, and judicial branches of the federal and state governments. The study pertains only to the restraints imposed by official legal authority, and not to those which may be the result of the influences exerted by non-official power groups such as trade associations, labor unions, large corporations, and the like.

Preliminarily, the article strives to distinguish between the positivist and the natural law concept of freedom, and suggests that the latter underlies much of the structure of legal control in this country. Next, an analysis is made of legally imposed limitations upon conduct arising out of those jural relations between men which are established by private agreement. The remedy for one injured by a failure of another to observe duties assumed by private agreement is, of course, the suit for damages for breach of contract. This contractual analysis is essentially a study of that most elastic concept, "freedom of contract," and of the expansion and diminishing of its content in response to the pressures of social change.

Thereafter attention is directed to the restraints which the law places upon voluntary action in noncontractual situations. This necessitates first a consideration of a number of facets of the law of torts, which decrees generally that a man, when placed in a relationship with his fellows, must act reasonably—and this entirely without regard to any agreement so to act. For example, he may not drive his automobile carelessly or let noxious fumes from his brick kiln destroy the trees in his neighbor's orchard. The penalty for failure to live up to these and the numerous other tort duties is payment of damages to the party injured by the dereliction. To see just how far the law has gone in laying down obligations of reasonable action, and to examine the trends in the formulation of these obligations, is the purpose of the section of the article dealing with the law of torts.

Consideration of the noncontractual field involves as another element a study of criminal law and social control. The law in certain fact situations imposes sanctions in the form of fines or imprisonment, or both, or even death, upon persons whose conduct has deviated from prescribed norms. An attempt is made to trace the developments in this branch of law within recent years.

The relationship between military law and freedom is also treated. Particularly in this age, when a great part of the country's productive energies and the services of millions of its young men are devoted to defense efforts, military law has such vast significance that its impact upon individual freedom cannot be overlooked.

Finally, that broad area of the law denominated "Civil Liberties" is dealt with. The study in this area relates principally to an analysis of the accommodations and adjustments which are constantly taking place between individual and governmental rights. Civil liberties is a field of law which is in constant ferment, and necessarily the analysis can be barely more than a description of present law. Hence, though some synthesis is made, little extrapolation into the future is attempted. Upon completion of the discussion of contracts, torts, criminal law, military law, and civil liberties, some general conclusions are offered concerning freedom under law in the United States, and a few thoughts for the future are ventured.

This article does not purport, of course, to set forth all the limitations upon voluntary action which the law imposes. Indeed, to do so would be to restate the entire body of the law from the viewpoint of individual freedom, a project which is obviously beyond the scope of the present study. But by focusing attention on developments in the more important areas of the law it is hoped that some insight into the whole field is achieved.

In substance then this paper strives to point out the more important restraints on freedom which the law recognizes and enforces, and thus, by a type of elimination process, to determine the sphere in which, legally speaking, the individual is free to operate as he chooses.

The Interaction of Law and Freedom in General

Before entering upon the discussion outlined above, it is well to get in mind a general notion of how the law bears upon individual freedom. The various analyses which appear in the succeeding sections will be better understood if we pause for a moment and review some of the more obvious interactions between law and freedom that constantly occur before our eyes. Many of these are so commonplace that we forget their importance.

In order to make matters a little more concrete, let us briefly consider the life of a typical American citizen. We shall call him Mr. Prudent Man, in honor of the standard of the imaginary "prudent man" by which the law constantly measures the actions of flesh-and-blood men.[2] Merely pointing out some of the multitude of ways in which the edicts of the law intermesh with the activities of Prudent Man will serve to bring into focus the magnitude of the average citizen's dealings with the law, and show at once how much effect the law has upon many of his actions.

When Prudent Man is born, it is obligatory that a certificate of his birth be filed. In early years the law decrees that his immunization against certain diseases take place. When he first begins to toddle about, he may become liable in damages—theoretically at least—if his uncertain and precarious steps should run him afoul of a hostile neighbor's garden.

At a given age Prudent Man is obliged to go to school. Moreover, by about this time, he has attained a sufficient use of reason to be liable for negligence if he injures someone through failure to use the care which can be expected of a child his age. Thereafter, throughout his life, negligence liability is a potential factor whenever he is placed in a position where injury to others may occur.

As a typical American lad, Prudent Man may early come in contact with the law of contracts. Though the contracts of a minor are, at his election, voidable as to him, they are binding upon the adult with whom the infant contracts and are binding upon the infant unless and until avoided. Perhaps Prudent Man's first contractual experience is when, acting as an agent, he goes to the corner store to buy cigarettes or a newspaper for his dad. Or, like many boys, he may have a newspaper route in which event he will make contracts with both the newspaper distributing agency and the various customers along the way. From then on Prudent Man will be dealing with the law of contracts during all the years of his earthly existence.

If he is so unfortunate in his youth as to commit a serious antisocial act, Prudent Man may come before one or another of the juvenile delinquency tribunals. In later life the criminal courts serve the same function. The average boy does not get so involved, however, and, if Prudent Man acts as he should, it will probably not be until his eighteenth year that he again comes into contact with the law. Then he will become liable for military training, and, if inducted into the Armed Forces, will be under the rule of military law for the period of his service.

Should Prudent Man decide, after his discharge from the service, to enter one of the professions, he will find himself subject to special obligations imposed by various administrative regulatory bodies, and will come within the operative ambit of a large body of case law built up in past years concerning the duties and obligations of members of his profession—the law of malpractice for instance. The same will be true if he should join some specialized occupational group such as the plumbing or electrical trade,[3] and, of course, whatever Prudent Man does for a living, he will be enmeshed in the complicated framework of tax law, and probably in the law of master and servant as well. Unemployment insurance and disability benefits laws and workmen's compensation statutes may also play their part at some time in his occupational life.

When Prudent Man marries he will have to go through legally prescribed preliminaries such as obtaining a marriage license, and taking a blood test. The marriage itself must take place before a person recognized by the law as competent to perform the ceremony, and the married state will carry with it well settled obligations to wife and children as established by the law of domestic relations. Furthermore, if Prudent Man rents an apartment or buys a house, real property law will become operative. On the other hand, should he purchase an automobile for the enjoyment of his household, he will become amenable to the laws of sales and automobile negligence, to the vast collection of traffic ordinances, and, in most states, to a Motor Vehicle Safety Responsibility Act with its various insurance provisions.

With the caution that his name indicates, Prudent Man will want to insure himself, his family and his property. To do so he will have to comply with the special laws relating to such matters. When he makes a will, the law will also be at his side, determining the validity and effect of the provisions he inserts. In his old age, Social Security laws and statutes requiring relatives to support indigent aged persons may come into play. Finally, after Prudent Man dies, a death certificate will have to be filed, and his estate will be distributed in accordance with applicable estate and tax statutes.

This brief sketch of the life of a typical citizen demonstrates how the law confronts him at every turn "from the cradle to the grave." Only the more important relationships between law and personal freedom have been indicated, but a moment's reflection will add hundreds of others. Bearing in mind this general picture of the interaction of law and freedom, let us turn now to a more specific analysis. The first step in that analysis is to try to clarify the meaning of legal freedom, a process that makes imperative a comparison of opposing views.

Positivist versus Natural Law Concept of Freedom

There are two basic concepts of legal freedom which have existed side by side and have struggled for supremacy during many thousands of years: one, the positivist concept, as it may be called; and the other, the natural law concept. The lines of distinction between the two are well marked.

According to positivism, the existence and limits of the individual's rights are determinable solely by the civil law. The necessary corollary to this proposition is that the only sanctions for invasions of such rights are the sanctions granted by the civil law. This view, which was perhaps best particularized during the French Revolution in the National Assembly's article of organic law,[4] has been well expressed in its modern formulation by Dr. Rommen. As he puts it, "Law, according to positivism, is only positive law, that is, statute law and such customary law as is recognized by the state. More precisely, positivism characterizes as law to be applied by the judge and alone to be considered by jurisprudence those norms only which are enacted as such by the factual and published will of the legislative organ in due conformity with constitutional law or which are explicitly or tacitly admitted by it."[5]

The results which often flow from application of the positivist concept may be illustrated by reference to the French Revolution. The leaders of the Revolution were apt to speak in glowing terms of the "rights of man." Yet, as is well known, the "rights" of those who disagreed with the ruling authority came to mean little or nothing—at least during certain phases of the Revolution, such as the Reign of Terror. Once the premise that man's rights came from the State was accepted, the Terror was a very logical process, for, if the State gave rights, it could take them away entirely, or limit them as it saw fit.

It is therefore obvious that under the positivist concept of legal freedom, the individual's rights are as variable and flexible as the winds of whim and caprice which shape the thoughts of the masters of the government. True it is that the positivist view need not necessarily result in a Reign of Terror. It is undeniable that it is *possible* for government to be administered in a benevolent way even when premised on the positivist idea. Soviet Russia, for example, is founded on the positivist concept of legal freedom. Yet it is *possible* for the Soviet leaders, if they wish to do so, to exercise their powers in a benevolent way. Overnight they *could* abolish slave labor, the secret police, and the suppression of religion.

But, practically speaking, the basic difficulty is that the positivist concept is generally not employed benevolently. Acceptance of it grants to the rulers of the nation unlimited power, and the heady wine of this unlimited power soon intoxicates. Whether the rulers are a select clique, or, as in a democracy, the people themselves, makes little difference. As applied in this context, the maxim that power corrupts is a sound one. It has been well stated that, "Juridical positivism disassociates law from dependence upon, or conformity with, any order transcending the legislator," and "invests the State with an absolute control over the citizen by endowing it with uncontrolled and therefore irresponsible power." [6]

Principles under positivism are never immutable. Standards of morality shift and change. The criterion for action tends to become expediency. The individual positivist may be, and often is, a good man, but he lacks the firm anchor of unshakeable principle. His quest for the good of the majority is rendered difficult by the fact that he lacks any clear-cut standard of what is good. The positivist system is apt to become concerned too much with the quickest method of getting things done rather than with the method that accords with unchangeable moral principles. Too often the end result is to substitute the lash and the guillotine in place of reasoned argument with dissenters. The sickening dictatorship of a Hitler or Stalin is not the necessary result of the positivist philosophy but it is often the final product thereof. As Pope Pius XII puts it, "[t]he belief that everything that is done officially is real law is 'an error which is at the base of State absolutism and which is equivalent to a deification of the state itself.' " [7]

It must not be supposed, however, that the proponents of the positivist approach to legal freedom are all disciples of dictatorship. Far from it. Even in modern America there are many scholars who advocate a philosophy of law which is essentially the positivist approach garnished with assertedly "democratic" spices and thus served more palatably. These present-day advocates insist that justice is wholly a matter of convenience or enactment, or, to put it another way, "law is the majority vote." [8]

Of course, the American positivists do not advocate concentration camps or the guillotine for those who disagree with them. Indeed they are, for the most part, sincerely—albeit in a misguided way—striving for the greatest good of the greatest number, and would be horrified to be placed in the same category with ruthless dictators past or present. However, there is no blinking the fact that they do espouse the same basic philosophy of law as have despots from time immemorial. Their error may be well-meaning, but it is nonetheless serious.

The Roman Catholic Church has always unequivocally opposed the positivist approach to legal freedom. In recent years Pope Pius XII has been particularly concerned with the resurgence of positivism. In *Summi Pontificatus,* his first encyclical, Pius spoke of the error of those who "seek to dispense the civil authority from observing any of those higher laws which have their origin in God," and in the 1942 *Christmas Message* he called for a constitutionalism which "gives man a right to juridical security, and accordingly grants him a sphere of rights immune from arbitrary attacks" by the State. Speaking to the members of the Roman Rota in 1949, the Pontiff reiterated that, "[t]he mere fact of a law being declared by the legislative power as an obligatory norm in the State, this fact alone and by itself, is not enough to create true law." [9]

The second approach to legal freedom, the natural law concept, is the one which the Roman Catholic Church has traditionally advocated. According to this concept, liberty is not simply something which a man enjoys by reason of the fact that he is a citizen of Great Britain or a citizen of the United States, but rather "an attribute which a man enjoys simply and solely *because* he is a man, a creature of rational nature, a PERSON with all that such a dignity embodies. . . ." [10] His rights and liberties are just as "natural to him as the circulation of his blood and the growth of his body cells. . . ." [11] As Maritain puts it, "Man's right to existence, to personal freedom, and to the pursuit of the perfection of moral life, belongs, strictly speaking, to natural law." [12]

This approach is embodied in the Declaration of Independence which declares that all men are created equal; that they are endowed by their Creator with certain unalienable rights; and that the purpose of government is to secure those rights. It is also the approach which is implicit both in our Constitution and the Bill of Rights. These fundamental charters of American liberty, richly steeped as they are in natural law, reflect the fact that the natural law concept of freedom is a keystone of our entire legal system. Indeed it is not too much to say that the natural law concept of liberty is the only one which is truly compatible with our system of government. Positivism is as alien to America as is that step-child of positivism, dictatorship.

It is, however, not within the scope of this paper to analyze further the theoretical foundation upon which our freedom rests. Such an analysis is more for the realm of philosophy than for that of legal analysis. The purpose here is mainly to see how in practice the various branches of the law carry through the theoretical concept of freedom and apply it in concrete fact situations. Accordingly, we turn to the first large area in which individual freedom and the law intermeshes, namely, the area of contracts.

Freedom and the Law of Contracts

We have adverted to the fact that throughout most of his life our hypothetical friend, Mr. Prudent Man, makes agreements with others which the law calls contracts. From the time at the age of six or seven when he goes to the corner store to buy a newspaper for his dad, he engages more or less continuously in business transactions of one sort or another and thus, consciously or unconsciously, makes contracts. Buying groceries, going to the movies, riding on the railroad—these and the thousand and one similar activities of every-day life involve Prudent Man in consensual transactions which have certain legal consequences defined in the law of contracts.

Although Prudent Man has a wide range of choice in deciding what kinds of agreements he makes with others, once he makes one, he is forbidden by law, as a general rule, to repudiate it. Therefore, his area of uninhibited action is cut down to a great extent by the compulsion which the law of contracts exerts to make him live up to his promises.

Of course the law of contracts is not as strict as the moral law. Sometimes Prudent Man may be able to avoid performance of a perfectly valid moral obligation because the civil law has made the claim unenforceable, under a statute of limitations (setting time limits to enforcement of rights), or a statute of frauds (requiring certain agreements to be in writing), or a technical principle like the doctrine of consideration. Such exceptions and a few others aside, the law of contracts will enforce legal agreements entered into between persons of adequate mental capacity.

Moreover, Prudent Man's field of free action is narrowed still further by the fact that the law of contracts does not always permit him to enter into agreements which he desires to make. An overriding policy of the law may confront him, if, for instance, he should wish to make an agreement which is offensive to a usury statute or opposed to some other statutory or common law precept.

Lawyers express Prudent Man's right to make contracts, and the limitations upon that right, in the phrase "freedom of contract" or "liberty of contract." This concept of freedom of contract is generally considered both by lawyers and laymen to be one of the most important pillars of the American legal system. Yet, surprisingly enough, its meaning has seldom been critically analyzed.[13] It behooves us, therefore, to recall to mind its background and history, and to gain some knowledge of its present status.

Historically, the growth of the law of contracts has been closely connected with the expansion of commerce. In a simple and primitive society there is little need for the making of contracts. In such a society, self-sufficient family groups or clans tend to follow accustomed ways with very little deviation, and there is not much bargaining within these groups or among different groups. Each family or clan hunts its own food, or raises it, and has little cause to make agreements with others to obtain the staples of existence. Similarly, each group provides its own shelter and clothing, and the other needs of the uncomplicated agrarian life.

With the development of commerce and the consequent beginning of interdependence among groups, the need for making and enforcing contracts grows. Different societies have diverse customs and varying ways of doing things. The only method of orderly dealing between people schooled in these different mores is by agreements freely made among individuals and groups. As Kessler has pithily expressed it, "Rational behavior within the context of [commercial and industrial] culture is only possible if agreements will be respected." [14] In a business society the reasonable expectations created by promises must receive the protection of the law, or else the society will suffer the fate of Montesquieu's Troglodytes who perished because they did not fulfill their promises.

Thus it is that in the history of the ancient Jews, Greeks and Romans, as well as in medieval Europe, we see the States giving greater scope to individuals in making contracts as commerce becomes more widespread. Cohen has pointed out, for example, that the growth and liberalization of the Hebrew law of contract in the Mishnah seems to have followed the expansion of commerce that came with the capture of their first seaport, Jaffa, by Simon Maccabaeus.[15] It may similarly be observed that the Hellenic law of contract enjoyed a great expansion after the change, under Cleisthenes, from tribal organization and after the great expansion of commerce that followed in the fifth century B.C. Analogous developments occurred in Ancient Rome and, around the time of the Crusades, in Europe.

Then, too, the expansion of the law of contracts in more modern times is directly traceable to the Commercial Revolution in Europe, following the opening of trade routes to India and America, and to the Industrial Revolution which came soon after. The scope of private agreements grew in steady ratio with the rise of business. However, at no time, either on the Continent or in England, did the State ever completely give up the power to define and regulate to some extent the making and the effect of these agreements. The State always maintained a reserved power in order to prevent the general interest of all its members from being jeopardized by improvident agreements made by a few.[16]

In these more recent centuries the rise of business was accompanied by developments in political and economic philosophy which contributed much to the formation of the freedom of contract concept as we know it today. Eighteenth century political and economic philosophy taught that governmental restraint was to be avoided as much as possible and that the government was best which governed least. The political and economic thinkers who built theories in accord with the practices of the growing commercial and industrial interests viewed the State as almost an instrument of oppression, and sought to limit its sphere of operation as much as possible. It is not far wrong to say, therefore, that our modern doctrine of freedom of contract developed as but one phase of the broad politico-economic theory of Adam Smith and others, commonly called *laissez-faire*.[17]

The notion of freedom of contract in Anglo-American law also had religious as well as political and economic origins. In the Middle Ages the Doctors of the Roman Catholic Church emphasized custom, rather than the contract of the parties, as the prime factor to be considered in determining fair prices and other incidents of commercial transactions. The Reformation, however, with its underlying philosophy of individual conscience as the final authority in human action, had the effect of broadening the operative area of personal motivation in many fields, including that of contracts. Especially is this true of Calvinism, which was predominantly the faith of the commercial classes. The tenets of that religion, as interpreted and applied in economic culture by John Knox, the leader of the Scottish Reformation, fitted in particularly well with the idea that individual choice should be the main factor in determining contractual responsibility. Knox, writing in the sixteenth century, anticipated in his politico-theological approach the fully developed rationalism of the two centuries which followed.

In sum, we see that the idea of freedom of contract, as that concept is commonly understood, had its genesis in the individualism which reached full bloom in the eighteenth century. This individualism had philosophic, political, economic and religious overtones, out of the blending of which grew the theory that a man was free to make agreements determinative of his economic destiny.

It is undeniable that freedom of contract has much to commend it. There can be little quarrel with the thought that man, as a free being, should have a great deal of power to agree with his fellowmen upon things that mutually concern them. But it is likewise undeniable, that such an individualistic philosophy can be carried too far, it is now generally conceded that it was carried too far in this country and in England.

As illustrative of the abuses which occurred from extending the theory of freedom of contract to extremes we may refer specifically to one legal field—that of the labor contract. Mr. Justice Harlan of the United States Supreme Court thus expresses the prevailing nineteenth century judicial view towards the labor contract:

> The right of a person to sell his labor upon such terms as he deems proper, is in its essence, the same as the right of the purchaser of labor to prescribe the conditions upon which he will accept such labor from the person offering to sell it. So the right of the employee to quit the service of the employer, for whatever reason, is the same as the right of the employer, for whatever reason, to dispense with the services of such employee. . . . In all such particulars the employer and the employee have equality of right, and any legislation that disturbs that equality is an arbitrary interference with the liberty of contract, which no government can legally justify in a free land.[18]

There is in that broad statement of freedom of contract a certain deceptive charm. The notion that employer and employee have "equal rights" to contract, or not to contract, with each other is appealing on its face to innate ideas of fairness. But when we examine the prevailing economic climate of the industrial society of nineteenth and twentieth century America, fallacies appear. It must be apparent that there existed in the nineteenth century, and even now still exists, a basic *inequality* in the bargaining power of the individual employee and the industrial employer. (The present discussion is not directly concerned with the effect of labor unions as instruments for minimizing such inequality.)

A laborer has certain skills to sell. If he is a weaver or a mechanic, he finds the market for his skills limited; so, likewise, is his mobility.

Perhaps there are one or two large concerns in the laborer's village or in a neighboring town to which he may sell his skills. The laborer must work if he is to eat, but the industrial establishment can go on without him. If he is not hired by one of a few nearby concerns, he can do nothing. But these concerns, if they do not hire him, can soon find someone else with the same qualifications. It is, of course, true that industry must have laborers, but it does not need any one particular laborer, whereas each individual laborer does need industry.

The very nature of an industrial society, it would appear, imposes this measure of duress upon the individual laborer. His freedom of contract, theoretically real, is factually to a great extent non-exercisable. The freedom, to be sure, exists in the same manner that the freedom to resist the highwayman's demand for one's money or one's life exists; but, as in the highwayman case, the exercise of the freedom is most difficult.

The inability or unwillingness to recognize these economic facts of life led the nineteenth century American jurists astray. It prompted them to decide cases on the basis of a theoretical freedom of contract, which if it had ever existed in reality, had certainly been swept away by the tides of industrialism. Examples of the judicial myopia of that time are legion, but only a few need be cited. One court stated that the remedy for the company store evil was "in the hands of the employee" since he was not legally compelled to buy from his employer.[19] This Court's error lay, as Dean Pound reminds us, in "[f]orgetting that there may be compulsion in fact where there is none in law." [20] Another court made a similar error, when, in holding against a statute prohibiting company stores and requiring miners to be paid weekly, it intoned that among our citizens "there is no inferior class, other than that of those degraded by crime or other vicious indulgences of the passions. . . ." [21] Of course, this court was correct to the extent that there is in this country no groups whose legal rights are inferior to those of other groups. But it overlooked the fact that there are vast economic gulfs between categories of our people, and that it was within the power of the legislature to attempt to ameliorate the lot of the less fortunate categories.

Still another bench went so far as to decree that, since men and women have equal rights, a woman must be allowed to enter into a contract to work as many hours a day as a man.[22] In like manner, various courts operating from this premise of theoretical equality, frowned upon statutes designed to aid laborers and called such legislation insulting to the manhood of laborers,[23] or degrading,[24] or putting laborers under guardianship,[25] or stamping them as imbeciles.[26] The highest tribunal of one State went to the extreme of striking down a municipal ordinance prescribing an eight-hour day on public works, as an infringement of the rights of persons to make and enforce their contracts.[27] Similar reasoning voided a statute making it illegal for an employer and employee to agree that the employee would not join or remain in a union.[28]

We see, therefore, that nineteenth century judicial thought placed extreme emphasis upon the desirability of absolute freedom of contract. Sir George Jessel expressed this emphasis when he said, "If there is one thing more than any other which public policy requires, it is that men of full age and competent understanding shall have the utmost liberty of contracting, and that contracts when entered into freely and voluntarily, shall be held good and shall be enforced by courts of justice." [29] Though Sir George said these words in deciding an English case, their philosophy was that of American law as well.

It was finally realized, however, that the abuses which stemmed from unlimited freedom of contract required some alterations and modifications in the concept. "Observation of results . . . proved that unlimited freedom of contract, like unlimited freedom in other directions, [did] not necessarily lead to public or individual welfare and that the only ultimate test of proper limitations [was] that provided by experience." [30] People began to realize that the unlimited freedom of contract of the *laissez-faire* system means in practice freedom for the strong and slavery for the weak.[31] Religious influences too played a large part in this awakening. It is not without significance, for example, that Pope Leo XIII in 1891 published the famed "Rerum Novarum" at just about the time of the turning point in the freedom of contract concept.

Hence, it is that during the past fifty years the tide has set strongly in a direction opposite to that of the nineteenth century. The effort has been to impose legal limitations on the bargaining power of the economically strong in order to put them on more of a parity with the economically weak. Illustrations readily come to mind of limitations upon contractual freedom which have evolved, at least in large part, as a result of this effort.[32] Usury laws are an example. Usury statutes are by no means a product of this century. They were well established in England even before freedom of contract assumed such a large role in British jurisprudence, and for the most part they continued on the English and American statute books all through the era when unlimited freedom of contract flourished, both here and abroad. But during the period when freedom of contract was regarded as the highest good, usury statutes were often made less stringent either by amendment or judicial interpretation. In a few cases they were repealed. In recent years the tendency has been the other way, and statutes aimed at the "loan shark" have flourished with renewed vigor.

Another important present-day restraint on freedom of contract appears in the Anti-Trust Laws. Some common law limitations on the right to make contracts in restraint of trade existed even during the highwater mark of liberty of contract, but the twentieth century has seen extensive federal legislation like the Sherman Act, the Clayton Act, and the Robinson Patman Act supplementing and greatly extending the common law rules. Many state legislatures have followed suit and passed laws designed to preserve free competition. The general effect of such legislation is to prevent business men from agreeing on cooperative measures such as price-fixing and patent licensing, which have the effect of unreasonably restraining trade or fostering monopoly conditions.

Somewhat analogous to Anti-Trust laws are the many statutes aimed at regulation of the issuance of corporate securities. The Federal Securities Act and the Securities Exchange Act, and the state "blue-sky" laws all limit to a marked degree the power of corporations to issue their securities on the basis of *caveat emptor* bargaining. Today it is the seller of securities who must beware. The seller can no longer contract freely with whomever he can induce to purchase his stocks or bonds. Detailed disclosure, far greater than that which the law of contracts demands, must be made as to the financial status of the issuing company and other relevant matters.

Public utility regulation has also markedly restricted the freedom of contract of those subject to it. Every state in the union has a public utility commission or similar body, charged with the fixing of rates for services like railroads, busses, trucks, electricity, gas, water, and the like, and no contract can lawfully be made changing the rates so fixed. The federal government too has entered this field. The Federal Power Commission, an administrative tribunal of fairly recent origin, sets rates for utilities engaged in interstate activities. The Interstate Commerce Commission, one of the oldest federal administrative agencies, dating back to the late years of the last century, fixes rates for carriers engaged in interstate commerce.

Nor is the abridgement of freedom of contract which these state and federal utility regulatory bodies accomplish limited solely to rates. Many other details of the furnishing of service come within their jurisdiction, and the very structure of corporations is often regulated, as for instance by the federal Public Utility Holding Company Act.

Abuses which arose from free contracting in the insurance field have led to much the same kind of regulation there. State after state has passed legislation providing for a Superintendent of Insurance or similar official to head up an administrative body which fixes insurance rates and keeps a weather eye peeled for possible abuses. Almost without exception, the major terms of insurance contracts are fixed by statute or by administrative regulation, with very little being left to the company and the policy-holder to agree upon. The day has passed when "fine print" clauses served as a trap for the unwary policy holder. Moreover, in recent years decisions of the United States Supreme Court have opened the way for federal regulation of much of the insurance field. While this regulation has not as yet materialized, it may well come on the scene in future years.

We have already seen that freedom of contract was, in past years, a concept of great power in the labor field. Here too the tide has turned. The change began in the early years of this century when the United States Supreme Court upheld a law which made it criminal to employ women more than ten hours a day in a factory or similar establishment.[33] Since that time numerous statutes limiting the working hours of men, women, and children, and specifying the conditions of labor, have been sustained. Minimum wage laws have been enacted federally and in the states, and have been uniformly upheld. "Yellow dog contracts," under which an employee agrees not to join a union, have been almost universally outlawed. The other broad expansions in the rights of labor which have occurred in the past twenty years are too well known to require restating here; most of them, it may be added, have been at the expense of the doctrine of freedom of contract. Whether these expansions have all been desirable from the standpoint of the nation as a whole, is a question with which it is not the business of this paper to deal. Many have felt that the pendulum has now swung too far the other way, and there is much evidence to sustain that view. But, be that as it may, it is perfectly clear that the contemporary concept of freedom of contract in the labor field is far different and less vital than that of fifty or seventy-five years ago.

If necessary, numerous other illustrations could be given to show not only the tendency of legislatures in recent years to limit freedom of contract when they determined that sound public policy required it, but also the concomitant tendency of courts to sustain such limitations unless clearly arbitrary or capricious. Recent war and defense emergencies, for instance, brought forth rent, eviction and price control legislation, and other similar laws which imposed restrictions hitherto undreamed of on the scope of private agreements. Such laws successfully resisted challenge in the courts. But the examples which have already been noted will serve to demonstrate the magnitude of the "legal revolution" which has occurred in this field.

The present situation may be briefly summarized. There are, first of all, many subjects upon which society will not permit people to contract at all. For example, a borrower cannot lawfully agree to pay usurious interest, and a husband and wife cannot lawfully agree to dissolve their marriage. Speaking more generally, no agreement criminal in nature or otherwise opposed to public policy will be sustained. Society also interferes with the making of contracts by prescribing their form or requiring in them the inclusion of certain terms, as in the case of insurance and public utility contracts, or in the case of contracts regulated by statutes such as the Uniform Sales Act, the Uniform Bills of Lading Act, and the Uniform Warehouse Receipts Act.

Yet, in spite of these interventions by society, and the many others to which reference has been made, it is probably true that the role of the private contracting parties still is larger and more important in contract law than that of the state. "Where the line is to be drawn between private autonomy and public authority has not been a static thing" in the field of contracts.[34] The line has shifted very far from where it was during the nineteenth century; where it will be drawn in years to come is part of the larger question of the role that the individual and the State will play in tomorrow's world.[35]

The best principle to be followed in tomorrow's law is reasonably clear. Private initiative in making contracts should be allowed as wide a sphere of operation as is compatible with the interests of society in protecting all its members. Freedom of contract should not again be permitted to become the wild and destructive force that it was in past years; neither should it be harnessed too tightly lest its power for good be rendered impotent. But how this general principle is to be satisfactorily translated into practice is a vast problem whose solution will be one of the serious problems of the law in years to come.

Freedom and the Law of Torts

Having dealt with freedom of contract, we turn now to another field in which adjustments are continually being made between individual action and the edicts of the law. This is the area controlled by the law of torts.

The word "tort" is not a term of easy definition. When either the lawyer or layman speaks of a "contract," it conjures up a mental image of fairly well defined nature, but not so with "tort." A tort may be very loosely spoken of as "unprivileged harmful interference with others."[36]

Yet this definition is inadequate in that in some sense breaches of contract and crimes also fall within it.

Rather than defining a tort as such, it is more useful to describe the scope of the law of torts. This can be done by referring generally to the common types of conduct which come within the realm of torts, such as assault and battery, false imprisonment, malicious prosecution, abuse of process, trespass to chattels, conversion, fraud, inducing breach of contract, interference with business rights, slander of title, negligence, nuisance, libel, slander, together with activities for which strict liability is imposed. Many of these terms are words of ordinary usage. In any event, it is unnecessary for present purposes to define them exactly.

Suffice it to say that the law of torts embraces this more or less miscellaneous collection of non-promissory wrongs (thus excluding breaches of contract) which result in damage, and to redress which the wronged person may bring a civil action, usually seeking damages only. Some of these wrongs are intentional ones, others are negligently caused, and still others possess neither the element of intent nor that of negligence. Frequently, a tort is also a crime; in such instances the offender is subject both to a civil suit by the individual injured and to a criminal suit by the State in which a penalty of fine or imprisonment may be imposed.

It has been said earlier that throughout his life, our mythical friend, Prudent Man, will be making contracts. It is impossible to exist in a civilized community without doing so. Thus the law of contracts places restraints upon an individual's activities. Similarly tort law limits the scope of his voluntary action. A man may not drive a car carelessly or emit noxious fumes from his factory to the detriment of his neighbor; the law of torts will hold him to account. The purpose here is to show in what ways the law of torts does impinge upon free action. To do that a brief historical analysis is necessary.

Historically, the law seems first to have concerned itself with acts committed against the safety or dignity of society. Holdsworth has shown this to be true of English law.[37] The effort of the early law everywhere was to substitute some form of legal action by the group in place of private vengeance and the blood feud. Since the safety and dignity of society were most outraged by acts of violence, the proscriptions of early law were generally directed against such acts. Moreover, the punishments involved were usually as violent as the wrongful acts themselves.

In English law, the next step in the historical process was to permit the wrongdoer or his kin to escape violent retribution by the payment of a sum of money, roughly proportioned to the gravity of the offense and the importance of the injured person. The group still was the prime mover in taking action against the offender, but the penalty recovered from him went to the injured party.

Out of this grew modern Anglo-American criminal law—the lawsuit by the State—and tort law—the lawsuit by the individual. Gradually the individual replaced the King as the plaintiff in the action for damages. The injured party still alleged that the defendant's action was committed *contra pacem Domini Regis* and *vi et armis,* but, beginning in the middle of the twelfth century, the injury to the peace of the realm was subordinated, in the action for damages, to the injury to the individual. At first this civil action covered only violence to the person, to land, and to goods, but gradually, through the centuries, remedies came to the fore for all those wrongs which we have previously listed as within the scope of modern tort law.

As would naturally be assumed, early English tort law was little concerned with the ethical aspects of the defendant's conduct. The primitive law of the twelfth century was not prone to inquire whether a defendant had struck down his neighbor intentionally, carelessly, or purely accidentally, because in any of those events the peace of the realm had been violently broken. The only question was, did the defendant do the act? Even self-protection was not considered by the courts as a defense either in criminal prosecutions or tort suits. "The man who has slain another in self-defense deserves, it is true, but also needs a royal pardon. . . . [S]elf-help is an enemy of law, a contempt of the king and his court. . . ." [38] In an England where the king was seeking to establish his authority among warring nobles, there was no room for other than direct and simple prohibitions, without any exceptions to them. Certain acts of violence were unlawful *per se,* regardless of why or how they happened.

The idea of liability based simply upon the doing of certain acts lost ground as England became less a nation of warring clans and more a united country. As the nation was unifying, the idea was correlatively developing that the individual was ethically responsible for his acts. This notion was fostered by the teachings of Christianity, as well as by the writings of Plato, Aristotle, and the Roman lawgivers whose tomes had been influencing English legal law for three hundred years, more or less, before the height of the Renaissance. Thus at the same time that the need for simple and quick community vengeance for unlawful acts was diminishing, the notion of personal responsibility was growing.

Under this newer concept it was logical to say that a man should be responsible in tort if he intentionally or carelessly harmed another person, but not otherwise. That is exactly what the law did come to hold. The development was a slow one. It was spurred by the economic necessities of the Commercial and Industrial Revolutions, as well as by the whole spirit of individualism which was the dominant tone of those Revolutions.

Thus it was, that by the early part of the nineteenth century, intent and negligence or "fault" became the touchstones of tort liability. And, although the older concept of liability without fault never entirely disappeared, it gradually fell into disuse. In a growing industrial society, the judges were not disposed to hold a manufacturer or supplier of goods liable without a showing of fault on his part, for to do so offended against the tenor of the times.

As we have seen previously, the nineteenth century was the highwater mark of freedom of contract. It was also, to coin a phrase, the highwater mark of "freedom of tort." Just as the individualistic *laissez-faire* spirit of the nineteenth century demanded that a man should have a great measure of freedom in making contracts, so too it demanded that he should have a great measure of freedom in his noncontractual actions.

But as freedom of contract was carried too far, so also was "freedom of tort." The nineteenth century limited tort liability sharply to intentional wrongs and negligent ones. It also tended to limit closely the category of persons to whom a defendant might be liable. If a manufacturer put on the market unwholesome food, he would be liable to the wholesaler to whom he had sold it if the wholesaler happened to be injured by using the instrument or eating the food. But of course it was usually the ultimate consumer who was hurt, and he, the courts ruled, could not sue the manufacturer. Perhaps such a rule was desirable as a kind of "protective tariff," saving the pioneers of mass production from excessive costs in order to foster industrial development in the early days of the nineteenth century, but clearly it was ill-adapted to the needs of the twentieth.

Then too, those touchstones of nineteenth century tort liability, negligence and intent, were not a complete solution to the problems of more recent years. Take the airplane for instance. What was the law of torts to do with it? Was the law to say that the airplane pilot and owner were responsible only if the pilot intentionally or carelessly crashed the plane? Or was the law to change its views and say that the risk of loss by airplane crash was to rest in all cases, including even those where no personal fault was present, upon the persons who put the plane aloft?

Other questions plagued the tort law of the twentieth century. What about industrial accidents? Hundreds of thousands of workers, mainly family breadwinners, were being struck down annually by industrial accidents. Sometimes the industrial establishment could be shown to be at fault, and a recovery achieved under conventional tort doctrines of negligence. But in many cases there was no fault by anyone, and, even if there were, it was often the fault of a fellow servant in which case the courts held the employer not to be liable. As a result many an injured laborer went totally uncompensated for an injury which disabled him totally or at the very least substantially reduced his earning power.

The law found the answers to these, and to other analogous modern tort problems, in what may be described as a tendency to return to the early theory of strict liability or liability without fault. Sometimes this change was accomplished legislatively as in the Workmen's Compensation Acts, and other times judicially, as in the ultra-hazardous activity rule which imposes strict liability for injuries occasioned by airplanes and similar highly dangerous instrumentalities. In some instances no definite solution has yet been found. The tort problems posed by artificial rain-making, for instance, have not yet been answered.

It is clear then that today, because we are living in an age of expanding tort liability, the freedom to do as we please is increasingly curtailed. The modern tendency is in the direction of imposing tort liability largely aside from "fault" or other delinquency and mainly for reasons of economic and social policy. This policy may be expressed as that of spreading losses from accidents over large groups in order to minimize the impact upon any one individual. Every citizen is becoming to a large extent his brother's keeper so far as accident law goes. In this respect the law may ultimately weave a new fabric which will bring within the purview of the law more of the moral obligations of justice and charity.

We have already mentioned Workmen's Compensation statutes. The overall effect of these is to make the employer liable, irrespective of his fault, for any injury to a worker which arises out of and in the course of employment. Since the employer knows he will be liable, he naturally procures insurance—in fact most compensation statutes require him to do so—and the economic effect is to spread the loss over all the premium-paying employers. Anyone who goes into business covered by a Workmen's Compensation law must assume this insurance cost. He has no choice about it. This is not to say that the system is a bad one. Indeed it is almost universally agreed that Workmen's Compensation Laws are a great social advance. But good or bad, they certainly do limit sharply the orbit of an employer's unrestricted action.

In no other field of the law of torts has the tendency towards increasing the scope of liability gone so far as it has in the area of industrial accidents. But the same trend is very evident elsewhere.[39] The nineteenth century law as applied to manufacturers and suppliers of goods has undergone a complete transformation. Today a manufacturer or supplier must exercise reasonable care in the manufacture, assembling or supply of any goods or instruments which will constitute a menace to life or limb if not made or maintained with care, and this duty extends to anyone likely to be harmed by the defective product while being used for the purpose intended. Moreover, particularly as to food products, there is a growing movement towards making the manufacturer or supplier absolutely liable, regardless of the degree of care he may have taken.

There has likewise been much broadening of the liability of land owners and occupiers. Whereas years ago there were not many serious dangers to be encountered on land, today power transmission lines and machinery of various sorts in farm and urban communities present new hazards which the courts have attempted to meet by imposing new and more onerous liabilities on owners and occupiers of land. Furthermore, increased recognition is being given in modern courts to emotional disturbance as an element of damage. The old rule that one could not recover for physical harm brought about through emotional shock without physical injury has been abandoned in most jurisdictions, and even those states which still nominally adhere to the "no liability without impact" rule have stripped the principle of much of its harshness by diluting it with frequent exceptions.[40]

Other widening vistas of liability are seen in the development within the past sixty years of the "right of privacy," that is, the right to be let alone and to pursue one's activities without subjection to the prying and publicizing of others. There we have the appearance of a principle which both expands and restricts freedom: it expands it by affording at least a modicum of protection from publicity to a man in carrying out his everyday affairs; at the same time, however, it restricts freedom to inquire into, discuss and publicize the affairs of others.

The ever-increasing use of liability insurance in recent years has been an important factor in the promotion of extensions in liability patterns.[41] The wider use of insurance has been both an effect and a cause. As more and more defendants are held liable, the need of potential defendants to insure grows greater. This is illustrated by the automobile field where the danger of an owner being subjected to a large verdict virtually compels him to insure. Again, as insurance becomes more widespread, juries realize that frequently it is not the individual defendant, but rather the insurance carrier who will bear the brunt of the verdict, and consequently tend to find for the plaintiff.

It seems clear, therefore, that present-day rules of tort law give the individual a much narrower scope of untrammeled activity than did those of fifty or a hundred years ago. Probably as a necessary result of the industrial society in which we live, the area of unrestricted action has been much limited. The only way in which the courts and legislatures have been able to effect a satisfactory adjustment of conflicting interests in that society has been by curtailing to an appreciable extent the free action of individual members.

It may be noted, however, that even these great expansions which have taken place in tort law have not made its obligations as strict as those decreed by the moral law.[42] In imposing affirmative obligations upon individuals, such as active duties to exercise care, tort law in the past required, and still seems to require as a *sine qua non,* the existence of some beneficial relationship between the parties concerned.[43] A manufacturer, for example, has an affirmative duty to prepare his product carefully in order to guard against injury to the consumers. This duty is grounded basically in the fact that the manufacturer may derive a benefit from his consumer. The same is true of the landowner's affirmative duty towards his business visitor, the railroad's duty towards its passenger, and the innkeeper's towards his guest. In all these instances, and in other similar ones, the duty which the law imposes is grounded upon the benefit. When these situations are analyzed in moral terms, it would seem that too much stress is placed by the law upon the existence of a *quid pro quo* and too little upon the real need of the community that further moral duties of justice and charity be enforced by the law.

Consistent and logical application of the benefit principle results in serious discrepancies between the duties at law and the duties which conscience dictates. It appears to be the law that, "No action will lie against a spiteful man who, seeing another running into a position of danger, merely omits to warn him." [44] The general rule applicable in this situation, and similar ones, has perhaps been best epitomized by a New Hampshire court:

> With purely moral obligations the law does not deal. For example, the priest and levite who passed by on the other side were not, it is supposed, liable at law for the continued suffering of the man who fell among thieves, which they might and morally ought to have prevented or relieved. Suppose A, standing by a railroad, sees a two year old babe on the track and a car approaching. He can easily rescue the child with entire safety to himself, and the instincts of humanity require him to do so. If he does not, he may, perhaps, justly be styled a ruthless savage and a moral monster; but he is not liable in damages for the child's injury or indictable under the statute for its death.[45]

The decisions based upon this doctrine have been truly shocking. It has been held that a physician will not be liable for a failure to attend a man who is in dire danger of death; [46] that a railroad may ignore a trespasser who has been injured, without the railroad's negligence, in operation of its train; [47] that a master need not rescue his servant's goods from the ravages of a flood though the master might easily do so; [48] that there can be no recovery for injuries to a child resulting from failure of those in charge of dangerous machinery to remove him from harm's way; [49] and that one may stand idly by and watch another drown [50] or bleed to death.[51]

It seems apparent that in these areas of clear moral obligation [52] the law of torts should impose a duty to act; [53] in those situations, at least, where one can readily aid another in saving life, limb or property, without danger or serious inconvenience, the law should add to the roster of affirmative duties that of humanitarianism.[54]

Summarizing our tort discussion, we see that the law has curtailed individual freedom in noncontractual situations to a considerable extent. In compelling one man to accommodate his actions to the rights of others, it consequently holds him liable for intentionally or carelessly violating such rights. Moreover, in recent years there has been a widespread extension in the scope of tort liability, and a concurrent decrease in individual freedom, through the development of liability without fault. This development has been most marked in the Workmen's Compensation field, but can be seen in other subdivisions of tort law as well. With these numerous extensions of liability we seem to be moving in the direction of law and morality. We have not yet translated all moral obligations into legal ones, and it would probably not be desirable to attempt to do so. There is a considerable need, however, to afford legal status to certain moral obligations, such as those heretofore discussed.

Criminal Law and Freedom

Closely allied to the law of torts is the law of crimes. The criminal law is obviously a large factor in restricting the individual's freedom to do as he wishes, and study of the compulsions which it exacts is an exercise of some profit. Our friend, Prudent Man, will probably not get seriously involved with the criminal law since by definition, he is an average citizen, and the average citizen is the law-abiding one. Nonetheless, it is always possible, and indeed does happen, that an innocent man is accused of crime. Furthermore, the mere existence of the criminal law places boundaries around Prudent Man's area of free action, and, as we shall see later, the broad scope of such law sometimes makes him technically a criminal.

The word "crime" is much more susceptible of reasonably exact legal definition than is its related concept, "tort." As we have already seen, the term "tort" has a multiplicity of meanings and includes many unrelated sub-concepts. But a crime is rather generally agreed to be simply "[a] positive or negative act in violation of penal law." [55] This "penal law," although in early days a part of the common law, is today almost entirely encompassed within a statutory framework, so that the modern "crime" is simply a transgression against a statutory prohibition. To punish such transgression and to deter others from committing like offenses, the law exacts retribution from the criminal in the form of a fine or imprisonment, or both, or, in some cases death. Crimes are often subdivided into "misdemeanors" and "felonies," terms which, speaking somewhat inexactly, refer respectively to less serious, and more serious crimes.

American legal scholarship has frequently stressed an underlying unity in the law of crimes and torts. Holmes went so far as to assert that "the general principles of criminal and civil liability are the same," [56] and Terry discussed both fields of law under the head of "Wrongs." [57] It may be admitted that there is a great similarity in terminology between the fields. Words like assault, battery, fraud and conspiracy appear in both, and in a few cases the words represent identical meanings, or nearly so. The basic difference between these two branches of the law appears to be that "penal law is concerned with social harms which include moral culpability as an essential element whereas torts deal with individual damage which need not have been effected by morally culpable conduct." [58] This statement, while subject to criticism since some crimes do not involve moral culpability, is true for all practical purposes.

It is not necessary, however, for us to delve deeply into the rationale of torts and crimes, and the distinctions between the fields. What is important here is the indisputable fact that criminal law, like the law of torts, places substantial limits upon the individual's free action. What these limits are and how they have changed and are changing is our concern.

It has already been observed that the Commercial and Industrial Revolutions had marked effects on the law of torts and contracts.

Less marked, perhaps, but still significant, was their impact upon the law of crimes. It may be worthwhile to recall to mind a few famous examples.

During the sixteenth and seventeenth centuries, the flow of gold into England became much greater with the vast increase in trade fostered by the Commercial Revolution. As overseas trade made financing essential, the goldsmiths, who had long functioned as depositaries for precious metals, about the middle of the seventeenth century began to make loans. In 1694 the Bank of England was organized in order to provide stability and safety for deposits, objectives which the goldsmiths had never been able to achieve. The widespread use of notes, checks and other instruments soon followed.

With the development of these new economic forces came changes in the criminal law. The Act of 1742, an embezzlement statute, was designed to protect the Bank of England, and applied to officials of that Bank.[59] A second embezzlement statute, passed in 1751, applied to officers and employees of the South Sea Company, and a third extended to employees of the Post Office.

The impact of the shifting economic climate was also felt in other subdivisions of the criminal law. The fantastic speculation in the securities of some of the seventeenth and eighteenth century trading companies, such as the Hudson's Bay, Levant, East India, Virginia, and South Sea Companies, and the great losses suffered in such economic crashes as the Panic of 1721, resulted in changes which strengthened the law of criminal fraud.

We are not, however, so much interested in these early examples of the criminal law's impact upon individual action, and such law's amenability to change, as we are in the situation as it exists in the present day. The past fifty years of the growth of criminal law have been in the general direction of greater restrictions upon individual conduct, particularly in the realm of economics, and it is this era that is most interesting for study purposes.

Fifty years ago the Criminal Code of almost every state in the United States was a relatively brief statute.[60] This statute had superseded entirely or to a considerable extent the common law of crimes which had existed fifty or seventy-five years earlier, but it still branded as criminal substantially the same types of conduct which the common law forbids, and little else.

The past half-century has brought great changes in these statutes of the 1900's. These alterations in widening greatly the area of conduct subject to criminal sanction, have cut down the realm of free activity. Probably, as Pound has suggested, the weakening of religious and familial institutions in America has had a good deal to do with this broadening of the scope of criminal law.[61] Such weakening has made it necessary for the State to come forward and substitute the rules of criminal law for the disciplines of religion and family.

One large domain in which the scope of criminal sanctions has substantially increased is that of "economic crimes." There are very few trades, professions or businesses today which are not subject to the provisions of one or more criminal statutes, generally enacted during the last fifty or sixty years.

For example, the businessman, especially in big business, is concerned with the criminal sanctions which form part of the Anti-Trust Laws. The common law imposed criminal liability only for monopolies in necessities of life,[62] but this liability proved inadequate to cope with the activities of the industrial giants which began to emerge after the Civil War. Soon state anti-trust statutes appeared on the scene, and in 1890 the Sherman Act was enacted by Congress. For enforcement, state anti-trust legislation, as well as the Sherman Act, and its later fellows relied in part on criminal sanctions.[63] Criminal prosecutions were never very successful, however, and as a practical matter were largely replaced by suits for injunctive relief. An injunction is much better suited to handle a business problem for it can direct future conduct whereas the criminal prosecution can only punish past activity.

The sanctions of criminal law have likewise appeared on a wide scale in recent years in banking and finance. Where fifty years ago only a few penal statutes, such as embezzlement and false report laws, existed in this field, today many statutes cover specific items of unsound banking practice. Bank failures led to the adoption of criminal legislation that made it possible to punish bank officials who knowingly received deposits while their banks were insolvent, as well as those who brought about insolvency through their fraud or negligence. It may well be queried whether these laws have been of much help in promoting sound banking; for such improvements as have come about in banking practices seem to be accounted for by tightened administrative regulation rather than more stringent penal sanctions.

Closely allied to developments in the banking field has been the growth of the criminal law in respect to stocks, bonds, and other securities. Laws were passed in most states, starting with Kansas in 1911, designed to insure registration of securities with state officials before sale, under pain of criminal punishment. Fraudulent registration was similarly made punishable criminally. As with the anti-trust laws, criminal enforcement was never very successful, and today the injunction has largely supplanted criminal penalties. In the federal field, too, criminal prosecutions are now seldom resorted to, although the Securities Act of 1933, the Securities Exchange Act of 1934, and the Public Utility Holding Company Act of 1935, all contain criminal provisions of one form or another.

Pure Food Laws on both federal and state level are further illustrations of economic and welfare legislation with criminal sanctions, as are anti-narcotic statutes like the Harrison Act and the Miller-Jones Act, both federal laws. The liquor traffic has undergone an almost complete cycle of criminal law regulation, but one, however, that began and ended in a very brief period. Only six states had prohibition in 1887, yet the unfortunate experiment of National Prohibition had begun by 1920. The experiment, of course, ended in the early 30's and since then regulation of the liquor trade has been effected mainly through federal tax measures and local controls of various sorts. The history of Prohibition in the 1920's is an illustration of how unwise prohibitory and penal legislation can stimulate the very crime which it seeks to suppress. Even now, the country has not wholly recovered from the gangsterism which followed in the wake of National Prohibition.

Other new crimes have been created to keep pace with the fast movement of modern life. The radio has led to the creation of criminal slander,[64] the telephone and telegraph have brought statutes prohibiting eavesdropping through these media, and stealing electricity has been made a crime.[65] Numerous special criminal laws have grown out of the invention of the automobile, such as "joy riding" larceny statutes, and reckless driving, automobile assault and homicide laws, as well as countless quasi-criminal traffic ordinances.

The idea of corporate criminality has also been a creature of relatively recent years. The early difficulty in imposing criminal liability upon corporations was occasioned by the notion that a corporation could not form the intent to commit a criminal act. Practical considerations have overcome this theoretical objection, and today it may be stated as a general proposition that a corporation is liable for any crime committed by its agents on its behalf, provided that the crime is punishable by a fine. Most criminal statutes have been amended to include a general section making a corporation liable to pay a fine in any case where a natural person would be subjected to imprisonment.[66] There has also been a substantial increase in the volume of criminal laws applicable to the corporate officials themselves, as for instance, those imposing penal sanctions for paying dividends out of capital.

What effect has this large scale growth in the domain of criminal law had on the freedom of the individual? It is perhaps not far from the truth to say, as Livingston Hall does, that one of the results of increasing use of criminal law in the business field "has been to make everyone a criminal." [67] So multitudinous are the criminal laws today that even an average citizen like Prudent Man can hardly go through life without committing some technical violations which are not prosecuted and which do not involve immoral conduct. This indiscriminate use of penal statutes is unfortunate because it tends to make people lose respect for the criminal law. It seems reasonably clear that criminal sanctions to have a real deterrent effect must be limited to the more serious offenses.

Yet, despite the vast increase in criminal legislation, there has not been, it would seem, a proportionate decrease in individual freedom. The business man, it is true, is much more restricted in his scope of operation than was his counterpart of fifty or seventy-five years ago; he has to watch his step closely or he will be violating the penal law. But outside of this special case, it may be doubted whether the individual's freedom has suffered any appreciable loss from the increase in the domain of criminal law; for although, under the vast mass of modern criminal legislation the average person may now and then become technically a "criminal," his freedom is, as a practical matter, little hampered by these measures.

We turn next in our discussion to an area of the law that is closely allied to criminal law. Namely, the field of military law, a field which has become of ever-increasing importance during the past few years.

Military Law and Freedom

So close is the relationship between criminal law and military law that, in one sense, military law may be viewed as but a specialized form of criminal law. However, its effects upon individual freedom are of sufficient importance to warrant an independent discussion of them.

In recent years the Armed Forces have become part and parcel of everyone's life. Some 15,000,000 Americans served in them during World War II, and those who remained at home had close friends or relatives in the service. This situation has continued, though on a modified scale, during the post-war years, and, so long as the forces of atheistic Communism stand poised for attack, it will continue. This is in sharp contrast to the days of the 1920's and 1930's when the Army and Navy were composed solely of professional military men, and it was unusual for the average person even to come in contact with a soldier or sailor. In view of this large part which the military system plays in everyday life, it behooves us to see what restrictions that system places on the freedom of those who are subject to it. Just what happens to the rights of our friend Prudent Man, when he enlists or is inducted into the military service?

The military services have their own system of criminal law which is entirely independent from the criminal law to which the civilian is subject. So far as the civil law goes, a soldier or sailor, generally speaking, has the same rights and duties as civilians; for example, a cause of action in tort or contract involving a serviceman is tried in the same state or federal court that would try it if a civilian were involved. But a serviceman who commits a crime, or an offense against military discipline analogous to a crime (such as absence without leave), is tried, except in rare instances, before a court-martial.

Up until very recent years the Armed Forces operated under a legal system that had its roots in the distant past.[68] During World War II the Navy was ruled by the Articles for the Government of the Navy, a statute that was not unlike Cromwell's Articles of some 300 years ago. The Army was governed by a law (the Articles of War) which still bore the imprint of an ancient Roman predecessor.

Despite its age, the military legal system was working reasonably well when World War II broke out, but an overhauling was clearly called for. This was made manifest during World War II when, under the pressure of wartime conditions and with the inevitable use of inexperienced personnel, abuses crept into the system. Various investigations in the closing days of the War and after its termination, disclosed some unfortunate occurrences. It appeared that sentences were sometimes imposed that were entirely disproportionate to the offenses. Moreover, there were instances where commanding officers influenced the decisions of courts-martial, especially in regard to sentences, and at times they reprimanded such courts for the imposition of "inadequate" sentences.

Another defect was the failure, in some cases, to employ legally-trained personnel to perform law work. A court-martial trial is just as complicated and involves just as many technical legal questions as a civilian one, but the Armed Services apparently took the attitude that any intelligent officer was qualified to act as defense counsel, trial judge advocate (prosecuting attorney), or law member (roughly equivalent to judge) in courts-martial. The Armed Forces did not recognize law as a profession in the same sense in which they recognized medicine. Although every physician taken into the service was given a commission and assigned medical duties, lawyer applicants were frequently told that there was no room for lawyers, as such, in a wartime military organization. When lawyers volunteered or were inducted, they were very often assigned non-legal duties. Yet later on the Armed Forces sometimes sought to excuse the failure to appoint lawyers to courts-martial by claiming that they were unavailable.

Finally, the investigating committees found that in the military legal system there was some discrimination against enlisted men. Minor misconduct, particularly, was at times overlooked in the case of officers but punished when enlisted men were involved. These deficiencies in the military legal system meant that the basic rights and freedoms of many of our soldiers, sailors and airmen were unnecessarily infringed upon during their period of service. It is well recognized that no military organization can operate properly without a partial sacrifice of the freedom of its members. The millions of civilians that became citizen soldiers during World War II expected some curtailment of their ordinary rights. But these defects in the military legal system made this curtailment much more extensive and arbitrary than it had to be.

To meet these and other difficulties, reform legislation was enacted after World War II, culminating in the Uniform Code of Military Justice which became effective in 1951 and applies to all services. The new Code supplants the Articles of War, the Articles for the Government of the Navy, and the Disciplinary Laws of the Coast Guard.[69] The main changes effected by the various reform laws are the following: (a) a mandatory requirement that trial counsel (prosecutor) and defense counsel in a general court-martial be lawyers; (b) the supplanting of the former law member of the general court-martial with a "law officer" who is not a member of the court, does not vote on its findings of guilt or innocence, and is much more akin to the civilian court's judge than was the law member; (c) the providing in statutory form of a comprehensive and well-defined penal law; and (d) the establishment of a single final appellate tribunal, the Court of Military Appeals, consisting of three civilian judges appointed by the President. In addition enlisted men, if available, may now serve on courts-martial when the accused is an enlisted man and he requests, in writing, their presence.

Probably the most important reform the Uniform Code of Military Justice introduces is the establishment of the Court of Military Appeals. The new Court is located for administrative purposes in the Department of Defense but it is entirely independent of military control. After less than a year of active operation, it was docketing cases at rates which indicate that it will have a yearly volume considerably greater than that of the United States Supreme Court, and at present, it is the busiest appellate tribunal in the country.

The Court's early decisions have shown a marked concern for the rights of servicemen. It established in one case [70] the concept of "military due process" which includes the basic procedural rights granted by Congress to the accused. Just as a denial of constitutional rights in a civilian court will constitute a deprivation of civilian due process, so also, the Court held, a denial of basic statutory rights in a military court will deprive an accused of military due process and furnish grounds for a voiding of any conviction. The Court further pointed out that in marking out the bounds of military due process, it would look to civilian cases as helpful guides. This bold and courageous decision in substance transplants to military law all the rights afforded by civilian due process which have a counterpart in the Uniform Code of Military Justice. The Court is to be congratulated for recognizing that in these difficult times, when, in some sense at least, every civilian is a soldier, every soldier should be a civilian so far as basic rights are concerned.

It may also be noted that the Court of Military Appeals has shown that it is more concerned—and properly so—with prejudice to the accused than with technical propositions of law. It has quite often reversed cases where material prejudice to the accused resulted from some legal error, even in the absence of proper objection to the error by the defense counsel in the court-martial proceeding itself. In thus taking cognizance of points not raised below, the Court has been more lenient towards accused persons than civilian appellate tribunals generally are. Finally, the Court has not hesitated in its opinions to criticize the actions of courts-martial where such criticism has been warranted.

In the light of these reforms our typical American, Prudent Man, is now assured the protection of his fundamental legal rights if he should become involved with military law during his term of military service. Should Prudent Man ever be accused of any serious military offense he will be brought before a military tribunal headed by a competent "law officer" (judge). The trial counsel (prosecutor) and the defense counsel will both be lawyers, and the guilt or innocence of Prudent Man will be determined strictly according to law. Moreover, even if he should be convicted by the court-martial, Prudent Man is assured the benefit of an appeal procedure under which he can ultimately carry his case to a civilian Court of Military Appeals, which it may be added, has shown a definite inclination to protect the freedoms of servicemen to the greatest extent practicable.

It must not be supposed, however, that these important strides forward in military law mean that the system is now perfect. A significant defect is the continued existence of "command control" or "command influence." The members, the law officer, the trial counsel, and the defense counsel of courts-martial are still appointed by the commanding officer, and the commanding officer is the initial reviewing authority of their decisions. Although practically all of the investigating committees which studied military justice after World War II recommended that the appointing and review functions, or at least part of them, be taken away from the commanding officer, nothing has been done on that score.

This criticism of the present system does not rest upon an assumption that commanding officers very often influence courts-martial. Certainly that is not the case. But World War II experience indicates that in some instances they did do so, and, unless the court-martial is divorced entirely from "command control," a possibility of the exercise of influence will continue to exist. It would seem that the appointing and review functions should be taken out of the chain of command, and given to an independent authority, such as, for example, the Judge Advocates General of the respective services.

In recapitulation, we see that when Prudent Man enters the service today, he is much more assured of the protection of his rights than was his brother who served in World War II. His freedom of action is necessarily circumscribed to a great extent by the exigencies of military life. But Prudent Man can now at least feel confident that he will be fairly treated, and will not lose his basic rights. Reform in military law has not progressed as far as it should, but the system is definitely marching forward.

In the discussion of military law it has been observed that Prudent Man is now given the protection of a "military due process" concept formulated by the Court of Military Appeals. The Court has analogized this concept to civilian due process. The next section of the paper deals with this latter concept, as well as with the many other doctrines embraced within the law of Civil Liberties.

Freedom and the Law of Civil Liberties

As we have seen, many branches of the law have important effects upon individual liberty. Prudent Man is constantly coming into contact with legal doctrines that impinge upon his free action. The next and final branch of the law to be considered, that of Civil Liberties, is, however, the one that most intimately and overtly deals with freedom. This branch has as its prime function the task of making adjustments and accommodations between man and man, man and the State, and Religion and the State. It is neither profitable nor necessary at this point to attempt to define with precision the term, "Law of Civil Liberties," which term refers generally to that branch of the law that governs the protection of personal rights—usually constitutional rights. As it is far easier to make the meaning clear by reference to specific cases, the ensuing discussion therefore, will follow this method.

Historically speaking, it seems always to have been true that the State exercised some control over rights of personal liberty, as, for example, over the right to speak one's mind. Seelman says that, "In a free country, speech and writing must be untrammeled. Our constitutions, federal and state, guarantee such freedom. But freedom is often attended by license. . . . The State which guarantees the freedom, punishes its abuse, and accords to the individual whose reputation has been attacked, remedies for the injury sustained." [71]

In the United States we have an almost unique system of protection of civil liberties. The Federal Constitution recognizes that Prudent Man possesses certain basic rights, among which are freedom of speech, press, and religion, and these freedoms may not be cut down by the Congress. In this respect our Constitution differs from those of practically all other nations, even the so-called "democratic" ones. Thus, although the Irish Constitution guarantees freedom of speech, assembly, and religion, it also provides that exercise of these freedoms is "subject to public order and morality." [72] While these words appear in themselves innocuous, and even at first glance desirable, they tend nevertheless, both to open the door to legislative intervention in the civil rights field and to curtail the power of the courts to invalidate liberty-restricting legislation. Similar "escape clauses" appear in the constitutions of Switzerland, Brazil, Argentina and Nicaragua. In the Soviet Union, such things as freedom of the press, speech, and assembly are "guaranteed" by the Constitution, but an Article of the document makes such "rights" dependent upon their being used "in accordance with the interests of the toilers and with the aim of strengthening the Socialist order." [73]

A few nations such as the Philippine Commonwealth, have followed the lead of the United States and have adopted Constitutions which enumerate rights, but contain no escape clause by means of which the legislature can undermine them. Of course, it is not to be assumed that the mere absence of an escape clause in the American Constitution necessarily assures that the liberty of Prudent Man is forever secure from legislative encroachment. Words like freedom of the press, freedom of speech, and freedom of religion are not self-defining, and the ultimate responsibility of giving them meaning falls in this country upon the courts, particularly the Supreme Court of the United States. Theoretically there is nothing to prevent the Supreme Court from defining Prudent Man's "freedom" to mean "slavery," and, if that Court would acquiesce in the attempt, it would not be impossible to establish a dictatorship in this country. But the point is, that with the type of Constitution we have and with the judiciary's traditional independence and respect for precedent, the establishing of a dictatorship is far less likely here than elsewhere.

Let us analyze more closely the field of civil liberties to try to determine just what these so-called "basic rights" of Prudent Man are, as well as the trends in their delineation. Every schoolboy knows that ours is a government of delegated powers. The federal government has only those powers expressly or impliedly delegated to it, whereas the states have all those powers (reserved powers) which are not expressly or impliedly delegated to the federal government. Moreover, the Constitution contains certain prohibitions against action by the federal and state governments, the most important of which are those contained in the first ten amendments to the Constitution, called the Bill of Rights, and much of the law of Civil Liberties has evolved as a gloss upon the simple language of these amendments.

The Bill of Rights was adopted in response to the demands of those who felt that the Constitution as originally written did not adequately safeguard the liberties for which the colonists had fought so hard and so long during the Revolution. Many felt that the Constitutional Convention had produced too strong a central government, and the Bill of Rights was adopted as a check upon this strength. The Bill of Rights, broadly speaking, "enjoined the Federal Government from abridging the rights of freedom of assembly, speech, press and religion, and from infringing the rights of persons accused of crime." [74] These prohibitions, it is important to note, were against federal action and not against state activity. The first ten amendments, as originally adopted, did not assure the ancestor of Prudent Man against the deprivation of his freedom by the States.

It was not until 1868, when the Fourteenth Amendment was adopted, that the Bill of Rights had any effect upon state action. This is not to say that from 1789 to 1868 there were no restraints on state action. There were numerous such restraints because the States inserted in their own Constitutions all or practically all of the guarantees set forth in the First Amendment. But a state guarantee was in no wise the equivalent of a federal one. Freedom of speech to a negro in the South might mean little if guaranteed only by the Alabama Constitution but much if guaranteed by the United States Constitution. The protection of federal tribunals and federal officials is often much more powerful and effective than that of state courts and state officers.

The Fourteenth Amendment provides in part that no state shall ". . . deprive any person of life, liberty or property, without due process of law." The vital question for the courts to determine was the meaning of this "liberty" which was protected by the Amendment. Did "liberty" mean all the rights granted by the Bill of Rights or did it mean something less or more than that? The answer was slow in coming forth, mainly because for many years after the adoption of the Fourteenth Amendment the courts assumed that its only purpose was the limited one of protecting the liberated negro in his recently acquired rights.

However, in 1925, with the Supreme Court's decision in *Gitlow* v. *New York*,[75] the Fourteenth Amendment took on a larger aspect. It was held that "freedom of speech and of the press . . . are among the fundamental personal rights and 'liberties' protected by the due process clause of the Fourteenth Amendment from impairment by the States." [76] Thus, the Supreme Court read into the Fourteenth Amendment, the protections of freedom of speech and of the press, guaranteed by the First Amendment and also indicated that such other protections of the Bill of Rights as were "fundamental" were secured against State abridgement. The Bill of Rights was no longer to be a restraint solely on federal action; its prohibitions were now to have at least some vitality as applied to the States. This new doctrine opened the way for a vast advance in protection of civil liberties. The problem in recent years has been to mark out the bounds of this new area of Constitutional protection which has been given to Prudent Man.

On the one hand, the Supreme Court has steadfastly refused, despite the efforts of Mr. Justice Black, to incorporate the Bill of Rights *in toto* into the Fourteenth Amendment, and has consistently ruled that the Bill cannot be used as a measure of "either the minimum or maximum content of the Fourteenth Amendment." [77] On the other hand, the Court has tended to expand the coverage of the Fourteenth Amendment, and in some instances has even embraced within it rights not prescribed in the Bill of Rights.[78]

The net result is that it is impossible to make more than a reasoned guess whether a given right which the Bill of Rights expressly recognizes is possessed by Prudent Man will be incorporated into the due process clause of the Fourteenth Amendment, and thus made invulnerable against state abridgement. The Supreme Court has left to itself a wide area of discretion in passing upon which of Prudent Man's rights are the "fundamental" ones secure against State action. It has, however, indicated that the rights enumerated in the First Amendment should have a preferred position so far as such inclusion is concerned.

In addition to this growth under the due process clause of the Fourteenth Amendment, civil liberties have also undergone expansion through the mechanism of a broader interpretation of the clause in that Amendment which guarantees equal protection of the laws.

This clause has been used increasingly by the courts as a weapon for striking down discriminatory legislation.[79] It has had particularly wide application in the field of education. Up until very recently the Supreme Court gave lip service approval to the doctrine of "separate but equal" educational facilities, although at the same time it struck down numerous instances of discrimination in education. Thus one decision held that a State's duty to furnish equal educational facilities was not complied with by offering to pay the tuition of a prospective negro student in a law school outside the state,[80] another, that a State Board of Regents was obliged either to enroll the negro plaintiff in its law school or else to admit no students until equal law school facilities had been established for negroes,[81] and still another, that a State must treat a negro student the same way as other students after admitting him to the graduate division of its University.[82] Finally, in a recent case the Court abandoned the doctrine of "separate but equal" as applied to the education field, and flatly ruled that the use of segregated classes violated the Constitution.[83]

The equal protection clause has been invoked in various other areas, but by far its best work has been done in the field of education. Whatever may be the race, creed, color or economic condition of Prudent Man, he is now assured of equality of treatment so far as tax-supported educational facilities are concerned, at least to the extent that the judicial system is able to guarantee such equality.

Thus we see that greater protection has been given to Prudent Man's civil rights through a broadened interpretation of the Fourteenth Amendment. This broadening has had the effect of making the Federal Constitution and the federal judiciary more effective barriers against state restrictions on civil liberties. The central government's intervention to protect civil rights has also had another important aspect, however, and this is a statutory one. The statute in question is the federal Civil Rights Act of 1866 as amended. It has been said that the Bill of Rights is ". . . a shield fashioned by a democracy for safeguarding individual freedom against governmental encroachment," and that the Civil Rights Section of the Department of Justice, which administers the Civil Rights Act, is the "sword" for the protection of this freedom.[84]

The Civil Rights Act was originally passed for the purpose of safeguarding the rights which the negro had won as a result of the Civil War. Through amendments added during the course of the years, the statute now punishes with fine and imprisonment any persons who conspire "to injure, oppress, threaten or intimidate any citizen in the free exercise of any right or privilege secured to him by the Constitution or laws of the United States . . . ," as well as any public officer who "under color of any law . . . willfully subjects . . . any inhabitant of any State, Territory, or District to the deprivation of any rights, privileges, or immunities secured or protected by the Constitution and laws of the United States. . . ."

Until recent years this statute was a "dead letter" law and almost never used. During the past decade, however, increasing awareness of its possibilities has become evident. The law's constitutionality has been sustained.[85] This means that the federal government now has available a criminal statute which can be effectively used to safeguard federal civil rights against encroachment by state officials or private persons. A major difficulty in the civil liberties field has always been the reluctance of state officials to prosecute offenders in situations where oppression of civil rights has taken place. Now the federal government can take a hand in striking at the activities of night riders and similar conspirators. If state officials decline to prosecute under the state criminal laws, the United States Attorney can enter the picture, and the services of the Federal Bureau of Investigation can be utilized. In appropriate cases the state officials themselves may be subject to federal indictment. Moreover, persons injured by the lawless acts can bring tort suits against their oppressors in the federal courts,[86] and obtain appropriate damages. While federal intervention under the Civil Rights Act has not yet materialized on a large scale,[87] this area is likely to be one of the most active battlefronts of civil liberties law in years to come.

Doubtless the most important, and yet at the same time one of the most confused areas of the law of Civil Liberties, is that dealing with Prudent Man's religious liberty. The First Amendment, as we all know, restrains the federal government from making any laws "respecting an establishment of religion" or "prohibiting the free exercise thereof." While the Fourteenth Amendment which restricts state action, makes no specific reference to religion, the Supreme Court has clearly held that the "fundamental concept of liberty" embodied in the Fourteenth Amendment embraces the religious liberty of which the First Amendment speaks.[88] Thus, neither the federal government nor the state may pass laws "respecting an establishment of religion" or "prohibiting the free exercise thereof." The problem is, however, to give specific meaning to this general language in the context of particular fact situations. While it is impossible, in the brief compass of this article, to give anything like adequate coverage to the multitude of religious freedom decisions, at least some criticism of the Supreme Court's views may be made.

Unfortunately the Supreme Court seems to have gone astray in at least one phase of the concept of religious freedom which it has constructed. This is in the area of the so-called "separation of Church and State." In a misguided effort to erect an "impregnable wall" between Church and State, it struck down in 1948 a system of "released time" for religious education in Illinois.[89] Admittedly, the Illinois system did involve some slight state participation in religious education in that religious classes were conducted on public school premises. However, there was no expense to the State for the services of the teachers, and participation in the program was voluntary.

More encouraging is the Court's very recent decision which upheld the New York City "released time" program.[90] The New York program differed somewhat from that in Illinois, the main distinction being that in the former State the religious instruction took place off the school premises. This latest decision of the Court shows that it is not following slavishly, as some feared it would, the principle of separation of Church and State.[91] The most rabid proponents of the separation principle would destroy any kind of cooperation between Church and State, and acceptance of their views would lead inevitably to the elimination of such well recognized cooperation ventures as tax exemptions for religious properties, chaplains in the Armed Services, and so forth. The Supreme Court seems to understand the absurdity of the views of the absolute separatists, and apparently is inclined to pursue what it regards as the middle way.

A field which is not always recognized as bearing on Civil Liberties is that of administrative law, that is, the law administered by the many federal, state and local quasi-judicial tribunals, such as the Federal Trade Commission, the New York State Liquor Authority, or the local Zoning Board. When one stops to think, it becomes apparent that these bodies exercise great influence on Prudent Man's freedom. There were about ten federal administrative agencies before the Civil War; at the outbreak of World War II there were over fifty. That War saw many other temporary ones spring up, some of which still remain with us. On the state and local level, too, the growth of administrative law has been phenomenal. Obviously the numerous decisions, rules, and regulations of these many bodies cannot help but affect the actions of Prudent Man.

The threat which administrative law poses to Prudent Man's freedom is a subtle one. It stems from the blending in one body of the investigatory, prosecuting and adjudicating function. An administrative agency investigates matters which come within its ambit and holds hearings at which evidence is presented by its legal staff, and the ultimate decisions are made by the same agency's hearing examiners or members. In one sense the police, the district attorney, and the judge are one and the same. One authority puts it this way:

> . . . Such bureaus all tend to regard their particular function one to enforce some paramount law overriding all other laws and constitutional guarantees. The bureaucratic officials are advocates against him, and at the same time judges of his cause. They not only prosecute the charge against him, but also decide the case. . . .[92]

Although that statement overstates the case, it does contain a germ of truth. It cannot be doubted that administrative agencies are a necessary element of modern government. The vast majority of the personnel of these agencies are fair-minded public servants. Nonetheless, abuses have occurred and will continue to occur so long as the functions of prosecuting and adjudicating are allowed to coalesce too freely.[93]

The Administrative Procedure Act, a federal statute passed in 1946, was an attempt to remedy the abuses which had been shown to exist in the administrative process. The Act strove to protect the rights of Prudent Man against the continuing inroads of administrative law: first, by trying to achieve uniformity of procedure among the various federal agencies; secondly, by attempting to separate the prosecuting and adjudicating roles, and providing a satisfactory method of review of decisions. The Act has achieved a fair measure of success in all these endeavors, although the administrative agencies themselves have now and then evidenced an unfortunate reluctance to go ahead with sorely needed reforms.

Other areas of Civil Liberties law might be here dealt with. Such problems as the right of labor to strike, picket, and boycott, the investigatory power of Congress, the power of Congress to combat subversion, and the treaty-making power of the Senate, all continue to pose many new and critical problems. But those questions that have already been discussed are enough to point up the nature of Civil

Liberties law today and its vital impact on Prudent Man's freedom. The problem in Civil Liberties law is, as it has always been, to reconcile the governmental interest with the individual interest—to safeguard the country, state and municipality while yet assuring to the citizen the greatest possible measure of freedom. This is a problem which, because it is never solved permanently, must be faced anew by each generation in the light of that generation's particular problems.

By way of summary we may say that the civil liberties situation today is reasonably encouraging. We seem well on the way to realizing the long-cherished ideal of equal rights for all citizens, without regard to race, creed, or color. Prejudice is by no means dead, but the law is doing its best to erase it. Although some dark clouds have appeared on the horizon in the areas of religious liberty and administrative law, the situation does not seem alarming. The Supreme Court has given too literal a meaning to the phrase, "separation of Church and State," but its upholding of the New York released time program shows that it is trying to find a workable middle way in its decisions on separation.

It is true that the Communists, their fellow-travelers, and even some sincere friends of civil liberties often assert that the recent program of Communist prosecutions, loyalty oaths, and the like, have put the nation on the road to dictatorship. But despite these frequent prophecies of doom, the fact remains that we have recently fought a great World War and are now engaged in a "cold war," and still the liberties of our friend Prudent Man remain intact. Certainly we must be careful that we do not weaken Prudent Man's civil rights at home while fighting communism abroad and subversion within the nation's borders.[94] Saying this is but to state the obvious. But it does not appear that we have weakened or are weakening his liberties by the steps which have been taken against Communist infiltration at home. Indeed by these measures we have only instituted precautions needed to safeguard from destruction the rights which Prudent Man has long held dear.

Conclusions

This paper has traced the impact upon individual freedom of the most important branches of the law. The story of Mr. Prudent Man has been told. We have seen how the laws of contracts, torts, and crimes impose numerous restrictions upon his desire to do as he wishes. The same is true of military law. Finally, we have noted that the law of civil liberties, through a long process of growth, has established for Prudent Man a basic residuum of rights secured by the Constitution against governmental invasion. Through analysis of these areas of the law it is hoped that the article has pointed up the extent to which, legally speaking, Prudent Man may act free from restraint.

No attempt is made in this concluding section to recapitulate or summarize the specific restrictions upon liberty which the various subdivisions of the law have constructed and which have been already discussed. Rather, the attempt is to state a few generalizations about freedom and American law.

Our nation has survived the storms, international and domestic, of more than a century and a half. Other countries, much older and for a time much stronger than it, have perished. Indeed, scarcely any other governmental system which was in existence at the time the United States was founded lives today. Yet we still have the same Constitution and, fundamentally, the same legal and political institutions that our forefathers established. Moreover, though economic freedom—at least in the *laissez-faire* sense—has probably declined somewhat, personal freedom has expanded considerably in this country since 1789. There is, for example, much more participation by the average citizen in government than there was at the time the nation was founded; the voting franchise has been greatly broadened and education today is much more widespread.

It is submitted that the American system of law has been the most important single factor in keeping the nation on an even keel for this long period of time. This legal system has been both flexible and resilient; although it has permitted change to occur, it has also allowed the basic structure to remain. Though bending with the winds of changing economics and politics, it has never broken.

Our system, of course, is based upon the common law, and therein lies its saving grace. The centuries-old tradition of the common law is that it alters and grows where necessary to accommodate to changing times; yet also respects precedent, and does not change its rules overnight or without weighty reasons.

We have then been fortunate enough to have in this country a system of law which embodies both a principle of change and a principle of stability. The existence of a written Constitution has brought additional strength to the principle of stability, and the Supreme Court established by that Constitution has made the changes which have become reasonably systematic ones.

Our aim for the future should be to improve the American legal system while yet retaining its basic virtues. To cries that the system is outmoded and the product of a bygone age, we should turn a deaf ear, always mindful of the fact that American law has safeguarded freedom as no other law in the history of mankind ever has. Yet we cannot be afraid of change. So long as change is progress and not merely change for the sake of change, it holds no terrors for American law.

It has been well said that "freedom without restraint or qualification destroys itself. . . ." [95] Freedom needs an organized framework within which to operate. That framework is the law. We can be proud of the task American law has accomplished in winning the battle of freedom for over a hundred and sixty years. We can be confident that American law will continue to win this battle in the future.

Freedom in the International Society

by DR. EDWARD D. RE
Professor of Law,
School of Law, St. John's University

I. INTRODUCTION

A. Thesis

Predicated upon the profound belief that the progress of man is truly progress and achievement only insofar as it permits a better fulfillment of man's true function here on earth, and since freedom is the necessary condition of all human progress, this article will undertake to discuss and evaluate the international protection of one aspect of that freedom, viz., the freedom enjoyed by the human person in the international society. It is the underlying philosophy of this paper that the end of man is the attainment of true happiness. It is the scholastic postulate that "the entire universe is ordained to man as a good, but man is ordained only to God as a last end." [1] It is founded upon the scholastic philosophy that man is a rational animal possessing a spiritual soul which endows him with intellect, will and other distinctly human capacities. This elevates man above brute nature, proclaims his dignity and indicates his destiny. This concept affects as well his relationship to society, both national and international, and renders significant the concept of freedom. It is clear, therefore, that any discussion of rights and freedom can only be in true perspective if it is founded upon an understanding of the true nature of man.

This discussion will deal primarily with the freedom of the individual in the international society as distinguished from the rights and prerogatives of States or nations. The rights of States will be discussed only insofar as they purport to vindicate rights of individuals.

The nature and basis for the freedom of the human person is accurately explained by Jacques Maritain. In his *Rights of Man and Natural Law* he writes: "The human person possesses rights because of the very fact that it is a person, a whole, master of itself, and of its acts, and which consequently is not merely a means to an end, but an end, an end which must be treated as such. The dignity of the human person? The expression means nothing if it does not signify that by virtue of natural law, the human person has the right to be respected, is the subject of rights, possesses rights. There are things which are owed to man because of the very fact that he is man. The notion of right and the notion of moral obligation are correlative; both are founded on the freedom proper to spiritual agents. If man is morally bound to the things which are necessary to the fulfillment of his destiny, obviously, then, he has the right to fulfill his destiny; and if he has the right to fulfill his destiny, he has the right to the things necessary for this purpose." [2]

These claims to rights and freedom are made by man by virtue of his very nature as a human person. They are the demands of the individual for those freedoms that are essential for the fulfillment of God's creative purpose. This article, therefore, will deal with man's natural aspirations here on earth. Freedom is the condition for the full realization of these natural aspirations.

B. Freedom and Rights

The discussion, in this connection, will deal with what may be termed "social freedom," i.e., man's freedom as a social being, and not freedom of the will, as such. This social freedom, which encompasses religious, civil, political and economic areas, has been defined as "man's self-determination in respect of his natural ends without hindrance from men or society." [3] In order to attain these ends man has been endowed with certain rights. His demand for freedom is therefore based upon these rights.

Since freedom implies the existence of certain rights that are to be universally respected, the measure of man's freedom will be coextensive with man's enjoyment of rights. A discussion of freedom, therefore, of necessity will be a discussion of the natural rights of man. By natural rights it is intended to refer to those rights of man traditionally called fundamental, inherent and inalienable rights. Natural rights include "all those moral powers, opportunities and immunities which the individual requires in order to attain the end of his nature." [4]

Ryan and Millar in their book, *The State and the Church,* distinguish natural rights from "civil rights" which belong to the individual as a member of the State. They say that "Natural rights are those which are derived from the individual's nature, needs and destiny. They are those moral prerogatives which the individual needs in order to live a reasonable life, and attain the end appointed for him by God." [5] Furthermore, these are not rights that belong more to one man than to another. They belong to all men regardless of station or condition. All human beings have the same "ethical worth, equal moral responsibility and identical eternal destiny." [6] These rights are also sometimes referred to as con-natural [7] rights because they belong to man by his very nature. They have been beautifully summarized by the American Declaration of Independence as being "Life, Liberty and the Pursuit of Happiness."

C. The State and Rights

These natural rights, indispensably enjoyed by man if he is to attain his true end or purpose, are not rights created by the State. Since man preceded the State, these rights are antecedent to the existence of the State, and therefore cannot be said to be derived from the latter. Again, this self-evident truth is beautifully expressed by the American Declaration of Independence in the statement that "all men are created equal," and "are endowed by their Creator with certain unalienable rights." According to the American's creed, as expressed in the Declaration of Independence, these rights are "unalienable" because their source is "the Laws of Nature and of Nature's God." Since they are derived from man's Creator and are therefore God-given, they cannot be "alienated" or taken away by the State. On the contrary, the State is the political organization or machinery through which these rights are realized and respected. Its aid is required to attain these rights.

That such is the true purpose of government can also be seen from the terminology of the Declaration of Independence. It declares that "to secure these rights Governments are instituted among men."

The State and the government, therefore, although not the source of the rights of man, exist to *secure* or *protect* these rights from invasion. In the words of John Locke, whose political philosophy found magnificent expression in the Declaration of Independence, "The end of government is the good of mankind." [8] In this connection it is relevant to quote the words of a capable American jurist: "The Constitution is misread by those who say that these rights are created by the Constitution. The men who wrote the Constitution did not doubt that these rights existed before the nation was created and are dedicated by God's word." [9]

Since this is the end and purpose of government, it follows logically and clearly that, "whenever any Form of Government becomes destructive of these ends, it is the Right of the People to alter or abolish it and to institute a new Government." In this respect, the lessons of history teach that the dictator and tyrant would do well to ponder the warning of Cicero that "Freedom suppressed and again regained, bites with keener fangs than freedom never endangered." [10]

D. Law and Rights

Just as the State is not the source of these natural rights, neither is the law. Rights exist independently of and apart from the law. The function of law is to recognize these rights and thereby afford the human being a legal protection of his natural rights. The legal system, of course, attains maturity and perfection not only by the recognition of these rights in response to man's demands, but also by ascribing to these rights their proper place. The law defines the limits within which these rights will be recognized and will be given effect through the organization of the State. The law, therefore, recognizes rights, defines the extent to which they will be given effect and also "it must devise the means by which they are to be secured." [11] "The ultimate purpose, the moral end of law is to safeguard these personal rights. . . . The maintenance, protection and promotion of the individual human being in his moral aspects constitutes the end of law." [12] In the words of Pope Pius XII: "The protection of this personal freedom is the purpose of every juridical order worthy of the name." [13] This concept is part of the great scholastic tradition of "the common good." Francisco Suarez, the eminent Spanish theologian, phrases it well when he asserts that "It is inherent in the nature and essence of law, that it shall be enacted for the sake of the common good." [14]

E. Family of Nations

It has been established that the principal purposes of the national State are to secure the rights of man and further his natural aspirations. Since there is no supra-national State it may be asked whether there exists some international community that is also concerned with the rights of man.

There can be little doubt that there has been for many centuries a community of nations. Because of cultural affinity, economic interdependence, or the fear of war, nations have always manifested gregarious tendencies in much the same manner as human beings. Writing in 1792, Thomas Paine referred to this unifying process as follows: "The mutual dependence and reciprocal interest which man has upon man and all the parts of civilized community upon each other, create that great chain of connection which holds it together." [15] Although nations have claimed to be sovereign and independent, they are, and in fact have been for centuries, interdependent and subject to precepts of law that comprise the body of international law. These rules and precepts, which have come into being by usage and acceptance over the ages, together with consensual agreements called treaties, contain the legal doctrines and standards which govern the community of nations. Although in earlier times as the common interests of nations became more apparent and numerous, treaties were generally confined to two or three contracting parties, entered into by many nations, thereby giving impetus to an international order. In fact, such treaties became so numerous and of such wide scope and acceptability that they have been referred to as "international legislation." [16] With the advent of the League of Nations and the United Nations there unfolds the modern era with international institutions and something approximating an international confederation—a *civitas maxima.*

However loose may be the structure, there are definite bonds which unite the family of nations into an international society. Since this society is an established fact there must be a law to govern it—*ubi societas ibi jus.*[17]

Writing about Suarez, whose contribution in this area has already been referred to, Westlake, an English scholar, wrote: "Suarez has put on record with a master's hand the existence of a necessary human society transcending the boundaries of states, the indispensableness of rules for that society, the insufficiency of reason to provide with demonstrative force all the rules required, and the right of human society to supply the deficiency by custom enforced as law, such custom being suitable to nature." [18]

In the light of the foregoing introduction, therefore, the purpose of this article may be restated to be an inquiry as to the concern and the efforts of the international society for the natural rights of man and freedom as its indispensable handmaid.

It is at this, the international, level that attention is particularly focused today. The rights of the person, the survival of the State and our very preservation as a race depend upon the success of a sane system of international cooperation. The greatest value to be preserved, therefore, is freedom in the international society.

II. The Individual in International Law

A. The "Persons" of International Law

Having determined the nature and source of natural rights and the required freedom to permit their enjoyment it seems necessary, as a threshold question, to ascertain the status of the individual in international law. This inquiry cannot be avoided in any discussion of freedom and human rights in the international society.

In view of the universality and magnitude of the efforts calculated to achieve universal respect for human rights, the status and relation of the individual to international law is today of especial importance. Since the definition of international law is to the effect that such a system of law concerns itself with the "precepts and principles that govern nations in their mutual dealings and relations," [19] the inquiry strikes at the very core of international law and organization.

To the non-lawyer it is probably strange, if not startling, that the "persons" of international law are States and not human persons. The leading authorities agree that international law or the law of nations is the name for that body of customary and conventional rules which is considered by civilized States to be legally binding upon one another in their mutual dealings. Oppenheim states: "The Law of Nations is a law regulating primarily the intercourse of States with one another, not that of individuals." [20] He explains that the conception of "International Persons is derived from the conception of the Law of Nations. As this law is the body of rules which the civilized States consider legally binding in their intercourse, every State which belongs to the civilized States, and is therefore a member of the Family of Nations, is an International Person." [21] The individual, therefore, traditionally has not been considered a subject of, but rather as an object of international law.

B. The "Sovereignty" of States

This notion is at least partially explained by the fact that international law developed gradually and primarily as a method or system for the regulation of the conflicting interests of States. Since the basic postulates of the system were the independence and sovereign equality of these States it was clear that no State could be bound by a rule of law unless it had consented thereto.[22] This consent was manifested either by a customary observance of a rule of conduct or by a formal contract called a treaty or convention. By virtue of its sovereignty, which recognizes no external or superior authority, a State possesses exclusive jurisdiction over its territory and all persons residing therein. Obviously under such a system the State was the principal actor. Only the State was capable of possessing substantive rights or the procedural ability to vindicate their violation before arbitral tribunals or an international court.

This concept of unlimited State sovereignty, at this writing perhaps well on its way into dilution if not extinction, is refuted by Pope Pius XII in a statement that has particular application here. On October 20, 1939, in *Summi Pontificatus* the Holy Father stated:

> The idea which credits the state with unlimited authority is not simply an error harmful to the internal life of nations, to their prosperity and to the larger and well-ordered increase in their well-being, but likewise it injures the relations between peoples, for it breaks the unity of supranational society, robs the law of nations of its foundation and vigor, leads to violation of others' rights and impedes agreement and peaceful intercourse.
>
> A disposition, in fact, of the divinely-sanctioned natural order divides the human race into social groups, nations or states, which are mutually independent in organization and in the direction of their internal life. But for all that, the human race is bound together by reciprocal ties, moral and juridical, into a great commonwealth directed to the good of all nations and ruled by special laws which protect its unity and promote its prosperity. Now no one can fail to see how the claim to absolute autonomy for the state stands in open opposition to this natural law that is inherent in man—nay, denies it utterly—and, therefore, leaves the stability of international relations at the mercy of the will of rulers, while it destroys the possibility of true union and fruitful collaboration directed to the general good.

C. The Individual and Nationality

Since there are many situations under which individuals derive benefits under international law it may be said that, at least in this limited sense, the individual is a subject of international law. Actually, the answer has been clear that, under the traditional view, whatever benefits or protections were enjoyed by the individual were not enjoyed by any right of his own, but only by reason of a right belonging to the State of which the individual was a national. The doctrine held fast: if a right had been violated it was the right of the State and the individual was still merely the *object* of that right; if the individual had been improperly treated this might have been a violation of some right of the State of which the individual was a national. Nationality, therefore, is the link between international law and the individual.

In the concrete, the doctrine would apply as follows: If a national of State A was in some way mistreated in State B, or was otherwise not granted rights appertaining to him by a treaty between the two states, the national of State A would complain to his own State which would in turn seek redress from State B. The theory and procedure was clear: the right violated was the right of the State and only the State could vindicate its violation. The national was merely a "beneficiary" of the right of the State, and hence, the explanation for the assertion that the individual is merely an *object* of international law.

Oppenheim thus correctly summarizes the traditional doctrinal view: "It is through the medium of their nationality that, individuals can normally enjoy benefits from the existence of the Law of Nations." [23]

The postulate that an individual can seek redress of a wrong suffered at the hands of a foreign nation only through the diplomatic channels of his own nation finds a wealth of expression in judicial decisions of the highest tribunals. The Supreme Court of the United States expressed itself quite clearly on the matter: In the leading case of *United States* v. *Diekelman* [24] it stated that "a citizen of one nation wronged by the conduct of another nation, must seek redress through his own government. His sovereign must assume the responsibility of presenting his claim, or it need not be considered. If this responsibility is assumed, the claim may be prosecuted as one nation proceeds against another, not by suit in the courts, as of right, but by diplomacy, or, if need be, by war." The identical view was expressed even more tersely by Judge Wallace of the United States Court of Appeals: "Foreign citizens can rely upon the intervention of their respective governments to redress their wrongs, even by resort, if necessary, to the arbitrament of war." [25]

Obviously, both quotations are founded upon the traditional and incomplete notion of sovereignty and State supremacy. Written many years ago, they are the expressions, it is hoped, of a past era. Concerning the remarks that a sovereign may resort to war to vindicate a right or otherwise redress a grievance, as has been stated elsewhere "it would be indeed sad if a court were to utter such a remark today." [26]

III. Effects of Traditional Doctrine

A. Right of State to Present Claim is Discretionary

The traditional concept that only States are persons in international law capable of possessing rights implies serious substantive and procedural consequences. In the first place, it tends to deify the State, thereby making the State an end in itself. Secondly, it obscures the fundamental truth that the State exists to secure the rights of individuals. Therefore, if a State chose to present a claim on behalf of its national it did so because it suited the pleasure of the State. In fact a State might assert a claim against another State on behalf of its citizen even if the citizen did not wish to present the claim. The state might decide to present the claim for the maintenance of its prestige notwithstanding the wishes of its national, even though under other circumstances it might decide not to assert the claim of another national who may have suffered grievous injury. On this very question, Mr. Frederick S. Dunn has observed that, "To give personality to the state rather than to the individual," may suggest "a cold indifference to the interests and welfare of the man on the street and is apt to arouse in him an equal indifference to the status of international law." [27]

This observation concerning the interest of the individual in international law may possibly have been true as of the time that Mr. Dunn wrote. It is hoped that since World War II and the Charter of the United Nations no person will regard international law as being cold and indifferent toward the individual and human rights. The Charter itself and the work of many organs of the United Nations will bear witness to the contrary.

B. Rights of States over Its Own Nationals

The foregoing has indicated that if a citizen of a State was mistreated by a foreign nation, his own nation through diplomatic channels could present a claim on his behalf. This would apply whether the injury was to his person or to his property. Thus, this responsibility of States is duty owed to *aliens,* i.e. citizens of other States. For example, if soldiers of State B, in the line of duty and without justification, shoot a citizen of State A, State B has breached its "responsibility" and is liable to State A.[28] Also if State B, arbitrarily were to confiscate the property of a citizen of State A, again State A could demand full indemnification on behalf of its citizen if it decided to present the claim. In these cases State B would be liable to State A since its official acts have constituted what is called a *denial of justice* for which it is internationally responsible.[29]

The foregoing have been cases where a State was responsible for its mistreatment of *aliens.* But if State B instead of having acted upon a citizen of State A had acted upon its own citizens would it still have breached an international responsibility? The traditional answer must be in the negative! Individuals have no rights, recognized by customary international law, as against their own State. This is said to be a matter of local concern or one of "domestic jurisdiction." The individual in his own State has enjoyed only the rights that have been secured by the positive law of that State and if that law did not protect him no international law was involved. Concerning this anomalous situation, Professor Oppenheim writes as follows in a footnote: "The somewhat paradoxical result of the existing position is that individuals, when residing as aliens in a foreign State, enjoy a measure of protection which International Law denies to the nationals of a State within its territory." [30]

Because of the present state of the law on this important matter specific treaties have been entered into for the protection of minority groups. In the absence of an applicable treaty, however, a State has been deemed privileged to treat its own citizens as it wished. This, of course, has meant that certain States have on occasions been able to persecute and mistreat, almost with impunity, minorities within their borders. It is, therefore, perfectly true that a person may have enjoyed greater rights abroad by virtue of the international law *denial of justice* doctrine, whereas his own State could have dealt with him "unhampered" [31] by any international law.

C. Humanitarian Intervention

In addition to the treaty method of protection of minority groups, occasionally some States have claimed what might be termed a right of *humanitarian intervention.* Professor Stowell, who has written a comprehensive study [32] on this phase of State practice, has defined humanitarian intervention as "the justifiable use of force for the purpose of protecting the inhabitants of another state from treatment so arbitrary and persistently abusive as to exceed the limits within which the sovereign is presumed to act with reason and justice." [33] He enlists the authority of many outstanding publicists who have supported the existence or development of a doctrine of humanitarian intervention as a positive principle of international law. Although he admits that other publicists have "looked askance at humanitarian intervention" he agrees with Professor Borchard who wrote that "where a state under exceptional circumstances disregards certain rights of its own citizens, over whom presumably it has absolute sovereignty, the other states of the family of nations are authorized by international law to intervene on grounds of humanity. When these 'human' rights are habitually violated, one or more states may intervene in the name of the society of nations and may take such measures as to substitute at least temporarily, if not permanently, its own sovereignty for that of the state thus controlled." [34]

As can be seen from The International Law of the Future, a monograph written in 1944 and sponsored by the American Bar Association, this doctrine of humanitarian intervention is well-recognized and has adherents. Principle 2 of this monograph states: "Each State has a legal duty to see that conditions prevailing within its own territory do not menace international peace and order, and to this end it must treat its own population in a way which will not violate the dictates of humanity and justice or shock the conscience of mankind." [35]

Serious reflection upon this doctrine of humanitarian intervention would indicate that, if it were to be abused by any nation, it could serve as a pretext for aggression and conquest. Fully aware of this possibility of abuse Professor Stowell observed that "the general and salutary attitude of suspicion with which every intervention upon the ground of humanity is regarded serves as a rough check upon its abuse." [36]

It is nevertheless relevant at this juncture to note the occasions on which that "right" to intervene has been either claimed or exercised. The first occasion would include cases of governmental *persecution* on such a scale as to amount to shockingly inhumane conduct. Unfortunately, the pages of history are replete with instances of religious intolerance that have been so flagrant and outrageous that they could not have been ignored by neighboring States.

A second occasion would be a systematic *oppression* of a people who wish to retain their language or other racial customs and institutions. This may be closely related to what is termed a people's right of self-determination. On this ground there is justification for the intervention of the American government in the Irish troubles of 1848. The instructions of Mr. Toucey, then Secretary of State *ad interim,* to Minister Bancroft are worthy of quotation. "It is the wish of the President and he instructs you to urge upon the British Government the adoption of a magnanimous and merciful course towards those men who have been implicated in the late disturbances in Ireland." [37]

A third type of situation that has led to humanitarian intervention has been the palpable violation of the laws of war in cases of rebellion or civil strife conducted with such brutality that they are referred to as uncivilized warfare or barbarous warfare. Writing on insurrection in 1880, Sheldon Amos stated that "Gross acts of inhumanity persisted in on either side may, on grounds of humanity, properly precipitate intervention." [38]

The fourth occasion, which is of a more general nature and hence may possibly include instances coming within one of the prior categories, deals with situations involving *gross injustice.* This *denial of justice* concept, which has already been alluded to, is generally applied to cases involving an unjustifiable restraint of a person's liberty, or the arbitrary confiscation of his property.

This claim on the part of some States to "intervene" when another has followed a policy of persecution or flagrant denial of human rights, unfortunately has never crystallized into an accepted right or legally established practice of States. In many instances this humanitarian intervention was little more than a registration of protest.[39] Although many cases can be found when a nation has protested against the persecution of minorities in foreign countries, often the protests were *vox clamantis in deserto.* Their ineffectiveness, which fundamentally was simply manifestations of humanitarian appeal, nevertheless served to indicate in striking fashion a basic weakness of the traditional concept of international law in relation to the individual. In fact, the untold abuses and atrocities that have been committed under the protective concept of "domestic jurisdiction" have led to a gigantic alliance of effort calculated to extend the traditional view and to bring the individual directly within the spheres of the protection of international law.

Many scholars who have given the subject profound thought hopefully suggest that the extension of the traditional concept would be a real step in the promotion of international peace. Professor Jessup is so convinced of this fact that he considers it to be one of the two keystones of a revised international order. Professor Lauterpacht,[40] writing in England, would agree with him that "international law, like national law, must be directly applicable to the individual." [41] This, of course, would be accomplished by means of treaties. All who agree with such views find strength and encouragement in the language of the Charter of the United Nations which enshrines fundamental human rights in an epoch-making document.

D. Stateless Persons

Since nationality is the link between international law and the individual, it has been well-established that a State may not present a claim against another State on behalf of a person who is not its own national. Therefore, under the traditional view, a *stateless* person has been helpless for the reason that no State could be found that could undertake to seek redress on his behalf. In fact, the bald and frightening statement has been uttered that a State "does not commit an international delinquency in inflicting an injury upon an individual lacking nationality, and consequently, no State is empowered to intervene or complain on his behalf either before or after the injury." [42] Furthermore, if a person is a national of two States and one of the two inflicts an injury upon him, one of the States cannot assert a claim against the injuring State, since, as a national of the State that inflicted the injury, no international law was violated. This situation is obviously a weakness to be corrected by treaties as a further refinement of the concept of international law.

IV. Extensions of Traditional Doctrine

A. Logical and Practical Weaknesses

From what has been said of the restricted traditional doctrine which regards only States as persons in international law, it is easy to understand why certain extensions or apparent exceptions have come into being. If a State were to present a claim against another State for an injury inflicted upon a citizen of the former, it would be said that "international law protects his state against injuries done to his state through him." [43] Mr. Dunn, who refers to the doctrine as a "legal fossil" that is "highly misleading and in large degree false," believes that it "explains, in part, why international law is held in such ill repute by laymen today." [44]

On the question of the present system for the prosecution of these international claims, Professor Borchard has indicated that inasmuch as the procedure involves the use of diplomatic channels this "political recourse obviously has great disadvantages." [45] "The very fact that it is associated with politics indicates one of its weaknesses. The success of the alien's remedy often depends upon the particular nationality he may enjoy, the strength of his State, the weakness of the defendant one, the political relations between the two States, the uncontrollable political disposition of his State to entertain his claim, and similar factors." [46] Although Professor Borchard did not favor the proposal that would have unqualifiedly allowed individuals to appear before an international judicial tribunal, he noted the serious inadequacy and disadvantages of the existing system.

The limitations of this body of international law dealing with the diplomatic protection of citizens abroad manifest themselves in several ways. Although the injury to the individual is said to be a violation of the rights of his State, the claim, however, is prosecuted by his State "on behalf of Mr. Individual Citizen," and whatever award may be made, is paid to the claimant State "on behalf of Mr. Individual Citizen." Also, as one would imagine, the important question of the measure of damages to be awarded is based upon the injury actually suffered by Mr. Individual Citizen. It is clear that the procedure reflects and perpetuates the legal fiction that the individual does not have rights in international law—that the rights legally belong to the State and that the individual is merely the beneficiary of the rights of the State of which he is a national.

B. Treaties of Humanitarian Appeal

Professor Lauterpacht, a champion of the recognition of the rights of individuals in international law, recently wrote that "Like various other tenets of the positivist creed, the doctrine that only States are subjects of international law is unable to stand the test of actual practice." [47] Positivists are undoubtedly "embarrassed to explain" [48] some of the deviations or extensions of the traditional doctrine.

At the outset it may be pointed out that, in recent years, only a relatively small number of treaties have dealt with the relations of States as political entities. The vast majority of treaties were concerned with the rights and privileges of individuals. They have dealt with the day to day activities of man, with matters of health, morals, trade, communication, the ability to travel from State to State, and a host of other matters dealing with the rights of human beings. In the light of the vast array of treaties which deal exclusively with humanitarian matters and which seek to secure man's natural rights, the doctrinal statement that an individual has no rights in international law is rendered empty and devoid of reality. When the theoretical veil of legal fiction is pierced, there unfolds the actual practice of States which reveals the many treaties that were entered into for a variety of humanitarian purposes. For example, treaties deal with the protection of racial and religious minorities, the abolition of slavery, the slave trade, forced labor, protection of refugees, protection of stateless persons, safeguarding health, securing humane conditions of work and many other areas of humanitarian appeal.

Although these activities of nations can be explained on the beneficiary theory of the rights of man, Professor Oppenheim, after referring to these treaties, remarks that "although none of these developments have had the legal effect of incorporating the fundamental rights of man as part of the positive law of nations, they are not without significance for this aspect of International Law." [49] Notwithstanding his professional restraint and conservatism, however, he concludes that "It is possible that the Charter of the United Nations, with its repeated recognition of human rights and fundamental freedoms has inaugurated a new and decisive departure with regard to this abiding problem of law and government." [50]

C. Offenses Against the Law of Nations

For many years international law has acknowledged the existence of certain crimes, such as piracy, of which only individuals can be guilty, which challenge the doctrine that individuals are not subjects of international law. Even the most cautious authors agree that "The offense of piracy derives its internationally illegal aspect from the will of the international society. . . . It signifies that what is so punishable must be regarded as internationally illegal, in the sense that it defies what the law of the international society is deemed itself to forbid." [51] The domestic law providing for the punishment of piracy refers to this crime "as defined by the law of nations." [52] The American statute, of course, is passed pursuant to the constitutional authority which expressly authorizes the Congress to "define and punish piracies and felonies committed on the high seas, and offenses against the law of nations." [53] It is significant that the Constitution expressly refers to "offenses against the law of nations."

Other crimes, similarly of an international nature, are slave trading, counterfeiting, blockade running and contraband carriage. It is clear, for example, that the *person* who runs a blockade or carries contraband has violated an international law and that no State is responsible for his act. The violator alone is liable. Nevertheless, in all these cases the argument is made that the individual is punished by a State for a violation of domestic law.[54] The argument contains a *non-sequitur,* because even though it be conceded that State action is required to punish the violator, it does not necessarily follow that the State is enforcing domestic law. The argument is vaguely reminiscent of the assertion made by the Austinian school of thought that international law is no law at all since there is no international executive to enforce it. Not only does it exaggerate the deficiencies and minimize the achievements of international law, but it also fails to appreciate the true meaning of "sanctions." [55] Although a particular State enforces the law, its authority and content stem from the family of nations. Following this latter line of reasoning, Professor Eagleton observes that "The pirate or the blockade runner, in fact, has rights as well as duties; he has a right not to be punished for what international law has not declared to be illegal." [56]

D. *Additional Examples*

Several additional examples may be mentioned simply to indicate that the artificiality of the traditional doctrine inevitably led to exceptions.

Although insurgents recognized as belligerent are not States, they are nevertheless recognized as "persons" in international law, and, as such, acquire rights and responsibilities. Most notably of all responsibilities they are bound by the obligation to conduct hostilities in accordance with the rules of international law.

Additional exceptions of entities that, although they are not States, enjoy international personality include such international bodies as the United Nations and the International Labor Organization. Another exception is the Holy See, which, although admittedly a person in international law, is devoted to purposes fundamentally different from those of ordinary States.

E. *Recent Significant Developments*

In an address delivered in 1941 before the American Society of International Law, Dr. Edvard I. Hambro, commenting on the fact that he had "learned in the classroom in the old days that international law was law between states," stated that the "old dogma seems to have lost support in the last years." [57] He also referred to certain exceptional circumstances when individuals appeared before international tribunals, and indicated how it may come to pass that individuals could appear before international tribunals not only as an accused but also as a claimant.

There can be little doubt that commencing with the Nurnberg trials a new chapter was opened in the never-ending pages of history: —individual responsibility was placed upon persons who committed the international crime of plotting world aggression. It is no mere manifestation of enthusiasm or advocacy when Judge John J. Parker stated that the International Trial at Nurnberg was a "triumph of international cooperation" and "gave vitality to international law." [58]

The Judgment of the International Military Tribunal, established by the Four Powers Agreement and the Charter annexed thereto, of August 6th, 1945, summarily dismissed as follows an objection based upon the traditional doctrine: "It was submitted that international law is concerned with the actions of sovereign States, and provides no punishment for individuals . . . these submissions must be rejected." It concluded the matter by stating that "Crimes against international law are committed by men, not abstract entities, and only by punishing individuals who commit such crimes can the provisions of international law be enforced." [59] The objection raised, of course, was doomed to fail, in view of Article 6 of the Charter which expressly provided for individual responsibility in cases coming within the jurisdiction of the tribunal. As a matter of interest, it is to be noted that there is considerable authority for the proposition that the Charter was merely declaratory of existing law insofar as the waging of aggressive war was a violation of international law.[60]

Perhaps the most noteworthy step in the establishment of individual responsibility for acts deemed internationally criminal is the recent Genocide Convention, which, prepared by the General Assembly of the United Nations as a treaty, was open to ratification by Member and other invited States. In accordance with its terms, after a ratification by twenty States on January 12, 1951, the convention became effective as the Signatory States that had also ratified the Convention. It defined the international crime of genocide as the commission of certain acts with intent to destroy, in whole or in part, a national, ethical, racial or religious group. Whereas the Nurnberg Judgment made the brutal treatment by a State of its own citizens a matter of international concern if connected with war or the preparation of a war of aggression, the Genocide Convention makes such acts internationally criminal whenever committed.

In addition to the humanitarian interest which motivated the Genocide Convention, it is significant here because it expressly imposes responsibility for any violation not only upon States but also upon individuals. It holds individuals liable "whether they are constitutionally responsible rulers, public officials or private individuals." [61] Insofar as the Convention imposes responsibility upon rulers and public officials it codifies the precedent established by the Nurnberg Trials. However, in extending responsibility to private individuals it gives effect to the expanding trend which departs from the traditional doctrine and makes the individual directly a subject of international law.

V. Monumental Declarations of the Rights of Man

A. The Individual and a Charter of Human Rights

The previous discussion has endeavored to demonstrate that through treaties of a humanitarian purpose, the concept of denial of justice, and the imperfect doctrine of humanitarian intervention, the international society and international law have always been concerned with the protection of the natural rights of individuals. It is undeniable that in many cases international law has placed responsibility directly upon the individual without resort to the fictitious procedural intermediary of the State. Although it is true that the Nurnberg precedent is authoritative solely on the question of the *duties* of individuals in international law rather than their rights, it is also true that it fortified the position of the individual as a *person* in international law. The Nurnberg trials, together with the unprecedented references to the individual in the historic United Nations Charter, have given immeasurable encouragement to the many scholars and statesmen that have maintained that international law should protect the rights of the individual.[62] Like Professor Jessup, these authorities would assert that the "modern law of nations" should be defined as the "law applicable to states in their mutual relations *and to individuals in their relations with states.*"[63] Although such a definition is probably an indication of something to come rather than an accomplished legal fact, there is no question that as a result of recent developments—particularly through the efforts of the United Nations—the international society has accepted responsibility for the drafting of an international bill of rights which attempts to assure every human being an irreducible minimum of protection of his natural rights.

Before embarking upon a discussion of the leading role of the United Nations in the promotion and the drafting of an international charter of human rights, it is proposed to point out several encouraging efforts, both official and unofficial, that have helped to make possible an international charter of such rights. Such a charter, if it is to be more than a mere grandiloquent statement of rights, involves problems of the greatest magnitude. Any such charter, which would possess the force of a multi-lateral treaty, truly international legislation, would raise tormenting issues. It would class, for example, with the exclusive jurisdiction of a State within its own territory.

Nevertheless, it would be the true test of the claim of international law to protect an individual even against his own State. Such a treaty, to be effective, would also have to cope with the problem of tribunals empowered to enforce a violation of the rights contained in such a charter. These problems, and many more, have in fact been raised in connection with the United Nations Covenant on Human Rights.

B. Early Statements on Human Rights

It is beyond the scope of this study to trace chronologically the many statements and declarations that proclaim the rights of man. Although many were written in glowing terms and indeed voiced noble aspirations, only a few, however, will be mentioned. Length of treatment will be afforded only to those efforts that, more or less directly, blazed an influential path that may be said ultimately to have culminated in the decisive efforts of the United Nations.

If one were constantly to bear in mind that rights imply duties, in that the right of one person is the duty of another, it will become more readily apparent that the Commandments contain a statement of rights. To the biblical examples of the just treatment of man may be added the observations of the philosophers of all civilizations. A thorough study of man's age-old struggle for the universal recognition of his natural rights would involve a study of civilization itself. It would be a study of many cultures which would reveal the contribution of many people.

C. The English Contribution

The overwhelming importance of English political thought can best be appreciated by an awareness of its direct contribution to the American system of government. This contribution played its initial role in the drafting of the constitutions for the various States prior to the Constitution of the United States and its initial amendments, dramatically called the "American Bill of Rights."

Of primary importance in English constitutional development, in the safeguarding of the rights of the individuals, was the practice of statutory enactment. Regardless of its historical vicissitudes, of unquestioned paramount importance stands the Magna Carta. Although the historic occasion in 1215 on the plains of Runnymede was originally of importance perhaps only to the barons and King John, it is from that humble beginning that the greatest traditions of political liberty have sprung. It doubtlessly served a purpose far nobler than any dreamed of by its draftsmen. Although, in 1215, it stood for the principle of limitations upon governmental power, its true greatness lies in the heritage that it helped create. As stated elsewhere, "The Great Charter, as the forerunner of bills of rights, stands as the classical monument of freedom. Magna Carta gave us the talismanic phrase *per legem terrae*. From this vague fiction sprang the concepts that school boys have come to know as the inalienable rights of man, to due process of law—trial by jury, freedom from unreasonable searches and seizures, protection against ex post facto laws and bills of attainder, habeas corpus—in short, Our Bill of Rights. . . . It represents the uncompromising principle of the supremacy of the law and equality before the law." [64] The thirty-ninth and fortieth sections of the Great Charter are worthy of quotation:

"39. No free-man shall be seized, or imprisoned, or dispossessed, or outlawed, in any way destroyed; nor will we condemn him, nor will we commit him to prison, excepting by legal judgment of his peers, or by the laws of the land.

"40. To none will we sell, to none will we deny, to none will we delay right or justice."

Magna Carta, and its subsequent confirmations, together with the Petition of Right (1627), the Habeas Corpus Act (1679), the Bill of Rights (1688) and the Act of Settlement (1700), are the keystones upon which rest the rights of Englishmen. It is to be noted that the basic rights of Englishmen are not guaranteed by any written organic constitution, such as that of the United States, but rather by specific parliamentary enactments which technically may be modified or repealed by parliament. The constitution of England is therefore said to be unwritten. The real binding authority of this "unwritten constitution" is explained by Lord Wright to be "the good sense of the people," [65] a thought related to the observation of Sir Cecil Carr to the effect that, although the legislature at Westminster has supreme authority in England, the "legislator would hesitate to tamper" with the monumental enactments previously enumerated "because their historical value entitles them to peculiar reverence." [66] These restrained statements simply mean that the Englishman will not tolerate parliamentary "tampering" with his rights of a free man. Commencing with Magna Carta, enactments such as the Habeas Corpus Act and the Bill of Rights, for example, acquired the authority of constitutional pronouncements. They imposed limitations upon governmental power and assured the individual against the infringement of his basic rights. Those safeguards, attained after centuries of toil and struggle, simply will not be relinquished.

D. French Declaration of the Rights of Man

The French Declaration of the Rights of Man and the Citizen, adopted in 1789 by the National Assembly of France during the revolution, will be treated separately because of two specific reasons: first, it represented the culmination of centuries of thought about a declaration of human rights; and secondly, because the declaration was a magnificent inspiration to peoples in countless nations, and particularly to the United States of America. The preamble and the first article of the declaration, which will be quoted, will give some idea of the nature of this document.

> The representatives of the people of France, formed into a National Assembly, considering that ignorance, neglect, or contempt of human rights, are the sole causes of public misfortunes and corruptions of Government, have resolved to set forth in a solemn declaration, these natural imprescriptible, and inalienable rights; that this declaration being constantly present to the minds of the members of the body social, they may be forever kept attentive to their rights and their duties; that the acts of the legislative and executive powers of government, being capable of being every moment compared with the end of political institutions, may be more respected; and also, that the future claims of the citizens, being directed by simple and incontestable principles, may always tend to the maintenance of the constitution, and the general happiness.
>
> For these reasons the National Assembly doth recognise and declare, in the presence of the Supreme Being, and with the hope of his blessing and favour, the following *sacred* rights of men and of citizens:
>
> I. Men are born, and always continue, free and equal in respect of their rights. Civil distinctions, therefore, can be founded only on public utility.

Although the Declaration of Rights contained seventeen articles, the first three are in effect the core of the rights which are clarified by the succeeding articles. Although Thomas Paine correctly asserted that in the preface to the Declaration of Rights "we see the solemn and majestic spectacle of a nation opening its commission, under the auspices of its Creator," [67] the French Declaration does not contain the perfection of expression found in the American Declaration of 1776 concerning the source of human rights. It will be remembered that the American Declaration does not merely acknowledge the existence of "God" and the "Creator" but expressly proclaims that men *"are endowed by their Creator with certain inalienable rights."* It is to be observed that, although the French Declaration is subject to criticism on this ground, the 1946 Constitution of the Republic of France makes no reference whatever to the Creator or a Supreme Being.

E. The American Contribution

Numerous references have already been made to the Declaration of Independence. Its importance, both nationally and internationally, cannot be overemphasized. It is also evident that the American Constitution has played an important role. The very opening phrase in the United Nations Charter, "We the People of the United Nations," was obviously inspired by the Constitution of the United States. This phrase is of particular importance because it demonstrates an effort and tendency to bring the international organization closer to the individual. It clearly evidences an awareness of the necessity of public support. Although unquestionably the Charter is a document agreed to by "Governments, through representatives assembled in the city of San Francisco," the phraseology marked a vast departure from that of the Covenant to the League of Nations which commenced with the traditional language of treaties, "the High Contracting Parties." [68]

It should be mentioned at this point, that notwithstanding the popular notion that the American Bill of Rights is contained in the first ten amendments to the Constitution of the United States, the provisions of those amendments comprise only a part of the constitutional guarantees of freedom for the American. In addition to the writ of habeas corpus, the prohibition against bills of attainder and *ex post facto* laws, the right to jury trial in federal criminal cases, and the provision eliminating religious tests for federal public office found in the Constitution itself, the rights guaranteed by the various State Constitutions should not be ignored. In fact, contributions made by the various states, even prior to the State Constitutions, cannot be ignored. They would include declarations such as the Maryland Toleration Act of 1649, and such colonial charters as the Rhode Island Colonial Charter of 1663.

In order to give some idea of the various declarations of rights found in the constitutions of the several states a few clauses of four state constitutions will be set forth:

A DECLARATION OF THE RIGHTS OF THE INHABITANTS OF THE COMMONWEALTH OF MASSACHUSETTS

Art. 1. All men are born free and equal, and have certain natural, essential and unalienable rights; among which may be reckoned the right of enjoying and defending their lives and liberties; that of acquiring, possessing and protecting property; in fine, that of seeking and obtaining their safety and happiness.

Art. 2. It is the right as well as the duty of all men in society, publicly, and at stated seasons, to worship the Supreme Being, the great Creator and Preserver of the Universe. And no subject shall be hurt, molested or restrained in his person, liberty, or estate, for worshipping God in the manner and season most agreeable to the dictates of his own conscience; or for his religious profession or sentiments; provided he doth not disturb the public peace, or obstruct others in their religious worship.

NORTH CAROLINA

That the great, general and essential principles of liberty and free government may be recognized and established, and that the relations of this state to the Union and Government of the United States, and those of the people of this state to the rest of the American people, may be defined and affirmed, we do declare:

Sect. 1. That we hold it to be self-evident that all persons are created equal; that they are endowed by their Creator with certain inalienable rights: that among these are life, liberty, the enjoyment of the fruits of their own labour, and the pursuit of happiness.

DECLARATION OF THE RIGHTS OF THE INHABITANTS OF THE STATE OF VERMONT

Art. 1. That all men are born equally free and independent, and have certain natural, inherent and inalienable rights, amongst which are the enjoying and defending life and liberty, acquiring, possessing and protecting property, and pursuing and obtaining happiness and safety. . . .

CONSTITUTION OF THE COMMONWEALTH OF VIRGINIA (of 1902)

Bill of Rights

A declaration of rights made by the good people of Virginia in the exercise of their sovereign powers, which rights do pertain to them and their posterity as the basis and foundation of government.

Sect. 1. That all men are by nature equally free and independent and have certain inherent rights, of which, when they enter into a state of society, they cannot, by any compact, deprive or divest their posterity, namely the enjoyment of life and liberty, with the means of acquiring and possessing property, and pursuing and obtaining happiness and safety.

F. Guarantees of Human Rights in National Laws

At the second session of the United Nations Economic and Social Council a resolution was adopted which requested the Secretary General to make arrangements for:

"(a) the compilation and publication of a yearbook on law and usage relating to human rights, the first edition of which should include all declarations and bills of human rights now in force in the various countries. . . ." [69]

In compliance with that resolution, the 1946 issue of the Yearbook on Human Rights contains the provisions concerning human rights that were in effect on December 31, 1946, in the constitutions and legislative enactments of all countries. A reading of many of these laws, which proclaim human rights in the most glowing terms, together with a reading of the daily newspaper accounts, which report the flagrant violation of human rights,[70] will indicate the great gulf between "paper guaranties" and the actual enjoyment of human rights. It could almost be said that an internationally enforceable covenant of human rights is unnecessary *if the stated rights were a reality in all the countries of the world.*

In a book review of *Les Constitutions Europeennes,*[71] a book which contains the texts of all continental constitutions in force on September 1, 1951, Professor Bernard Schwartz made the following comment:

> Bills of Rights occupy the place of honor in all of the new European Constitutions. Yet, it is common knowledge that, on much of the continent, individual liberties have never been more restricted. . . . The European preoccupation with the formal provisions protecting human rights appears often to blur the true picture, by erecting a legal facade behind which rights continue to be systematically violated. It is machinery for enforcement and not provisions in texts above, which is important.[72]

The vast contrast between "the law" as proclaimed in constitutions and its actual application or operation is not limited to Europe. Mrs. Clagett, writing on the laws of Latin America, admits frankly that the ". . . actual operation of institutions in some instances has been a far cry from the legislators's original design. . . ." [73] She continues: "We all know, for example, that despite constitutional and legal guaranties to the contrary, more than once has an entire bench of the highest court of the land been deposed and replaced by incumbents more friendly to the government, without benefit of removal or appointment through the regular channels provided by law." [74]

VI. Unofficial Efforts for a Charter of Human Rights

A. Efforts of Scholars

It has been shown that provisions on human rights are usually contained in either the constitutions or the general laws of the various States. The reader was also reminded of the fact that reading of these constitutions and statutes would not always give a true picture of the actual respect for human rights in many countries. Flagrant violations, however, always resulted in a renewed interest in the movement for an effective Bill of Rights to be enforced by the family of nations.

Even in a cursory treatment of the preliminary steps that gave impetus to the movement for a universal charter of human rights, mention must be made of the efforts and contribution of certain unofficial organizations and individuals. At the outset one would have to review in a position of honor all the adherents of natural law and natural rights who realized that the natural rights of man and an effective international law were only possible if there existed limitations on the absolute sovereignty of the State. Moreover, these same men made it clear that since the welfare of the human person was the primary and ultimate goal of the State, international law had to serve a dual purpose. First, it had to safeguard the State from external aggression; secondly, it must assure the individual that his natural rights would not be violated even by his own State.

The difficulties inherent in such a project, however important or even indispensable, are apparent. Professor Lauterpacht, who has made an invaluable contribution in having drafted single-handed an International Bill of Rights, referred to these difficulties in the following scholarly language: "Any attempt to translate the idea of an international bill of rights of man, into a working rule of law is fraught with difficulties which disturb orthodox thought to the point of discouragement." [75] Of course, like others, Professor Lauterpacht refers to the difficulties arising out of the agreement (or lack of agreement) as to the content of such a bill and the methods of enforcement. Nonetheless, many scholars, statesmen, and religious leaders have endeavored to draft such a bill. Many formulations of "essential" rights were made. For example, the following simple statements of "inalienable" rights are found in a book by Neil MacNeil.[76]

The right to life
The right to think
The right to eat
The right to raise a family
The right to worship God
The right to vote

Many others could be reproduced. All men of good will gave of their time and effort to help realize a time-honored noble aspiration.

B. Contributions of Organizations

Of the several notable charters that were drawn subsequent to the First World War, one particularly worthy of note is the Declaration of The International Rights of Man, adopted in New York in 1929 by the Institute of International Law. The preamble follows:

> The Institute of International Law, considering that the juridic conscience of the civilized world demands the recognition of the individual's rights exempted from all infringement on the part of the State;
>
> That the Declarations of Rights inscribed in a great many constitutions and notably in the American and French constitutions of the end of the eighteenth century, enacted laws not only for the citizen, but for the human being;
>
> That the Fourteenth Amendment to the Constitution of the United States declares that no State shall "deprive any person of life, liberty, or property without due process of the law, nor deny to any person within its jurisdiction the equal protection of the laws";
>
> That the Supreme Court of the United States, in a unanimous decision, ruled that, by the terms of this amendment, it applied within the jurisdiction of the United States "to all persons without distinctions of race, color or nationality, and that the equal protection of the laws is a guarantee of the protection of equal laws";
>
> That, moreover, a certain number of treaties explicitly provide for the recognition of the rights of man;
>
> That it is all important to spread throughout the entire world the international recognition of the rights of man. . . .[77]

Its six well-drawn articles provide for the right to life, liberty, property, worship, language and nationality. Article 5 proscribes "all discrimination, direct or indirect."

This Declaration should be read together with the "Statement of Essential Human Rights" prepared by a special committee of the American Law Institute in 1946. Since the membership of the Committee represented many cultures and countries, it seems remarkable that the Committee reached agreement on such an extended and detailed statement of essential Human Rights. The Preamble to the Statement reads as follows:

PREAMBLE

Upon the freedom of the individual depends the welfare of the people, the safety of the state and the peace of the world.

In society complete freedom cannot be attained; the liberties of the one are limited by the liberties of others, and the preservation of freedom requires the fulfillment by individuals of their duties as members of society.

The function of the state is to promote conditions under which the individual can be most free.

To express those freedoms to which every human being is entitled and to assure that all shall live under a government of the people, by the people, for the people, this declaration is made.

Its 18 articles deal with the following rights and freedoms:

Article 1—Freedom of Religion
Article 2—Freedom of Opinion
Article 3—Freedom of Speech
Article 4—Freedom of Assembly
Article 5—Freedom to Form Associations
Article 6—Freedom From Wrongful Interference
Article 7—Fair Trial
Article 8—Freedom From Arbitrary Detention
Article 9—Retroactive Laws
Article 10—Property Rights
Article 11—Education
Article 12—Work
Article 13—Conditions of Work
Article 14—Food and Housing
Article 15—Social Security
Article 16—Participation in Government
Article 17—Equal Protection
Article 18—Limitations on Exercise of Rights [78]

Although extended discussion on the two preceding declarations does not seem warranted a few observations are in order.

First, both declarations recognize the primacy of the individual in the international society.

Second, both declarations speak in terms of the duty of the State toward the individual. Whereas the 1929 declaration speaks of the *duty* of every state to *recognize* the rights of every individual (except article 1 which speaks of the duty to accord to every one the protection of the law), the 1946 Statement speaks of the duty of the State to *protect* all rights and freedoms.

Third, although both declarations acknowledge the importance of the rights of man "throughout the entire world," the 1946 declaration states at the outset that there is a relationship between the freedom of the individual and "the peace of the world."

Fourth, although both declarations may be said to include the natural rights of man, the 1946 statement goes beyond these rights and includes such "rights" as the right to education, work, and social security.

Professor Quincy Wright, who was a member of the committee that drew up the 1946 statement, named in 1941 in "A Conference of Experts in International Relations," the following six freedoms that in his opinion should be included in an international declaration:

> First, the freedom of opinion and religion.
> Secondly, the freedom of communication, including the freedom to use the press and the radio.
> Thirdly, the freedom of trade and economic enterprise.
> Fourth, freedom from economic exploitation.
> Equality before the law is a fifth basic right.
> Sixthly, there should be no denial of civil rights because of race, religion, or nationality.[79]

The discussion that followed at the 1941 conference indicated clearly that there were basic differences in the "rights" that were being grouped together. For example, in reply to a question whether he would include "social security" in a list of essential human rights, Professor Wright stated:

> There is a difference between saying there are certain freedoms of which the State cannot deprive the individual no matter how poor a State is, and saying you must give this person a certain degree of comfort, a radio, and so on. If you attempt to guarantee social security, the court will continually be running up against an impossibility: Conditions may have arisen so that the State cannot give the economic security it would like to give all its citizens.[80]

The distinction made indicates a definite awareness of the concept that certain rights are "natural" and inalienable. These are the rights "of which the State cannot deprive the individual no matter how poor a State is."

In this connection it may be interesting to list also the rights that were considered to be fundamental by President Truman's Committee on Civil Rights. This Committee which emphasized the American heritage that extols the "individual person," enumerated and restated the following rights found in the Declaration of Independence and the Constitution:

1. The right of safety and security of the person;
2. The right of citizenship and its privileges;
3. The right to freedom of conscience and expression;
4. The right of equality of opportunity.

Sadly enough, this Committee proceeded to show that, in practice, the actual treatment of minorities in the United States does not always accord with the high standards established in the constitution and laws.

The completely secular nature of the foregoing declarations is made apparent when they are compared with the "Declaration of Human Rights" [81] drafted by the National Catholic Welfare Conference and with the "Seven Principles" signed by 147 Catholic, Jewish and Protestant leaders. This latter declaration called a "Pattern for Peace" was released to the press Oct. 7, 1943.[82] Both the Catholic Preamble and the "Seven Principles," because of their philosophical accuracy and brevity of expression, will be reproduced in full.

CATHOLIC PREAMBLE

We present for the consideration of all men of good-will the following postulates of a just peace as embodying the principles of the moral law and their prime applications to world problems of our day. To our mind they express the minimum requirements of a peace which Christians can endorse as fair to all men. They are the foundation on which Catholics in a free world can work from deep motives of Christian justice and charity for the building of a better social order.

SEVEN PRINCIPLES

1. The organization of a just peace depends upon practical recognition of the fact that not only individuals but nations, states and international society are subject to the sovereignty of God and to the moral law which comes from God.

2. The dignity of the human person as the image of God must be set forth in all its essential implications in an international declaration of rights, and be vindicated by the positive action of national govern-

ments and international organization. States as well as individuals must repudiate racial, religious or other discrimination in violation of those rights.

3. The rights of all peoples, large and small, subject to the good of the organized world community, must be safeguarded within the framework of collective security. The progress of undeveloped, colonial, or oppressed peoples toward political responsibility must be the object of international concern.

4. National governments and international organization must respect and guarantee the rights of ethnic, religious and cultural minorities to economic livelihood, to equal opportunity for educational and cultural development, and to political equality.

5. An enduring peace requires the organization of international institutions which will: a) develop a body of international law; b) guarantee the faithful fulfillment of international obligations, and revise them when necessary; c) assure collective security by drastic limitation and continuing control of armaments, compulsory arbitration and adjudication of controversies, and the use when necessary of adequate sanctions to enforce the law.

6. International economic collaboration to assist all states to provide an adequate standard of living for their citizens must replace the present economic monopoly and exploitation of natural resources by privileged groups and states.

7. Since the harmony and well-being of the world community are intimately bound up with the internal equilibrium and social order of the individual states, steps must be taken to provide for the security of the family, the collaboration of all groups and classes in the interest of the common good, a standard of living adequate for self-development and family life, decent conditions of work, and participation by labor in decisions affecting its welfare.

VII. The United Nations and Human Rights

A. The Dawning of a New Era

The outbreak of World War II, a calamity in no small measure provoked by a nation that ruthlessly denied fundamental human rights to a segment of its population on account of race or religion, ushered in an era of unprecedented world-wide interest in the natural rights of man. Along the arduous age-old path of man's struggle to achieve his natural rights several milestones have been indicated. Magna Carta, the French Declaration of the Rights of Man, and the American Declaration of Independence all remain as inspirational guides that paved the way for a universal charter of human rights. Such a charter would probably have remained a mere romantic dream for many years to come were it not for the establishment of the United Nations. Although it is true that the first purpose of the United Nations is the maintenance of international peace, it is the United Nations Charter that dramatically reaffirms man's faith in "human rights and fundamental freedoms." In a recent address, Dr. O. Frederick Nolde, underscored this "revolutionary step" taken by the framers of the United Nations charter, because, "in addition to collective security, they recognized the observance of human rights as an imperative cornerstone on which world peace and justice must be built." [83]

It may be said that this new era for the international protection of human rights dawned with the historic meeting of President Franklin D. Roosevelt and Prime Minister Winston Churchill in the Atlantic Ocean on August 1, 1941. Although the specific purpose of the meeting was to state to the world "certain common principles in the national policies of their respective countries on which they have their hopes for a better future for the world," the Atlantic Charter, which resulted from that meeting, spearheaded a new movement for human rights and gave renewed hope of freedom to oppressed peoples everywhere. Paragraph six of that charter declared that, "after the final destruction of the Nazi tyranny, they hope to see established a peace which will afford to all nations the means of dwelling in safety within their own boundaries, and which will afford assurance that all men in all the lands may live out their lives in freedom from fear and want." This document was essentially of a political nature and hence it mentioned only freedom from fear and want. President Roosevelt had made a more complete statement on human freedoms in his annual message to Congress on January 6th of the same year. In this address, President Roosevelt advanced his now famous "Four Freedoms." He stated:

> In the future days, which we seek to make secure we look forward to a world founded upon four essential human freedoms.
>
> The first is freedom of speech and expression—everywhere in the world.
>
> The second is freedom of every person to worship God—in his own way everywhere in the world.
>
> The third is freedom from want—which, translated into world terms, means economic understandings which will secure to every nation a healthy peacetime life for its inhabitants everywhere in the world.
>
> The fourth is freedom from fear—which, translated into world terms, means a world-wide reduction of armaments to such a point and in

such a thorough fashion that no nation will be in a position to commit an act of physical aggression against any neighbor—anywhere in the world.

Significantly enough, President Roosevelt added that the "essential human freedoms" outlined were not a "vision of a distant millennium. It is a definite basis for a kind of world attainable in our own time and generation."

B. World War II Declarations of Human Rights

In the Preamble of the Washington Declaration of January 1, 1942, the nations then at war with Germany, already called "the United Nations," declared their adherence to the principles of the Atlantic Charter and added the following significant statement: "Being convinced that complete victory over their enemies is essential to defend life, liberty, independence and religious freedom, and to preserve *human rights* and justice in their own lands as well as in other lands. . . ." [84] This was the first occasion when the "United Nations" voiced their concern for the human rights of all people everywhere in the world. On November 1, 1943, from the historic Moscow meeting, there emanated a concrete statement of human rights. "Freedom of speech, of religious worship, of political belief, and of public meeting, shall be restored in full measure to the Italian people." This statement is particularly noteworthy since human right provisions were actually inserted in the Peace Treaties that followed World War II. From the Teheran Conference of December 1, 1943, resulted a declaration that the participating nations were "dedicated to the elimination of tyranny and slavery, oppression and intolerance."

It can be seen from the foregoing declarations that during World War II there occurred a crystallization on an international plane of the demands for the international recognition of human rights. It seemed almost conclusive that the family of nations had been convinced that gross violations of human rights on the part of any nation was a matter of international concern and not one of "domestic jurisdiction." [85]

With the Dumbarton Oaks Proposals of 1944 the "United Nations" began seriously to prepare for the peace that was to come and to propose a charter for the world organization that was to be called the United Nations. These proposals, that directly preceded the United Nations Charter, included the following purposes: (1) "to maintain international peace and security"; (2) "to develop friendly relations among nations and to take other appropriate measures to strengthen universal peace"; (3) "to achieve international cooperation in the solution of international economic, social, and other humanitarian problems."

In Chapter IX, Section A (1), dealing with economic and social cooperation there is found a phrase that may soon have a glorious history. It states that "With a view to the creation of stability and well-being . . . the Organization should . . . *promote respect for human rights and fundamental freedoms.*"

C. Human Rights Provisions in the United Nations Charter

Notwithstanding the pressure from many groups and organizations, the United Nations Conference on International Organization which convened in San Francisco on April 25, 1945, rejected the proposals to include a Bill of Rights or a Charter on Human Rights in the United Nations Charter.

On June 26, 1945, when the Charter was finally completed, although it did not contain an international Bill of Rights, it was replete with references which clearly indicated the organization's concern over the universal recognition and respect for human rights.

The United Nations Charter expressly mentions matters of human rights seven times. In addition thereto Articles 56 and 87 also affect human rights although they do not expressly mention them. A reading of the Charter indicates that the human rights provisions are woven throughout the charter and clearly manifest a genuine concern over human rights everywhere in the world.

The Preamble states: "We the people of the United Nations determined . . . to reaffirm faith in fundamental human rights, in the dignity and worth of the human person, in the equal rights of men and women . . . have resolved to combine our efforts to accomplish these aims."

Article 1 states: "The Purposes of the United Nations are: . . .

3. To achieve international cooperation in solving international problems of an economic, social, cultural, or humanitarian character, and in promoting and encouraging respect for human rights and for fundamental freedoms for all without distinction as to race, sex, language or religion";

Article 13 states: "1. The General Assembly shall initiate studies and make recommendations for the purpose of . . . b. promoting international cooperation in the economic, social, cultural, educational, and health fields, and assisting in the realization of human rights and fundamental freedoms for all without distinction as to race, sex, language or religion."

Article 55 states: "With a view to the creation of conditions of stability and well-being which are necessary for peaceful and friendly relations among nations based on respect for the principle of equal rights and self-determination of peoples, the United Nations shall promote: . . . c. universal respect for and observance of human rights and fundamental freedoms for all without distinction as to race, sex, language, or religion." In this connection *Article 56* should also be noted since it expressly states that "All Members pledge themselves to take joint and separate action in cooperation with the organization for the achievement of the purposes set forth in Article 55."

Article 62, which deals with the functions and powers of the Economic and Social Council, states that the Council ". . . may make recommendations for the purpose of promoting respect for, and observance of, human rights and fundamental freedoms for all."

Article 68 states: "The Economic and Social Council shall set up commissions in economic and social fields and for the promotion of human rights, and such other commissions as may be required for the performance of its functions."

Article 76, which deals with the "International Trusteeship System," states: "The basic objectives of the trusteeship system, in accordance with the Purposes of the United Nations laid down in Article 1 of the present Charter shall be: . . . c. to encourage respect for human rights and for fundamental freedoms for all without distinction as to race, sex, language or religion, and to encourage recognition of the interdependence of the peoples of the world."

Notwithstanding the many declarations on human rights in the Charter, it cannot be said that even cumulatively they comprise an effective guarantee of the natural rights of man. Particularly, there is absent in the Charter any definition of "human rights and fundamental freedoms." It contains no statement which gives some indication as to the source of these "human rights," and, in this regard, the Charter does not attain the perfection of the Declaration of Independence. Moreover, although the Charter speaks of the "universal respect for, and observance of, human rights and fundamental freedoms" it does not acknowledge a principle or method whereby the provisions for *observance* may be rendered effective. It is evident that although the Charter intended to stimulate and give impetus to the recognition of human rights everywhere in the world, it did not itself contain an international Bill of Rights or otherwise provide for measures of enforcement. On the other hand, it is also obvious from the provisions reproduced herein, and particularly from Article 68 which mandatorily enjoins the Economic and Social Council to establish a commission for the promotion of human rights, that the United Nations would not be carrying out one of its express purposes and principles if it did not go forward and take action to *promote respect for* and *observance of* these rights. Not only is the United Nations charged with such a duty, but by Article 56, the *Members themselves* pledge to take joint and separate action to achieve the purposes of Article 55 which include "universal respect for, and observance of, human rights and fundamental freedoms for all without distinction as to race, sex, language, or religion." Therefore, as of the moment that the Charter of the United Nations became effective several conclusions were appropriate regarding the concern of the international society for human rights:

First: The international society finally and perspicuously declared its concern for the individual and his rights;

Second: Vague platitudes and glowing phrases were not enough. A Commission on Human Rights was to be established to give reality to the human rights provisions of the Charter;

Third: It seemed clear that this commission would draft a specific International Bill of Rights of Man—a fulfillment of the cries of many centuries;

Fourth: It seemed also clear that the work of the Commission would not cease with the drafting of an International Bill of Rights. Such a bill would be destined to have the effective force of a treaty;

Fifth: The matter of respect and observance of human rights, and consequently their violation, ceased to be a question solely within the "exclusive jurisdiction" of a given nation. Although the charter did not give the United Nations the right to intervene directly, matters of human rights were recognized to be of legitimate concern for the United Nations which represented the international society;

Sixth: Although no effective machinery for the enforcement of the human rights provisions was established, all of the Member nations solemnly pledged themselves in a treaty to respect and observe human rights and fundamental freedoms;

Seventh: Henceforth, human rights and fundamental freedoms are *legal rights* cognizable under international law, and

Eighth: Subject to the limitation of the Charter, pursuant to which the United Nations are not authorized to "intervene in matters which are essentially within the domestic jurisdiction of any state," [86] the effective enforcement of these rights is also a matter of concern for the international society. It should be indicated at this point that the "domestic jurisdiction" clause does not preclude the United Nations or any of its organs from taking action *short of intervention.* For example, on a petition alleging a violation of fundamental human rights, the organization and its organs may investigate and make appropriate recommendations either to the United Nations or to the particular State concerned. This simple expedient would surely serve to focus world public opinion upon the incidents in question. Moreover, it must be remembered that the "domestic jurisdiction" clause does not apply to cases in which the Security Council, pursuant to Chapter VII of the Charter, proceeds to take measures of enforcement after having determined "the existence of any threat to the peace, breach of the peace, or act of aggression." [87]

D. *United Nations Commission on Human Rights*

In the pageant of human rights, the pages of history will unmistakably record the leading role of the United Nations. With respect to the recognition of the dignity of the human person, the Charter truly represents "a new departure in history." Mr. Winant, a member of the Economic and Social Council, in 1946, correctly indicated that "International action in the basic field of human rights is a new departure in history." The keynote was set by the Charter; an international Bill of Rights and methods of implementations seemed to be attainable in this generation.

On June 26, 1945, the day on which the United Nations Charter was signed, a Preparatory Commission of the United Nations was created to make arrangements for the first session of the General Assembly. This Commission recommended to the Economic and Social Council that it should create at its first session five commissions, one of them being the Commission on Human Rights. The Preparatory Commission defined in general terms the primary functions and general purposes of the Commission on Human Rights as follows:

> In general, the functions of the Commission (on Human Rights) would be to assist the Council to carry out its responsibility under the Charter to promote human rights. The studies and recommendations of the Commission would encourage the acceptance of higher standards in this field and help to check and eliminate discrimination and other abuses.
>
> In particular the work of the commission might be directed towards the following objects:
>
> (a) Formulation of an international bill of rights;
> (b) Formulation of recommendations for an international declaration or convention on such matters as civil liberties, status of women, freedom of information;
> (c) Protection of minorities;
> (d) Prevention of discrimination on grounds of race; sex, language or religion; and
> (e) Any matters within the field of human rights considered likely to impair the general welfare of friendly relations among nations.

At the first session of the Economic and Social Council a "nuclear Commission on Human Rights," created by a resolution dated February 16, 1946, was completed on June 21, 1946, at which time the Council also established the Commission on Human Rights. At the first meeting of this important Commission, consisting of 18 members (organized pursuant to the mandate of Article 68 of the Charter), Mrs. Eleanor Roosevelt was elected Chairman. The Commission on Human Rights, an organ of the Economic and Social Council, is assisted by three subsidiary bodies: a sub-commission on Freedom of Information and the Press; a sub-commission on the Prevention of Discrimination and the Protection of Minorities; and a Drafting Committee whose scope was limited to the drafting of an "International Bill of Human Rights."

The pattern for the assigned project was orderly and understandable. There would first be drawn a "Draft Declaration on Human Rights" which would be followed by a "Draft Covenant on Human Rights," and "Measures of Implementation." The draft covenant and the measures of implementation together would form the "International Bill of Rights." Since this bill potentially could help achieve "the irreducible guarantee of unity, peace and prosperity, law, justice and tranquility," [88] no other endeavor was more worthy or more important.

VIII. United Nations Declaration of Human Rights

A. Approval of Declaration by General Assembly

The task of drafting an International Bill of Rights has been accurately referred to as the Commission's "first and most important task." [89] The Commission embarked immediately upon its assigned venture. It decided that the Bill of Rights would contain two parts. The first would be a *Declaration* which could be approved through action of the Member States of the United Nations in the General Assembly. In the words of the Commission, this Declaration would have *great moral force,* since it would in effect say to the peoples of the world "this is what we hope human rights may mean to all peoples in the years to come." The second part of the Bill of Rights would be a *covenant* which would be in the form of a treaty to be presented to the nations of the world for adoption and ratification. This covenant, once ratified or adopted by a nation would become legally binding. The signatory nations, if necessary, would thereby be obligated to change their national laws wherever such laws did not conform with the provisions or standards established in the covenant.

The first results of the labors of the Commission on Human Rights, the "Universal Declaration of Human Rights," were presented to the General Assembly in its 1948 meeting in Paris. Commenting on this fact, the then Secretary of State Marshall stated: "It is entirely fitting that this General Assembly, meeting in France which fired the hearts of men with the Declaration of the Rights of Man in 1789, should consider in 1948 the approval of a new declaration of human rights for free men in a free world." [90]

The Universal Declaration of Human Rights was overwhelmingly approved by the General Assembly on December 10, 1948. Only the Soviet bloc abstained.[91] The resolution of the General Assembly proclaimed the Declaration "as a common standard of achievement for all peoples and all nations." Commenting upon the significance of the Declaration, Mrs. Roosevelt asserted: "We stand today at the threshold of a great event both in the life of the United Nations and in the life of mankind. . . . This Declaration may well become the international Magna Carta of all men everywhere." [92] December 10th was unquestionably destined to become Human Rights Day throughout the world.[93]

B. Nature and Content of the Declaration

Although in the past, specific declarations of rights were usually framed with particular abuses in mind, and to remedy specific grievances, the Universal Declaration of Human Rights may be regarded as the first all-embracing official codification of the rights of man. The general purpose of the Declaration was to depict in rather simple terms practically the entire broad range of human rights. It was clearly the first concrete step calculated to fulfill the pledge contained in the Charter to "promote universal respect for, and observance of human rights and fundamental freedoms for all without distinction as to race, sex, language, or religion." [94]

The Declaration, containing a Preamble and thirty articles, is not limited to the basic civil and political rights which may be said to characterize the "American Bill of Rights." Rather, in addition to certain miscellaneous provisions, such as the right of asylum, the Declaration includes economic and social rights such as the right to work and the right to education.

The importance of the Declaration cannot be minimized; for the first time in history the greater part of the world agreed on basic human rights. Not only does it unmistakably recognize the rights of the individual in the international society, but it also clearly fulfills the implied promise of the Charter which acknowledged international responsibility. Following the path of the Charter, it was the second powerful wedge driven into the ever-widening crevices of the traditional doctrine which excluded the individual from the scope of international law.

The keynote of the moral fiber of the Declaration is set by the phrase "the inherent dignity of man." Its preamble declares:

> Whereas recognition of the inherent dignity and of the equal and inalienable rights of all members of the human family is the foundation of freedom, justice and peace in the world, . . . Whereas . . . The advent of a world in which human beings shall enjoy freedom of speech and belief and freedom from fear and want has been proclaimed as the highest aspiration of the common people, whereas it is essential . . . that human rights should be protected by the rule of law. . . . Whereas the peoples of the United Nations have in the Charter reaffirmed their faith in fundamental human rights, in the dignity and worth of the human person and in the equal rights of men and women and have determined to promote social progress and better standards of life in larger freedom, . . .

> Now therefore The General Assembly, Proclaims this Universal Declaration of Human Rights as a common standard of achievement for all peoples and all nations, to the end that every individual and every organ of society, keeping this Declaration constantly in mind, shall strive by teaching and education to promote respect for these rights and freedoms and by progressive measures, national and international, to secure their universal and effective recognition and observance, both among the peoples of Member States themselves and among the peoples of territories under their jurisdiction.

The thirty articles of the Declaration proclaim the right to life, liberty and security of person, freedom from slavery, torture, cruel, inhuman or degrading treatment or punishment, freedom from arbitrary arrest, detention or exile, right to a fair and public hearing by an independent and impartial tribunal, presumption of innocence, protection against ex post facto laws, freedom from arbitrary interference with one's privacy, family, home or correspondence, freedom to leave any country, freedom of movement and residence, right of asylum from persecution, equal rights as to marriage, right to own property, freedom of religion, expression, assembly, association, right of people to have their will serve as the basis of the authority of Government, right to work, right to join trade unions, right to rest and leisure, right to social security, right to education, right to participate in the cultural life of the community, right to equality before the law, and freedom from discrimination.

As may be gathered from the several quotations from the Preamble, the Declaration does not contain any statement pertaining to the source of the rights that are proclaimed. In this essential respect the Declaration is inferior to the American Declaration of Independence, and has failed to follow the magnificent example of the American document. Of course, no explanation is required in pointing out that any reference to God, or to the fact that man is endowed by his Creator with natural and inalienable rights, was anathema to the Soviet bloc.[95] Therefore, on this fundamental basis which concerns the nature and source of human rights, Mr. Holman, former President of the American Bar Association, is correct in his disappointment and adverse criticism of the Universal Declaration of Human Rights. However, although it is true that the American concept of a Bill of Rights has been that of a "Bill of Prohibitions" against the encroachments of the government upon the inalienable rights of man, this ground alone would not warrant a complete condemnation of the Universal Declaration. It would be entirely proper to enumerate the God-given rights that are beyond the pale of governmental infringement, and, to add thereto, those rights that are rendered necessary because of the modern age. The enumeration of certain rights, other than *natural rights,* in a declaration of rights is not a mandatory ground which justifies either criticism or a minimizing of its importance, provided the distinction as to the nature of the various rights be borne in mind. It seems illogical to assert that the inclusion of social rights necessarily results in establishing "a collectivist concept of government for all the peoples of the world." [96]

In order that the reader may more readily perceive the underlying concepts which pervade throughout the Universal Declaration of Human Rights a few important sections will be set forth.

Article 1 proclaims the equality of man in the following terms: "All human beings are born free and equal in dignity and rights. They are endowed with reason and conscience and should act towards one another in a spirit of brotherhood." *Article 2* proscribes discrimination by declaring: "Everyone is entitled to all the rights and freedoms set forth in this Declaration, without distinction of any kind, such as race, color, sex, language, religion, political or other opinion, national or social origin, property, birth or other status." [97] *Article 3* declares that "Everyone has the right to life, liberty and security of person."

Concerning marriage, *Article 16* provides:

"1. Men and women of full age, without any limitation due to race, nationality or religion, have the right to marry and to found a family. They are entitled to equal rights as to marriage, during marriage and at its dissolution.

"2. Marriage shall be entered into only with the free and full consent of the intending spouses.

"3. The family is the natural and fundamental group unit of society and is entitled to protection by society and the State." [98]

Article 18 spells out freedom of worship in the following terms:

"Everyone has the right to freedom of thought, conscience and religion; this right includes freedom to change his religion or belief, and freedom, either alone or in community with others and in public or private, to manifest his religion or belief in teaching, practice, worship and observance."

Article 26 provides for the right to education in three subdivisions:

"1. Everyone has the right to education. Education shall be free, at least in the elementary and fundamental stages. Elementary education shall be compulsory. Technical and professional education shall be made generally available and higher education shall be equally accessible to all on the basis of merit.

"2. Education shall be directed to the full development of the human personality and to the strengthening of respect for human rights and fundamental freedoms. It shall promote understanding, tolerance and friendship among all nations, racial or religious groups, and shall further the activities of the United Nations for the maintenance of peace.

"3. Parents have a prior right to choose the kind of education that shall be given to their children."

To judge from the vastness of the rights and freedoms proclaimed in the Universal Declaration on Human Rights, its adoption, as a *common standard of achievement* by nations representing the greater portion of the world's population, is nothing short of a phenomenal achievement. Indeed, it is significant that not one country ventured to cast a negative vote!

C. *Moral and Legal Effect of the Declaration*

In any appraisal of the Declaration it must be clearly understood that, from its inception, it was not cast in the form of a treaty. Its basic character is that of a *declaration* and not of an international covenant or treaty. As stated just prior to its adoption by the chairman of the Human Rights Commission and the United States Representative to the General Assembly: "It is not and does not purport to be a statement of law or a legal obligation. It is a declaration of basic principles of human rights and freedoms, to be stamped with the approval of the General Assembly by formal vote to its members, and to serve as a common standard of achievement for all peoples of all nations." [99] Nevertheless, after its approval by the General Assembly, the Declaration enjoys the respect and authority of a *resolution* of the General Assembly. The legal effect of the Declaration, therefore, depends upon the nature and effect of a *Resolution* of the General Assembly. Since the General Assembly, by the provisions of the Charter, may merely *discuss, consider* and *recommend,* it is clear that under the Charter the resolution does not have the force of international law. Nevertheless it is unquestionable that these resolutions carry great weight. Surely, the various organs of the United Nations consider the resolutions of the General Assembly to be more than mere exhortations. The Declaration, therefore, although not a legally binding treaty is nevertheless, an "authoritative interpretation" of the human rights provisions of the Charter. It is manifestly a solemn expression of an international public policy.

The affirmative contribution of the Declaration to world thinking has been to awaken the whole world to "a human rights conscience," which, although perhaps yet subdued, has been highlighted and crystallized by the world-wide discussions on the work of the Human Rights Commission. Even those individuals who were critical of the Declaration, and even more so of the subsequent Covenant on Human Rights, played an important role in focusing public attention upon the work of the United Nations in the field of human rights, a task of the utmost and unquestioned importance.[100] To accomplish it, millions of copies of the Declaration, translated into over thirty languages, have been distributed by the United Nations and its various agencies. Many non-governmental agencies have aided in the world-wide program of publicity and education. The Declaration, thereto, has already served as a "powerful incentive in its own right. Progressively, nations have felt themselves called upon to refute, to explain, to defend, or to remedy any reported deviation from the requirements which the standard (of the Declaration) places upon them." [101] Clearly then, the moral effects of the Declaration by far exceed its binding authority. Its moral persuasiveness has already borne fruit in certain provisions of various international agreements, in the peace treaties, and in the national constitutions and legislation of several countries.

The reaction to the Universal Declaration of Human Rights should properly be regarded as the result of one phase of the work of the United Nations. It is true that the United Nations, with the help of national groups both governmental and unofficial, has vitally contributed to the creation of the "human rights conscience" referred to previously. Its contribution has not been limited to the work of the Economic and Social Council and the Human Rights Commission. All of its organs, within their respective jurisdiction, have promoted the movement for the protection of human rights. For example, the International Law Commission, established November 21, 1947 by resolution of the General Assembly, included a most significant human rights provision in its draft, *Declaration on the Rights and Duties of States,*[102] which was considered by the General Assembly to be "a notable and substantial contribution towards the progressive development of international law." It proclaimed in Article VI that "Every State has the duty to treat all persons under its jurisdiction with respect for human rights and fundamental freedoms, without distinction as to race, sex, language or religion." Although this declaration is not internationally binding, it involves a revolutionary conceptual and doctrinal departure from the principles of international law which have left to the discretion of the State the treatment that it must accord its own citizens. Referring to Article VI of this Declaration, Professor Hans Kelsen has commented that it "has no basis in general international law." [103] Insofar as the Declaration affects the "rights" of a State over its own citizens within its jurisdiction, the comment is unquestionably true. Formerly, any statement concerning the duties of States as against individuals would have been limited to "aliens" or "foreigners." The language heretofore might have read "A state is responsible if an injury *to an alien* results from a denial of justice." [104] Under the present trend not only is the international protection not intended to be limited to aliens, but also, no discrimination will be tolerated on account of "race, sex, language or religion."

IX. Regional Declarations on Human Rights

A. United Nations Efforts Supplemented by Regional Charters

It has been indicated that the Universal Declaration of Human Rights was the first concrete contribution of the Commission on Human Rights. Its adoption by the General Assembly, however, did not mean that the work of the Commission was completed. To the contrary, its work had merely begun. The execution of the initial plan required the drafting of a *Covenant on Human Rights,* that is, an international treaty on human rights that would be submitted for approval and ratification to the Member States. The Commission labored diligently on this difficult and momentous project. After much discussion and revision it succeeded in drafting a Covenant on Human Rights. The Covenant, because of its importance and the criticism that it has generated, will be treated separately. Prior to a discussion of the Covenant, however, it is interesting to note that efforts to draft a broad charter of human liberty have not been limited to the United Nations or the type of organizations previously mentioned in this article. In addition to the inclusion of human rights provisions in the peace treaties and in other international covenants and declarations, the efforts of regional organizations have paralleled or supplemented those of the United Nations. Specifically, mention will be made of the 1948 "American Declaration of the Rights and Duties of Man," and the 1950 "European Convention for the Protection of Human Rights and Fundamental Freedoms."

B. American Declaration on Rights and Duties of Man

At the Ninth International Conference of the American States, which met in Bogota, Colombia, between March 30th and May 2nd, 1948, a resolution was passed adopting the "American Declaration of the Rights and Duties of Man." [105] This Declaration, which preceded the adoption of the Universal Declaration by the General Assembly (December 10, 1948), in strict legal effect is not unlike the Universal Declaration. It does, however, serve to emphasize the fact that United Nations' efforts in the field are not exclusive. There is no doubt that these regional efforts will advance the date when men and women everywhere will achieve "better standards of life in larger freedom."

The Preamble to the American Declaration of the Rights and Duties of Man is preceded by a very significant statement of principles. This prefatory statement declares that:

> WHEREAS:
>
> The American peoples have acknowledged the dignity of the individual, and their national constitutions recognize that juridical and political institutions, which regulate life in human society, have as their principal aim the protection of the essential rights of man and the creation of circumstances that will permit him to achieve spiritual and material progress and attain happiness;
>
> The American States have on repeated occasions recognized that the essential rights of man are not derived from the fact that he is a national of a certain state, but are based upon attributes of his human personality;
>
> The international protection of the rights of man should be the principal guide of an evolving American law. . . .

This statement not only acknowledges the dignity of man, but also refers to the *spiritual* progress of man, and to the fact that the rights of man are not derived from the State of which he is a national. Although again there is no statement as to the Divine origin of the "essential rights of man," there is a recognition that they are "based upon attributes of his *human* personality." This prefatory statement also declares that "The affirmation of essential human rights by the American States together with the guarantees given by the internal regimes of the states establish the initial system of protection considered by the American States as being suited to the present social and juridical conditions. . . ."

The Preamble declares that "All men are born free and equal, in dignity and in rights, and being endowed by nature with reason and conscience, they should conduct themselves as brothers one to another."

At this point it is observed that this Preamble speaks of man being endowed *by nature* with reason and conscience. This phraseology is perhaps the only reference in any of the modern multi-national documents on human rights that approximates the concept beautifully expressed in the American Declaration of Independence. That which refers to *nature* as a source of rights or other human attributes is obviously a compromise between those who wish to employ the language of the Declaration of Independence and those who oppose any reference to God, or the Creator. The spirit of compromise, however, in the Universal Declaration of Human Rights, prevailed to the extent that even the phrase "by nature" was ultimately eliminated.[106]

In addition to a statement on the interrelation of rights and duties, the Preamble declares that "Duties of juridical nature presuppose others of a moral nature which support them in principle and constitute their basis." This statement, which concerns duties of a "moral nature," precedes the following noteworthy declaration: "Inasmuch as spiritual development is the supreme end of human existence and the highest expression thereof, it is the duty of man to serve that end with all his strength and resources."

The American Declaration contains thirty-eight articles, and is divided into two chapters, the first of which deals with rights; the second, with duties. Like the Universal Declaration, the Chapter on Rights includes a host of human rights. In terse sentences the American Declaration proclaims the traditional rights of life, liberty, security of person, religion and expression. It also proclaims the right to establish a family, freedom of movement, assembly, inviolability of the home, preservation of health, transmission of correspondence, education, work, recreation, "social security which will protect him from the consequences of unemployment, old age . . . ,"[107] and other rights such as those surrounding a person accused of crime and the right of asylum.

Article 29, which is the first of the ten articles dealing with duties, states: "It is the duty of the individual so to conduct himself in relation to others that each and every one may fully form and develop his personality." Article 20 states that every person must aid, support, educate and protect his minor children, and that "it is the duty of children to honor their parents always, and to aid, support and protect them when they need it." The duties listed include the duty to acquire an elementary education, vote, obey the law, military service, hold public office, cooperate with respect to social security, pay taxes, work and refrain from political activities limited to citizens.

Although the American Declaration of the Rights and Duties of Man, except as previously indicated, does not differ materially from the Universal Declaration, nevertheless, by its inclusion of duties in such a Declaration it does highlight the difference in the various types of rights; everyone, for example, has both the right and duty to work.

C. Convention of the Council of Europe

Perhaps the most challenging phenomenon on the modern scene of the international protection of human rights is the convention for the Protection of Human Rights and Fundamental Freedoms signed at Rome, Italy, on November 4, 1950. This Convention is a formal treaty signed by thirteen governments, all members of the Council of Europe. It is not only significant because it is the first legally binding treaty which expressly purports to effectuate the aims of the Universal Declaration of Human Rights, but it is perhaps more important because it has ventured into the heretofore unexplored regions of modes of implementation by establishing a European Commission on Human Rights, and a European Court of Human Rights.

The Preamble of the Convention, which refers to the aims of the Universal Declaration of Human Rights, and to the aim of the Council of Europe, which is the achievement of greater unity between its members, declares that "one of the methods by which that aim [of greater unity] is to be pursued is the maintenance and further realization of Human Rights and Fundamental Freedoms." The Members of the Council of Europe, therefore, reaffirm "their profound belief in those Fundamental Freedoms which are the foundation of justice and peace in the world," and agree that they "shall secure to everyone within their jurisdiction" the rights and freedoms defined in the Convention. The phrase, "to everyone within their jurisdiction," is very significant because it was deliberately selected in preference to less inclusive language. In addition, it can leave no doubt that the rights enumerated in the convention are not limited to either "nationals" or "aliens"—the signatory nations must secure those rights to *everyone*. Article 14 adds that "The enjoyment of the rights and freedoms set forth in this Convention shall be secured without discrimination on any ground such as sex, race, color, language, religion, political or other opinion, national or social origin, association with a national minority, property, birth or other status."

Although the Convention generally enumerates all of the rights proclaimed in the Universal Declaration of Human Rights, the Convention is more specific and defines many of these rights. Although the method of detailed definition will doubtlessly prove to be helpful in the actual administration of the Convention, it has been pointed out that there is in it always "the danger of unintentional omissions which may later be construed as deliberate exclusions." [108] Actually, the convention introduces a necessary element of precision into the broad statements of rights proclaimed in the Universal Declaration; for a reading of any one of the Articles in the European convention states the limitations that may be legitimately imposed on the right secured. For example, Article 2 which states that "Everyone's right to life shall be protected by law," has the following explanatory text: "no one shall be deprived of his life intentionally save in the execution of a sentence of a court following his conviction of a crime for which this penalty is provided by law." Subdivision two of the article adds the following qualifying grounds:

> Deprivation of life shall not be regarded as inflicted in contravention of this Article when it results from the use of force which is not more than absolutely necessary—
> (a) in defence of any person from unlawful violence;
> (b) in order to effect a lawful arrest or to prevent the escape of a person lawfully detained;
> (c) in action lawfully taken for the purpose of quelling a riot or insurrection.

The true step forward in the European Convention is the venture into the realm of enforcement. Article 13 provides that "Everyone whose rights and freedoms as set forth in this Convention are violated shall have an effective remedy before a national authority notwithstanding that the violation has been committed by persons acting in an official capacity." Article 24 authorizes a signatory of the Convention to refer to the Commission on Human Rights any alleged breach of the provisions of the Convention by any other signatory nation. The Convention unqualifiedly departs from the traditional doctrine that an individual has no *locus standi* in international law, by giving to individuals the right to petition for a redress of grievances. Article 25 provides that the Commissioner may receive petitions "from any person, non-governmental organization or group of individuals claiming to be the victim of a violation by one of the High Contracting Parties of the rights set forth in this Convention. . . ." To guard against the abuse of this right of petition it is provided that there must first be an exhaustion of all domestic remedies, and that the Commission cannot deal with a petition that is anonymous or manifestly ill-founded.[109]

As indicated previously, the Convention creates a European Court of Human Rights.[110] Article 19 states that the European Commission of Human Rights and the European Court of Human Rights are set up to "ensure the observance of the engagements undertaken by the High Contracting Parties." It is evident that the two most important innovations of the European Convention are the granting to individuals the direct access to an international organ, and the creation of an international court, with jurisdiction to sit in judgment on nations accused of violating any of the human rights secured by the Convention. Since these two innovations are truly revolutionary the signatory nations were not willing *ipso facto* to be bound by them.

In relation to the individual petition, therefore, it was provided that the nation against which a complaint has been filed has to declare that it "recognizes the competence of the Commission to receive such petitions." [111] Since the signatory nations have not automatically subjected themselves to the jurisdiction of the Court of Human Rights, Article 46 provides that "Any of the High Contracting Parties may at any time declare that it recognizes as compulsory ipso facto . . . the jurisdiction of the Court in all matters concerning the interpretation and application of the present Convention." Hence, it can be seen that the true means of implementation require additional action on the part of the members to the Convention. Nevertheless, the establishment of the Commission on Human Rights is real progress because in any event the members are automatically subject to its jurisdiction when a matter is referred to it by another member nation.[112] The creation of a Court is also welcomed, even though it has optional jurisdiction. It is a regional development that cannot be ignored. It is hoped, of course, that all of the governments that signed the convention will take the two additional steps by accepting the right of the individual to petition, and the compulsory jurisdiction of the Court. The permanent effective contribution of the Convention, therefore, has probably been best expressed by Dr. Robertson who wrote that "The success and importance of the convention will depend largely on the number of states which are prepared to express their faith in the rule of law by taking these two further steps." [113]

X. United Nations Draft of Human Rights

A. Reaction to Covenant on Human Rights

From one standpoint, the drafting of a legally effective international charter on human rights, such as the United Nations Covenant on Human Rights, might be considered as the culmination of years of diligent labor and struggle. From another viewpoint, particularly that of an individual or group whose human rights may have been shockingly violated, the drafting of such a covenant would merely be the first effective step toward the ultimate realization of the rights secured in the covenant. With the fruition of the efforts to draft such a covenant, one fact, however, became crystal-clear. If ever there was a question that much was still to be done to make such a legally binding covenant a living reality, the debates, criticisms and vigorous opposition to the United Nations Draft Covenant on Human Rights removed any possible doubt.

At a rather early date the draftsmen of the Covenant became aware of the staunch opposition, which prevailed in some circles, to any international effort calculated to inject the element of legal enforceability into the movement which favored the international protection of human rights. It hardly seemed wise or necessary to oppose or complain against any *Declaration* of human rights as a standard of achievement, but when drafting of a legally binding treaty was seriously undertaken, many voices, echoing some traditions of the past, spoke sharply against such a covenant. Apparently it seemed that no objection needed seriously to be voiced against a mere Declaration which simply proclaims a goal, perhaps to be achieved in some distant millennium far removed from the neat status quo of today. The seriousness of the efforts to bring about a realization of that goal in the present day, however, became an alarming threat to those who opposed international enforcement of human rights. The ideological battle could no longer be postponed; it had to be waged immediately in the halls of the United Nations, in Congress, in committees, in bar associations, in gatherings everywhere.

In an address before the American Society of International Law, Mr. Sandifer, of the Department of State, referring to the Universal Declaration of Human Rights, had accurately pointed out that, from the standpoint of the rights proclaimed by the Declaration, it was not a revolutionary document. To the contrary, it was stated that from the viewpoint of its contents, the Declaration was "in fact a modest undertaking." What was new, Mr. Sandifer indicated, was the fact that 58 nations had agreed on the Declaration as a standard of achievement.[114] As soon as the first draft Covenant on Human Rights was completed by the United Nations Commission on Human Rights it was apparent that universal agreement upon a *treaty, as distinguished from a declaration,* was more difficult to be obtained. Clearly the process of publicity, education and discussion had reached its peak.

B. The Problems of the Draftsmen

The best evidence of the difficulties encountered by the Commission on Human Rights can be found in a statement issued in September 1952 by Dr. Charles Malik, its Chairman and Minister of the Republic of Lebanon. Speaking for the Commission he stated: "We began with the somewhat naive, albeit sincere, determination to work out an International Bill of Rights and, in the initial impulse of our inexperience, we saw the completion of this task just around the corner. . . . We completed the first step in 1948, and many of us thought the other two steps would be forthcoming in speedy succession. We have been grappling with them now for four years, and while much indeed has been accomplished during this time, the end is not yet in sight. We have all been sobered by the realization of the truly formidable task assigned to us."[115]

During the period referred to by Dr. Malik several drafts were submitted by the Commission. One of the ever-recurring problems dealt with the content of draft covenant in relation to the *kind* of rights that properly should have been included in such a document. With each draft that was submitted, suggested changes and recommendations were invited. The question that required a definite solution was concerned with whether the Covenant should include merely the traditional civil and political rights, or whether it should also include economic, social and cultural ones. It seemed at first that the least resistance would be encountered if the Covenant was limited to the rights traditionally found in existing national charters and constitutions. For example, in 1949, a committee of the American Bar Association reported that it would approve a Covenant on Human Rights which embodied rights relating to life, property, protection against torture, slavery, forced labor, arbitrary arrest or detention, protection against imprisonment for failure to fulfill a contractual obligation, freedom of movement and residence, freedom to leave a country, freedom to return to one's country, right to a fair and public hearing before an independent and impartial tribunal, protection against *ex post facto* laws, right to recognition as a person before the law, freedom of religion, assembly and to form trade associations, and equal protection of the law.[116]

After the 1950 session of the Commission on Human Rights, the Commission submitted a revised draft of a covenant to the Economic and Social Council for its consideration. The Covenant submitted at that time embodied only basic civil and political rights comparable to those secured by the Constitution of the United States; and in contrast to the Universal Declaration, it did not include the so-called economic and social rights.[117] This revised draft, which contained many of the changes proposed by the United States to the first draft, did not provide for any means whereby complaints could have been filed by or against individuals who allegedly deprived others of rights secured by the Covenant. Concerning this particular draft the General Assembly on December 4, 1950, adopted three resolutions. After commending the Commission for its work and calling upon the Economic and Social Council to request the Commission to continue to give priority to the Draft Covenant, the first resolution stated that the Draft then submitted did not contain certain basic rights. It was indicated that additional rights were to be added and that it was desirable to define both the rights and their limitations with the greatest possible precision. Among other things, the first resolution expressly provided for the inclusion in the Covenant of economic, social and cultural rights and an explicit recognition of equality of men and women in the enjoyment of rights. Pursuant to this resolution, therefore, the Council was instructed to request that the Commission include a clear statement of the economic, social and political freedoms provided for in the submitted Draft.

The second resolution requested the Commission on Human Rights to include in the Covenant an article that would expressly provide that the Covenant would be applicable equally to a signatory metropolitan State and to all territories, be they non-self-governing, trust or colonial, which are administered or governed by such a State.

The third resolution invited all States and interested organizations to adopt December 10 as Human Rights Day and invited all States to report annually through the Secretary-General on the observance of that day.[118]

Surely the difficulties encountered served to inject a note of caution and sobriety into the initial enthusiasm of the Commission. Since the views of the majority of the Commission concerning the content of the Covenant were not shared by the General Assembly, the task of drafting a Covenant had to be keyed to the instructions of the General Assembly.

C. One or Two Covenants

Although it became clear then the international bill of rights about to be drafted was to have included both the traditional civil rights and economic, social and cultural rights, a problem was presented as to whether all of them were to be included in one Covenant, or whether two Covenants would have better served the purpose. Since the 1950 General Assembly decision was in favor of one containing all rights, the Commission continued to work on the basis of that understanding. In 1951, however, the General Assembly reversed its policy on the matter and instructed the Commission to draft two Covenants. Although they were to include as much common language as possible, and were to be drafted with equal care, they would nevertheless be two separate documents capable of being adhered to separately and independently. Since the Commission receives its instructions, ultimately, from the General Assembly through the Economic and Social Council, it proceeded to execute the new directive.

D. Shifting Emphasis from Civil to Economic and Social Rights

Since its inception, and concurrently with the new policy which called for the drafting of two covenants, Dr. Malik writes that a "quiet revolution" had occurred in the Commission. In the first years of existence of the Commission it was thought that the more important function dealt with the inclusion of the civil and political rights. It seemed that what had to be guaranteed was freedom from discrimination, arbitrary arrest and freedom of religion and speech. Speaking for the Commission Dr. Malik wrote: "It never occurred to us that anything else was as important as these." [119] Yet, a transition had occurred which resulted in a shifting of emphasis from the civil and political rights to the economic, social and cultural rights. Dr. Malik explained the three steps in this change of emphasis to be as follows: First, it is stated that although the civil and political rights are of primary importance, the economic, social and cultural rights also have their place; the second step involves the imperceptible shift from the view that both groups are of equal importance; the final step is to say that the civil and political rights cannot really be enjoyed if the economic and social rights are not first guaranteed. On such reasoning it may be concluded, therefore, that the social and economic rights are of greater importance. Unfortunately, Dr. Malik may be correct when he writes that "What goes on in the Commission is but a reflection of what goes on in the wide world." [120] In this shift of emphasis one may perceive the dangerous and insidious tendency whereby materialism can seriously disturb the natural order by destroying a true sense of values.

XI. Covenant on Economic, Social and Cultural Rights

A. Preamble and Source of Rights

Pursuant to the instructions received the Commission on Human Rights has drafted two Covenants on Human Rights. One deals with the "Economic, Social and Cultural Rights," and the other with the "Civil and Political Rights." Although each draft Covenant commences with a Preamble, the same Preamble is used. It reads as follows:

> The State Parties hereto,
>
> Considering, that, in accordance with the principles proclaimed in the Charter of the United Nations, recognition of the inherent dignity

and of the equal and inalienable rights of all members of the human family is the foundation of freedom, justice and peace in the world,

Recognizing that these rights and freedoms derive from the inherent dignity of the human person,

Recognizing that, in accordance with the Universal Declaration of Human Rights, the ideal of free men enjoying freedom from fear and want can only be achieved if conditions are created whereby everyone may enjoy his economic, social and cultural rights, as well as his civil and political rights,

Considering the obligation of State under the Charter of the United Nations to promote universal respect for, and observance of, human rights and freedoms,

Realizing, that the individual, having duties to other individuals and to the community to which he belongs, is under responsibility to strive for the promotion and observance of the rights recognized in this Covenant,

Agree upon the following articles. . . .

Following an article dealing with the self-determination of peoples, the Preamble to the Covenant on economic, social and cultural rights contains fifteen articles. Since the Preamble adopted much of the language of the Universal Declaration, and therefore, both evidence the same moral fibre, what has been said previously about the Declaration also applies to the Covenant. It is extremely important to note, however, that Dr. Malik, in reference to the phrase "recognition of the inherent dignity and the equal and inalienable rights," asserts that it "stresses the notion that these rights belong to the nature of man." He also asserts that the recital in the Preamble "recognizing that these rights derive from the inherent dignity of the human person . . . refutes any notion that an external power such as a benevolent government or even the United Nations, 'granted' man these rights." He concludes that "It is difficult to think of a stronger or more adequate language with which to express the law of nature." [121] Although these statements, coming from the chairman of the Commission on Human Rights, are indeed welcomed and help alleviate some of the fears of those who are profoundly interested in the philosophical basis of the Covenant, it is apparent that "stronger" and more "adequate" language *could have been selected.* It is true that the word "inalienable" connotes an inability to take away those rights. It can not be asserted, however, that a statement that rights "derive from the inherent dignity of the human person" necessarily implies that they are God-given and of Divine origin. It is not fair to say that to raise such a question is to quibble over words. Although the statements of Mr. Malik, that rights are not derived from the State or the United Nations, are reassuring, if such a concept was to be expressed, surely the language of the American Declaration of Independence could have served as a starting point. In fact, the phraseology of the Covenant, on the question of the source of the rights secured, has caused serious thinking persons to have grave doubts concerning the "philosophy behind the proposed covenants." [122] These doubts are well founded when one considers the statements made by some of the proponents of the covenants. For example, on one occasion it was stated that there was no substance to the discussion as to the source of human rights. In answer to former Governor Miller of New York, who criticized the Covenant on this score, Judge Proskauer replied: "And all this discussion about whether Human Rights come from God Almighty or from nations—I cannot find any real substance in that. I do not think that it makes any difference whether you philosophically think that God gave these rights or that nations gave them. . . ." [123] Obviously there is a vast difference as to the underlying philosophy. People such as Governor Miller and Judge Burke, whose philosophy is founded upon the understanding of the Divine origin of natural rights, would not agree that the underlying philosophy is not important. In the words of Judge Burke: "How could they [rights] be inalienable if the source of those rights is the State? If the State is the source of human rights, what is to prevent the State from taking them away?" [124] It is clearly impossible, therefore, to agree that the matter of underlying philosophy is not a matter of importance.

B. Content and Scope of Covenant

Article I provides that each State that is a party to the Covenant "undertakes to take steps, individually and through international cooperation, to the maximum of its available resources, with a view to achieving progressively the full realization of the rights recognized in this Covenant by legislative as well as by other means." It also provides that the parties to the Covenant "undertake to guarantee that the rights enunciated in this Covenant will be exercised without destruction of any kind, such as race, color, sex, language, religion, political or other opinions, national or social origin, property, birth or other status." Together with Article II, pursuant to which States "undertake to ensure the equal right of men and women to the enjoyment of all economic, social and cultural rights," these provisions are designed to prevent discrimination on any basis whatever.

The substantive articles dealing with the economic, social and cultural rights, include the right to work, to "just and favorable conditions of work," [125] to "form and join local, national and international trade unions," [126] to "social security," [127] to special protection "to motherhood and particularly to maternity," [128] children and the family,[129] to "adequate food, clothing and housing," [130] to "an adequate standard of living," [131] to health,[132] to education,[133] and to science and culture.[134]

A reading of the vast scope of the "rights" guaranteed will indicate the reason for the need of Article I pursuant to which a State undertakes *to achieve progressively* the full *realization* of the rights recognized in the Covenant. However, although the "available resources" of a State may make it impossible immediately to realize the rights enunciated in the Covenant, it is clear beyond any doubt that to the extent that any right is enjoyed it cannot be exercised on a discriminatory basis. For example, Article XIII recognizes "the right of everyone to education." Although it is entirely understandable that in a particular State there may not be enough available facilities for all children,[135] yet to the extent that facilities are available all children must be admitted without discrimination on any ground.

Since 1948, when the Commission on Human Rights was able to agree on Article XVII of the Universal Declaration, which proclaims the right to private property, all attempts to include the right to private property in the Draft Covenant proved unsuccessful. The French Delegation advanced a proposal on the right of property but from the many objections and difficulties raised it was obvious that the inclusion of a provision on the right to private property was hopeless. The right to private property has suffered in the wake of the present ideological conflict torturing the world. It would have been unthinkable for those countries that have pursued the policy of nationalization of property without adequate or effective compensation to include any provision dealing with private property and the rights of its owners. As has been stated elsewhere, "The issue basically involves one's philosophy concerning the right to own private property." [136] Although it is still true that "Since Magna Carta, in England and in countries whose jurisprudence is based upon the heritage of the common law, the due process of law concept is too firmly imbedded in the municipal law of those countries to tolerate any appropriation of private property without adequate compensation," [137] it is startling to observe "the extent to which the non-communist world has been communistically softened or frightened." [138] Dr. Malik adds that "It seems incredible that in these economic matters, which reflect indeed much more than mere economic divergencies, the Western world is so divided on itself as to be incapable of presenting a common front against communism." [139]

XII. Covenant on Civil and Political Rights

A. Nature of Rights Secured—The Covenants Compared

Unlike the phraseology of the Covenant dealing with the economic, social and cultural rights, Article 1 of the Covenant on Civil and Political Rights uses mandatory terms calculated to ensure the present enjoyment of the rights established. The so-called economic, social and cultural "rights" are really statements of objectives to be achieved "progressively." In the Covenant on civil and political rights, however, Article 1, Subdivision 1 states that "Each State Party hereto undertakes to respect and to ensure to all individuals within its territory and subject to its jurisdiction the rights recognized in this Covenant, without destruction of any kind, such as race, color, sex, language, religion, political or other opinion, national or social origin, property, birth or other status." Although this is a clause against discrimination of any kind, what is significant is the fact that a State by signing would *presently undertake to respect and ensure* the rights stated in the Covenant to *all individuals*. The provision is mandatory and applies to nationals and aliens alike. Subdivision 2 of Article 1 places the burden for observance of these rights by States as follows: "Where not already provided for by existing legislative or other measures, each State undertakes to take the necessary steps, in accordance with its constitutional processes and with the provisions of this Covenant, to adopt such legislative or other measures as may be necessary to give effect to the rights recognized in this Covenant." This subdivision places upon a State the obligation of bringing its national legislation up to the standards established in the Covenant in those States where such a standard is not provided for by existing law. Subdivision 3 of Article 1, again in terms of present duty, specifies further the obligation of the States. It provides that each State undertakes:

(a) To ensure that any person whose rights or freedoms as herein recognized are violated shall have an effective remedy, notwithstanding that the violation has been committed by persons acting in an official capacity; (b) To develop the possibilities of judicial remedy and to ensure that any person claiming such a remedy shall have his rights thereto determined by competent authorities, political, administrative or judicial; (c) To ensure that the competent authorities shall enforce such remedies where granted.

Article 1 in its entirety, therefore, leaves no doubt that actual rights are ensured, and that they are to be enjoyed today by everyone. If they are not presently enjoyed in a country, steps must be taken by the appropriate agency of the State to conform to the standards of the Covenant. Furthermore, there must be an effective remedy for any violation of these rights. Although possibilities for a "judicial remedy" are to be "developed," by part (a) of Subdivision 3 of Article 1, any person whose rights have been violated "shall have a remedy" which must be enforced by competent authorities.[140] Clearly, the draftsmen of the Covenant were well aware of the basic difference between the natural rights restated in the Covenant on Civil and Political Rights, and the rights proclaimed in the Covenant on Economic, Social and Cultural Rights. Under the Covenants, although all States would bind themselves to *strive to achieve* all of the rights of the Covenant on Economic, Social, Cultural Rights, no State could deprive anyone in its jurisdiction of the basic civil and political rights proclaimed in that Covenant.

B. Scope of Rights Secured

The Covenant, containing eighteen articles, secures the right to life, liberty and security of persons, peaceful assembly, freedom of thought, conscience and religion, freedom of expression, freedom of association, and freedom from slavery, torture and cruel or inhuman treatment.

Other rights are also proclaimed. Article 8 forbids imprisonment on the ground of inability to fulfill a contractual obligation. Article 9 proclaims the liberty of movement and the freedom to choose a residence. Article 11 declares that "All persons shall be equal before the courts or tribunals," and sets forth with particularity the rights of a person accused of crime. Although Subdivision 1 of Article 12 prohibits *ex post facto* laws, Subdivision 2 states that "Nothing in this Article shall prejudice the trial and punishment of any person for any act or omission, which, at the time when it was committed, was criminal according to the general principles of law recognized by the community of nations."

The Covenant is emphatic, perhaps even to the point of undue repetition, in its condemnation of discriminatory practices. In addition to Article 1 pursuant to which each State undertakes to respect and ensure all rights to all individuals within its territory without distinction of any kind, Article 18 provides:

"All persons are equal before the law. The law shall prohibit any discrimination and guarantee to all persons equal and effective protection against discrimination on any ground such as race, color, sex, language, religion, political or other opinion, national or social origin, property, birth or other status."

The rights contained in this Covenant are historic and traditional. All who would favor an International Bill of Rights would favor likewise the inclusion of these rights, since they are indeed basic and natural. The Covenant has done no more than to stress the fact that discrimination will not be tolerated, and has subjected previous formulations to greater refinement.

The rights enunciated in this Covenant are not set forth in general terms. They are specific and often contain a statement of the allowable limitations. For example, the Covenant does not simply provide that "Every one shall have the right to freedom of thought, conscience and religion." Article 14, which proclaims this right, goes on to say that "This right shall include freedom to maintain or to change his religion or belief, and freedom, either individually or in community with others and in public or private, to manifest his religion or belief in worship, observance, practice and teaching." Subdivision 2 provides that "No one shall be subject to coercion which would impair his freedom to maintain or to change his religion or belief." Subdivision 3 provides for a legal limitation on the rights prescribed as follows: "Freedom to manifest one's religion or beliefs may be subject only to such limitations as are prescribed by law and are necessary to protect public safety, order, health, or morals or the fundamental rights and freedoms of others."

Freedom of speech and expression, set forth in Article 15, also illustrates the particularity employed in the drafting of the various rights. It states in Subdivision 1 that "Everyone shall have the right to hold opinions without interference." Subdivision 2 states that "Everyone shall have the right to freedom of expression." It clarifies this by adding that "this right shall include freedom to seek, receive and impart information and ideas of all kinds, regardless of frontiers, either orally, in writing or in print, in the form of art, or through any other media of his choice." Subdivision 3 acknowledges that the exercise of the rights in paragraph 2 "carries with it special duties and responsibilities." It adds: "It may therefore be subject to certain restrictions, but these shall be such only as are provided by law and are necessary, (1) for respect for the rights or reputation of others, (2) for the protection of national security or of public order, or of public health or morals."

C. Inalienable Nature of Certain Rights

Although it cannot be said that the Covenant possesses a clear statement of its philosophical basis, such as is found, for example, in the Declaration of Human Rights drafted by the National Catholic Conference, the Covenant does unmistakably indicate that certain rights are inalienable. The proof of this awareness is not found solely in the Preamble which speaks of the "inalienable rights of all members of the human family," but also in the specific provisions of Article 2. This article states the circumstances under which a State may derogate from its obligations under the Covenant. Subdivision 1 provides: "In time of public emergency which threatens the life of the nations, and the existence of which is officially proclaimed, the States Parties hereto may take measures derogating from their obligations under this Covenant to the extent strictly required by the exigencies of the situation, provided that such measures are not inconsistent with their other obligations under international law and do not involve discrimination solely on the ground of race, color, sex, language, religion or social origin."

Although the preceding Subdivision authorizes a legitimate derogation from certain rights, Subdivision 2 states that "No derogation from Articles 3, 4, 5, 7 (paragraphs 1 and 2), 11, 12 and 13 may be made under this provision." The Articles from which no derogation can be made, even under the extreme circumstances described in Subdivision 1, cover the following rights:

Article 4 covers the right to life; Article 5 ensures freedom from torture or cruel, inhuman or degrading treatment or punishment; Article 7 covers the right to liberty and security of person; Article 11 declares that "all persons shall be equal before the courts or tribunals," and specified the rights of persons accused of crime; Article 12 prohibits retroactive criminal laws (*ex post facto* laws);

Article 13 states that "Everyone shall have the right to recognition everywhere as a person before the law."

Article 3 contains two important subdivisions: Subdivision 1 states that "Nothing in this Covenant may be interpreted as implying for any State, group or person the right to engage in any activity or perform any act aimed at the destruction of any of the rights and freedoms recognized herein or of their limitations to a greater extent than is provided for in this Covenant."

Subdivision 2 is of particular importance because it specifically answers one of the major objections aimed against prior drafts of the Covenant. It states that "There shall be no restriction upon or derogation from any of the fundamental human rights recognized or existing in any contracting State pursuant to law, conventions, regulations or custom on the pretext that the present Covenant does not recognize such rights or that it recognizes them to a lesser extent." This provision conclusively answers the objection that has been so vigorously voiced that, by adopting the Covenant, Americans would lose the rights presently guaranteed by the Bill of Rights of the Constitution.[141]

XIII. Some Criticisms of the Covenants on Human Rights

A. Fundamental Opposition to an International Bill of Rights

Although the truly final drafts of the Covenants on Human Rights have not yet been completed, some of the major criticisms can nevertheless be stated in brief. On certain matters the lack of agreement, if not strong opposition, was felt even within the ranks of the Commission itself. On the all-important issue of methods of implementation, for example, the proposed provisions that the Covenant grant to individuals and organizations the right to file complaints alleging violations of rights were promptly rejected.

Since it seems clear that the criticisms that were aimed at the prior drafts of the Covenant will also be voiced in opposition to the present draft Covenants, they will be stated as representing opposition to the adoption of the latest available drafts. In fact, it is fair to assume, that, in some circles the opposition will be intensified insofar as the new International Bill of Rights will contain a Covenant on Economic, Social and Cultural Rights. Even those groups that seemed favorably disposed to a Covenant on Human Rights embodying rights relating to life, liberty and the other traditional rights, opposed a Covenant dealing with "so-called economic and social rights." [142] In a Committee Report of the Section of International and Comparative Law of the American Bar Association, the view was expressed that the nations of the world at this time are not in a position "to take on the mandatory obligation to provide social and economic rights—if rights they are." [143] It was added that "Social and economic rights must await an evolutionary development of world opinion." [144] It is suspected that those who agree with the views expressed in this Committee report will still object to the Covenant on Economic, Social and Cultural Rights, notwithstanding the fact that the draftsmen were well aware not only of the applicability of the evolutionary process but also of the fact that these "rights" are presently *objectives* that should be achieved at the earliest possible time. This awareness is made crystal clear by the exactitude of the phraseology of Article 1 of the draft Covenant pursuant to which the States undertake *to take steps to achieve a full realization* of the rights enunciated. It will be remembered also that the Article mentions (as a possible limiting factor) the "available resources" of the States. Furthermore, by the language "with a view to achieving progressively the full realization of the rights recognized" in the Covenant it wishes to give impetus to the necessary evolutionary process. The Covenant would in all events play a part in influencing attitudes helpful in reducing existing discrimination.[145]

Perhaps the most basic criticism of the draft Covenant stems from the firm belief that such a Covenant is improper in the present status of international relations. Those that share this view feel that a Covenant on Human Rights would be an invasion into the internal life of a nation. In the language of the Charter of the United Nations, they say that such a Covenant would interfere with a matter "essentially within the domestic jurisdiction" [146] of a State. This argument stems from the traditional doctrine that international law is the law between States, and therefore it cannot concern itself with individual human rights. More specifically, it represents the view that it is improper and not within the purview of international law to concern itself with the relations of State with its own citizens.[147] In reply to the foregoing arguments and criticisms it has been pointed out that a Covenant on Human Rights would merely be an implementation of the mandate of the Charter of the United Nations. The Charter contains more than mere exhortations on the matter of human rights and, therefore, such a Covenant is a necessary offshoot of the principles and purpose of the United Nations calculated to *promote* and *encourage* respect for human rights and fundamental freedoms.[148] In this connection one would do well to keep in mind the words of Professor Jessup who writes that "It should at the outset be agreed that the Charter of the United Nations creates rights, for individuals, rights which are stated in the basic instrument in general terms and which are to be defined more precisely in an International Bill of Rights." [149] Under this interpretation of the Charter of the United Nations, respect for human rights and the taking of action in furtherance of their observation and realization is obligatory.

A second source of criticism stems from the belief that there is no connection between the observance of human rights and the maintenance of international peace. This argument has been emphatically answered by the limpid statement that it "ignores history." [150] It can also be shown that although Subdivision 1 of Article 1 of the Charter of the United Nations declares that a purpose of the United Nations is "To maintain international peace and security," such is not the only purpose. Subdivision 3 of Article 1 states that another purpose is "To achieve international cooperation in solving international problems of an economic, social, cultural or humanitarian character, and in promoting and encouraging respect for human rights and for fundamental freedoms for all without distinction as to race, sex, language or religion." The Charter, therefore, codifies what seems apparent to so many others, namely, that under the Charter, matters of human rights are of international concern. It is beginning to become apparent that in some circles the words "domestic jurisdiction," may become the new shibboleth to attain the results formerly made possible by the use of such words as "State equality," "sovereignty" and "sovereign equality." [151]

B. Constitutional Objections to Covenant on Human Rights

Another objection is predicated upon the assumption that an International Bill of Rights would be unconstitutional in the United States because it goes beyond the treaty-making power of that country, which consequently, it is thought, could not ratify it. Those sharing this view also maintain that such a treaty is beyond the realm of the federal power because it would involve an invasion of the rights of the various states of the United States. This latter view, in a federal state such as the United States of America, implies that matters of human rights are of local concern and are not a proper subject of national legislation or international treaty.[152] Since this objection stems mainly from certain leaders of the American Bar Association it is of particular interest to note that in 1944, in a very useful monograph prepared by the American Bar Association entitled *The International Law of the Future,* it was stated, as previously indicated, that "Instances are numerous in which states have assumed obligations with respect to the treatment of their own nationals." [153]

In order to appreciate this particular objection and the seriousness with which it is urged, several matters should be mentioned. The first pertains to Article VI of the Constitution of the United States which states: "This Constitution, and the Laws of the United States which shall be made in Pursuance thereof; and all Treaties made or which shall be made, under the authority of the United States, shall be the supreme Law of the Land; and the Judges in every State shall be bound thereby, any Thing in the Constitution or Laws of any State to the contrary notwithstanding."

Although under this clause of the Constitution treaties are the *supreme law of the land,* it is not legally correct to believe that all treaties, when ratified, *ipso facto* become part of the law of the land in the sense that their provisions must be given effect by the courts.[154] The distinction between "self-executing" and "non-self-executing" treaties is well known to constitutional lawyers. This distinction found expression in the celebrated case of *Foster v. Neilson,*[155] wherein Mr. Chief Justice Marshall distinguished between a treaty provision that "operates of itself," and one that states that something more shall be done, in which event "the legislature must execute the contract, before it can become a rule for the court." [156] Professor Wright explains that a self-executing treaty refers to a treaty "which imposes an obligation upon the United States of such a character as to be applied by the courts," whereas, the obligation of a non-self-executing treaty "is of such a character that execution belongs not to the courts but to the Congress, the President, or the treaty-making authority." [157] In other words, the non-self-executing treaty may very well impose a duty on the Congress to pass laws to implement the provisions of the treaty. However, the courts are not bound to apply the treaty provisions until such time as the implementing statute is actually passed.

In spite of the clear phraseology of Article 1 Subdivision 1 of the draft Covenant on Economic, Social and Cultural Rights, and Article

1 Subdivision 2 of the draft Covenant on Civil and Political Rights, it has been seriously maintained that the Covenant will be "self-executing," and hence, if ratified by the United States will become ready-made law for the whole nation.[158] Under the latter Article, a State undertakes *"in accordance with its constitutional processes . . .* within a reasonable time *such legislative or other measures as may be necessary to give effect* to the rights recognized in this Covenant." This language manifestly involves an undertaking to enact legislation, where and if necessary, to give effect to the rights affirmed in the Covenant. Furthermore, the view that the Covenant will not be a self-executing treaty has been accepted by the United States Government. Mr. John N. Cates, Jr., writing in the Department of State Bulletin, stated that it was "clear beyond any possible doubt that the provisions of the Covenant will not become part of our domestic law until the necessary domestic legislation has been enacted." [159] Mr. Cates adds that "The rights of individuals would be preserved and protected not under the Covenant but under the domestic legislation adopted." [160]

This objection was dramatically highlighted by the California case of *Sei Fujii v. The State of California.*[161] In this case the District Court of Appeals of California held that a California statute which prohibited aliens ineligible to citizenship from acquiring land within the State of California was in "direct conflict with the plain terms" of the human rights provisions of the United Nations Charter,[162] and hence land granted to a Japanese did not escheat to the State. The *Sei Fujii* case was not the first to raise the question of the effect of the Charter provisions upon domestic law. In a Canadian case entitled *Re Drummond Wren,*[163] a landowner succeeded in having a covenant declared invalid which forbade the sale of his land to "Jews or persons of objectionable nationality." The Canadian court held that the covenant was invalid as repugnant to the public policy enunciated in the United Nations Charter, a treaty to which Canada was a party. It was the *Sei Fujii* case, however, that caused much alarm in the United States as to what might occur in the United States if a Covenant on Human Rights was ratified. If a decision such as *Sei Fujii* was possible under the Charter and the Declarations, without a binding treaty on human rights, it was clear to those who opposed the Covenant, that with a binding treaty terrible things would happen to the "rights" of Americans.

Actually, there was no doubt among constitutional and international lawyers that the California District Court had misconstrued the provisions of the Charter.[164] Under the *Foster v. Neilson* doctrine the human rights provisions of the Charter were not self-executing, and apart from any action taken by the Congress to implement them, it was not for the court to apply those provisions in the decision of the case. The *Sei Fujii* case was appealed to the Supreme Court of California where the statute which denied to aliens ineligible to citizenship the right to own realty was declared invalid as being inconsistent with the equal protection clause of the Fourteenth Amendment.[165] Notwithstanding the fact that the lower court opinion has thereby been completely overturned, it has been stated that "the movement for the protection of human rights would have been spared what has proved rather an embarrassment than an aid," [166] had such a decision never been rendered.

Moved by their distrust of the treaty power and of the executive power in foreign affairs, the opponents of the Covenant have urged a constitutional amendment designed to limit the treaty power and that of the President. This proposed amendment, spearheaded by Senator Bricker and certain members of the American Bar Association, has received serious consideration by bar associations throughout the country. The Association of the Bar of the City of New York, in an exhaustive report by the Committee on Federal Legislation and the Committee on International Law,[167] concluded that the proposed amendment was undesirable and unwise on the score that since "no treaty need be self-executing . . . no constitutional amendment is needed to afford protection in this field." [168] Judge Manley O. Hudson, in an address before the American Society of International Law, stated frankly that he did not "share the alarm" felt by some of his colleagues in the American Bar Association and hoped that "they will find time to re-study the whole matter with perhaps more attention to the vast structure of the actual instruments" being concluded by the United States.[169] Professor Dickinson, who refers to the proposal to amend the constitution by imposing limitations on the treaty power, holds that "These are counsels of exaggeration and fear to which we can ill-afford to listen." [170]

The problem of a proposed constitutional amendment has nevertheless become extremely acute. In view of the crippling effect that such an amendment could have upon the power of the President in world affairs, its adoption would be nothing less than disastrous. This has been recognized not only by Bar Associations but by

President Eisenhower as well. Since one of the proposed treaties that has led to the proposed Bricker Amendment is the United Nations Covenant on Human Rights, Secretary of State Dulles, recognizing this fact, in order to attempt to forestall action on the Bricker Amendment, has promised that the United States would not sign such a covenant. For the obvious purpose of dissuading the Senate from adopting the proposed amendment Secretary Dulles, before the Senate Judiciary Committee, promised that the United States would not sign either the United Nations Covenant on Human Rights or the United Nations Covenant on the Political Rights of Women. This statement, emanating from the Secretary of State, who speaks with the authorization of President Eisenhower, is most discouraging to the proponents of an international Bill of Rights. What is more important is the fact that it may seriously place in jeopardy American leadership and may call into question the American sincerity of purpose in the cause of human rights.[171]

On this important question it is submitted that Professor MacChesney has correctly stated that the basic issue is "whether this country is presently prepared to adopt a Covenant containing minimum standards of human rights and to take international responsibility for the effective implementation of these standards." [172] The argument that the Covenant would lower the American standard of rights presently enjoyed under the Constitution, also cannot withstand the force of examination and scrutiny. It is elementary that the goal is to raise the level of human rights wherever it is lower than the standard established by the Covenant. It is preposterous to assume or otherwise intimate that an obligation under any treaty would violate constitutional rights. It has been stated officially that the Covenant could not by its specific provisions reduce any of the present rights enjoyed by Americans under the Constitution.[173] The goal, obviously, is not to detract from rights presently enjoyed by individuals anywhere, but rather, to assure a minimum protection to individuals everywhere. Perhaps the best evidence in support of this allegation that the Covenants would lower the existing standard of rights, is the lack of a provision in the Covenant protecting private property.[174] Assuming that the Covenants were to be adopted it would be nothing short of absurd to urge that the protection afforded private property by the Fifth and Fourteenth Amendments would thereby be repealed. The purpose is to ensure rights where they are not presently enjoyed, and not to lower the standards of those countries where human rights are made inviolate by a constitutional provision.

XIV. Conclusions

A. Concern over Human Rights

The preceding survey was designed to demonstrate the tremendous concern that the international community has shown in the field of human rights. Regardless of whether it can be said today that the individual is a subject of international law, it is apparent that a whole body of international law is evolving for the exclusive benefit of the individual. Whether the individual is regarded as the subject or object of international law seems relatively unimportant provided the individual is assured, at the very least, his natural rights. This assurance, to be effective, must be more than the protection presently afforded only to nationals abroad. The existing doctrine that an injury to an individual is internationally an injury solely to the State of which the individual is a national should be extended.[175] The individual should be legally competent effectively to vindicate a violation of his own rights above and beyond any claim that may be asserted by the State because of the injury to what has often been called its "national honor."

History has shown that the protection of nationals abroad is only part of the broader problem of the protection of the individual. Although the law may be said to be inadequate and archaic in this branch, there is at least a basis for a minimum protection where a national of one State unjustifiably suffers an injury at the hands of another State. The more crucial problem deals with injuries inflicted by a State upon its own citizens and nationals. It is in this area that effective international machinery is lacking; that humanitarian intervention dared to venture; and that the United Nations, through the Covenant on Human Rights, has proposed to afford *to all individuals everywhere* a minimum protection of their basic human rights. Notwithstanding the voices of those that oppose international intervention in the field of human rights an irretractable cornerstone has already been laid in the new structure of international protection of human rights. Although the evolutionary process commenced many years ago, with the establishment of the United Nations a new peak was reached in international cooperation. International recognition of human rights had become a reality with the adoption of the Charter of the United Nations. Although the foundation was firm much remained to be done.

B. Foundations of Effective Action

When the entire problem of the international protection of human rights is dispassionately evaluated, several conclusions emerge as indispensable conditions if human rights are to be guaranteed everywhere in the world.

The first would involve a recognition of the fact that there is a definite relationship between respect and observance of human rights and the maintenance of international peace. As expressed by former President Truman: "So long as the basic rights of man are denied in any substantial portion of the earth, men everywhere will live in fear of their own rights and their own security." [176] From this fundamental fact it also becomes clear that the protection of human rights can no longer be regarded as a matter of "domestic jurisdiction" or local concern. Not only has the community of nations been vitally interested in human rights, but it has now become apparent that their observance is one of the conditions for the maintenance of peace.

A second condition for the effective protection of human rights everywhere involves the drafting and universal acceptance of an International Bill of Rights. This is made necessary to assure individuals everywhere that, regardless of the existing state of the law in a particular country, certain basic rights are to be enjoyed by people everywhere in the world. It is no answer to say that this project is unnecessary because the constitutions and laws of most countries provide for basic natural rights. As indicated previously, these rights may be denied a whole segment of a population. Even if these rights are found in local laws they are not always enforced. It may, therefore, become necessary to invoke an international protection. Although it is to be regretted that from a reading of the present draft Covenant on Human Rights one does not see a perfect statement of the fundamental basis of the rights proclaimed, the Commission on Human Rights is on the right path in its efforts to draft an International Bill of Rights. There is no question that much remains to be done before even a minimum of agreement is reached on matters of implementation or enforcement. Nevertheless, the path is clear and the duty cannot be shirked. Although it is unlikely that the time is ripe for a Court of Human Rights, with compulsory jurisdiction to hear cases of violations of human rights provisions, such a court still remains as a goal to be achieved. Although the goal is presently probably far distant, it may include a court with power to declare illegal national laws in violation of the International Bill of Rights. Part of this ultimate goal may include the right of the individual to have access to such an international tribunal after having exhausted the remedy afforded by the country involved. Again, it is not responsive to say that agreement cannot presently be had on such proposals. It is admitted that the world is dealing with an evolutionary process. Yet, it is the duty of all those that can help to lend assistance to this worthwhile aspiration. This aspiration can never be achieved without some form of effective international organization. There is no doubt that the United Nations provides the necessary international organization. Its effectiveness depends entirely upon the good-will of its Member-States which in turn depends upon the support of the people. In this manner, there can develop a definite sense of sincere respect, if not loyalty, for the international organization that is striving to promote the observance of fundamental human rights everywhere in the world. This project, not only needs, but deserves, the backing of world public opinion. World public opinion should strongly support the efforts of the United Nations in the present project for the promotion and recognition of human rights. The world community cannot ignore inhumanities anywhere in the world. To do so would turn back the pages of history. It would mean that the world has failed to learn the lessons of history that were so costly and heartbreaking.

C. World Leadership

As has been indicated, although much remains to be done, much has already been accomplished. With the dawning of the realization that freedom has no frontiers [177] new horizons were opened to the international community. It now remains to complete the work that has already taken root. The work is of the utmost importance. Few undertakings can claim a more noble goal than the one that seeks to assure man his natural rights and to free him from misery and bondage.

In this undertaking the United States cannot falter in its position of leadership. All will agree that the position of the United States entails a grave responsibility. It is no exaggeration to say that "We stand at the crossroad of our civilization." [178] This leadership, which cannot be shirked, must be both material and moral. There must be continuing efforts to ameliorate the underlying religious and philosophical foundations of an International Bill of Rights. Yet, if complete success cannot be achieved in the beginning, the efforts cannot be relaxed nor can people of good will join the ranks of the obstructionists. There can be no decline in the spirit of reconciliation. The ideological conflict must be waged with sincerity of purpose. The natural rights adherents must raise high the torch of enlightenment. Although the spirit of compromise is the indispensable lubricant of international relations and all understanding, it can never be misunderstood as a compromise with principle. There is no compromise with the basic thesis that natural rights are God-given and hence, cannot be withdrawn by any State. What is presently maintained, however, is that if a violation of this unalterable principle is committed by any State, the international society will undertake to vindicate the rights of the individual. Whereas formerly there existed no effective remedy, it is now proposed to give the individual a status recognized by the international community even against a person's own country. The fundamental issue should not be made to suffer in a sea of legal irrelevancies. For the United States, the simple question is presented whether it will continue in its role to elevate the standard of the inalienable rights of man. There can be no doubt that "Our good faith as a member of the United Nations, as a champion of individual liberty is being judged by our readiness to cooperate." [179] Cooperation is indeed the minimum requirement for the United States, a country that has historically earned its position of leadership. It cannot now suffer an adverse judgment in the eyes of the people of the world.

Economic Systems and the Individual

by Dr. Arpad F. Kovacs
Professor of History,
Graduate School, St. John's University

The Commercial Revolution and Mercantilism

The collapse of the Western Roman Empire and the waves of barbarian invasions destroyed trade and industry in Europe and in the Mediterranean. When international trade, after the Crusades, revived again, the strategically located Italian city states became its middle-men. Venice and Genoa were the focal points, the New York and London of their times. Here the luxury articles of the East were exchanged for the gold of the West. But this trade was small in volume because of transportation difficulties over the caravan routes and Alpine passes. However, in spite of its diminutive quantities, it brought tremendous riches. "Venice was built on pepper," ran a contemporary saying.

After the discoveries of Columbus and Vasco da Gama, a great geographical shift took place. Henceforth trade with the Far East sought the Atlantic sea coast wherefrom it could reach India and the spice islands directly by boat. The new centers of this direct trade developed first in Portugal and Spain, then successively in the Netherlands, France, and England.

The character of this new western trade differed in many ways from the commerce of the Italian city states. It ceased to depend on caravan transportation. It became entirely water-borne. Bulkier articles could be carried on the large sail boats plying between Western Europe and points overseas. By the end of the sixteenth century, due to her strategic location, the Netherlands emerged as the center of this activity. What Venice and Genoa were to the Levantine trade, Antwerp and Amsterdam became to the new colonial trade. Antwerp rose especially fast in importance.

> Thither flocked . . . bankers and merchants, attracted by its favorable location at the crossroads of the old and new trade routes. By the middle of the sixteenth century, more than a thousand foreign merchants—German, Spanish, Portuguese, English, Danish, and Italian—were residing at Antwerp. Every week, two thousand wagons came into the city, to exchange wares with the four hundred ships which daily entered its harbor. A Venetian ambassador of the time declared that as much business was done at Antwerp in a fortnight as at Venice in a year.[1]

Not only greater quantities of goods could be brought in now from the old areas of trade, but also new types of goods appeared as a result of ample cargo space in the holds of ocean-going vessels, in contrast to the scanty space afforded by camel backs or mule packs. The large volume and cheap water-borne transportation gradually reduced the price of colonial goods so that more people could buy them. Unlike before, when international trade was essentially a luxury trade, the new colonial goods like tobacco, sugar, tea and cotton became *articles of mass consumption.*

In consequence the markets grew steadily in size, requiring larger capital, entirely new credit operations, warehousing and distribution. This vastly enlarged commercial activity caused such fundamental changes in the economic life of Western Europe that the overall effect was nothing less than revolutionary. It was during this commercial revolution that modern capitalism and modern economic institutions like joint stock companies, produce and stock exchanges, mass marketing techniques, credit operations, etc., developed and that an influential and numerous middle class arose.

The Middle Ages were permeated with religious motives even in the field of economic activities. Man and his salvation, rather than profit and riches, was the principal aim. Commerce and industry were in the hands of the guilds. They too were deeply imbued with the religious spirit and strictly banned profiteering or competition. They were functional organizations aiming at supplying the needs of the community. Beyond that they would go only when they sent their products to the great fairs. The price charged was to be a just price or the cost plus a fair amount of profit. This would seldom allow them any luxuries. Some of the guilds did grow rich, however, but only as organizations. The individual members, as a rule, could not amass wealth at the expense of the other members. Rich merchants or industrialists in the guild-controlled world of the Middle Ages were a great rarity and developed only at the end of the period. Some cities with exceptionally favorable strategic locations rose to great power and their merchants and craftsmen became princes of wealth. But such cases as the Hansa towns, the Italian, Flemish and Dutch city states were the exceptions. Their wealth was due as much to political and military as to commercial and geographical factors.

In the average medieval town, service was the motto, a mutual service for the benefit of all. He who would work mainly for profit or financial aggrandizement could find a place in it only with difficulty, if at all. The social ideal of this world was not the successful business man; the very atmosphere of the Middle Ages was inimical to it. Work then was a way of life and not a means to attain riches. The profit motive spurred human activity only in exceptional cases. The vast majority of the people sought the attainment of riches and rewards of a spiritual rather than of a worldly kind.

The discoveries jolted the medieval world out of its comparatively stable and quiet conditions. The fabulous tales about the newly discovered world acted as a stimulant to enterprise and thought alike. Although there were vast resources to be tapped and great wealth to be amassed by individuals or private companies, the state, however, quickly laid its heavy hand on the new sources of wealth, and the new trade gradually settled into well regulated grooves. The governments encouraged exports to obtain gold, but imports were curtailed or altogether forbidden in order to stop the flow of money outside the national boundaries. The more gold and precious metals that could be accumulated, it was held, the stronger would be the national economy and the power of the state. "I believe," said Colbert, the great minister of Louis XIV, King of France, "that agreement is fixed upon the principle that it is only the abundance of money in the state that determines its greatness and power." [2] That gold could provide everything, was the common belief, as exemplified by the might of Spain, which could obtain so much of the precious metals in the Americas. By the middle of the seventeenth century it appeared that aside from mines, colonial and foreign trade were the only means to get it.

Trade, however, as it was looked upon during the seventeenth century, was something unchangeable and constant. The idea of progress was as yet insufficiently understood; nor was expansion recognized as a general movement benefiting all. The view prevailed that expansion could take place only at the expense of some one else.

> The commerce of all Europe is carried on by ships of every size to the number of 20,000, and it is perfectly clear that this number cannot be increased, since the number of people in all the states remains the same and consumption likewise remains the same; and that of this number of ships the Dutch have 15,000 to 16,000, the English about 3,000 to 4,000 and the French 500 to 600. . . .
>
> It must be added that commerce causes a perpetual combat in peace and war among the nations of Europe, as to who shall win the most of it. . . .
>
> Commerce is a perpetual and peaceable war of wit and energy among nations. It is carried on by 20,000 vessels and this number cannot be increased. Each nation works incessantly to have its legitimate share of commerce or to gain an advantage over another nation. The Dutch fight at present, . . . with 15,000 to 16,000 ships, a government of merchants, all of whose maxims and power are directed solely toward the preservation and increase of their commerce, and much more care, energy, and thrift than any other nation.
>
> The English with 3,000 to 4,000 ships, less energy and care, and more expenditures than the Dutch.
>
> The French with 500 to 600.
>
> Those two last cannot improve their commerce save by increasing the number of their vessels, and cannot increase this number save from the 20,000 which carry all the commerce and consequently by making inroads on the 15,000 to 16,000 of the Dutch.[3]

The result of such views could only be a war of all against all. Consequently, desperate struggles raged between Spain and England, Holland and Portugal, Holland and France, and finally between France and England for the final hegemony. These wars inevitably fostered national feeling. The new middle class, increasing steadily in number and wealth, embraced the new national feeling and supported king and government with fervor. With the "my country right or wrong" attitude, the national monarchs could easily make this strong and wealthy class rally behind their thrones in support of the national cause.

> The chief impulse that the Commercial Revolution brought to the growth of national states came from the rise of the middle class and their alliance with the monarchs in the attempts to destroy the anarchy and decentralisation of the feudal system.[4]

We have seen that after the great discoveries of Columbus and da Gama the center of weight of European civilization shifted to the Atlantic sea coast. Before the shift, the city states dominated trade and industry. Hence the early tendency of the shift, aside from seeking strategic location, was to settle among the cities of the Netherlands. But cities were now small vessels to hold forces whose energies were generated by world-wide influences. The advantage of the territorial states of Western Europe was that they offered a broader base for the new forces. Since trade after the discoveries was going to spread out over large markets with goods for mass and not luxury consumption, the national territorial state was a much more logical receptacle for it than the tiny units of the cities. The future belonged to them. In the struggle of these giants for final supremacy in the new world the city states were eliminated.

And yet there were a great number of them. In Flanders and Italy there were "star clusters" of city states. "Between the Italian and Flemish cluster, across Swabia and the Rhineland, there stretched a star-riband of looser mesh and lesser luminosity in the likeness of the milky way. . . ." [5]

In this huge centralized organism, represented by the kingdom-state or national territorial state, the guild societies of the towns quickly withered away. The guilds in fact lost their local character and became nation-wide in scope. In the next chapter of Western history, the problem was to discover how the new Italian and Flemish way of life could be lived, on the kingdom-state scale, by the Western World as a whole.[6]

In the early days of the towns the local market absorbed all their activities. Because the medieval town had natural limits, i.e., sustenance, no further aims had to be served. The national state, on the other hand, expected the guilds to work harder in order to accumulate surplus for export, assure the flow of gold, and increase the power of the king. The state recognised no such natural limits as the medieval town; it was not satisfied with sustenance. Primarily, it aimed at unlimited expansion "because its objective was not sustenance but gold." [7] As an economic system Mercantilism was an advance only insofar as through the national state it enlarged the scope of activities. "Mercantilism simply extended to a wider area of the state the economic feeling of the town." [8]

> Generally it may be said that Mercantilism is of greater interest for what it attempted than for what it achieved. It certainly paved the way for its successors, and the discussions which went on throughout the seventeenth and early eighteenth centuries eventually bore fruit, although chiefly through the criticisms they called forth. Great change in the society which most statesmen had taken over from the Middle Ages did not occur; that was reserved for their successors.[9]

If then Mercantilism merely enlarged the scope of the medieval town, if it was more an attempt than an achievement, what, therefore, is the significance of the Commercial Revolution?

The city state was stamped out but the intellectual vigor and the new outlook stimulated by the contact and interaction of so many cultures after the discoveries could not be stamped out. As in ancient Greece, after her discoveries in the Mediterranean, the curiosity of the West to discover more and to inquire into wider fields remained as strong as ever. In fact, it was the new individual who became the most significant result of all the upheavals of these revolutionary times. He was "economic man," the precursor of the self-made man of the industrial revolution and the "rugged individualist" of the nineteenth century. Economic man would no longer fit into the calm tempo of life as it had existed in the guild society of the medieval town. He would think in terms of world-wide colonial trade or nation-wide markets. Success for him would mean riches which now, since the Reformation, would in many cases be considered as a sure sign of belonging to the select, to those few who were predestined to enjoy even higher rewards in the hereafter. The unity and simplicity of Christian society were gone. Its firmament, formerly dotted with star clusters of city states was now rent apart by huge national ones, bent upon aggrandizement, power and military glory.

After 1688, England was engaged in a long struggle with France over supremacy in the colonial world. In this bitter struggle which is often called the "Second Hundred Years War," France lost her overseas empire and Great Britain emerged as the undisputed lord of the Seven Seas. In 1815 she was a world power. Her position at that time compares well with the position of the United States in 1919. Neither the England of 1815 nor the United States of 1919 had a serious rival. And both of them were in the midst of a tremendous industrial revolution.

The First Industrial Revolution

There are several reasons why the first Industrial Revolution took place in England. Perhaps in the first place should be mentioned her abundant mineral resources, especially coal and iron; secondly, her insular position, which saved her from being overrun by hostile armies. It prevented her also from wasting a great deal of her national energies in maintaining huge armies for defense. Instead, by cleverly manipulating the balance of power in Europe, she was able to direct her national energies into colonial expansion. She became, as a result, the greatest trading nation with a large and wealthy middle class furnishing an ever increasing market for industrial goods.

The heavy industries played a large part in this development, especially metallurgy and mining. In the latter, one of the greatest problems was to pump the water out of the shafts and tunnels. At first, animal power was used to drive the pumps; later in the eighteenth century, Newcomen's atmospheric steam engine found wide application. It was a clumsy affair using about thirteen tons of coal a day to provide seventy-five horsepower. In 1775 there were 130 of them.[10]

In this year also, Watt's steam engine was first installed to pump water for strictly industrial purposes. The water, pumped into a reservoir, was led to fall over a wheel, which in turn drove the industrial machinery of the plant of the Boulton Manufacturing Company, near Manchester. Watt's engine was built in this plant which had many skilled craftsmen of the metal working trades. Other firms and other nameless craftsmen helped to make the success of this engine possible, so that it emerged as the symbol of British know-how. Also the better steel which could be produced by this time, the better casting and machining methods and all the minor skills, products of decades of slow improvements and experimentation, had to be fused together, in the accomplishment of the greatest and most significant single act of the industrial revolution.

Henceforth the Watt-Boulton combination, that is, the steam engine, driving a pump which filled a reservoir, spread rapidly in England. Such machines raised water to drive works of various kinds or the bellows and forge hammers of the steel industry. "If Watt had done no more than this, he would have established a claim to a place in the front rank of British inventors." [11] But he refused to rest on his laurels. His mind remained busy until he developed a device whereby the reciprocating movement of the piston could be turned into the rotative movement of a fly wheel. Through a transmission belt the power of his engine could be directly applied to the driving of machinery. He took out the first patent in 1781. In this same year, Boulton, his business partner wrote to the inventor: "The people of London and Birmingham and Manchester are *steam mill mad*." [12] It was, indeed, a correct estimate of the situation.

Watt's invention and the improvement of his engine came at a time when inventors were busy in other fields of industry. In textiles especially, one invention or improvement followed the other. The new textile machinery quickly became the other factor which, together with Watt's engine, was responsible for the industrial revolution. But other industries joined the parade. As a result of a new casting method in metallurgy, a great demand arose for steam power, because hardware of all kinds could now be mass produced. Earthenware followed suit and found wide acceptance by the growing middle class.

> Once the new goods were on the market, their use became general in a very short time, and there grew up in connection with their production, a kind of industrial system as novel as the goods themselves. Just as in the early twentieth century the appearance of the automobile was followed by the rapid extension of its use and by the development of an almost new industrial setup for manufacturing it, so in the eighteenth century popular response to the appearance of cotton cloth, cast iron, and earthenware dishes led to the rapid development of their manufacture. This in turn brought reduced prices which led to still further extension of sales.[13]

This large scale meeting of the steam engine with production machinery was the very heart and soul of the industrial revolution. It produced a new, radically different form of manufacturing, the steam mill, which brought to the factory an army of workers to serve the machines. This gave rise to new social classes: the new type of capitalist, usually self-made men, who had carved out a career for themselves amid this surging welter of new conditions; and the army of industrial proletariat whose life was degraded and always on the brink of misery as the helpless victims of the new order. Mechanization spread rapidly because competition was fierce. In 1801 Watt's patent expired and other firms began to build steam engines. By 1815 there were several thousands of them in operation. Between 1820 and 1830 the true mechanical engineer began to appear and with him came the precision tools of the modern industrial age. In half a century, ending in 1830, the pig iron production of the country increased by more than ten-fold, reaching almost 700,000 tons of annual production. In this year, when practically the entire industrial plant of England became mechanized, another event occurred, heralding a new phase of the industrial revolution: the first all-steam railroad was put into operation between Liverpool and Manchester. The railroad age had begun.

> It is difficult to calculate the effect of transportation upon the areas they serve. But it is basic to the development and functioning of national economy even to agriculture which remains subsistence farming without it but with such excellent means of transportation agriculture turns into a great source of wealth to the whole nation and every product of husbandry becomes an article of national value in the support of a large population.[14]

England at the beginning of the railway age had an excellent network of transportation routes which were the objects of study and admiration of foreign travelers. This network consisted of 4,000 miles of canals and navigable rivers and 21,000 miles of turnpikes which spread over an area not larger than one-fourth of France or the state of New York. These routes, excellently maintained, turned England into a closely integrated industrial neighborhood. In the manufacturing districts of the kingdom the growth of the industrial cities in 1820-1830 attained the maximum rate of growth which in some cases was phenomenal.[15]

It was a pulsating and robust economy full of expansive energies. Into it was thrown the exciting idea of a new means of transportation with unheard-of speeds and efficiency. No wonder that the coming of the railroad was greeted with enthusiasm, soon to turn into wild speculation. At first, however, there was no agreement whether the railroads, well known in the mining districts, where they had been hauling coal, should be horse-drawn or operated by steam. It was the force of habit and tradition because the coal cars, run on rails, which connected the mines with the canals, were drawn by horses.

The founders of the Baltimore and Ohio railroad in the United States were facing a similar dilemma. They decided to solve their problem by sending commissioners to England to study the operations of both types of transportation. The Stockton and Darlington mine railroad, which used both systems, offered excellent testing grounds for the American observers. They reported on February 4, 1829, that they boarded a train which went downhill with a load of seventy tons. Then the locomotive stopped and pushed back the train uphill with a speed of ten miles an hour. The report continues:

> We rode upon the wagons, counted the revolutions of the locomotive engine wheels, and marked the time, so as not to be mistaken as to the velocity. In addition to this, each quarter of a mile is marked upon the road by a post.[16]

There could be no question about the superiority of the locomotive in rail traction. In this same year the Rainhill trials of the newly built Liverpool-Manchester railroad furnished additional proofs. Stephenson's famous "Rocket," which won first prize in these trials, became the symbol of the new age in transportation. So many railroad schemes were promoted that the feverish speculation ended in the panic of 1837. After that, however, solid railroad building became a reality. By the end of 1843 there were nearly 2,000 miles open to traffic. Five years later there were 5,000 miles in operation. This tremendous progress, stimulated a great extension of business.

> Investment in the past had been in terms of thousands of pounds each. . . . The new railroad companies which applied for charters in the three years from 1844 to 1847 had an authorised capital of 180,138,901 Pounds.[17]

The railroads not only encouraged financial operations and mobilization of capital on such gigantic scales, but also promoted manufactures of all kinds. Railroad construction required a huge number of crossties, gravel, masonry, pipes for drainage and culverts, bridges, stations, round houses, repair shops and an enormous amount of rails. For the building of the locomotives and cars they needed more iron and steel, lumber, upholstery, glass, and a hundred and one other things.

England indeed went through a series of unprecedented booms. Directly, producers of every kind of material needed in railroad building participated in them; indirectly, the entire national economy profited greatly from this transportation revolution. Wherever a new line was built, gangs of construction workers spent their payrolls. In 1849 employment figures reported to Parliament show that 188,000 men were at work on lines not yet open.[18] Speculation raised prices of land and realty values by leaps and bounds as towns found themselves at the hubs of the ever increasing railroad network. England was entering upon her brightest period of economic development. She was already the most powerful nation in the world. She was now going to be the wealthiest by organizing the economy of a vast colonial and free trade empire spanning the entire globe.

The Consequences of the First Industrial Revolution

Not least of the many consequences of the industrial revolution of England was the rapid rise of a new and influential class, the self-made men who were mostly behind these startling innovations in industry and transportation. If, in the majority of cases, they were men of humble origins, their children certainly acquired a different status in society.

> Where, then, did the industrial capitalists originate? As in eighteenth-century England, they came largely from the yeomanry, or the independent farmer class. All one has to do is compare the names of those who were becoming important in manufacturing in the 1850's and later in the 1870's: and it at once becomes apparent that next to no transfer took place.[19]

The great French Revolution was preceded by a philosophic movement. The Enlightenment had conditioned the minds of the people of France for the radical change carried out by the National Assembly and the Convention. Voltaire, Rousseau and the Encyclopedists were the precursors of the Jacobins. The liberal movement in Britain had a similar intellectual vanguard in that group of philosophers known as the Classical Economists. Adam Smith, who started the school, was followed by Malthus, Ricardo, James Mill and others. They set the pattern of thought which insisted on clearing away the obstacles before free enterprise which, just as free thought and human reason were to accomplish the same miracles half-a-century earlier in France, was now preparing to usher in a new millennium. In England the new age of mechanical wonders stimulated men's imaginations and quickened the pulse of public action. The Classical Economists became immensely popular.

> . . . their notions were widely popularized, and their general views as much the order of polite conversation in British parlors as Rousseau's notions of the state of nature had been in the French salon of

half a century before. The bourgeois entrepreneur had replaced the noble savage of the previous century as the recipient of idealized admiration.[20]

The result of this agitation was the parliamentary reform of 1832, a great victory for the middle class. But much had to be done yet. Trade and industry had to be freed from the shackles of an antiquated system of state controls. It was not an easy task. With the abolition of the Corn Laws the first great breech was laid in the Chinese wall of Mercantilism. Many more measures followed, so that by 1860 practically all commodities could enter or leave Britain without paying duty. Free trade became an accomplished fact.

It was one of the great revolutions of history. Like the "Silent Revolution" of the United States which has fundamentally changed the everyday life of the masses in this country this great transformation wrought both by the industrial revolution and free trade in Great Britain was working with relentless force, but without causing catastrophic upheavals. It derived its strength mainly from the triumph of the new middle class which now set out to reshape the mother country and the empire. It was the triumph of the self-made man, the product of the Industrial Revolution.

The credo of this movement was freedom, but freedom of a kind motivated by the effort of the strong to exploit resources, natural as well as human resources. Elbow room for those who had tough elbows. The new technology, particularly, as related to the machine harnessed to steam power, had given a tool to the strong and the rich with which they could unlock nature's forces, open the sides of mountains, penetrate the jungle and the prairie, build steam ships and railroads, and connect it all in a swift and efficient system of transportation, with the result that Great Britain became the hub and the workshop of the world.

It was a gigantic undertaking which called for hundreds and thousands of enterprising men who would some day become captains of industry or members of the board of directors. The world was wide and its treasures unfathomable. The call was irresistible. Like the Jacobins of the French Revolution who set forth to carry the torch everywhere in the world, the self-made men of this revolution set out to organize trade and industry everywhere. British know-how was in high demand. In India alone, millions and millions of profits were waiting for those who would bring the capital and engineering talent. All the Latin American republics were open for enterprise.

Canada, Australia, even the United States needed capital and help, let alone the more backward areas like the whole Near East. If the urge was great, the zeal equally matched it.

England thus became the workshop of the world. From her factories, manufactured articles of all kinds were sent to the five continents to be exchanged for raw materials. As the Classical Economists, notably Adam Smith, had pointed out in advance, a great division of labor developed under the stimulation of free competition. Production of raw materials naturally sought only soils and climates of optimum conditions. Elsewhere the competition of prices made it uneconomical. Argentina became the meat supplier of England, Australia of her wool, the United States, cotton, Canada, wheat, Portugal, wine and Denmark, butter and eggs.

The mother country was not only the workshop which clothed and supplied the world with industrial goods, she exported know-how as well as capital. Great Britain became the banker and the chief industrial and engineering consultant of the world. The building of railroads, harbors and industrial plants, the organization of credit and insurance operations called for it all. More and more investments were made abroad. In 1850 they amounted to one and a half billion dollars. This sum rose to six billions by 1875 and to ten billions in 1900.[21] These huge investments, huge in terms of nineteenth century monetary values, poured back a steady flow of dividends, which, in turn, were reinvested. It was this enormous circulation of gold, tapped constantly in the City, which made Britain so wealthy.

> The cities were growing fast as were the numbers engaged in manufacturing. One of the most notable features of changing incomes and positions was the great increase in the middle and professional classes, and as an evidence of increasing wealth the number of domestic servants rose from 900,000 in 1851 to 1,500,000 in 1871, although . . . the cost of maintaining them had much increased.[22]

After 1875 agriculture began to decline. Overseas competition made it unprofitable. A good measure of England's wealth was that her aristocracy could turn their great estates, the main food producing areas, into parks, game preserves, and play grounds.

It was a free world as far as economics were concerned. Any one who had the ability could succeed in it. And he who had actually succeeded received the unqualified recognition of society. The Victorian age believed in equality of opportunity but not in the equality of man. Like its manners, its social gradations were also stiff, rigidly maintained and rigidly observed by the population.

> My Lord and My Lady insisted no more on their precedence of rank than did the butler and housekeeper. If in great houses physicians and surgeons, except the most renowned, were expected to dine in the housekeeper's room and not with the family, on the other hand, the etiquette demanded by the servants among themselves was quite as strict. In houses with large staffs, the under servants, even if they had their meals with the upper, were not allowed to speak in their presence, and after the meat course, the upper ones would adjourn to the housekeeper's room for their pudding and wine, leaving the first footman to preside for the remainder of the meal in place of the august butler.
>
> The details might vary from house to house but the main point is that the gradations of precedence of the master class were not resented but copied and insisted upon among the working class themselves.[23]

Such society had little understanding for those who could not make good, and they were left in their self-condemning position. The social ideal of the age was the successful industrial leader, who now found it possible to join the ranks of the titled and privileged members of society. It could have no feeling for those who "by their very unsuccess have proved their worthlessness." This philosophy, in spite of its belief in progress along social, political and economic fields, thoroughly materialized western thinking. In losing the concept of man as a creature made to the likeness of God, it increasingly saw man with no higher destiny than the economic. It measured freedom as a physical power rather than moral power and "identified progress by the height of the pile of discarded moral and religious traditions." [24]

This system began by asserting the rights of man and of the individual. Both the American and the French revolutions vehemently insisted on it. No one realized, however, that the Industrial Revolution would give tools into the hands of individuals which might enable some of them to rise above the average, amass huge fortunes, and finally acquire great influence and eventually political power. It was a rapid revolutionary transformation. In changing the rights of the individual into the rights of the *rugged individual,* it encouraged a system which loudly proclaimed a freedom which the strong too often turned into license. As for the non-rugged, they were left too frequently the freedom to starve.

This system, as it spread in the wake of the Industrial Revolution, carried its philosophy, its prejudices, its disregard for the weak and the poor, and its adulation of success all over the world. It spread its parliamentary institutions, its free competition and the works of its classical economists everywhere. It had its missionaries who were usually followed by the flag which in turn was followed by marines. Unlike the guilds of the Middle Ages, it sought not to satisfy human needs, but rather to attain profit. Because of its competitive spirit it had a voracious acquisitive tendency. "If you don't get in," was the saying, "somebody else will, so you might just as well do it yourself." There was no limit to it, at least not in the moral sense. It was a free for all for the strong. It sought self-justification in success. It lacked social sense and knew no distributive ethics. Its doctrine was made to serve the interests of the rich. Freedom was its slogan but in reality it was by wealth, for wealth, of wealth. No wonder that the Holy Father condemned it in the sharpest terms.

> For the ancient workingmen's guilds were destroyed in the last century, and no other organisation took their place. Public institutions and the laws have repudiated the ancient religion. Hence by degrees it has come to pass that workingmen have been given over, isolated and defenceless, to the callousness of employers and the greed of unrestrained competition. The evil has been increased by rapacious usury, which, although more than once condemned by the Church, is nevertheless, under a different form but with the same guilt, still practiced by avaricious and grasping men. And to this must be added the custom of working by contract, and the concentration of so many branches of trade in the hands of a few individuals, *so that a small number of very rich men have been able to lay upon the masses of the poor a yoke little better than slavery itself.*[25]

The word of the Pontiff, sounded at a time when Liberalism reigned supreme, remained for a long time the voice in the wilderness. This was a revolution driven forward by the incentive of dazzling success made possible by the new tools of the machine and speed age. Self-made man pushed even the state aside to have more elbow room. All he asked from the state was military and police protection. Otherwise it was to be a struggle for the survival of the fittest in which the prevailing biological theories gave the successful justification along scientific lines. But the theory of the survival of the fittest could easily be carried over and applied to the international field.

Germany could not introduce the industrial revolution on a large scale before the problem of unification was solved. This came in 1870. With it Bismarck introduced a parliamentary system and moderate forms of liberal institutions. The stage was set for building up an industrial plant. Coal and iron were available in large quantities. In Great Britain the industrial revolution was essentially the work of human dynamos who could operate with the speed of the railroad and the telegraph and the mass production techniques of modern factories. Germany, too, began to produce her human dynamos, who soon began turning out products in greater mass, in faster tempo. The late start of that country gave her the advantage of more advanced techniques. She could offer her products at lower prices and soon Britain found out that trade preferred to follow the price list and not the flag. Undersold and driven out of markets which hitherto had been considered her monopolies, the British quickly drew the conclusion and splendid isolation was abandoned. Rival alliances rose and henceforth it remained merely a matter of time when the two leading industrial and imperialist nations in Europe would appeal to the force of arms.

The American or Second Industrial Revolution

At the turn of the century America was already the greatest industrial power in the world. On the eve of the second industrial revolution her steel production surpassed that of England and Germany put together and the total value of her industrial products reflected the high productivity and standards developed in the nineteenth century. Hand in hand with this vast industrial plant went her agriculture, forestry and mining, furnishing a wealth of food and raw materials. At the same time, immigration reached record figures. Cheap labor was coming in at the rate of a million a year. These people, eager to avail themselves of opportunities in a country where opportunities were unlimited, increased her productive capacity and enlarged the consumer market. It was a land of plenty for all.

Industry in Europe in many respects was still ahead of the United States especially in quality products. Britain was still leading the world in the mechanical arts and Germany, ahead of all, had solved the problem of teaming up science with technology. But in one respect the United States was superior to all European countries, in her mass production techniques. This is best reflected in agriculture. In Europe the average yield per acre was much higher than in America, because Europe had plentiful cheap labor. The American economy from the earliest times was handicapped by lack of labor. This was especially true west of the Appalachians where abundance of land, the great fertility of the soil, and the thinly spread population over vast areas discouraged the growth of large numbers of poor people eager to work for low wages. Even in the oldest sections of the country the absence of poverty was obvious and striking to European observers. When Lord Howe's army landed on Long Island in the spring of 1776

> the British and Hessian invaders marvelled at the orchards, meadows, fields and well-filled barnes. As former peasants or slum dwellers, they exclaimed at the opportunities of a country in which a poor man could aspire to own a farm. Even more wonderful to these newcomers, accustomed to the bounties of nature being reserved for the gentry, was the privilege of every American to catch a string of bass, shoot a few canvas-back ducks, or pick a bucket of wild berries.[26]

Later the rapidly growing cities on the east coast received waves of poor immigrants who, at least for some time, remained paupers and slum dwellers. But they could always migrate West, where they could start an independent existence. The poor, in other words, during the early days of the nation, were the exception and not the rule, as in Europe. This country has never known the peasant type of village dweller which formed the bulk of Europe's population. As soon as a European peasant set foot on American soil he caught the spirit of individual independence, the spirit of initiative and self-reliance. Consequently, even though he stayed in the East to earn his living, he was no longer the same downtrodden proletarian, resigned, as he would have been in the old world, to his fate. He too, like other fellow-workers, became restless, eager to improve his lot. This restlessness, which caused a large turnover in American factories, was aggravated by the constant land booms and waves of migrations. Huge numbers of replacements were broken-in, only to be lost again. The tendency was naturally to replace them by machines. These, however, require skilled operators. It was important therefore to break up every operation into simple components where skill was not required. This "unskilled component" was later one of the basic factors in the development of mass production techniques. It serves also to explain why Europe could not develop such assembly line methods like the present American industrial system. The European method of apprenticeship produced highly skilled all-round men in all trades. Such people would have indignantly rejected the unskilled component principle. They were master craftsmen, conscious of their status and able to perform all the operations required from raw material to finished product. No such traditional obstacles existed here.

The resulting market was large, not only in the physical sense, but also, and mainly, in its purchasing power. With the absence of peasantry in the country and large scale pauperism in the cities, the market was able to buy more in spite of the low density of the population. The American farmer produced cash crops. The European farmer, operating on a much smaller acreage was forced to be self-sustaining. He had little surplus to sell, whereas the American farmer sold his products for cash and purchased his needs for cash instead of producing them at home. Soap for instance ceased to be a home product in this country at a time when more than half of the population still lived on farms. It was much simpler to buy factory-made soap which could be produced in great mass and at a low price as the by-product of the stock yards. But it could not have been mass-produced so cheaply had the market not existed for it. In Europe factory-made soap remained a luxury article bought only by the upper and middle classes. The mass of the people used the home-made product.

This could also be applied to canned goods, but even more so to ready made clothing. No other industry has demonstrated it so tellingly as the shoe and clothing industry that mass-produced articles in this country did not run against mass acceptance. In Europe ready-made clothes were frowned upon to such an extent that they could not break down sales resistance. Here they became the prevailing brand gradually increasing in quality to such an extent that it rivalled the custom-made product.

Without such an attitude the mass-produced auto would have been unthinkable. In 1909 Henry Ford announced "any customer can have a car painted any color that he wants so long as it is black." Moreover, the chassis would be the same for all of these black cars. In Europe any manufacturer stating such a policy to abolish diversity would have promptly ruined himself. In this country, so long used to standard products and appreciating them for their low price and high quality, the announcement was taken with satisfaction and soon the black "Lizzies" became the landmark of the American countryside. Not only was Ford's famous Model-T car accepted with good-natured enthusiasm but also the idea of everybody owning a car. In Europe, where the auto was the plaything of the rich, the mass of the people never even thought of owning one. Here the public accepted it eagerly and plunged into the new venture with a spirit bordering on recklessness. And it was taken for granted that everybody could have a car and indeed should have one. Why not? No country had so much equalitarian optimism and so much sporting spirit which made the auto, the plaything of the leisure class of Europe, the everyday article of necessity and pleasure of the masses in the United States.

The first industrial revolution, technologically speaking, had not been completed in Great Britain until every line of industrial production was mechanized. That is until steam power and machine methods were introduced in the entire industrial plant of the nation. The second industrial revolution in this country meant a similar uniform application of a new principle, the assembly line. When assembly line methods or the continuous flow principle of production pervaded every line of manufacture we may say that the second industrial revolution completed its full cycle.

But the assembly line alone would not have created such revolutionary changes as we have witnessed in this country during the period following World War I. Without the automobile the assembly line would have come slowly. It was the motor car which brought it upon the scene with the momentum and effect of a revolution. The automobile and the assembly line thus became twin brothers whose mutual relationships have so fabulously accelerated the pace of our economic progress that we speak of it as a revolution. Not only in industry, but also in politics and social relations, it was truly a revolution which affected our daily lives, our standards and habits which we now designate the American way of life. So different, so high in its standards of living is the United States that it has become, of all the nations, the richest and mightiest, most admired and most envied if not the most hated on earth. It has created "Homo Americanus," a species of a special kind.

Henry Ford was not the inventor of the idea of mass-production. His stroke of genius was to apply it to the automobile. Mass-production techniques were well known in his time. It was his epoch making contribution to combine them so that the final result was the assembly line. It originated from his experiments in bringing the work to the workingman, who from now on would not be moving around but stay in line because the belt would bring the work piece to him. It was always the same work piece on which the men had to fit a part, always the same identical part. These were all interchangeable and manufactured to fine tolerances. They fitted exactly the same way. And there were many parts in an automobile. Altogether about five thousand pieces. Yet they all had to fit exactly the same way in spite of the fact that they were mass-produced. They all so much represented unskilled components that at any point of the assembly line any one of them would fit wherever it was intended to fit. This was the staggering task solved by Ford so superbly.

Yet the capstone was still missing in the arch which rose on the four wheels of the motor car; it was an economic arch which was to support the world's highest standard of living. Henry Ford put the capstone in it when he announced his minimum wage policy as the principal expression of his theory of high purchasing power. Without it the second industrial revolution was unthinkable. It was the *sine qua non* of the new era which was dawning on the American scene, in which assembly lines of all kinds were to pour forth not only cars but other goods of the greatest variety and abundance. But without a multitude of people with incomes high enough to absorb this cataract of goods at the end of each conveyor belt, the assembly lines would stop. When moving, they would be producing wealth; when standing, they would be producing unemployment of the most appalling proportions. America was yet to learn this lesson. At the time of Henry Ford's announcement of the minimum wage policy there was scepticism and mockery. Cartoonists depicted floor sweepers arriving to work in limousines and who, with fat cigars in their mouths, would grab their brooms and go to work—why yes, they would be getting five dollars a day when the prevailing rate was two dollars! The implications of the minimum wage were not fully understood. It presented a problem too complex for the times. The age was still steeped in the thinking of the nineteenth century, in the conditions created by the first industrial revolution. They were not favorable to a "philosophy of abundance." Free enterprise or *laissez faire* created an economic or social atmosphere for the survival of the fittest. It was still a raw age with both cut-throat competition prevailing and devious ways to avoid it in restraint of trade. The market was a prize to conquer and capture and not to serve. The attitude toward labor was exploitative. A minimum wage theory was, in consequence, taken as another manifestation of Henry Ford's eccentricities which would soon collapse under their own weight.

The first industrial revolution developed around the textile industry, one of the oldest manufactures in human history. It created no new commodity. Steam power and machine methods merely speeded up the output; the automobile was a different matter, but the public failed to realize the eventual and tremendous consequences of everybody moving around on wheels. However, it became increasingly apparent that adjustments would have to be made requiring the greatest efforts of all from the government down to the humblest worker, and that assembly lines unloading mountains of goods every day would require a new economic system fundamentally different from anything existing hitherto.

The problem, however, was too complex to be understood and there was no chance to analyze it coolly while there was still time. In 1914, the same year in which Henry Ford announced his minimum wage policy, World War I broke out. For the time being the country's energies were absorbed by it. When the war ended, the second industrial revolution broke upon the country with the violence of a storm. For years to come, although it created great psychological effects, its meaning remained obscure.

The First World War in itself caused revolutionary changes not only in the United States but also throughout the world. It ended the primacy of Europe in the constellation of world power. It caused a financial shift which suddenly made the United States the financial center of the world. The realization of her incomparable power dawned upon the world after the unconditional surrender of the enemy. America's enormous industrial power became the object of admiration by foe and friend alike. All this inevitably reacted upon the country and created a sense of exhilaration. America after the armistice faced the future with boundless confidence.

A new discovery was made! During the war, the assembly line proved to be an instrument of superior productive power and capacity. With comparative ease it could be converted to the production of any other article like tanks or airplanes and could pour forth these new items with the same efficiency and low price as it could produce automobiles. The instrument of fabulous bounty was here. America went wild and plunged into the revelries of the "Roaring Twenties." The story of insane real estate booms, wild promotions and still wilder stock exchange speculations is too well known to be described here in detail. It is more important to know what the underlying factors were which fed the minds of the people on seemingly irrefutable and recurring evidence that an ever growing prosperity was here to stay.

The driving of a car is an exhilarating experience giving a sense of power and independence to the driver.

> Someone has said that the Asiatic, long accustomed to humiliation at the hands of the lordly white European, will endure it no longer after he has once sat at the controls of a tractor or a bulldozer. Similarly the American who has been humbled by poverty, or by his insignificance in the business order, or by his racial status, or by any other circumstance that might demean him in his own eyes, gains a sense of authority when he slides behind the wheel of an automobile and it leaps forward at his bidding, ready to take him wherever he personally may please. If he drives a bus or a huge truck trailer his state is all the more kingly, for he feels himself responsible for the wielding of a sizeable concentration of force.[27]

It was, therefore, difficult, to resist the temptation to acquire a car, whether new or used, depending on the means of the individual. It did not take many years before the vast majority of adults had one.

> The result of all these developments was a headlong rush to buy cars on the part of innumerable people to whom the idea of becoming automobile owners would have seemed fantastic only a few years before. In 1915 there were less than 2.5 million cars registered in the United States. By 1920 there were over 9 million; by 1925 nearly 20 million; by 1930 over 26.5 million.[28]

Henry Ford alone could not satisfy the demand. A number of other companies entered the field and an avalanche of cars descended upon the market. Competition became fierce, prices went down, quality went up. New models came out every year or were featuring improvements of all kinds. Soon the temptation of owning a car changed to the temptation of owning the latest model.

An assembly line which is capable of turning out several thousands of cars a day is like a tree. Its branches are the sub-assembly lines which unload the main parts of the car like the engine, the body, etc., to the main assembly line. The sub-assembly lines have their own branches, which, in turn, have to be fed by a continuous flow of small parts, analogous to the leaves of the tree. The automobile concern often finds it simpler to order some of them outside, instead of manufacturing them at home. Sub-contracting has become a tremendous industry as a consequence, because, even if we take a small item like an electric cigarette lighter, to supply them all to an automobile firm of the size of the Ford Motor Company requires a volume of several hundred thousands of them annually. Considering furthermore that thousands of parts go into the making of a car, the number of special suppliers may also run into the thousands.[29]

In this way the main assembly lines affected a vast variety of businesses stimulating industrial activity all along the line. Aside from this general effect upon business, the manufacture of cars created entirely new industries. The distribution, sale, repair and servicing began to employ thousands and thousands of people. New roads were being built with feverish haste to satisfy the rising demand. The construction industries were booming. The demand for lubricants and fuel rose in steep curves and a gigantic oil industry was born. Tires called for millions of tons of rubber which created a practically new industry. Steel manufacturing was stimulated, as was plate glass, upholstery and paint. Tourism increased by leaps and bounds, for when America decided to go on wheels, movement became general in the country. To provide accommodations to this army of travelers grew into a major industry. The business of financing installment buying spurred credit activities and insurance of all types stimulated that line of business. So much stimulation brought on so much new activity and job opportunities that there seemed no end in view. American life was being transformed rapidly. More cars meant more industries, more industries meant more work, more work meant more purchasing power which meant more cars again. It looked like a circle which continuously returned to itself, continuously enlarging itself in the process. The car seemed to be the magic boot strap by which the country would never endingly keep on lifting itself into higher and higher standards. No wonder that people lost their balance of judgment and declared that there would be no end to this expanding prosperity. In anticipation of bigger and better things to come, values began to rise fantastically and the public, drugged by more and more irresponsible talk, began to live in a fool's paradise of fictitious wealth. Never was there such a frenzy of speculation. It looked as if speculation itself had been put on a super assembly line.

And yet the foundations were very shaky. The total income of the country in 1928 was large enough to guarantee a fair amount of well-being to each family. Actual distribution of wealth, however, was far from being satisfactory. The per capita income in 1928 was 749 dollars. This multiplied by five gives 3,745 for the average family unit which, in 1928, with much higher purchasing power of the dollar, would have amounted to a decent income. But there was no way of making this a reality. The country believed in rugged individualism more than ever which was a dangerous thing at a time when the assembly lines were pouring a flood of goods on the market. Purchasing power was the thing to create and not individual wealth. But no method of redistribution of wealth was known, nor would this age have tolerated any such attempt. Instead of increasing mass purchasing power, it was syphoned off the market. Instead of broadening the base of the market, it was narrowed down.

In the period of highest prosperity, that is between 1921 and 1929 incomes of over 100,000 dollars increased by 597 p.c., and incomes of over a million by 2343 p.c., whereas incomes of over 5,000 dollars a year only 92 p.c. This did not solve the threatening problem of overproduction. Sixty per cent of all American families of 1929 had an income of 2,000 dollars a year or less. This was the line of demarcation below which purchasing power to support the assembly lines vanished. This was the principal problem in the United States.[30]

And yet in a world wrecked by war and unable to recover from its devastation, the United States stood alone like a happy oasis in the desert, though most of it proved to be a mirage. The collapse was inevitable. When it came in 1929 in America, the rest of the world, still shaky from the ravages of the war, crashed down on this country. The loss of billions of foreign investments and war loans deepened the effect of the slump. The mirage of never-ending prosperity vanished and America was facing ruin. The shock had a terrific psychological effect as boundless optimism gave way to dark despair.

The period between September 1929, when the great crash started, to March 1933, when President Roosevelt began the New Deal, was a time of bewilderment and of divided counsel. For four years there was a continuous decline of employment and of prices. Doom settled upon the country because no satisfactory diagnosis could be given of the unprecedented collapse of the economy. Therefore, no cure could be found which might bring about quick recovery. Indeed there was no recovery to speak of during the six years of the New Deal between President Roosevelt's inauguration and the outbreak of the War in Europe in 1939. The remedy, if there was any, acted mainly along psychological lines. President Roosevelt could inspire hope with his vigorous leadership and energetic though ineffective measures. Even though improvements fell far short of expectations, there was relief for the unemployed. The upward curve of economic activity began slowly to rise but broke again sharply in the recession of 1937. Criticism now took courage. It was indeed the paradox of the age that while people were starving in the cities, the government ordered that crops be plowed under and animals slaughtered and buried in order to create scarcity. For scarcity, it was argued, as the result of the operation of the law of supply and demand, would increase prices, which, in turn, would stimulate production. The plan, however, failed and in spite of frantic efforts and lavish spending for pump priming purposes, no appreciable change was noted. Consequently, the enormous productive capacity of the country with all its assembly lines, the symbols of abundance, remained idle because of lack of purchasing power. It was a vicious circle which could not be broken until World War II arrived with its fabulous orders for armaments. America suddenly became the arsenal of democracy. The huge plants and millions of farms were called upon to arm and feed the world threatened by conquest. The country's productive capacity, as if by magic, was brought to life and the miracle of American production followed. When the smoke cleared away and the enemy lay prostrate, the world again looked at this country with envy and amazement.

In the heat of the political and ideological struggle stirred up by the Great Depression and the New Deal, a few things stand out clearly. In the orgy of speculation followed by World War I, nothing was done to assure a systematic broadening of the purchasing power of the masses. While the economic pyramid was rising fast, due to the productive capacity of the assembly line, its base was not being widened. It toppled over. The New Deal could not build a new foundation and reconstruct the pyramid on it in a few years. Only the total effects of World War II calling for exceptional efforts all along the line could accomplish this gigantic feat. The New Deal, with its labor legislation and farm relief, had paved the way for it. The New Deal erected the framework and World War II filled it with substance. Perhaps the enormous national debt left behind gives some idea of what that substance was.

In the light of all that has happened since World War I, it is evident that the captains of industry who after the Civil War seem to have dominated the American economy as well as the political destinies of the nation are definitely a type of the past. The second industrial revolution calls for new types of leaders much more conscious of the social purposes of production than their predecessors who were bent on selfish control, on cornering the market for quick profits, or on establishing exploitative monopolies.

In the new world brought about by the second industrial revolution, rugged individualism in the service of personal gain has no place in the economy. The nation has become too closely knit, too massively integrated to allow excesses of this kind. Personal achievement is still possible but not in disregard of the need of closely integrating every economic advance with the general social and economic requirements of the nation.

The Great Depression was caused by this lack of integration which calls for the most delicate and most balanced type of leadership. It could not be forthcoming during the fourteen years from 1919 to 1933 because the problem was not understood nor was there much inclination to understand it. Little could be accomplished in the following six years because by that time the *malaise* was far beyond human power to cure it quickly. But the years following World War II with their prosperity and sober views give us a clue for a better understanding of our complex economic system.

In a letter, dated July 7, 1952, written to the president of a Catholic social organization in France, the Holy Father made one of the most important pronouncements since the Encyclical *Quadragesimo Anno,* issued in 1931. The Pontiff's letter refers to this close integration of the economy not in the United States but generally speaking.

> Since employers and workers have a common interest in the healthy prosperity of the national economy, "why should it not be legitimate to give workers a just share of responsibility in establishing and developing this economy?" the Pope asked.
>
> How the fruits of labor are to be distributed is too weighty a matter to be left to the "free play of blind economic forces," he went on and requires intervention by the state as a coordinator.[31]

Coordination is the question and the dispute rages about its degree. The factors of the problem are:

1. The enormous and steadily rising productive capacity created by the second industrial revolution, and

2. How to distribute this wealth of goods coming off the assembly lines which now have been adopted as the standard manufacturing method from the loaf of bread to the ten-thousand ton victory boat.

The first factor has been a natural phenomenon, the result of a combination of elements inherent in the American scene. It arrived as a result of forces generated by typical American conditions. When it did appear its implications were not understood, the full significance of its revolutionary effects was submerged in the frenzy of jubilation over victory and ever-increasing prosperity. When, at last, the catastrophe of the Great Depression drove home the lesson that the emphasis in the new era was on distribution rather than profit, much controversy arose on problems and methods of effecting the former. Should there be a radical departure from the traditional American way of free enterprise? Should the state direct all the coordination or exercise only its supervisory functions and arbitrate disputes? Early, under the New Deal, the state had to intervene quickly, and, although the effort was only partly successful, the fact that the state did step in with great determination to act as a guarantee that further deterioration of conditions will be stopped, produced a great psychological effect.

When World War II made the wheels of industry hum as never before, and when after the war prosperity continued in spite of predictions to the contrary, the controversy tended to give more weight to the traditional American ways of free initiative. *Étatism* seems to have been accepted only as a temporary emergency measure.

In the historical perspective, the American, or, as we may call it, second Industrial Revolution, emerges with a mark of distinction for more than one reason. In the past some of the greatest civilizations foundered because they were unable to abolish the deep gap which from time immemorial has separated the rich from the poor. The Athenian Empire, after Pericles, broke down because she exploited the member states of the Delian League, which she had to do in order to keep her own poor proletariat happy. Rome offered bread and circuses to her own "poor white trash," but even these meager largesses were too much and they exhausted the resources of the empire. The French Revolution broke down in bloodshed because Robespierre's "Republic of Virtue" could not be established on a solid foundation of material plenty. Virtue alone could not satisfy the enfranchised and clamorous proletariat of Paris; there were too many hungry mouths to feed and the surpluses were scanty. Lastly, England's labor government struggled in vain to translate Socialism into economic plenty. The only plentiful thing was austerity.

Only the American social and economic system was capable so far in history to correct everybody's fortune. The first Industrial Revolution created a proletariat of appalling poverty and misery. To epitomize its effects, it made the rich richer and the poor poorer; it created industrial and financial capitalism, with its robber barons; it gave rise to socialistic movements of all kinds, reaching its acme in the Marxian type of bitter class struggle. In the industrial world, another large estate rose up, composed of armies of destitute and entire have-not nations.

In this gloomy picture the second Industrial Revolution in the United States stands out as a unique accomplishment. It wiped out the fourth estate in this country by raising its members into the middle class. America has achieved the dream of a classless society not because the proletariat seized power, as Karl Marx thought it should, but because the assembly line has produced such surpluses that there is plenty for all who can and care to work. High standards have become uniform in American society. To any foreign observer this is only too obvious. Class consciousness has vanished from the American community. A Jacobin come alive in this country today would proclaim every Main Street a *Place de la Concorde* where the only discord he could see would arise from the lack of parking space.

But, perhaps the greatest significance of the transformation of the American social scene arising out of this revolution is the amazing improvement in the social status of the laboring man who has been raised to that of the middle class as a full-fledged citizen. The stigma which had always been attached to the lowly types of menial work, has been wiped out. Literally a new type of man has been produced in the country non-existent before in the history of the world. Let's call him *faute de mieux, Homo Americanus* in contradistinction to *Homo Sibiricus* produced by the Soviet type of civilization.

Homo Americanus of the ditch-digging variety operates a behemoth machine which requires high skill and technical knowledge. He is an engineer sitting at the controls. The scrub woman of tomorrow might become a technician directing electronic devices from a switchboard. The proverbial hewers of wood and carriers of water have disappeared because *Homo Americanus* has developed higher occupational standards and with it higher occupational classifications and nomenclatures corresponding to the general rise of the fourth estate in economic standards to the ranks of the middle class and even higher.

But if this rise to the middle class has become so universal, it might be argued, mass must have diluted quality and the gain is merely quantitative. The transformation has certainly been revolutionary, and such sudden changes in social and economic conditions, it is to be remembered, do cause great dislocations in standards of quality and quantity; for the adjustments along institutional lines always lag behind. This cultural lag is a great drawback but one that seems to be inevitable. Among the first problems to be solved in the early days was the mastery of the crude methods of mass-production. Then came the refinements and now we see that quantity and quality rise at a steady tempo which shows an annual average of 2-5 per cent, depending on external factors of stimulation. But, whereas the rise in quantity may be measured, the increase of quality is a matter of speculation.

> . . . improvements in quality almost completely fail to assert themselves although they constitute, in many lines, the core of the progress achieved—there is no way of expressing adequately the difference between a motorcar of 1940 and a motorcar of 1900 or the extent to which the price of motorcars per unit of utility has fallen. . . . Moreover, even if we had the means of measuring the change in the technological efficiency of industrial products, this measure would still fail to convey an adequate idea of what it means for the dignity or intensity or pleasantness of human life. . . .[32]

The point of the preceding pages has been to show that all this tremendous change could happen only in the United States, where, because of special conditions, among which were large space, free institutions, high purchasing power and uniform standards, conditions were uniquely favorable for such startling developments. Although the British Empire had an even larger base, nevertheless, it lacked homogeneity. No mass market could develop there where conditions differed as greatly as in the case of India or Australia, Egypt or Canada; and the home base was too small in comparison to the total area of the economic empire.

In contrast the home base encompassed by the United States, as well as the "imperial" market, were both large and identical. To organize this space called for extraordinary efforts which were not hampered by rigid forms of tradition. It was done by a free people who plunged with courage and enthusiasm into this experiment. The result was the second Industrial Revolution. Aside from these basic factors, other circumstances hastened the process. The two world wars, for example, accelerated the shift of the economic center from Western Europe to the United States. Without them the revolution might have developed somewhat slower and without all the glamor and drama which accompanied the sudden rise of the United States as the world's foremost industrial, financial, and military power.

But eventually it would have come. The European powers were bound to lose their comparative position in leadership to those nations which had space, immense natural resources and uniformity of conditions. A country like France, even without the ravages of two world wars, could not have kept the pace of economic development. Even today, despite technological advances, she is too small an economic unit to provide a market necessary to stimulate mass production. She could not go through the same evolutionary processes which have led the United States to her industrial revolution. She lacked the broad base to rear a superstructure of that magnitude. That goes equally for Germany. Hence the efforts of the Western European powers to form an economic unit, a sort of United States of Europe to establish a large, uniform market as the foundation of assembly lines.

On the other hand, Russia has enough space to provide this foundation. It was this seemingly endless *Lebensraum* which tempted Hitler to gamble on military conquest. It is her inestimable natural resources which have been driving her Bolshevik rulers to prepare new five-year-plans for the industrialization of the country. The aim is to copy the United States and overtake her in productive capacity as a pre-condition of military strength. Will the mere fact that Russia has space and resources, homogeneity and compactness, suffice to launch her on the road toward material abundance? Will the fact that, as a result of the Bolshevik Revolution, she started out with a slate wiped clean of all hampering traditions, help her along? She has more space, more resources and greater manpower than the United States. Let us look into this problem which seems to be the central one of our age.

The Soviet System and the Race Between Russia and the United States

We have seen that a special set of conditions in the United States has produced a special kind of civilization. We have seen that space and great resources had much to do with it; that the evolution of the American economy finally reached its culmination in the assembly line; that during World War I it was found that the assembly line method of production could be adapted to any armament or piece of equipment; that any article to be mass-produced had to be taken apart to its smallest component and manufactured separately, after which it was put on subassembly lines, which in turn had to be brought together and assembled on the main assembly line; that all the operations on all the lines had to be reduced to their unskilled components, after which any worker, skilled or unskilled, could perform it; and that finally, the assembly line would pour forth a tremendous volume of goods. This in World War I and II was true of both small arms and the heaviest type of equipment.

For all these reasons it should be easy to adopt an assembly line system to a purely military economy where the cataract of goods rolling off the conveyors is absorbed by a huge army instead of a civilian market. This, for example, explains the astonishing performance of Russia in accomplishing her industrial progress without going through the automobile age. After thirty-six years of Bolshevik rule she has still no highway system worthy of mention. In fact, she did not even go through the first industrial revolution. She plunged right into the second. She built up an enormous industrial plant which is capable of turning out first class products. World War II has shown that her army could fight with weapons in many instances superior to those of Germany; and the Korean conflict has given us additional proofs. The MIG plane, the flak guns of her ground forces and her tanks indicate very progressive engineering and very advanced techniques. We hear, moreover, that she has produced the atomic bomb and that she is introducing automatic machinery in her mines and factories. In other words she is beyond the mere assembly line stage. She is introducing automatic methods of production which try to eliminate human work by substituting electronic controls. This is as high a stage of industrial development as it is possible to attain at the present.

But let the record speak for itself. In 1944, that is in the last full year of the war, when large parts of Russia were devastated, the Soviet industry produced, according to Stalin himself

> Up to 40,000 planes, more than 30,000 tanks, self-propelled guns and armored carriers, up to 120,000 guns of all calibers and up to 100,000 mortars. . . . Up to 450,000 light and heavy machine guns, over three million rifles and over two million tommy guns.[33]

This indicates a vast number of assembly lines and a very well developed industrial system with mines, railroads and a vast organization and controls. These figures, which represent one year's production, compare very well with production quantities in the same period in Western Europe and the United States.

> The figure for planes compares almost exactly with German production in 1944, a peak year, and is almost 40 per cent above the British peak of 26,500 aircraft in 1944, in which, however, nearly 30 per cent were medium and heavy bombers, planes larger than the Russians were making in quantity.[34]

As to tanks, the Russian effort was also very impressive in comparison to other production figures. The Soviet output in the single year of 1944

> was about two-thirds larger than the total German output *during the entire war,* about 20 per cent larger than the British production during the entire war, and more than three-quarters as large as American production in the peak year of 1943.[35]

Evidently very great emphasis was laid on this type of equipment. But artillery, always a favorite weapon of Russian armies, fared even better. One hundred thousand guns were turned out in this year, a figure which compares with the West in the following impressive way:

> Including naval guns in the case of Britain and the United States, the Soviet production of artillery in 1944 was about six-sevenths of the combined British and American production of all guns in the two countries' peak years of 1942 and 1943 respectively. Soviet mortar output in 1944 was about as large as British production *during the entire war* and only ten per cent less than *the entire American production* from July 1940 to July 1945.[36]

In an economy so thoroughly saturated by military considerations and run by military discipline, not profitability, but only production enters into the calculations. How much it costs to the economy or to the nation is entirely beside the point. Like Prussia in the eighteenth century, Russia is completely subordinating her national life to the support of a military organization so huge that it absorbs all the national energies. Although unquestionably there are great problems of organization, management and efficiency of production, nevertheless, neither bankruptcy nor depression ever threatens such an economy. Everybody is driven ahead to make superhuman efforts.

It is like building the pyramid in the times of Pharao. Then, too, great problems of organization, management and efficiency must have arisen, although the technological conditions were still so primitive that not even the wheel was known. The pyramids were built, nevertheless, and they were built very well; but no economy was served by it. On the contrary, the entire national economy was subordinated to the pyramid.

So it is in the communist economy where the pyramid is power, mostly of a military and police nature. In building up this power the assembly lines are kept busy day and night. Technically speaking, the assembly line, at least the visible portion of it, is the same in the totalitarian states as in the West. In the United States we see a huge distribution system of transportation lines, wholesalers and retailers who form, so to speak, a direct continuation of the assembly lines, integrating them with the national economy. Through this the vast stream of goods reaches the smallest hamlet. In Russia the army takes care of it all.

But we have seen that an assembly line must be fed by myriads of little parts daily entering the sub-assembly lines to take final shape on the main stem. Where do these masses of little parts flow from? It is here that we find the main difference between the American and the Russian type of economy now copied feverishly by China and imposed on all the Eastern European satellite countries.

As we have seen, in the United States there is a vast number of sub-contractors who supply the assembly lines. As independent business men, employing from a few to hundreds or thousands of workers, their greatest asset is their extreme flexibility which springs from freedom and independence. Such plants may supply only one assembly line, or several of them manufacturing a variety of products. They may be producing only a few tiny parts or quite complicated components for a major assembly line far away from their own establishment. There are thousands of such places in this country, some of which die off early; some just plod along; some grow into giant organizations. Through them, just as well as through all the assembly lines for which they work, circulates the life blood of the American economy.

They are the products of free enterprise. Their success depends essentially on the business acumen, inventiveness, drive, and energy of the owners or managers who may have to solicit orders in order to sell their products. They may compete fiercely with each other or may be tied down by a tight contract as the dependency of an assembly line. But always it is by their own free will that they are engaged in business, and not coercion or bureaucratic promotion. Always their motive is to make money, but in an emergency this motive may easily change into something much higher than mere profit-seeking. If working for a great cause, as they have shown several times, they can produce miracles by pooling all their resources, spiritual and physical.

If we compare this situation with that prevailing in totalitarianism, we find great differences. In Russia, where small shops run by private owners are unthinkable, the supply system can never be the result of competition or spontaneous growth. It may be the result of long experimentation but never of private initiative. No assembly line in Russia had grown from tiny seeds like Ford's plant. They are born in the board rooms of huge planning committees and arise as gigantic factories right from the blueprint stage. Such a system is clumsy, bureaucratic and lacks vigor, quick adaptability, inventiveness and initiative, which characterize the American way of doing things. Our sub-contractors may differ in size and capacity but they are a sturdy lot because competition automatically weeds out the incompetent. It is the purge of free enterprise, a more healthy and bloodless process than the communist purge. If their incentive is not only profit but primarily the winning of a great cause they form an unbeatable team among themselves and in conjunction with the big assembly lines, because with their flexibility they can unite high purpose with collective action, the speedup with ever diminishing costs, and mass methods with highly individualistic initiative.

This is *Homo Americanus* at his best who has evolved the system of mass-production not merely as a technological device, not merely as an economic procedure, but practically as a social principle. He has not applied it merely to the making of automobiles and appliances. The wheat farmer in Kansas, the suburban real estate developer, the aircraft factory, the shipyard or the diesel-electric plant all follow the same principle. When the country was called upon in World War II, after the fall of Malaya, to turn out synthetic rubber on a large scale, the problem was solved in due time. When atomic energy had to be produced, the mass production principle was introduced in laboratory research, in the mass manufacture of precision instruments and last but not least in precision construction where tons of materials had to be shaped, poured, or moulded to microscopic tolerances. It was all done on schedule.

> Most startling, however, is the application of the principle to military organisation. Of all pre-industrial types of organisations, the Army was the most highly formalised and apparently the most rigid. But the great Allied invasions of World War II were prepared and carried out as mass-production processes, with each officer doing only one highly specialised and largely mechanical task. He was seldom shifted from operation to operation, nor did he usually know where his piece fitted into the total. This application of the mass-production principle to the conduct of war was one of the most important contributions this country made to victory.[37]

And finally the success of the Berlin air lift was born out of the same social principle. It was certainly the most spectacular assembly line in history.

Social coordination for promoting mass-production has become a national characteristic. And yet the individual has not suffered in the process. The American people have not tended to develop an ant-heap-like mentality. Far from it! Individualism still thrives and there is still room for the development of rugged creative talent. The rewards may not be princely fortunes. It would not meet more with social sanction which was so lavishly bestowed upon it in the previous century. It is the incomparable strength of American society that side by side with collective organization for mass-production it could produce the highest type of individualism. Such a society, even if partly destroyed, by an atomic attack, would again and again restore its creative powers. Initiative and resourcefulness rising spontaneously out of nowhere, combined with collective action as a response to leadership, are its principal assets.

This is unthinkable in Russia, where collectivism operates not as a spontaneous social force but something imposed upon the masses from above. Initiative is reserved only for a few top officials and discouraged elsewhere. The assembly line and the mass-production principle are not an indigenous product but an importation, an artificial plant, which can be maintained and kept producing with enormous effort and wasteful practices.

The managerial class in Russian society [38] live under conditions which are appalling to a Western observer. The terror of the purge, of degradation into the ranks, of banishment to Siberia, or sudden liquidation is constantly stalking them. Production norms are always higher than what is physically possible to squeeze out of the plant and the crew. Material shortages plague them continuously, as a result of which, they have to resort to black market operations in order to feed the plant. This, in turn, forces them to juggle the books and create false balances, a practice which exposes them to blackmail and extortion; because black market operations and false statements draw heavy punishments if discovered. And the coming and going of inspectors and controllers is continuous. Their material rewards and social status are relatively high, but they have no freedom, no set hours of work, and their time, in fact, their whole life, belongs to the state. Their status as citizens and individuals is nil. They are the slaves of efficiency and fulfillment of production norms. At the same time, while they are driven mercilessly, they in turn have to drive the workers. But a lot can be squeezed out of slaves. In a society where standards are very low, even little rewards will produce great effort. The housing conditions of present-day Russia are so subnormal, crowding in the big cities so horrible, that the promise of improvement, or of a small apartment, acts as an extraordinary incentive.

Among the many methods of spurring workers on to superhuman efforts, Stakhanovism is a most cleverly conceived device. If a worker can turn out production in figures high above the maximum norms, he may receive rewards similar to the managerial class. This tricky method is the bunch of straw dangled in front of the starved mule, while the purge is the whip which works from the opposite end. During the 36 years of Bolshevik rule, a new generation has grown up which knows nothing except the standards they were born in. With promises and some rewards, with discipline and the routine life of the barracks, this generation is going around its tasks in the huge treadmill of Russia dreaming about the time when communism will eventually attain the earthly paradise they have heard about so much since their childhood. They do not realize that they are expecting the impossible because the Bolshevik system, by its very nature, will forever remain Paradise Postponed.

On the material side, however, on the production line, impressive results are obtained just the same. According to the Fifth Five Year Plan which will end in 1955 enormous accomplishments will be chalked up by the Soviet economy. In the light of Russia's record in the second World War it is worth while to examine the broad outline of this plan, the main emphasis of which is, as in all the preceding plans, on heavy industry, electric power and heavy transportation. No concessions are made to the consumer because a slave economy will never recognize the needs of the slave beyond food, clothing and some shelter. Russians will have no luxuries at the end of this plan nor presumably at the end of others following after. But there will be bigger and better tanks, bigger and better guided missiles and atomic bombs.

By 1955 Russia and her European satellites will be turning out 68 million tons of steel, 640 million tons of coal and 250 billion kilowatt hours of electric power. "This is what Western Europe is producing this year," [39] that is in 1952. In comparison the output of the United States in these three key items in 1952 was steel 108 million tons, coal 540 million tons, and electric power 395 billion kilowatt hours. This shows that Russia's industrial situation will compare very favorably, at least along these basic materials, with that of the United States. But that is not the most important consideration. We have to take the historical point of view to appreciate these figures.

Russia was no industrial power at the turn of the century, while Western Europe and the United States could look back upon a long record of industrial expansion. When finally Czarist Russia began to make some progress in building up her industrial plant, World War I, which was successively followed by revolution and the long civil war, set her back over a decade.

> It was in 1929 that the industrial revolution really got going in Russia—Stalin style. In just over twenty years it has put Russia into second place as an industrial nation. In the process it has completely changed the pre-1930 economic balance of power in the world.[40]

These figures do not include production of China, a huge country which may be considered as having arrived at the stage of industrial development at the present moment that Russia reached in 1929. Where will she be two decades from now with her enormous resources in material and in population and with Russian help? Or is it perhaps that China is too great an emptiness even for Russia to fill it up completely and that the Chinese hole will just drain Russian resources? One might just as well say that the free world outside of the Iron Curtain is too great a void for the United States to fill and that constant aid sent to Western Europe and elsewhere will merely sap the strength of this country.

If aid means the sending of experts and technicians, Russia is well situated. She has been making gigantic strides in increasing the annual production of expert personnel. The number of graduates in Russian technical and other specialized secondary schools are growing with frightening acceleration. Her engineering schools turned out 50,000 graduates in 1953 as against 19,000 in the United States.[41] With so many experts she will be able to prod along China to step up her production. And China's cooly society is admirably suited to the Bolshevik experiment. Once the intellectuals are liquidated or forced to conform, Chinese society will become an eldorado of Stakhanovism, where the common people from time immemorial have known nothing better than the sixteen-hour work day and the proverbial handful of rice for wages. The world has already had an opportunity to see in Korea what communist fanaticism and discipline can make out of peaceful Chinese peasants. If this vast country will be fully on the march, Bolshevism will have an inexhaustible reservoir of Janissaries and Stakhanovites.

It is hardly better in Russia and in the satellite countries, where the rank and file are reduced to a toil and drudgery on small rations, so hard to believe in the western world. A spirit of militancy pervades everything. There are fronts like the steel front or the wheat front or the other innumerable fronts of production and there are shock troops and storm brigades who lead the assault and there are victories and defeats and casualties. There are extra norms to fulfill and extra sacrifices to perform. Discipline is harsh and the purges are many. The worker has no say. His unions are mock organizations to extort more contributions from him to the state, his merciless employer. The common man in Russia has no civilian status and his existence is not far removed from that of the slave. If he grumbles, slows down, or rebels, he is removed to the concentration camp where formal slavery is his lot.

For the hard worker and faithful follower, there are medals and distinctions, citations, and other military types of rewards, just as every army has for its heroes. In Russia, such medals and ribbons are pinned on miners, railroad workers or steel mill operators, and they are called the heroes of production. And well they might be considered heroes, because often the conditions under which they are forced to work are extremely dangerous.

Russian economy is an eternal battle waged with an inhuman drive and with fanatical endurance. The speedups never cease, the sacrifices become daily routine. It is a militant society regimented from tender youth to old age. There is little difference for the Russian people whether they serve in civilian life or in the army. Conditions are the same. Thirty-six years of such rule have produced a new type of man, *Homo Sibiricus,* who knows no moral standards or ethical principles having never learned or practiced religion. Deprived of any opportunity to learn civilized conduct, he is like an intelligent beast hitched on to the programs of ambitious five year plans, bending his back to fulfill ever increasing norms. He knows no higher desires except those which arise out of immediate physical needs. He is fed, however, promises and a philosophy of social existence which remain forever a distant Nirvana. He is incredibly tough and capable of endurance both as a worker and as a soldier which would quickly exhaust or ruin western man. At the same time he is highly expendable on the work front as well as on the war front. It is an ant society with an impersonal, inhuman authority and discipline. Its members know no individualistic initiative. That quality is suppressed in them from early youth. They are mere cogs made of the hardest steel in a vast machinery, and more and more ant-like humans of this *Homo Sibiricus* variety are being produced now in the satellite countries of Europe and in China, who will be even more expendable in the hands of their Russian masters than the Russians themselves.

The short term implications of all this are a slow progress; but the long term implications, with the ever accelerating tempo of production, are terrifying.

The Great Challenge

The industrial revolution affected different societies in different ways. In Great Britain it led to free trade which in turn produced a widespread division of labor by spontaneous integration. In the United States it resulted in the development of the home market under protectionism to such an extent that a further consequence has been the second industrial revolution.

The Soviet regime in Russia, by the medium of five year plans precluded from the beginning the spontaneous operation of the economic, social and political forces, which the industrial revolutions brought to life elsewhere. Instead, only the technology of it was accepted but under the strictest control and subordinated to military purposes. It has so far been frighteningly successful. It has aroused the admiration of many people in the West but particularly among backward nations. They see only the great technological advances made by Russia, herself a backward nation not so long ago. They do not calculate the cost in human values. Nor is there a way of formulating any realistic appraisal of it because of the Iron Curtain. This gives Russia a great propaganda advantage over the free world and that is her great challenge to the United States. She may show only the positive achievements of her economy to the outside world whereas our free institutions allow anyone to study the seamy sides of our system.

And the accomplishments of Russia, as it has been shown on the preceding pages, have been monumental. It makes an inspiring record to backward nations. For this reason the Chinese experiment will be watched with even greater interest in all the backward areas in the world but especially in Asia. If the Chinese should successfully repeat the Russian performance and introduce a large scale technological revolution, the leadership of the West will be put on the hardest trial. The world has witnessed the impact of Japan's success in peace and war, which, among other effects, brought about the collapse of the colonial idea. Chinese successes might mean the isolation of the western world unless the United States and her few allies will accomplish miracles of leadership.

As yet, the world outside of the Iron Curtain is in no immediate danger. But the race is on. It will not be only on a military and an industrial basis, but also a totalitarian rivalry in the sense that the totality of the world will be involved for the totality of control over man's resources and man's mind.

Each side will try to undermine the other's solidity and unity. Each side, at the same time, will strive to preserve a united front. The western world is infinitely more handicapped in this respect than the Soviet world. In the latter there are only two huge units, Russia and China. If they can keep their Communist solidarity the rest matters little because Russia's superiority over the Eastern European satellites is crushing.

The West on the other hand consists of a variety of units forming a conglomeration at best. Leadership over this heterogeneous world has been thrust suddenly upon a reluctant and hesitant nation without experience and without a taste for such a task. Through a series of very fortunate circumstances the United States has achieved standards so high that she is separated from the rest of the world by a gap difficult to eliminate. The desire is naturally great to keep these high standards and live in splendid isolation. "The American people's dream has been to disentangle America from the Old World in order to build an Earthly Paradise in the New World." [42] But the world wars inextricably entangled her with the rest of the world. No retreat is possible. In fact an isolated America would eventually be engulfed by a red avalanche.

> In order to make the United States or any other part of the world safe for democracy, the whole world under present conditions has to be made safe for democracy. This psychological readjustment is an excruciating experience, and the fact that the necessity for it comes from an increase of power and from a great victory is an aggravation of the malaise.
>
> Yet we Western peoples no longer have a choice. We are bound to unite with one another, considering that we have no intentions of allowing ourselves to go under, and that our downfall would be the inevitable penalty of a continuing disunity.[43]

The world is on the threshold of a new industrial revolution. The first and the second both were the results of the combination of a new source of mechanical power and new techniques of production, transportation and communication. There were various other corollaries arising from scientific advances and improvements. The three main elements were, however, power, manufacturing techniques and movement of persons, freight and thought. Their end results, since they speeded up everything, were in their cumulative effects great dynamism and expansive energies.

The third industrial revolution will be a similar combination of power, manufacturing techniques, and movement. Power furnished by atomic energy, manufacturing techniques by the transmutation of matter and movement of everything, including ideas, faster than ever. The turning point has not arrived yet. In the first, such a turning point came when Watt perfected his steam engine so that through a fly wheel steam power could be directly transmitted to machines. This happened in 1781. In the second, such a turning point came when Henry Ford perfected the assembly line, reduced the price of his car, and America began to move on wheels. This was in 1909, the coming of the Model-T car.

Such a turning point has not come yet in atomic energy, although the atomic age dates from December 2, 1942, when the first reactor was started at the University of Chicago. Eleven years later atomic energy is still in a primitive stage and serves exclusively military purposes. Like the old Newcomen steam engine which was used only for pumping or the early cars which were only toys in the hands of the rich. An industrial revolution begins when the invention is turned to serve a fundamental social or economic purpose. Not even the commercial revolution could get fully into its stride until trade shifted from the old luxury articles to goods of mass consumption.

When will atomic energy come to this turning point? This seems to be very important because in the great race between the two worlds outside and inside of the Iron Curtain the immediate aim will be to arrive at this point first. What has been accomplished so far? Great advances have been made in the matter of power. Already private companies in the United States are showing great interest in producing electricity by atomic power. The Navy has now launched the first atomic submarine; and already engines are being built for the first atomic aircraft carrier. In other words, atomic propulsion is a fact. It is not economical but the Navy is not interested in this. The great advantage of atomic propulsion is the saving of space by eliminating the necessity of carrying fuel and storage batteries. Atomic fuel, which occupies no space comparable to the old fuels, makes it possible for the submarine to stay under water for more than two months without refueling.

The difference between the first and the second industrial revolutions expressed in simple technological terms was the ratio between engine weight and power output. Watt's steam engine, which could produce only a few horsepowers, weighed several tons. Modern gasoline motors reduced this ratio to less than half a pound per horsepower. This made flying possible. Atomic energy will reduce this ratio to an infinitesimal sum because, theoretically, a lump of uranium not larger than a man's fist could drive an ocean liner several times around the world. No wonder that the Navy is anxious to have her vessels powered by such a magic source of energy.

A full scale industrial revolution will be accomplished with the atom only when the breeding principle will be operating in great variety and on a large scale. Breeding is the transmutation of matter. This is being done already by the great reactors in Hanford, Washington, where uranium is transformed into the man-made element of plutonium.[44] The aim now is twofold: first, to produce more plutonium than the amount of uranium being used up in the process;

secondly, to produce heat for industrial purposes during the same process. The experiments are now in the pilot plant stage.

The production of electricity with simultaneous breeding and propulsion of seagoing vessels, is therefore an accomplished fact. But the third Industrial Revolution is not here yet. All that has been done so far is not economical and is supported by military necessity. The economical stage will have arrived when electricity is manufactured cheap enough so that its sale alone will be profitable; for plutonium in a strictly civilian economy would be useless. Furthermore, the breeding principle will have to be extended to other elements. In other words, the transmutation of matter will have to become a general manufacturing process able to produce a variety of useful materials like the synthetic chemical and plastic industries. Finally, atomic propulsion will have to be extended to all kinds of transportation on land, sea, and in the air. Only then will the third Industrial Revolution be in full swing. How soon this will materialize is a matter of speculation. But there is no question that the communist bloc of nations will strive with all their power to achieve this stage of atomic development at least as soon as the free nations. The race will go on along these lines with ever increasing speed and pressure. In fact, the side which will accomplish most, may obtain a preponderance so great that appeal to arms may not be necessary. The menace of the communist bloc, therefore, which forces the free world and especially the United States, to speed up this scientific race, may, in the long run, become very beneficial. Mankind may share in the wonders of the full atomic age decades sooner than without this pressure.

In contrast to *laissez faire* the new age of this impending revolution will be characterized by control and central regulation. It will not be the age of the self-made man in industry, but rather the age of the scientist, who, operating in the huge super-laboratories maintained by governments and super-universities, will turn out other scientists. The inventions and improvements produced by science and large corporations under government supervision, may be applied by private business in the rough-and-tumble of free enterprise but not without certain fundamental controls exercised by the state. At best it will be a supervised economy and the question is to what extent will this supervision be imbued with the spirit of social responsibility for the betterment of man, and to what extent it will promote man's spiritual needs. But control will be inevitable due to the very nature of the atom, for without the strictest supervision catastrophic explosions or mass contaminations could take place.

Life, however, will be very different. The individual in the atomic age may live on a much higher plane as regards material comforts than it is possible for us to imagine just as it would have been very difficult a hundred years ago to imagine the forms in which man in the automobile age was going to live. We are only on the threshold of a superscientific age which may banish disease, establish large scale weather control, produce a variety of new materials in such abundance that there will be plenty for all. The great question is whether man will be able to rise to moral heights commensurate with his scientific accomplishments or whether he will allow the atom to become the tool of his Neanderthal inheritance?

God gave free will to man to work out his own salvation. The trouble is that in the process man often forgets that his destiny can never be fulfilled in his material existence.

Freedom and Labor

by DR. WALTER L. WILLIGAN
Professor of History and Social Studies,
Graduate School, St. John's University

INTRODUCTION

Discordant concepts of freedom are the key to modern industrial conflict. In the pursuit of freedom, labor unions have waged war against employers and these same employers have organized themselves to protect their freedom from the hands of so-called despotic labor organizations. Basically this conflict is between an established-power interest, management, desiring to retain its power and privileged position and an emerging-power interest, organized labor, determined to have a share in establishing wages and working conditions.[1] The specific freedoms which each side advocates and the argumentation presented are evidence of the struggle between both parties to attract the support of the American people in order to solidify their respective power positions.

The development of modern enterprise has placed the control and direction of the American economic system in the hands of management. For years management has had the exclusive power to determine wages, hours and working conditions. These powers were enforced by withholding from the working man his means of subsistence, namely, employment. The power of the management class has been limited by competition and economic factors, but these factors have not, within the range of these limits, restricted management's ability to fix wages and determine the hours and conditions of work. Such decisions have been management's alone, while the power of the worker until recent times, has been negligible.

To support this position management has consistently appealed to economic freedom. An analysis of economic and social data for the past fifty years, such as the publications of employer groups, convention resolutions, speeches and writings of important managers of industry, government investigation reports, as well as the experience across the bargaining table, indicates that according to management, economic freedom encompasses in its definition, freedom of enterprise, freedom of contract and freedom of property. Other freedoms such as those of speech and press, and freedom from arbitrary arrest have elicited less attention until the passage of the Wagner Act and the seizure of industrial plants by the Federal government during World War II.

Large segments of management still believe that economic freedom is the safeguard of other forms of freedom.[2] Harry A. Bullis, Chairman of the Committee on Economic Policy of the Chamber of Commerce of the United States, wrote that, "Economic freedom depends upon the diffusion, dispersal and fragmentation of economic power among millions of private enterprises and tens of millions of individual economic decisions to buy, to sell, to save and to invest." [3] In fact, economic freedom touches each exchange of goods and services, the ownership of property and every contractual arrangement involving these economic affairs.

Economic freedom is curtailed whenever a person is prohibited from using his talents and his property to produce and sell anything he desires at whatever price is agreeable to him and to the buyer. If he is prohibited from doing this by another person or by any combination of persons who are not direct parties to the transactions, his freedom is thereby transgressed. Management holds to the idea that it makes no difference, in so far as economic freedom is concerned, under what name the act of restriction is paraded; or who does the prohibiting, be it a corporation, a cooperative, a labor union or the government.[4]

The employer class associate their power, enjoyed for generations, with the universal concept of freedom. Any challenge to this power appears to be a challenge to liberty and freedom. The American industrialist who enjoyed the right to refuse to recognize unions, to deny collective bargaining, to discriminate between employees because of union activity, considered the ability of a union to close down his business as a threat to his freedom.[5] He also considered the government to be oppressive when it used its power to protect organized labor in these activities, or ordered an election in his plants to determine the collective bargaining agents with whom, thereafter, he must negotiate.

Organized labor believes that such appeals by management for freedom have been made for the purpose of maintaining the "status quo" as regards the distribution of power. Philip Murray, as President of the C.I.O., said, "The C.I.O. cannot lend comfort to a system which provides approximately seventeen or eighteen billion dollars worth of net corporate profits to American business." [6] Speaking before the 14th Constitutional Convention of the C.I.O., Walter Reuther stated, "We have to work at the complete destruction of the economic and moral double standard that industry operates on." He added that, "The future of peace and the future of freedom in the world in which we live, cannot be made secure if we go on trying to divide up economic security in the world. Freedom and peace are only possible if their future is protected by the economics of abundance, and we have to fight the forces of monopoly and scarcity in order to realize the abundance that our resources made possible, and then translate that abundance into tangible human values." [7]

Management has placed particular stress on the freedom of enterprise. Phelps Adams states that, ". . . the American system of free enterprise, on its record indisputably is the most progressive and completely democratic form of capitalism yet devised by man. It is the only economic system which provides investor, producer and consumer with freedom of choice and opportunity." [8] H. W. Prentis Jr. believes that, ". . . No individual eager to help preserve our American Liberties can possibly justify the denial to industry of the right to champion free enterprise." [9] The editors of *Fortune* magazine point out that, "All in all, the Free Enterprise campaign is shaping up as one of the most intensive 'sales jobs' in the history of industry. . . . More to the point, it is absorbing more and more of the energies expended by the top men in U. S. Management." [10]

Labor contends that the application of this concept of freedom means power for management to dictate wages, hours and working conditions, power to suppress unionization of employees as well as the right to discriminate in hiring and firing. Furthermore, the leaders of industry desire that freedom of enterprise be exercised by industrialists while the enterprise of labor organizations be restrained.[11]

The insistence upon freedom of contract also represents a struggle for power; the interpretations offered by management would insure continued unchallenged control over industry by employers; the position taken by labor would result in the enhancement of its position at the expense of management. Our present labor laws aim at establishing real freedom of contract for employees as well as for management. The National Labor Relations Act was designed to restrict the exercise of freedom previously enjoyed by management. Professor Bryon R. Abernethy questions whether management can rightfully identify this lost freedom with the general freedom of contract. Labor supporters think not. They reason that by restricting the freedom of employers, the freedom of all is actually enlarged.

Freedom of property is supported by management in its struggle to retain industrial power. Management argues that little progress could have ever occurred anywhere in the world without the right of a person to own private property and continued progress requires full protection of this right. Nine-tenths or more of the economic welfare in the more prosperous nations of the world results from the use of the accumulated tools of production rather than from human effort unaided by these tools. The material means that are necessary for economic prosperity and for cultural progress will not be accumulated except as the person who saves them is assured of continuing rights to their possession.[12]

Labor and management believe in freedom of property but the concept means different things to both parties. Management believes that freedom of property means the right to acquire, possess and use property. It means the freedom of those now owning productive property to use that property as they see fit. Such an interpretation would give the employer the right to deny to workers access to the means of production as well as the possession of that individual property necessary for the fulfillment of the worker's obligation to himself and his family.[13]

Labor desires freedom of property which will give the worker an equal opportunity to acquire, possess and use property. The worker wants certain limitations on the freedom of the use of property by the current owners. He wants the power to command a greater share of the product of his work. Labor, moreover, wants freedom of property to include freedom and protection for the only kind of property that most workers have—their jobs. This concept would include the right of a worker to his job as a property right; a right to be protected by governmental action, if necessary, even at the expense of restricting the rights of owners of corporate property.

Workers believe in freedom of enterprise, freedom of contract and freedom of property but not on the terms of definition as supplied by management. Herein is the key to much of modern industrial conflict. Can these divergent concepts of freedom sought by labor and management be reconciled? To resolve this problem it is imperative not only to evaluate management's concepts of freedom, but also to analyze the growth, development and effect of those basic freedoms for which labor has struggled. They are freedom of association, freedom to bargain collectively and the freedom to strike.

Freedom of Association

In his economic life, the workingman strives constantly to secure those facets of economic freedom necessary for the satisfaction of the constant and universal desire for fulfillment which is rooted in his nature.[14] This striving implies that its goal is to be an economic emancipation which will release the workingman from the bonds of material nature. It is a spiritual and intellectual dynamism which has motivated man down through the ages to demand greater and greater satisfaction of his material wants so that he may be free to enjoy and to develop his higher faculties.

Some of the important facets upon which economic freedom rests are the sufficiency of private property, the reception of just wages for honest work rendered, the payment of just prices, the access to the means of production as a guarantee of continuous employment, and the realization of a position of status established upon the principle of human dignity. To achieve these facets of economic freedom the workingman has many alternatives of choice. At one period of history his alternatives of choice are wide, for he secures his private property, his wages, his job and a position of status through his own individual efforts; at another period of history he narrows his field of individual choice by delegating the attainment of these objectives to organized groups which in turn are to guarantee to him their fulfillment.

Many of the problems facing the worker are manifestations of his freedom of choice in economic activity. Engaging in a strike is a concrete example of the freedom of the employee not to work; the lockout, on the other hand, is evidence of the employer's corresponding privilege not to hire. Strikes, picketing, boycott, union security, demands for a guaranteed annual wage, industry-wide bargaining are phenomena which have arisen as a result of voluntary employer-employee relations in an economic society characterized by a predominantly free labor market. This condition has distinguished the American labor movement from that of other countries.

In practically the entire colonial period the interests of the small merchant, the employer, and the journeyman were identical. It was not until after the Constitution of 1789 and the elimination of market barriers which each colony had erected against others, that a new phase began to appear with its wholesale markets, its credit system and its creation of the merchant capitalist. In many instances the capitalist's profit was the margin between the prices he paid for labor and the prices he received for his product. The wage earner, on the other hand, received a stipulated income for exertion. During the 1830's these conditions drove the wage earners as such into a conscious union with fellow laborers in self-defense against their bosses. The Holy Father, Pius XI, declared, "Each class must receive its due share and the distribution of created goods must be brought into conformity with the demands of the common good and Social Justice. For every sincere observer is conscious that the vast differences between the few who hold excessive wealth and the many who live in destitution constitute a grave evil in modern society." [15]

For many years the development of the American economy provided for the unlimited application of individual initiative, liberty and freedom. As the principles of specialization and mass production techniques were introduced into the American industrial process, however, it became more and more difficult for the worker to secure economic fulfillment on his own. Helpless to resist oppression and exploitation by the selfish, inhumane type of employer, the workers organized themselves so that by collective action they could force these employers and managers of large industry to pay just wages and provide fair conditions of employment. The American workers objected to leaving their rights to the mercy of arbitrary discipline and discharge, and their wages and hours of labor subject to the rigors of unmitigated competition.[16] Consequently, they chose labor managers whom they felt they could trust to protect their interests in signing contracts with business managers whom they could not control.

To achieve the facets of economic freedom it was necessary for the workers to enjoy freedom of association. That they should exercise this freedom to organize into unions without employer interference has not only been recognized in Catholic Social Thought, but has also been supported by a developing public opinion in the United States. Leo XIII pointed out in his Encyclical, "The Conditions of Labor," that, "Workmen's Associations should be so organized and governed as to furnish the best and most suitable means for attaining what is aimed at, that is to say, for helping each individual member to better his condition to the utmost in body, mind and property." [17]

In their endeavor to secure these rights, unions attempted to combine into one organization all the men employed or capable of being employed at a given trade. The immediate goal of union policy is to achieve basic minima of real wages consistent with continued employment and stability of business.[18] In spite of management's reluctance to face these needs, union campaigning has secured higher wages, job security, as well as health and disability insurance, hospitalization and medical care benefits.

The recognition of the union involves the recognition of the principle of collective bargaining. Freedom of association and freedom to bargain collectively are correlative. Unions hold that workingmen would have a nominal but not a real freedom of contract if they were prevented from contracting collectively instead of individually. Acceptance of this principle has been reflected in the growth of union membership. In recent years this growth has come about through a continuous penetration of unionism into new sectors of the country. The "growth cones" of unionism began with the skilled trades, then spread from them to the semi-skilled, to unskilled manual occupations, to white collar workers, and finally to governmental civil service workers.[19]

The managers of industry, however, consistently refused to recognize this concerted drive for freedom of association. They refused to alter their industrial relations policies and voluntarily recognize the right of workers to form unions for the purpose of collective negotiation. This attitude was unusual in the light of the ample warnings that if industry did not act in view of the changed economic relationships, the Federal government would be compelled to do so. Starting in 1885, a long list of government commissions and agencies reported favorably in behalf of the process of collective bargaining. In 1898, the United States Congress passed the Erdman Act, which provided that discriminating against union activity on the nation's railroads was a misdemeanor. Although this Act was declared unconstitutional, the Railway Disputes Act of 1926 again supported the principle of union organization and the process of collective bargaining. In fact, between the years 1890 and 1914, fourteen states enacted state legislation patterned after the Erdman Act. During World War I, the War Labor Board recognized the right of collective bargaining and forbade discrimination because of union activity. Secret elections were conducted to determine collective bargaining agents. This policy was continued by the Norris-La-Guardia Act of 1932, which contained a statement supporting the right of workers to full freedom of association, self-organization, and designation of representatives to negotiate the terms and conditions of employment.

Changed conditions in the labor market gave an added impetus to this movement. During the 1880's, gainfully employed persons increased by one-third. The individual had a good chance to rise to a skilled position or to become a straw boss, foreman, or superintendent. These favorable opportunities created by rapid industrial expansion made men more interested in rising to better jobs than in getting better conditions on their present jobs. When the opportunities for advancement disappeared during the depression of the thirties, however, the need for organization was intensified.[20] Because alternative job opportunities were no longer available, workers took an intense interest in union organization and in collective bargaining as a means of controlling layoffs and establishing greater job security. The Federal government recognized these conditions and legislative support was given to the exercise of these rights.[21]

In the field of industrial relations, the period from 1933 to 1935 was characterized principally by the operation of the National Recovery Administration. Guaranteeing the right of self-organization to workers and freedom from interference, coercion and intimidation by employers, Section 7A of the Act was the focal point around which labor relations converged.

The National Association of Manufacturers, with the cooperation of other employers' associations, opposed the rise of bona fide unions for genuine collective bargaining under the protection of Federal legislation.[22]

In 1935 the Wagner Act was passed. This law contained a statement of employee rights as well as certain employer obligations. Section 1 declares it to be the policy of the United States to encourage "the practice and procedure of collective bargaining" and "to protect the exercise by workers of full freedom of association, self-organization and designation of representatives of their own choosing, for the purpose of negotiating the terms and conditions of their employment or other mutual aid or protection." Section 8 makes it illegal for employers to "interfere with, restrain or to coerce employees in the rights guaranteed in Section 7; . . . to aid or support the unions of employees; . . . to discriminate against employees in layoffs, promotions or other conditions of employment because of the employee's membership or activities in a union; . . . to discharge or otherwise discriminate against an employee because he has filed charges or given testimony under this Act." Furthermore, "the employer must bargain collectively with the duly-designated representatives of his employees." [23]

The Wagner Act did much in removing the paralyzing fear of employer retaliation. Today the worker enjoys freedom of association and freedom of assembly. His union meetings are no longer dispersed by hired thugs. He cannot be discharged from his job for urging his fellow workmen to join a union. Court injunctions, citizens' committees, arrests for alleged vagrancy or other trumped-up charges, running organizers out of town, and similar expressions of vigilantism as revealed by the Senate Investigation Committee on Violations of Free Speech and Rights of Labor, have been removed from our labor-management relations.

In the well-known Jones and Laughlin Case in 1937, the Supreme Court agreed with the government position in holding that Congress is justified in protecting employees in their right to organize and to elect representatives of their own choosing for collective bargaining or for other purposes without restraint or coercion by their employers.[24]

Government policy implemented by such court decisions enabled the Wagner Labor Relations Act to achieve its basic purpose—the recognition of the worker's right to form associations for collective bargaining.[25] This established policy definitely aided the development of union growth. In 1935, when the Act became law, union membership stood at approximately 3,900,000. In 1947, when the Taft-Hartley Act was passed, union membership was close to 16,000,000.

Freedom of Collective Bargaining

Once the legal recognition of freedom of association and the freedom of collective bargaining had been obtained, the American workers increased their efforts to make the exercise of these freedoms effective by developing a labor union structure similar in organization and power to that developed by American industry.

As American enterprise continued to grow to mammoth proportions, labor was forced to adapt its organizational structure to meet these changed conditions. In order to bargain effectively with managerial boards who controlled far-flung industrial empires, unions were forced to place the responsibilities for collective bargaining negotiations in the hands of national union officers. Collective agreements which previously affected only the fringe of the American economy now had a firm grasp upon the very heart of our economic system. There are now for example more than 200 national unions controlling the bulk of organized workers in the United States. In 1953, the following eight national unions claimed a membership of over 4,600,000 members exercising influence over a wide range of industry: [26]

Union	*Membership*
United Steel Workers (CIO)	1,100,000
United Automobile Workers (AF of L)	100,000
Machinists Union (AF of L)	699,298
Brotherhood of Teamsters (AF of L)	1,000,000
United Electrical, Radio and Machine Workers (CIO)	390,000
United Mine Workers (Independent)	600,000
Brotherhood of Carpenters (AF of L)	750,000
United Automobile, Aircraft and Agriculture Workers (CIO)	1,350,000

These national unions have a predominative influence over the entire labor movement; they have consistently attempted to extend their jurisdictional power over wide competitive areas. Their present development represents the third stage in the growth of the bargaining process. The first stage was characterized by individual-employer agreement; the second, was the development of the small union and the individual managerial enterprise bargaining over terms of employment; and the third and present stage is the development of large unions and large managerial units bargaining for vast segments of our American economy. Although phases of all three stages of development exist at the present time in our economy, the third, however, is now the most significant; here the relationships of individuals can be fully understood only in the context of the collectives to which the individuals belong. Interactions between individuals and small groups on a face to face basis are qualitatively different from those between individuals as members of highly complex organized groups.[27] In labor-management relations, individuals are representatives of their respective groups. In this group role, the individual is constantly subject to "in-group" and "out-group" pressures.

The present stage of collective bargaining has developed into one of the most effective devices for securing higher wages and guaranteeing union security. Employers put up less resistance to wage demands when they know that all employers are going to be subjected to the same rise in costs. The more employers the wage agreement covers, the less will be the competitive position of any one employer within the industry and the easier it will be to shift higher wages to prices.

In some major industries, such as the Steel Industry and the Automobile Industry, the establishment of national wage and labor patterns has the effect of an industry-wide master contract. The steel workers, for instance, will first make a settlement with one of the largest producers of steel (U. S. Steel), and the terms agreed to will then become a pattern or standard for the industry under the union's jurisdiction. This pattern is then applied to all contracts signed with large and small firms, no matter where situated. Differentials between large industrial metropolitan centers and small industrial areas as well as big and small producers are gradually eliminated.

The boards of directors of our large industries, in spite of the tremendous power and control which they exercise throughout their widely-scattered plants, object to the present development of industrywide bargaining. They maintain that the "increasing tendency of strong international unions to exercise central control by formulating policy at the top and applying it evenly across plants of a whole industry, give certain unions a monopoly grip which is doing great harm to our country." [28] These industrial leaders insist that, ". . . if we, as a nation, want to have genuine collective bargaining as the basis of labor-management relations in a free society, we must repudiate industrywide bargaining, which involves governmental intervention and opens the door to government domination of labor-management relations, with the loss of long-cherished rights by organized labor and industry." [29]

Another current trend in the collective bargaining process is the expanding range of subjects to be included within the proper sphere of the negotiators. In order to meet the possibilities of an economic recession with its concomitant unemployment, many leaders of organized labor are now demanding a guaranteed annual wage. This principle is considered to be the last big innovation that organized labor will demand for some years to come. The guaranteed annual wage is a continuation of labor's historic drive for security and a symbolic demand on the part of the "blue collar" workers for equality both with managers and professional and white collar workers.[30] The United Automobile Workers' Convention adopted Resolution 24 in March of 1953 which stated that, "We have seen repeatedly how financial responsibility can convert management to social responsibility. A sound guaranteed annual wage plan will arouse management's social conscience and stimulate its social ingenuity by putting pressure on its pocketbook nerve. The guaranteed annual wage will compel management to take steps in its plants to end the instability of employment for which it is directly responsible. It will lead management to cooperate more readily in developing national economic measures designed to maintain full employment and full production by eliminating the causes of instability over which the individual plant managers have no control. . . ." [31]

While variable in its proposed details, the guaranteed annual wage concept aims to require management to set up a fund which is to make up the difference between state-contributed unemployment insurance benefits and an amount equal to three-fourths of a worker's annual earnings. The expenses of such guarantees are to be considered part of the cost of overhead. Labor believes that with established incomes, workers could plan expenditures, thus permitting the expansion of consumer goods industries. The labor advocates admit that guaranteed annual wage would create short run costs and burdens to industry; nevertheless, they reason that high cost labor has spurred management to more efficient planning and mechanization. The mass production unions have readily accepted large scale technological improvements in exchange for improved grievance systems, seniority, pensions and welfare benefits. Labor believes that this latest proposal is the capstone to those guarantees necessary to secure stabilized production and greater security at higher levels of employment.[32]

Industrial leaders reject the concept of the guaranteed annual wage as being economically and socially unsound. Prior stabilization of production or sales, or both, must be achieved before formal commitment by industry can be made. Wage payments must be based on production and sales. The guaranteed annual wage is in fact a proposal "to narrow the differential between wages and [unemployment] benefits to such an extent that the incentive to work would be lessened, and in some cases destroyed, and unemployment for some would be a desirable situation." [33]

In cases where the workers are represented by a national industrial union, the guaranteed annual wage would presuppose agreement between labor and management on the aggregate man-hours of employment that an industry can support, and the number of workers among whom the guaranteed employment has to be allocated. The accuracy of such a forecast would be an important factor in determining the continuance of such guarantees and their value to different classes of workers. There is a real danger that rigidity in the labor force would result from the inability of industry to hire additional workers because of the burden of additional guaranteed overhead. This condition would tend to freeze employment among the older workers, and reduce the employment opportunities for younger workers. These and many other basic decisions must be worked out before the guaranteed annual wage can effectively be placed as an obligation upon industry.

The Freedom to Strike

In our American experience a pre-requisite to collective bargaining is the right to strike. Without the possibility of a strike, there would be little reason for an employer to make concessions to a union. In fact, a strike is a continuation of the bargaining process by other methods. To many Americans, the strike epitomizes the union for headlines are made by such industrial disputes, which are the sensational aspects of union activity and managerial reaction. Impartial examination of the evidence reveals, however, that in comparison either to man-days worked or to the number of collective agreements negotiated, strikes are surprisingly few. Slanted reporting and propaganda have not kept the lay mind informed of the constructive contributions of unions.

It is estimated that between 98 and 99 per cent of the contract negotiations conducted in the United States each year result in agreement without a strike. The Bureau of Labor Statistics reports that from 1935 to 1939, the average annual number of man-days lost in the United States because of strikes was 16,000,000 or 0.27 per cent of the total annual estimated work time. In 1946, the worst strike year, man-days lost were 116,000,000 or 1.43 per cent of the annual estimated working time.[34]

In spite of the relatively few strikes which have marred labor-management relations, the occurrence has generated much controversy on the part of labor, management and the public who are inconvenienced by this form of industrial warfare. When a labor leader or the governing board of a national labor union calls for a strike, the worker's emotions are immediately aroused. Believing that security against arbitrary management can only be obtained through support of their union, the members are willing to undergo privations, dwindling savings accounts and a hostile public opinion. Since 1932, managerial leaders have continually renewed the demand for revisions of the Wagner Labor Act, blaming their difficulties with labor on an Act, which they insist interferes with their economic freedom.

In times of national emergency, an action which normally would be accepted as usual practice, becomes surcharged with emotion in the minds of the general public. Indignation developed against organized labor in the year 1946 because of the large number of strikes which took place and the publicity given to the figure of 116,000,000 man-days work lost.[35] On four different occasions during 1946, nation-wide strikes paralyzed essential industries. The public utility strikes, like the lengthy strike of electric light and power workers in Pittsburgh, aroused hostile anti-labor feeling to an all-time high. Tremendous pressure was placed upon Congress to amend the Wagner Act and restore some balance in the labor-management structure by placing curbs upon the exercise of labor power as well as to afford protection to individual union members. The Federal government was asked to modify its position of openly supporting union organization. It now was to assume an attitude of neutrality. To achieve these objectives the Taft-Hartley Act was passed on June 23, 1947, over the veto of the President and the vehement protest of organized labor.

With several important modifications, the Taft-Hartley Law retained the five unfair labor practices contained in the Wagner Act. Employers were given the right of free speech; they could give expression to any new arguments or opinions as long as there was no actual threat or reprisal, force or promised benefit. The Labor Board could no longer reinstate workers with back pay who were discharged for cause. A modification of the disestablishment of company unions, as well as the right of employers to ask for elections when a union seeks recognition, was also provided. Employers were granted the privilege to sue unions in Federal Courts for breach of contract.[36]

Section 8 of the Taft-Hartley Act attempted to define unfair union practices. The law defines any attempt of the union to restrain or coerce employees' right to bargain collectively through representatives of his own choosing as well as the right to refrain from such activity except where a union shop has been authorized by law. This provision had the effect of outlawing the closed shop. It is unlawful for unions to make illegal demands for union security, such as demanding that an employer discriminate against an employee for non-union membership in cases where no union security contract exists. Union shop agreements had to provide a thirty-day waiting period before new employees would be required to join the union, dismissal from which could be only for non-payment of dues or initiation fees. Unions were also restrained from refusing to bargain, engaging in illegal boycotts, excessive jurisdictional disputes, charging excessive initiation fees and "feather-bedding." Added to these many provisions were others which required loyalty affidavits, financial accounting, restrictions on political contributions, and regulations covering contributions and administration of welfare funds. In order to protect the workers from the arbitrary power of labor leaders, changes were made in election procedures, compulsory check-off, and discriminatory practices against minorities.

The Taft-Hartley Law was written by those who for the most part were antagonistic to organized labor. This fact has resulted in an emotional attitude of mind on the part of labor leaders who can see no value in the present law.

All complicated pieces of social legislation which apply fixed standards and procedures to dynamic social phenomena develop inequities and contradictions. In recognition of this problem many modifications of the Taft-Hartley Law have been proposed by labor and management. Among the important pro-union modifications suggested are: (1) the mitigation of secondary boycott prohibitions; (2) curtailment of the power of employers to break unions by provoking a strike and then hiring strike breakers as permanent replacements; (3) provision for union security in the construction, amusement and maritime industries by requiring employees to become members of the union seven days after beginning employment; (4) the elimination of loyalty affidavits; and (5) the simplification of financial and membership reports.[37] The pro-employer modifications of the Law would (1) restrict the making of new demands while a contract was in force; (2) strengthen the freedom of speech clause for employers; (3) improve regulations for union dues check-off; (4) impose higher standards for the conservation of union welfare funds; and (5) provide for the right of a state to establish and maintain its own labor relations law.[38]

One of the fundamental reasons for the passage of the Taft-Hartley Act was the necessity of finding some means to protect the community from stoppages of the flow of essential commodities and services. The Wagner Act had succeeded in reducing strikes called because of organizational disputes from 60 per cent in 1937 to 22 per cent in 1945.[39] Entire industries, however, were involved in industrywide or pattern bargaining over such economic issues as wages, hours and working conditions. Consequently, the man-days lost increased three-fold. Through the instrumentality of procedures and prohibitions, the Taft-Hartley Law sought to narrow the freedom to strike by placing special restrictions on actual or threatened strikes or lockouts which may result in a national emergency. In order for such a work stoppage or threatened stoppage to be subject to these restrictions, it must affect an entire industry or a substantial part of an industry that is engaged in trade, commerce, transportation, or communication in interstate or foreign commerce, or in the production of goods for such commerce, provided that in each case the national health or safety would be imperiled.

If the President is of the opinion that such an actual or threatened strike or lock-out will imperil the national health or safety, he is authorized to appoint a Board of Inquiry to investigate and report on the issues involved without, however, making any recommendations. One copy of the report is to be filed with the Federal Mediation and Conciliation Service and the contents made public.

After receiving the report, the President may direct the Attorney General to ask for an injunction from a Federal District Court having jurisdiction of the parties to the dispute. If the Court finds that the threatened strike or lock-out in such an industry will imperil the national health or safety, it may grant an injunction. In addition, the Court may issue whatever orders are deemed appropriate.

After the injunction is issued the parties to the dispute are required, during the next sixty days, to try to settle their differences with the assistance of the Federal Mediation and Conciliation Service. During the same time the President is authorized to reconvene the Board of Inquiry. At the end of the sixty-day period, a further report is required to be made by the Board to the President, which he must make available to the public. This report must include a statement of the employer's last offer of settlement.

Within fifteen days following the end of the sixty-day period, the National Labor Relations Board must hold an election to determine whether or not the employees involved in the dispute wish to accept the final offer or settlement made by their employer. The results of the election are then certified to the Attorney General, who must request the Court to discharge the injunction. After the Court has granted this request, a report of the entire proceedings must be made to Congress by the President, with such recommendations as he desires to make.[40]

The national emergency provisions of the Taft-Hartley Law have proved most unsatisfactory. These provisions do not forbid national emergency strikes, but merely provide for their postponement. No ultimate sanctions are provided for, after the cooling-off period has elapsed. Fact-finding reports are ineffectual in arousing a sustained public opinion strong enough to force a settlement of labor disputes.

An unfortunate experience with these provisions took place in 1951. In December, 1950, a contract between Philip Murray's steel workers' union and the industry, supplied the fifth round of wage increases, a maintenance of membership provision, the check-off and a no-strike pledge for 1951.[41] The contract contained no provision for an increase cost of living adjustment. Hence, the contract had to be rewritten for 1951. Negotiations between Mr. Murray and the leaders of the steel industry broke down. President Truman submitted the controversy to the Wage Stabilization Board, which, after two months' discussion, issued a report containing 3,000 pages of testimony, calling for wage increases and a union shop clause. The steel industry refused to accept the recommendations of the Wage Stabilization Board, and insisted that no wage increase could be granted unless the Office of Price Administration increased the price of steel to the consumer. The steel industry's objection to the union shop was an attempt to reverse a principle recognized in law for the past fifteen years. The idleness of 60,000 steel workers cost the country eighteen million tons of vitally needed steel. In desperation, President Truman seized the steel industry on April 8, 1952. Both parties were forced to sign a contract which satisfied neither labor nor management and did not provide a satisfactory answer to the problem of eliminating national emergency strikes in our basic industries.[42]

The economic impact of a single industrywide strike has had so many repercussions throughout the American economy that it is imperative that some solution, acceptable to labor and management as well as protective of the public interest, be devised.

A case study of the chain reaction set up by the 1949-1950 bituminous coal strike is illuminating. The immediate effect of the prolonged idleness within the bituminous coal industry was on the miners themselves. The workers had to bear the brunt of the prolonged idleness and loss of income. The time lost in actual strikes from September 19, 1949, to the date of settlement, March 5, 1950, was 23,790,000 man-days lost; assuming an average daily pay of $14.46, the time lost because of strikes alone cost the miners approximately 370 million dollars.[43] Assuming again that on the average, 325,000 men were made idle during the strike period, these workers sustained a pay loss of about $1,200 each. In the final strike settlement, miners were awarded a pay increase of 70¢ a day. The average worker, therefore, would have to work 1,714 days to make up the loss sustained because of the strike.[44]

The indirect effects of this coal strike were felt throughout the entire economy. On February 11, 1950, Governor Dewey of New York appointed a Solid Fuels Administrator with broad powers to ration coal and to take action to curtail the use of coal. On February 6, 1950, a "modified brown-out" was ordered to conserve coal used by public utilities. The same order directed "local and regional administrators to set up a system of priorities for deliveries of solid fuels from dealers' stocks." Deliveries were restricted to customers who had only a week's supply on hand. Mixtures of lower grade coals with better grades were also ordered.

The Wheeling Steel Company closed its Denwood Works on February 8, 1950, and operations were curtailed at the Steubenville plant. These cutbacks threw 8,000 employees out of work. On February 27, 1950, the *New York Times* reported that "More than 40,000 steel workers have already been laid off because of coal shortages." In the first week of March, the Jones and Laughlin Company's Pittsburgh plant was practically at a standstill. Blast furnaces, open hearths and finishing mills were closed. The Carnegie-Illinois Division of the United States Steel Company had cut coke production to 50 per cent of capacity, and later cut it to 25 per cent. Steel ingot production at the Carnegie-Illinois plant was down to 53 per cent of capacity.

According to *Business Week* of March 4, 1950,[45] the Tennessee Coal, Iron and Railroad Works in Birmingham, Alabama, had closed its entire Ensley Works. Tin and plate mills at Fairfield and Bessemer, Alabama, were shut down and only the rolling mills were running. State employment figures for Alabama showed that 40,000 workers in addition to the 34,000 striking miners had been laid off.

Railroads of the country were also hard hit by coal shortages. This was particularly true of "coal-carrying" railroads, such as the Chesapeake and Ohio, the Pennsylvania, and the Norfolk and Western.

The *New York Times* of January 31, 1950, reported that between 600 and 700 coal-burning passenger trains had been withdrawn from service or limited in their runs, and that the cut was likely to go deeper if coal output did not rise. Effective February 10, 1950, the Chesapeake and Ohio Railroad gave notice that 1,032 of its employees in the mechanical departments would be laid off. At the same time, the Pennsylvania Railroad laid off 1,500 employees and the Norfolk and Western laid off 500 employees.

The experience of the coal strike of 1949-1950 is indicative of the fact that the right to strike may be used as a weapon in the struggle for power. Freedom to strike is a weapon through which organized labor may capture power from organized management.

Management contends that "the right to strike should never be permitted against the supply of products or services affecting the safety, health and welfare of the people until adequate precautions have been taken to safeguard the community and the nation against an inadequate supply of such products or services." [46] Labor, in contrary fashion, insists that the limitation by management of the freedom to strike would eliminate the effectiveness of such freedom. In view of the fact that the freedom and welfare of all American citizens is more significant than the exercise of such freedom by either labor or management, a new definition is needed for the conditions under which the freedom to strike may be exercised.

Freedom in a Union

The growth of union structure and industrywide collective bargaining, while securing many benefits, has also raised many serious problems for the worker. Labor unions are pyramidal in their power structure. Union members constitute the base of the pyramid while labor leaders occupy the middle and upper tiers. This condition is seen in the financial and operational control of union administration. The union member is overwhelmed by the gigantic size and impersonality of the organization which is to represent his interests. In the last twenty years the American Federation of Labor has attained a membership of 8,500,000. Approximately 20,000 full time officials are needed to serve the national unions, with a corresponding number working for 70,000 local unions and central labor bodies, bringing the total to an estimated 500,000 persons. This rapid growth in so short a time creates serious problems of managerial continuity and executive staff work as well as a need for leadership training programs within the union structure. Consultation with the members of a union of one million members becomes a mere formality. In the early days of labor organization, unions were composed of voluntary members who joined willingly and continued to support their locals because they believed that the union protected and promoted their interests. Today, workers are compelled to join and to support a local in order to hold a job and thus earn a living. In a closed shop no one can secure a job unless he is already a union member. In a union shop, he cannot maintain his job unless he becomes a union member, or at least proffers union dues. In either case, continuous employment in organized enterprise is open only to union members.

The union argument holds that the rule of the majority is "The American Way"; that in view of the fact that unions secure high wages and benefits for the American worker, all should share in the costs of this endeavor by supporting the union. Critics of the union position maintain that compulsory unionism attacks the very foundation upon which American society has been built, namely, the recognition of the rights of the minority and of individuals which must be maintained, rights which the majority must not be permitted to impair or destroy.[47]

Today, many serious-minded persons both within and outside the ranks of organized labor are questioning the value of compulsory union membership which is contained in many industrywide collective bargaining agreements. They feel, for example, that such practice is depriving the American workingman of his right to earn a livelihood as well as his freedom to work at a trade of his own choosing. A person should be free, not only to join or not to join, but also, once he has joined, to withdraw. The association organized should be sufficiently large to accomplish its purpose, but not a monopolistic goliath which absorbs the individual and destroys his integrity.[48]

The American worker is no longer able to curtail the power of the anonymous national labor union board which legislates collective bargaining agreements for him. He no longer can control the national union's extensive taxing power. Minorities lose their potency when political machines entrench themselves in such unions.

The exercise of freedom demands that democratic procedures be introduced into the union structure so that union leaders will be responsive to the will of the union membership. There has developed the precedent of long tenure of office by national union officials, such as John L. Lewis of the United Mine Workers, David B. Robertson of the Locomotive Firemen, and Sidney Hillman of the Amalgamated Clothing Workers, all of whom held the office of president for more than twenty-five years. Daniel Tobin of the Teamsters' Union and William Mahon of the Street Railway Employees held office for more than forty years. Robert P. Brindell of the New York Building Trades Council, and Joseph P. Ryan of the ousted International Longshoremen's Association had themselves elected for life. Because of their ability to secure substantial gains for the union membership in terms of wages and working conditions some of the above leaders have been popular with the rank and file of their unions. Most of these leaders, however, have been able to perpetuate their office-holding because of astute political maneuvering within their unions and in successful stifling of opposition by keeping minorities in complete subjection.

The problem of preserving the freedom of the individual union member can be clearly perceived when one recalls the dictatorial power of a leader such as Robert P. Brindell, who in the years 1918 to 1920 formed an alliance with Tammany Hall and the local building contractors. The unions were permitted to work only for members of this group. Those contractors who refused to join were unable to secure workers and hence were forced either to sign up or to go out of business. Brindell was thus enabled to levy tribute on both workers and employers. In one year he collected more than $500,000 in strike insurance from employers and is said to have extracted a similar amount from the 115,000 building trade workers in the New York City area.[49]

There is, unfortunately, a low degree of active participation on the part of the workers in the local affairs of their union. Here is a focal point where the worker loses the exercise of much of his freedom and his integrity as a person. When an inactive majority is controlled by an active minority, the exercise of freedom is seriously curtailed and a labor monopoly develops. To be free, a man must maintain and defend his right to be responsible for his freedom. Attendance at union meetings varies from two to eight per cent. During a strike the attendance may go as high as eighty per cent and if voting is made easy, such as polling at the place of work, ninety per cent often exercise their franchise. Otherwise, only sixty per cent will show enough interest to incommode themselves in order to vote.[50]

This apathy on the part of union members frequently leads to the development of tyranny, organized violence, defiance of government labor boards, calling of national emergency strikes in vital industries, diversion of union funds for improper purposes, and the suppression of union elections. Decent well-meaning members of labor unions abhor these practices. In many instances such conditions have produced a labor dictatorship no longer answerable to the rank and file of the American workingmen.

Labor unions have not been immune to functional disorders in their internal and external relationships. The infiltration of racketeers into organized labor has been concentrated in the New York and Chicago areas. The transportation and dock unions have been particularly singled out for this activity. Some experts estimate that in the mid-thirties about two-thirds of the union members in Chicago were paying tribute in one way or another to the Capone organization. However, racketeering is a law enforcement problem, and would not reach its present proportions if it was not carried on in collusion with local political organizations and business interests.

Unfortunately, the many attempts of union locals to remove mob control and racketeering practices are not so widely known or publicized as are the sensational instances of union dereliction. After twenty-five years of lethargy, the states of New York and New Jersey, backed by Congressional investigating committees, have taken action to remove racketeering and dictatorial union practices from the New York and New Jersey waterfronts.

A unique experience in the field of union administration and effective membership participation is revealed in a study, issued by the New York State School of Industrial and Labor Relations under the direction of Professor Maurice F. Neufeld, concerning the operation of Local 3 of the International Brotherhood of Electrical Workers. Local 3 is a New York City industrial federation which has developed from a faction-torn band of 7,000 members in 1932 to its present membership of 30,000. As an institution, Local 3 was begotten in strife and nursed in turmoil. Strikes, picket lines, brutality, violence, corruption, indictments, courtroom battles and jail sentences mark its growth. The decent elements in Local 3, however, were able eventually to overcome the triple obstacles of internal strife, anarchy within the industry itself, and the anti-union spirit of the times. The solution offered by Local 3 and by those contractors who bargain collectively with the union took the form of strong internal union discipline and a unified employer's association cooperating with the Local. The fruit of these developments is a comprehensive job control.[51]

The governmental structure and administrative forms and processes of Local 3 are geared to meet the basic needs of the industry within which the union must operate. The discipline imposed upon its own members and upon its employers is aimed to prevent chaos in an industry where cutthroat competition had flourished in the past, and through collective bargaining to secure conditions under which both the union and the contractors could thrive.

As in many other institutions faced with the problem of effective control, the reins of the administrative process in Local 3 are tightly held by an elected official in whose person responsibility is centered. Within the Local, the delegation of authority and responsibility devolves, in clear-cut fashion, to assistant-business managers who are appointed by the business manager himself. This security-wrought system of organization and management is meshed in logical fashion with the administrative arrangements of the Joint Industry Board.[52] The Joint Industry Board maintains an elaborate system of record-keeping in order to provide its contribution to the prevention of chaos in an industry which without protective controls could quickly generate conditions of intolerable proportions. These arrangements seek to obtain the prosperity of the contractors, with an equitable distribution of jobs among union workers at a rate of pay and under working conditions and benefits commensurate with their training and skill.

Local 3 has established a series of committee arrangements and membership meetings and activities which it is hoped will answer the democratic needs of the members. Decisions taken by the leaders are ratified at meetings conducted regularly at all craft and industry levels. Attendance is maintained by subjecting all those who are absent to a fine. Elections of local-wide officials are conducted by an impartial outside agency and opposition candidates are given an opportunity to place their names on the ballot. The operations of Local 3 consequently point the way to new and effective democratic forms as contrasted to the traditional concepts of union operation and management. The leaders of this Local are realists who do not believe that the intricacies of policy formation and the execution of them for a complex industry, as contrasted to policy approval, can be thrashed out in membership meetings where thousands of workers are present. They distinguish between the administrative and the broadly legislative function. Moreover, they believe that certain expert functions such as financial control, should be executed by persons trained for that specific purpose. Their stated objective is to preserve in their divisional and class officers and committees a creative type of democratic activity as a protective safeguard for the exercise of freedom by the union members.

Experiences such as those in Local 3 are indicative of the possibilities of leadership which the decent law-abiding unionist may attain in preserving his freedom as a member of a union. It is on the local level of union activity that many of the undemocratic practices now existent in the labor movement can be removed.

The problem of freedom within the union structure is of paramount importance. The protection of individuals and minorities operating within a group demands a democratization of procedures. Ever since the end of the feudal era, society has seen the progressive atomization of the individual and the dissolution of his social ties. The present trend is toward institutional or organizational development. In the economic realm the individual can protect his individual rights and freedoms only through group action. The continuing problem is not to limit collective action but how to make collective action responsive to individual needs and the common good.

The Dynamics of Economic Freedom

Industrial strife will continue to plague American society so long as the leaders of labor and management fail to agree upon a sound and mutually acceptable definition of freedom. Management has deep convictions appertaining to freedom of enterprise, freedom of contract and freedom of property. Labor, likewise, has deep-seated convictions concerning freedom of association, freedom of collective bargaining and the freedom to strike. Each side is convinced that if their conceptualization of freedom is compromised, they thereby would encourage a threat to their own survival. Consequently, labor and management all too frequently view the attitudes, actions and policies of each other with mutual suspicion.

In every industrial negotiation, the leaders of each group are trying not merely to resolve a specific problem, but also endeavoring to solve their difficulties in such a way as to preserve their own power structure intact. They struggle to preserve the familiar methods for achieving their respective goals. They desire to act as they have always acted; in ways which their respective groups have come to accept as effective and proper. They struggle to preserve the ideas, symbols and ritual which reinforce such behavior. Even when they appeal to a specific freedom, using the same words, the meaning for each differs.[53]

Labor and management have forgotten the fundamental truth, that freedom is a postulate of the human person, arising from his very nature. Both parties have failed to realize that the exercise of the various external freedoms is necessary for the proper development of a human person. This proper development, moreover, demands that the exercise of freedom must be shared, shared to that degree which permits cooperative effort toward a common goal.

This mutual sharing requires the acceptance of the principles of cooperation and subsidiarity of association. There is an immediate need for a detailed working out of cooperative activity on all levels. From the single factory and the union local to the great federations of business and labor, there should be a realization of common concerns and general responsibilities.[54]

If the exercise of freedom is open only to one group, then that group is merely defending a privilege. If freedom is to be available to all, one group cannot exclude another group from similar rights to enhance its own welfare. Economic freedom is that freedom which best promotes the economic interests of all and not the self-interest of the holders of economic power.

Collective bargaining should be directed toward cooperation for the welfare of all. Barriers to cooperation are many and varied but not insurmountable. Labor will have to overcome its fear that cooperation would destroy job security and dilute the loyalty of workers to their union organization; management will have to divest itself of the notion that cooperation is synonymous with the limitation of its functions and responsibilities.[55]

Case studies reveal that the number of unions and employers who are attempting to integrate the principle of cooperation into their industrial relations has increased to that point where such practice is now considered a definite trend. Indicative of this is the agreement of the United States Steel Corporation and the United Steelworkers of America for quarterly conferences to discuss problems arising out of the application, administration and interpretation of their contract. These meetings are not for the purpose of modifying the contractual provisions agreed upon, but to develop cooperative, good industrial relations.[56] At the Botany Worsted Mills in Passaic, New Jersey, the company and the Textile Workers Union of America have established a school to train company supervisors and union shop representatives in the technical procedures affecting their relationships. The UAW-CIO and the Chrysler Corporation agreed that "The Union and the Company disapprove and will discourage their members or representatives to use or issue statements in their official papers, hand bills, newspapers or other literature which are inconsistent with amicable industrial relations between the parties. Each party will encourage collective bargaining in good faith to achieve full industrial harmony." [57] In Minnesota the A.F. of L. employees ran a series of advertisements stating, "We believe in private enterprise, not government in business. We want the boss to make money and expand his business. When he can expand, he needs more of us. . . ." [58] Today "human relations" programs instituted by management are placing more emphasis upon the dignity of the worker and the need for better teamwork and communication in the plant.[59]

In spite of this trend, cooperation as a social process has failed to achieve the concord necessary to a sound social order because the social structure necessary for effective cooperative activity has not been established. Both labor and management have the means for pressing their special interests and claims, yet the institutional organization necessary for the attainment of common interest goals is lacking.

The exercise of freedom also demands the specific application of the principle of subsidiarity. This principle would give our economic society the organic structure necessary for the enjoyment and exercise of freedom. Men are to be joined not merely in terms of what separates them but in terms of what unites them. This cooperative process should be committed to self-governing (socio-economic) groups which would represent the different economic interests in our society. These groups are to be functional rather than mere interest or pressure groups. They are to be more than present day labor unions or employers' associations. They must be groups which could carry on quasilegal functions seeking the common good in their particular areas. A multiplicity of these buffer groups, hierarchically arranged, must be established with the maximum exercise of power at the lower levels, while higher groups are called into action only when needed to coordinate and regulate economic relationships.[60] According to the principle of subsidiarity, freedom would be enjoyed if these higher groups did not arrogate to themselves functions which could be performed by smaller groups. These groups, large and small, should not be considered organs of the state. Their independence is essential for the safeguarding of freedom. They should exercise many powers now assumed by the government in default of other ways of procuring the common good.

In the United States many authorities urged the adoption of the Industry Council Plan as a feasible application of the principle of subsidiarity to our economic system. The Industry Council is to be a public body, an intermediary between government and private enterprise, made up of the democratically chosen representatives of employers and workers in a given industry. They are to be guided, but not dictated to, by government officials. The Industry Council members are to be empowered to fix wages, hours, working conditions and prices for their industry in cooperation with similarly constituted bodies from other occupations.[61]

According to the supporters of this program, economic life is meant to be an organized and democratic partnership for the general welfare rather than a harsh competitive struggle for individual or group advantage. Consequently, the industries, the professions and extractive occupations, as mining and agriculture, must voluntarily enter into an organized system of economic cooperation among themselves and with government to establish a rational and moral economic order. The Industry Council is to be a social institution, a conceptualization of society in which the individual achieves the fullest expression of his freedom in an orderly relationship to social groups.[62]

The application of the principle of subsidiarity in the form of the Industry Council Plan would necessitate changes in motivation as well as modification of our complicated systems of status, prestige and authority. These Industry Councils cannot exist as effective social organizations until they are integrated into the social structure of the society in which they are to be adopted.

Neither the universal adoption of the principle of cooperation nor the principle of subsidiarity of association will insure the enjoyment of freedom by labor and management, unless there is also a considerable change in human hearts and ideals. Catholic Social Thought insists that the codes of manners and ethics which govern the day-to-day relationships of individuals and groups must recognize the moral law. Consequently, the exercise of freedom in our modern economic society demands a reformation of morals and ethics, a reformation based on reason and on principles flowing from the nature of man and society.[63] This reform does not imply a revolution or overthrow of the present economic system but rather an evolution toward an ordered, organic society. One of the greatest students of the labor problem in America, Monsignor John A. Ryan, believed that, "The rich must cease to put their faith in material things and rise to a simpler and saner plane of living, the middle classes and the poor must give up their envy and snobbish imitation of the false and degrading standards of the opulent classes, and all must learn the elementary lesson that the path to worthwhile achievement leads through the field of hard and honest labor, . . . that the only life worth living is that in which one's cherished wants are few, simple and noble. For the adoption and pursuit of these ideals the most necessary requisite is a revival of genuine religion." [64]

Freedom and Education

by Dr. Daniel C. Sullivan
Professor of Education,
Graduate School, St. John's University

International emergencies tend invariably to intensify the controversy concerning academic freedom. Today's "cold war" is no exception. It has centered public attention on the teacher and his freedom in a democratic society. The greatest tension generates over the question: Should a democratic society permit teaching destructive of its values and its truths?

This is obviously a limited view of the subject. It overlooks, for instance, student freedom in education, and a host of other problems. However, since most current controversy is concerned with the teacher and freedom, this, therefore, will be the subject matter of this paper. The freedom to seek truth wherever it may be found; freedom to teach within the educational institution; freedom of the teacher to make extra-mural utterances; to participate in extra-mural activities; these are the important elements in any consideration of the teacher's academic freedom.

The first of these elements is sufficiently safeguarded so that it warrants no consideration here. The other two have enough in common so that any reference to one may be safely applied to the other. However, because of the tremendous concern over freedom to teach in the schools of America, the second of the three elements will be given major attention in this discourse.

It should be added, by the way of introduction, that unlike most expositions concerning academic freedom, the freedom of the teacher at the secondary level will be considered. That this is of as much concern to the public as it is to the academic world is readily understood when one notes the increasing number of investigations and dismissals involving secondary school teachers. Consequently, whatever is said here pertaining to the freedom of the teacher applies also to all levels of education.

This paper will not present a rehash of such *causes célèbres* as the dismissal of the professors at Washington University in Seattle and those at Rutgers University in New Jersey, the refusal of the faculty at the University of California to sign the loyalty oath, the Bertrand Russell case, the dismissal of certain New York City teachers on secondary and collegiate levels, and many others. These have had their full share of professional as well as lay treatment, not only in the press but also in the court, classroom, and lecture hall. Space does not permit more than a passing reference to them. Furthermore, too often they emphasize only the emotional, hysterical and illogical manner in which certain elements attempt to rationalize their false interpretation of academic freedom.

Any accurate determination of the meaning and limitations of academic freedom revolves about three prime issues: (1) the function of the academic institution and of education; (2) the nature of the academic calling; (3) the natural limitations placed upon the teacher's academic freedom in the fulfillment of his function.

The Function of the Academic Institution

International tension today is not only producing apprehension with respect to political affairs, but also a growing sensitivity to the role of the school in transmitting to each new generation of students values inherent in a democratic way of life. Because of this it is necessary, before the freedom of the teacher can be assayed, to consider the function of the school, and particularly of the university, in America.

Universitas, as employed in the Middle Ages was a legal term, which derived its meaning from the *corpus juris civilis,* and denoted an association taken as a whole, i.e. in its corporate sense. In this sense when referring to a school the term *universitas* does not refer to the sciences or material taught, but rather to the group pursuing these studies, the body of teachers and students: *universites magistrorum et scholarium.*

It is in the manner and reason for the development of higher schools that their function is best seen. During the eleventh and twelfth centuries a number of causes were at work which resulted in a new type of higher school. The older monastic and cathedral schools are generally considered to be the basis out of which arose the Universities modified by such influences as Saracenic culture, the Crusades, and, most important, the new method and activity of the Schoolmen. These undoubtedly influenced the origin and development of the Universities as great centers of education.

Another factor influencing the development of the Universities was the increased specialization of learning. A large mass of learning had developed around subjects of greater interest to man, intellectually and practically. This resulted in the tendency for these schools to specialize in the study of law, medicine, and theology, a course of action that had the salubrious effect of bringing thousands of students to the great centers of learning. In this is seen the major reason for the Universities' existence.

As time modified the early purpose of the institutions, they broadened their function to the extent that today they serve three functions: (1) to train in the profession; (2) to disseminate a general education; (3) to promote research.

The function of higher education in America is further clarified by reference to the *Report of the President's Commission on Higher Education,* which lists the following as the objectives of the college and university: to give a fuller realization of democracy in every phase of living; to educate for international understanding and cooperation; to educate for the application of creative imagination and trained intelligence to the solution of social problems; and to the improvement of the administration of public affairs.[1] Although this may not be a complete description of the function of American institutions of higher learning, it does, however, contain certain elements which place a limit upon the teacher's freedom in these schools.

Inasmuch as education is the transmission of the intellectual and cultural heritage of one generation to the next, the schools, which are the principal educational agents, act as arteries through which pass this heritage. As such the American schools—on all levels—are veritable fountains of youth for American democracy. In the final analysis it is the school which will be mainly responsible for sustaining the intellectual, cultural, and spiritual ideals of a democracy.

This being the case, once again, it is possible to realize why institutional purposes place limitations upon academic freedom.

In a similar vein the then President of Harvard, John Conant, writing about the function of schools in America stated:

> The student in high school, college, and in graduate school must be concerned, in part at least, with the words "right" and "wrong" in the ethical and mathematical sense . . . the primary concern of American education today is not the development of the appreciation of the good life in young gentlemen born to the purple. It is the infusion of the liberal and human tradition into our educational system. Our purpose is to cultivate in the largest possible numbers of our future citizens an appreciation of both the responsibilities and benefits which come to them because they are Americans and free.[2]

The importance of this function of American educational institutions is further emphasized by a resolution adopted by the National Educational Association at St. Louis in July 1950.

> All schools have an obligation to teach the rights, privileges, and responsibilities of living in a democracy. The responsibility of the schools is to teach the value of our American way of life, founded as it is on the dignity and worth of the individual, our youth should know it, believe in it, and live it continuously.

In summarizing the function of Education generally and that of the university particularly, it may be said that the pursuit of truth, the deepening of the intellectual life of the student, raising the cultural level of the community and region are of major concern. In addition, these educational agencies are established to prepare future citizens for their place in the American democratic society.

Educational institutions in America, regardless of their levels, attempt to realize in some degree the functions mentioned. In addition, it should be kept in mind that all schools should direct their efforts toward ". . . the whole aggregate of human life, physical and spiritual, intellectual and moral, individual, domestic, and social, not with a view of reducing it in any way, but in order to elevate, regulate, and perfect it, in accordance with the example and teaching of Christ." [3]

Probably the finest statement of the objectives of institutions of higher learning is found in Cardinal Newman's sermon on "Intellect, The Instrument of Religious Training." Considering the fact that it is necessary to clarify the purposes of educational institutions in order to establish the basis for determining the extent and limitations of academic freedom, a careful reading of his statement makes it very obvious why these limitations are necessarily imposed upon the teacher's freedom. Although it specifically refers to Catholic institutions, there is, nevertheless, sufficient reason to warrant its inclusion here. It gives weight to the argument that institutional purposes place limitations upon academic freedom regardless of the prevalence of a church's influence in establishing these goals. The fact remains that all educational institutions in America have been established in accordance with principles inherent in a religious way of life. According to Newman, the object of the Catholic Church in establishing universities is "to reunite things which were in the beginning joined together by God, and have been put asunder by man." He states further: "Some persons will say that I am thinking of confining, distorting, and stunting the growth of intellect by ecclesiastical supervision. I have no such thought. . . . I wish the intellect to range with the utmost freedom, . . . I want the same roof to contain both the intellectual and moral discipline." [4]

In accomplishing these ends, the university, particularly, according to one educator ". . . must hold fast to its primary function in the imparting of wisdom and the discovery of truth." It must, furthermore, "be conservative in the etymological sense; it is the guardian of culture of the intellectual world. While in no wise unfriendly to new discoveries, it should be unwilling to pick up its academic robes and run pell-mell after every pedagogical piper that pipes in the market place. It is not progress for the university, even in a democracy, to lower its drawbridge for the howling mobs clamoring for admittance under the leadership of science." [5]

The functions of higher education indicate the school's responsibility to promote inquiry and advance human knowledge in all areas pertaining to man's welfare. In the natural sciences, social sciences, philosophy, and religion in which the scholar investigates man's relation to outer nature, to his fellow men and to ultimate realities, the university functions to provide not only the facilities for this research but the opportunities to express and publish his findings. However, as with its other progress, the institutions of higher learning must also limit the extent to which the members of the academic community may go with respect to their personal findings and opinions of their research. These limitations, it will be seen, do not, as some would maintain, hamper or impede the search for truth or its exposition. They do, however, guard against the charlatan, the subversive, and the dilettante in the fields of research and teaching, at the same time giving the true research worker and teacher ample leeway in his endeavors to help the university fulfill its purpose.

As was stated at the beginning of this section of the paper, the importance of academic freedom, its meaning, and delimitations are most clearly perceived in the light of the purpose for which educational institutions are established. Similarly, the proper function of the academic calling will further enhance a more complete understanding of the limits placed upon the teacher's and scholar's academic freedom.

The Function of the Academic Calling

Being a teacher in a democratic culture whose principles are derived from the moral law and involve a consideration of the worth and dignity of the individual, there is a more serious function to be performed. The pupil is not merely existing as a citizen and subject of a country, he is even more so as a citizen and subject of the kingdom of God: he is destined for both time and eternity. As a consequence the basic responsibility of the teacher is to help his pupil not only to obtain his best welfare in this life, but also to obtain his eternal happiness in the next. It must be from the fact that each individual has four sides to his nature that the only true function of the teacher can be derived.

Each is a child of God with a supernatural destiny; a social being, a citizen living in society; an individual with personal needs and wants; and finally, each is a person who has to make his way in the world. These aspects of the individual's nature clarify the function of the academic calling. Their's is the task of assisting each individual to a fuller realization of his religious, social, avocational, and vocational needs.

These general aims of the teacher in American schools are the concern of all levels of the educational ladder. Since, however, the question of academic freedom is more related to higher education an exposition of the specific function of the teacher in these latter schools is required.

The most prevalent statement relevant to the primary function of university teaching and research is: ". . . to deal at first hand, after prolonged and specialized training, with the sources of knowledge; and to impart the results of their own and of their fellow-specialists' investigation and reflection, both to the students and general public, without fear or favor." [6]

However, it must be maintained that this statement of the A.A.U.P. cannot be accepted, without reservation, as the function of the academic community. And when one reads further from the same source that teachers should be: ". . . no more subject to the control of trustees than are judges subject to the control of the President, with respect to their decisions," [7] then it is understandable wherein lies the cause of so much confusion concerning the freedom of the teacher.

Such statements would lead one to believe that teaching, on any level, is a right, whereas, in truth, it is a responsibility. Moreover, as such, the teacher in fulfilling his functions is not free to the extent that the trustees' policies can be ignored; nor can the teacher pass on to his students his personal opinions with impunity, particularly if there has been any attempt to ignore the complete sources of truth.

The teacher in institutions of higher learning is responsible for teaching truth for purposes previously stated. In this he must recognize not only the social heritage but also that body of objective truths made known to man by divine revelation—truths which all must accept; teacher and pupil, for right living and eternal salvation as well as for right thought.

Because of this the teacher in American schools cannot subscribe to a philosophy which accepts no tradition, recognizes no authority outside of himself in fulfilling his function. Neither may he proclaim the right to express himself untrammeled by any limitations except those derived from his own judgment and individual interpretation. The nature of the individual, of an educational agency in a democracy preclude any possibility of unlimited freedom for the teacher in fulfilling his function regardless of the level of education.

Speaking of any school, it is the faculty that in the long run shapes its aims—its products. As Pius XI says, ". . . good schools are the result of good teachers." [8] It is they who carry on research, it is they who keep in constant touch with advances in their special fields, and it is they who instruct the students who crowd the schools, the colleges, the universities. It is the individual member of each faculty who is responsible for the training of his students to use their minds, to make thoughtful judgments; in short, to become as was indicated earlier, good citizens, intelligent human beings whatever their life work may be.

This function is only fulfilled, when, as was stated, all sources of truth are recognized and when there is a realization that the teacher's function within democratic schools cannot be spoken of in terms of the A.A.U.P. statement without qualification.

Finally with reference to the teacher the remarks of one leading American educator will suffice. He maintains that the ideal Christian teacher:

> . . . must be conversant with all the errors in his field, with all the arguments of his adversaries, and, at the same time, he must be able to answer them effectively and be convinced of the truth of his response. Of most importance, he must have the zeal and courage not to leave any doubt in his students' minds as to what he believes and what they should believe, if they are to remain within the framework of Christian doctrine and practice.[9]

It is evident from this and preceding remarks concerning the teacher's function that there are implied limitations with reference to the teacher's freedom; and by no stretch of the imagination can one deduce from the functions of educational agencies or the teachers therein an unbridled license for the latter in fulfilling his purpose. Within this conceptual framework, i.e. the ambient of the university, the college, and lower schools, and that of the teacher, the answer to the question: "To what extent is the teacher free in the instruction of his students?" is found and will be specifically answered in the following section.

Academic Freedom—Meaning and Limitations

Without laboring the point, it should be evident that the function of the educational institution and the role played by the teacher who is responsible for implementing that function are factors which condition the meaning and extent of academic freedom. Consequently, from the previous exposition, it should be possible to define academic freedom, to state what academic freedom is not, and to ascertain the limitations within which the teacher will be permitted to exercise his freedom. This more or less resolves itself into a question of determining the proper extent of freedom of teaching between the two extremes of unrestricted freedom and a total lack of freedom.

It can be assayed at this point that academic freedom does not mean freedom of the teacher or research worker in an educational institution to investigate and discuss the problems in his field, to disseminate his personal findings or opinions without consideration of the political, social, ecclesiastical authorities, or consideration of the administrative officials of his institution.

Nor can one truthfully deduce from previous statements, with reference to institutional and teacher function, that academic freedom means as the late Dr. Nicholas Murray Butler would have the academic community believe, "the right to search for truth unhampered by shackles of political, religious, or scientific beliefs or opinions." [10] Farther in this same source he states that this freedom should be limited by "common morality, common sense." Like too many statements concerning the meaning of academic freedom, this too suffers from vagueness, being furthermore presumptuous and paradoxical. If there are to be no shackles, if this vague freedom is to be unhampered, why then should common morality and common sense be limitations?

Furthermore, if one were to remain aware of the true functions of educational institutions and their teachers, academic freedom could not be construed to have the unlimited freedom attributed to it by the Civil Liberties Union. In their proposals in behalf of academic freedom is found the statement to the effect that there should be "no limitations on classroom discussion relevant to the subjects taught." [11] Academic freedom is not license—it does not guarantee to any teacher the right to teach whatever he pleases, nor to impose on the immature, the unwary, the uncritical, his own intellectual idiosyncrasies.

What academic freedom is and is not is well stated by Tyler and Cheyney in the following passage:

> Academic freedom, with its resulting measurable security of tenure, is not a special immunity or prerequisite gained by the act of adopting the teaching profession. It is for the community a guarantee of securing to society the best service of men of advanced knowledge and thought; for institutions a means of attracting and retaining men and women of superior ability; for teachers and investigators a privilege to be deserved by the exercise of a just measure of both freedom and self-restraint, by supporting and living up to the best standards of their profession.[12]

Hence, academic freedom is not so undefined in its limitations as to permit Willard S. Elsbree's statement to the effect that: ". . . it is difficult to see how the school can provide experience in democratic living for pupils without freedom of teaching"; [13] nor the statement of Oscar Shaftel, former Professor of English at Queens College, New York, who upon being accused of being a member of the Communist Party replied: "This inquisition is a bludgeon against academic freedom, the time-tried system by which the academic profession . . . accepts the responsibility of what should be taught, and how, and by whom." [14]

With respect to this and many similar statements by educators in defense of the inviolability of the academic community, one educator put it quite bluntly when he stated that for unadulterated rubbish the above statement would be hard to beat.[15] He goes further, and, as few have in the past, properly places the problem which has been greatly responsible for the present intense interest in academic freedom. He says that there is no question of academic freedom involved but that the question pertains to membership in the Communistic Party. To establish a connection between this question and the interpretation of academic freedom one would have to be double-jointed intellectually.[16] It is patent that there is no problem of academic freedom involved in a refusal by a Board of Education or University Trustees to allow a Communist to teach in their schools. As a matter of fact there would be considerable loss of academic freedom if a Communistic system of education were prevalent in America today.

These false interpretations of academic freedom have been responsible for the dishonesty of those who pay lip service to one set of principles while teaching their students, under a smoke screen of academic freedom, such principles as those basic to agnosticism, atheism, extreme liberalism, or Communism. It is definitions such as the above that have been used as a shield behind which are found not only incompetent members of the academic community, but more serious for the youth of America, those who would advocate an entirely different way of life—a Godless way of life. And it is behind such interpretations of academic freedom that certain elements within the academic community defend their rights to refuse to sign loyalty oaths, to refuse to divulge membership in subversive organizations, to teach opinions and personal beliefs as truth.

Because of a vociferous few who have used academic freedom for these selfish purposes, the term becomes a fetish and a cult. Furthermore, the intellectual world is witnessing a foolhardy attempt to bring into being that which has neither form nor substance, is subject to no standard, has neither limitations nor definition. This condition has unfortunately resulted in so much confusion and misunderstanding among teachers and the lay public that one educator maintains that this fetish of academic freedom—unlimited and undefined—has become the soft under-belly of the American way of life, and that the sooner it is armor-plated by some sensible limitations the sooner will the future of America be secured from fatal consequences.[17]

Academic Freedom, not unlike other freedoms, has limitations placed upon it. Freedom is not an exclusive consideration in human life, nor can it be made an absolute criterion in the field of education without disturbing the order of reality. There are duties and responsibilities in life: purposes, loyalties, disciplines, and binding agreements that claim each, regardless of his life-calling. Free expression has never been an absolute right. Expression is curtailed at all times in the interest of truth, decency, and national security. Members of the teaching profession, as well as those in other fields of human endeavor, must realize that freedom taken by itself and for itself leads to negation and anarchy—might well under present conditions lead to Communism.

The fact that limitations are necessary in determining the extent of freedom to teach should never be interpreted to mean that the teacher is restrained from the discussion of controversial issues or is afraid to acquaint himself with erroneous and unorthodox opinion. Furthermore, these limits, if properly understood, in no way prevent the teacher from presenting the facts and known truths concerning Communism.

Limitations of Academic Freedom

That academic freedom has attendant and inseparable limitations, that its claim may be extended beyond all reason, is granted. How then shall the moral and rational interpretation be made? How shall the teacher and the student be protected from either undue restrictions on the one hand and undue license on the other? To this question many answers have been given—answers which run the gamut from extreme totalitarianism that assuming powers of omniscience and temporary omnipotence, insists that the members of the academic community have no freedom outside the dictates of the state, to those among the academic community whose interpretation of academic freedom is nothing more than license to do as one pleases. The correct answer is found at neither of these extremes but rather in terms of the limitations that were implied in the previous discussions of the function of educational institutions and the function of the academic calling.

Specifically it is possible to group the limitations upon academic freedom under the following categories, following the suggestion of Redden and Ryan: (1) the obligation to teach the truth; (2) the American way of life; (3) the immaturity of the student; (4) the policies of the institution; (5) the boundaries of one's field of specialization.[18]

The obligation to tell the truth: Anyone considering the meaning of academic freedom must primarily concern himself with the meaning of freedom. Freedom means neither license nor the right to do what one must. Its true meaning, as Bishop Fulton Sheen states is ". . . the right to do whatever you ought, and ought implies purpose and law. We are free in the law and not outside of it. We are most free when we obey the nature of things and not when we disobey them." [19]

In the creation of man God gave him a spiritual soul, one of whose faculties, the intellect, has for its proper object the seeking of truth. Since the nature of the student's mind is therefore to know truth, then the academic freedom of the teacher is initially and basically limited by this proper object of the mind. Consequently the teacher must above all else present the truth. In presenting error, teaching opinion as truth, the teacher is doing an injustice both to his own intellect and that of the student.

In times like these when error is so often accepted as truth, when the right to teach error is being protected by recourse to some vague and erroneous interpretation of academic freedom, the fundamental power of the mind to grasp truth needs vigorous restatements. It is not a fact that truth is not verifiable unless it can be put to the test of the microscope; it is not a fact that there is no knowledge beyond the senses; nor is it a fact that truth is relative; that there are no absolutes. The acceptance on the part of certain elements within the academic community of the erroneous conclusion that truth is relative and their right to teach truth as such protected by recourse to academic freedom has resulted in their students' being indoctrinated with an inane philosophy of change for change's sake.[20]

Throughout the ages the fabric of education has been the result of the teachers' consecration to seek and to teach truth, that is truth as it is and not some substitute, dictated by tyranny. The dedication to teach truth does not permit the teacher to use his position of authority to commit his students to his views or to use his position to indoctrinate if demonstrable truth is absent.

When the latter is absent and opinion is being presented then because of its nature, it is the duty of the teacher to label it as such. It is customary for Americans to want to know what they are buying, so too in the realm of education one must label his wares. Is what is being presented truth, or is it opinion, or probable opinion, or is it error?

This interpretation permits the presentation of error but labelled as such. It will permit the discussion of Communism, but, truthfully, as a stark reality, in its stark nakedness. This does not permit the presentation of Communism as the many-volumed Soviet Republic Encyclopedia would. This would be demonstrable error and would consequently do violence to the students' intellects which seek truth. It would, furthermore, challenge the known truth, and the teacher has no right to play false with realities.

It also permits the presentation of any controversial issue, but again so labelled. Democracy may not be the best form of political organization, but as far as political thought has advanced today it is the nearest thing to the truth. While the teacher, then, is free to discuss and present its limitations, its weaknesses, he is not permitted, even in the name of academic freedom, to indoctrinate his students with a Communistic philosophy as a better alternative.

In presenting controversial issues, the teacher must keep in mind his responsibility for the rectitude both of his thoughts and his actions. He is no less obliged to think according to the truth than to act according to the truth. Consequently, truth must be taught as certain and error as error; where as opinion must, by the same token, be so labelled. This still provides the teacher with ample leeway to pursue truth wherever it might be, to discover what is new and to sustain what is old.

If truth, let alone common decency and morality, did not bound the freedom of the teacher, there would be no limit to how far certain individuals would go in their teaching. It is not merely protection against the teaching of false political ideologies that is being sought, but protection against the false philosophy of morality as espoused by such as Bertrand Russell and others. It is only academic freedom, when limited by truth, that can prevent the teaching of untruth as truth or opinion as fact, and the indoctrination of students by those who hold chairs in universities, not for the purpose of seeking and presenting truth but rather for fostering personal opinion and personal philosophy, regardless of their false bases.

The teacher's academic freedom, limited by the obligation to seek and teach the truth, rather than imposing any undue restrictions upon him, does prevent such cases as those mentioned above and at the same time protects the prior rights of the student in his seeking truth through the instrumentality of academic community. The latter must, in addition, not only recognize its obligation with respect to the truth, but must also recognize all sources of truth, not only reason but revelation as well. Any system of education which would exclude God and His revelation as a source of truth would become in the words of Pius XI, "a den and not a temple."

For man to attain his ultimate goal the knowledge of truth is strictly necessary. Consequently, inasmuch as the student has a right to know any and all truth that can be known through reason, then it follows that the teacher is morally bound to present nothing but the truth to his students. Furthermore as John Curran states:

> It is evident that man can have no right to knowledge of anything but the truth. It is self-evident that the mind of man has no right to error. The mind is made to know the truth. Error is an imperfection of the mind and of its nature impedes man from activity toward his goal.[21]

In the final analysis the teacher is limited very definitely in his freedom of teaching by having to answer the inquiries: "Is the matter being taught true or false?", and if false, "May one prudently suppose that a good and not an evil will eventuate from its exposition?" The limitation here then, upon academic freedom, is the true and the good. It is the teacher above all who must in these critical times accept the challenge of Christ to all those who reject and despise truth: "For this was I born, and for this came I into the world, that I should give testimony to the truth." [22]

It follows, therefore, that to teach what is true and to receive instructions in what is true is academic freedom in the only true sense. And when it comes to defining what is the truth the teacher must seek the guidance not only of reason but of supernatural revelation that has come from God.

The American way of life: As is indicated from the Christian principles of the Founding Fathers of this country, the American way of life cherished and defended for centuries, the sanctuary of countless millions who elsewhere have suffered religious and political persecution and economic degradation, is very definitely dedicated to such tenets as are contained in the Bill of Rights and the Constitution. These principles, basic as they are to American prosperity and individual well-being, must be protected by, as well as disseminated to, each new generation.

Inasmuch as the freedoms, loyalties, privileges, and responsibilities of the American way of life are not entirely inborn, education is essential for their propagation. Consequently, American democracy has a right to expect of its educational institutions a dedication to this task, not only on elementary and secondary levels but on the levels of higher education as well. All educational agencies must be dedicated to the task of inculcating in each individual the loyalties and allegiances necessary for the survival and perpetuation of this democratic way of life.

That the educational institutions are aware of their dedicated purpose is evident from the following statement of the Committee of Academic Freedom and Tenure of the Association of American Colleges: "The American College . . . views itself as none other than a part of that American society which gave it birth and which it now exists to preserve. . . . The colleges are fully aware of their stake in the preservation of a free society and recognize their responsibility to protect its ideals against any and all movements to subvert them." [23]

It follows that the teacher in his school is not there because of an unqualified right, but because he feels a responsibility to inculcate democratic ideals in young people. Furthermore, this function of education and the teacher to preserve the American way of life places a further limitation upon academic freedom. The teacher has no right to teach the overthrow of this democratic form of government, nor right to advocate that in its place there should be a Communistic type of economic and political organization.

This places a member of the academic community, who is a member of a subversive group, in a paradoxical and possibly an immoral predicament. He is assuming the responsibility of employment in an institution dedicated to the preservation and advancement of the American way of life, while at the same time dedicating himself to the cause that advocates its overthrow. Under these circumstances, such individuals have gone beyond the limits of academic freedom and can no longer be considered members of the teaching profession in good standing.

There are, however, some who would have the American people believe that membership in the Communistic Party need not be a factor in barring anyone from teaching. They maintain, without any proof whatsoever, that such membership would not affect the teaching of music, art, science, nor would it be harmful to the student's concept of the democratic way of life, if such teaching were confined to those and similar subjects.

The answer to this is found in Communistic literature. It is evident that a Communist has surrendered his right to deviate from the party line on all questions of political and social policy. This political surrender of that for which a school, and particularly a university stands, disqualifies the individual for teaching. For the same reason one cannot approve of the idea that anyone may teach if he is circumspect in his teaching, and if his teaching brings a greater good to the community in the field of his specialty, providing he was innocuous in his political allegiance. As with all such thoughts, there is nothing innocuous about any Communistic teacher's political allegiance.

The fact is that membership in the Communist Party is a matter of being dedicated to a set of principles. Whereas the American teacher is dedicated to the American way of life and to the task of developing future citizens who possess an understanding of the principles basic to this way of life, those who are affiliated with Communism are dedicated to uphold and propagate principles diametrically opposed to the American way.

Specifically and unequivocally, these believers in Communism, regardless of color, red or pink, are dedicated to uphold the teaching of Marx, Lenin, Stalin, *et al.* The principles of these individuals must be accepted *in toto* by their followers. It is not a matter of accepting some and rejecting others. One must, if he is in any way a follower of Communism, accept their teaching which includes a denial of the spirituality of man, denies the existence of God, denies the dignity of man; furthermore he must accept and teach the Communistic object of world domination and the spread of Stalinism; he must teach that the individual must lose himself in working for the advancement of the state. To him the individual is merely an item of human fodder with which to feed the totalitarian appetite of the state.

Furthermore, the Communist Party's ideological journal, *The Communist,* makes it quite clear that a party member, regardless of his special subject as a teacher, cannot be innocuous in his approach. They are told that the Communist teacher cannot afford to ignore the fact that he comes in contact with the children of the masses, that he is responsible for training these children and he must mobilize other teachers in this fight to spread Communism. He is told to take advantage of his position, without exposing himself, and to give his students a working-class education. This, then, would not lead one to believe that a Communist teacher would dare refrain from spreading his poison even in the music class. Likewise under these conditions it is obvious that academic freedom loosely defined and unlimited can do the greatest harm to the American way of life by becoming a ready cloak for the protection of subversives in the school.

Considering the function of education in the American culture and the dedicated purpose of the teacher, it follows that his freedom is limited by any obligation to teach democratic principles. It also follows that the teacher who is in any way affiliated with an organization upholding an antithetical philosophy is not qualified to teach or do research in American schools, and as a consequence that there is complete justification for asking the teacher if he is a member of a subversive organization. The fact that belonging to the Communist Party has not been declared illegal, that the Communist Party has not been outlawed does not alter the situation. It still remains a fact that Communistic principles are detrimental to the American way of life and are, furthermore, not based upon truth. Neither academic freedom nor tenure affords protection for treason, anymore than academic freedom should afford one protection in the dissemination of error regardless of whether it is in the field of political science, economics, or philosophy.

There is no need for the true scholar or teacher dedicated to preserve the American way of life, to fear any limitations upon his seeking and teaching truth; neither should he fear inquiries concerning his affiliations. It is the weak, the incompetent, and the political and moral subversives who, in order to protect themselves, hide behind the cloak of academic freedom. Such inquiries when properly conducted can in no way impair the vigor of school autonomy or curtail the freedom in education when such education is dedicated to truth and the democratic way of life.

Former United States Senator Herbert O'Conor makes the inquirers' position quite clear. It is his contention that although educators are entitled to think as they please, they have no right however, to depart from the principle that change in a government must be attained through orderly and legal processes, all within the framework of the American Constitution. For that reason, he feels, there should be no toleration of those few teachers who advocate directly or indirectly the forceful and violent overthrow of the American form of government.[24]

None of this should be misinterpreted to imply that error labelled as such should not be presented at various levels of education. As has been stated previously, the school should teach about other forms of political and economic organizations. However, the teacher must be mindful that teaching about Communism does not mean advocating Communism. Such advocacy cannot be tolerated in American schools.

The limitation placed upon the teacher by accepting a position in schools established to perpetuate the American way of life, leaves without justification the refusal of the professor at the University of California to sign a loyalty oath. The cry that such oaths jeopardize academic freedom is sheer nonsense. This is not a matter of the teacher's freedom but one of citizenship, just as it was in the case of the professors at University of Washington, Rutgers University, Brooklyn College, etc., who refused to divulge affiliation, if any, in the Communist Party. Any educational institution or government agency which did not seek to locate and rid itself of individuals dedicated to anti-American ideologies would be abdicating its rights and sacred duties.

Because these individuals seeking protection from an ill-defined and unlimited concept of academic freedom are, nonetheless, employed to teach American youth, those who employ them and pay them have a right to know not only their professional qualifications but also—and even more important—their attitude toward this country and the American way of life. For this reason, therefore, members of a faculty who refuse to give an account of their position in matters of community and national interests cannot be defended by an appeal to academic freedom. This is particularly true when such an explanation is called for by duly constituted governmental or school bodies acting within the limits of their authority.[25] Academic freedom immunizes teachers neither from an examination of what they teach nor from any consideration of their loyalty to the American way of life. Academic freedom cannot be a sanctuary for propagandists, communistic indoctrinators, or pseudo-intellectuals who teach error as truth, particularly in the field of ethics.

Just as the teacher is limited in his freedom to teach by his dedication to impart nothing but the truth, in like manner he is limited in his teaching by a dedication to instill in his pupils those principles from which the American way of life has been derived. To teach anarchy, to indoctrinate young minds with erroneous ideologies can no more be protected in the name of academic freedom than can the stressing of error as truth.

Academic freedom is no exception to the rule that sets of rights and privileges entail corresponding duties and responsibilities. This principle imposes a great obligation upon the teacher. He must be honest, have integrity, cherish scholarship. But above all there must be no question of his loyalty to truth and the principles upon which the American system of government has been founded; one of these principles being freedom within the law and not outside of it.

The importance of this particular limitation upon the teacher's freedom was admirably stated by Dwight D. Eisenhower upon the occasion of his inauguration as President of Columbia University. "Indeed," he said, "academic freedom is nothing more than a specific application of the freedom inherent in the American way of life." To this should be added the fact that "academic freedom ends where the undermining of democracy begins."

The immaturity of the students: Education may be defined in part as the influence exerted by a mature person upon the immature through instruction, example, and discipline. The immaturity of the average student forces the teacher to relinquish certain elements of his freedom when he assumes responsibility for the student's knowledge of truth, goodness, and beauty. The teacher must, furthermore, realize that his knowledge, experiences, his position of authority over those less mature than he often limit the student's equal rights unless certain limits are placed upon the teacher's freedom.

Because at most levels on the educational ladder, the student's character is still in the formative stage and his intellectual powers as yet in their developmental stages, it is imperative that the teacher present scientific truths with discretion, and that he introduce new concepts gradually with due consideration for the background of each student.

It is, however, in the matter of controversial issues that the teacher must limit his freedom when presenting these topics to immature students. For in these areas where opinion is more prevalent than fact, it is possible for certain elements of the academic community to take advantage of their position to teach opinion, and at times, error as truth. Here the teacher is particularly admonished to be cognizant of the immaturity of his students and to refrain from indoctrinating them with his own opinions before they have had opportunities of analyzing other aspects of the issue.

The degree of maturity of the student not only places upon the teacher the responsibility of considering the difficulty of the material but also limits him in his manner of presentation. At certain stages of his mental growth the student habitually credits as truth any authoritative statement by the teacher. This is a substitutional function of authority and contributes to the exercise of freedom rightly determined.

This important limitation upon academic freedom, particularly with respect to method at certain levels, determines the extent to which discussion will be allowed; the extent to which the student will be permitted to reach independent conclusions. The exercise of mental and moral discipline, of authority over the pupil is a God-given responsibility. Accordingly, any system of education which overlooks this fact is derelict in its duty. In addition a system which permits free discussion at too early a stage in the student's development sets out deliberately to foster the spirit of self-determinism. This does an injustice to the student because it sends him forth inclined toward the same false philosophy of life upon which it is based, i.e. a philosophy which denies the absoluteness of truth.

The teacher must use judgment and discrimination in instructing students, who because of their relative immaturity lack the background of knowledge, experience, and reflection to evaluate properly facts, detect fallacies, and foresee results. Under the circumstances it is unfair of the teacher to take advantage of his position and influence to mold prematurely the thoughts of his students in those areas alien to the teacher's special training or foreign to the policies of the institution. Furthermore, because of their immaturity the students should not be compelled to listen to offensive and injurious remarks, moral or spiritual, just because they are forced to attend certain educational courses.

Thus the teacher's freedom is limited by the immaturity of his students; by the fact that specific obligations to the student rest upon the teacher because of the student's immaturity, and by the added fact that the teacher must respect the degree of development of the student's intellect, the proper object of which is truth.

Policies of the institution: As was seen in greater detail in the previous section of this paper, educational institutions are established for specific purposes—such purposes being determined by the state, church, or individuals. The policies of the trustees, therefore, have a limiting effect upon the teachers they employ, as well as upon the students who attend the schools.

As with a person, so likewise is it with institutions: the school is not fancy free, footloose to teach what it pleases, how, and when it pleases. As a part of society, it must take for its purpose the policy which is dedicated to it by those responsible for its establishment. Because it has a dependence as well as an independence, the members of the teaching profession employed in schools established by those interested in perpetuating the American way of life are consequently limited in their freedom of expression.

The teacher, of course, must be free to use all his powers of thought and education, but subject to the exercise of like rights of others, particularly his students; free to express his ideas wholly or in part. His academic freedom is the right to express these ideas to his students—while under the obligation to remember that the students are not really his. He must always remember that they are entrusted to him by their parents and the community and they enroll themselves for certain specific purposes, among which are the pursuit of truth, the increase of knowledge, and the improvement of character—purposes which, incidentally, are established by the very nature of the student and implemented in his behalf by institutional policy.

There are those, however, within the academic community who declare that no donor—and this would include the state and its citizens—has a right to interfere with the teacher's freedom of expression. If such a theory were justified in the name of academic freedom, it is easy to imagine how society could be placed at the mercy of every educational charlatan and dispenser of extreme liberalism. A Communist, who is interested primarily in the destruction of the American system, would under those circumstances, feel quite safe in teaching his philosophy, safe from the sanction of either scholastic or civil authority. This could quite possibly be the consequence of unlimited freedom, unrestrained by institutional policy.

The teacher must in general be in harmony with the policies of the college or institution in which he is teaching. A member of the academic community who is aware of the Christian beliefs of his employer can scarcely assume freedom of teaching gives him the right to undermine or publicly attack Christianity; a man who teaches or desires to teach in the average school which believes in monogamy can hardly expect the institution to go through a long legal fight to discharge him when he publicly professes and teaches his belief in free love. Under these and similar circumstances the appeal to academic freedom appeals more to one's sense of humor than to one's sense of fair play or what is right.

Therefore, when in opposition to the wishes of the institution, or without its consent, a professor persists in presenting to the students theories which are false and antithetical to the policies of the university, or persists in presenting matters deemed false by the majority of the most intelligent minds of the ages, the individual has abused his position and his acts justify his dismissal.

This follows from the fact that the institution has a right to employ whom it pleases. It, furthermore, has a right and a duty to protect the interests of its students and their parents who send them to these schools aware of the political and moral views of the institution. It is one thing to allow a man to speak his mind, another to give him an audience. The American educational system was established for a particular purpose, and as such, cannot permit on its faculties individuals who hold views detrimental to the fulfillment of that purpose.

Unlike membership in the social order, wherein the individual participates more because of necessity than choice, membership in the academic community is a matter of volition and as such carries with it certain obligations. Consequently, irrespective of one's definition of academic freedom its privileges and responsibilities arise in part from the nature of the professional community and seat of authority within the academic community—in this instance the school or college which employs the individual. As a matter of fact members of the academic community are members of either public or private institutions and are granted special privileges only because they have agreed to furnish special services for the good of the individual and society.

The fact that academic freedom is limited by institutional policies in no way warrants the fears expressed in the following statement by Frank Karelsen:

> It has been argued by those who support the action taken by the University of Washington in discharging the Communist professors, that Communists have no right to teach in schools whose ends they disavow. This is a dangerous philosophy. If this philosophy prevails and we allow to teach only those who agree with current ends or policies of an administrator, education will become static, and change and evolution, which are necessary for progress, will end.[26]

Nor the fears found in the writing of the ultra-liberal Harold Laski to the effect that,

> Nothing is more dangerous to academic freedom than a situation where teachers . . . stand uncertain whether to speak at all, fearing the censure of those who at the moment are able to define the accepted mores of a community. This right to speak fearlessly is jeopardized in American universities by the present climate of opinion.[27]

As a matter of fact the extent to which academic freedom is limited by institutional policies and dogma is rarely understood by those who decry the loss of academic freedom and profess to see it hampered and restricted by administrators. If these sorcerers of academic doom honestly appraised the results of institutional discipline they would find that it imposes no strictures on either the definition or discussion of controversial issues. These individuals have for their gospel, subjectivity; for their excuse, progress. However, progress to chaos and anarchy is not in keeping with the best that Greece and Rome and Christianity have to offer.[28]

Furthermore, as one educational administrator remarked concerning the teacher: ". . . we expect him to keep abreast of the latest advances in his own field. We expect him to aid the thinking of his students by presenting both sides of the question, to stimulate their interest in learning more by challenging their opinions, to encourage in them a burning thirst for truth." [29] In discussing principles and methods of government it would be absurd for a teacher to ignore communistic and fascistic systems. In dealing with labor problems the teacher must not only dwell on the right to work unmolested but consider also the demands for a job with a living wage. Controversy limited only by the desire to seek the truth, by competence, institutional policy and the maturity of the students is the very lifeblood of advancing the boundaries of knowledge. This certainly does not indicate any undue curtailment of the teacher's function nor does it give any reason for fear on the part of faculty members.

It is evident that educators, in dealing with the supposedly ticklish problems of academic freedom, rarely have the courage and forthright clarity of perception to speak as did the Reverend Cyril Meyer, C.M., when he referred to Congressional investigations and institutional policies: "If those who are responsible for running our colleges and universities only made up their minds what basic truths their institutions stand for, and had the courage to make these the boundaries of the academic freedom of their faculty members, there would probably be no need for such investigations." [30]

As Buckley states, after seeing what he claims is possible when institutional policies are ignored: ". . . academic freedom must mean the freedom of men and women to supervise the educational activities and aims of the schools they oversee and supervise." [31]

The boundaries of the teacher's field: While the teacher is permitted, within the bounds established by the previous discussion, wide latitude in his field of special interest, he is, however, definitely limited when expressing himself concerning matters outside his subject. He is even more definitely limited when such expression concerns a matter of controversy beyond the scope of his professional training. The teacher, in spite of his position of authority and eminence, is not all things to all men; he is not to put himself in the position of the "headless rider" and ride off in all directions. Unfortunately, at times, the constant protracted contact that the teacher has with successive generations of adolescents has given him an authoritarian psychology which may quite unconsciously extend to regions in which the teacher is less (or not at all) competent.

Because of this limitation no teacher may claim as his right the privilege of discussing in his classroom controversial topics outside of the field of his special subject matter. The teacher is morally bound not to take advantage of his position by introducing into the classroom provocative discussion of irrelevant material not within the field of his specialization.

The proper function of the teacher is to deal, after prolonged study and training, with the sources of knowledge and to impart the results of these studies to his students and the general public. In this he has ample freedom of expression. However, because his is a position of trust and public interest his pronouncements are carefully noted and believed. This places upon him the responsibility of remaining in his chosen field lest his opinions concerning problems in other fields be taken as facts. To avoid this situation the teacher is restricted to teach and to seek the truth in the field in which he is especially prepared and for which he is employed by the school's trustees. In this field, and this field alone, is the teacher permitted to present controversial issues and to pursue inquiry, subject, of course, to limitations previously enumerated.

Conclusion

Once again due to tensions, particularly of an economic-political nature, the question of intellectual freedom, of the freedom of the teacher and of the scholar to express their views and do research has become a burning issue. The result has been to create in the minds of some elements of the academic world the fear that academic freedom is unduly restricted.

This hubbub, created by extreme intellectual liberals, has forced the academic community to re-evaluate the freedom it should have in order to teach the accumulated heritage and to continue the seeking for new truths. If, however, during this re-evaluation, academic freedom is falsely interpreted to mean freedom without restraint, freedom to teach without the presence of limitations, then it is possible that America may lose the accumulated values of her civilization and the faith which is the source of that civilization.

Behind much of the furor created by the discussion of academic freedom and evident from the cases and incidents which have brought the matter to the fore has been the question of the teacher's membership in the Communistic party and the extent to which he has been influencing his students in that direction. A mere cursory glance at the literature pertinent to this topic leaves no doubt that if the question of Communism were removed few cases would remain for consideration, and these would be so professional as to be of little popular interest. Note, for instance, the excellent article by Whittaker Chambers who, in answer to the question: "Is academic freedom in danger?", confines his attention to the Congressional investigation of Communists within the academic community. He notes incidentally, that most of the fuss at the present time is, strangely enough, the result of the appearance and questioning of approximately one hundred educators out of the considerably more than one million educators, professors, instructors, and teachers in the United States. With respect to this he wisely remarks: ". . . that about 150 teachers called as witnesses, out of more than one million teachers in the nation scarcely add up to a witch hunt." [32]

As a matter of interest one of the shrewdest countermoves of Communism in the American schools is the propaganda, abetted by would-be liberals, by means of which the Communist have attempted to create fear within the academic community. They have tried to upset the equilibrium of the educational world by maintaining that any attempt to foster loyalty oaths or question members of the academic community about their philosophies is an abridgement of the academic freedom.

This is quite evident in the publication of the correspondence between William Frauenglass, a teacher, who refused to answer a question inquiring of his membership in the Communist Party, and Albert Einstein,[33] the scientist. Unfortunately and unwisely, because his reply was eagerly used by those who were seeking unrestricted academic freedom as a cloak, Dr. Einstein upheld the teacher's reluctance to answer such inquiries because they impinged upon his academic freedom. Here is another instance where the teacher's freedom is mistaken for a question of citizenship.

Probably the best answer to Dr. Einstein is found, once again, in the report of the President of Rutgers University:

> It follows that for the members of a university faculty to refuse to give a rational account of their position on vital community issues not only cannot be defended by an appeal to academic freedom, but in fact cuts the ground from under academic freedom itself. This one weapon of defense is gone, and the entire academic community must suffer accordingly.[34]

Because the stakes are so high these subversive elements within the academic community make wild claims and petty complaints in the name of liberty, crying out for all to hear about the infringement upon their academic rights—never, however, their responsibilities. The elementary issue, the fundamental philosophy, and the ever legal question is always left out, not because of ignorance but because of voluntary evasion.

It is still a fact that at all times, and especially during such times as these, the university in particular and the school in general remain a shelter for the freedom of inquiry, freedom to teach, freedom to publish. This, however, implies responsibility and competence within the academic community. To confuse competence with Communism, with ultra-liberalism, is beyond the realm of possibility; it is, to say the least, ridiculous. To correlate conspiracy with free speech, dissecting opinion and academic freedom is the height of intellectual folly. The gist of the matter is that a greater degree of academic freedom is neither needed nor justified. Truth, in spite of all that has been said in other places, has not been endangered in educational institutions; strangely enough a high degree of liberality has prevailed.

The more than one million members of the teaching profession who do not see any undue infringement or feel any undue limitations upon their freedom to teach have the pleasant experience that seldom—very seldom—does the scholar get into difficulty because of his views or teaching. On the other hand, if the subversives in the educational institutions of America, seeking protection by recourse to unlimited and unrestricted academic freedom, are not exposed then, as Whittaker Chambers so aptly and fearfully puts it: "all freedom will become academic—merely academic."

The American public, the parents of the students in American educational institutions, must always be aware of the fact that the teacher's task is a sacred and dedicated one, dedicated by an overwhelming majority of the academic world to the task of perpetuating the American way of life and the promulgation of truth in all fields of human welfare. If the public and minor elements of the teaching profession feel that this purpose of the academic community is being carried on in an atmosphere of fear it is a fear more talked about than real. Within the framework of the limitations previously considered discussion is not stifled and controversial issues are freely discussed. These limitations, let it be emphasized, permit considerably more freedom of honest inquiry and pursuit of truth than could be conceived of in institutions dedicated to totalitarian-Godless ideologies.

Freedom in Relation to the Expression of the Beautiful

by Rev. Denis K. O'Regan, O.P.
*Department of Philosophy,
Providence College, Providence, R. I.*

Heraclitus is supposed to have said: "No man swims twice in the same stream." Such are the stern demands of our modern cult of freedom that today there would probably be a sign in front of that stream reading: "Swimming twice in this stream is positively forbidden." Possibly the medieval scholastics wrote better than they knew when they defined freedom as *negatio determinationis ad unum*. For today if there is anything we are determined about, it is that we are not going to be determined to anything. That this determination extends to the realm of the beautiful is evident from the loud clamor that immediately arises at any censure of representations denoted, be it ever so vaguely, as artistic.

In this era in which, in the words of Protagoras, "Man is the measure of all things," one might be so free as to bring up two problems in relation to the expression of the beautiful, or, to put it more specifically, in relation to artistic expression. These problems are: (1) Is there any objective norm of reality to which artistic expression must conform? (2) Supposing such an objective norm, are there restrictions upon what may be represented? Needless to say, there is no point in answering the second question, if the answer to the first question is negative. And actually, today, a great deal of the fervid objection to any kind of censorship as to the subject matter of artistic representation would appear to stem from an at least tacit, negative answer to that first question. This Heraclitean world is presumed to be in a state of happy flux, with no fixed laws of nature, and, least of all, no fixed norms of morality. These latter are merely *tabus* which the enlightened transcend.

The erasure of any line between reality and fantasy, with its consequent "no-holds-barred" attitude in artistic expression, gives rise to an education such as that pictured by St. Augustine in his *Confessions*. Here man, and what is worse, man and his vices, have supplanted nature.

> I was forced to learn the wanderings of one Aeneas, forgetful of my own, and to weep for dead Dido, because she killed herself for love; the while, with dry eyes, I endured myself dying among these things, far from Thee, O God, my life. . . . In them [the vanities of pagan literature] indeed, I learnt many a useful word, but these may as well be learned in things not vain; and that is the safe path for the steps of youth. But woe is thee, thou torrent of human custom! Who shall stand against thee? How long roll the sons of Eve into that huge and hideous ocean, which even they scarcely overpass who climb the cross? Did not I read in thee of Jove the thunderer and the adulterer? Both, doubtless, he could not be; but so that the feigned thunder might countenance and pander to real adultery. And now which of our gowned masters lends a sober ear to one who from their own school cries out: "These are Homer's fictions, transferring things human to the gods; would he had brought down things divine to us!" Yet more truly had he said, "These are indeed his fictions; but attributing a divine nature to wicked men, that crimes might be no longer crimes, and those who commit them might seem to imitate, not abandoned men, but the celestial gods." And yet, thou hellish torrent, into thee are cast the sons of men with rich rewards for compassing such learning. . . . Yet, O my God (in whose presence I now without hurt may remember this), all this unhappily I learnt willingly with great delight, and for this was pronounced a hopeful boy.[1]

It is our purpose in this paper to show that the exaltation of human freedom has inevitably been mirrored in artistic expression. The abuses of the one will necessarily be reflected in the other. On the other hand, the concept of an ordered, governed universe will necessarily carry with it certain canons of artistic expression. Perhaps throughout one should bear in mind the fatal danger of confusing human freedom with divine freedom. Divine freedom is something actual, the freedom of being all that ever may be. Human freedom, on the other hand, is not in itself an ultimate perfection but a condition, the condition which allows man to *choose* himself to be united to the divinity, the source of all that is. To worship that freedom as an end in itself, is to worship indetermination, formlessness, that state of being which is but one step removed from absolute nothingness.

Ars gratia artis. The independence of the arts is so stressed today that it requires some temerity even to raise the question of whether they are subject to control; such is our tyranny of "freedom," that one scarcely feels free to do it. Their emancipation from all rules, from metaphysics, from morality, seems so sacrosanct that the question of their being an effect of current standards of ethics, or of being responsible for repercussions upon morality, is deftly put aside with all the hauteur that artistic snobbery can summon. Even the great Greeks, Plato and Aristotle, are severely castigated for their would-be subjection of the artist to the censors of the state. Art is above all that sort of thing—in a world of its own. Plato and Aristotle are suspected of professional jealousy, the jealousy of the philosopher who sees his sway over the people supplanted by that of the poet and has recourse to state suppression.

Whence comes this state of affairs? An examination of the evolution of art will show that it has kept pace very faithfully with the evolution in human thinking from the Renaissance on. Deep at the root is the more and more open rejection of any absolute order of things in favor of human freedom—a freedom which, alas, now finds itself subject to the blind whims of evolving matter. This freedom involves, of course, the rejection of metaphysics with its concept of universal, objective being absolutely governed by divine causes. Metaphysics has been reduced to the status of a parlor game for Ph.D's. In a generally pragmatic outlook, art plays the role of means of forming the masses on practical issues, issues which themselves are considered to be subject to change and evolution. The arts become something like the empirical sciences. Not scholastic "form," but rather "structure" is considered paramount. Since there is no ultimate end, the means are the thing. The same idea is contained in our unconscious feeling in the realm of transportation that if we get there faster, we somehow get there better.

Today any intrinsic intelligibility in nature is denied. It is like, in the words of Einstein, a clock whose face we see but whose works we can only guess at. But this view of the unintelligibility of nature has been paralleled by an increasing devotion to man himself as the center of all things. The earth has been moved out as the physical center of the universe, but, in a move far more anthropocentric than anything ever contemplated by the ancients, man, a very small portion of that earth, has been moved in as its intelligible center. Because of its peculiar place midway between the purely intelligible and the purely sensible, so appropriate to man, art has kept pace with this shift. One may see this in detail in Sorokin's *Social and Cultural Dynamics,*[2] where the fluctuations of systems of art and systems of ethics are seen to go side by side. A progress to non-being through self-assertion is the trend.

The decline of art from objective intelligibility, with its concept of order in the universe and God at the pinnacle of that order is fairly evident. In the Middle Ages, art was essentially sacred in that the form embodied in matter was not the end of the contemplator, since that form had a further purpose, to raise him above the material object. Anatomical accuracy was not so important as the idea conveyed. Technique was visibly animated by devotion. This is manifest in the works of Fra Angelico where the devotion of the painter has somehow imprisoned in his paintings a celestial dignity and serenity for which purely artistic virtuosity is no substitute. Already in Raphael one feels that the purely human is beginning to pierce through the sacred subject. His subjects are entitled "Madonnas," but they are also equally good likenesses of Italian ladies of the Renaissance.

It would seem that only in Michaelangelo in the Sistine Chapel does there linger in the faces of his human characters that wistfulness for the divine. They are not self-centered humans, but men and women whose gaze rests beseechingly and trustfully upon God. Once the purely human came into focus in art, sacred subjects such as the Holy Family became gradually supplanted by temporal subjects, kings, queens, dukes and duchesses. With the ascendency of the bourgeoisie, "solid citizens" became the subject matter, as in the Flemish school. Where opulence and magnificence continued to reign, the human subjects were often apotheosized into heavens filled with obliging cherubs, as in the Venetian school. Then came revolution, with the Goddess of Reason, and Liberty standing at the barricades, and romanticism supplanted classicism. Henceforth there is to be not even the pretense of the divine; the stage is occupied by the purely human, the purely terrestrial. One sees it in the misty landscapes of Turner, in the pleasant sunlit parks of the French. Turner connotes perhaps a certain nostalgia, a certain feeling that there must be something more beyond, while the French grasp a sunny afternoon, an episode in a life. What comes before, what is to follow? *Qui sait?* In the words of Lamartine:

> *L'homme n'a point de port, le temps n'a point de rive;*
> *Il coule, et nous passons.*

Material "structure" has replaced scholastic "form." Media and form have become more or less identified. End is denied inasmuch as art is the expression of an evolving society. With man's discovery of himself as the focus of interest in the Renaissance, and the encouraging outlook furnished by cosmologists such as Laplace of a universe intelligible to man without the "hypothesis" of God, there was indeed a happy devotion to the reproduction of sensible nature —housewives, cows, trees, waterfalls. But the series of social upheavals that have ensued have rendered the face of nature somewhat grim. Now "realism" becomes synonymous with the sordid, the brutal, the soulless. Because nature since the time of Kant is found inscrutable, and since Darwin and Marx increasingly menacing, it is not, therefore, surprising that art should seek refuge in fancy. If the universe is unintelligible, then why not art? Consequently, serious attention is paid to something like "Dadaism," where a deliberately meaningless word is used to denote a consciously meaningless art. But is it meaningless? It does mean that man feels that whatever intelligibility there is derives not from nature, but from himself. Therefore, he freely creates worlds of his own, and, as one who strolls through the Museum of Modern Art will experience, pleasantly defies you to penetrate them.

Obviously, if the universe is irrational, it is futile to invoke "rational" arguments in criticism of modern art, of statues with holes through their middles, of bits of tin dangling on wires, where if one finds an obvious meaning the artist has failed. An elusive, fluid, unintelligible, inexpressible something, symbolic of a world in flux, is the aim. There is at least one consoling thought, that is, that man is not happy about being nothing more than the top bubble on the cosmic soup. People like Jean-Paul Sartre say they wish there *was* a God because they are tired of carrying the world on their shoulders. In the meantime, if art can express nothing genuinely and perennially intelligible—because there is nothing to express—then it is better not to argue but to wait.

But supposing that the universe is indeed intelligible, then art as a refuge for subjective intelligibility in an unintelligible world has no role to play. But *is* it art? Because modern art forms have nothing in common with the Venus de Milo or Gothic cathedrals, does this mean that art had hitherto not existed? Because art is now "emancipated," does this mean that it is beyond the critique of men who lived seven hundred years or two thousand years before ladies turned up in portraits with not one eye, but both eyes on the same side of their faces? It is true that neither Aristotle nor the scholastic writers referred to the "fine arts" as such, dividing arts as they did into the mechanical and the liberal. But was this an oversight on their part—or are the fine arts already adequately accounted for in their division? The latter is the belief of such contemporaries as Sister Mary Gonzaga Odell, O.P., in her *Theory of Criticism of Fiction in Its Moral Aspects According to Thomistic Principles.*[3] In a like vein, we shall endeavor to derive from Thomistic principles a plausible *rationale* for the fine arts.

In the beginning we suggested that there was a two fold problem involved in a treatment of the fine arts. Need they conform to some objective norm of reality? And, supposing that they do so, are there any further restrictions to be imposed? The whole answer which will be proposed may be summed up in the two words with which St. Thomas expresses the guide of all human activity: *recta ratio.* In art, there must be *ratio,* referring to the intellect; and this *ratio* must be *recta,* referring to the will.

As is well known, the pursuits of man as man are of two sorts, either speculative, where the end is to know something, or practical, where the end is either in doing something or producing something. These two latter intellectual virtues are called prudence and art. Prudence is concerned with a practical judgment concerning something one should do in the moral order. Its activity of itself does not extend without. Art, on the other hand, is concerned with a practical judgment concerning something to be made. Its term is normally in some external production—a bed, a chair, a boat, a statue, even an exquisite round of golf. Art is not prudence, yet it will be seen that the nature of *recta ratio* relates them.

However, supposing art to consist in production, where lies the distinction between the fine arts and the purely mechanical arts? This difficulty is proposed by A. W. Levi as follows: "If art is simply production, no more, no less, then it becomes possible to identify, at least for practical purposes, the artist and the artisan. And so there arises no necessity to make the separation between the lower arts and the fine arts. This distinction, viewed historically, is a product of the high Renaissance, unknown to the medievals. Their practice in this matter was to follow the ancients, who it is true, did distinguish the servile from the liberal arts, but the basis of this distinction was only the corporal labor involved." [4]

If the ancients and the men of the Middle Ages did not distinguish the artist and the artisan, they seem to have fared rather well in their own crude way, producing such works as the Victory of Samothrace and the Cathedral of Chartres which seem destined to remain perennially unequaled and inimitable. It would seem that the "artisan" of the Middle Ages was indeed an artist, to judge from the beautifully illumined Books of Hours which our own era can admire but not duplicate, while the magnificent form of Michaelangelo was initially inspired by that of Greece.

We must remember that men like Aristotle and St. Thomas were familiar with all the fine arts which we know today. And in honesty we should perhaps even admit that great art was a more familiar sight to them than it is to us. The glories of the past which we admire today were fresh and new to them. In the passage from A. W. Levi quoted above, one has the impression that the fine arts must be segregated from amongst the mechanical arts, since, like the mechanical arts, they involve physical labor. But if one is seeking in someone like St. Thomas some inkling of where the fine arts would be for him, one feels impelled to locate them, not in the realm of the mechanical arts, but in that of the liberal arts. And this is a significant distinction which throws light upon the whole medieval concept of art, a concept which, not surprisingly, is more lofty than the most modern pretensions. Just as the men of the Middle Ages are maddeningly more rational than the moderns, so also is their concept of art more exalted.

"All men by nature desire to know." In this brief, initial sentence of Aristotle's *Metaphysics,* we have the key to human nature. Man would sooner know than act or produce, and so we have movie stars outranking generals in the public eye. The man who composes a symphony is more revered than the man who built a steam engine. Aristotle points up our innate desire to know by underlining the fact that of all our senses, that which we cherish most is not the most practical or the most necessary for life, but the most knowledgeable, namely, the sense of sight. And it is upon this note, rather than upon that of lack of manual labor, that the liberal arts assume their identity above the mechanical arts. They are liberal arts because they lead to knowledge. Thus St. Thomas writes of that liberal art which is logic in his exposition of the opening lines of the *Metaphysics:*

> Therefore, when a number of arts had been discovered as to utility, certain of which are for the necessities of life, as are the mechanical; certain others for the introduction into other sciences, as are the logical sciences: those artificers are to be called wiser, whose sciences were not discovered for the sake of utility, but for the sake of knowledge itself, as are the speculative sciences.[5]

Here, too, it is not superfluous to mention, since we are speaking of freedom, that the liberal arts are not called liberal or free because they are studied by free men or citizens, but primarily because the speculative sciences which they introduce are free, that is, not servile or existing for the sake of something else, but for their own sake.

One might well wonder what logic has to do with the fine arts. But we have already seen that art transcends the purely mechanical, the strictly utilitarian, when it leads to knowledge. And it is, in the words of St. Thomas expounding Aristotle, among the logical arts that the fine arts find their place: "Sometimes one's thought alone inclines to one part of a contradiction because of some representation, as when a man is brought to abominate some food if it is presented to him under the form of something abominable. To this is ordained the *Poetics:* for it is the task of the poet to induce one to something virtuous by means of some representation. All these things pertain to *Rational Philosophy* [or logic]." [6] If all the fine arts are essentially reducible to the subject matter of the *Poetics,* and the *Poetics,* in turn, are part of Rational Philosophy or Logic, i.e., ordained to the art of grasping the truth through reasoning, then the fine arts are ultimately concerned with the communication of truth, and to be judged accordingly. What is peculiar to them in the realm of the communication of the truth?

The fact that the truth to be grasped is not presented as the conclusion of a syllogism, but induced through a *representation.* An example of this may be seen in billboard advertising, where automobile drivers are induced to drive carefully through the representation of an accident that occurs to non-careful drivers. Here the representation occupies the role of a major premiss: "Whoever does not drive carefully has accidents." The minor premiss is usually supplied by words, such as: "This might be you," conveying the thought: "I perhaps do not drive carefully." The conclusion, as in all syllogisms, follows automatically: "I may have an accident if I don't watch out." It is to be noted here how the particular, or singular representation in art takes on the role of a universal—a fact implied in Aristotle's statement that poetry is more philosophic than history.

But does Aristotle really embrace the concept of all the fine arts in his *Poetics?* As is well known, the *Poetics* is not about poetry, but rather about "things to be made," artistic creations, as the Greek *poietika* signifies. Although it concentrates on the drama, it lays down principles common to the arts in general: painting, sculpture, music, the dance, poetry and theater. Undoubtedly, even the novel which does *not* require rime or even meter could be fitted in under poetry. What have all these arts in common? "[They] are all, viewed as a whole, modes of imitation." [7] Some use "color" (painting) and "form" (sculpture); others use "rhythm" (the dance), "language" (poetry), and "harmony" (music), separately or all combined as in "Tragedy and Comedy" (the theater).[8] And what is it that is imitated? "The objects the imitator represents are actions, with agents who are necessarily either good men or bad—the diversities of human character being nearly always derivative from this primary distinction, since the line between virtue and vice is one dividing the whole of mankind." [9] Thus even the dancer, "by the rhythms of his attitudes, may represent men's characters, as well as what they do and suffer." [10]

But what is the point of all this imitation? First, "imitation is *natural* to man from his childhood, one of his advantages over the lower animals being this, that he is the most imitative creature in the world, and learns at first by imitation." Secondly, "to be learning something is the greatest of pleasures not only to the philosopher but also to the rest of mankind, however small their capacity for it. . . . The reason for the delight (in seeing a work of art, whose imitation pleases) is that one is at the same time learning—gathering the meaning of things." [11] In a word, the artist represents actions which are morally good or bad. The aim, even when the imitation is not evident—"if one has not seen the thing before"—is that the beholder should learn. Learn what? Learn what truly good and evil actions are. And since the fulfillment of morals is not in knowing but in doing, the final outcome should be to lead the beholder to perform good actions and eschew evil ones. And thus St. Thomas says that "it is the task of the poet to induce one to something virtuous by means of some representation."

If such is the aim of fine art—an aim which Aristotle attributes to it not by any arbitrary *fiat,* but rather as arising from the very nature of man—then such art must be *true,* if by it men are to learn; and even if objectively true to reality, since its aim is to induce to the *good,* it must also be in accord with moral reality. Thus in Michaelangelo's *Last Judgment,* on the wall of the Sistine Chapel, the figures were originally represented as unclothed, which undoubtedly corresponds to the reality. But since this was considered to deter from the effect intended, they were later ordered clothed. Thus freedom in art, as in every realm, is subordinate to the true, *and* to the morally good. It is not enough that it be true objectively, but it must also take into consideration the reality of human nature, the condition of the beholder, if it is not to be perverted. Needless to say, this latter, the estimation of the condition of the beholder, which may vary from individual to individual, lies within the realm of prudence, which must make correct judgments as to individual cases.

Initially, however, we are concerned with art's subjection to truth. Logic is concerned with the presentation of that truth which is the result of reasoning. Some truths are unvaryingly and perpetually true, such as, for instance, the truths of the triangle, and that is the realm of science. Others, such as those truths concerned with human society, may vary, and that is the realm of art. For example, art inciting to revolution, such as Beaumarchais' *Le Barbier de Seville,* may at one time be true to the moral situation, at another not. Thus today there is art which incites to Communism, and there is art which rises against it. They cannot *both* be true. Over all, the fact remains whether the artist admits or not, art does spur man on to moral judgment, and the artist is thereby responsible for the truth or falsehood which he induces. Should he make that appear true which is not, make vice lovable and virtue odious, then he has failed as an artist to induce to the good through representation; and has become instead a sophist, that is, one who deals in that which *appears* to be true, but is not. St. Augustine once wrote that, since truth can be variously expressed, philosophy must not be hostile to poetry, for the latter can express truth under a figure.[12] Not only did Aristotle and St. Thomas not neglect the fine arts, rather they attributed to them a role and purpose in human life to which a man could wholeheartedly and justifiably devote himself.

Although art is represented in terms of the sensible individual—

Shakespeare's *Hamlet,* Michaelangelo's *David*—nevertheless, that which it has to convey is of universal significance. We have maintained that art is endowed, by its very nature, with moral purpose. But moral actions are singulars. If it was right for Judith to kill Holofernes, would it be right for Mrs. Eisenhower to kill Malenkov? Each situation is determined as to its moral status not by universal principles alone, but by circumstances which must vary with every occasion. Consequently, the artistic representation, taken in its individuality, cannot be simply reimposed in reality. If John Smith slew his uncle, following Hamlet's example, even if deemed right, it would not *ipso facto* dispense John Smith from further justification. Consequently, the value of art lies in the degree in which it transcends the singular and conveys principles of perennial validity, although the adaptation to circumstance still remains. Hence the words of Aristotle that "poetry is something more philosophic and of graver import than history, since its statements are of the nature rather of universals, whereas those of history are singulars." [13] Why should this be, when the one is real and the other only possible? The difference lies in the fact that, historically, good may come about through evil, as the birth of Solomon through the murder of Urias, but if it does it is accidental to what precedes. Yet it might be seized upon as a justification for a like act, as Theodosius justified his massacre by the murder of Urias by David.

Whereas in poetry and art in general, the artist, if he has control over the situation, may rightly bring good from good and evil from evil as, to quote the example of Aristotle, "the statue of Mitys at Argos killed the author of Mitys' death by falling down on him when a looker-on at a public spectacle." [14] Such is the classic example of "poetic justice." By inculcating in the beholder in such manner the principles that good will ultimately triumph and evil be ultimately avenged, the artist is strengthening true moral principles, which are to be eventually the motives for singular actions. In this vein, it might be well to add that sacred subjects, such as the Crucifixion, are of themselves universal principles since they express immediately universal truth emanating from the universal cause, as the love of the Redeemer for all mankind.

Consequently, far from moving in the purely corporeal sphere of the useful arts, far from the accent being on the paint, the stone, the material technique, the artist's prime concern is not with the fleeting, the ephemeral, but with relating that which he represents to something unchanging, universal. What is a landscape if it does not somehow suggest the Creator? What is a human face if one does not sense therein an immortal soul created to enjoy happiness with God? Thus St. Thomas writes: "Every creature is made as a witness to God, inasmuch as every creature is a certain witness to the divine goodness. The magnitude of the creature is a certain witness of the divine power and omnipotence; its beauty of the divine wisdom." [15] Such a consideration does not disembody human beauty, but rather enhances it. It is no longer simply a happy accident, but the deliberate expression of the divine wisdom and love. Does it diminish one's admiration for the human body to reflect that the Second Person of the Trinity, God Himself, has chosen to assume it for all eternity? And why? In the words of St. Thomas:

> . . . to show the greatness of God's benignity towards us. For it is evident that the rational soul is more conformed to God than flesh, and it would indeed have been a great sacrament of love if the Word had assumed a human soul, as conformed to Himself, but also to assume flesh distant from the simplicity of His nature, was the sign of a much greater, nay, inestimable love.[16]

The artist cannot but have an exalted concept of human beauty on reflecting that this beauty is mirroring divine wisdom, that it is a beauty forever assumed by God Himself.

Although it is natural to think of art in terms of the expression of the beautiful, this would not seem to be quite the point which is characteristic of all fine art. Else how explain these words of Aristotle: "Though the objects themselves may be painful to see, we delight to view the realistic representations of them in art, the forms, for example, of the lowest animals and of dead bodies"? [17] These words are further corroborated by St. Augustine: "Why is it that man desires to be made sad, beholding doleful and tragic things, which yet himself would by no means suffer? Yet he desires as a spectator to feel sorrow for them, and this very sorrow is his pleasure." [18] It is evident that all fine art must take its rise from a sensible representation. Yet sensible beauty, as the passages above demonstrate, is by no means indispensable to artistic pleasure. The pleasure, therefore, must appeal basically to man as man, to man as an intellectual creature, to man who by nature desires to know, not in a purely sensible way but completely. This does not mean the exclusion of sense, but rather sensible reality seen in its ultimate relation to supreme and immaterial reality.

Man does not perceive this ultimate reality directly, but in the *order* underlying sensible things his mind is elevated to grasp what he can of it through effects. Not surprisingly, then, does St. Thomas say in the opening lecture on the *Ethics,* commenting on the words of Aristotle that it is the part of the wise man to order: "Wisdom is the greatest perfection of reason, whose property is to know order. For even though the sensitive parts know some things absolutely, to know the *order of one thing to another* belongs solely to intellect or reason." [19] And in every great work of art, even though sensible beauty be not always found, there is always found order. This gives an inkling of why, of all the senses, we reserve the word "beautiful" solely to the objects of those senses which are foremost, not in the necessities of existence, but in conducing to intellectual knowledge. We do not speak of a "beautiful taste," a "beautiful smell," or of something "beautiful to the touch." But we do speak of "beautiful sights," and "beautiful sounds." Thus when we enjoy something sensibly beautiful it can only be because there is in that sensible thing something which appeals to the *intellect,* whose property is *to know order.* Even though we do not avert to it, in the pleasure of physical beauty our minds have been captivated by a reflection of the divine wisdom for which they were made. Whence St. Thomas writes: "But beauty regards the power of knowing; for those things are called beautiful which please when seen. Whence the beautiful consists in right proportion, since sense is delighted in things rightly proportioned, as in things like to itself, for *sense, too, is a certain reason,* as is every cognoscitive power." [20]

Since the sensible in the fine arts is ultimately ordained to reason, whose property is to know the order of one thing to another, it is only proper that artistic creation should be placed by St. Thomas in the realm of Rational Philosophy or Logic, which is the art or science of learning "to discourse from one thing to another . . . in a way which is orderly, easy and without error." Wherever the artist has made that order brilliant, it is to this above all that we reserve the word: *Beautiful!* But it is not enough that the order be brilliant; it must also be *without error.*

In speaking of the objectivity of art, we can well employ the division of logic into formal and material. In reasoning, the premisses may well be ordered to the conclusion as to form, but that is not enough, for the premisses themselves must first be ordered to reality as to their matter. So, too, in art; that which is represented may be ordered to a certain conclusion. But should that which is represented not be derived from reality, the art is misleading. This appears to be a favorite device of Hollywood, and even the theater. Some historical personage whose name has a scandalous attraction—for example, Salome, or Henry VIII—is selected. Box office is assured. Then to placate the censors, the nature of the character is altered—Salome is really trying to save John the Baptist—and then everything else goes. Salome can dance all she wants, and how she wants, because it is for a good cause.

What has happened? In cold syllogistic terms we have something like this: Whoever tries to save the life of another is good. But Salome tries to save the life of John the Baptist. Therefore Salome is good. The major is beyond cavil, so the artist need not establish it. But he does set out to establish the minor in his representation. And from it follows in the mind of the beholder a false conclusion. But of course the beholder must *know* that it is false! But does he? So much of one's history is derived from the movies, and other like popular means of communication, that the line between truth and fiction is indiscernible. The beholder may well walk out of the theater thinking to himself: "Salome was a pretty good girl after all. All this talk about her is just one more example of how puritans frown at anyone who really has life."

Or the misleading conclusion may be even more subtle. One might represent the story of David and Bethsabee according to the facts: David's illicit love of Bethsabee; his murder of Urias by having him placed where the fighting was thickest and abandoning him there; his ultimate taking of Bethsabee as his queen and the birth of Solomon eventually crowned by him out of line of succession. Urias is the tragic figure in this story, a good and brave man, devoted to his king, whom a cruel fate befalls through no fault of his own. Bethsabee, in the words of Scripture, was "very beautiful." David was the anointed of God and the hero of Israel. Should Urias be represented as good but colorless, and David romantic rather than lustful, the sympathies of the audience would lean towards the adulterer, and the Scriptures would become the means of inculcating the Nietzschean ethic of the superman, beyond good and evil. Such are the dangerous perversions of art if instead of representing reality, it merely reveals man's own subjective wish of how he would like reality to be. We are speaking of freedom in the representation of the beautiful. If a man is not free to lie, neither is art free so to represent.

All this implies, needless to say, that art in its representation is an imitation of reality. Should it not be, then the beholder cannot be genuinely said to learn, since he would be learning what is not. But suppose reality is intrinsically unknowable, a doctrine universally touted since Kant decided that we knew *phenomena,* that which appears, but not *noumena,* things in themselves? Then surely art is its own master, free as the wind. Or suppose that we do know reality, but that reality itself is ever changing, ever evolving, that change is its very nature. Then surely nothing may be represented as permanently good or permanently bad. What may once have been considered evil, may now be considered permissible, and the artist is free to represent it as such. We live in a relativistic world today, where even though we do not agree with someone, as, for example, with Stalin's defense of the liquidation of three million kulaks, nevertheless we bend over backwards in a spirit of cosmic "de gustibus non disputandum," to the extent that it becomes quite proper for the ex-President's wife to shake warmly the hand of the Soviet Foreign Minister.

If society should reach the point where truth is considered unattainable and such seems to be the doctrine today of "Academic Freedom" in actual practice namely, that while truth is attainable, no one may state that it irrevocably has been—there is little point in losing sleep over a parallel freedom in art. That would be like criticizing Nero's violin technique while Rome is going up in smoke. Rather, the burden of this paper has been that art parallels thought in general, that, as the mind goes, so will art go. In this sense it certainly is not free no matter how it might struggle to emancipate itself. It is thus because art is innately an expression of how the world looks to man. It varies from words only in the mode of its expression. And just as words represent thought, and thought reality, so, too, art represents thought and through it reality, or what one chooses to take for reality. In a word, it is imitative.

But cannot one take the tail of a fish and the body of a woman and create a mermaid, or the legs of a goat and the body of a man and create a satyr? Here, too, the elements all come from reality. Here, too, one should remember that art is not limited to the actual, but may embrace the possible, as in a novel. Its only barricade is the impossible, that which cannot be. The only way the representation of the impossible may be justified, other than in jest, is by the denial of the impossible, the denial of the principle of contradiction, of truth and falsehood. Still art remains an imitation, even if only the imitation of an impossible universe. In the outlook of Aristotle and St. Thomas, however, that imitation which is art is an imitation of a world that is both intelligible and, in its destiny, permanent. Art is the *recta ratio factibilium,* whether the *factibilia* be in the utilitarian order, such as saws and houses, or representations ordained to knowledge, such as paintings or statues. The word *ratio* in scholastic terminology has a wide range, but it centers around the reason or the essence of the thing, be the thing an object or an action.

In an art such as golf, the *factibile* is, let us say, the stroke. The art of golf seeks the true *ratio,* the right, or *recta ratio* of that stroke. When it is found, possibly simply by experience, it can be checked and found to be an imitation of nature. That is, the longest, straightest, drive in golf will be that which is most perfectly in accord with the physical laws governing distance in a straight line. In the fine arts, while the *ratio* as always is derived from nature, the *recta,* since here the aim is to induce to virtuous action, will be such only if the representation, true to life though it may be, *does* induce to virtuous action. For, in the words of St. Thomas, "every artist intends to endow his work with the best disposition, not absolutely, but by comparison to the end. . . . As the artisan who makes a saw for sawing, makes it out of iron; and does not care to make it out of glass, which is a more beautiful material, since such beauty would be an impediment to the end." [21] So, too, if in Michelangelo's *Last Judgment* the bodies of the just, while more strikingly beautiful unclothed, nevertheless distract in that state from the awe which the representation is intended to convey, then the end requires that they be clothed. Thus art, while not free to misrepresent reality any more than one is free to lie, is further not free, even if it is representing reality, to represent it in a way which detracts from, rather than induces to, virtuous action.

But if art is an imitation of nature—so natural to man who is by nature imitative and learns by imitation—is it simply a copy, a photographic reproduction? In that case art would not only not be free, it would be slavery, slavery to the photograph. But art is not mere imitation. We have the words of Aristotle: ". . . Generally art partly completes what nature cannot bring to a finish, and partly imitates her." [22] How does art complete as well as imitate? One might take, for example, the case of shelter. A cave provides shelter by nature, but man, employing what he has learned from nature, goes farther and builds a house. So, too, in the fine arts, if their basic delight is in man's desire to know, then the artist will so imitate nature as, if possible, to make it more intelligible. In painting a portrait, he will not slavishly imitate the exterior, but by accenting this and de-emphasizing that, endeavor to capture something of that which lies beneath, endeavor to make his subject more intelligible. This is the universal process by which man goes to the nature of things through his senses, and when that process is rendered more easy, there is that delight of the mind for which the word "beautiful" seems so appropriate. Thus we find St. Thomas saying, in his expositions of Aristotle, "As Aristotle says most beautifully. . . ."

In this process, man is creative and thus free. As St. Thomas says in his introduction to the exposition of the *Politics,* just as all of nature may be considered a work of art of the Creator, so, too, every work of art may be considered a creation.[23] As nature proceeds from the mind of God, so art proceeds from the mind of man. Just as men are free to use different words and combinations thereof to express what they see, so also may the artist use different techniques to express what he sees. The importance of his role may be seen from Aristotle's statement that in allocutions before general audiences it is the metaphor which is supreme. And what is the metaphor but the conveying of an idea through a graphic image? But just as the speaker must use his metaphors to convey the truth, so must the artist use his representations. The very fact that he is expressing the intelligible through sensible forms, a task which can never be performed with complete adequacy, leaves him liberty since he must use imagery which does not pretend to be a completely adequate representation. It uses, as St. Thomas says: *Quasi quibusdam similitudinibus.*[24]

To repeat, art is imitative of nature.

> The principle of those things which are made according to art is the human intellect, which according to a certain likeness is derived from the divine intellect, which is the principle of natural things. Whence it is necessary that the operations of art imitate the operations of nature; and that those things which are according to art, imitate those things which are in nature.[25]

Here St. Thomas is not talking of building a ship or building a house, but of that work of art which is "more eminent than all those which can be known and made by human reason," namely, the state. If that work of art which is the human state must imitate nature, certainly the parts of that whole, individual men, must imitate nature in their art. It is in any case useless to labor the point, since every work of art, exotic or esoteric though it may seem, is dependent upon sense knowledge which is, in fact, of nature.

But something can be said of the degree of that imitation, something which has bearing upon the freedom of art. The most perfect of imitations is that in which the exemplar and the image, although distinct, have numerical identity of nature, as is true of the divine Persons, the Father and the Son. A lesser imitation is that of human generation, in which the son is the image of his father as to specific likeness, though not numerical identity of nature. All other imitations in which the image is not of like species with the exemplar—and which occurs only in the generation of living things—have only an accidental, not essential likeness with the exemplar, as the accidental figure of a statue imitates the substantial form of a man. The figure of the statue is indeed accidental, because as far as the substance of the statue is concerned, it is only inert matter.

In a word, the relation of a work of art to that which it represents is not that of substantial form to substantial form, but rather that of accidental figure to substantial form. And since these accidental figures which bear a resemblance to the substantial form, are not proper accidents of that form—for example, there is no one particular shape of the human body that may be said to be the *only* shape proper to man—there is a certain liberty in choosing the accidental forms with which one wishes to convey the object of the representation. Even though the majority of men might have hair, one is free to represent them as bald. We have gotten to feel that busts of Julius Caesar, for instance, would hardly look right any other way.

A further point which should perhaps not be omitted in speaking of the imitative nature of art, is that somehow artistic creation seems eminently human. For man is made in the image of God, the Divine Artist, who from the contemplation of His Own divine mind produces creatures in resemblance of the divine perfections. So, too, if man is in the divine image, it is fitting that he, also, from the contemplation of his thought should produce works in the image of that thought. In human generation, where the generative powers do not belong to man as man but as animal, and where, it must be remembered man does not produce the whole human being, but only the body disposed for the soul, thought is not required. But in a work of art it is, since the work of art is the representation of that which man as man has conceived. It is true that there is this difference: the human mind, unlike the divine mind, is not the sole measure of that which is produced. For all that is in the human mind, as even the staunchest of idealists would admit, is derived from the divine mind either directly, or indirectly, through nature. Should it have been received directly, there is then lacking any sensible imagery by which it may be recognized by others, and one has "words which it is not given man to speak," that which "eyes have not seen, nor ears heard." But as to those works of art which man can produce, so connatural are they to human nature, that it is a commonplace that an artist may treat his artistic creations like his own children. Speaking of how benefactors love their beneficiaries, because they are the men whom they have "made," Aristotle writes: "This is what happens with craftsmen, too; every man loves his own handiwork better than he would be loved by it if it came alive; and this happens perhaps most of all with poets; for they have an excessive love for their own poems, doting on them as if they were their children." [26]

Art, then, necessarily imitates nature, in that it is a representation of human thought, which in turn is a representation of reality. If reality is an illusion, or is unintelligible, to worry about whether art should imitate nature, would be equivalent to plucking the patient's eyebrows while he is dying of a heart attack. The question of whether truth is attainable, or whether there is such a thing as truth, is a crucial question which art, following rather than regulating human thought, cannot settle. It does perhaps perform a service, however, when by its own aberrations it indicates the aberrations of human thought. But then the object of concern should be not the work of art but rather the artist and the society which produced him.

We have endeavored to establish here that art imitates nature, and that just as nature is true because it conforms to the exemplar in the divine mind, so likewise human art must be true by conforming to nature or reality. This obligation lies upon it since its connatural function is to give knowledge to man, to induce him to virtue, a function which is indeed noble. And just as the function is noble, so is the responsibility to represent the truth a heavy one, the responsibility which lies upon all men to express that which is true, since man, being a social animal, naturally looks to others to teach him and instruct him. We have pointed out that inasmuch as art cannot perfectly imitate the exemplar, or employ proper accidents in representing that which it chooses to represent, is there any *one* facial expression or composition or technique which *alone* can express bravery or love or sorrow? It enjoys freedom in choosing the means of its expression. And here may it not be suggested paradoxically that the artist of the Middle Ages employed that freedom to a far greater extent than the supposedly freer artist of the Renaissance.

Take, for example, the statues of the Middle Ages of the Blessed Virgin holding her child in her arms and compare them to Raphael's lovely *Madonna of the Goldfinch.* Although the latter may resemble more closely the Blessed Virgin and her Child in a purely human way, one nevertheless becomes so engrossed with the beauty of the Madonna as a woman of the Italian Renaissance at its best, with her gentle aristocratic countenance and with admiration for the grace of the Italian landscape in the background, one does not think of the Madonna as the Queen of Heaven. But in the statues of the Middle Ages, the artist uses his freedom to make you know that the Blessed Virgin is the Queen of Heaven: he puts a crown on her head. Her Child is not holding in his hand a goldfinch, but the orb of the universe. As a result, one in looking at such statues, at the happy, receptive smile upon the face of the Mother with her crown upon her head, at the friendly Child balanced on His Mother's hip, one feels confidence and hope in that Mother's benignity and in the power of her intercession. By his freedom the artist of the Middle Ages has done what the artist of the Renaissance nominally professes to do, but often does not, he has led us by his representation to an act of virtue—to hope and prayer.

But if the artist enjoys liberty in representing that which is true, choice of means in representing the intelligible through the sensible, is there no further restraint upon him? Is it enough that his subject be true to life? And by this "true to life" we obviously do not mean a servile copy. A bleak photograph of a tree conveys: "Here is everything that is material in a tree." An artist tries to convey: "Here is what the tree *means.*" And not to me as though my feelings were the laws of the universe, but to me as groping for the invisible things of God in the things which are made. It is not enough that someone strike *me* as hideous for me to represent him as such; he must be *objectively* hideous. This does not mean that he must be visibly hideous. Rather the freedom of the artist lies in making that visible which to the naked eye is invisible, as was the wont with

Rembrandt. How unlike the "freedom" of the Renaissance is Titian's *Sacred and Profane Love,* wherein *both* the ladies look alike. But supposing the work of art to be true with all due liberty of expression, supposing the artist has captured the *ratio* of his subject; has he also attained the *recta ratio?* Is his work *right,* not in the sense of being true to life, which is presupposed, but in the sense of right for being conducive to virtue?

All art has some purpose since it is impossible for a man to act as a man without acting for a purpose. That there is a right one is undoubted; yet, because a man's will is free, he may choose some other purpose. Needless to say, it will always be proportioned to the artist's view of the ultimate end, whether that end be considered to be matter evolving blindly, or an immaterial intelligent divinity. That art should give pleasure is no distinctive end for art. Whatever is in accord with the principles of the beholder, be they true or corrupt, will give him pleasure. Thus the mere fact that a representation pleases does not make it right. The artist cannot decide what must please, but he knows that whatever representation is in accord with the end of the beholder will please him, since delight or pleasure is nothing other than the appetites coming to rest in that which it desires as an end or good.

We have already maintained that the ultimate end of both the artist and his art, is to induce to something virtuous through his representation. The reason for this may be simply restated. The artist intends to communicate some truth, a truth which is not already self-evident; otherwise there would be nothing added by the representation. This places fine art in the realm of rational philosophy, concerned with the process of reasoning, by which man goes from what he knows to what he did not know.

But the artist is not concerned with conveying universal speculative truths, which are best conveyed by nude demonstrations, but with conveying truths concerned with the life of man. And since life consists in action, art is concerned with human actions. The truth that it conveys is of some action as good and desirable, or some action as evil and therefore to be avoided. Not that the representation need represent an action; it may be only a human figure. But it arouses delight or distaste, arouses a spiritual motion towards something as good or away from something as evil. In this sense we have the purging or catharsis of the passions as in great tragedy, wherein one is led to love the good and hate that which is evil. The perversion of this consists in rendering vice delectable and virtue odious, as in that era of the "mad twenties" when adolescents grew to love the suave movie gangsters and to look down upon the uncouth "flat-foots."

Since the end is that which first impels us to move in the moral order, it is equivalent to a principle in purely speculative matters, and consequently is not proved. The end is in the realm of indemonstrable first principles. Just as one does not prove the principle of contradiction upon which all reasoning depends, so one does not prove the end. The principle of contradiction is defended by showing the impossibility of not holding it. The true end is established from false ends not by creating that end but by perceiving, through the study of human nature what that end, perfective of that nature, must be. Here, because the end is not something immediate and sensible one can err, and it becomes the task of speculative thought to establish what that end must be. But even when once established in the speculative order, its attainment in the practical order is not automatic. The reason for this may be seen in the difference between the intemperate man and the incontinent man. The intemperate man is the man who has the vice of intemperance, who gets drunk because he likes to get drunk and enjoys it. "But there is a sort of man who is carried away as a result of passion and contrary to the right rule—a man whom passions master so that he does not act according to the right rule, but does not master to the extent of making him ready to believe that he ought to pursue such pleasures without reserve." [27] And this is the incontinent man. One does wrong because he likes it, the other does wrong not because he deliberately wants to, but because he is swept off his feet. This fact, clearly perceived by Aristotle, brings out that even should we know and desire to pursue that which is right, we may be influenced by our passions to pursue that which is wrong.

Consequently, it is perfectly possible that a work of art may be true to life and intended for a right end, and the beholder may have the same right end, yet there may be in that work of art that which so arouses the passions as to carry the beholder away from the right end. Thus a story of adultery intended to show its tragic consequences may fail in its purpose if the beauty of the adulteress is such as attracts the beholder more than he is deterred from the vice. The beauty of the human body, since it is that of the highest sensible creature, undoubtedly surpasses all other sensible beauty. Yet the contemplation of that beauty in man's present state, as is well known, may lead not to perception of the goodness of the Creator mirrored therein but to illicit desires. This the artist must face in choosing the mode of his representation. It must not only have the *ratio* of the thing, but the *recta ratio;* the ratio so expressed as to induce to that which is virtuous; a *ratio* which harmonizes with a *right will.*

Although the result of art is to influence towards singular actions, this singularity is not that of the art work itself, which necessarily, as all things existing, is singular, and represents singulars. But the fact that it may be dealing with some singular person, such as Hamlet, and destined to influence singular actions, does not mean that its meaning is singular. It deals with universals. As Aristotle says in the *Poetics:* "By a universal statement I mean one as to what such or such a kind of man will probably or necessarily say or do—which is the aim of poetry, though it affixes proper names to the characters." In other words, the work of art conveys what the brave man or the loving wife *in universali* would do. Just as no one can anticipate the ultimate circumstances which determine the goodness or badness of a moral act, so the circumstances of time and place contained in the work of art are accidental if the work is to have lasting significance, the significance of that which is universally true. So it is with all moral principles which, universal in themselves, only come into action as clothed with singular circumstances. That is why art need not be of the actual, but it suffices that it be of the possible, since the singular circumstances are unessential. For example, it is not essential that a representation of the Blessed Mother have her arrayed in clothes which she may have actually worn. But although one aims at a universal message, and such circumstances do not count, it is a message, nonetheless, resulting in singular actions. This does, of course, imply, that art intends to communicate. That it does may be seen by the fact that even if the artist should create only for himself, even then he intends his art to convey something if only to himself, as the hermit might fashion a crude crucifix to remind him of his Redeemer.

We have spoken of art as inducing to virtuous action. This would exclude from art its being a purely contemplative end, that which is known for itself, as are the speculative sciences. For the role of art is to represent reality "by certain similitudes," and the end of a similitude is not the similitude but that which the similitude represents. Yet its midway place between the universal and the singular, and its partaking of both, makes it peculiarly proper to man's nature, which partakes of the material and the intelligible. Herein lies its special perfection and also its danger. St. Thomas speaks of reason being "seduced" by its similitudes.[28] Possibly he means no more than that reason is attracted rather than convinced, the role which he assigns to this form of reasoning in the introduction to the exposition of the *Posterior Analytics*. But the very fact that the intelligible which is expressed may not be seen with unequivocal clarity in the sensible, indicates that one may be drawn in the wrong direction. Thus, the expression of human beauty, alas, may draw not to reverence but to lust, as Daniel said to the elders: "Beauty hath deceived thee, and lust hath perverted thy heart."

The artist has indeed freedom in choosing the means by which he will represent that which he has conceived. He is a creator in the sense that he reproduces not simply the external surface of things which strikes the eyes, but rather those things as understood by him. But the means of that expression must also recognize the realities of human nature in the beholder. No matter how one cares to explain it, there *are* sensible sights and sounds capable of moving the passions against reason which if used as the dominant motivation by the artist result in the total failure of his art to realize its purpose. But this susceptibility may vary from man to man, from nation to nation, from era to era, since it is not uninfluenced by environment and upbringing. Thus, in discerning what are the *right* means, prudence must be invoked, that virtue which makes correct judgments as to what is to be done in particular cases. The artist has indeed a grave responsibility in that in creating his work of art he must endeavor to know what sort of sensible impression it will create upon the beholder should it be a matter to which the passions are susceptible. And even if he is sure that the matter is appropriate for the majority of beholders, what of a possible minority for which it is not? Some writers such as Mauriac, appear to have solved this problem by referring it to the prudence, not of the artist, but of the beholder. It is up to them to make a prudential judgment whether to behold or not to behold. Then, too, how distinguish between scandal which is genuine and scandal which is pharisaical? One cannot go wrong by invariably following the *tutior via,* the "safer way."

But by this much of life, much of beauty is necessarily excluded. For those who accept life as a time of trial, a time when a man must forego often that which is good in itself because of his own weakness, this point of view makes sense. It is not a denial of beauty, nor a dislike for beauty, but just one more sacrifice until that happy day when the vale of tears is left behind and man is all that God meant him to be. Certainly none was more susceptible and sensitive to the beautiful than the saints, yet this seems to have been their way. Those who have taken a loftier, "I-can-take-it-or-leave-it-alone" attitude have often found the truth of Pascal's words: *Celui qui fait l'ange, fait la bête.* This is not simply a logical consequence of those who accept the doctrine of original sin and its consequences with regard to the mind's mastery over the passions, but it is a fact noted by such men as Aristotle who stated regretfully that "most men follow their senses." [29]

There is a school of thought which would disassociate art from morality on the basis that content is unimportant, unessential, and that technique is all. Artistic judgment is to be based on the media of the arts, such as color, line, harmony, etc. Form becomes structure, and so it is the organization of the matter rather than the matter as organized which has, it is thought, artistic appeal. Since, then, the essence of a work of art in this doctrine consists in structure, anything falling outside of structure is indifferent; and from this standpoint, therefore, a complete separation of art from morality occurs. But this is more wishful thinking than actuality. But because the content of art, whether one wishes to abstract from it or not, has definitely a moral effect, it moves one to action. True, art may not have a moral effect which is good, but even should the effect be bad, it is still a moral effect. This is instinctively recognized by all.

Why do Communist governments ban certain expressions of art, certain types of music? They hold to no such morality as those who insist upon the moral responsibility of art. Yet, at the same time, they do not concentrate on technique, on structure, but instead, are acutely aware of content, and of its influence. The importance of content is noted by Aristotle where he points out how "in painting, . . . the most beautiful colours laid on without order will not give one the same pleasure as a simple black-and-white sketch of a portrait." The question, therefore, is not really whether structure and technique may replace content, but rather that of whether norms may be set for content; in a word, whether the moral effect of art is subject to control. What the end is to which that moral effect should lead is not here in question, or need it be. We are faced rather with the *de facto* situation that every society recognizes the moral effect of art, and that consequently those in control of that society will deliberately seek to control that art. A recent modernistic work commanded in Mexico was refused precisely, not for its advanced technique, but for its very anti-capitalistic motif. If the artist, modern though he might be, amoral, perhaps in the conventional sense, were indifferent to content, then why did he select a content which would undoubtedly cause protest?

Granted the influence of content, has the state a right to regulate it? This question is really none other than asking whether in addition to the personal prudence of the artist in seeking the means proper to attaining a good end, and the individual prudence of the beholder who must decide whether even if for others the work is beneficial, it is so to him, there is not also a communal prudence, a prudence which decides whether the work is for the common good. In a society which is considered purely contractual, where men are considered to obey so-called "moral" laws not because they are in the nature of man, but because otherwise peaceful cohabitation would be impossible, there can be no intrinsic reason for the regulation of art, but only extrinsic coercion. Thus the police might be called in to quiet an all-night carousal not because it is wrong but because it is keeping the neighbors awake. In this vein certain movies are banned not because of any moral judgment but because of the indignation that they might provoke among a certain religious or racial group. Such a society supposes itself to be basically libertarian in every respect, including art. But in reality it is basically tyrannical. Since there are no objective norms of judgment, whoever has the power to impose his will will feel free to impose it. Such is the tyranny over art in Soviet circles, under a regime which pretends that there is no immutable truth, no ultimate end above man to which he must subordinate himself.

But in a society which does recognize an ultimate end for man, which recognizes God, and which recognizes that man attains his destiny not as an isolated individual, but as a social being, the social influence of art, beheld as it is by man, will naturally be the concern of those whose duty is to see that everything should be conducive to man's last end. That is why the state has a right to regulate education in order that the citizens, who by nature attain their end in common pursuits, may have those communal pursuits ordained to the ultimate end. If a state believes in God, it has the duty to see that its component parts, the citizens, be led to that which is the good of all, the common good. In a word, if all men have a common ultimate end, and they are going to attain that end as social beings, where no one individual can dictate the norm, then that norm must be laid down by that which represents the community, the state. Thus the regulation of art by the state, at least in a negative way, while it will always be a *de facto* situation under any regime, is also a normal situation in a regime devoted to a true common good. Far from debasing art, this is a recognition of its very genuine role in the formation of the citizen. What this role is, is aptly expressed by Aristotle in the *Politics,* where he discusses the part played by music in education. Speaking of liberal education, education in things worthwhile for their own sake, he says:

> Amusement is needed more amid [these] serious occupations than at other times . . . and they [these amusements] should be our medicines, for the emotion which they create in the soul is a relaxation, and from the pleasure we obtain rest. . . . And therefore our fathers admitted music into education, not on the ground either of its necessity or utility . . . [but] for intellectual enjoyment in leisure.[30]

And what is said here of music could be said also of the other fine arts such as painting and dancing or the theater. They afford enjoyment which is conducive to, rather than deterrent from intellectual activity, something which rugged sports, for example, would not do. Its moral role may be further seen in the words: "Since then music is a pleasure, and virtue consists in rejoicing and loving aright, there is clearly nothing which we are so much concerned to acquire and to cultivate as the power of forming right judgments, and of taking delight in good dispositions and noble actions." [31] Speaking of painting and sculpture, Aristotle goes on to say:

> The habit of feeling pleasure and pain at mere representations is not far removed from the same feeling about realities; for example, if anyone delights in the sight of a statue for its beauty only, it necessarily follows that the sight of the original will be pleasant to him. The objects of no other sense, such as taste or touch, have any resemblance to moral qualities; in visible objects there is only a little, for there are figures which are of a moral character, but only to a slight extent, and all do not participate in the feeling about them. The connexion of them with morals is slight, but in so far as there is any, young men should be taught to look, not at the works of Pauson (in which the personages are worse than we are), but at those of Polygnotus (whose personages are better than we are), or any other painter or sculptor who expresses moral ideas. On the other hand, even in mere

> melodies, there is an expression of character. . . . Enough has been said to show that music (and, if to a lesser extent, painting and sculpture) has a power of forming the character, and should therefore be introduced into the education of the young.[32]

These are in addition to the 3 R's and physical exercises. The words of St. Thomas concerning these thoughts are not without interest: "If music can make men better as to morals, it is to be learned because of this: for it cannot make men better as to morals, except through the habit of judging and delighting concerning those things which are according to reason." [33] And in general, "we see that upon changes made by sensible things according to every sense we are moved to moral passions or actions either good or bad, which is because of some likeness, since in all there is found some likeness of them." [34] Not just any type of music is to be given to the young, "but as it is useful to the republic." [35] "For all things concerning the young are to be measured and determined according to their usefulness to the end of the republic, which is the perfect good according to the intellect." [36] If music and the arts in general are as they should be, "those using them are more inclined to virtue and good ways, and being so inclined will act more according to reason, and acting according to reason easily attain to the happiness which consists in the most perfect operation of man according to his supreme power with respect to its most perfect object. Which is God, blessed for ever and ever." [37] Thus ends St. Thomas' exposition of the *Politics*.

As is evident from the above, although the arts play a role in the communication of purely intelligible truth, and as such are the object of contemplation, that is not their primary or connatural role. For whereas the purely intelligible is better conveyed by the speculative sciences, the main function of art is in the realm of practical truth, since, by virtue of its sensible representations it influences the passions. These passions are moved by that which is similar to them in art. Thus, the artist can influence the passions towards moral actions which are according to right reason. Such is its influence that art can even transform the passions, from joy to sadness, or from sadness to joy, where right reason requires. This is its purgative role, the *catharsis*. Consequently, it is the moral as pleasing which is the principle of art, not the moral as moral. From this aspect we may see how the morally bad may coincide with the beautiful, not as bad, but because the beauty represented moves the passions to that which is morally bad, as pleasing and connatural to one of such character.

The delicate balance of art may be seen from the further fact that since art influences the passions, and the passions may vary in the same individual, the same thing may not be pleasing not only to all men, but not even to the same man all the time.

But the main point is that, supposing an objective and permanent reality, art, to be anything, must be in conformity with that reality and influence towards actions in conformity with right reason. Thus moral principle is inseparable from art. Our subject has been that of freedom in relation to the expression of the beautiful. We have said that "the expression of the beautiful" is synonymous with "art," since art primarily seeks the beautiful—if the ugly is represented it is a sort of disillusionment at the fleetingness of the beautiful. In the expression of art we have said that one is not free to distort reality any more than one is free to lie. Even more, the artist will necessarily express in art his concept of reality, since art is by nature an attempt to communicate that which is not already self-evident or immediately existent. It will be the world as it seems to the artist. Whether he sees it as it is, is basically a philosophical question, of the solution of which art, as an expression, is only a consequent.

Likewise, art as the expression of a view of reality will necessarily exert an influence, since it moves the passions, which in turn influence action. We have stated that even when the artist has expressed that which is objectively true, he cannot absolve himself from considering whether his representation is right, since the representation of the true, as experience shows, may not only influence one towards right reason, but against it. The attainment of the perfect measure is the matter of prudence. We have also said that this prudential element is not only a personal one, but devolves also upon the state as having care of the common good. Thus art even if satisfactory to the prudence of the artist, and such for several individuals, nevertheless because of its social nature, because it may be viewed by many, is subject to control by the state, as is the education of the citizen in general.

Here the protests of the artist are useless, because no matter how anarchistic his philosophy, it is a fact that every state, whether tyrannical or democratic, whether moral or amoral, recognizes the influence of art upon communal action and will therefore seek to control it in favor of the end of the state. And we have stated that in the good state, the ideal state, because of its very communal nature, it should be supervised if only to the extent of insuring that it does not go against that end. This concept of the state, of course, is that of the state in keeping with human nature, where man, by nature a social animal, attains his end better than if solitary. Thus its end is indeed freedom, the intent to free man from everything which prevents him from attaining true happiness and enslaves him. "Whence," St. Thomas says, "the legislator must care for the good disposition or upbringing of the young," in which art plays a role, since they are the future of the state.[38]

The freedom of the artist, then, is no different than that of the freedom of the children of God. It is the freedom, absolute, and untrammelled, to seek for ultimate happiness according to right reason. The artist seeks it as a man, and, as men naturally love each other, strives to encourage and help others along that way. He enjoys real freedom in his expression, since it is up to him to discern the best means of conveying the intelligible through the sensible. This freedom seems to have been more the property of the Middle Ages than the Renaissance, and to have produced a higher, in the sense of more humanly beneficial, art. To represent the Son of God with the orb of the universe, rather than a goldfinch, in His hand is at once freer *and* truer. Here we see art, as St. Thomas says, "seducing" the mind towards those things, such as the Son of Man holding the universe in the palm of His hand—as He does, which reason cannot, because they are divine, clearly grasp.

In conclusion, we may gain an inkling of how beauty pervades the universe and how divine it is, from these words of St. Thomas commenting upon Dionysius:

> All things which in whatever way pertain to harmony proceed from the divine beauty . . . and thus are because of the divine beauty the *concords* of all rational creatures, for those concord as to intellect which agree in the same opinion; and the *friendships,* as to affection; and the *common causes,* as to act or anything extrinsic; and universally all creatures, to what extent they are united, have this by the power of the beautiful.[39]

Part V

Freedom and Theology

Freedom and Theology

by VERY REV. FRANCIS J. CONNELL, C.SS.R., S.T.D., LL.D.
*Dean, School of Sacred Theology,
Catholic University of America*

INTRODUCTION

To understand adequately the significance and the scope of this study on "Freedom and Theology," one must have a clear concept of what is meant by *theology,* as this word is used in the Catholic Church. The word itself is derived from two Greek words, *Theos* (God) and *logos* (word, or study). Literally, therefore, theology is *a study of God.* More completely, in the traditional Catholic usage of the word, theology is defined as *a science concerned with truths about God and about created things in their relation to God.*[1] Considered in its proper sense, therefore, theology is a *scientific* treatment of religious truths, as distinct from a simple or devotional treatment of these truths.[2] Like every genuine science, theology has certain fundamental principles on which it bases its conclusions. *Natural* theology has for its principles those truths about the Creator and His relations to His creatures which can be discovered by human reason through the use of its inherent ability, such as the existence of a personal God, His infinite perfection, His eternity, etc.[3] *Supernatural* theology is based on the truths contained in divine revelation, God's special message to His human creatures.

Theology is called *speculative* when it presents doctrine not directly concerned with human conduct, such as the doctrine of the Holy Trinity. Speculative natural theology is called *theodicy;* speculative supernatural theology is called *dogmatic theology.* Theology is called *practical* when it discusses doctrines relative to the way in which men should or should not act if they wish to observe the laws of morality. Thus, practical theology discusses the obligation to make restitution when one has injured another's property, the malice of perjury, etc. This practical phase of natural theology is known as *ethics,* of supernatural theology as *moral theology*.

In this chapter we are discussing human freedom as proposed and explained by *supernatural Catholic theology,* and we are limiting ourselves to that aspect of freedom which concerns religious belief and practice. Since the discussion centers mainly about human conduct, it is primarily a problem of moral theology. While the attitude of the Catholic Church in reference to religious freedom is the object of frequent objections and attacks, the treatment of this topic here presented is not primarily polemical or defensive, but is rather expository, because it is thought that the most effective refutation of the charges brought against the Catholic stand on this matter is a clear and logical explanation of the church's teaching on freedom, particularly as applied to religious belief and practice.

To understand the Catholic attitude toward freedom in the field of religion, one must clearly perceive the great difference that exists between *physical* liberty and *moral* liberty. The former consists in the *power* to perform a certain action, the latter in the *right* to do something. Only this latter form of liberty deserves to be called freedom in the true sense. Any intelligent and honest person will perceive and admit this distinction, at least in relation to the norms of right and wrong commonly recognized in human legislation. A robust gangster may have the physical strength necessary to overcome a peaceful citizen and to despoil him of his possessions; hence we can say that he has the physical liberty either to rob the man or to abstain from robbing him. But he has no right to commit this crime; hence, he does not possess the moral liberty to exercise his brute strength against the person and the property of a fellow man. It would be an utter misuse of terms to say without any qualification that the gangster enjoys *freedom* to perpetrate the evil deed.

Using this same distinction, the Catholic Church teaches that a person possesses freedom in the strict sense to accept and to practice only that form of religion which is in conformity with the commands of the Creator. According to Catholic belief, that religious system is *supernatural,* based on God's gratuitous communications with His human creatures, manifesting truths which human reason of itself could not discover. If, in the sphere of civil life, a person cannot be said to be free (morally) to transgress the laws of his country, surely one cannot be said to possess true freedom to disobey laws which the Creator has laid down concerning the belief and the cult which He requires from those creatures whom He has made the noblest of earth's beings, by endowing them with intelligence and free will. To assert that in their relations with God men are entirely free to believe any doctrines that may appeal to them and to practice any form of worship they may choose, without concerning themselves with laws that God may have promulgated on this matter, is entirely illogical, and is most inconsistent when those who make this statement would emphatically reject the use of the term *freedom* to designate the merely physical liberty which one may possess to break laws emanating from human legislators.

We shall discuss the subject of freedom in the sphere of religion as it is expounded in Catholic theology under the following headings:

1. The Idea of Religion,
2. The Place of the Catholic Church in the Field of Religion,
3. Freedom of Conscience,
4. Freedom of Worship,
5. Religious Freedom and the State,
6. Religious Freedom in the United States, and,
7. Freedom of Religious Thought Within the Catholic Church.

The main sources for this study are God's own communication to men, known as divine revelation; the official pronouncements of the Catholic Church (particularly those proclaimed by the Popes); and the teachings of approved Catholic theologians.

1. The Idea of Religion

The word *religion* is derived undoubtedly from the Latin language, but from what particular root is uncertain. Some say it comes from *relegere* (to read over or think over divine things), others find its origin in *religare* (to bind one again to God), others derive it from *re-eligere* (to choose God again after losing Him by sin).[4] In general, religion is a moral bond or union between man and God, embracing certain doctrines or beliefs that are accepted by man as true, and certain ethical principles that form for him a norm of proper conduct. In Catholic theology the term *religion* is also applied to a particular virtue which inclines a person to believe the doctrines and to fulfill the duties pertinent to the worship of God. In this sense we refer to one who is habitually faithful to his duty of worshipping God as a *religious* person. Religion as a virtue is regarded by Catholic theologians as one aspect of the cardinal (principal) moral virtue of justice, inasmuch as it inspires one to render to God the homage due to Him, and the object of justice is to give to others what is due to them.[5]

There are many views as to the nature and the origin of religion, taken in its more general sense. They can be reduced to two principal categories. According to some, religion is essentially a subjective and personal attitude, fashioned by man himself. According to this concept, every individual may establish a relation between himself and the divinity in a way that appeals to him personally, without regard to any objective and absolute standards. Those who hold this view are inclined to regard religion as essentially an emotional feature of human life, derived from the desire to find consolation in sorrow or courage in difficulties, etc. Explaining this interpretation of religion, Fr. Walter Farrell, O.P., says: "Religion is described as an emotional outburst, satisfying the side of man's nature that escapes knowledge. It is a matter of feeling, of religious sense, of religious experience. Consequently it is as varied and independent as the emotions of each individual; it is strictly personal." [6]

According to the other school of thought, religion is fundamentally something objective, something based on facts extrinsic to man himself, not dependent for its validity on the personal desires and feelings of individuals. In this concept of religion, the doctrines which it proposes about God and His relation to men are absolute and unchangeable truths which all human beings should accept, and the obligations which it imposes have universal binding force. The exponents of this view admit that there can be justifiable differences in the way in which men and women make religion a reality in their lives, in the sense that some persons will emphasize certain truths more than others, and some will be more inclined toward certain acts of worship than toward others. But this difference of attitude involves no diversity in the doctrines of religion themselves or in the general obligations religion imposes on human beings.

Those who take this objective attitude toward religion are fully aware that individual human beings may in perfect sincerity misinterpret or fail to perceive some of the doctrines of religion, or may make honest mistakes in their endeavor to discover their religious duties. Such errors are inculpable, and do not render those who commit them less worthy in the sight of God. Yet, they remain errors despite the good faith of such individuals. Their sincerity does not render the false doctrines they accept objectively true, or the misunderstanding of their religious duties objectively good.

As is very evident, the choice which a person makes between these two concepts of religion will have an important bearing on his attitude toward freedom in religious belief and worship. If one interprets religion as essentially something subjective, arising from emotional factors and personal traits, he will logically hold that different forms of religion, even though mutually contradictory, are equally good and beneficial. From this it would follow that every individual has full and unlimited moral freedom to believe and to practice any religion he prefers, without any restrictions save such as are needed for the protection of the rights of others and the maintenance of proper social order. According to this notion of religion, a person has full freedom to change from one system of doctrine and worship to another for reasons of personal preference, and no moral fault is involved in the change.

However, if a person believes that objectively constituted facts form the basis of religion, it is vitally important for him to accept and to practice the true system of religious belief and cult. Certainly one who takes this attitude will admit that the condition of those persons who assent to erroneous doctrines and practice a manner of worship that is not in accord with the prescriptions of God (however sincere they may be) is by no means as fortunate as the condition of those whose belief and worship are conformable to objective facts and to the laws laid down by the Almighty.

The attitude of the Catholic Church regarding the nature of religion is definitely and immutably in favor of this second view. The Church teaches that the doctrines about God and about creatures in their relation to God that constitute the intellectual aspect of religion are factual and unchangeable, independent of the subjective feelings and the personal inclinations of different individuals. Some religious tenets, the Church holds, can be perceived by human reason, without any special assistance from without. Thus, the Vatican Council, held in 1870, condemned those who assert that "the one true God, our Creator and Lord, cannot be known with certainty by the natural light of human reason, through those things that are made." [7] Moreover, it is commonly held by Catholic theologians that other truths of a religious nature can be demonstrated by unaided reason, such as the perfection and the eternity of God, and the spirituality and immortality of the human soul.[8]

However, there are religious doctrines which have been made known to men by God through the supernatural mode of communication called revelation. Some of these doctrines transcend the native powers of the human intellect, such as the doctrine of the Holy Trinity, according to which God, though one in nature is three in Persons—the Father, the Son and the Holy Spirit. Although the intelligence of man is unable to discover and clearly understand this sublime tenet, it is fully reasonable to believe it through faith, motivated by God's authority, since there is convincing proof that He has revealed it and that He can neither be deceived nor deceive. A doctrine of this kind is known as a supernatural mystery.[9]

Furthermore, because many persons would find it difficult or even impossible to acquire an adequate knowledge of even natural religious truths by their own intellectual powers, God has deigned to include in the content of divine revelation some of these doctrines of the natural order, such as His eternity and omnipresence,[10] and the immortality of the human soul.[11] All these doctrines, both those that are within the competence of man's reasoning powers (natural religious truths) and those that by their nature surpass human intelligence (supernatural religious truths), make up the body of religious truths which must be accepted by all men, either because they are known with certainty by the light of natural reason or because they have been communicated by the Creator to His creatures with the obligation of believing them on His authority.[12]

Similarly, according to the tenets of the Catholic Church, the norms of conduct which men are bound to observe as a duty of conscience are objective rules, irrespective of the personal desires and inclinations of each individual. Some of these are based on the very nature of man, as God has created him. For example, man is destined to live as a social being, passing his days in the company of other human beings, aided by others and in turn aiding them toward the proper pursuit of life. Hence, that type of conduct which will promote social life, such as truthfulness, obedience to lawful authority and regard for the property of others is objectively good and obligatory on all men, whether they desire it or not. On the other hand, such actions as tend toward the destruction of proper social life, such as falsehood and treason to one's country, are objectively bad and prohibited, and men cannot make them good by thinking they are good or desiring that they be good. Similarly, man by his very nature is a rational being, composed of a spiritual soul and a material body in such wise that the soul is adapted to rule the body and to control its activities within the bounds of moderation; hence, gluttony and drunkenness are intrinsically wrong, and temperance is intrinsically good. Again, man is a creature of God, so that his very nature demands that he adore his Creator, and abstain from such deeds as perjury and blasphemy. The code of right and wrong which is based on man's very nature is unchangeable, as is human nature itself. It is called the natural law because it flows necessarily from the nature of man as designed and fashioned by God Himself; and consequently it is truly the law of God, an essential element of the homage which the Creator demands from His creatures.[13]

The natural law, at least as regards its most fundamental precepts, can be discovered by human reason. Even if the human race had never been raised to the supernatural state, men would have been bound by the natural law.[14] However, since human beings have been destined to a supernatural goal, superior to their natural end, God has communicated through supernatural revelation certain commandments over and above the natural law, such as the obligation to observe the Sabbath Day, imposed by the Almighty on the Jewish people in pre-Christian times (which, however, has been abrogated with the establishment of Christianity) and the obligation to receive Baptism imposed on all mankind through the Son of God, Jesus Christ. These commandments, added to the natural law, and made known through revelation, constitute the divine-positive law. As in the case of natural religious truths, so the obligations contained in the natural law have been, in great part, included by God in His revealed messages to mankind. For, if men were left entirely to their own reasoning powers to determine the content of the natural law, they would go astray in many points. Hence, God has confirmed many of the prescriptions of the natural law by a positive revealed statement—for example, the prohibition of divorce (in the sense of a dissolution of the marriage bond). The decalogue, or ten commandments, promulgated to the Jewish people through the prophet Moses are entirely a matter of natural law, with the exception of the third commandment: "Remember thou keep holy the Sabbath Day." [15]

Since the doctrines concerning God made known by reason represent objective facts, not mere emotional attitudes of individuals, all men are bound to accept them. Similarly, since the obligations of the natural law arise from human nature, common to all men, all are bound to fulfill them. Moreover, since the Creator has the right to prescribe that all His creatures shall believe His statements and obey whatever precepts He may add to the natural law, all men are bound to embrace revealed religion, if it can be shown that God has revealed religious truths and moral obligations for the entire human race. Hence, in this supposition, the practice of religion on both the natural and supernatural (revealed) plane becomes an obligation incumbent on every human being.

However, religious belief and worship also constitute a right—indeed, the most fundamental of human rights since it is through the acceptance of religious truths and the fulfillment of religious obligations that one conforms his conduct to the will of his Creator and Sovereign Lord and thus attains to the goal of human life, the eternal possession of God in the life beyond the grave. The right to perform the duties imposed by religion is so basic and personal a right, that no human authority, whether domestic (a parent) or social (a civil government) may lawfully prevent a person from exercising this right. The most wicked deed that civil rulers can perpetrate is to legislate against the practice of religion by the citizens subject to their jurisdiction or to punish them for observing their religious duties. It should be noted, however, that a person has a strict claim to the physical freedom to practice religion contingently on his moral freedom to do so. In other words, a human being has a real right to exercise religious worship only in as far as it is conformable to objective truth and to the will of God. No one possesses genuine freedom to set himself against the form of religious belief and cult prescribed by the Almighty. A person has no more right to profess a false religion than he has to purloin his neighbor's goods. Actually, in both cases his pretended right or freedom of conduct amounts to an enslavement of his personality—enslavement to error and to the evil of defying the Ruler of the universe. It is vitally important that this true idea of "freedom of worship" be grasped, else the phrase will be open to all manner of erroneous interpretations. This point will be explained later in greater detail.

Men are bound to practice religion, not only as individuals, but also as social beings. In other words, organized society, or the state, has the obligation to acknowledge and to venerate Almighty God. This duty is to be fulfilled by those who govern the state. Not only as private persons, but also as civil rulers they must worship the Most High. As in the case of private individuals, those who hold authority in government must conform their official religious conduct to objective standards. If God has manifested His will that a certain form of religious worship be accepted officially by those who rule their fellow men, civil rulers in their official capacity must accept this system of religion, and are not free to substitute a different species of belief or cult. Furthermore, in their legislative enactments they are not at liberty to decree practices at variance with the laws of God, whether contained in the natural law or in the divine-positive law.

The attitude of the Catholic Church regarding the obligation of civil rulers to honor God in their official capacity and to regulate their official conduct in accordance with the teachings and laws of the particular religion which He Himself requires from His human creatures is thus expressed by Pope Leo XIII: "It is a public crime to act as though there were no God. So, too, it is a sin in the State not to have care for religion, as something beyond its scope, or as of no practical benefit; or out of many forms of religion to adopt that one which chimes in with the fancy; for we are bound absolutely to worship God in that way which He has shown to be His will. All who rule, therefore, should hold in honor the holy Name of God, and one of their chief duties must be to favor religion, to protect it, to shield it under the credit and sanction of the laws, and neither to organize nor enact any measures that may compromise its safety." [16]

In his Encyclical, *Quas primas,* on the Kingship of Jesus Christ, Pope Pius XI thus spoke of the duty of civil officials to profess and to practice the revealed religion which God requires from all mankind: "Nor is there any difference in this matter between individuals and societies, both domestic and civil; for men joined in society are no less under the power of Christ than individuals. . . . Therefore, let the rulers of nations not refuse to fulfill by themselves and through their people the public duty of reverence and homage, if they wish to promote and to augment the prosperity of their country, while preserving uninjured their authority." [17]

2. The Place of the Catholic Church in the Field of Religion

Jesus Christ, who lived in Palestine almost two thousand years ago, preached a system of religious doctrine and a moral code which He claimed came from God. In confirmation of this claim He worked many miracles, extraordinary deeds surpassing all the powers of created nature, such as the instantaneous cure of lepers and of blind persons and the raising of the dead to life.[18] His most astounding miracle was His own resurrection from the grave on the Sunday following the Friday when He had expired on a cross on Mount Calvary. This miracle He had announced previously as the very touchstone of his religion.[19] The historical authenticity of these miracles, related in the four Gospel narratives of Matthew, Mark, Luke and John, can be established just as scientifically and convincingly as other contemporary facts which all scholars admit without any hesitation, such as the wars of Julius Caesar and the succession of the Roman Emperors.[20]

Now, since miracles by their very nature surpass all created forces, they can originate only in God as their principal cause, although He may perform them through a creature as an instrument of His power. Furthermore, the all-truthful God would never work a miracle under such circumstances that it would be normally interpreted as the confirmation of a false religion. Accordingly, in the miracles wrought by Jesus Christ in corroboration of His religious teachings we have an irrefutable proof that the doctrines He proclaimed are approved by God and, hence, are infallibly true.[21]

Among the religious tenets taught by Jesus was the doctrine of the Holy Trinity—the doctrine that God, though one in nature is three in persons, the Father, the Son and the Holy Spirit.[22] Furthermore, Jesus claimed that He Himself was the Second Person of the Holy Trinity, the true Son of God, equal in all respects to the Father and the Holy Spirit.[23] He had taken to Himself a human nature, thus becoming true man, without any derogation or diminution of His divine nature and powers. In the language of Christian tradition, there was thus established between the Person of the Son of God and a human nature, received from the Virgin Mary, a hypostatic, or personal, union.[24] He is *one* divine Person with *two* distinct natures, the nature of God and the nature of man. Hence, even in His human nature, Jesus Christ, being a divine Person, is worthy of adoration, and is endowed with sovereign power over all mankind, both individuals and organized societies. He is, in very truth, even as man, "Ruler of the kings of the earth." [25]

While He was on earth, Jesus Christ established a religious society, which He called His Church, promising that it would not be overcome by hostile powers, but would endure until the end of time.[26] He bade the little group of disciples whom He had chosen as His special companions—the apostles, as they are called—to go through out the entire world, preaching His doctrines and summoning all men to accept His religion. According to His commission to the apostles, all men have an obligation to believe His doctrines and to enter His religious society by the reception of Baptism. He declared that those who would believe His doctrines would be saved, while those who would not believe would be condemned.[27] He visualized His Church as a universal society and, designating His followers as sheep and Himself as the good shepherd, He clearly stated His desire that there be only one sheepfold.[28]

This same notion, that the Church of Christ is a necessary means of salvation for the entire human race, so that all are bound to enter the Church, was frequently emphasized by the writers of the early Christian centuries. Thus, St. Cyprian, who lived in Africa about the year 250, wrote: "He cannot have God as his Father, who does not have the Church as his mother." [29] And the brilliant St. Augustine, referring to a certain bishop who had left the Church, declared: "Outside the Catholic Church he can have everything except salvation. He can have honor, he can have the sacrament, . . . but never except in the Catholic Church will he be able to find salvation." [30]

Therefore, it has been stipulated by Jesus Christ, the Son of God and the Ruler of all men that all human beings shall join His Church in order to attain to eternal salvation. Hence, while men have the physical freedom to reject this ordinance of Christ, they do not have the right, the moral freedom, to oppose it. For, undoubtedly, if God has commanded that all His creatures shall accept and practice one particular form of religion, all men must obey this command if they would fulfill the destiny assigned to them, the attainment of everlasting happiness in the life beyond the grave.

Since we have the assurance of Christ, the Son of God, that His Church will endure until the end of time, it is evident that this Church is still in existence in the world. It is vitally important for every human being to recognize this Church and to seek membership in it, since this is a necessary means of obtaining eternal happiness. Undoubtedly, if God requires all men to join this Church, He has provided means whereby it can be discerned by all earnest seekers. In other words, it must be possible for a person of good will to discover, among the many organized forms of Christian worship now existing in the world, the one true Church, the only society established by Jesus Christ, the particular organization which all men are bound to enter in the quest for eternal life.

A thorough and impartial investigation will reveal that only the Catholic Church, the Church which recognizes the Bishop of Rome as its supreme spiritual head, possesses the qualities characteristic of the religious organization founded more than nineteen hundred years ago by Jesus Christ. There are various ways of establishing this fact. The most common method is the use of the four *notes* (distinguishing marks), designated as unity, holiness, universality and apostolicity. This procedure consists in demonstrating that the Church as Christ founded it possessed these four qualities, and that they are found in the Catholic Church alone of the Christian groups that exist throughout the world. Unity, or oneness, of doctrine, cult and government was surely characteristic of the religious society established by Jesus. He made it clear that all His followers were to accept all the doctrines that He taught, participate in the same rites, such as Baptism and the Holy Eucharist, and submit to the spiritual government of the apostles (and their successors, since the Church was to endure until the end of the world) to whom He said: "He who hears you, hears me; and he who rejects you, rejects me." [31] The Church of Christ was to be holy—not in the sense that all its members would be models of virtue, for He Himself clearly indicated that there would be sinners in the Church [32]—but in the sense that the Church would always uphold ideals of Christian virtue, and afford abundant means of leading a holy life and be successful in sanctifying many souls. The Church of Christ was to be universal, or catholic; its mission was for all nations and eventually it was to be found throughout the entire world. Finally, the Church instituted by Christ was to be apostolic, in that it was to be administered by the apostles after the departure of the Master from earth, and after their death by their lawful successors. For, since the Church was destined to endure until the end of time, it must have been the will of Christ that the apostles would have successors. Indeed, the history of the

Church from the very beginning indicated that through the ceremony of the imposition of hands, the apostles planned to pass on to other men the sacred power they themselves had received from Christ.[33]

Now, among the many Christian religious bodies in the world today the Catholic Church is distinguished in a unique manner and degree by the possession of these same four characteristics. The Catholic Church is one in faith, worship and government; the standards of virtue it proclaims (such as the obligations of married life) remain untouched by the materialism of the age, and the holiness of millions of its members manifests the sanctifying power of the Church, despite the fact that many Catholics are wicked; the Catholic Church is surely spread throughout the entire world; and it is an undeniable fact that the bishops of the Catholic Church are the successors of the apostles in their ecclesiastical ministry and authority down through the centuries. No other Christian organization can lay a just claim to these characteristics. Indeed, as far as their origin is concerned, most of the non-Catholic religious denominations began only in the sixteenth century or subsequently.[34]

Even the succession of bishops in the see of Rome alone will show the identity of the Catholic Church with the Church established by Jesus Christ. For He chose the apostle Peter to govern the Church as its supreme pastor after His ascension into heaven.[35] Now, from the earliest centuries of Christianity it was recognized that the successor of Peter is the bishop of Rome. Peter himself became bishop of Rome, and the Church recognized that subsequently the bishop who succeeded him in that see became by that very fact the spiritual head of all Christians.[36] And down through the past nineteen centuries there has been an unbroken chain of bishops in the see of Rome, acknowledged by the Catholic Church as the lawful successors of St. Peter and the earthly vicars of Jesus Christ. In other words, from St. Peter, on whom Christ said He would found His Church, down to Pope Pius XII in our own days the line of Roman bishops keeps the Catholic Church identical with the Church established by the Son of God.

Other arguments for the claim of the Catholic Church to be the same Church that Christ established can be found in what are known as moral miracles, such as the endurance of the Church, despite persecution and opposition down through the centuries. The fact that the Catholic Church has survived such difficulties is a sign that the Church has received special divine assistance, enabling it to remain in existence in circumstances that would have brought destruction to any purely natural society. God's special protection of the Church indicates that it is the one true Church. Furthermore, just as physical miracles, such as the instantaneous cure of the sick, attested to the divine mission of Christ Himself, so many well authenticated miracles have taken place in connection with the Church's teaching and worship, pointing to the Catholic Church as the organization which Christ established and in which He wills all men to be incorporated.[37]

The Catholic Church claims the prerogative of infallibility in the exercise of its teaching office, and this claim rests on the words of Jesus Christ. When He sent the apostles into the world to preach His religion, He assured them that He would be with them "even to the consummation of the world." [38] Evidently this promise extended also to the successors of the apostles, the bishops of the Church, and coming from the lips of a Divine Person, this assurance must reasonably be interpreted as a guarantee that He would preserve His authorized teachers from error in the fulfillment of their task. For, undoubtedly it was His will that His teachings in the full splendor of their truth, should be available to men as long as the human race endures. A similar conclusion can be deduced from Christ's promise that the gates of hell shall not prevail against His Church.[39] Surely, if the whole Church fell into error, as could happen if the official teachers did not enjoy a divinely guaranteed preservation from error, it could be said that the gates of hell had prevailed against the Church.

For this reason Catholics believe that the doctrinal pronouncements of their Church, when proclaimed with the full measure of the Church's teaching authority, are infallibly true. Of course, not every statement of the Church is pronounced with the requisite qualifications for an infallible declaration. To merit the prerogative of infallibility, a doctrine must be concerned with a matter of faith or morals, must be proclaimed with the full measure of the Church's teaching authority, and must be intended as a definitive and final decision for all the members of the Church. Such a statement can be made by the Pope speaking most solemnly—or *ex cathedra,* as the technical phrase describes it [40]—or by the bishops of the Church in conjunction with the Pope. The bishops can exercise this prerogative, either when they meet in a general council under the headship of the Pope, or when they are unanimous (or practically unanimous) in teaching some doctrine of faith or morals in their respective dioceses throughout the world.[41] When the Church teaches infallibly a doctrine contained in divine revelation, the assent given to it by the members of the Church is an act of divine-catholic faith; when the doctrine is not contained in revelation but is connected with it, the assent is called ecclesiastical faith.[42] But Catholics are also bound to accept with religious assent even those doctrines that are not taught with the protection of infallibility, but are proclaimed authoritatively by the Church.[43]

The logical conclusion from the Catholic Church's claim to be the one true Church established by the Son of God, and to be authorized to teach His doctrines with infallible certainty is that all human beings are obliged to be affiliated with the Catholic Church in order to be saved. This is an obligation that is imposed on mankind, not by the Church itself, but by the Son of God, the Ruler of all mankind, who established the Church as a necessary means of attaining to eternal salvation.

In other words, no human being enjoys the *moral* liberty, in which alone is true freedom, to remain outside the Catholic Church or to establish or join any other religious organization in preference to the Catholic Church. To many persons this unqualified and uncompromising stand of the Catholic Church appears most arrogant and overbearing, and their immediate reaction is a vehement denunciation of the Church's claims. It is true, in view of the commonly accepted notions about "freedom of religious worship," the average American is likely to be startled and aroused when he hears of a religious society that asserts definitely: "You must join me under penalty of eternal damnation." But to become enraged against the Catholic Church because of this claim is most unreasonable, for the question at stake is not whether the claim of the Catholic Church *seems* autocratic; the point to be considered is whether or not the Catholic Church *is* justified in making this claim. The answer to this question is to be sought, not in a surge of emotion, not in an angry denunciation of the Catholic Church, but in a scholarly and objective study of the arguments on which the Church relies to support its claim to be the one and only Church established by the Son of God, the Church which all are bound to enter as a means of reaching the goal of eternal happiness. If the Church's claim is valid—and Catholics believe that the validity of this claim can be established by solid, logical arguments—then the attitude of the Church on religious liberty, however autocratic it may appear, is entirely consistent and is authorized by God Himself. Surely, anyone who admits the existence of a personal God must agree that He has the right to make one particular form of religion obligatory on all His human creatures; and if He has made a decree to this effect it is supremely audacious for any human being to say: "I shall practice religion in the manner I choose, whatever laws God may have enacted on this matter." The most vital question to be answered by every person who is really concerned with his own eternal happiness is whether or not the Almighty has established the Catholic Church as the one religious society which all men are gravely obliged to enter.[44]

The doctrine just expounded is briefly proposed in the axiom: "Outside the (Catholic) Church there is no salvation." It is unfortunate that in recent times a group of Catholics proposed an erroneous interpretation of this doctrine, for which they were reproved by the Holy See.[45] But it is also unfortunate that some Catholics, in their desire to emphasize the error of this group, went so far as to repudiate the doctrine that outside the Church there is no salvation. This doctrine is an article of Catholic faith, defined by the Fourth Council of the Lateran in the year 1215.[46] It is simply a mode of stating the doctrine explained above, that Jesus Christ made His Church a necessary means of salvation for all mankind. But, it does not mean that only those who are *actually* members of the Catholic Church can be saved. As will be seen in the following section, a person in all sincerity can erroneously judge that he is not bound to enter the Catholic Church, or even that he would commit sin by entering the Catholic Church. Such a person would not be deprived of the opportunity of saving his soul merely because he is not an actual member of the Catholic Church. But the axiom is truly applicable to him, inasmuch as he is not *outside* the Catholic Church in the fullest sense of the word. On the contrary, because of his willingness to conform his conduct to God's law as he perceives it, such a person is connected with the Catholic Church *by desire* (at least implicit in his wish to do what God has commanded), and can attain to eternal salvation if he obtains or recovers sanctifying grace (by an act of divine charity or perfect contrition, or by valid sacraments which may be at his disposal). Nevertheless, even this individual, if he does gain heaven, has been saved through the Catholic Church as an essential means, inasmuch as the desire he has to fulfill all that is necessary for salvation implicitly linked him with the one true Church which Christ established.[47]

The firm conviction which the Catholic Church has ever maintained, that it is the only true and authorized Church, empowered to carry the message of Jesus Christ to the people of all nations, has moved the hierarchy of the Church at all times to send missionaries to all lands in order to convert the inhabitants to the Catholic faith. Ordinarily, the Church seeks to secure the approval of civil rulers before establishing itself in a country, but, as far as strict right is concerned, the Church believes that it is not dependent on the governments of nations in the performance of its spiritual tasks, preaching, administering the sacraments, establishing dioceses and parishes, etc. For the Church has received its commission from Christ Himself, the King of kings, the Ruler of all nations; and His authorization to the rulers of the Church to announce His message and to establish His religion throughout the entire earth supersedes all civil legislation. Hence, in a land where the civil laws forbid the exercise of Catholic worship (as took place in England in the sixteenth century and is taking place in some of the lands dominated by Communistic tyranny today) Catholic priests and bishops have no qualms of conscience in defying civil legislation and continuing to celebrate Mass and administer the sacraments and preach Catholic doctrine. In such circumstances Catholics are convinced that the laws of the land forbidding Catholic teaching and worship are null and void because they are opposed to the ruling of God Himself. Consequently, when they are placed in such a situation Catholics follow the principle laid down by St. Peter and the other apostles, when they were brought before the Jewish Sanhedrin on the charge of preaching in the name of Jesus. The answer of the apostles was: "We must obey God rather than men." [48]

Because of its conviction that it has received its mission directly from God, the Catholic Church claims the right of certain immunities from civil legislation when such immunity is needed for the proper fulfillment of the Church's task of laboring for the salvation of mankind. Thus, the law of the Church prescribes that the members of the clergy shall not be liable to military service.[49] When the laws of a country refuse to grant the Catholic clergy any exception in this matter—as was the case in the World Wars on the part of some European governments—the Church accepts the situation as best it can, and seeks at least the assurance that the members of the clergy will not be employed in those functions of military service that involve bloodshed.

Similarly, the Church claims for her clergy immunity from such duties as serving on a jury,[50] though again in regions where this is not recognized the Church makes the best of the situation. The basis of these exemptions is the commission given to the Church by the Son of God to provide mankind with the means of attaining eternal salvation; and since this objective is far superior to the primary purpose of civil government, which is to procure the temporal happiness of the citizens, the right of the Church to those immunities that are necessary for the proper conducting of its ministerial activities is correctly regarded as superior to civil jurisdiction. The selection of the particular immunities required for the due pursuance of its functions is made by the Church in its canon law, and can vary in accordance with the different conditions of time and place. But the right of immunity is fundamentally divine in its origin.[51]

It is also a tenet of the Catholic faith that in matters involving the marriages of those subject to her jurisdiction through valid baptism, the Church possesses the right to make laws, affecting even the validity of such marriages, to the exclusion of civil laws, which can affect only the merely civil effects of marriage (such as the disposition of inheritance, the registration of the marriage in the city archives, etc.). [52] The basis of this claim is the fact that the marriage of all baptized persons is a sacrament, and consequently is subject to the exclusive authority of the Church. It is just as incongruous for civil legislators to claim competency over the sacrament of Matrimony (apart from its merely civil effects) as it would be for them to demand the right to make laws concerning the administration and the reception of the Holy Eucharist or Extreme Unction.

It should be noted that in asserting its claims to certain prerogatives independently of the authority of civil governments on the ground that it has the right and the duty to function throughout the entire world as the divinely established and obligatory way to salvation for all men, the Catholic Church is actually defending the most fundamental of all personal rights—the right to the means necessary to attain to the supreme goal of human life, the eternal possession of God. The Church can never forget that the very reason of its existence is to provide all men with these means, and it is bound to take a stand, as far as circumstances permit, against any attempt to hinder men from joining the Church and enjoying therein in full measure the abundant spiritual benefits available to the members. From this standpoint, the Catholic Church is the most ardent supporter of human freedom that exists in the world.

It must be repeated, that no argument against the Catholic Church's stand can be found in a sneer or in an angry retort that the claims of the Church are preposterous. They would be indeed preposterous if the fundamental Catholic doctrine that the Catholic Church is the one true Church of Jesus Christ were erroneous. But, if this doctrine is true, all the rights of the Catholic Church described above must logically be admitted. And it is the most important duty in the life of every human being to inquire honestly and thoroughly if this fundamental tenet of Catholicism is true, because it is intimately connected with his eternal lot beyond the grave.

3. Freedom of Conscience

The word "conscience" is used by many persons to signify a purely emotional attitude toward the moral aspect of a certain action, a *feeling* that this action is morally good or bad. The result is that such persons are very likely to determine their standards of conduct through sentiment. To them right and wrong are not objective factors, but purely subjective notions. Consequently, such persons will readily change their judgments on what they should do or should not do in accordance with their current whims and moods. It is difficult to argue on problems of morality with those who favor subjective and emotional reactions as the norms of right and wrong, because their decisions are not subject to the rules of logic.

In the proper sense, conscience is an *intellectual* act, a reasoned judgment concerning the moral aspect of a particular action which one has himself performed or is thinking about performing in the future. Feelings of pleasure or displeasure, of joy or sadness, may be produced by conscience, since the emotional side of human nature is closely connected with the spiritual faculties of intellect and will. But these sensations are only secondary factors; the essential feature of conscience is an act of practical judgment, elicited by the intellect.

If conscience concerns an act which one has already performed it is called *consequent* conscience. It is in this sense that a Catholic speaks of "examining his conscience" in preparation for confession. Consequent conscience approves or reproves us for our past conduct. If, however, conscience is concerned with an action the morality of which one is trying to decide with a view to performing it or omitting it in the future, conscience is called *antecedent*. The judgment of conscience which one passes in such a situation may be that the act is obligatory, or that it is forbidden, or that it is permissible (though not of obligation) or that it is commendable (as the better course). Hence, we distinguish four types of conscience:—commanding, forbidding, permitting and counselling.

Theologians also distinguish two kinds of conscience from the standpoint of the firmness of assent to the judgment that is passed—*certain* and *doubtful* conscience. There are several schools of thought among Catholic scholars as to the degree of probability for liberty that one must have before he can act with a safe conscience in the face of a probable obligation. These points do not pertain to the matter we are discussing save for a general principle admitted by the theologians of all schools—namely, that there is an obligation incumbent on one who is in doubt whether or not he is subject to some law to make inquiries for the purpose of acquiring certainty whether or not he is actually bound by the law. A pertinent application is this: If a person is in doubt whether or not the Catholic religion is the true and divinely established religion for all mankind, he is bound in conscience to investigate the claims of the Catholic Church. One who would neglect to make inquiries in such a situation would show himself gravely negligent regarding his eternal salvation.[53]

More relevant to the discussion on freedom of conscience in religious matters is the distinction of conscience into *correct* and *erroneous conscience*. A correct conscience is one that passes judgment on a moral problem in accordance with the objective morality of the case—namely, a conscience that declares good an action which actually is good, or bad an action which is truly bad. An erroneous conscience is one that judges as good an act which is morally evil, or as bad an act which is morally good. As is evident from experience, a person may have an erroneous conscience. People often make mistakes in passing judgment on the moral aspect of an action. We often hear the statement that in such an event one may and even should follow his conscience, even though it is erroneous. But such an unqualified statement does not take into consideration another very important distinction: that of the erroneous conscience into the *inculpably* erroneous conscience, and the *culpably* erroneous conscience. The former type is had when one has come to an incorrect decision through no fault on his own part, when he has given due reflection to the moral aspect of an action and yet has come to an erroneous decision. A person may and (if it commands something as obligatory) should follow an erroneous conscience, if it is inculpably erroneous. Such a conscience excuses one from the guilt of formal sin when his conscience propounds as good and permissible something that actually is bad. For he is acting reasonably in this case, inasmuch as he has honestly and sincerely used for the discovery of truth the intellectual power which God has given him to guide his conduct, to serve as the proximate norm of morality for him personally. It is on the basis of his honestly formed conscience that every human being will be judged by the Almighty, when the soul appears before Him after death. Hence, the person who has done something which was objectively bad because an inculpably erroneous conscience told him it was good, will be rewarded by God; but, on the contrary, one who, with an inculpably erroneous conscience, judged a certain deed to be obligatory and yet deliberately refused to perform it, will be punished by God, even though the action in question was objectively evil.[54]

But the case is very different when a person has a culpably erroneous conscience. This means that he has fallen into an error of judgment regarding the morality of some action the performance of which he is contemplating. The error has been due to his own fault, because of his failure to take prudent and adequate measures to find out the correct solution of the problem. Or, he may have been guilty of that deplorable psychological process known as rationalization, forcing his mind to pass a judgment that something is morally good, though in the depths of his soul he knows that it is morally bad. Sometimes, too, a person may develop a culpably erroneous conscience by fostering prejudices; and while it must be admitted that sometimes one may be unaware that he is thus actually influenced in his judgments, it is also true that one may at times realize that he is the victim of an unjustifiable prejudice that is warping his conscience, and yet refuse to take any measures to remedy the situation.

As must be fully evident, the condition of one who maintains a culpably erroneous conscience about the morality of his actions is very different from that of the person who acts at the dictate of an inculpably erroneous conscience. One who performs an action that is objectively evil cannot be regarded as innocent if he was led astray by a culpably erroneous conscience. It is the duty of one whose erroneous attitude is due to his own fault to correct the defect as soon as possible by making a thorough, honest and unprejudiced examination of the moral problem that faces him. Only after he has fulfilled this duty can he safely proceed to act with the consciousness that he has done what God demands of him in the matter of properly forming his conscience.[55]

Furthermore, it should be emphasized that even an inculpably erroneous conscience does not make an action good, in the true sense of the word, when the action is objectively sinful. It exonerates the individual who makes the judgment from *formal* sin, sin as far as his personal responsibility is concerned. It renders his action *subjectively* good when his inculpably erroneous conscience pronounces it such. But if the action in question is *objectively* evil, it is not rendered *simply good* because of his sincerity, merely because his conscience dictates it to be such. God will not punish a person for doing something objectively wrong in such circumstances, for God can discern the good subjective disposition of the individual which inspired the action. But human authorities must act on the presumption that a person is sufficiently aware of the moral aspect of his free acts, and hence, they are not to be blamed if they punish a person for conduct that is objectively illicit, even when he protests that he acted in all sincerity and good faith. It is only when he gives adequate proof that he honestly believed in conscience that he was permitted (or obliged) to perform a certain (objectively bad) action that he can reasonably claim immunity from civil penal laws.

Moreover, however guiltless a person may be in his judgments on moral matters, he can justly be prevented from performing external actions which are objectively wrong, particularly when such actions infringe on the rights of others. The man who sincerely believes from religious motives that he would commit a sin by procuring blood transfusions for his sick child can be lawfully commanded by the civil authorities to provide this remedy for the child. If he refuses, the authorities themselves may have this remedy given, despite the father's protests. However honest he may have been in arriving at his erroneous judgment (which actually gives him a *subjective* right and obligation to refuse the remedy to the child), he certainly has no real or objective right to take this stand and may be imprisoned, if necessary, in order that he may be deterred from following his inculpably erroneous conscience. Even when the rights of others which are impugned are of a spiritual rather than physical nature, this principle can be applied. Thus, a man who sincerely believes that he has a right (and perhaps even a duty!) to distribute obscene pictures can be justly prevented from this procedure by the civil law, which is surely justified in impeding those who would work moral harm to the citizens.

Hence, however sincere a person may be in passing judgment on his own conduct, he cannot be said without qualification to have a *right* to do something that is objectively wrong. He may be said to have a *purely subjective* right to the action; but not a right as such, because a true right is an objective thing. In the words of the theologian, Fr. Merkelbach, O.P.: "As regards an invincibly erroneous conscience, although in the internal forum a man may and should follow it, he has not truly and properly a right to this, because a true right is based on the objective relations of things; but he has only a putative right (*jus existimatum*). Especially he has no right to follow his conscience in an external act. An authority may not punish him if it is *proved* that he followed the dictate of conscience; but an authority may prevent him from following it in an external manner." [56]

When we apply these principles to the matter of religious belief, we find the basic rules on "freedom of conscience." If a person, after an adequate and honest study of the various religions, is convinced that a certain system of religious doctrine is true, he may accept it. If he is convinced that he is bound in conscience to profess and practice this religion, he commits a sin by neglecting to follow out the dictates of his conscience. This principle is valid even when the religion in question is objectively false, for in that event the person is bound to follow an invincibly erroneous conscience. Furthermore, anyone who would endeavor to induce this individual to reject his religion or to accept another *against his conscience* would be guilty of a grave transgression of the law of God, for he would be trying to lead this person into subjective or *formal* sin. It must be remembered that we are considering the case of one who adheres to the conviction that his religion is true without any fear that it may be false.

For this reason Catholic theology teaches that a non-Catholic who, with an inculpably erroneous conscience, believes his religion to be true is performing a good deed in the sight of God by continuing to practice that religion. St. Alphonsus de Liguori, the outstanding authority in Moral Theology, thus expresses this truth, quoting the Jesuit theologian, Busembaum: "When those who have been reared in heresy are persuaded that we [Catholics] reject and distort the word of God, that we are idolaters, etc., they cannot in conscience hear us as long as this conviction lasts, and they are the victims of invincible [inculpable] ignorance, since they do not doubt that they are on the right way." [57] If a person in this frame of mind is honestly and unhesitatingly convinced that a certain non-Catholic religion is the only true religion, which he is bound in conscience to accept, he would commit a (subjectively) grave sin by entering the Catholic Church—for example, for some worldly motive, such as a favorable marriage with a Catholic.

Catholics are fully aware that there are many persons perfectly sincere in their conviction that Catholicism is a false religion and that their affiliation with some non-Catholic denomination in which they have been brought up is pleasing to God or even obligatory. How many there are who, because they have heard false and prejudiced accounts of the Catholic Church and Catholic teaching since their childhood, are absolutely certain that Catholics believe absurd doctrines and practice degrading superstitions! Now, while Catholics regret that these men and women entertain such erroneous ideas about the Catholic faith, they are fully aware that there is no subjective guilt in their opposition to Catholicism. If these persons retain their inculpably erroneous conscience until death and never seek membership in the Catholic Church, they can nevertheless be saved through their implicit (or unconscious) desire of the true Church, joined to divine charity, love of God because of His infinite goodness.

An official pronouncement of the Holy Office on the true meaning of "Outside the Church there is no salvation" contains these statements:

> Among the commandments of Christ that hold not the least place is that by which we are commanded to be incorporated by Baptism into the Mystical Body of Christ, which is the Church, and to remain united to Christ and to His Vicar, through whom He Himself in a visible manner governs the Church on earth. Therefore, no one will be saved who, knowing the Church to have been divinely established by Christ, nevertheless refuses to submit to the Church or withholds obedience from the Roman Pontiff, the Vicar of Christ on earth.
>
> Not only did the Saviour command that all nations should enter the Church but He also decreed that the Church is to be a means of salva-

tion, without which no one can enter the kingdom of eternal glory. In His infinite mercy God has willed that the effects necessary for one to be saved, of those helps to salvation which are directed toward man's final end, not by intrinsic necessity but only by divine institution, can also be obtained in certain circumstances when those helps are used only in *desire* or *longing*. . . . Therefore, that one may obtain eternal salvation it is not always required that he be incorporated into the Church *actually* as a member, but it is necessary that at least he be united to her by *desire* and *longing*. However, this desire need not always be explicit, as it is in catechumens; but when a person is involved in invincible ignorance God accepts also an implicit desire, so called because it is included in that good disposition of soul whereby a person wishes his will to be conformed to the will of God. . . . But it must not be thought that any kind of desire of entering the Church suffices that one may be saved. It is necessary that the desire by which one is related to the Church be animated by perfect charity.[58]

Hence, it would be a serious sin for a Catholic to coerce or to induce a person to join the Catholic Church against the sincere dictates of his conscience, and thus to commit a formal (subjective) sin. For it is God's will that everyone shall follow his own conscience after he has sincerely and adequately tried to form it correctly, even though actually he has arrived at an erroneous decision. Doubtless there have been instances in the history of Christianity when undue pressure was brought to bear on some individuals to persuade them to become Catholics against their convictions and their desires; but such instances do not reflect the true Catholic attitude relative to convert-making. Pope Pius XII expressed the official stand of the Church on this matter when he said: "Whenever it happens, despite the invariable teaching of this Apostolic See, that anyone against his will is compelled to embrace the Catholic faith, Our sense of duty demands that we condemn the act." [59]

On the other hand, the Catholic Church has never considered it wrong to present arguments for the truth of the Catholic religion to those who profess other religions, even though they are sincere and honest in their convictions. The Church adopts this procedure by virtue of its divine mission to "preach the Gospel to every creature." [60] In following this course the Church does not aim to induce anyone to become a Catholic against the sincere dictates of his conscience, but rather strives to persuade him of the validity of the claims of Catholicism so that he will enter the Church with a right conscience. For it is a great misfortune to be deprived of membership in the society which the Son of God established for all men, even though one may be inculpably convinced that his form of religion is pleasing to God. Pope Pius XII stated this truth in these words:

> From a heart overflowing with love We ask each and every one of them [non-Catholics] to be quick and ready to follow the interior movements of grace, and to look to that state in which they cannot be sure of their salvation. For even though unsuspectingly they are related to the Mystical Body of the Redeemer in desire and resolution, they still remain deprived of so many precious gifts and helps from heaven, which one can enjoy only in the Catholic Church. . . . With persevering prayer to the Spirit of love and truth We wait for them with open arms to return, not to a stranger's house, but to their own, their Father's house.[61]

It must always be borne in mind that the principle that a person has a subjective right to profess a religion that is objectively false presupposes that this individual has an *inculpably* erroneous conscience. One who deliberately neglects to study the claims of the Catholic Church when he has the opportunity of doing so and suspects that Catholicism is the only true religion can no longer lay claim to even a subjective right to continue tranquilly and unquestioningly in the profession and practice of a religion that he now fears may be false. He is then fostering a culpably erroneous conscience, which it is his duty to rectify as soon as possible.[62] While it would ordinarily be unjust to ascribe such an attitude to any particular individual, it is undeniable that there are some persons in the world who are in this frame of mind and yet are trying to justify themselves in refusing to investigate the claims of the Catholic Church because they dislike the obligations that Catholicism imposes on its adherents. They are guilty of a deplorable form of self-deception inasmuch as they are striving to stifle the voice of conscience that is urging them to examine the basis of the Catholic religion for the sake of their eternal salvation.

In judging the possibility of an inculpably erroneous conscience in reference to the obligation to be a member of the Catholic Church a distinction must be made between those who have never been affiliated with the Church and those who have been educated in Catholicism and have subsequently rejected it. In the words of the Vatican Council: "The condition is by no means the same of those who have adhered to Catholic truth through the heavenly gift of faith and of those who, led by human opinions, follow a false religion." [63] Those who have never been members of the Catholic Church, or at least have never received adequate instruction in the Catholic religion even though they were affiliated with it, can easily be presumed to be victims of an inculpably erroneous conscience and to be free from subjective guilt when they refuse to become Catholics or when they sever their connection with the Church. They may be definitely hostile to the Catholic religion because of the calumnies and distorted accounts about the Church they have frequently heard; hence, it never occurs to them that they have any obligation to make further inquiries about Catholicism.

But those who have enjoyed the privilege of membership in the Catholic Church and have received sufficient instruction in the teachings of the Church and in the arguments for the divine origin of the Catholic religion (the motives of credibility) are presumed to be guilty of subjective or formal sin if they reject their membership in the Church. In other words, it is reasonable to suppose that their decision to leave the Church was a definite defiance of their conscience or a dictate of a culpably erroneous conscience. In either case they are guilty of formal sin. Theologians commonly teach that the sin which brings about the rejection of Catholicism on the part of such persons is not necessarily a direct violation of the virtue of faith. It is possible that some other evil habit has caused this spiritual tragedy, such as insolent pride or degrading sensuality. In consequence of such a habit of grave sin a person may deprive himself of the graces he needs to be loyal to the Catholic Church and darken his intellect so that the light of supernatural truth no longer is perceptible and thus come to the conclusion (which may be a sincere conviction as far as his present impaired mental attitude is concerned) that Catholicism is false. But even in this instance his defection is due to previous sinful practices and consequently is "culpable in cause," in the language of theology.[64]

Thus, the basic reason for the presumption that any adequately instructed Catholic who renounces affiliation with the Church—whether he rejects all religion or joins another religious society—is the principle that God will not allow anyone to suffer the grave spiritual losses that separation from the Catholic Church entails unless this person himself has been gravely unfaithful to God. St. Augustine, in his work *De natura et gratia,* propounded this principle in the terse phrase: "God will not desert [one who has received the gift of the true faith] unless He is first deserted." [65] This axiom was repeated by both the Council of Trent and the Vatican Council.[66]

It does not necessarily apply to a Catholic who never received adequate instruction in the faith, since from the intellectual standpoint in the field of religion he is like one who was never a Catholic, and hence might require, to keep him in the Church, an extraordinary grace which God will not infallibly grant.

Because of this reasonable presumption the Catholic Church does not hesitate to inflict severe spiritual punishments on those of her members who renounce their allegiance to the Church and its teachings, even though they may protest that they are acting in perfect sincerity. For example, the Church imposes the penalty of excommunication on those who defect from her membership by apostasy, heresy or schism.[67] In this respect the Church is only following the legal principle accepted by all public societies—that one who has had sufficient opportunity of knowing the law is deserving of punishment if he deliberately violates it, even though he protests that he sincerely believes himself justified in doing so. If every citizen when accused of a crime could assure himself of immunity from punishment by merely claiming subjective guiltlessness, penal legislation would be rendered worthless. The gangster charged with carrying concealed weapons could assert that he sincerely believed the prohibition not intended for such law-abiding citizens as himself; the murderer could claim that he felt himself urged by a divine inspiration to plunge a knife into the heart of his victim. If common sense tells us that an appeal to the "right of conscience" in such cases is utterly unjustifiable, why should we object to the Church's attitude in regarding as guilty and punishing those who have transgressed the law of God by abandoning the religious system divinely enjoined on all mankind —at least, when they are sufficiently instructed to realize they are doing wrong?

In a word, a judge cannot read the conscience of the prisoner brought before his tribunal, and while admitting the possibility of an invincibly erroneous conscience on this latter's part, he will presume him to be subjectively guilty of objective transgressions of the law as long as he had sufficient intelligence to realize what he was doing. This is particularly true in the matter of treason. The citizen who turns against his own country and gives loyalty and assistance to a hostile nation may plead in defense that allegiance to his own government is now contrary to his conscience and that he believes the triumph of the hostile power would be for the betterment of his people; but despite his protests the authorities of his own land will condemn him as a traitor and punish him accordingly. If everyone could betray his country with the assurance that, when discovered and convicted, he could win freedom from punishment merely by pleading "freedom of conscience," those citizens of a nation who desire to perpetrate the heinous crime of treason would not hesitate to use every method possible to overthrow their own government. Loyal citizens would never sanction such a procedure nor deem it unjust for their civil rulers to inflict the severest penalties on the culprits without asking them if they felt justified in their subversive activity.

Now, since it is God's command that all the members of the Catholic Church maintain loyalty to the Church as long as they live, defection from the Church by a Catholic sufficiently instructed to be aware of his obligation to remain a Catholic is a serious transgression of God's law. It is an act of treason no less than defection from loyalty to one's country in order to aid a hostile power. Even if it is done openly and the apostate or heretic does not engage in active opposition to the Church, it is a positive blow against ecclesiastical unity. Above all, it is an indication that the guilty person did not use the means to guide himself and to obtain spiritual strength in his religious problems, such as counsel and prayer and the reception of the sacraments. If he had not neglected such measures he would not have abandoned the Catholic faith, for "God does not desert, unless He is first deserted." Accordingly, the Church does not regard it as unjust to condemn one who thus renounces allegiance to the Catholic faith and to the Church of which he was a member, and to penalize him by the privation of spiritual benefits, such as the right to Christian burial and the right to act as godparent for a Catholic child.[68]

In previous centuries it sometimes happened that governments of countries in which there was an intimate union of Church and State regarded the renunciation of membership in the Catholic Church as a form of treason and punished it severely, sometimes even with the infliction of the death sentence. Beyond doubt, there were many instances of injustice and of barbaric cruelty under this system, particularly in connection with the Spanish Inquisition. But the principle underlying the claim of the civil government to punish citizens who were disloyal to the Catholic religion was substantially the same as that which is used today to justify governments in punishing those who violate their obligation of civil allegiance. Because of the close union between Church and State heretics were foes of the State as well as of the Church; hence, they were liable to punishment as traitors. The *Catholic Encyclopedia* thus explains this point, so vital to the understanding of the harsh treatment meted out to those who abandoned their allegiance to the Catholic Church in medieval Catholic lands:

> Everywhere and always in the past men believed that nothing disturbed the common weal and public peace so much as religious dissensions and conflicts, and that, on the other hand, a uniform public faith was the surest guarantee for the State's stability and prosperity. The more thoroughly religion had become part of the national life, and the stronger the conviction of its inviolability and divine origin, the more disposed would men be to consider every attack on it as an intolerable crime against the Deity and a highly criminal menace to the public peace. . . . In the middle ages the Catholic faith became alone dominant, and the welfare of the Commonwealth came to be closely bound up with the cause of religious unity. King Peter of Aragon, therefore, but voiced the universal conviction when he said: "The enemies of the Cross of Christ and violators of the Christian law are likewise our enemies and the enemies of our kingdom, and ought therefore to be dealt with as such." [69]

In a somewhat similar vein a contributor to the *Dictionnaire de catholique* explains the punishments inflicted by civil rulers in connection with the Inquisition:

> The severity of the code should not astonish us too much. The doctrines and the practices which they represent were conformable to the idea which the people of the middle ages entertained on justice. Those who exercised civil authority had not only the mission to protect the social order but also the mission to defend the interests of God in this world. They regarded themselves in very truth as the representatives of the divine authority here below. The affairs of God were theirs; consequently it belonged to them to avenge insults against the Divinity.[70]

At any rate, those Protestants who express horror at the persecution of non-Catholics by Catholic governments should bear in mind that similar tactics were employed against Catholics by governments allied to Protestant denominations in post-Reformation times. As Winfred E. Garrison, himself a Protestant, expresses it:

> There was no such flowering out of religious liberty and toleration in the Protestant countries as might be expected by those who think of Protestantism as the source of all our modern principles and practice of religious liberty. That religious liberty did slowly develop in Protes-

> tant countries and that the toleration of dissent became general are due to the fact that the Protestant churches developed away from the church-type and toward the sect-type. . . . Once [Calvin] settled in Geneva, he turned his attention to the organization of a political state which would give concrete embodiment to that faith and to the moral code which went with it—both of course drawn, as he believed, direct from the sacred oracles. In undertaking this enterprise he was assuming, as the Roman Catholic Church had always done, and as Luther did in Germany and Zwingli in Zurich, and as the English reformers were about to do in England and John Knox in Scotland, that the religion of a state must be uniform and that it was entitled to the cooperation of the civil power both for its maintenance and for the suppression of all variations.[71]

The Protestant historian Schaff declares:

> To the great humiliation of the Protestant churches religious intolerance and even persecution unto death were continued long after the Reformation. In Geneva the pernicious theory was put into practice by state and church, even to the use of torture and the admission of the testimony of children against their parents, and with the sanction of Calvin. Bullinger, in the second Helvetic Confession announced the principle that heresy could be punished like murder or treason.[72]

The fact that Protestant governments persecuted Catholics is not, in itself, proposed as a positive argument in favor of the restriction and punishment of heresy by Catholic governments. The basic argument for this latter is the doctrine that Jesus Christ established one religion for all mankind which must be accepted both by individuals and by governments. However, the fact that the leaders of Protestantism were just as vigorous in their opposition to the Catholic Church as were Catholic authorities of Church and State toward those who opposed Catholicism is at least an *argumentum ad hominem,* and as such it should suffice to answer those who denounce the Catholic Church as the enemy of freedom and extoll Protestantism as the champion of "liberty of conscience."

It must be recalled that punishment for heresy is justifiable only in the case of those who are reasonably presumed to have been guilty of subjective or formal sin by their defection from the Catholic Church. The case of those who have been reared from infancy in some non-Catholic denomination is very different. They are presumed to be in good faith, to be free from subjective guilt in their refusal to enter the Catholic Church; hence, punishment should not be inflicted on them as long as this presumption holds. In fact, the

Church law states that those whose ignorance excuses them from grave fault in conscience do not actually incur ecclesiastical penalties for sins which have such penalties attached to them in Church legislation.[73] The civil laws of lands where Church and State are united are supposed to refrain from imposing any punishment on those who have been brought up in non-Catholic religions. When this rule has been violated the authorities responsible for such action have exceeded the bounds of their legitimate power.[74]

As will be explained later,[75] this does not mean that a Catholic state necessarily regards itself as obliged to permit non-Catholics to propagate their doctrines to the spiritual detriment of the Catholic citizens or to perform public religious rites that may be equivalent to propaganda or may be the occasion of dissension or disorder.

4. Freedom of Worship

The expression "freedom of worship" is sometimes understood as synonymous with "freedom of conscience," but an accurate distinction should be drawn between them. Freedom of conscience refers merely to the right to accept a religious creed; freedom of worship implies the right to manifest one's religious belief externally through specific forms of cult, preaching, writing, etc., and particularly the right to propagate religious tenets with a view to induce others to accept them. Having discussed the attitude of the Catholic Church toward freedom of conscience, we shall now consider freedom of worship in this exact sense.

No human being possesses complete moral freedom of worship in the sense that he is at liberty either to render external homage to Almighty God or to refuse such homage, according to his own good pleasure. Everyone who has attained the use of reason is strictly bound to worship God externally. For man is a composite of a material body and a spiritual soul, both gifts of God; hence, in body as well as in soul man must render homage to his Creator. Internal worship is, of course, the more important factor. Indeed, external acts of cult, if not accompanied by inward sentiments of intellect and will, constitute the most despicable type of formalism and hypocrisy. But to assert that it suffices to worship God merely with the spiritual faculties indicates a failure to recognize the unity of human nature and man's inherent inclination to express through his bodily powers the thoughts and desires of his soul. The doctrine of the Quietist,

Michael Molinos, that "everything sensible that we experience in the spiritual life is abominable, foul and unclean" was condemned by Pope Innocent XI in 1687.[76] It is one of the basic tenets of the Quakers, or Society of Friends, that external religious rites are to be discarded.[77]

The commonly accepted Catholic doctrine on external worship is thus expressed by St. Thomas Aquinas:

> We show reverence and honor to God, not for His sake, because in Himself He is full of glory to which nothing can be added by a creature, but for our own sake. For, by the fact that we honor and reverence God our mind is subjected to Him, and in this consists its perfection, for everything is perfected by being subjected to its superior, just as the body is perfected by being animated by the soul, and the air by being illuminated by the sun. But the human soul, to be joined to God, needs to be led by sensible things. For, "the invisible things of God are clearly seen, being understood by the things that are made" as the Apostle says (Rom., 1:20). Hence, in divine worship it is necessary to use some corporal things in order that by them, as by certain signs, the mind of man may be aroused to spiritual acts, by which it is joined to God. Hence, religion has internal acts, as principal acts which *per se* pertain to religion, and exterior acts as secondary acts, ordained to the interior acts.[78]

Furthermore, man is a social being, ordained by his very nature to associate with his fellow men and to join with them in expressing the yearnings and convictions of his soul. Hence, since the duty of adoring God is deeply implanted in man's soul, it is in accord with his nature that at times he join with other men in acknowledging God as the Creator and Father of mankind. In a word, man's obligation to worship God externally demands communal as well as individual acts of exterior cult. Thus, it is the view of some good theologians, including St. Thomas Aquinas, that even if the human race had not been elevated to the supernatural plane and received supernatural revelation, men would have been bound by the natural law itself to the act of public worship known as *sacrifice*.[79]

However, from this it does not follow that every individual is free to select any form of external worship that may appeal to him as a suitable form of religious cult. For, in the first place, only that type of worship should be given to God which expresses true doctrines. God is the God of truth; hence, only that expression of homage which is founded on true ideas concerning His nature and attributes can be pleasing to Him. Thus, religious cult based on the erroneous notion that God is cruel and unjust and rejoices in the sufferings of His creatures is forbidden to men by the natural law itself. For this reason, human sacrifice, such as was offered by certain primitive people, was objectively insulting to the Most High, despite the good faith of those who participated in this form of worship.

Moreover, when it is quite evident that God Himself demands a certain kind of external worship, it is the duty of those whom the Almighty obliges to render this homage to give Him this determined species of cult. Such was true of the Mosaic ritual worship in pre-Christian times. The Almighty, through His prophet Moses, specified in great detail the type of worship He required of His chosen people, the Jewish race.[80] A greater latitude in the choice of external worship was permitted to the nations foreign to the Jewish people—the gentiles—though for them also the principle held that worship must be based on truth.

Similarly, in the New Law, established by the Son of God, Jesus Christ, certain specified acts of divine worship have been imposed on all mankind. Thus, Christ commanded that all are to receive Baptism and the Holy Eucharist, and that those who sin gravely after Baptism must receive pardon from the apostles or from their successors in the Christian ministry. He bade the apostles (and their successors in the Christian priesthood) to perpetuate the rite He celebrated at the Last Supper, whereby He changed bread and wine into His own body and blood as a sacrificial offering to God and a sacrament for the spiritual nourishment of His followers.[81]

Since these commands were issued by a divine Person, men must obey them and conform their manner of celebrating religious cult to these prescriptions. For a human being to claim for himself the right to exercise a form of worship different from that specified by God Himself or the right to abstain from ritual observances divinely established for all men would indicate an egregious failure to grasp the fundamental principle that the creature is bound in all things to obey his Creator. Even when the deviation from God's prescriptions is due to inculpable ignorance or error on the part of those who participate in unauthorized cult, the manner of worship cannot be objectively pleasing to the Almighty, although the sincerity of those who perform it will be acceptable in His sight.

Since Jesus Christ established His Church as the one religious organization which all men are bound to join and the only religious society approved by God, this Church—which is the Catholic Church

—is authorized to legislate as to the form of public worship which is to be offered to God, to the exclusion of other forms of worship established by any individuals or organizations. Although the Church may not modify the substance of the ritual observances instituted by Christ Himself, the sacrifice of the Mass and the sacraments, it may, however, embellish these forms of worship by adding certain accessory rites and prayers, such as the use of candles, incense, vestments, etc.[82] Furthermore, the Church has established certain ceremonies, known as sacramentals, ordained to draw down divine blessings by virtue of the Church's own prayers on those who employ them.[83] In thus determining the manner of external cult that is to be employed by mankind, the Church believes that it is acting through the authorization of its Divine Founder, Jesus Christ.

The principle upheld by the Catholic Church in regard to freedom of worship is similar to the principle the Church proposes regarding freedom of conscience, explained above. Just as no one has a real right, from the objective standpoint, to accept a doctrinal and moral religious system different from that which God Himself has prescribed, so no one has a real objective right to practice any form of religious worship at variance with the type of worship which the Son of God has approved and commanded. This includes those rites and ceremonies which He Himself explicitly established as well as those prescribed by His Church which He commissioned to legislate on this matter. No human being has a real right to reject God's plan regarding the type of external homage that is to be rendered to Him or to substitute a different form of worship contrary to the divine prescriptions or to the rules laid down by the Church, the only divinely authorized religious society in the world.

It is important to note here the distinction between *public* and *private* worship, as these terms are defined by Catholic theologians and canonists. By public worship is meant those acts of religious cult which are recognized by a religious society as its approved or ritual forms of prayer or adoration. By private worship is meant those acts of homage which individuals perform unofficially, without regarding them as "church functions." As is evident, the distinction between these two is not easily perceived at times. In practice, even the professional theologian sometimes finds it difficult to determine whether a certain act of external worship is to be classified as public or private. But in many cases there is no difficulty in drawing the line between these two. Thus, for example, the administration of a sacrament is an act of public worship, even though only the minister and the recipient are present. On the other hand, the recitation of the Lord's Prayer by a large group of persons in a private home or in an auditorium in connection with a civic function is to be accounted an act of private worship.

The Catholic Church regards all public worship conducted under the auspices of non-Catholic religious societies as objectively unlawful and contrary to the will of God. This is a logical consequence of the Church's belief that only that cult which has been approved or authorized by the one religious society established by Jesus Christ—which the Catholic Church believes itself to be—has the approval of God Himself and is objectively pleasing to Him. Consequently, the Church forbids Catholics to take any active part in public non-Catholic worship.[84] By active participation is meant the reception of the sacraments, joining in the prayers, singing of the hymns, marching in church processions, etc. Sometimes acts of non-Catholic worship contain doctrinal statements or implications that are contrary to Catholic faith, and in that event active communication would be by its very nature sinful. But even when no unorthodox doctrine is expressed in a public religious service, active participation is forbidden because the authorization of the Catholic Church, the only legitimate religious organization in the world (as far as the divine law is concerned), is lacking. In the words of Fr. John Bancroft, C.Ss.R.:

> Even though a form of cult exercised by a non-Catholic religious body contains nothing false, it is not a legitimate act of religion, because that body has no authority to prescribe religious acts, as a body existing against the order of things established by Christ.[85]

Those non-Catholics who perform acts of public religious worship not approved by the Catholic Church with sincerity and devotion, convinced that they are rendering homage pleasing to God, are rewarded by the Almighty for their good will. Beyond doubt, there are persons in this category whose subjective sentiments are far more pleasing to God when they take part in the religious services of their particular denomination than are the interior dispositions of many Catholics in their attendance at Mass or other forms of Catholic worship. But that does not render acts of worship not lawfully authorized in the plan of Jesus Christ objectively good and conformable to the will of God.

For a just reason a Catholic may participate *passively* (or merely materially) at public religious functions under non-Catholic auspices.[86] A person participates passively when he is present at a religious service without joining in the hymns, prayers, etc. As a matter of courtesy he may and should be decorous and respectful, rising or sitting with the congregation, keeping silence, etc. A good reason for such passive participation in a non-Catholic religious service would be present when a Catholic wishes to attend the marriage or the funeral of a non-Catholic closely united to him by the bonds of blood or friendship, or when a Catholic in civil office is supposed to be present at such a function in his public capacity. Sometimes, however, circumstances could be present which would preclude even passive attendance—for example, if the non-Catholic friend were a divorced person attempting another marriage in defiance of the laws of God. In such a case even the mere presence of the Catholic at the ceremony would ordinarily be interpreted as an approval of the invalid union, and hence would constitute a form of scandal. It could also be a species of co-operation in the sin of the contracting parties. The same would be true in the case of a marriage between a Catholic and a non-Catholic in a non-Catholic church, which would be invalid because of the failure of the Catholic to observe the ecclesiastical law requiring the presence of an authorized priest, besides two witnesses.[87] Fr. Davis, S.J., states: "Assistance at a mixed marriage in a Protestant church would not be tolerated, since this would be co-operation in violating a serious church law that forbids mixed marriages without dispensation, and such a marriage would now be invalid [because a priest did not officiate]." [88]

However, the question is different when the case involves only private worship. A Catholic is free to participate in private acts of worship with persons of other religious beliefs, provided these acts do not express or imply anything contrary to Catholic doctrine. The Church has legislated no prohibition against this manner of participation. Thus, Catholics may join in the grace said at meals by the members of a non-Catholic family. Or, they could recite the Lord's Prayer with persons of other creeds at the opening of a school session or at a civic gathering, as on Memorial Day. In this vein an instruction of the Holy Office, concerning the "ecumenical" movement—the movement toward the "reunion" of all Christians—informs bishops that when there take place meetings of Catholics and non-Catholics to discuss efforts toward reunion "there is nothing blameworthy in the common recitation of the Lord's Prayer or of a prayer approved by the Catholic Church, by which these meetings are opened or concluded." [89]

Since Catholics regard all forms of public non-Catholic worship as contrary to the divinely established order which decrees that only those acts of worship are lawful which have the approbation of Christ's Church, Catholics logically conclude that they may not give direct or formal co-operation toward such an act of worship. This rule extends not only to active participation in the forbidden cult (already considered) but also to the act of inviting others to perform worship of this nature. Thus, a Catholic priest could not lawfully request a non-Catholic clergyman to come to his town and to establish a church of his denomination there, since this would be formal co-operation toward a form of cult which the priest himself consistently regards as opposed to the command of God.[90]

The case is different when only *material* co-operation is involved—that is, some action which in itself is morally permissible, even though the person wishing to conduct non-Catholic worship finds in this action an occasion or a help toward his activities. Thus, if a nurse in a Catholic hospital summons a non-Catholic clergyman at the request of a patient, merely stating that the sick person desires to see him, she is co-operating only materially toward any religious rites the minister may perform on the occasion of the visit. According to Catholic moral principles, material co-operation toward another's unlawful action may be lawfully given, provided there is a sufficient reason for such co-operation. The factors to be considered are the gravity of the matter involved and the measure and proximity of the assistance afforded toward the activity of the principal agent. Thus, the nurse just described is justified in summoning the non-Catholic clergyman because a hospital is presumed to extend such service to its patients. However, when the co-operation is very intimately connected with the act of non-Catholic worship, Catholics naturally are deterred by conscientious motives from giving it, apart from extraordinarily grave reasons. Thus, a priest could not be expected to provide a non-Catholic clergyman with altar-bread to use for his communion service, which the priest holds in conscience to be opposed to God's law.[91]

Many would denounce the Catholic ideas on freedom of worship, as they do the Church's notions on freedom of conscience. Certainly, the attitude of the Catholic Church on this matter is radically different from the stand taken by the average American on freedom of worship; he believes that everyone is fully at liberty to select and to exercise any form of religious worship he desires. As will be shown later, this is perfectly correct as far as the civil laws of the United States are concerned, and American Catholics are fully in agreement that for our land this is the most practical system, the one best adapted to peace and harmony among our citizens.[92] But, from the standpoint of the law of God, it is not correct to say that a person has a real right, or moral freedom, to exercise any form of religious cult in opposition to God's expressed will. If God has decreed that only that form of worship is permitted to human beings which His Church authorizes, then it follows logically that other forms of worship are not objectively pleasing to Him. Human beings may have the *physical* freedom to select a manner of worship at variance with God's prescriptions; but true freedom consists in the *moral* liberty, the genuine right, to follow a certain course of action. It is from such principles that Catholics deduce the conclusion that the limitation of the rights of human beings to the exercise of worship approved by the Catholic Church is in no wise a limitation of true freedom.

5. Religious Freedom and the State

As was previously stated, organized society has the obligation to acknowledge God and to testify its homage to Him.[93] This means, at least, that those who occupy posts of authority and responsibility in civil government are *per se* bound sometimes to perform acts of religious worship in the name of the state, asking God's protection and blessing on the people, and thanking Him for favors. Those who rule in any organized society have received their authority from God, as St. Paul tells us.[94] Hence, in their official capacity they must acknowledge their dependence on the Creator and seek from Him guidance and strength in the performance of their duties. In the words of Pope Leo XIII: "Rulers must ever bear in mind that God is the paramount Ruler of the world, and must set Him before themselves as their exemplar and law in the administration of the State." [95]

However, like the private individual, civil rulers in their official duty of honoring God must seek the one true religion and be guided by its teachings in their official conduct. Some few Catholics in recent years have maintained the opinion that the state as such is not bound by any religious or moral obligations save those which can be known by reason—in other words, the natural law. According to this view, the laws laid down by Jesus Christ—divine-positive laws, as they are called—would not bind the rulers even of nations essentially Catholic. However, this view cannot be reconciled with authoritative statements of Sovereign Pontiffs and with the practice of the Church. For example, Pope Leo XIII made this statement:

> The Creator and Redeemer of human nature, the Son of God, is King and Lord of the world, and holds absolute sovereignty over men, both as individuals and as members of society. . . . Therefore, the law of Christ ought to hold sway in human society and in communities so far as to be the teacher and guide of public no less than private life. . . . The security of the State demands that we should be brought back to Him from Whom we ought never to have departed, to Him Who is the Way, the Truth and the Life, not as individuals merely, but as human society through all its extent. Christ Our Lord must be reinstated as the Ruler of human society. It belongs to Him, as do all its members.[96]

The same Pope also asserted of the Word Incarnate: "Not only Catholics and as many as have received Christian baptism validly, but men, individually and universally, have been made for Him a purchased people." [97]

In a similar vein, Pope Pius XI, in his majestic Encyclical on Christ the King wrote:

> Nor is there any difference in this matter between individuals and societies, both domestic and civil, for men joined in society are no less under the power of Christ than individuals. . . . Therefore, let the rulers of nations not refuse to fulfill by themselves and through their people the public duty of reverence and homage, if they wish to promote and to augment the prosperity of their country, while preserving uninjured their authority.[98]

From this it follows that the rulers of nations are *per se* bound to acknowledge the Church which Jesus Christ established and to grant this Church the free exercise of the rights which it received from Our Divine Lord. Such a right is the Church's claim to have exclusive authority over the marriages of baptized persons, since such marriages are sacraments, and the Church is deputed to legislate for what pertains to the sacraments. In the words of Canon Law: "The marriage of baptized persons is governed, not only by divine law but also by canon law, saving the competence of the civil power over the merely civil effects of marriage." [99] Again, the Church claims certain *exemptions,* such as the exemption of its clergy from the obligation of military service.[100] Such privileges, the Church believes, are basically divine in origin, contained in Christ's general prescription that His Church shall be endowed with the means necessary for the proper fulfilment of its spiritual activity.[101]

In this recognition of the Catholic Church as the true Church by the civil government and the acknowledgment of the Church's spiritual claims is to be found the essential factor of the "union of Church and State" which Catholic theology proposes as *per se* the desirable condition that should exist between these two powers. Other features of this union, such as subsidy of the clergy, have sometimes been introduced in Catholic nations; but the fundamental element is the acknowledgment by the government that the Catholic Church is the Church established by the Son of God for all mankind and the acquiescence to the Church's claim to the free exercise of its ministry in fulfilling the mission imposed on it by Christ, to labor for the sanctification and the salvation of all men. It is an acknowledged principle of the Catholic Church that at least this essential element of union *per se* be realized between the State government and the Catholic Church in all nations. In the words of Pope Pius XII, in an address to jurists on December 6, 1953: "In principle, that is, in theory, she [the Church] cannot approve complete separation of the two powers." [102]

An exemplification of union between Church and State is found in the Concordat between the Holy See and the Spanish government, signed on August 27, 1953. The opening articles of this document state:

> The Catholic Apostolic Roman religion will continue to be the sole religion of the Spanish nation and will enjoy the rights and prerogatives which are due it in conformity with the divine law and the canon law. The Spanish State recognizes in the Catholic Church its character of a perfect society and guarantees it the free and full exercise of its spiritual power as well as its jurisdiction. It also guarantees the free and public worship of the Catholic religion.[103]

The question naturally arises as to the attitude which a government that accepts the Catholic Church as the only true Church and makes the Catholic Church the established Church of the nation should adopt toward non-Catholic groups.

Logically, the government must look on such religious societies as professing erroneous beliefs and exercising forms of religious worship that are not authorized by God and objectively are opposed to His will. However, this does not mean that any government which recognizes Catholicism as the established religion is bound or even permitted to persecute or to punish those who profess some form of non-Catholic religion, at least if they have been brought up in this religion, so that their separation from the Catholic Church is presumably due to no fault on their part. Such persons are to be allowed to follow what is reasonably supposed to be their conscientious conviction regarding the profession and the practice of religion. Any attempt on the part of the State or of private individuals to coerce them into accepting the Catholic religion against their sincere beliefs should be severely condemned, as Pope Pius XII explicitly declared in the Encyclical "Mystici corporis." These points have been explained previously.[104]

However, a government that acknowledges Catholicism as the one true religion and recognizes the privileges granted to the Catholic Church by Jesus Christ is not acting inconsistently if it restricts the attempts of non-Catholics to propagate their religious beliefs or to exercise their religious worship in public fashion so that it would be likely to arouse conflict and discord. Moreover, as experience has shown, attacks on Catholic faith and practice can be presented in so persuasive a manner that some members of the Church, incapable of perceiving their errors, will be induced to renounce their Catholic allegiance. Hence, a Catholic state, desirous both of protecting its citizens from the grave misfortune of the loss of their Catholic faith and preserving peace and harmony, could be justified in restricting non-Catholic propaganda and influence, in order to preserve its people from the danger of losing their Catholic faith. This is the justification adduced by General Franco for the restrictions and limitations imposed on Protestant propaganda in Spain. The General made this statement in connection with the Concordat between his country and the Holy See:

> In Spain the few who do not practice the Catholic faith rarely practice any other positive religion. Heterodoxy here has always been like an exotic plant which has been forced without roots among Spaniards, even in the propitious days of the Republic. It is for this reason that we make a public statement of the dogmatic principles on which the Church is based and defend the Catholic unity of our nation.
>
> The principle of religious unity does not conflict with the private practice of their faith by isolated Spaniards or foreigners residing in

> Spain who belong to non-conformist churches, and with the maintenance of the *status quo* in the African colonies. In any case, tolerance of various cults and beliefs does not mean freedom of propaganda, which foments religious discord and disturbs the sure and unanimous possession of truth and its practice in our country. We can allow dissidents in our country to practice their faith in Spain, but not to proselytize and mislead Catholics in the face of popular opinion when almost the whole nation wants to preserve its Catholic unity at any price.[105]

In a nation whose government acknowledges the Catholic religion as the one true religion, legislation could be lawfully directed against non-Catholic propaganda exercised through preaching or publications, the use of the mails to spread attacks on the Catholic Church, etc. Similarly, public religious demonstrations hostile to Catholicism could be prohibited. All such efforts to weaken the allegiance of the citizens to the Catholic faith, especially of those who have not sufficient intellectual acumen to pass judgment on the arguments presented by non-Catholics, are logically regarded in a Catholic nation as harmful to the spiritual and temporal welfare of the people, and hence are justly banned. Moreover, in a Catholic country the government could justly forbid divorce, campaigns for contraception, euthanasia, etc., even though some of the non-Catholic citizens might regard such procedures as morally permissible. Catholics believe these to be against the natural law, and hence do not hesitate to make use of legal measures to oppose them, just as in the United States there are laws forbidding polygamy, even though the adherents of some religious sects regard polygamy as conformable to God's law.

As is very evident, the procedure whereby the Catholic Church would receive the special recognition from the government as the true Church of Christ could be put into operation only in a nation that is predominantly Catholic—that is, a nation in which the great proportion of the citizens are Catholic and Catholic traditions have become a part of the national life. In such a country the government would *per se* have an obligation to recognize the divinely granted rights of the Catholic Church, for, as Pope Leo XIII asserted:

> It is a public crime to act as though there were no God. So, too, it is a sin in the State not to have care for religion, as something beyond its scope, or as of no practical benefit; or out of many forms of religion to adopt that one which chimes in with the fancy; for we are bound absolutely to worship God in that way which He has shown to be His will.[106]

However, circumstances may dictate a different procedure as the better course. Thus, as will be seen more fully in the discussion on freedom of religion in the United States, the mere fact that Catholics would attain predominance of numbers in a country does not necessarily mean that they would be obliged to give the Catholic Church a place of privilege. Furthermore, even in a distinctively Catholic country, circumstances may be present that suggest as the better policy complete toleration of non-Catholic churches, to the extent of allowing them equal rights with Catholics in the matter of public worship, propaganda, etc. Reasons that would justify this policy of toleration would be, for example, the well-founded fear that any discriminations might bring about bitterness and dissension among the citizens, or that some non-Catholics, as a result of the restrictive measures, might enter the Catholic Church, not through conviction but rather for motives of expediency. This last would be a grave evil, because it would be a formal sin on the part of those who would thus act against their conscience, even though objectively it would be a good deed. Catholics regard it as a great blessing for a non-Catholic to enter the Catholic Church through conviction that it is the true religious society, but they deplore the entrance of a non-Catholic through a feigned conversion for the purpose of gaining some temporal advantage.

When the rulers of a Catholic country weigh all the circumstances and come to the conclusion that the evil results of a policy of discrimination against erroneous religious propaganda would surpass the good effects, they may (and even should) abstain from making restrictions against non-Catholics, and allow non-Catholic sects the same liberty of action that is enjoyed by the Catholic Church. Such a policy of complete toleration is followed in Eire, though that part of Ireland is composed to the extent of more than 95% of Catholics. The official statement of the Church on this subject, proclaimed by Pope Leo XIII, was this:

> The Church indeed deems it unlawful to place the various forms of divine worship on the same footing with the true religion, but does not on that account condemn those rulers who, for the sake of securing some great good or of preventing some evil, patiently allow custom or usage to sanction that each form of religion have its place in the state. And, in fact, the Church is wont to take earnest heed that no one shall be forced to embrace the Catholic faith against his will, for, as St. Augustine wisely reminds us, "Man cannot believe otherwise than of his own free will." [107]

A more recent declaration on this important matter was given by Pope Pius XII, in an address to Catholic jurists on December 6, 1953. The Holy Father was considering the matter of religious toleration, particularly in connection with a juridical community of sovereign states. In this important address he asserted:

> Reality shows that error and sin are in the world in great measure. God reprobates them, but He permits them to exist. Hence, the affirmation: religious and moral error must always be impeded, when it is possible, because toleration of them is in itself immoral, is not valid *absolutely and unconditionally*. . . . The duty of repressing moral and religious error cannot, therefore, be an ultimate norm of action. It must be subordinate to higher and more general norms, which in some circumstances permit, and even perhaps seem to indicate as the better policy, toleration of error in order to promote a greater good.[108]

Hence, to say that a civil government, from the very fact that it is legally *empowered* to suppress erroneous religious propaganda, is *obliged* to follow this policy is not a Catholic doctrine. The toleration of such erroneous propaganda may be the lesser of two evils; and if this is evident, the Catholic civil government is bound to tolerate false propaganda in preference to seeking whatever advantages may result from the policy of repression. Consequently, to say that according to Catholic doctrine the Catholics of a nation in which they have acquired the predominance of the legislative power are *obliged* to restrict non-Catholic propaganda is utterly false. On the other hand, it would be false to assert that in all instances it would be wrong for a Catholic state to limit non-Catholic propaganda, for Pope Pius XII definitely refers to the granting of freedom to non-Catholic denominations by Catholic governments as a *toleration*. By proposing the question whether positive repression of false propaganda is *not always a duty* [109] he clearly indicates that *sometimes* it may be a duty. For, the Sovereign Pontiff definitely states "that which does not correspond to truth or to the norm of morality objectively has no right to exist, to be spread or to be activated." [110] As far as God's law is concerned, a false religion has no right to exist or to be propagated.

In recent times there have been frequent and vigorous protests from many persons in the United States against the restrictions placed on the religious activities of Protestants in certain Catholic countries, especially Spain. Some Catholics have united their voices to this protest. However, as far as the *principle* involved in this policy of repression of propaganda is concerned, the teaching of the Church is clear. Since the Catholic Church is the one true Church of Jesus Christ, having the right to recognition as such by civil governments, a civil government which acknowledges the Church as the only divinely authorized religious society has *per se* the right to restrict the activities of those who would undermine the faith of the Catholic citizens.

As far as the *application* of this principle to concrete cases is concerned, higher and more general norms must be considered, as Pope Pius XII states—namely, the duty to choose the lesser of two evils and to procure greater good through toleration. In some countries which are distinctively Catholic, both in tradition and in population, such as Spain, the governments consider that certain restrictions on non-Catholic activities are expedient; and it should be noted that Article VI of the Spanish Charter, dealing with the limitations of public non-Catholic religious functions, is approved in the final protocol of the Concordat between the Spanish government and the Holy See.[111] However, Catholics could discuss the situation in Catholic countries which have accepted this policy, from the standpoint of its practical application at the present day. As the present author wrote in 1944:

> Reasons for the policy of complete toleration on the part of Catholic states have been augmented in recent times, when international relations have become more intimate and governments must regard themselves obligated to some degree toward the people of other lands as well as toward their own citizens. Accordingly, if it is foreseen that the granting of full civil rights to all religions within its own national territory will be beneficial to citizens of other nations, a Catholic country could be justified in adopting this policy. Indeed, a Catholic would not be inconsistent with any principle of his faith if he held that in the circumstances that prevail at the present time, it would be the most feasible plan to have complete religious toleration throughout the entire world. But it must ever be remembered that a Catholic cannot advocate such a plan on the basis that all religions have a genuine, God-given right to exist. Such a right belongs only to the one religion founded by Jesus Christ for all men.[112]

The duty of Catholic rulers in determining whether or not complete toleration should be accepted as the policy for their particular countries, Pope Pius XII thus explains:

> Before all else the Catholic statesman must judge if this condition is verified in the concrete—this is the "question of fact." In his decision

> he will permit himself to be guided by weighing the dangerous consequences that stem from toleration against those from which the community of nations will be spared if the formula of toleration be accepted. Moreover, he will be guided by the good which, according to a wise prognosis, can be derived from toleration for the international community as such, and indirectly for the member state. In that which concerns religion and morality he will also ask the judgment of the Church. For her only he to whom Christ has entrusted the guidance of His whole Church is competent to speak in the last instance on such vital questions touching international life; that is, the Roman Pontiff.[113]

It is supremely inconsistent for non-Catholics to condemn the policy of discrimination adopted in some Catholic countries toward those who are not members of the Catholic Church and yet to express no complaint regarding governments which discriminate against Catholics. For example, in England the Anglican Church is the established church of the nation, and receives from the government special favors which are not granted to other religious organizations. Moreover, by the law of the nation a Catholic is excluded from the office of King or Queen. The Swiss Federal Constitution forbids the members of the Society of Jesus to exist as a corporate body in that country.[114] By the law of Sweden the King and the most important members of his cabinet must be adherents of the Evangelical Lutheran religion. Moreover, in Sweden Catholics may not establish monasteries or convents, for "the fear of cloisters as centers of Roman Catholic propaganda lies deep in the Swedish soul." [115]

Catholics willingly admit that the Protestants of those lands in which a particular denomination exerts the balance of power are acting consistently with their conscience if they believe that their religion is the only true one and in consequence restrict the propaganda activities of persons of other beliefs. But why do those who denounce the governmental policy of Catholic lands, restricting the efforts of non-Catholics toward propaganda, limit their attacks to these countries, and refrain from mentioning parallel restrictions placed by some Protestant governments against Catholics?

6. Religious Freedom in the United States

The first amendment of the Constitution of the United States (embraced in the "Bill of Rights") stipulates that "Congress shall make no law respecting an establishment of religion or prohibiting the free exercise thereof." This ruling meant that there was to be no specially favored religious group under the federal government, no "established" church of the United States. To interpret this amendment as forbidding any governmental favor to religion as such, as a "wall of separation" between government and the acknowledgment and worship of the Almighty, is certainly putting into the words of this enactment a meaning far different from that intended by those who passed it. They intended to protect the equality of all religious groups before the law; they surely did not intend to legislate against the support of religious ideals and practices in the United States, provided no particular church was specially favored.[116] It should be noted that this enactment of the Bill of Rights had reference only to the federal government, not to the government of the individual States. Consequently, some of the States maintained established churches for a considerable period after the formation of our national government. It was only in 1868, with the passing of the fourteenth amendment, which guarantees to all citizens the same privileges and immunities as citizens of the State that they enjoy as citizens of the United States, that full and equal freedom of religious worship was assured to all the people of America.

The Catholic citizens of the United States have always approved the policy of religious freedom as established by the first amendment to the Constitution for our country. For, in a country like the United States, where the religious affiliations of the citizens are so many and so varied, a system of perfect equality for all religious groups is the only practical policy if peace and harmony among the citizens are to be attained. Indeed, as was stated above, and corroborated by the words of Pope Pius XII, circumstances can be present even in a definitely Catholic country that will suggest or even impose a policy of complete toleration of all religious groups. Since the establishment of our nation American Catholics, including many prominent members of the hierarchy, have praised the policy of equality and freedom in regard to different religions as exemplified by our government as the most desirable for the United States.

Frequently the charge is made that if Catholics ever gained the balance of the voting power in the United States they would be obliged by their principles to give special favor to the Catholic Church and to impose restrictions on the religious activities of their non-Catholic fellow citizens. This charge, as is evident from what has been stated above, is utterly erroneous. Catholics have no *obliga-*

tion to seek special privileges for their Church in a land where the bad results of such a procedure would surpass the good effects; and certainly if there is any land where that would be the case, it is the United States, even if a very great proportion of our people eventually became Catholics. Such a radical change of a policy that has worked out successfully since the birth of our nation would inevitably cause grave harm to the unity of our people. In fact, even from the standpoint of the Church's own advantage it would seem to be a poor procedure, in view of our distinctively American characteristic of reluctance to be coerced into following any course of action. For, in the supposition that non-Catholics were limited in their efforts for the spread of their religion, they would surely be less favorably inclined to study the claims of the Church than if they were given the same opportunities for public worship and for the spreading of their teachings that are at present enjoyed by all the citizens of our country.

In view of all these considerations, Catholics in the United States can assert without any hesitation or mental restriction that, as far as they are concerned, the policy of complete religious freedom and of full governmental impartiality toward all religious groups will continue, whatever the future may bring in the way of an increase of the Catholic population in our land. No one, indeed, can give any absolute assurance as to what course of action will be followed by those who will be living a century or a thousand years hence. But American Catholics can truthfully make these two statements to their fellow citizens of other religious beliefs: First, there is no principle of the Catholic faith which obliges the Catholics of a nation to restrict non-Catholics in their religious practices whenever Catholics obtain sufficient political power to put such a policy into effect. In the words of Pope Pius XII: "The duty of repressing moral and religious error cannot be an ultimate norm of action. It must be subordinate to higher and more general norms, which in some circumstances permit, and even perhaps seem to indicate as the better policy, toleration of error in order to promote a greater good." [117] Second, as far as can be foreseen now, there would always be cogent reasons in the United States for the maintenance of the present system of complete equality for all religious bodies even in the (most improbable) supposition that Catholics ever attained sufficient voting power to change this policy and procure special privileges for the Catholic Church. Thus speaking of the definition of religious freedom given in our Constitution, Cardinal Stritch of Chicago has made the statement: "We accept it as the only practical definition in the circumstances in which we find ourselves and *foresee in our future*." [118]

Unfortunately, whenever the possibility that at some future time a particular church may seek a place of special privilege in the United States is discussed, the only church that is considered is the Catholic Church. Many Catholics have become accustomed to this one-sided view of the problem, and in consequence always approach it in a purely defensive attitude. They seem to believe that if they can prove satisfactorily that Catholics have no desire to change our Constitution in the matter of religious liberty, the discussion has been adequately terminated. Seldom do they retort to those who seek the assurance that the Catholic Church will not try to restrict the liberty of non-Catholics, if the way is ever opened to such a procedure: "What assurance can any particular non-Catholic sect give us that if they ever became sufficiently powerful to legislate themselves into a position of special favor, they would not use their ballots to make their church the established church of the United States, and to restrict the activities of Catholics?" Certainly, there is at least as much reason to believe that this would happen, at least in the case of certain Protestant groups, as there is to fear that Catholics would adopt this course of action in a parallel situation.

Indeed the history of the United States gives more reason to fear a Protestant *coup* of this kind than one conducted by Catholics. For, as was stated above,[119] even after the federal government of the United States came into existence some of the States continued to maintain established churches and to restrict the civil rights of Catholics. For example, until 1815 all the citizens of Massachusetts were obliged to pay taxes for the support of the Congregational Church, the established church of the State. There were legal discriminations against Catholics in North Carolina until 1835, and in New Jersey until 1844. New Hampshire excluded Catholics from certain high office until 1876, despite the fact that the Fourteenth Amendment, passed in 1868, extended to the citizens of every State all the rights of the federal Constitution.[120]

When we consider such examples of discrimination by Protestant groups against Catholic citizens of the United States, we have reason to wonder if similar restrictions would not arise in the event that some particular Protestant denominations would gain the ascendancy in our country. At any rate, it surely seems inconsistent for Protestants in the United States to charge Catholics with designs to limit the civil rights of their non-Catholic fellow citizens, when instances of such legal discrimination in the past have come from Protestants, not from Catholics.

7. Freedom of Religious Thought Within the Catholic Church

Many non-Catholics have the idea that the unity of faith claimed by Catholics signifies that all Catholics are in full agreement on all religious and theological questions. This is an erroneous notion of the unity of faith, as Catholics attribute it to their Church. There are many questions on religious subjects on which Catholics—and especially Catholic theologians—disagree. What is meant when we speak of unity of faith in the Catholic Church is that all Catholics acknowledge in their Church a principle of unity, the magisterial authority of those who have received from Christ the mission to teach all men the doctrines of religion, comprehending both speculative tenets and the rules of good conduct. All Catholics accept the teachings of those authorized by God to propose religious truth.

The fullness of teaching authority resides in the Pope. He is the successor of St. Peter whom Jesus Christ appointed chief of the apostles and His own visible representative in the government and guidance of the Church when He Himself was about to ascend into heaven. For Our Lord said to this apostle: "Thou art Peter, and upon this rock I will build my Church, and the gates of hell shall not prevail against it," [121] and also gave to Peter the sacred commission: "Feed my lambs. . . . Feed my sheep." [122] Unquestionably Christ willed that the authority He gave to Peter should be transmitted to Peter's successors; and from the earliest centuries it was recognized that those who succeed Peter in the Roman See are also his successors in the primacy of the Church.[123]

Since Christ willed that His Church should continue to teach His doctrines until the end of time, in the fullness of truth, He naturally provided a means of preserving these teachings unmixed with error down through the centuries. According to Catholic belief this divinely constituted means is the infallibility of the Pope. The Council of the Vatican, in 1870, solemnly declared that the Pope, when he uses the fullness of his teaching power to propose definitely a doctrine of faith or morals that must be held by the entire Church is protected from error by the divine assistance promised to him in St. Peter. In such a case the Pope is said to speak *ex cathedra.*[124]

The bishops of the Catholic Church are the successors of the other apostles, just as the Pope is the successor of St. Peter. The bishops also possess the prerogative of infallibility—not individually, but as a group united with the Pope. The divine assistance, protecting them from error, is bestowed on the bishops when they definitively proclaim a doctrine of faith or morals, either assembled in general council or fulfilling their teaching office in their respective dioceses throughout the world. This latter is known as the *ordinary and universal magisterium.*[125]

The infallible pronouncements of the Pope or of the bishops (in union with the Pope) may propose doctrines contained in divine revelation (Scripture and divine tradition) or doctrines not contained in divine revelation but intimately connected with it. An infallible pronouncement proposing a doctrine as revealed is accepted by Catholics with divine-catholic faith. Such, for example, is the doctrine solemnly proclaimed by Pope Pius XII—that the Blessed Virgin Mary has been assumed, in body as well as in soul, into heaven.[126] A doctrine which is connected with divine revelation, but not contained in it, when proposed infallibly is accepted by Catholics with ecclesiastical faith, according to the more common view of theologians, although some believe that this, too, is to be believed with divine-catholic faith.[127]

At any rate, Catholics are bound in conscience, under penalty of grave sin, to hold all doctrines proposed in the manner required for an infallible statement, by the Pope alone or by the Pope with the bishops, for in these circumstances God protects the teaching authority of the Church from making any erroneous statement. A baptized person who doubts or denies any doctrine of divine-catholic faith thereby becomes a *heretic;* one who rejects the Christian faith entirely is an *apostate.*[128] By falling into heresy or apostasy, at least when this is expressed externally, a person cuts himself off from membership in the Church, the Mystical Body of Christ.[129]

Some doctrines are proclaimed by the Church authoritatively, though not infallibly. Such, for example, are official statements on matters of faith or morals issued by the Congregation of the Holy Office or by the Biblical Commission. These bodies are entitled to teach with authority but do not possess the prerogative of infallibility. Similarly, some of the statements of the Pope in Encyclical letters, addresses to various groups, etc., are authoritative without being infallible, inasmuch as the Pope, in pronouncing them, did not intend to speak with the fullness of his teaching authority, or *ex cathedra*. It must not be supposed, however, that Catholics are free to reject such pronouncements. On the contrary, they must be accepted with religious assent, a form of acquiescence based on the virtues of religion and obedience. Theoretically, it is possible for an error to be found in statements of this category; hence, a Catholic who is deeply versed in the subject treated in a pronouncement of this kind might be convinced that a mistake has been made in an authoritative non-infallible decision. In such case he may withhold his assent, and in the meantime communicate his arguments to the Holy See. But such an occurrence must be regarded as a very rare exception, since the greatest care is exercised by the Pope (or the Congregation in question) to make such statements most accurately. Moreover, the assistance of the Holy Ghost is not lacking even in such non-infallible pronouncements of the Church.[130] In his Encyclical *Humani generis* Pope Pius XII reproved those who refuse to accept the doctrine enunciated in Encyclical letters on the ground that it is not taught infallibly.[131]

Evidently, freedom of belief is not permitted to Catholics in the same way that it is usually claimed by Protestants, who accept the principle that private interpretation of God's message is permissible, and consequently differ widely in their religious beliefs even within the same denomination. But Catholics, convinced that the assistance of an all-wise and all-truthful God is bestowed on the teaching authority of their Church, do not regard it as an infringement of their freedom to be bound to accept doctrines the truth of which is guaranteed by God Himself.

Although Catholics are not free to reject the doctrines proposed to them authoritatively by the Church (even though not infallibly), there is a wide range of religious problems on which they are perfectly free to hold divergent opinions. Anyone who studies Catholic theology will learn that there are many different ways of explaining the manner in which divine grace influences the soul without impairing man's free will, any of which a Catholic may accept and defend.[132] Similarly, there are countless theological explanations as to the manner in which the Mass fulfills the required conditions for a true sacrifice.[133] In the field of moral theology there are innumerable points of difference among theologians concerning the application to concrete cases of the general principles of morality accepted by all Catholics.[134]

Similarly, on many questions of the natural sciences related to theological doctrines [135] Catholics enjoy full liberty of discussion. For example, in the Encyclical *Humani generis* Pope Pius XII declared that, although it would be rash in the present state of scientific investigation to declare as a proved fact that the human body has developed from some lower form of life, yet scientific research and discussion on this topic are freely permitted.[136] The implication is that if it will ever be proved that evolution of the human body did take place, Catholics will be at liberty to accept it unhesitatingly as a scientific fact, in no wise incompatible with the teaching of the Church. Then it will be evident that the scriptural statement that God formed the body of the first man out of the dust of earth [137] is to be understood metaphorically, as signifying that through the divinely established laws of nature a lower form of animal life developed until the Creator judged it a suitable body for a rational soul, and accordingly substituted a spiritual soul in place of the animal's irrational principle of life, and thus made the first man to God's image and likeness.

Conclusion

Catholics are fully aware that their concept of freedom in the matter of religion, and religious worship, and the relation between the state and the church differ radically from that which is current among most non-Catholics at the present day, at least in the United States. The point of difference centers mainly in the fundamental notion of freedom itself with relation to God. Has a human being the right to choose a religious belief or exercise a form of worship according to his own choice, if God has commanded all men to accept a definite religious creed and practice a form of worship determined by Himself and by the authorities of a Church which He has established for the entire human race? Catholics answer this question in the negative; and it is impossible to see how anyone who believes in a personal God and admits His sovereign jurisdiction over all men can give a different answer. To ascribe freedom of belief and worship to a creature in defiance of the command of the Creator is a distortion of the notion of freedom. For the most perfect freedom a creature can enjoy is the right to choose and to follow that course of conduct which is laid down for him by the Creator. This is the freedom which St. Paul calls the "freedom of the glory of the sons of God." [138]

Notes

The Initial Freedom

1. From a statement of the Administration Board of the National Catholic Welfare Conference. April 14, 1945.
2. St. Thomas Aquinas, *Summa Theologica,* L, 76, 2 ad 1.
3. *Ibid.,* I, 76, 1 ad 5.
4. Owen Bennett, *Notes on Metaphysics,* Chaska, Minn., 1952.
5. *Cf. Summa Theol.,* I-II, 8, 1, c.
6. St. Augustine, Book I, Chap. I, p. 3 (tr. by Frank Sheed), Sheed & Ward, New York, 1952.
7. Gerard Manley Hopkins, *Poems,* New York, 1948, p. 70.
8. *Cf. Summa Theol.,* I-II, 13, 6, c.
9. St. Thomas Aquinas, *De Anima,* III, 1, 16.
10. *Cf. Summa Theol.,* I-II, 13, 6, c.
11. *Ibid.,* I, 14, 8, c.
12. *Loc. cit.*
13. *Ibid.,* I, 19, 4, c.
14. *Ibid.,* I, 19, 8, *Sed contra.*

Freedom of Autonomy—The Terminal Freedom

1. *QQ. Disputatae De Veritate,* Turin, 1927.
2. *Ibid.,* q. 22, aa. 5-6; q. 24.
3. *Ibid.,* q. 22, a. 4.
4. *Ibid.,* a. 5.
5. *Cf.* Odon Lottin, *La Théorie du Libre Arbitre Depuis S. Anselme Jusqu'à S. Thomas d'Aquin,* n.p., 1929, p. 142; *De Veritate,* q. 22, a. 6.
6. *De Veritate,* q. 24, a. 2.
7. *Cf.* Lottin, *op. cit.,* p. 145; *De Veritate,* q. 24, a. 1.
8. *Cf. De Veritate,* q. 24, a. 2.
9. *QQ. Disputatae De Potentia Dei* (Eng. Tr. *On the Power of God* by English Dominican Fathers), London, 1934, q. 10, a. 2 ad 5, III, p. 186.
10. *Cf. De Veritate,* q. 24, a. 1 ad 20.
11. *Ibid.,* q. 22, a. 5 ad 3; also q. 23, a. 4; *De Potentia Dei,* q. 10, a. 2 ad 5; *Contra Gentiles,* III, c. 139; *Summa Theologia* I, q. 82, a.1.
12. Yves Simon, *Traité du Libre Arbitre,* Liege, 1951, p. 128.
13. *QQ. Disputate De Malo,* q. 6, a. unic., Turin, 1927.
14. *Cf. supra,* pp. 60-61 and note 9.
15. *Cf. De Malo,* 1. c.; also *Summa Theol.,* I-II, qq. 9-10.
16. *Cf. Summa Theol.,* I-II, q. 61, a. 1.

17. *Ibid.,* q. 55, a. 4; St. Augustine, *De Libero Arbitrio,* II, 19.
18. Jacques Leclerq, *Les Grandes Lignes de la Philosophie Morale,* Louvain, 1947, p. 381.
19. *Cf.* Karl Menninger, "What the Girls Told," *Saturday Review,* XXXVI (Sept. 26, 1953), 21 sqq. (Review of Kinsey Report).
20. Simon, *op. cit.,* p. 132.
21. *Cf.* Leclerq, *op. cit.,* p. 383.
22. *Summa Theol.,* I-II, q. 65, a. 1.
23. *Cf.* Henri Renard, *The Philosophy of Morality,* Milwaukee, 1953, p. 180.

Freedom of Thought

1. Plato ascribes this teaching that man is the measure of all things to Protagoras. *Cf.* Plato, *Theaet.* 152A.
2. *Cf.* Edward Hugon, *Metaphysica,* Paris: 1907, I, 160 ff.; 179.
3. *Cf.* Benedict Henry Merklebach, *Summa Theologiae Moralis,* Paris: 1938, I, 87; D. O'Connell, "Christian Liberty," *The Thomist,* XV, April 1952, 221.
4. Spatial limitations have required the adoption of several expedients in addition to the assumptions made. Thus, definition and exposition are emphasized rather than argumentation.
5. *Cf.* St. Thomas, *In Meta.,* Bk. V, 1. 22, n. 1129; Bk. VI, 1. r, nn. 1223 ff.; Bk. IX, 1. 11, n. 1895; *In Periher.,* Bk. I, 1. 3, nn. 6, ff. In scholastic philosophy logical truth is a quality of man's judgments, the second act of the intellect, as opposed to simple apprehension, the first act of intellect attaining ultimately to the nature of things. *Cf.* St. Thomas, *In Meta.,* Bk. VI, 1. 4, nn. 1233, 1238; Bk. IX, 1. 11, nn. 896 ff.; *De Anima,* Bk. III, 1. 11, nn. 746 ff.; *De Veritate,* q. 1, aa. 3, 9.; *Contra Gentes,* Bk. I, c. 59. *Summa Theol.,* I, q. 16, a. 2.
6. *Cf.* St. Thomas, *Summa Theol.,* I-II, q. 76, a. 2; II-II, q. 2, a. 1; I, q. 101, a. 1 ad 2um; *De Veritate,* q. 14, a. 1.
7. By criterion is meant a means, rule, standard, or measure through which man can distinguish one thing from another. Accordingly, criterion of truth is a standard by which true judgments may be distinguished from false. Should there be a series of subordinated criteria, there must be one which is final and to which the last appeal must be made. This is the ultimate court of appeal, the final criterion. *Cf.* Joseph Gredt, *Elementa Philosophiae,* St. Louis, 1931, II, p. 96 ff.
8. *Cf.* Celestine Nicholas Bittle, *Reality and the Mind,* Milwaukee, 1936, pp. 292, 293.
9. *Ibid.,* p. 298.
10. *John,* 8:34.
11. St. Thomas, *Posterior Analytics,* Bk. I, 1. 1, *Proemium,* n. 5.
12. *Loc. cit.*
13. *Cf.* St. Thomas, *In Ethic. ad Nicomach,* Bk. I, 1. 3, n. 36.
14. *Cf.* St. Thomas, *Post. Analyt.,* Bk. I, 1. 1, n. 6; *Summa Theol.,* I-II, q. 57, a. 6, ad 3um.
15. *Cf.* St. Thomas, *Post. Analyt.,* Bk. I, 1. 5, nn. 2 ff.; *Summa Theol.,* I, q. 2, a. 1.
16. For a discussion of the various causes of the knowledge of first principles and all immediate truths, see St. Thomas, *Post. Analyt.,* Bk. I, L. 30, n. 5. Consult also the notation of the Leonine editors on this text, Notad., p. 259.

See also St. Thomas, *In Meta.,* Bk. IV, 1. 6. See also Francis Xavier Maquart, *Elementa Philosophiae,* Paris, 1938, I, 189 ff.

17. *Cf. Post. Analyt.,* n. 6, 7.
18. *Cf.* Aristotle, *Metaphysics,* Bk. IV, c. 3, 1005b 32 ff.; St. Thomas, *In Meta.,* Bk. IV, 1. 6, nn. 59 ff.
19. *Loc. cit.*
20. Owing to the complexity of the matter and to the dispute in regards to the validity of scientific laws discovered by induction, we have not treated of induction in this paper. For an argument in favor of their validity consult Maquart, *op. cit.,* I, 191 ff. For a summarized statement of John of St. Thomas' partially negative position see Jacques Maritain, *An Introduction to Logic,* New York 1937, pp. 271 ff. See also J. M. Marling, "The Dialectical Character of Scientific Knowledge," in *Philosophical Studies in honor of the Very Rev. Ignatius Smith, O.P.* (Ed. by John Ryan), Westminster, Maryland, pp. 3-12.
21. We have not treated of sense knowledge nor intellectual knowledge of particular contingent events. Both these knowledges are certain in proportion to their proper necessity: the natural necessity of the sense to report its object when sensed and as sensed; the hypothetical necessity of contingent facts of experience to be what they are and not otherwise when they are being experienced.
22. *Cf.* St. Thomas, *Summa Theol.,* III, q. 27, a. 4, ad 2um.; III, q. 30, a. 4 ad 2um.
23. *Cf. Ibid.,* I-II, q. 32, a. 8; I, q. 12, a. 1; I, q. 105, a. 7; *II Sent.,* d. 18, q. 1, a. 3; *Contra Gentes,* III, c. 101. For a more complete account of doubt, both natural and methodical, see my "Portals of Doubt," *The Thomist,* VIII (1945), 293 ff.
24. *Cf. De Veritate,* q. XIV, a. 1; *Summa Theol.,* II-II, q. 2, a. 1.
25. *Cf. Ibid.*
26. *Cf. In Meta.,* Bk. I, 1. 2.
27. *Cf. Ibid.,* Bk. III, 1. i.
28. Aristotle, *Topics,* Bk. I, c. 2, 101a 35-36.
29. *Cf. Ibid.* The immediate purpose of topical reasoning is to enable one to argue from probable premises in such a way that he may avoid contradicting himself in arguments. A second use is to enable the arguer to meet his opponents on the ground of their own opinions and convictions.
30. *Cf.* Aristotle, *Prior Analytics,* Bk. I, c. 1, 24 a 20-25; St. Thomas, *Post. Analy.,* Bk. I, 1. 4, and 1. 19.
31. *Cf.* Aristotle, *Topics,* Bk. I, c. 1, 4 b 30; c. 10, 104 a 9-15; St. Thomas, *Proemium to Post. Analy.*
32. *Cf.* St. Thomas, *In Meta.,* Bk. IV, 1. 1; John of St. Thomas, *Cursus Philosophicus,* Vol. I, Logica, II, P.Q.I. *De Logica,* a. 5. It is not always necessary to use logical intentions in dialectical reasoning. The common principles, as opposed to proper principles, of real being are also dialectical "not because they proceed from logical terms, but because they proceed in the manner of logic, namely from commons and probables." St. Thomas, *On Phys.,* Bk. III, 1. 7.
33. *Cf.* St. Thomas, *De Trinitate,* q. 6, a. 1.
34. The elements of John Dewey's thought used in this paper were taken from his *Logic; The Theory of Inquiry; Human Nature and Conduct; Democracy and Education; Education and Experience.*
35. Vincent Smith, *Idea Men of Today,* Milwaukee, 1951, p. 209.

The Acts of Freedom

1. *Cf.* Joseph Gredt, *Elementa Philosophiae Aristotelico-Thomisticae,* Friburg, 1937, II, 473.
2. It is called "subjective indifference" because it is present in man, or more exactly, in the faculty by which man chooses, the will. It is distinguished from "objective indifference" which was listed as the second requisite condition, which is present in an object which is not wholly desirable.
3. *Cf.* John of St. Thomas, *Cursus Philosophicus Thomisticus,* Taurini, Italy, 1937, III, 387.
4. Hubert Gruender, *Experimental Psychology,* Milwaukee, 1932, p. 476.
5. *Ethics,* Bk. 3, ch. 7 (1113 b 7 ff.).
6. "It is not only things pertaining to the will that the will desires, but also that which pertains to each power, and to the entire man. Therefore man wills naturally not only the object of the will, but also other things that are appropriate to the other powers, such as knowledge of truth, which befits the intellect, and to be and to live and other like things which regard his natural well-being—all of which are included in the object of the will as so many particular goods." St. Thomas Aquinas, *Summa Theologica,* I-II, 10, 1.
7. "Man of necessity seeks happiness, which, according to Boethius, consists in the perfect state of the assembly of all good things. I say, however, of necessity, as regards the determination of the act because man can not will the opposite; not, however, in regard to the exercise of the act because every one can then not will to think of happiness, because the very acts of the intellect and will are particular ones." St. Thomas, *De Malo,* q. 6, art. 1. *q.v.* Reginald Garrigou-Lagrange, *God: His Existence and His Nature* (tr. by Dom Bede Rose), St. Louis, 1934, II, 293-4.
8. The soul is of a substantial nature while potencies are in the genus of predicamental accident. A predicamental accident is a class of reality which requires a subject in which to inhere, as distinguished from a substance which can exist by itself. The soul is a substance for it is one of the essential, constituent elements of a composite, which is a substance. Although the human soul is a substance complete in itself, for it can exercise some operations in a non-organic way, it is not a complete substance in the order of species, for the soul is only one of the essential elements of man. The faculties which are in the category of quality, inhere in the soul as subject. Here it must be stressed that the term "accident" as applied to the faculties, is not to be confused with another type of "accident," the Predicable accident, which is a classification of the relationship that exists between a universal idea and its inferiors, where the former predicates something that merely happens to be possessed by the subject, such as, John is rich. Not everything that is in the category of accident, as distinguished from substance, is of such a nature that it merely happens to belong to something. So, for example, the human faculties of intellect and will are not substantial because they must inhere in man, but they are not something that man just happens to have. They are an essential part of human nature.
9. Objective concept, as distinguished from a subjective concept, refers to the object or reality which is represented by the idea. The latter refers to the mental representation, the idea itself. In judging, we pronounce upon the

agreement or disagreement of the *things* for which these concepts stand. When I judge "the leaf is green," I do not primarily affirm that my *idea* of leaf agrees with my *idea* of green, but that the subject *leaf* has the quality *green.*

10. If we consider the subjective concepts, the mind formulates its affirmative or negative enunciations by comparing and *combining* concepts, and so from this point of view, there is always uniting or composition. *q.v.* Jacques Maritain, *An Introduction to Logic,* New York, 1937, pp. 82-93.
11. *Q.v.* Brother Benignus, *Nature, Knowledge and God,* Milwaukee, 1947, pp. 200-203.
12. Metaphysical concepts are distinguished from two other types: mathematical and physical concepts. Mathematical include objects which cannot exist but which can be thought of as existing, without matter—our ideas of number and extension. Physical concepts include objects which can neither exist, nor can they be thought of as existing, without matter. "Man," for example, can neither exist, nor can he be thought of as existing, without matter, for the idea of "animality" and hence materiality, is one of its essential notes.
13. *Q.v.* Garrigou-Lagrange, *op. cit.,* p. 292.
14. *Q.v. Summa Theol.,* I, q. 82, art. 4.
15. *Q.v.* Aristotle, *Ethics,* VI, 2 (1139 a 26). Also *Summa Theol.,* I-II, q. 57, art. 5 ad 3.
16. *Q.v.* Garrigou-Lagrange, *op. cit.,* p. 300.
17. Richard P. Phillips, *Modern Thomistic Philosophy,* London, 1934, II, p. 291.
18. *De Meta,* IV, 2 (1013 b 9).
19. Phillips, *op. cit.,* p. 289.
20. *Summa Theol.,* q. 9, art. 4.
21. *Ibid.,* art. 6.
22. *Ibid.,* q. 14.
23. *Ibid.,* q. 15, art. 1.
24. *Ethics,* VI, 2 (1139 b 4). *Q.v. Summa Theol.,* I-II, q. 14, art. I ad 1.

The Proper Concept of Freedom in Individual Acts

1. "For when the gentiles, who by nature have not law, fulfill the requirements of the law, these though they have not the law, are a law unto themselves, showing as they do demands of the law to be written in their hearts" (*Romans,* 2:14-15).
2. John MacGuinness, "De Gratia," *Commentarii Theologici,* 3rd Ed., Dublin, 1910, p. 473.
3. Jacques Maritain, *Freedom in the Modern World* (Tr. by Richard O'Sullivan), New York, 1936, p. 39.
4. St. Thomas Aquinas, "Treatise on Law," *Summa Theologica,* Ia-IIae, qq. 90-97, q. 90, art. 1.
5. *Ibid.,* q. 90, art. 3.
6. *Ibid.,* q. 93, art. 1.
7. *Ibid.,* q. 90, art. 1.
8. *Hebrews,* 13:14.
9. The common opinion of Thomistic Philosophers teaches that the *proximate rule* of morality and the immediate determinant of moral freedom *is right reason;* while the supreme rule is the *eternal law. Cf.* Henri Grenier,

Thomistic Philosophy (Tr. by J. P. O'Hanley), Charlottetown, P. E. I., Canada, 1948, III, p. 89. Right reason may be defined as human reason based on a complete understanding of human nature in its essential relationships and constituents toward God, ourselves, and our neighbor.

10. John F. O'Hara, "Archbishop Emphasizes Obedience to Natural Law at Bar Association Mass." Philadelphia *Catholic Standard and Times,* March 14, 1952, pp. 1, 7.
11. *Loc. cit.*
12. "Man, therefore, can offend against the Natural Law only under penalty of not obtaining his natural end. The obviousness of this fact is probably the cause of its frequent denial by people—people who would never fail to follow the maker's direction in the use of inanimate things. An automobile, for instance, must be used according to its maker's directions if it is to attain the end for which it was manufactured. It cannot be used as a pile driver or a row boat without disastrous results. So, too, man must follow the direction of his Maker if he would attain his proper end. If he embraces something his reason tells him is evil he violates the end of his nature." (*Loc. cit.*)
13. *Loc. cit.*
14. *Ibid.,* p. 7.
15. John McCann, "The Purpose of Liberty," American Catholic Philosophical Association, *Proceedings,* XVI (1940), 133-134.
16. *Ibid.,* p. 134.
17. Grenier, *op. cit.* III, p. 476.
18. *Loc. cit.*
19. *Cf.* Frederick G. Hochwalt, "Human Rights," *China Missionary Bulletin,* III (1951), 571-2.
20. Francis J. Connell, "The Catholic Church and Freedom of Speech," *Catholic University Bulletin,* XVII (1949), 4.
21. *Loc. cit.*
22. *Ibid.,* p. 4.
23. Schenck vs. United States, 249 *U.S.* 47; 39 *S. Ct.* 247; 63 *L Ed.* 470.
24. "A lie is intrinsically evil because it involves using a natural faculty in a way that is directly contrary to its natural end or purpose. The primary purpose of the faculty of speech is to manifest to others one's thoughts and judgments. Since we are by nature obviously destined to live, not each in utter seclusion, but with other human beings, God evidently intended us to exchange ideas with them, and the means given us for this is the faculty of speech. The right use of this faculty is to reveal to others the thoughts of one's mind. To employ this faculty in order to manifest as the thought of one's mind what is not the thought of one's mind is contrary to the primary end of speech." (Edwin Francis Healy, *Moral Guidance,* Chicago, 1942, p. 245.)
25. *Summa Theol.,* IIa-IIae, q. 73, art. 2.
26. "Honor and a good name are far superior in value to material possessions. And just as one has the right in strict justice to possessions received by inheritance or acquired through personal initiative and industry so one has the right in strict justice to the honor and good name obtained naturally or as a result of personal activity. Each person has a *connatural* right to the esteem which is accorded people because of their natural dignity as human beings and because of the gifts and qualities nature has bestowed

on them. Thus every person has the right to be esteemed as good until proved to be bad. And each person has the connatural right to acquire *special* honor through extraordinary personal achievement, so long as his endeavor does not violate the rights of others or harm the common good of all. Similarly, each person has the *acquired right* to retain the honor and good reputation he has been able to build up for himself among his fellow men as a consequence of his personal achievements." (Celestine Nicholas Bittle, *Man and Morals*, Milwaukee, 1950, p. 392.)

27. Connell, *op. cit.*, pp. 4-5.
28. *Ibid.*, p. 5.
29. *Cf.* "Purpose of art, movies defined—Martin Quigley asserts moral perfection is their end," *Tablet,* Mar. 13, 1953, p. 20, cols. 1-3.
30. *Cf.* "Television backs a code of ethics," New York *Times,* Oct. 20, 1951, p. 21, col. 1.
31. "Taking into account every conceivable possibility, comic books present the details of how to commit crimes, how to conceal evidence, how to evade detection, how to hurt people." *Ladies' Home Journal,* LXX (1953), 215.
32. "The peak of immorality of comic books . . . is the glorified justification of the individual's right to mete out justice. The sock on the jaw—in the comic books—takes the place of the decision of the Supreme Court." Dr. Ralph S. Banay, "2d Psychiatrist Joins Attack on Comic Books," New York *Herald Tribune,* Jan. 4, 1948, Sec. 2, p. 11, col. 2.
33. Connell, *op. cit.*, p. 5.
34. Kenneth E. Appel, "How Parents Change Children into Mental Misfits," *Your Life* (Dec. 1944), p. 88.
35. *Cf.* Fredric Wertham, "What Parents Don't Know About Comic Books," *Ladies' Home Journal,* LXX (1953), 214.
36. *Ibid.*, p. 217.

Freedom and Government

1. Learned Hand, "Freedom and the Humanities," *Bulletin* American Association of University Professors, XXXVIII (1952-3), 522.
2. The six "most important" of man's God-given prerogatives or rights as listed by Pius XI are: "the right to life, to bodily integrity, to the necessary means of existence; the right to tend toward his ultimate goal . . . ; the right of association and the right to possess and use property." *Divini Redemptoris* (March 19, 1937).
3. See *Ibid.*, wherein is said: "Above all other reality there exists one supreme Being: God, the omnipotent Creator of all things, the all-wise and just Judge of all men. . . . Man has a spiritual and immortal soul. He is a person, marvelously endowed by his Creator with gifts of body and mind. . . . God alone is his last end, in this life and the next . . . he has been endowed by God with many and varied prerogatives."
4. "Society . . . cannot defraud man of his God-granted rights . . . nor can society systematically void these rights by making their use impossible." (*Ibid.*)
5. "God . . . destined man for civil society according to the dictates of his very nature . . . society is a natural means which man can and must use to reach his destined end." (*Ibid.*)
6. *Loc. cit.*

7. A contemporary re-affirmation of the vitality and the validity of the principle of the separation of power may be noted: "The contest between the three departments in national, state and local governments still goes on from day to day with varying results, but with all of the skirmishes, sometimes none too edifying, the goal remains constant—a government of law rather than of official will or whim."

   The same writer believes that the continuation of freedom for Americans, and indeed for the world is conditioned on adherence to this basic principle of American government: "On respect for the doctrine of the separation of powers, not as a technical rule of law but as a guide to the sound functioning of government, rests not only the stability of this nation but of every other nation and the freedom not only of our own citizens but of the citizens of every other country." Arthur T. Vanderbilt, *The Doctrine of the Separation of Powers and Its Present-Day Significance.* Lincoln, Nebraska, 1953, *passim.*
8. Alfredo Rocco, "The Political Doctrines of Fascism," *International Conciliation,* CCXXIII (1926), 403.
9. Pius XI, *op. cit.*
10. *Loc. cit.*
11. Charles Coppens, *A Brief Text-Book of Moral Philosophy.* New York, 1924, p. 185; Leo XIII, *Rerum Novarum.*
12. Coppens, *op. cit.,* p. 187.
13. "When . . . government usurps the rights of individuals, it becomes a form of tyranny, quiet submission to which is not patriotism, but slavery." (*Ibid.*)
14. *The New York Times,* November 8, 1953.
15. Charles A. Beard, *The Republic.* New York, 1943, p. 237.
16. Barron vs. Baltimore, 7 *Peters* 243.
17. Congregationalism was not finally disestablished in New England until 1838.
18. Prudential Insurance Company vs. Cheek, 259 *U.S.* 530.
19. Gitlow vs. New York, 268 *U.S.* 652.
20. Pollock vs. Williams, 322 *U.S.* 17.
21. Hirabayashi vs. U.S., 320 *U.S.* 100; but see Truax vs. Corrigan, 257 *U.S.* 332 for an earlier contrary opinion.
22. Takahashi vs. Fish and Game Commission, 334 *U.S.* 410.
23. Plessy vs. Ferguson, 163 *U.S.* 551.
24. Missouri *ex rel.* Gaines vs. Canada, 305 *U.S.* 337. In 1948, in Sipuel vs. Board of Regents, 332 *U.S.* 631, and Fisher vs. Hurst, 333 *U.S.* 147, the ruling was repeated with regard to Oklahoma, and in 1950 was reaffirmed with regard to Texas, Sweatt vs. Painter, 339 *U.S.* 629.
25. Paul C. Reinert, to the faculty of the University of Colorado. *The Tablet,* March 14, 1953.
26. Near vs. Minnesota, 283 *U.S.* 708.
27. *Ibid.,* p. 716.
28. Schenck vs. U.S., 249 *U.S.* 52.
29. 54 *Stat.* 670, Sect. 2(a).
30. Dennis et al. vs. U.S., 341 *U.S.* 494.
31. *Cf.* Hague vs. C.I.O., 307 *U.S.* 496.
32. *The New York Times,* April 21, 1953.

Freedom and the Law

1. This thought is well expressed by Lawrence Vold, "The Functional Perspective for the Law of Torts," 14 *Nebraska Law Bulletin* 217, 226 (1936): "Where law is not available or is ineffective to control the conduct involved in the activities of competing persons or groups with sharply conflicting interests, the alternative that practically results is physical violence. . . ." See also John A. Ryan and Francis J. Boland, *Catholic Principles of Politics,* New York, 1950, p. 172: ". . . [T]he true liberty of human society does not consist in every man doing what he pleases, for this would simply end in turmoil and confusion, and bring on the overthrow of the State; but rather in this, that through the injunctions of the civil law all may more easily conform to the prescriptions of the eternal law." Professor Sutherland frames the same basic idea in this way: "Sooner or later to all who study the law comes the sobering realization that no freedom can be absolute. Reconciliation of liberty and security is a recurring necessity for every generation." "Freedom and Internal Security," 64 *Harvard Law Review* 383, 414 (1951).
2. It is interesting to note that "[t]he reasonable or 'ordinary' man of the (common) law is by definition a free man." Richard O'Sullivan, "The English Tradition in Law and Politics," *The Catholic Mind Through Fifty Years 1903-1953* (ed. by Benjamin L. Masse), New York, 1952, p. 414.
3. "Today licenses are required for the practice of at least seventy-five occupations in one or more states. Practitioners in fourteen fields are licensed in all states: accountants, architects, attorneys, chiropodists, dentists, embalmers, engineers, nurses, optometrists, osteopaths, pharmacists, physicians, teachers, and veterinarians." Council of State Governments, *Occupational Licensing in the States,* 1952, p. 28.
4. Patrick A. O'Boyle, D.D., "Liberty Under Law" (Address delivered to the Guild of Catholic Lawyers at the Red Mass in St. Andrew's Church, New York City, September 14, 1949), 10 *Jurist* 1, 2 (1950).
5. *The Natural Law* (translated by Thomas R. Hanley), St. Louis, 1949, p. 247.
6. Francis J. Powers, *Papal Pronouncements and the Political Order,* Westminster, 1952, p. 142.
7. Address delivered to the members of the Roman Rota in 1949.
8. Judge Burke has pithily summarized the views of the modern positivists in "A Law Above the King" (Address at the Mid-summer Meeting of the New York State Bar Association, 1949), 21 *New York State Bar Association Bulletin* 278, 282-284 (1949).
9. Powers, *op. cit.,* p. 143. This is essentially what Saint Thomas had in mind when he wrote: "As Augustine says, that which is not just seems to be no law at all. Hence the force of a law depends on the extent of its justice. Now in human affairs a thing is said to be just from being right, according to the rule of reason. But the first rule of reason is the law of nature. . . . Consequently, every human law has just so much of the nature of law as it is derived from the law of nature. But if in any point it departs from the law of nature, it is no longer a law but a perversion of law." Anton C. Pegis, *Basic Writings of Saint Thomas Aquinas* (*Human Law*), 2 vols., New York, 1944, II, 784.
10. O'Boyle, *op. cit.,* p. 3.
11. *Loc. cit.*

12. *Man and the State,* Chicago, 1951, p. 100.
13. Jennings goes so far as to say that, ". . . broad as are the implications and far-reaching as are the inarticulate premises which underlie the doctrine of 'freedom of contract' there has been but little unified growth since its inception." "Freedom of Contract—Inquiries and Speculations," 22 *California Law Review* 636, 651 (1934).
14. "Contracts of Adhesion—Some Thoughts About Freedom of Contract," 43 *Columbia Law Review* 629 (1943).
15. Morris R. Cohen, "The Basis of Contract," 46 *Harvard Law Review* 553, 556 (1933).
16. W. S. Holdsworth, *A History of English Law,* 14 vols., Boston, 1926, VIII, 100 ff.
17. Adam Smith, *Wealth of Nations* (ed. by Edwin Cannan), New York, 1937, bk. IV, ch. IX, p. 651.
18. Adair v. United States, 208 *U.S.* 161, 174, 175 (1908).
19. State v. Fire Creek Coal & Coke Co., 33 W. Va. 188, 190, 10 S.E. 288, 289 (1889).
20. Roscoe Pound, "Liberty of Contract," 18 *Yale Law Journal* 454, 463 (1909).
21. Frorer v. People, 141 Ill. 171, 186, 31 N.E. 395, 399 (1892). The Court further stated: "Those who are entitled to exercise the elective franchise are deemed equals before the law, and it is not admissible to arbitrarily brand, by statute, one class of them, without reference to and wholly irrespective of their actual good or bad behavior, as too unscrupulous, and the other class as too imbecile or timid and weak to exercise that freedom in contracting which is allowed to all others." *Loc. cit.*
22. Ritchie v. People, 155 Ill. 98, 40 N.E. 454 (1895).
23. Godcharles v. Wigeman, 113 Pa. St. 431, 6 Atl. 354 (1886). Said the Court: ". . . [I]t is an insulting attempt to put the laborer under the legislative tutelage, which is not only degrading to his manhood, but subversive of his rights as a citizen of the United States." 113 Pa. St. at 437, 6 Atl. at 356.
24. State v. Goodwill, 33 W. Va. 179, 10 S.E. 285 (1889).
25. Braceville Coal Co. V. People, 147 Ill. 66, 35 N.E. 62 (1893). The court expressed its view in these words: "They would by the act, be practically under guardianship; their contracts voidable, as if they were minors; their right to freely contract for and to receive the benefit of their labor, as others might do, denied them." 147 Ill. at 74, 35 N.E. at 64.
26. State v. Goodwill, *supra* note 24; Frorer V. People, *supra* note 21.
27. *Ex parte* Kuback, 85 Cal. 274, 24 Pac. 737 (1890).
28. Gillespie v. People, 188 Ill. 176, 58 N.E. 1007 (1900).
29. Printing Co. v. Sampson, L. R. 19 Eq. 465 (1874).
30. Samuel Williston, "Freedom of Contract," 6 *Cornell Law Quarterly* 365, 374 (1921). Expressive of the more modern view is Kessler's statement to the effect that ". . . freedom of contract must mean different things for different types of contracts. Its meaning must change with the social importance of the type of contract and with the degree of monopoly enjoyed by the author of the standardized contract." *Op. cit.,* p. 642.
31. See Robert L. Hale, "Bargaining, Duress, and Economic Liberty," 43 *Columbia Law Review* 603, 626 (1943).
32. Illustrations are found in Jennings, *op. cit.,* p. 636.
33. Muller v. Oregon, 208 *U.S.* 412 (1908). The Court wrote: "It is undoubtedly true, as more than once declared by this court, that the general right to contract in relation to one's business is part of the liberty of the individual

protected by the Fourteenth Amendment to the Federal Constitution; yet it is equally well settled that this liberty is not absolute and extending to all contracts, and that a state may, without conflicting with the provisions of the Fourteenth Amendment, restrict in many respects the individual's power of contract." *Ibid.,* p. 421.

34. See Hugh Evander Willis, "Key to Understanding the Law of Contracts," 34 *Kentucky Law Journal* 165, 170 (1946).
35. One possible method of judicial "policing" of contracts is suggested in the final draft of the Uniform Commercial Code approved by the Commissioners on Uniform State Laws and the American Law Institute on September 15, 1951. The Code provides in 2-302: "If the court finds the contract or any clause of the contract to be unconscionable it may refuse to enforce the contract or may strike any unconscionable clauses and enforce the contract as if the stricken clause had never existed." See the discussion of the clause by Frederick A. Whitney, "Some Effects of the Uniform Commercial Code on New York Law—A Symposium (Contracts)," 26 *St. John's Law Review* 3, 24, 25 (1951).
36. Vold, *op. cit.,* p. 217.
37. Holdsworth, *op. cit.,* II, 44.
38. Frederick Pollock and Frederic W. Maitland, *The History of English Law,* 2d ed., 2 vols., London, 1899, II, 574.
39. See the discussion by Harold F. McNiece and John V. Thornton, "Is the Law of Negligence Obsolete?", 26 *St. John's Law Review* 255 (1952), and Harold F. McNiece and John V. Thornton, "Automobile Accident Prevention and Compensation," 27 *New York University Law Review* 585 (1952).
40. Harold F. McNiece, "Psychic Injury and Tort Liability in New York," 24 *St. John's Law Review* 1 (1949).
41. Fleming James, Jr. and John V. Thornton, "The Impact of Insurance on Law of Torts," 15 *Law and Contemporary Problems* 431 (1950).
42. The moral duties which are discussed in this section of the text are, in the main, duties of charity. Thus, morally speaking, "[i]n a neighbor's extreme temporal need we must help him at our own grave but not extreme inconvenience. In his grave need we must help him but not to our own serious harm. In his ordinary need we are not obliged to help everyone, but must help some at some time." Henry Davis, *A Summary of Moral and Pastoral Theology,* New York, 1952, p. 34.
43. Harold F. McNiece and John V. Thornton, "Affirmative Duties in Tort," 58 *Yale Law Journal* 1272 (1949).
44. Gautret v. Egerton, L.R. 2 C. P. 371, 375 (1867).
45. Buch v. Amory Mfg. Co., 69 N.H. 257, 260, 44 Atl. 809, 810 (1898).
46. Hurley v. Eddingfield, 156 Ind. 416, 59 N.E. 1058 (1901).
47. Union Pac. Ry. v. Cappier, 66 Kan. 649, 72 Pac. 281 (1903).
48. Matthews v. Carolina & N.W. Ry., 175 N.C. 35, 94 S.E. 714 (1917).
49. Buch v. Amory Mfg. Co., *supra* note 45.
50. Osterlind v. Hill, 263 Mass. 73, 160 N.E. 301 (1928).
51. Riley v. Gulf, C. & S. F. Ry., 160 S.W. 595 (Tex. Civ. App. 1913).
52. See note 42 *supra.*
53. Pound has well said: "Legal precepts sometimes are, and perhaps sometimes must be, at variance with the requirements of morals. Yet such a condition is not something of which the jurist is to be proud. It is not a virtue in the law to have it so." *Law and Morals,* 2d ed., Chapel Hill, 1926, p. 38.

54. For experiences with affirmative duties under systems of law other than the Anglo-American, see Note, "The Failure to Rescue: A Comparative Study," 52 *Columbia Law Review* 631 (1952).
55. Henry Campbell Black, *Black's Law Dictionary,* 4th ed., St. Paul, 1951, p. 444.
56. *The Common Law,* Boston, 1946, p. 44.
57. Henry Taylor Terry, *Some Leading Principles of Anglo-American Law,* Philadelphia, 1884, p. 538.
58. Jerome Hall, *General Principles of Criminal Law,* Indianapolis, 1947, p. 213.
59. Jerome Hall, *Theft, Law and Society,* 2d ed., Indianapolis, 1952, p. 65 f.
60. Livingston Hall, "The Substantive Law of Crimes—1887-1936," 50 *Harvard Law Review* 616, 617 (1937).
61. *Criminal Justice in America,* New York, 1930, p. 13 f.
62. Livingston Hall, *op. cit.,* p. 623; Arthur M. Allen, "Criminal Conspiracies in Restraint of Trade at Common Law," 23 *Harvard Law Review* 531 (1910).
63. S. C. T. Dodd, "The Present Legal Status of Trusts," 7 *Harvard Law Review* 157, 164-169 (1893).
64. See, *e.g., California Penal Code* § 258 (1951); *North Dakota Revised Code* § 12-2815 (1943); *Oregon Compiled Laws Annotated* § 23-437 (1940). It may be noted, however, that "[o]nly a few states have seen fit to make specific the application of the criminal sanctions against libel . . . to defamation by radio." Donald H. Remmers, "Recent Legislative Trends in Defamation by Radio," 64 *Harvard Law Review* 727, 740 (1951).

    In the California statute, criminal slander is defined as ". . . a malicious defamation orally uttered, whether or not it be communicated through or by radio or any mechanical or other means or device whatsoever, tending to blacken the memory of one who is dead, or to impeach the honesty, integrity, virtue or reputation, or disclose the actual or alleged defects of one who is living, or of any educational, literary, social, fraternal, benevolent or religious corporation, association or organization, and thereby to expose him or it to public hatred, contempt, or ridicule."
65. See Livingston Hall, *op. cit.,* p. 634 f.
66. See, *e.g., New York Penal Law* § 1932.
67. Hall, *op. cit.,* p. 622.
68. For a fuller discussion of the developments in military law in recent years see Harold F. McNiece and John V. Thornton, "Military Law from Pearl Harbor to Korea," 22 *Fordham Law Review* 155 (1953).
69. An excellent analysis of the reform legislation is found in Edward D. Re, "The Uniform Code of Military Justice," 25 *St. John's Law Review* 155 (1951).
70. United States v. Clay, 1 CMR 74 (1951).
71. *The Law of Libel and Slander,* Albany, 1933, p. 1.
72. Art. 40, § 6(1); Art. 44, § 2. Of course, American freedom is also impliedly subject to public order and morality. But the absence in our Constitution of a specific escape clause serves as at least some check upon unwarranted legislative encroachments upon freedom.
73. See A. Nove, "Some Aspects of Soviet Constitutional Theory," 12 *Modern Law Review* 12, 24 (1949).
74. Alison Reppy, "Constitutionalism—Safeguard of American Freedom," 18 *Brooklyn Law Review* 159, 162 (1952).

75. 268 *U.S.* 652 (1925).
76. *Ibid.*, p. 666.
77. See Paul G. Kauper, "The First Ten Amendments," 37 *American Bar Association Journal* 717, 718 (1951).
78. New York State Ice Co. v. Liebman, 285 *U.S.* 262 (1932); Allgeyer v. Louisiana, 165 *U.S.* 578 (1897).
79. See Joseph Tussman and Jacobus tenBroek, "The Equal Protection of the Laws," 37 *California Law Review* 341 (1949).
80. Missouri *ex rel.* Gaines v. Canada, 305 *U.S.* 337 (1938).
81. Sipuel v. Board of Regents of the University of Oklahoma, 332 *U.S.* 631 (1948).
82. McLaurin v. Oklahoma State Regents for Higher Education, 339 *U.S.* 637 (1950).
83. Brown v. Board of Education of Topeka, 347 *U.S.* 483, 74 Sup. Ct. 686 (1954); Bolling v. Sharpe, 347 *U.S.* 497, 74 Sup. Ct. 693 (1954).
84. Robert K. Carr, *Federal Protection of Civil Rights: Quest for a Sword*, Ithaca, 1947, p. 210.
85. Screws v. United States, 325 *U.S.* 91 (1945).
86. See Picking v. Pennsylvania R.R., 151 F. 2d 240 (3d Cir.), *rehearing denied*, 152 F. 2d 753 (3d Cir. 1945).
87. *Cf.* the opinion of one writer that, "[i]t is doubtful if much can be done by way of existing federal statutes to implement effectively the Civil rights of individuals," because, in his view, the Supreme Court takes the position, "that civil rights lie within the realm of state power and that any federal attempt to encroach on that power is to be viewed narrowly and suspiciously." Eugene Gressman, "The Unhappy History of Civil Rights Legislation," 50 *Michigan Law Review* 1323, 1357 (1952). These statements seem unduly pessimistic.
88. Cantwell v. Connecticut, 310 *U.S.* 296 (1940); Murdock v. Pennsylvania, 319 *U.S.* 105 (1943).
89. People *ex rel.* McCollum v. Board of Education, 333 *U.S.* 203 (1948).
90. Zorach v. Clauson, 343 *U.S.* 306 (1952).
91. It has been said that "[t]he Judges of the United States Supreme Court seem to be in agreement that the First Amendment to the Constitution rests upon the premise that it, 'has erected a wall between the Church and State which must be kept high and impregnable,'" but do not agree ". . . upon the height, width and other dimensions of this wall when applied to the particular set of facts in each case." S. Leo Ruslander, "Religious Liberty as Judicially Defined," 13 *University of Pittsburgh Law Review* 666, 677 (1952).
92. Clarence T. Case, "Administrative Bureaus and the Lawyers," 9 *Missouri Bar Journal* 21 (1938).
93. Netterville warns: "If administrative law as we know it is to endure in our free society, it must grow up and function in the well disciplined and consciously restrained atmosphere of our constitutional environment." "The Administrative Procedure Act: A Study in Interpretation," 20 *George Washington Law Review* 1, 87 (1951).
94. O'Brian poses the question: "May it not well be that the greatest danger to our institutions lies not in the threats of foreigners but in our own weakness in yielding to emotion and our increasing readiness to minimize and disregard the fundamental rights of the individual?" "New Encroachments on Individual Freedom," 66 *Harvard Law Review* 1, 26 (1952).

95. Charles B. Nutting, "The Framework of Freedom," 5 *Journal of Legal Education* 131, 133 (1952).

Freedom in the International Society
(Written in April, 1953)

1. Francis Joseph Powers, *Religious Liberty and the Police Power of the State,* Washington, D. C., 1948, p. 35.
2. Jacques Maritain, *Rights of Man and Natural Law,* New York, 1943, p. 65.
3. Johannes Messner, *Social Ethics,* St. Louis, 1949, p. 220.
4. John Augustine Ryan and Francis Joseph Boland, *Catholic Principles of Politics,* New York, 1940, p. 104.
5. John Augustine Ryan and Morehouse Millar, *The State and the Church,* New York, 1922, p. 276.
6. Jacopo Banchi, *Vita Sociale,* Vicenza, Italy, 1932, p. 4. Translation mine.
7. John Elliott Ross, *Christian Ethics,* New York, 1951, p. 193.
8. John Locke, *Two Treatises on Civil Government,* New York, 1884, p. 311.
9. Irving Lehman, Chief Judge of the New York Court of Appeals, "The Moral Foundations of Law" (Address delivered November 12, 1944), New York *Law Journal,* November 15, 1944, p. 1291, col. 7.
10. Marcus Tullius Cicero, *De Officiis,* London, 1853, bk. II, VII, 24.
11. Roscoe Pound, "Interests of Personality," 28 *Harvard Law Review* 343 (1915).
12. Anton-Hermann Chroust, "Law and Morals," 25 *Boston University Law Review* 348, 362-364 (1945).
13. Allocution delivered January 8, 1947, New York *Times,* January 9, 1947, p. 8, cols. 3, 4.
14. Francisco Suarez, *De Legibus ac Deo Legislatore,* I, vii, secs. 1, 4.
15. Thomas Paine, *Rights of Man,* London, Bonner ed., 1949, p. 134.
16. See Manley Ottmer Hudson, ed., *International Legislation,* 4 vols., Washington, D. C., 1931, I, xii, sec. 2; F. N. Keen, "International Legislation," 27 *Journal of Comparative Legislation and International Law* 78 (1945).
17. Banchi, *op. cit.,* p. 513 "Man is always the beginning and end of social organizations. . . . But because of certain common characteristics of nature men constitute a family, and because of others comprise a State; consequently all human persons, bound by a common thread of nature (commune quoddam vinculum) form a great family which consists of all peoples on earth—which is called *humanity.*" Translation mine. See Pius XI, *Mortalium Animos* (encyclical on Religious Unity), January 6, 1928, as reprinted in Francis J. Powers, *Papal Pronouncements on the Political Order,* Westminster, 1952, p. 172.
18. John Westlake, *Chapters on the Principles of International Law,* Cambridge, 1894, p. 27 f.
19. Authorities are cited in Edward D. Re, "International Law and the United Nations," 26 *St. John's Law Review* 144, 147 (1947).
20. Edward Oppenheim, *International Law,* 7th ed., 2 vols., New York, 1948, I, 6.
21. *Ibid.,* p. 113.
22. On the concept of "sovereignty" see penetrating discussion and authorities cited in Jacques Maritain, *Man and the State,* Chicago, 1951, pp. 28-53. "The two concepts of sovereignty and absolutism have been forged to-

gether on the same anvil. They must be scrapped together." *Ibid.,* p. 53. For a summary of the great part played by the Holy See in international law see Walter George Smith, "Law, International," *Catholic Encyclopedia,* vol. 9, special ed., pp. 73 ff.

23. Oppenheim, *op. cit.,* I, 583.
24. United States v. Diekelman, 92 *U.S.* 520 (1876).
25. Underhill v. Hernandez, 65 Fed. 577, 579 (2d Cir. 1895).
26. Edward D. Re, *Foreign Confiscations in Anglo-American Law,* New York, 1951, p. 77. See Pius XII, *Christmas Message,* 1944, Pius XII, Address to delegates of the fourth annual Congress of World Movement for Federal Government, April 6, 1951, both as reprinted in Powers, *Papal Pronouncements on the Political Order,* p. 173.
27. Frederick S. Dunn, "The International Rights of Individuals," *American Society of International Law Proceedings,* Washington, D. C., 1941, p. 16 f. For some of the "defects" of international law see P. E. Corbett, *Post-War Worlds,* New York, 1942, pp. 99 ff.
28. For examples see Edwin M. Borchard, *Diplomatic Protection of Citizens Abroad,* New York, 1915.
29. See Edward D. Re, "The Nationalization of Foreign Owned Property," 36 *Minnesota Law Review* 323, 327 (1952). See Harvard Law School Research in International Law. "Responsibility of States for Damage Done in Their Territory to the Person or Property of Foreigners" (Draft Convention prepared in anticipation of the First Conference on the Codification of International Law, The Hague, 1930), 23 *American Journal of International Law, Supplement* 133 (1929) art. 9: "A state is responsible if an injury to an alien results from a denial of justice. Denial of justice exists when there is a denial, unwarranted delay or obstruction of access to courts, gross deficiency in the administration of judicial or remedial process, failure to provide those guaranties which are generally considered indispensable to the proper administration of justice, or a manifestly unjust judgment. An error of a national court which does not produce manifest injustice is not a denial of justice." *Ibid.,* p. 134.
30. Oppenheim, *op. cit.,* I, 584.
31. Philip Caryl Jessup, *A Modern Law of Nations,* New York, 1950, p. 100.
32. Ellery C. Stowell, *Intervention in International Law,* Washington, D. C., 1921.
33. Ellery C. Stowell, *International Law,* New York, 1931, p. 349.
34. Borchard, *op. cit.,* p. 14.
35. American Bar Association Journal, *The International Law of the Future,* Chicago, 1944, pp. 35 ff.
36. Stowell, *International Law,* p. 352.
37. See *ibid.,* pp. 352 ff. for other incidents of a similar nature. See also examples of Papal Arbitration when the Pope became the arbitrator between nations and the power to which appeals were made when the laws of justice and morality were flagrantly violated by States either in relation to aliens or their own subjects. Bede Jarrett, "Papal Arbitration," *Catholic Encyclopedia,* vol. 11, pp. 452 ff.
38. Sheldon Amos, *Political and Legal Remedies of War,* New York, 1880, p. 158.
39. Philip C. Jessup, "The Defense of Oppressed Peoples," 32 *American Journal of International Law* 116 (1938). *Cf.* Amos Shartle Hershey, *The Essen-*

tials of International Public Law and Organization, New York, 1927, p. 239. "Forcible interference in the internal affairs of another State has been justified on ground of humanity in extreme cases like those of Greece, Bulgaria, and Cuba, where great evils existed, great crimes were being perpetrated, or where there was danger of race extermination. The humanity of our time, combined with an increasing desire for justice and a growing consciousness of interdependence and international solidarity, will doubtless make interventions more frequent in the future than they have been in the past." For the views of Pius XII on Assistance to victim nations and sanction against aggression see *Christmas Message,* 1948, as reprinted in Powers, *Papal Pronouncements on the Political Order,* p. 174.

40. Hersh Lauterpacht, *An International Bill of Rights of Man,* New York, 1945; Hersh Lauterpacht, *International Law and Human Rights,* New York, 1950.
41. Jessup, *A Modern Law of Nations,* p. 2.
42. The United States of America v. The United Mexican States, *General Claims Commission, United States and Mexico* 191 (1931).
43. Clyde Eagleton, "The Individual and International Law," *American Society of International Law Proceedings,* 1946, p. 24.
44. Dunn, *op. cit.,* p. 14.
45. Edwin M. Borchard, "The Access of Individuals to International Courts," 24 *American Journal of International Law* 359, 362 (1930).
46. *Loc. cit.*
47. Lauterpacht, *International Law and Human Rights,* p. 9.
48. Clyde Eagleton, *International Government,* New York, 1948, p. 120.
49. Oppenheim, *op. cit.,* I, 584.
50. *Loc. cit.*
51. Charles Cheney Hyde, *International Law Chiefly as Interpreted and Applied by the United States,* 3 vols., Boston, 1947, I, 768.
52. 18 *United States Code Annotated* § 1651.
53. *United States Constitution,* art. I, § 8(10).
54. See Fred K. Nielsen, Discussion following Eagleton, "The Individual and International Law," *American Society of International Law Proceedings,* 1946, p. 37.
55. See Elihu Root, "The Sanction of International Law," *American Society of International Law Proceedings,* 1908, p. 14; Miriam Theresa Rooney, *Lawlessness, Law and Sanction,* Washington, D. C., 1937.
56. Eagleton, *International Government,* p. 121.
57. Edvard I. Hambro, "Individuals Before International Tribunals," *American Society of International Law Proceedings,* 1941, p. 22.
58. J. J. Parker, "The International Trial at Nurnberg," *The John Randolph Tucker Lectures—1949-1952,* Lexington, Va., 1952, p. 95. See Robert H. Jackson, "The Trials of War Criminals," 32 *American Bar Association Journal* 319 (1946).
59. See Robert H. Jackson, *The Nurnberg Case,* New York, 1947.
60. See Parker, *op. cit.,* p. 104.
61. United Nations General Assembly, "Convention on the Prevention and Punishment of the Crime of Genocide," art. 4, 45 *American Journal of International Law, Supplement* 7, 8 (1951).
62. For a list of authorities see Eagleton, *International Government,* p. 123 f.
63. Jessup, *A Modern Law of Nations,* p. 17.

64. Edward D. Re, book review of Faith Thompson, *Magna Carta: Its Role in the Making of the English Constitution,* 24 *St. John's Law Review* 185, 187 (1949).
65. Liversidge v. Anderson, (1942) App. Cas. 206.
66. Sir Cecil Carr, "Human Rights and Fundamental Freedoms in the United Kingdom," 1946 *Yearbook on Human Rights* 318 (1947).
67. Paine, *op. cit.,* p. 82.
68. See Edward D. Re, "International Law and the United Nations," 21 *St. John's Law Review* 144, 145 f. (1947).
69. *Journal of the Economic and Social Council,* First Year, no. 29, 1946, p. 521.
70. See United States, Department of State, "Evidence of Violations of Human Rights Provisions of the Treaties of Peace by Rumania, Bulgaria, and Hungary," *Publication 4376A* (submitted by the United States to the Secretary-General of the United Nations Pursuant to the Resolutions of the General Assembly of November 3, 1950).
71. Boris Mirkine-Guetzevitch (Dean of the Faculty of Law and Political Sciences of Ecole Libre des Hautes Etudes).
72. 27 *New York University Law Review* 886, 887 (1952).
73. *The Administration of Justice in Latin America,* New York, 1952, p. vii.
74. *Loc. cit.*
75. Lauterpacht, *An International Bill of the Rights of Man,* p. 3. For Professor Lauterpacht's suggested draft of an International Bill of Rights of Man see Lauterpacht, *International Law and Human Rights,* p. 313. This draft follows in general outline the one Professor Lauterpacht proposed in 1945. It includes not merely personal rights, but also political, social and economic rights.
76. Neil MacNeil, *An American Peace,* New York, 1944, p. 48 f.
77. Reproduced as an appendix in Maritain, *The Rights of Man and Natural Law,* p. 115.
78. Committee of the American Law Institute, "Statement of Essential Human Rights," 243 *The Annals* 18 (1946).
79. A Conference of Experts in International Relations, *The World's Destiny and the United States,* 1941, p. 106 f.
80. *Ibid.,* p. 120 f.
81. This declaration which was submitted by the American Hierarchy to the United Nations Committee on Human Rights in January 1947 is reproduced in Francis P. LeBuffe and James V. Hays, *The American Philosophy of Law,* 4th ed., New York, 1947, p. 116.
82. 41 *Catholic Mind,* 45-46 (1943).
83. O. Frederick Nolde, "Human Rights and the United Nations," 25 *Academy of Political Science Proceedings* 171 (1953).
84. These historic documents can be found in United States, Department of State, "Toward the Peace," *Publication 2298,* Washington, D. C.
85. See report of Commission to Study the Organization of Peace. One of the articles states: "Nations must accept certain human and cultural rights in their constitutions and in international covenants. The destruction of civil liberties anywhere creates danger of war. The peace is not secure if any large and efficient population is permanently subject to a control which can create a fanatical national sentiment impervious to external opinion." "Preliminary Report and Monograph," *International Conciliation,* New York, 1941.
86. *United Nations Charter,* art. 2(7).

87. *Ibid.*, art. 39. Article 2(7) which contains the principle of nonintervention in matters "essentially within the domestic jurisdiction of any state," also declares: "[b]ut this principle shall not prejudice the application of enforcement measures under Chapter VII."
88. Wilfrid Parsons, "A Declaration of Human Rights," *The Catholic Mind Through Fifty Years, 1903-1953* (ed. by Benjamin L. Masse), New York, 1952, p. 626.
89. Mrs. Franklin D. Roosevelt, "The Struggle for Human Rights," 19 *Department of State Bulletin* 457 (1948).
90. George Marshall, "No Compromise on Essential Freedoms" (Address before the Third Regular Session of the General Assembly, Paris), 19 *Department of State Bulletin* 432 (1948).
91. For the votes on each article of the Declaration, see 1948 *Yearbook on Human Rights* 465 (1950). The vote on the whole Declaration was: *"in favor:* 48 votes; *against:* nil; abstaining: 8 votes."
92. Mrs. Franklin D. Roosevelt, "General Assembly Adopts Declaration of Human Rights," 19 *Department of State Bulletin* 751 (1948).
93. Elizabeth Ann Brown, "Fifth Session of the General Assembly," 24 *Department of State Bulletin* 175, 177 (1951).
94. *United Nations Charter,* arts. 55(c) 56.
95. See Frank E. Holman, "International Proposals Affecting So-Called Human Rights," 14 *Law and Contemporary Problems* 479, 483 (1949).
96. *Ibid.*, p. 480.
97. Article 7 emphasizes this by stating "[a]ll are equal before the law and are entitled without any discrimination to equal protection of the law."
98. See Article 25(2) that states that "[m]otherhood and childhood are entitled to special care and assistance."
99. Roosevelt, "General Assembly Adopts Declaration of Human Rights," 19 *Department of State Bulletin* 751. See James Pomeroy Hendrick, "Progress Report on Human Rights," 19 *Department of State Bulletin* 159, 160 (1948): "Report of the Commission on Human Rights on the Second Session of the Commission." December 2-17, *United Nations Document,* E/600, 1947, p. 19.
100. For criticism of the Declaration and the Covenant on Human Rights, see Holman, "International Proposals Affecting So-Called Human Rights," 14 *Law and Contemporary Problems* 479; Frank E. Holman, "An International Bill of Rights, Proposals Have Dangerous Implications for U.S.," 34 *American Bar Association Journal* 984 (1948); Carl B. Rix, "Human Rights and International Law; Effect of the Covenant Under Our Constitution," 35 *American Bar Association Journal* 551 (1949); Frank E. Holman, "President Holman's Comments on Mr. Moskowitz's Reply," 35 *American Bar Association Journal* 288 (1949).
101. See Nolde, *op. cit.*, p. 176.
102. See "Resolution of Sixth Committee of the General Assembly," *United Nations Document,* A/1196, December 3, 1949, p. 18. Resolution was adopted by the General Assembly on December 6, 1949. *United Nations Document,* A/P.V. 270, December 6, 1949.
103. Hans Kelsen, "The Draft Declaration on Rights and Duties of States—Critical Remarks," 44 *American Journal of International Law* 259, 269 (1950).
104. Harvard Law School Research in International Law, *loc. cit.*
105. This was Resolution XXX, Pan-American Union 38 (1948); 43 *American Journal of International Law, Supplement* 133 (1949).

106. George A. Finch and Myres S. McDougal, "Discussion Following Session of American Society of International Law," *American Society of International Law Proceedings,* pp. 79, 83 (1949); Holman, "International Proposals Affecting So-Called Human Rights," 14 *Law and Contemporary Problems* 481; Judge Harold P. Burke's extemporaneous remarks following his address "A Law Above the King," 21 *New York State Bar Association Bulletin* 278, 286 f. (1949); addresses by Nathan L. Miller and Joseph M. Proskauer, "Human Rights and International Law," 21 *New York State Bar Association Bulletin* 333, 340 (1949).
107. Art. XVI, 43 *American Journal of International Law, Supplement,* 133, 136 (1949).
108. A. H. Robertson, "The European Convention for the Protection of Human Rights," 27 *The British Yearbook of International Law* 145, 152 (1951).
109. "Convention for the Protection of Human Rights and Fundamental Freedoms," arts. 26, 27, 45 *American Journal of International Law, Supplement* 24 (1941).
110. *Ibid.,* art. 38.
111. *Ibid.,* art. 25.
112. See *ibid.,* arts. 20-37, particularly art. 24.
113. Robertson, *op. cit.,* p. 163.
114. Durward V. Sandifer, "The International Protection of Human Rights: The United Nations System," *American Society of International Law Proceedings,* 1949, p. 62.
115. "Human Rights in the United Nations," 13 *United Nations Bulletin* no. 5 (September 1, 1952), reprinted in *United Nations Publications* 1/26, p. 1 (1952).
116. American Bar Association, *Proceedings of the Section of International and Comparative Law,* Chicago, 1949, p. 195.
117. See *Universal Declaration of Human Rights,* arts. 22-29.
118. See "Draft, International Covenant on Human Rights" (Fifth Session of the General Assembly), 24 *Department of State Bulletin* 175, 177 (1951).
119. Malik, *op. cit.,* p. 12.
120. *Loc. cit.*
121. *Loc. cit.*
122. See Burke, *op. cit.,* p. 287; see interesting discussion in Maritain, *Man and the State,* pp. 76-107, wherein the author endeavors to show that "men mutually opposed in their theoretical conceptions can come to a merely practical agreement regarding a list of human rights." "As the International Declaration of Rights published by the United Nations in 1948 showed very clearly, it is doubtless not easy but it is possible to establish a common formulation of such *practical conclusions,* or in other words, of the various rights possessed by man in his personal and social existence. Yet it would be quite futile to look for a common *rational justification* of these practical conclusions and these rights." *Ibid.,* p. 76.
123. Proskauer, *op. cit.,* p. 345.
124. Burke, *op. cit.,* p. 286 f.
125. *Draft Covenant on Economic, Social and Cultural Rights,* art. 6 (Reproduced in *United Nations Publications* 1/26, p. 13).
126. *Ibid.,* art. 7.
127. *Ibid.,* art. 8.
128. *Ibid.,* art. 9(1).

129. *Ibid.,* art. 9(2)(3).
130. *Ibid.,* art. 10.
131. *Ibid.,* art. 11.
132. *Ibid.,* art. 12.
133. *Ibid.,* art. 13.
134. *Ibid.,* art. 15.
135. *Ibid.,* art. 13(2)(a) states: "It is understood: That primary education shall be compulsory and available free to all."
136. Re, "The Nationalization of Foreign-Owned Property," 36 *Minnesota Law Review* 333.
137. Re, *Foreign Confiscations in Anglo-American Law,* p. 7.
138. Malik, *op. cit.,* p. 9.
139. *Loc. cit.*
140. *Covenant on Civil and Political Rights,* art. 1(3)(c), (Reproduced in *United Nations Publications* 1/26, p. 16).
141. For the human rights guaranteed in the United States, see Zechariah Chafee, "Federal and State Powers Under the U.N. Covenant on Human Rights," 1951 *Wisconsin Law Review* 389, 400 ff. (1951).
142. American Bar Association, *Proceedings of the Section of International and Comparative Law,* 1949, p. 197.
143. *Loc. cit.*
144. *Loc. cit.*
145. Monroe Berger, *Equality by Statute,* New York, 1952, p. 191.
146. *United Nations Charter,* art. 2(7).
147. See Holman, "An International Bill of Rights, Proposals Have Dangerous Implications for U.S.," 34 *American Bar Association Journal* 984; Rix, "Human Rights and International Law; Effects of the Covenant Under Our Constitution," 35 *American Bar Association Journal* 551; Holman, "President Holman's Comments on Mr. Moskowitz's Reply," 35 *American Bar Association Journal* 288.
148. The arguments of the critics of the Covenant are ably answered by Myres McDougal and Gertrude C. K. Leighton, "The Rights of Man in the World Community: Constitutional Illusions Versus Rational Action," 14 *Law and Contemporary Problems* 490 (1949).
149. Jessup, *A Modern Law of Nations,* p. 137.
150. American Bar Association, *Proceedings of the Section of International and Comparative Law,* 1950, pp. 112, 116.
151. See McDougal and Leighton, *op. cit.,* p. 507.
152. See American Bar Association, *Report of Special Committee on Peace and Law Through United Nations,* Chicago, September 1, 1949, p. 7.
153. American Bar Association Journal, *The International Law of the Future,* p. 36.
154. See materials cited in McDougal and Leighton, *op. cit.,* p. 490; Alison Reppy, "Constitutionalism—Safeguard of American Freedom," 18 *Brooklyn Law Review* 159 (1952); see authorities cited in Note, "The Human Rights Provisions of the U.N. Charter and Local Courts," 25 *St. John's Law Review* 41 (1950).
155. Foster v. Neilson, 2 Pet. 253 (U.S. 1829).
156. *Ibid.,* p. 314.
157. Quincy Wright, "National Courts and Human Rights—The Fujii Case," 45 *American Journal of International Law* 62, 63 f. (1951).

158. See American Bar Association, *Report of Special Committee on Peace and Law Through United Nations,* Chicago, September 1, 1949, pp. 7, 9. "Government by treaties is a new concept." *Ibid.,* p. 4.
159. John Cates, Jr., "Expanding Concept of Individual Liberties," 25 *Department of State Bulletin* 1059, 1063 (1951).
160. *Loc. cit.* See James Simsarian, "Proposed Human Rights Covenant," 22 *Department of State Bulletin* 945, 946 (1950).
161. 217 P. 2d 481 (1950). See 44 *American Journal of International Law* 590 (1950).
162. Arts. 55, 56.
163. 1945 O.R. 778, 1945 4 D.L.R. 674. See Paul Sayre, "United Nations Law," 25 *Canadian Bar Review* 809 (1947).
164. See materials cited in Wright, *op. cit.,* p. 62; Charles Fairman, "Finis to Fujii," 46 *American Journal of International Law* 682 (1952).
165. Sei Fujii v. State of California, 242 P. 2d 617 (1952). See Fairman, *loc. cit.*
166. Fairman, *loc. cit.*
167. Association of the Bar of the City of New York, Committee on Federal Legislation and Committee on International Law, *"Report on 'Joint Resolution Proposing an Amendment to the Constitution of the United States Relative to the Making of Treaties and Executive Agreements' (S. J. Res. 130),"* New York, 1952. See also "Committee Report," 8 *The Record* 167 (1953). "The amendment proposed by S. J. Res. 1 would place so many impediments upon our conduct of foreign affairs as to constitute a grave threat to our future in the modern world. We oppose the adoption of S. J. Res. 1." *Ibid.,* p. 191.
168. *Ibid.,* p. 40.
169. Manley O. Hudson, "Some Problems Under Current Discussion," American Society of International Law Proceedings, 1952, pp. 2, 11. As one might imagine there is no unanimity of opinion on these matters in the American Bar Association. See "International Law Report Arouses Debate" (Proceedings of the House of Delegates: Mid-Year Meeting, 1953), 39 *American Bar Association Journal* 337, 343 (1953).
170. Edwin D. Dickinson, *Law and Peace,* Philadelphia, 1951, p. 142. See Edward D. Re, book review of Dickinson, *Law and Peace,* 27 *St. John's Law Review,* 201, 303 f. (1952). See Richard A. Edwards, "The Constitution, the Treaty Power, and Juridical Isolationism," 14 *University of Pittsburgh Law Review* 199 (1953). "The principal example of existing juridical isolationism has found expression in opposition to the efforts of the United Nations Commission on Human Rights to prepare international covenants for the improvement of civil rights protection throughout the world."
171. "Treaties and Civil Rights," Editorial, New York *Herald Tribune,* April 8, 1953; Editorial, New York *Times,* April 12, 1953, p. 12.
172. Brunson MacChesney, "International Protection of Human Rights in the United Nations," 47 *Northwestern University Law Review* 198, 219 f. (1952).
173. Cates, *op. cit.,* p. 1061. William W. Bishop, Jr., "The Structure of Federal Power Over Foreign Affairs," 36 *Minnesota Law Review* 299, 310 (1952).
174. See American Bar Association, "Committee Report," *Proceedings of the Section of International and Comparative Law,* 1950, p. 118.
175. See Jessup, *A Modern Law of Nations,* p. 116.
176. "Toward Common Goals of Peace," 17 *Department of State Bulletin* 80 (1947).

177. See Carlos P. Romulo, "Natural Law and International Law," 3 *Natural Law Institute Proceedings* 127 (1949).
178. John G. Winant, "Pursuit of Happiness in the Economic and Social World," 14 *Department of State Bulletin* 975 (1946).
179. Cates, *op. cit.*, p. 1063.

Economic Systems and the Individual

1. Carlton, Joseph Huntley Hayes, *The Political and Cultural History of Modern Europe,* 2 vols., New York, 1937, I, 90.
2. Frederick Louis Nussbaum, *A History of the Economic Institutions of Modern Europe,* New York, 1948, p. 320.
3. Thomas Corwin Mendenhall et al., *Ideas and Institutions in European History* 800-1715, New York, 1948, p. 320. Memorandum written by the chief minister Jean Colbert for the use of the King of France in 1669.
4. Harry Elmer Barnes, *History and Social Intelligence,* New York, 1926, p. 159.
5. Arnold Joseph Toynbee, *A Study of History,* 6 vols., New York, 1934-1939, III, 346.
6. *Ibid.*, p. 351.
7. Nussbaum, *op. cit.*, p. 74.
8. *Ibid.*, p. 65.
9. Eli F. Heckscher, "Mercantilism," *Encyclopedia of the Social Sciences,* Vol. 10, pp. 333-339, New York, 1933.
10. Frederick Charles Dietz, *An Economic History of England,* New York, 1942, p. 354.
11. Thomas Southcliffe Ashton, *The Industrial Revolution 1760-1830,* New York, 1948, p. 69.
12. Dietz, *op. cit.*, p. 358.
13. *Ibid.*, pp. 334-335.
14. The words of Adam Smith as quoted by William T. Jackman, *The Development of Transportation in England,* 2 vols., London, 1916, I, 213.
15. See the statistical tables in Adna Ferrin Weber, *The Growth of Cities in the Nineteenth Century,* London, 1899, p. 53.
16. Edward Hungerford, *The Story of the Baltimore and Ohio Rail Road 1827-1927,* 2 vols., New York, 1928, I, 93.
17. Dietz, *op. cit.*, p. 415.
18. John Harold Clapham, *An Economic History of Modern Britain,* 3 vols., Cambridge, England, 1939, I, 406.
19. Louis Morton Hacker, *The Triumph of American Capitalism,* New York, 1944, p. 265.
20. Harry Elmer Barnes, *An Economic History of Western Europe,* New York, 1942, p. 422.
21. William Leonard Langer, *The Diplomacy of Imperialism,* 1890-1902, 2d ed., New York, 1951, p. 73.
22. James Truslow Adams, *Empire on Seven Seas,* New York, 1940, p. 186.
23. *Ibid.*, p. 157.
24. Fulton John Sheen, *Communism and the Conscience of the West,* New York, 1948, pp. 7-8.
25. Leo XIII, "Rerum Novarum," in *Social Wellsprings* (Ed. by Joseph Husslein), Milwaukee, Wis., I, 168.
26. Lynn Montross, *The Reluctant Rebels,* New York, 1950, p. 168.

27. Frederick Lewis Allen, *The Big Change,* New York, 1952, p. 130.
28. *Ibid.,* p. 124.
29. "Chrysler for instance, does business with 1,400 suppliers." (Evan Benner Alderfer and Herman Edward Michl, *Economics of American Industry,* New York, 1942, p. 158.)
30. Allen, *op. cit.,* p. 144.
31. New York *Times,* July 23, 1952.
32. Joseph Alois Schumpeter, *Capitalism, Socialism and Democracy,* 3d Ed., New York, 1942, p. 66.
33. New York *Times,* October 28, 1952.
34. *Loc. cit.*
35. *Loc. cit.,* Italics mine.
36. *Loc. cit.,* Italics mine.
37. Peter Ferdinand Drucker, *The New Society, The Anatomy of the Industrial Order,* New York, 1949.
38. The following characterizations of Russian social conditions are based on the four admirable articles published under the collective title "How Much Strength Behind the Iron Curtain," in *Fortune,* XL (February, 1953).
39. "Russia Doubles Her Industry in Five Years, Rivals Europe," *Business Week,* October 18, 1952, p. 165.
40. *Ibid.,* pp. 164-165.
41. New York *Times,* June 8, 1953, p. 30.
42. Arnold J. Toynbee, "The Siege of the West," *Foreign Affairs,* XXXI (1953), 286.
43. *Loc. cit.*
44. Arpad F. Kovacs, "The Economic Consequences of Atomic Energy," *Implications of Atomic Energy,* Brooklyn, 1950, pp. 93-125.

Freedom and Labor

1. Bryon Robert Abernethy, *Liberty Concepts in Labor Relations,* New York, 1943, pp. 1-7.
2. Vada Horsch, *N.A.M. Past and Present,* New York, 1951, pp. 9-10.
3. Harry Bullis, *Free Markets and Free Men,* Chamber of Commerce of the United States, Washington, D. C., 1953, p. 21.
4. Floyd Arthur Harper, *Liberty, A Path to Its Recovery,* Irvington on Hudson, N. Y., 1949, pp. 25-26.
5. *Cf.* Vervon Orval Watts, *Union Monopoly: Its Cause and Cure,* 1953.
6. Philip Murray, *Address,* May 10, 1948, Ralph Woods, *The Business Man's Book of Quotations,* 1951, New York, p. 311.
7. Walter Reuther, Address to 14th Constitutional Convention of the C.I.O., Dec. 4, 1952, *C.I.O. Proceedings,* 1952, pp. 481-490.
8. Phelps Adams, *The Free Enterprise System,* National Association of Manufacturers, New York, 1952, p. 5.
9. H. W. Prentis, *Tripodism,* National Association of Manufacturers (folder) n.d.
10. "Is Anybody Listening?", *Fortune,* XLII (Sept., 1950), 78.
11. Solomon Barkin, "A Trade Unionist Appraises Management Personnel Philosophy," *Harvard Business Review,* XXVIII (Sept., 1950), 59-60.
12. Harper, *op. cit.,* pp. 28-36.

13. *Cf.* Peter Drucker, *New Society, the Anatomy of the Industrial Order,* New York, 1949.
14. Ernest Kilzer, "The Duty and the Right to Work," *Social Concepts and Problems,* Collegeville, Minn., 1936, pp. 48-53.
15. Pius XI, Encyclical "Quadragesimo Anno," *The Five Great Encyclicals,* New York, 1939, p. 142.
16. John Maurice Clark, *Guideposts in Time of Change,* New York, 1949, p. 59.
17. Leo XIII, *Encyclical,* "The Conditions of Labor," *The Five Great Encyclicals,* New York, 1939, p. 27.
18. Virgil Michel, *Human Rights,* St. Paul, Minn., 1936, pp. 42-45.
19. John T. Dunlop, "The Development of Labor Organizations," in Richard Allen Lester and Joseph Shister, *Insights into Labor Issues,* New York, 1948.
20. Sumner H. Slichter, "The Development of National Labor Policy," *Studies in Economics and Labor Relations,* University of Pennsylvania Bicentennial Conference, Phila., 1941, p. 142.
21. Orme W. Phelps, "Public Regulation of Trade Unions," *Twentieth Century Economic Thought,* New York, 1950, p. 565.
22. Walter Luke Willigan and John Joseph O'Connor, *Social Order,* New York, 1941, p. 153.
23. U. S. Bureau of Labor Standards, "Federal Labor Laws and Agencies," *Bulletin* No. 123, Aug. 1950, pp. 5-26.
24. National Labor Relations Board vs. Jones and Laughlin, 301 *U.S.* 33-34.
25. Bowden Will, "Freedom For Wage Earners," The American Academy of Political and Social Science, *Annals,* CC (1938), 185-209.
26. U. S. Bureau of Labor Statistics, "Directory of Labor Unions," *Bulletin* No. 1127, Washington, D. C., 1953.
27. William Lloyd Warner and Josiah Orne Low, *The Social System of the Modern Factory,* New Haven, Conn., 1947, pp. 68-87.
28. National Association of Manufacturers, *Compulsory Arbitration,* New York, 1951, p. 9.
29. *Ibid.,* p. 10.
30. David Bell, "The Next American Labor Movement," *Fortune,* XLVII (April, 1953), 120.
31. United Auto Workers, "Resolution No. 24," *Annual Convention Proceedings,* March 1953.
32. Abraham David Kaplan, *The Guarantee of Annual Wages,* Washington, D. C., 1947, pp. 233-243.
33. Chamber of Commerce of the United States, *The Economics of the Guaranteed Wage,* Washington, D. C., 1953, p. 32.
34. *Cf. Monthly Labor Review*—Data published each month in Table E.
35. Sumner Slichter, "The Taft Hartley Act," *Quarterly Journal of Economics,* LXIII (1949), 1-31.
36. U. S. Bureau of Labor Standards, "Federal Labor Laws and Agencies," *Bulletin* No. 123, August 1950, pp. 5-26.
37. *Cf.* "Text of Eisenhower's Message Seeking Amendments in Taft Labor Law," *New York Times,* Jan. 12, 1954, p. 9, col. 6-8.
38. Chamber of Commerce of the United States, *Policy Declaration,* Washington, D. C., 1953, p. 81.
39. National Labor Relations Board, *Eleventh Annual Report,* Washington, D. C., 1946, p. 2.
40. Department of Labor, *Labor-Management Relations Act of 1947,* Title 11, Sections 206-210, Washington, D. C., N.E.

41. Robert Drinan, "The Fruitless Steel Dispute," *Social Order,* II (1952), pp. 291-297.
42. *Cf.* Leo Wolman "Lessons of the Steel Strike," reprint from *The Freeman,* II (Sept. 22, 1952).
43. *Cf.* United States Department of Labor, "Current Labor Statistics," Table C-2 Gross Average weekly earnings of production workers in selected industries, *Monthly Labor Review,* 1953.
44. Table A-3, "Production Workers in Mining and Manufacturing Industries," *Loc. cit.*
45. "The Coal Squeeze Spreads," *Business Week,* March 4, 1950, p. 21.
46. Chamber of Commerce of the United States, *Policy Declarations,* Washington, D. C., 1953, p. 79.
47. Donald R. Richberg, "Free Men vs. the Union Closed Shop," *The Freeman,* I (July 16, 1951), 2-8.
48. *Cf.* Pius XII, "Christmas Message," December 1952, reprint by *The Tablet,* 1953.
49. *Cf.* Harold Seidman, *Labor Czars,* New York, 1938.
50. Leonard Sayles and George Strauss, "What the Worker Really Thinks of His Union," *Harvard Business Review,* XXXI (June 1953), 94.
51. Maurice Newfield, *Day In, Day Out with Local 3, I.B.E.W.,* Ithaca, New York, 1951.
52. *Ibid.,* pp. 28-33.
53. Edward Wight Bakke, *Mutual Survival,* New York, 1946, pp. 80-81.
54. John Cronin, *Catholic Social Principles,* Milwaukee, Wis., 1950, pp. 200-253.
55. *Cf.* United States Department of Labor, Bureau of Labor Standards, *The President's National Labor-Management,* Nov. 5-30, 1945, Summary of Committee Report, *Bulletin* No. 77, 1946.
56. Earl Bunting, "Industrial Relations Move Ahead," Reprint of *Industrial and Labor Relations Review,* Vol. 1, No. 2, January 1948, p. 240.
57. *Ibid.,* p. 241.
58. *Ibid.,* p. 242.
59. *Cf.* Paul Pigors, *Effective Communication in Industry,* New York, 1949.
60. Oswald Von Nell-Breuning, *Reorganization of Social Economy,* Milwaukee, Wis., 1936, p. 206.
61. *Cf.* Jerome Toner, "Christian Conception of Labor Management Relations," in Augustine Osgniach, *Must It Be Communism?,* New York, 1949, p. 300 seq.
62. Joseph P. Fitzpatrick, "The Industry Council Plan as a Form of Social Organization," *American Catholic Sociological Review,* XIV (1953), 146-156.
63. Mary Lois Everdt and Gerald Schnepp, *Industrialism and The Popes,* New York, 1953, p. 23.
64. Cronin, *op. cit.,* p. 730.

Freedom and Education

1. George Frederick Zook, *Higher Education for American Democracy,* New York, 1948, p. 8.
2. James Bryant Conant, *Report of the President of Harvard University to the Board of Overseers,* pp. 16-17.
3. Pius XI, *Christian Education of Youth,* p. 36.

4. John Henry Newman, *Sermons Preached on Various Occasions,* London, 1900, pp. 12-13.
5. William Joseph McGucken, *The Philosophy of Catholic Education,* New York, 1948, p. 28.
6. American Association of University Professors, *Bulletin* VIII (1922) 490 ff.
7. *Loc. cit.*
8. Pius XI, *The Christian Education of Youth,* Washington, D. C., 1931, p. 33.
9. John A. Flynn, "The Christian Teacher," *Thought Patterns* (St. John's University), III, 60.
10. Nicholas Murray Butler, "Academic Freedom," *Educational Review,* XLVII (1914), 201.
11. David Edison Bunting, *Liberty and Learning,* Washington, D. C., 1942.
12. Henry W. Tyler & Edward Cheyney, "Academic Freedom," *Annals,* American Academy of Political and Social Science, II (1938), 118.
13. Willard Slingerland Elsbree, *American Teacher,* New York, 1939, p. 542.
14. Cyril Meyer, *The Tablet,* May 30, 1953, p. 14.
15. *Loc. cit.*
16. *Loc. cit.*
17. Hunter Guthrie, "The Sacred Fetish of Academic Freedom," *Vital Speeches,* XVI (1950), 633.
18. John D. Redden & Francis A. Ryan, *Freedom Through Education,* Milwaukee, 1944, p. 182.
19. Fulton John Sheen, *Education As the Guardian of the American Heritage,* 84th Convocation of Board of Regents, Albany, N. Y., Oct. 20, 1950.
20. Flynn, *op. cit.,* p. 60.
21. John W. Curran, "Freedom of Thought," National Catholic Educational Association, *Bulletin,* XLVIII (1951), 152.
22. Joseph V. Kerr, "Truth and Freedom," *Thought Patterns,* III, 54.
23. New York *Times,* January 11, 1953.
24. Herbert R. O'Connor, "Academic Freedom—A License for Subversives," *Tablet,* June 6, 1953, p. 13.
25. Lewis W. Jones, *Statement on the Heimlich-Finley Cases,* Rutgers University, January 24, 1953, p. 9.
26. Frank E. Karelsen, Jr., "A Layman Looks at Academic Freedom," *School and Society,* LXIX (1949), 241-44.
27. Harold J. Laski, "Liberty on the American Campus," *Nation,* CLXIX (1949), 182.
28. Flynn, *op. cit.,* p. 60.
29. Meyer, *op. cit.,* p. 14.
30. *Loc. cit.*
31. William Buckley, *God and Man at Yale,* Chicago, 1951.
32. Whittaker Chambers, "Is Academic Freedom in Danger?", *Life,* XXXIV (June 22, 1953), 90-92.
33. New York *Times,* June 12, 1953.
34. L. Jones, *op. cit.,* p. 9.

Freedom in Relation to the Expression of the Beautiful

1. St. Augustine, *Confessions* (tr. by Edward Pusey), London, 1910, Bk. I, 20, 24-27.
2. Pitirim Aleksandrovich Sorokin, *Social and Cultural Dynamics,* 4 Vols., New York, 1937.

3. Sister Mary Gonzaga O'dell, O.P., "A Theory of Criticism of Fiction in its Moral Aspects According to Thomistic Principles." Catholic University, 1941.
4. A. W. Levi, "Scholasticism and the Kantian Aesthetic," *New Scholasticism,* VIII (1934), 203.
5. St. Thomas Aquinas, *In Metaphysicam Aristotelis Commentaria,* 3d Ed., Torino, Italy, 1935, I, lect. 1.
6. St. Thomas Aquinas, *In Libros Posteriorum Analyticorum Expositio,* Torino, Italy, n.d., I, lect. 1.
7. Aristotle, *Poetics,* London, n.d., Ch. 1, 1447a.
8. *Loc. cit.*
9. *Ibid.,* Ch. 2, 1448a.
10. *Ibid.,* Ch. 1, 1447a.
11. *Ibid.,* Ch. 4, 1448b.
12. *Contra Academ.* III, 1, 7.
13. Aristotle, *op. cit.,* Ch. 9, 1451b.
14. *Ibid.,* Ch. 9, 1452a.
15. St. Thomas Aquinas, *Super Evangelium S. Joannis Lectura,* Cap. 1, lect. 4.
16. *Ibid.,* Cap. 1, lect. 7.
17. Aristotle, *op. cit.,* Ch. 4, 1448b.
18. St. Augustine, *Confessions,* Bk. III, 2.
19. St. Thomas Aquinas, *In Decem Libros Ethicorum Aristotelis Ad Nichomachum Expositio,* I, lect. 1.
20. St. Thomas Aquinas, *Summa Theologia,* I, q. 5, a. 4, ad 1.
21. *Ibid.,* I, q. 91, a. 3, c.
22. Aristotle, *Physics,* II, Ch. 8, 199a.
23. *In Libros Politicorum Seu De Rebus Civilibus Commentaria,* I, lect. 1.
24. *Scriptum Super Libros Sententiarum,* Prol., q. 1, a. 5, ad 3.
25. *In Libros Politicorum Seu De Rebus Civilibus Commentaria,* I, lect. 1.
26. *Ethics,* IX, Ch. 7, 1167b.
27. *Ibid.,* VII, Ch. 8, 1151a.
28. *Scriptum Super Libros Sententiarum,* Prol., q. 1, a. 5, ad 3.
29. *Ethics,* I, Ch. 5, 1095b. "Now the mass of mankind are evidently quite slavish in their tastes, preferring a life suitable to beasts."
30. *Politics,* VIII, Ch. 3, 1338a.
31. *Ibid.,* VIII, Ch. 5, 1340a.
32. *Ibid.,* 1340b.
33. *In Libros Politicorum Seu De Rebus Civilibus Commentaria,* VIII, lect. 2.
34. *Loc. cit.*
35. *Ibid.,* lect. 1.
36. *Loc. cit.*
37. *Ibid.,* lect. 3.
38. *Ibid.,* lect. 1.
39. *In Librum Beati Dionysii De Divinis Nominibus Expositio,* Cap. 4, lect. 5.

Freedom and Theology

1. J. Pohle, "Theology," *Catholic Encyclopedia,* Vol. 14, p. 580, New York, 1910. Many Catholic authors limit theology in their definition to supernatural theology.

2. *Cf.* Joseph Fenton, *The Concept of Sacred Theology,* Milwaukee, 1941. Chapter 8, "The Scientific Character of Sacred Theology."
3. S. Lortie, *Elementa philosophiae christianae,* Vol. 2, p. 329: "Theologia naturalis definitur *scientia de Deo lumine naturali rationis comparata.*"
4. *Cf.* Pietro Parente, *Dictionary of Dogmatic Theology* (tr. by Emanuel Doronzo), Milwaukee, 1951, p. 240.
5. *Cf.* St. Thomas Aquinas, *Summa Theologiae,* P. II-II, Q. 80.
6. Walter Farrell, *A Companion to the Summa,* New York, 1945, III, 297.
7. *Cf.* Henry Denzinger and Clement Bannwart, *Enchiridion Symbolorum,* St. Louis, 1942, n. 1806. Hereafter cited as *DB.*
8. *Cf.* Lortie, *op. cit.,* II, 146 ff.; 380-90.
9. *DB,* nn. 1642, 1669, 1785, 1789.
10. I *Timothy,* 6:16; *Acts,* 17:28.
11. *Matthew,* 22:31, 25:46.
12. The ceremonial worship proclaimed by God through the Prophet Moses was obligatory only on the Jewish people. Precepts of this kind have passed away with the establishment of Christianity. But the truths about Himself revealed by God in both the Old and New Testaments must be accepted by all human beings.
13. *Cf.* John Augustine Ryan, *The Norm of Morality,* Washington, D. C., 1946.
14. When we say that men have been raised to the supernatural state, we mean that they have been destined by God to share His own happiness in the life beyond the grave, by seeing Him face to face. God was not bound to grant this destiny to men; He could have ordained them to a purely natural happiness. In that supposition, men would have been bound by the precepts of the natural law only. *Cf. DB,* n. 1026.
15. *Exodus,* 20:2-17; *Deuteronomy,* 5:6-21.
16. *Acta Sanctae Sedis,* XVIII (1885), 163-64. Hereafter cited *ASS.*
17. *Acta Apostolicae Sedis,* XVII (1925), 601. Hereafter cited *AAS.*
18. The numerous miracles wrought by Jesus Christ are related in the four Books of the Gospel contained in the New Testament, written by Saints Matthew, Mark, Luke and John.
19. *Matthew,* 11:2-6; *John,* 10:37-38; 2:18-19.
20. On the authenticity of the Gospels see Parente, *op. cit.,* pp. 113-14; Anthony Charles Cotter, *Theologia fundamentalis,* Weston, Mass., 1940, pp. 99-158; E. Gutwenger, "The Gospels and non-Catholic Higher Criticism," *A Catholic Commentary on Holy Scripture* (Ed. by Bern and Orchard, et al.), London, 1953, p. 752 ff.
21. *Cf.* Cotter, *op. cit.,* pp. 275-88; *DB,* n. 1790.
22. *Matthew,* 28:19; *John,* 14:16; 15:26.
23. *Mark,* 16:61-62; *John,* 8:58; 10:30-38.
24. *DB,* nn. 148, 259, 462; Parente, *op. cit.,* p. 127.
25. *Apocalypse,* 1:5, *DB,* nn. 2194-96.
26. *Matthew,* 16:18, 28:20.
27. *Mark,* 16:16.
28. *John,* 10:16.
29. *De unitate ecclesiae,* n. 6, P. L., *Patrologiae Cursus Completus* (Ed. by J. P. Migne), Paris, n.d., IV, Col. 503.
30. *Sermo ad Caesareensis ecclesiae plebem,* n. 6, P. L., *ibid.,* XLIII, col. 695.
31. *Luke,* 10:16.
32. *Cf. Matthew,* 3:12; 13:47 ff.

33. *Acts,* 6:6; 13:3; I *Timothy,* 4:14; 5:22; II *Timothy,* 1:6.
34. *Cf.* Gustave Thils, *Les notes de l'eglise,* Gembloux, 1932; Parente, *op. cit.,* p. 174.
35. *Matthew,* 16:16-19; *John,* 21:15-17; *Acts,* 1:15.
36. *Cf.* Glez, "Primaute du pape," *Dictionnaire de Theologie Catholique,* Paris, 1936, XIII (1936), col. 247-343; *DB,* n. 1824.
37. *DB,* n. 1794; Cotter, *op. cit.,* pp. 430-502.
38. *Matthew,* 28:20.
39. *Matthew,* 16:18.
40. *DB,* n. 1839; Parente, *op. cit.,* p. 142.
41. Codex Juris Canonici, Canon 1323, Hereafter cited *Codex; Cf.,* Dublanchy, "L'eglise," *Dictionnaire de Theologie Catholique,* Paris, 1939, IV, col. 2175-2200.
42. This is the more common teaching. Some theologians believe that divine-catholic faith is to be given to all the infallible pronouncements of the Church so that the concept of strictly or merely ecclesiastical faith has no validity. *Cf.* J. Fenton, "The Question of Ecclesiastical Faith," *The American Ecclesiastical Review,* CXXVIII (1953), 287-301.
43. This will be explained more fully later (p. 474).
44. *Cf.* Francis J. Connell, *Freedom of Worship,* New York, 1944.
45. *Cf. The American Ecclesiastical Review,* XXVII (1952), 307-315; *Cf.* J. Fenton, "The Holy Office Letter on the Necessity of Salvation," *ibid.,* pp. 450-61.
46. *DB,* n. 430.
47. *Cf.* J. Fenton, "The Meaning of the Church's Necessity for Salvation," *The American Ecclesiastical Review,* CXXIV (1951), 124-43; 203-21; 290-302.
48. *Acts,* 5:29.
49. *Codex,* Canon 121.
50. *Loc. cit.*
51. Alfredo Ottaviani, *Institutiones juris publici ecclesiastici,* Rome, 1947, n. 196.
52. *DB,* 974, 1559, 1560; *Codex,* Canons, 1816, 1038.
53. *Cf.* F. J. Connell, *Outlines of Moral Theology,* Milwaukee, 1953, pp. 38-48.
54. *Cf.* Benedict Henry Merkelbach, *Summa theologiae moralis,* Paris, 1938, I, n. 208.
55. *Ibid.,* n. 209.
56. *Ibid.,* n. 211.
57. St. Alphonsus, *Theologia moralis,* Rome, 1905, Lib. II, cap. 2, n. 9.
58. *Cf. The American Ecclesiastical Review,* CXXVII (1952), 312-314.
59. "Mystici corporis," *AAS,* XXXV (1943), 243; (transl. NCWC, n. 101).
60. *Mark,* 16:15.
61. Encyclical "Mystici corporis," *AAS,* XXXV (1943), 243; (transl. NCWC, n. 100).
62. *Cf. supra,* p. 22.
63. *DB,* n. 1794.
64. *Cf.* Christian Pesch, *Compendium theologiae dogmaticae,* Friburg, 1935, III, n. 391.
65. *De natura et gratia,* Cap. 26, n. 29; P. L., *Patrological Cursus Completus* (Migne), Vol. XLIV, col. 261.
66. *DB,* n. 1794.
67. *Codex,* Canon 2314.

68. *Codex,* Canons 1240, 765. It should be noted that the Church considers herself empowered to inflict penalties of a temporal order also on those who are disloyal to the Catholic faith, such as fines or imprisonment. But the Church most probably does not possess the right to inflict capital punishment. *Cf.* Ottaviani, *op. cit.,* nn. 176-77.
69. Joseph Blotzer, "Inquisition," *Catholic Encyclopedia,* New York, 1913, VIII, 35.
70. Vacanard, "Inquisition," *Dictionnaire de Theologie Catholique,* Paris, 1927, VII, col. 2065.
71. Winfred Ernest Garrison, *Intolerance,* New York, 1934, pp. 119-120. *Cf.* Ray Allen Billington, *The Protestant Crusade: 1800-1860,* New York, 1938.
72. Philip Schaff, *History of the Christian Church,* New York, 1907, V, p. 524.
73. *Codex,* Canon 2218. This canon states that those things which excuse one from imputability (including inculpable ignorance) also excuse from penalties—even in the external forum, if the inculpability of the error be proved.
74. Theoretically it would not be unjust to punish one who is evidently staying out of the Church through his own fault, while fully aware of his duty to become a Catholic. In practice it would be imprudent for any Catholic government to adopt such a measure, since it would easily lead to the coercion of non-Catholics to join the Catholic Church against their conscientious conviction.
75. *Cf. infra,* p. 164.
76. *DB,* n. 1250.
77. James F. Loughlin, "Friends," *Catholic Encyclopedia,* New York, 1913, VI, 304.
78. *Summa theologiae,* II-II, Q. 81, a. 7.
79. *Ibid.,* Q. 85, a. 1.
80. These precepts are found chiefly in the Books of *Exodus* and *Leviticus.*
81. *Matthew,* 28:20; *John,* 20:23; I *Corinthians,* 11:24-26.
82. *DB,* n. 931.
83. *Codex,* Canon 1144.
84. *Ibid.,* Canon 1258, 1.
85. John Raymond Bancroft, *Communication in Religious Worship with non-Catholics,* Washington, D. C., 1943, p. 14.
86. *Codex,* Canon 1258, 2.
87. *Ibid.,* Canons 1094, 1099.
88. Henry Davis, *Moral and Pastoral Theology,* London, 1945, I, p. 286.
89. *Instructio S. Officii ad ordinarios loci de motione oecumenica,* Dec. 20, 1949.
90. *Cf.* Merkelbach, *op. cit.,* I, n. 763.
91. *Ibid.,* nn. 762, 765.
92. *Cf. infra,* p. 452 ff.
93. *Cf. supra,* pp. 427-28.
94. *Romans,* 13:1.
95. *ASS,* XVIII (1885), 162.
96. *ASS,* XXXIII (1900), 279-84.
97. *ASS,* XXXI (1898), 648.
98. *AAS,* XVII (1925), 601.
99. *Codex,* Canon 1016.
100. *Ibid.,* Canon 121.
101. Ottaviani, *op. cit.,* n. 196.

102. *Ci riesce,* transl., *The American Ecclesiastical Review,* Vol. 130, n. 2 (Feb., 1954), p. 137.
103. NCWC news release, Sept. 1, 1953.
104. *Cf. supra,* pp. 438-41.
105. NCWC news release, Nov. 6, 1953.
106. *ASS,* Vol. XVIII, p. 163.
107. *Ibid.,* p. 172.
108. *Cf. The American Ecclesiastical Review,* Vol. 130, n. 2 (Feb., 1954), p. 134.
109. *Ibid.*
110. *Ibid.*
111. *Cf.* statement of Cardinal Play Deniel, Primate of Spain, in NCWC news release, Nov. 6, 1953.
112. *Freedom of Worship* (Paulist Press, N. Y., 1944), p. 13.
113. *Ci riesce,* transl. *The American Ecclesiastical Review,* CXXX (1954), 135.
114. NCWC news release, Nov. 6, 1953.
115. N. Hedin, "Religious Freedom in Sweden," *American Swedish Monthly,* August, 1951.
116. *Cf.* Wilfrid Parsons, *The First Freedom,* New York, 1948.
117. *Ci riesce,* transl. *The American Ecclesiastical Review,* CXXX (1954), 134.
118. NCWC news release, Oct. 24, 1953.
119. *Cf. supra,* pp. 452-53.
120. *Cf.* Garrison, *op. cit.;* Michael Williams, *Shadow of the Pope,* New York, 1932. "In all the State Constitutions which had been written and adopted from 1776 to 1787, with the exception of Virginia, election to high office was barred to Catholics. By virtue of these early State Constitutions, South Carolina declared the Christian Protestant Religion to be the established religion of the State; The Massachusetts Constitution permitted the taxation of Catholics and other non-Protestants for the support of Protestant teachers of religion; and in six other States—North and South Carolina, Georgia, Pennsylvania, New Hampshire and Vermont—only Protestants could hold office . . . New York applied the test oath to all its citizens. This barred Catholics because the oath contained an abjuration of all foreign allegiance 'ecclesiastical as well as civil,' and was done for the express purpose of excluding Catholics from public office. New Jersey allowed only those who professed their belief 'in the faith of any Protestant Church' to hold office." *The Church in United States History: America's Debt to Catholics,* Huntington, Indiana, 1937, pp. 67-70.
121. *Matthew,* 16:18.
122. *John,* 21:16-17.
123. *DB,* n. 1826.
124. *DB,* n. 1839.
125. *Codex,* Canon 1323.
126. Apostolic Constitution, *Munificentissimus Deus,* transl. *The American Ecclesiastical Review,* CXXIV (1951), 1-17.
127. *Cf. supra,* pp. 436-37.
128. *Codex,* Canon 1325, 2.
129. Encyclical *Mystici corporis, AAS,* XXXV (1943), 202.
130. *Cf.* E. Benard, "Doctrinal Value of the Ordinary Teaching of the Holy Father," Catholic Theological Society of America, *Proceedings* (1951).
131. *AAS,* XLII (1950), pp. 567-68.
132. *Cf.* George Van Noort, *Tractatus de gratia Christi,* Hilversum, Holland, 1934, nn. 63-76.

133. *Cf.* George Van Noort, *De Sacramentis, I,* Hilversum, Holland, 1927, nn. 457-475.
134. When theologians agree unanimously to a point of doctrine for a considerable period, their view should be regarded as certain, since it has received at least the tacit approval of the Church.
135. Scientific topics which have no relation to faith or morals are not the concern of the Church.
136. *AAS,* XLII (1950), 575.
137. *Genesis,* 2:7.
138. *Romans,* 8:21.